THE PROTECTED
MALAY STATES
1874–1895

THE MALAY STATES
1895

0   50   100
MILES

KEDAH

KELANTAN

Penang

TRENGGANU

Parit Buntar

S. Krian

S. Perak

PERAK

TAIPING

Kuala Kangsar

Batu Gajah

S. Perak

S. Kinta

Kuala Lipis

S. Tembeling

P. Pangkor

Tapah

Telok Anson

S. Lipis

PAHANG

Kuantan

S. Bernam

Kuala Kubu

S. Semantan

S. Pahang

Kuala Selangor

S. Selangor

Temerioh

PEKAN

SELANGOR

KUALA LUMPUR

SUNGEI

Klang

Kajang

K. Klawang

S. Langat

SEREMBAN

Kuala Pilah

Langat

UJONG

NEGRI SEMBILAN

Port Dickson

Tampin

S. Linggi

MALACCA

Malacca

S. Muar

JOHORE

SINGAPORE

—·—·— State Boundary
++++ Railway, completed 1895
------ Railway, projected 1895
● Chief district headquarters
○ Residencies
▨ Straits settlements

MP

DEPARTMENT OF GEOGRAPHY, SCHOOL OF PACIFIC STUDIES, A.N.U.

THE PROTECTED MALAY STATES
1874-1895

EMILY SADKA

KUALA LUMPUR
UNIVERSITY OF MALAYA PRESS
SINGAPORE
1968

SOLE DISTRIBUTORS
Oxford University Press, Ely House, London W.1.
GLASGOW NEW YORK TORONTO MELBOURNE WELLINGTON
CAPE TOWN SALISBURY IBADAN NAIROBI LUSAKA ADDIS ABABA
BOMBAY CALCUTTA MADRAS KARACHI LAHORE DACCA
KUALA LUMPUR SINGAPORE HONG KONG TOKYO

● *University of Malaya Press Kuala Lumpur 1968*

The University of Malaya Press
is a joint enterprise of the University of Malaya
and the University of Singapore.

PRINTED IN JAPAN BY GENERAL PRINTING COMPANY LTD., YOKOHAMA, JAPAN

TO MY FATHER
AND MOTHER

ACKNOWLEDGEMENTS

PART of the research on which this book is based was originally undertaken in the preparation of a thesis presented for the degree of Doctor of Philosophy to the Australian National University in 1960. Subsequent research in Malaya was made possible by the generosity of the Australian National University, for which I express my thanks. I wish also to acknowledge the constant and patient help of the staffs of the Arkib Negara, Malaysia; the Kuala Lumpur Book Club; the National Library, Singapore; The Library of the University of Singapore; the Public Record Office, London; the National Library of Australia; and the Library of the Australian National University. Without their assistance in providing material in microfilm and photostat, the research could not have been undertaken. I am grateful in particular to Haji Abdullah Sulaiman of the Arkib Negara for assistance in transliterating Jawi manuscripts into Romanized Malay. The translations into English are my own. To my colleagues, and particularly Professor Wang Gungwu of the University of Malaya, I express my thanks for their encouragement and suggestions. Finally, I should like to thank Miss Susan Rule, who helped to check the script, and Mrs. Lamberts and Miss Gawronski, who typed it.

E.S.

Kuala Lumpur
October 1966

Illness prevented me from seeing the book through the press, and I am deeply grateful to William and Margaret Roff who did this for me.

Perth   E.S.
May 1968

CONTENTS

ABBREVIATIONS

ANM	Arkib Negara Malaysia
AR	*Annual Report*
CO	Colonial Office
CS	Colonial Secretary
EPO	*Enquiry as to the Complicity of Chiefs in the Perak Outrages*
FMS	Federated Malay States
JIA	*Journal of the Indian Archipelago and Eastern Asia*
JMBRAS	*Journal of the Royal Asiatic Society, Malayan Branch*
JSBRAS	*Journal of the Royal Asiatic Society, Straits Branch*
PCM	*Perak Council Minutes*
PGG	*Perak Government Gazette*
PRO	Public Record Office, London
SCM	Selangor Council Minutes (Unpublished)
SGG	*Selangor Government Gazette*
Sel/Sec.	Selangor Secretariat Papers
SS	Straits Settlements
SSGG	*Straits Settlements Government Gazette*

INTRODUCTION

IN 1879 a Victorian woman traveller braved the dangers and discomfort of the west coast of Malaya in order to make a journey into the Malay states. On the first stage of her journey, from Malacca to Seremban in the state of Sungei Ujong, she took thirty hours to cover sixty miles, travelling continuously by launch, *prahu*, and on foot. At long intervals her party came upon signs of habitation; there is one description, which might be written today, of 'a very large Malayan-Chinese village' with 'a lane of much decorated shops, exclusively Chinese, succeeded by a lane of detached Malay houses, each standing in its own fenced and neatly-sanded compound under the shade of coco-palms and bananas'. There was a brief hint of the security and order of the outside world when the party halted for a few hours at a lonely police station, its walls hung with rifles, *krises* and handcuffs, 'with which a "Sam Slick" clock, an engraving from the *Graphic*, and some curious Turkish pictures of Stamboul, are oddly mixed up'. But for the most part the journey lay along a silent river bordered by jungle, profoundly still, empty of human life except for an infrequent paddler in a dug-out canoe.[1]

Today the journey from Malacca to Seremban may be accomplished in two hours by bus over a smooth road, and the noises are of motor traffic, or Malayan dance tunes from somebody's transistor. The road goes through settled country all the way, the traditional delicate green checker-work of rice fields, Malay villages hidden among palms and fruit-trees, orderly acres of plantation rubber. The bus finally enters a small, busy town, and comes to a halt in a terminus of concrete and brick, lined with coffee-stalls, provision shops and advertisements. The jungle has been pushed to the foothills and is now a distant indigo haze on the horizon; to busy, incurious town minds, it scarcely exists.

Between the two journeys there lie many years of administrative planning, designed to bring about just such a material development. British rule—the 'Residential system' as it was known to contem-

[1] Isabella Bird [Mrs. Bishop], *The Golden Chersonese and the Way Thither*, London, 1883, pp. 162–83, *passim*.

poraries—was introduced between 1874 and 1895 into the west coast states, Perak, Selangor and Negri Sembilan, and the east coast state of Pahang. Reasons of imperial policy and strategy played their part in the assertion of British control over these states; but it was the local administrators who moved most strongly for intervention, and their motives were economic. The western Malay states already had an industry—tin-mining—and a mining labour force of Chinese, and from the 1840's onwards the tin output of these states began to boom. The administrations in the Straits Settlements hoped, by judicious government, not only to encourage existing mining enterprise but to intensify it by attracting European capital, management and machinery, and to establish a large plantation agriculture. Between 1874, the year in which British Residents were first introduced, and 1895, when the four states were federated, the first of these aims was accomplished and the second was on the way to realization. An administrative system was developed, a communications system laid down, immigration, labour and land policies formulated and put into practice; in short, the basic institutions of modern Malaya were established. The population structure changed as a result of large-scale immigration of Chinese and Malays and the beginnings of indentured Indian immigration; and with the development of new lines of communication, settlement patterns changed also.

This study deals with the formation of British policy and the development of the structure of government in the protected Malay states. The term 'British rule' used of the form of administration of these states during the period, is itself a challenge to conventional interpretations, which represent the British officers as advisers to the Malay Rulers, through whom the government of the country was carried on. The interpretations break down on investigation, but the theory of government, the way in which it developed, and the realities which it covered remain to be discussed. The study describes the accommodation reached between fact and fiction, the manner in which it was established, the way in which the Secretary of State for the Colonies, the Governor of the Straits Settlements and the Residents exercised authority in the states nominally under advice, and the part played by Malay Rulers and chiefs and local authorities in the government of the states. Finally, it considers the policies evolved to carry out programmes of economic development and social change.

The Residential system was first established in Perak and Selangor (and the minor state of Sungei Ujong) and had developed there for the greater part of the period before its extension to Negri Sembilan and Pahang. The great bulk of the material, also, comes from Perak and Selangor. The study therefore deals largely with the system of government as it was established in these two states. But while there are important differences in economic conditions and development between Perak and Selangor on the one hand, and Negri Sembilan and Pahang on the other, the generalizations about basic policy and the structure of government are applicable to all the states.

I

THE MALAY STATES UP TO INTERVENTION

OF the states with which this study is concerned, Perak, Selangor and
Negri Sembilan lie to the west of the main mountain range which
runs down the centre of Malaya from the Siam border to Malacca.
The northern-most state is Perak, lying between latitudes 6° and
3°40′ north. In 1874 the Krian river to the north provided a common
boundary with the Malay state of Kedah and the British settlement
of Province Wellesley;[1] the Bernam river to the south marked the
boundary between Perak and Selangor. Selangor, lying between
latitudes 3°40′ and 2°30′ north, extended in 1874 from the Bernam
river in the north to the Langat in the south-east; in the south-west
it extended southwards along the coast to include the Lukut and
Sungei Raya valleys, but after British intervention these valleys, and
the whole coastline south of the Sepang river, were given to Sungei
Ujong, and Selangor received in exchange the whole Langat valley
to its southern watershed.[2]

The Negri Sembilan (literally, 'Nine States'), a confederation of
petty states which at one time included Sungei Ujong and was to
include it again by an agreement reached under British auspices,
comprised the hinterland of Malacca as far as the Pahang border on
the north, Johore on the east, and Selangor on the west. It was
drained by the southern-most tributaries of the Pahang river in the
north, by the upper reaches of the Muar in the east and centre, and
by the Linggi in the west. The state of Sungei Ujong, which had
independent relations with the British and was separately administered during the period under study, lay between Selangor and the
rest of the Negri Sembilan. The delineation of its western boundary
has already been described. On the north it was separated from the

[1] By the Pangkor Engagement of 1874, the Perak-Province Wellesley boundary
was redrawn a few miles south of the Krian river.
[2] Boundary Agreement between Selangor and Sungei Ujong, 10 February 1878,
W. G. Maxwell and W. S. Gibson, *Treaties and Engagements affecting the Malay
States and Borneo*, London, 1924, pp. 212–13.

confederate state of Jelebu by the Jelebu range, between the upper Linggi and the upper Klawang; on the east it was separated from the confederate state of Sri Menanti by the Linggi-Terachi watershed, and from the confederate state of Rembau by the Linggi-Pedas watershed.

Pahang, the only east coast state to come under British control during the period, embraced most of east-central Malaya, between latitudes 4°45′ and 2°30′ north, and between the central mountain range and the China sea. In the Endau river to the south she had a common boundary with Johore; in the central watershed, she had a common boundary with the Negri Sembilan, Selangor and Perak; in the north she had a common boundary with the Siamese-dominated states of Kelantan and Trengganu. Pahang is the largest state in the Peninsula, with 13,873 square miles compared with 7,890 for Perak, 3,166 for Selangor, 2,550 for Negri Sembilan including Sungei Ujong, and 660 for Sungei Ujong.[1]

The west coast states are in close proximity to the territories which then constituted the Crown Colony of the Straits Settlements. The north-west of Perak was contiguous with Province Wellesley and was about eight hours by coastal steamer from Penang. The steaming distance between Klang, in central Selangor, and Malacca Town, about 100 miles southward in the British settlement of that name, was about twelve hours. Further south, the Linggi river for six miles from its mouth constituted a common boundary between Sungei Ujong and Malacca, and the Linggi estuary was some twenty-five miles distant from Malacca town; and Malacca itself was 150 miles and twelve hours' steaming distance from Singapore. By contrast the chief township of Pahang (Pekan), was 250 miles distant from Singapore, and isolated from it for five months in the year by the north-west monsoon, which closed the east coast between October and February.

In the nineteenth century the ranges and valleys of Malaya were still covered by equatorial rain forest, intersected by rivers which were the natural highways and obvious lines of settlement. Each state

---

[1] The figures give the modern areas of the states, and have been taken from M. V. del Tufo, *Malaya: A Report on the 1947 Census of Population*, Kuala Lumpur, 1949. The area of Perak has been slightly increased in modern times by the return of a small enclave on the west coast known as the Dindings, transferred by Perak to the Straits Settlements in 1886 and returned in 1935; but the area involved was less than 200 square miles. The Sungei Ujong figure is taken from Dickson to Knutsford, of 10 July 1890, forwarding *AR* States, 1889, C. 6222, no. 1.

consisted essentially of one or more river systems. The Perak river, flowing 200 miles from its source near the Siam-Perak border to its mouth in the extreme south of the state, formed with its eastern tributaries the main thread of settlement; the Pahang river system, the largest in the Peninsula, formed the main settlement area of that state; Selangor comprised the settled valleys of the Bernam, Selangor, Klang, Langat and Lukut rivers; the centre of Sungei Ujong lay in the upper reaches of the Linggi, and settlement in Negri Sembilan followed the upper Muar and its tributaries. The estimates of Malay population advanced before British intervention are pure guesses and are reproduced here only because they indicate the kind of information available to Straits officials on this question. Newbold, writing in the 1830's, estimated the (largely Malay) population of Perak at 35,000; in 1861, Governor Cavanagh estimated it at 50,000; in 1879, a census taken by *penghulus* (Malay village headmen) numbered the Malays at 59,682, including slaves and bondmen, and the first official census, taken in 1891 after twelve years of peace and steady immigration, placed it at 96,719.[1] In 1824, Anderson estimated the population of Selangor at about 6,000, of whom the great majority must have been Malays;[2] in 1875, after eight years of fighting, the estimate by Swettenham (the Assistant Resident) was of the same order.[3] In 1884, a census taken by penghulus placed it at 17,097, and in 1891 the official census placed it at 26,546.[4] The Malay population of Sungei Ujong (excluding Lukut and Sungei Raya) was estimated

[1] T. J. Newbold, *Political and Statistical Account of the British Settlements in the Straits of Malacca*, London, 1839, vol. i, p. 418; speech by Clarke, Straits Settlements Legislative Council Proceedings, 15 September 1874, C. 1111, enclosure in no. 72; *Census of the State of Perak, 1891*.

[2] J. Anderson, *Political and Commercial Considerations Relative to the Malayan Peninsula*, Prince of Wales Island, 1824, pp. 190–202. Anderson's figures include 1,000 for Lukut, which became part of Sungei Ujong after 1878.

[3] Report of the Assistant Resident, Selangor, 8 April 1875, C. 1320, enclosure 2 in no. 28. Between August 1874 and April 1875, Swettenham went up the Bernam, Selangor, Klang, Langat and Lukut rivers, visiting 'every town and village in the Sultan's country, except Ulu Bernam'. He estimated the total population of the coast districts (excluding Kuala Selangor) at 2,500, and these may be taken as largely Malay. He also gave 700 as the figure for the Malay population of Kuala Lumpur, and 400 as the combined Malay and Chinese population of Ulu Selangor. The Malay population of the Kuala Lumpur suburbs, Kuala Selangor and Ulu Langat would probably not have been less than 2,000, so that according to Swettenham's estimate, 5,000 would probably be the figure for the Malay population in 1875. It should be remembered however that his estimates were impressionistic and were made after several years of war and depopulation.

[4] *AR* Selangor, 1884; Census of Selangor for 1891, *SGG*, 11 December 1891.

by Swettenham at about 2,000 in 1878; the 1891 census placed it at 9,341.[1] The same census placed the Malay population of Negri Sembilan at 35,377, and that of Pahang at 50,527. The following table shows the approximate density of the Malay population of each state for various years, on the basis of figures given above.

Density of Malay population to the square mile

Year	Perak	Selangor	Sungei Ujong	Negri Sembilan	Pahang
1879	7.4	—	—	—	—
1884	—	5.4	—	—	—
1891	12.6	7.5	14	17.5	3.5

In 1891, after many years of British rule, during which there had been a considerable Malay immigration, the density of Malay population in Perak, Selangor and Sungei Ujong was only a little over eleven to the square mile; the figure for 1874 was certainly much less. The population was unstable; it was extremely sensitive to political events, and a common response to oppression, invasion or civil war was flight,[2] so that for political or other reasons there were internal shifts of population, and there was also a constant inflow of settlers from Indonesia (mainly Sumatra) and from the Siamese-dominated Malay states to the north. New districts were opened up; in North Perak about the middle of the country, the lower Krian and Kurau, later to be a rich rice-producing area, was brought under cultivation by Malays infiltrating from Province Wellesley, Kedah and Patani; in Selangor the settlements at Cheras, Semenyih and Beranang were established in the third quarter of the century, the last two being settled initially from Sungei Ujong.[3]

---

[1] Assistant CS for Native States, Audit Report on Native States for 1877, C. 2410, enclosure in no. 6, Anson to Hicks Beach, 6 March 1879; *AR* Sungei Ujong, 1893. The 1891 census figure is exclusive of Jelebu. Swettenham's estimate is almost certainly an understatement, based probably on the Malay population near the mines.

[2] In 1874, the Colonial Secretary, then visiting Selangor, described the desolation on the Selangor river, and the rapid reversion to jungle of an area which had been populous and cultivated three years before. The people had fled during the wars for possession of the valley, 1871–3. Most of them had gone to Bernam, the next valley to the north. Birch, Journal of a Visit to the Native States of Selangor and Perak in March and April 1874, Swettenham Papers, ANM item 72.

[3] 'W.S.', 'Traditions of Ulu Langat', *Selangor Journal*, vol. v, no. 19 (28 May 1897), pp. 305–9.

In addition to this internal immigration, there was a large inflow from the islands of the Indonesian archipelago. In Perak the foreign immigrants—the Bugis particularly—were the principal traders in the state; a Bugis trader, Nakhoda Trong, was a partner in the syndicate which leased the farm of the Perak river customs duties in 1874. There were settlements of Rawas and Mandelings from northeast Sumatra; a Rawa, Che Abdul Karim bin Ibrahim went with a Sumatran following to open up Selama in the 1870's, and during the British occupation of Perak in 1875–6, Rawas, Mandelings and Bugis helped the British in their military operations in the north. Much of North Perak was settled by Malays from across the border; Krian by settlers from Province Wellesley and Kedah, Ulu Selama and Ulu Perak by settlers from Patani.[1] In 1879, a census of the Malay population of Perak gave the number of foreign Malays as 9,274 out of a total free Malay population of 56,632.[2] In Selangor the population was even more mixed. Part of Selangor had once been tributary to the kingdom of Malacca, and there had probably been settlements of Malacca Malays between the Klang and Selangor rivers from the middle of the fifteenth century. Towards the end of the seventeenth century, the Bugis settled on the Klang and Selangor, and in the middle of the eighteenth century a Bugis prince became the first Sultan of Selangor and established the present dynasty. There were important Bugis and Sumatran trading communities in Kuala Lumpur and Klang;[3] it was a quarrel between them that precipitated the Selangor wars of 1866–73. In Kuala Selangor there were also foreign Malay communities; in 1875 the Resident of Selangor described the population as consisting of Menangkabaus, Mandelings, Rawas, Bugis and Chinese.[4] There was a *Dato' Dagang* (chief of foreigners) in Langat, and in Ulu Langat, according to the accounts of British officers from the earliest years of intervention, the

[1] W. E. Maxwell, 'A Journey on Foot to the Patani Frontier in|1876', *JSBRAS*, no. 9 (June 1882), pp. 8–20; W. E. Maxwell, 'The Law and Customs of the Malays with reference to the Tenure of Land', *JSBRAS*, no 13 (June 1884), p. 98; E. Sadka, 'The Journal of Sir Hugh Low, Perak 1877', *JMBRAS*, vol. xxvii, part 4 (November 1954), pp. 56, 58.

[2] *Census of Perak, 1891*. The unfree numbered 3,050.

[3] A Malay traveller has described the population of Klang in 1872 as a heterogeneous collection of Malays, Arabs, English, Chinese, Eurasian, Klings, Bengalis, Hindus, and native-born (*peranakan*) of Penang, Malacca, Singapore and Kedah—about 3,000 in all. See Mohammed Ibrahim b. Abdullah, *Kesah Pelayaran [Account of Travels]*, Johore, 1956, p. 46.

[4] Report of Resident at Selangor, 16 March 1875, C. 1320, enclosure in no. 27, Clarke to Carnarvon, 27 April 1875.

agricultural population consisted largely of Malays from Sumatra.[1] Negri Sembilan, traditionally settled by Menangkabau Malays, had absorbed into its clan system colonies of immigrants from Malacca, Java and Acheh; and at the end of the eighteenth century, a Bugis chief had established a settlement on the lower Linggi under the patronage of the territorial chief of Sungei Ujong.

The nucleus of settlement was the village, commonly founded by the head of a family and his kindred by blood and affinity. The Selangor records for the 1880's and 1890's are full of instances of such foundations, established by headmen who brought in their families and followers, organized their economic life and helped them initially with loans; in some cases the headmen obtained government recognition in the shape of a penghulu appointment and salary. The settlements varied in size from the hamlet of half a dozen houses and twenty-odd inhabitants to the long-established village of two or three hundred houses and a thousand inhabitants, the centre of the district and the headquarters of the district chief.

The people lived in an age-old economic pattern of subsistence agriculture based on rice cultivation, both dry rice cultivated in shifting patches on hillsides (*ladang*), and wet rice cultivated in permanent fields (*bendang*). Fruit and vegetable gardens and coconut plantations provided other elements in their diet; coconut products and bamboo provided most of their household utensils; housing materials—timber and thatch, rattan and bamboo—came from the jungle. The economy was not entirely self-contained, however; there was usually a local exchange of surplus food-crops and livestock, and there was an export of jungle produce (rattans, *gutta*, firewood, *atap*, precious woods), and for centuries there had been an important export of tin and gold. This sustained a trade cycle, in which the tin export was balanced by the import of trade goods, mainly textiles, ironware, tobacco, salt and opium.

On this social and economic basis, a number of autonomous political structures were built, each river system forming a separate unit with its own ruling family.[2] The variety of organization and political affiliation may perhaps be illustrated by a brief survey of the political systems of Negri Sembilan and Perak. Negri Sembilan, a feder-

---

[1] See e.g., Supt. of Police to Resident, 28 June 1876, Sel/Sec. 102/76, and 30 November 1878, Sel/Sec. 426/78.
[2] J. M. Gullick, *Indigenous Political Systems of Western Malaya*, London, 1958, provides a full and valuable account.

ation of small states to the north of Malacca, was settled from the sixteenth century onwards by colonies of Menangkabau Malays. Though subject to the overlordship of the Malacca Sultans, and to interference from the Portuguese, Dutch and Bugis invaders of Malaya, they were able to preserve in essentials the tribal organization of their homeland. Society in district and village was divided into clans and lineages counting descent and entailing property in the female line. The leaders of society were the clan and lineage headmen; the family heads and enfranchised clansmen at each level of the kinship structure played a part in the election of leaders at higher levels. Above the clan system was an essentially territorial authority, the district chief; in the four major districts or states—Sungei Ujong, Johol, Jelebu and Rembau—he had the title of *Undang* (lawgiver). The chiefs claimed authority by virtue of descent from the founding clan, but they were probably descendants of local governors appointed by the Sultans of Malacca, and originally were probably outside the clan organization. (Till the end of the eighteenth century, for example, the chiefs of Sungei Ujong, the largest of the states, succeeded in the male line.)[1] By the early nineteenth century the territorial chiefs had accommodated themselves to the prevailing social pattern; eligibility to office descended in the female line, and the special status of the chief's clan was expressed in terms appropriate to the clan organization of society; in a higher bride price, for example, and a higher reparation scale for injuries. The clan's title to ownership of the soil was justified in a manner consistent with the matrilineal descent system by a myth linking the clan with an aborigine ancestress from whom it claimed inheritance of the whole country.

While each lineage and clan headman had jurisdiction only within his own kin group, the chief's jurisdiction covered all the clans in his territory. But his powers were limited by the rights of the clans. No decision affecting them could be made except in council with the clan headmen; no engagement with a foreign power was valid unless it bore their seals. The territorial chief acted as a court of appeal and had sole jurisdiction over certain serious crimes; he alone might award the death penalty, and he was the final authority on the cus-

[1] J. M. Gullick, 'Sungei Ujong', *JMBRAS*, vol. xxii, part 2 (1949), p. 17. The territorial chiefs of Sungei Ujong, Johol, Jelebu and Rembau were given their hereditary titles and seals by the Sultans of Malacca-Johore. From the evidence of seals and genealogies, Wilkinson dates these creations from the beginning of the eighteenth century. R. J. Wilkinson, 'Notes on the Negri Sembilan', *Papers on Malay Subjects*, 1st Series, History, part 5.

tomary law. But he might not reach beyond the clan headmen to initiate a suit against an individual clansman; the latter must be dealt with first by his own lineage and clan heads, and sent to a higher authority only if the case presented special difficulty or involved a major crime. The special claims and jurisdiction of the territorial chiefs and the rights of the clans were held in uneasy equilibrium by a body of customs expressed in folk sayings known to every peasant. The history of the settlement, the respective land rights of the waris[1] and the other clans, the jurisdiction, dues and ceremonial privileges of the territorial chiefs and the clan and lineage headmen, the laws of property and inheritance, were embodied in cryptic images, universally understood and universally quoted.

Outside this system was a form of Malay kingship, introduced for political reasons by the states in combination, but standing in fundamentally hostile relationship to their clan organization. Malaysia had been in contact with India for 2,000 years and had assimilated the principles of Hindu kingship; royal dynasties with legendary Hindu affiliations had been established in various parts of the archipelago for many centuries. Sovereignty was not necessarily expressed in the exercise of political power, nor in any concentration of government machinery; it was venerated as a sacred symbol of group unity. The person of the *Raja*[2] was sacrosanct. Certain colours, architectural devices, robes and furnishings were reserved to him; there was a special vocabulary used of royalty, and his greatness was symbolized also in the *kebesaran* or regalia, which consisted of historic jewels, weapons, robes and other accoutrements, the royal drums, ritual ornaments and vessels and articles of magic workmanship. The unity of the Raja with his kingdom was expressed in symbolic ownership of the land, of natural phenomena and of rare and strange creatures.

In the late eighteenth century, the Negri Sembilan accepted a

[1] *Waris*—literally inheritors; used generally to mean any descent group with a right to office or inheritance. In Negri Sembilan the term *waris negeri* was used to distinguish the clan of the territorial chief; elsewhere the term was used of the male descendants of former Sultans, who provided candidates for the succession.

[2] The Hindu term *Raja* is the generic term for ruler and is still the title of the Raja of Perlis; it is also the title of the male and female descendants of a ruler. It has been generally superseded, as a title of the ruler, by the Arabic *Sultan*. The Malay designation is *Yang di-Pertuan* ('He who is made Lord') usually shortened to *Yam Tuan*. At this time the Rulers of Perak, Selangor and Pahang had already assumed the style Sultan; the Ruler of Negri Sembilan however continued to be known as *Yang di-Pertuan Besar*, or *Yam Tuan Besar*.

Menangkabau prince as their Raja. The traditional explanation is that they wanted a royal leader to help them against the Bugis invaders; another possible explanation is that the Sultans of Johore, hitherto suzerain over Negri Sembilan, were themselves under Bugis control and no longer effective or even accessible as arbitrators, and that the chiefs wanted someone closer at hand to settle their disputes and validate their authority. They entered into a convention with the Raja, establishing him as a ceremonial and ritual head outside the power structure; he enjoyed a ceremonial precedence as nominal head of the confederacy, certain sovereign powers of jurisdiction, and a prescribed income; but he did not own the soil, nor might he levy taxes, nor interfere in the internal affairs of the states; and in an effort to prevent a royal dynasty from forming, the territorial chiefs imported their first four Rajas in succession from Sumatra. The inevitable happened; there were royal efforts to establish a dynasty in Negri Sembilan and minor dynasties in Rembau and Jelebu. These attempts involved the aspiring *Yam Tuans*[1] in endless conflicts with the territorial chiefs. In 1869, on the death of the *Yam Tuan Besar*, the succession, always precarious, broke down altogether and with it the unity of the confederacy; the royal candidates (who were cousins) continued to live in the districts forming the royal appanage of Sri Menanti, their claims unresolved; the *Yam Tuan Muda* of Rembau was confined to his district of Tampin, on the border of Malacca; the Yam Tuan of Jelebu continued to struggle in vain for recognition. The attempt to establish a constitutional kingship in the Negri Sembilan had apparently been too much even for the Malay political genius, with its capacity for compromise, adjustment and absorption.

The Negri Sembilan structure clearly shows the difficulty of maintaining a balance between the competing sources of authority, the tribal representative, the territorial chief and the Yam Tuan. The relationship between the first two was finally stabilized by custom, which defined the rights of both. The Yam Tuans on the other hand never succeeded in establishing control over the Negri Sembilan. They remained in theory and practice constitutional symbols with no authority outside the royal district.

In the other riverine states, of which Perak was a type, the clan

---

[1] *Yam Tuan Besar* was the popular title of the ruler of Negri Sembilan (see previous note); *Yam Tuan Muda* the title of the aspirant rulers of Rembau and Jelebu.

organization—if it had ever existed—had long since disappeared. Kin affiliations, it is true, remained an important feature of the power structure. Kin groups split off to found new settlements; influence was concentrated in certain lineages which monopolized office; protection by the kin group was a vital feature of social organization. But the pyramid of control was based on territorial and not kin divisions. The country, as in the Negri Sembilan, was fragmented into districts, each occupying a stretch of the main river or tributary, and each ruled by a district chief. But the power of the chiefs was not limited, as in the Negri Sembilan, by tribal custom to which the chiefs themselves adhered. The autocratic control of the chief was free of any sanction the ra'ayat[1] could use against him, except the sanction of flight. In a country where people were much scarcer than land, where a village could be dismantled and packed in boats in a matter of days, Malay peasants were mobile and there was always the danger that oppressed groups might cut at the foundation of the chief's power by leaving his district. But the threat of flight, and the suicidal protest of the amok, were the only sanctions the ra'ayat could apply against extreme exploitation.

At the apex of the structure stood the Sultan. According to tradition, the first Sultan of Perak ascended the throne about 1528 and was a son of the last Sultan of Malacca, expelled by the Portuguese in 1511; and according to tradition, the earliest holders of the majority of the Perak offices of state were descendants of the family of Malacca Bendaharas.[2] It appears certain that the royal office and the major offices of state were imported into Perak after the break-up of the Malacca Empire, and that the original title-holders came to Perak as the Sultan's followers.[3] They thus appear to have been mutually dependent from the start; the Sultan depended on the support and counsel of the title-holders, and in turn legitimized their authority. Though conflicts arose from time to time between the Sultan and the chiefs, and though the chiefs might work to replace an individual Sultan, no chief ever dreamt of removing the sultanate, the symbol of order and the legal source of his own authority.

The Sultan's familiar role was to symbolize unity and order in the state. His resources, derived from the revenues of a royal district, from gifts, and from customs duties collected at the main river mouth,

[1] The peasants.
[2] The chief ministers of the Malacca Sultans.
[3] For an account of the Perak Constitution, see Appendix 1 below.

enabled him to maintain a court and a royal household, but they did not permit administrative or military control of the districts. The Sultan was theoretically the owner of the soil, and the arbiter of life and death; appointments to office, concessions and revenue monopolies were in his gift, and theoretically transferred no permanent or hereditary right. But ownership of the soil had only a symbolic importance in a country where land was much more plentiful than people; appointments and commissions were usually confirmations of power already established, and were in practice if not in principle hereditary. Furthermore, custom secured to the chiefs a degree of control over the sultanate, giving them a share in the determination of the succession, and requiring their consent to all important state decisions and to foreign treaties.[1] The one sphere in which the Sultan's prestige received unchallenged expression was in ceremonial life. Here his status was affirmed by an elaborate system of protocol and tabu which maintained, by ritual observance, sumptuary restrictions and special forms of address, distinctions between ruler and subject which were in danger of being blurred by the intimacies of Malay village life.

The constitution and ceremonial of the Perak Court, and the titles and functions of the officers of state, were borrowed from Malacca practice, which again derived from Hindu ideas of kingship and government grafted on to Malay society during the pre-Islamic era. The state offices were ranked in multiples of four, a pattern which recurred in other Malay states and in Burma, Siam and Cambodia, and is thought to derive from Hindu cosmology. First came the four great chiefs, nearest the audience hall of the Sultan; then the eight major chiefs, then the sixteen—the last rank consisting of deputies and successors-designate of the four and the eight. The offices bore elaborate titles and administrative responsibilities which may have had some meaning in the great port kingdom of Malacca, but which had very little in a small agricultural riverine community. By the middle of the nineteenth century hardly anything remained of these functions except a residue of ceremony and symbolism which bore little relation to duties actually performed. They were in fact titular

[1] Treaties between Perak and the Dutch East India Company, executed in 1650 and 1655, were sealed by officers of the first rank and by the Laksamana (R. O. Winstedt, 'History of Perak', *JMBRAS*, vol. xii, part 1 (1934), p. 142). The Pangkor Engagement of 1874, whereby the chiefs accepted Raja Abdullah as Sultan, and accepted a British Resident, was sealed by three officers of the first rank and four of the second. Maxwell and Gibson, op. cit. pp. 28–30.

honours bestowed in recognition of local influence, and were usually associated with local rights of taxation and control, which consolidated the chief's influence in his district.

The chief exercised direct personal control over his district. His headquarters consisted of a self-sufficient household of about fifty followers, established in a palisaded compound in the chief village of his district. Here dependents of various kinds dealt with the affairs of his family, his following, his fields and mines, and his district generally. His family provided him with secretaries and accountants, who worked in return for their keep and either a small allowance or the opportunity to find pickings in their various occupations. Free volunteers and mercenaries in search of a patron made up his guard; debt bondmen and slaves provided him with domestics, boatmen and attendants of all kinds, while bondwomen provided nurses and servants for his household, and mistresses for his male followers. Slaves and bondmen also worked in the fields and gardens to feed this unproductive household. Labour needs that could not be provided within the household were met by the institution of forced labour (*kerah*), whereby the male inhabitants of each village were liable to answer any call from the chief to work on public or private undertakings, from clearing rivers and paths to poling boats and running messages.[1]

Control over the neighbouring villages was maintained through the village headmen or penghulus. These were usually hereditary appointments held in most cases by a member of one of the founding families of the village. Length of residence and association with the village, wealth, piety, all affected the choice of the penghulu. The appointment was made formally by the Sultan,[2] but this was usually a confirmation of a local choice, in which the qualifications of the candidates, the feeling of the villagers and the approval of the chiefs all played a part. The penghulu, who was sometimes a family connexion of the chief, was the link between chief and village. He collected the chief's taxes on a small commission basis (he was otherwise unpaid), he recruited and supervised the labour levies, he kept the chief informed of affairs in the village and referred all serious crime to him. In a crisis of authority he could count on the chief's support.

[1] See F. A. Swettenham, *The Real Malay*, London, 1900, p. 143, for an account of a chief's household.

[2] Report of Resident of Perak, 2 April 1875, C. 1320, enclosure 1 in no. 26. Clarke to Carnarvon, 26 April 1875.

But he was far more than merely the agent of his patron. He represented a practical compromise between outside control and village leadership. He was part of the village society and economy. He kept the peace, arbitrated in village quarrels and punished small crime with the help of other village worthies, the elders of families and the lay officers of the mosque.

Two British Residents with an intimate knowledge of the Malays—Swettenham and Clifford—have likened the relationship between chief and people to that between members of an old Scottish clan; 'they will do his bidding and take harsh treatment from him more contentedly than from anybody else'. Malays, speaking for themselves through their own folk sayings, are more cynical. Still, it is possible to understand what the Residents meant. For generations, chiefs and people had lived in close daily contact between the same narrow horizons; they had in common a local attachment of great importance. Also the chief, while often oppressing his people, did provide them with a shield in their quarrels with other groups. Where the safeguards of the clan system had disappeared and the rule of law had not yet developed, the chief provided a primitive social protection, though there was little protection from his own arbitrary decisions.

The economic resources of the Sultan and chiefs were extremely varied, but they derived mainly from two sources; services extracted from slaves, bondmen and kerah levies, and taxes on production and trade. Cultivation for subsistence was not taxed as a rule, nor was a capitation tax generally exacted. The Sultan's chief source of revenue was the collection of customs duties at the mouth of the Perak river. The chiefs had their own customs stations on their stretches of river; according to one British observer, 'every chief in his own place took something'. Some of the collections were leased to other Malays or to Chinese or Europeans; others were entrusted to agents who collected on a commission basis, so that the revenue collection ramified endlessly and gave profit to large numbers.[1]

In Selangor, as in Perak, control of the districts was in the hands of territorial chiefs, who derived economic power from similar sources, but the conquest of Selangor by Bugis princes was comparatively recent; the ruling Sultan in 1874—Abdul Samad—was only the fourth of his line. The Klang and Selangor rivers had formerly been subject to Malacca, and had been governed by headmen appointed by the

[1] See Appendix 1 for details of the Perak revenue system.

Malacca Sultans; but though there were occasional references
(c. 1874) to commoner officers of state, and though two of them were
included in the list of Selangor state pensioners drawn up after 1876,[1]
territorial power was in the hands of various members of the Bugis
royal family. In 1870, the Bernam, Selangor and Lukut rivers were
in the hands of Selangor rajas; Klang, which had once been a royal
district, was in the hands of Tengku Zia'u'd-din, the Sultan's son-in-
law,[2] and the Sultan himself had been driven by the disturbances of
1866–73 to take up his residence in Langat. (In 1833, when a full
establishment of penghulus was set up for Selangor, more than half
the appointments were held by rajas.)[3] The Bugis rajas ruled a predominantly Sumatran population; they dealt with their subjects, in
some cases by appointing local headmen, in others, by placing their
own relations in authority; and in each of the townships of Kuala
Selangor, Kuala Langat and Kuala Lumpur, a Dato' Dagang
('chief of foreigners', or synonymously 'chief of traders'), was placed
in charge of the foreign Malay population.[4] Thus in Selangor, a

[1] Braddell, citing Newbold, mentions four officers of state in 1874; the Penggawa Permatang, Penggawa Tuah, Penghulu Aroo and Orang Kaya Kechil
(Report of Proceedings at Salangore, 18 February 1874, C.1111, enclosure in no.
3, Clarke to Kimberley, 24 February 1874). Of these, the Dato' Aru appeared as
a member of a court appointed by the Sultan to try the Jugra pirates in February
1874, but none of the four appear by title after 1874 either as state pensioners or
holders of appointments. In 1881, an applicant for a state pension claimed to be
one of four officers—the Dato' Kaya, the Dato' Engku, the Dato' Mentri and the
Dato' Naga—formerly possessing jurisdiction over the Klang valley (To' Naga
to the Governor, 12 September 1881, Sel/Sec. 381/1881). Winstedt mentions a
To' Engku of Klang c.1700, a relative of the Johore Bendaharas (R. O. Winstedt,
'History of Selangor', *JMBRAS*, vol. xii, part 3 (1934), p. 3). After 1880 the Dato'
Kaya and the Dato' Engku Klang became state pensioners, living in retirement in
Singapore; the others do not appear by title in the lists either of pensioners or
penghulus. To' Engku Klang had also disappeared from the lists of pensioners by
1891.
[2] See below, p. 34.
[3] SCM, 2 September 1883.
[4] In Kuala Lumpur in the 1860's there was a Dato' Dagang, privileged to levy
$1 on each bhara of tin exported from the district ('AbdulSamad b. Ahmad, [ed.],
Kenang2an Selangor, [*Recollections of Selangor*], *Kuala Lumpur, 1937*, p. 5).
In 1877 the tax was commuted for a pension (Swettenham, Report on the Accounts of the Native States for 1877, C. 2410, enclosure in no. 6). This Dato'
Dagang was probably Haji Mohammed Tahir, a resident of Klang, pioneer
coffee planter, and Malay contractor in the Klang and Kuala Langat districts.
His descendants still live in Kampong Jawa in Klang. There was also a Dato'
Dagang Nakhoda Allang in Kuala Selangor (Sel/Sec. 143/77), and a Dato'
Dagang Abu Said in Kuala Langat (Sel/Sec. 181/76 and 89/77). Under Malay
rule the Dato' Dagang appears to have been placed over Malay settlers of many
different places of origin, a situation which caused much dissatisfaction (SCM, 12

state where the population was heterogeneous in the extreme, where the ruling class was recently immigrant and the district chiefs of royal birth, there do not appear to have been the same links, deriving from kin connexions and common territorial origin, that existed between the district and village heads in Perak.

Pahang had been more closely associated than any other state with the old empire of Malacca-Johore, with certain consequences for her political structure.[1] The first Sultans of Pahang, established in the fifteenth century, were descended from the line of Malacca Sultans, and after the capture of Malacca by the Portuguese, the Pahang Sultans continued to acknowledge the suzerainty of the Sultans of Johore and to be installed by them. The suzerainty of Johore was interrupted by an Achehnese invasion in the seventeenth century, and the succession of Pahang kings ended; but on the Achehnese withdrawal in 1641, Pahang again came under the rule of the Johore dynasty. In the eighteenth century, a line of Bendaharas, descended from Johore Sultans, was established in Pahang. They were the *wakil mu'tallak* (fully accredited representatives) of the Johore Sultans, owed allegiance to them and were installed by them, but they were virtually independent rulers. The Anglo-Dutch Treaty of 1824, which divided the Riau-Johore empire into British and Dutch spheres of influence, removed the Pahang Bendaharas still further from their acknowledged suzerains, who were now in the Dutch sphere. In 1863, Ahmad, brother of the ruling Bendahara, took office by right of conquest and was installed as Bendahara by his own chiefs; in 1882 he assumed the title of Sultan, and in 1884 was proclaimed by his chiefs with the style of Sultan Ahmad Mu'atham Shah.

Like the Perak office holders, those in Pahang were arranged in groups of four (*orang besar berempat*), eight (*orang besar berlapan*), and sixteen (*orang kaya enambelas*), but there were considerable differences between the two states in the relative powers and dignities of the chiefs of the first and second rank. Since Pahang was nominally part of the dominions of Johore, the Johore court offices of Bendahara and *Temenggong* (also found in Perak) were not duplicated in Pahang till a separate Pahang sultanate was established in 1884, when

June 1877). The different trading communities were also represented by their own *ketuas* (headmen) but these do not appear to have had official appointments. In 1877 Nakhoda Allang was pensioned off, and Abu Said banished for misconduct and their appointments abolished.

[1] This account is taken largely from W. Linehan, 'History of Pahang', *JMBRAS*, vol. xiv, part 2 (1936), pp. 1–256, *passim*.

these titles were bestowed on relatives of Sultan Ahmad.[1] The great officers of Pahang, the orang besar berempat, were territorial chiefs.[2] Their titles date back at least to the eighteenth century; and though they owed allegiance directly to the Bendaharas, it is possible that they were ruling their districts under the Sultans of Johore before the advent of the Bendaharas. Between them, they held the tributaries of the Pahang (except the Tembeling) to the southern, eastern and northern borders of the state; their districts were larger than those of any Perak chief, and within them they held absolute power over their subjects, while in their turn they owed their ruler the usual obligations to military assistance, ceremonial attendance, counsel and tribute.

The orang besar berlapan, who held districts for the most part within the territories of the four major chiefs, were neither as powerful nor as well established as the orang besar of the same rank in Perak. Though according to Pahang custom they formed, with the orang besar berempat, the foundation on which the ruler's power rested, the majority possessed no long-established tradition, and in only one case does the record of title-holders go back as far as the eighteenth century.[3]

There was in addition to these three ranks of chiefs, a class of *orang besar raja* (the raja's great men) who owed their position directly to the ruler's favour. The Pahang war of succession provided opportunities for the emergence of such men, and one of them, Imam Perang Indera Gajah, was rewarded with a large district, and approached the greatest of the chiefs in importance. The Sultan at Pekan was assisted by secretaries and advisers without titles, but with an influence well known to the British in particular, and much deplored by them. Sultan Ahmad had shown during the Pahang War a mil-

---

[1] The earlier Bendaharas of Pahang were Bendaharas of the joint kingdom of Johore-Pahang.

[2] The chiefs and their districts were the Orang Kaya Indera Maharaja Perba (To' Raja) of Jelai, the Orang Kaya Indera Segera of Temerloh, the Orang Kaya Indera Pahlawan of Chenor, and the Orang Kaya Indera Shahbandar. The jurisdiction of the last-named extended from Luit to Bebar. Linehan, op. cit. appendix iii, pp. 188–97.

[3] This was the Orang Kaya Setia Wangsa (or, as he was occasionally styled, the Orang Kaya Setia Lela) of Lipis, in the district of the Maharaja Perba. Another of the eight, the Orang Kaya Setia Perkasa Pahlawan of Semantan achieved prominence in the reign of Ahmad because of the services rendered by the then holder during the Pahang War. The Lipis and Semantan chiefs, particularly the former, at this time wielded an influence close to that of the major chiefs. Ibid. pp. 197–9.

itary skill and capacity for leadership which kept him more effectively in control of his chiefs than the rulers of Perak and Selangor; and while the complaints of British officers in the last two states were of social disruption, civil war and local oppression, their chief complaints in Pahang were of a degree of oppression and extortion by the *budak raja* (young men of the Sultan's following) beyond that experienced elsewhere. But despite the stronger hold of the Sultan of Pahang over his chiefs, he was as dependent as the rulers of Perak and Selangor on the traditional modes of government through territorial chiefs.

In nineteenth-century Malay society, the old pattern of small, self-sufficient peasant communities, living by internally regulated custom, was essentially preserved, but with important changes. Tribal controls had long been superseded by the personal rule of local chiefs, and though society was still partitioned into small local loyalties, all were in principle united under a single acknowledged head of state. A social and political formula appropriate to these conditions had long been established, it had weathered many strains, and there seemed no reason why it should not persist indefinitely. But already in the neighbouring world, social and economic forces were gathering which were to change the foundations of life and government in the Malay states.

TIN AND THE CHINESE

For a thousand years or more, Malaya's chief interest for foreign traders lay in her mineral and particularly her tin supplies. Old mines, ascribed by modern Malays to 'the Siamese', are thought by some scholars to be the work of colonists who brought an Indo-Chinese bronze culture to Malaya about 2,000 years ago. Tin is mentioned as a staple of commerce from the ninth century; in the fifteenth century it was the chief support of the trade of Malacca. According to sixteenth-century Portuguese writers, there was a standard tin currency from Java to Lower Burma, and all transactions at Malacca were made in tin or gold.[1]

All the states in the Peninsula have been mentioned at various times as tin exporters; but probably because of their proximity to

[1] R. O. Winstedt, *The Malays; a Cultural History*, London, 1953, pp. 112–13; Tomé Pires, *Suma Oriental*, 2 vols. Hakluyt Society, 1944, vol. i, p. 94, n. 1; vol. ii, pp. 260–1, 275.

Malacca, the west coast states were the most prominent. The country from Linggi to Kedah was known as the 'tin lands' and provided Malacca with a large tin tribute. After the fall of Malacca, the Portuguese, and later the Dutch, tried to secure a monopoly of the tin of these states. Dutch treaties with Perak, Selangor and the Linggi states provided for the enforced sale of all tin to the Company at a buyer's price, and Dutch forts commanding the Perak and Selangor river mouths enforced compliance.

Until the nineteenth century, tin mining was a Malay industry, controlled by members of the royal and chiefly families. They enjoyed a large part of the profits, either by direct ownership of the mines, or by levying tribute on production and export. The carriage of the tin was also in their hands. The Malacca Sultans and Bendaharas took part in trading ventures as a matter of course; in the seventeenth century, Dutch records describe the large trading expeditions of the Sultan of Kedah, carrying tin to the Coromandel coast; and even in the 1860's, Malay rajas and chiefs still had a share in the tin trade and the return trade in miners' provisions. There was no attempt by the Portuguese or Dutch, in the period of their ascendancy, to take a direct part in the industry, or stimulate its development beyond occasional loans to rulers on the security of the tin supplies. They appeared content to siphon off the produce, and it was of course contrary to their monopolistic practice to permit individuals in their colony to trade directly with the Malay tin producers. Tin-mining therefore remained a local industry, financed internally from the resources of the ruling class.

In the nineteenth century the whole picture changed, in a way which meant not only a revolution in the tin industry, but a fundamental change in the structure of society. Between 1786 and 1819, British settlements were established in Penang, Malacca and Singapore,[1] and the tin trade was thrown open to private individuals. The great development of the Straits Settlements, the expansion of population and trade stimulated a search for new fields of enterprise; and Chinese finance, labour and mining techniques were introduced into the Malayan tin industry. European and Chinese merchants in Malacca, the natural outlet for the tin of Lukut, Sungei Ujong and other parts of the Negri Sembilan, appear to have been the first to engage in large-scale investment in the mines. At first their invest-

[1] The English East India Company took Malacca from the Dutch in 1795; they returned it in 1819, but resumed it permanently in 1825.

ments took the form of advances of money, rice and opium direct to the chiefs,[1] who in turn provided the miners with these necessities, bought the tin at a favourable price, and resold it at a profit.[2] The advances to the chiefs, and their interest in the industry as investors and traders, continued throughout the period of Malay rule; but in the 1830's production in Sungei Ujong and Lukut was already passing into the hands of Chinese management and labour.[3] In the 1840's and 1850's great new tin fields were discovered at Larut in Perak, and Kuala Lumpur in Selangor, and their development was entirely in Chinese hands. While continuing their advances to the chiefs, the Chinese traders in the settlements advanced direct to Chinese mine-owners and mine-managers in the fields,[4] the Malay chiefs tapping the flow of wealth from the mines by drawing an agreed tribute.

Investment was accompanied by the introduction of Chinese mining methods and machinery which made possible, for the first time, the full-time employment of a large labour force, recruited by mass

[1] The development of the Larut fields was initiated by a Malay chief, 'Che Long Ja'afar, who advanced money to the Chinese miners in his district. It was only in his son's time (c. 1858–74) that the Chinese worked the mines with their money (Evidence of Ah Kwee, Report of Larut Commissioners, 21 February 1874, Swettenham Papers, no. 72). In Selangor also, the advancers were initially Malays. In 1839 Raja Juma'at, son-in-law of the Sultan of Selangor, became surety for his father-in-law for $169,000 owed to Malacca merchants (Irving, Memorandum on the Lukut grant, 17 January 1879, CO 273/98). The loan was almost certainly made as a speculation on the development of tin land. In the late 1840's the Sultan again borrowed from Malacca merchants—one Eurasian and three Chinese—to prospect on the upper Klang; and in the 1850's his son-in-law borrowed money from two Malacca Chinese and with $30,000 began to prospect in the same area; the discovery of the Kuala Lumpur fields followed. S.M. Middlebrook, 'Yap Ah Loy', JMBRAS vol. xxiv, part 2 (1951), pp. 17–18 and 102, note. 6.

[2] An example of the way in which some chiefs exploited the miners is given in an account of Chinese mining in Patani, just across the Perak border. The agreement enforced the sale of all tin to a Patani chief at about half the local market price, and gave him the right to supply provisions at favourable rates (W. E. Maxwell, 'A Journey on Foot' pp. 58–59.).

[3] Newbold, writing in the 1830's, refers to the massacre of 1,000 Chinese miners in Sungei Ujong by Malays in 1828 and the despatch of 400 more miners to the state by Malacca merchants in 1830; he also mentions a rebellion by 300 400 Chinese miners in Lukut in 1834, against their Malay masters. Newbold, op. cit. vol. ii, pp. 33, 96–97.

[4] Braddell, in a historical account of British relations with Sungei Ujong, states that Malacca traders, who had advanced money, rice and opium to the chiefs on account of tin supplies, began advancing direct to the miners c. 1840. Proceedings of Government relating to the Native States in the Malayan Peninsula, C.1320, enclosure in no. 8, Clarke to Carnarvon, 29 December 1874.

Chinese immigration. Malayan tin is alluvial, occurring at the base of hills flanking the main mountain range. The ore appears as heavy granules in a stratum of gravel and sand, six to thirty feet under an unproductive soil overburden, and mining consists simply of removing the overburden and lifting and washing the tin sand. Malay mining consisted of breaking down the soil sides of the tin working and shovelling the pay dirt into a stream of running water; the particles of ore fell to the bottom while the earth was carried away by the stream. It was a simple process which cost little initial outlay, but was wasteful both of tin and labour. It was a method adapted to work in small valleys and along hillsides; it was not adapted to deep excavations which in the Malayan climate would in any case have been under water for most of the year. Working therefore tended to be distributed over a large number of small, shallow mines which were soon exhausted; it was carried on intermittently by a few Malays at a time, usually in addition to their other occupations.[1]

The Chinese introduced an ingenious hydraulic device, used to irrigate rice fields in South China,[2] which enabled them to drain the mines and at the same time direct the drainage waters into long wooden gutters where the ore was washed. It consisted of an endless chain of wooden troughs revolving round a wheel turned by muscle-power—or more commonly, in Malayan tin mines, by water-power. The equipment was simple and cheap enough, but it enabled the Chinese to make deep excavations (typical of Chinese mine workings) reaching down to the ore strata at low levels, and providing regular work for a large and specialized labour force. The tin was smelted in clay or brick ovens many times more efficient in their use of labour than the Malay oven.[3] The rest of the equipment consisted of wooden hoes, baskets for the ore, notched wooden beams giving access to the mine floor, and a palm-leaf shed to house the miners.

The introduction of these methods made possible a great expansion in the industry. The interest of Malacca traders in the Negri Sembilan fields was soon followed by heavy investment in Selangor, and the dis-

[1] R. O. Winstedt, 'Malay Arts and Crafts' in Wilkinson, *Papers on Malay Subjects* (1st Series), Industries, part 1, pp. 27–33. Swettenham describes one disused Malay mine in Kuala Selangor, dating from about 1800, which possessed an elaborate system of dams and sluices for washing the ore, but such works were exceptional. Report of the Assistant Resident, Selangor, 8 April 1875, C.1320, enclosure in no. 28, Clarke to Carnarvon, 27 April 1875.

[2] D. H. Grist, *Rice*, London, 1953, p. 28.

[3] Wong Lin Ken, *The Malayan Tin Industry to 1914*, Association for Asian Studies Monographs and Papers, no. xiv, Tucson, 1965, pp. 45 and 50–52.

covery of rich deposits in Larut in 1848 began a tin rush from the neighbouring settlement of Penang. In the 1830's, Newbold estimated the tin output for Selangor at about 1,200 *bharas* annually, mostly from the mines of Lukut, Klang and 'Langkat'. In 1872 the Kuala Lumpur field, which had first begun exporting in 1859, was alone exporting 1,000 bharas a month.[1] In the 1830's, Perak production came mainly from mines on the Kinta, Batang Padang, Bidor and upper Perak rivers, and Newbold estimated the annual export at roughly 3,000 bharas. In 1871, Penang's yearly import from Larut alone was about 11,000 bharas.[2] The value of the tin imports in proportion to total imports into Malacca for this period shows a spectacular rise. Between 1825 and 1835 the tin imports from the Malay states (i.e. from the Negri Sembilan and Selangor mines) into Malacca averaged 91,158 sicca rupees out of an average of 1,123,187 sicca rupees for all imports; in 1870, after the field at Kuala Lumpur had come into production, the tin import was $898,178 out of a total for all imports of $2,260,875.[3]

These economic changes took place in conjunction with a social change of even greater importance—the first large-scale immigration of the Chinese into the Malay states. Before the nineteenth century the Chinese colonies in Malaya were small settlements of merchants, established during the long history of trade with China. The oldest recorded community was that of the Malacca Chinese founded during the rule of the Malay Sultans. This was probably the first, and certainly the largest of many such settlements all over the Peninsula— licensed communities of traders and craftsmen living usually in the Sultan's village at the river mouth. In the 1830's there was hardly an

[1] Newbold, op. cit. vol. i, p. 425; Petition of Malacca Traders to Singapore Chamber of Commerce, 27 July 1872, C.1111, enclosure in no. 1, Ord to Kimberley, 6 November 1872. Bhara=3 piculs=400 lbs.

[2] Newbold, op. cit. vol. ii, p. 23; *Straits Daily Times*, 19 March 1872. The figure of 10,000 bharas a year for the Larut export to Penang c. 1870–2 is supported from other sources. The Penang trade figures for 1870 put the import from the Malay states (excluding Siam) at 13,000 bharas; this probably included the Perak river export of about 3,000 bharas (Revenue figures for Penang for 1870, in C.1038 of 1875, *Statistical Tables relating to the Colonies and other Possessions of the United Kingdom*). In 1874, when the mines were brought into working order under British administration, after the troubles of 1873, the average production for the last four months of the year was 840 bharas a month. Report of the Asst. Resident, Perak, for 1874, appendix iii, C.1320, enclosure in no. 20.

[3] Newbold, op. cit. vol. i, p. 149; Revenue figures for Malacca for 1870, C.1038 of 1875. The actual figure given for the total value of Malacca's imports in 1870 was £452,475 sterling, and this has been converted into dollars at the rate of 4s to $1.

important river-settlement in Malaya or south Siam which did not have such a community, well-established, accepted and reasonably prosperous, living in one quarter of the Sultan's township. These were permanently settled communities, whose founders had inter-married with Malaysian women and had thereby established a hybrid type characteristic of Malayan society; sentimentally attached to a mother culture, but soon acquiring the patina of a new environment, and sharing with the 'local-born' of other races, a common fund of new experience. These settlements—particularly that of Malacca—formed the nucleus of the Straits Chinese community, long-estab-lished, prosperous, enjoying a stable family life, yet most adaptable and responsive to new influences and new cultural forms.

In the nineteenth century, this leisurely, stable type of settlement was succeeded by a new immigration pattern—the wholesale importa-tion of adult male labourers. They came mostly from the maritime provinces of Kwangtung and Fukien in south China, the traditional place of origin of Chinese immigrants to South-East Asia. They were recruited in Macao, Hong Kong and South China ports by coolie-brokers, stowed in junks under slave-trade conditions and shipped to the Straits as indentured labour. On arrival they were bound to mine-owners for a year or more, until the cost of their initial advances had been worked off. They were then free to try independent mining or trading if they were exceptionally fortunate, or to continue, as most of them did, to work in the mines as wage or contract labour.

On leaving China, the immigrants were cut adrift from all the normal bases of authority and all their family and neighbourhood bonds. They came to a strange country where language barriers cut them off from communication with all but their fellow-Chinese; and with these, their only links were associations based on clan member-ship or common place of origin in China. The fortunate were helped by prosperous clansmen and relations; but the majority had no con-tacts except with employers and fellow immigrants. In the hard and dangerous conditions of the Malay states, the mine dormitories pro-vided the only shelter and protection they knew. Their domestic lives and social activities revolved round their work. They lived near the mines in large dormitories (*kongsi*-houses)[1]—atap sheds housing

---

[1] *Kongsi:* any joint association for common social, economic or political ends. An excellent description of a mining kongsi-house is to be found in J. C. P[asqual], 'Chinese tin-mining in Selangor', *Selangor Journal*, vol. iv, no. 2 (4 October 1895) and vol. iv, no. 10 (24 January 1896). See also Swettenham, *The Real Malay*, op. cit. pp. 54–55.

twenty to a hundred men and run by the mine-manager. The barest needs—shelter, a suit of clothes and a rice allowance—were provided free. Everything else was provided by the mine-owner at a considerable profit. The government records make matter-of-fact reference to the incidents of the miner's life, the gambling booth, the opium shop, the arrack shop, the brothel, the pawnshop and the home for destitutes. In this pattern of hard work, barrack life and barrack companionship and amusements, thousands of Chinese lived and died in the second half of the nineteenth century, initiating the profound changes in Malayan life and society which have continued ever since.

The size of the Chinese mining population in the 1870's has been the subject of various estimates, but there was no count made before British intervention, and the population, like most pioneer mining populations, fluctuated wildly with changes in the tin price and the productivity of the fields. It was also much affected by political conditions; in the decade before British intervention, the continuous troubles in the Malay states made life and work precarious and caused large internal migrations. It is therefore impossible to establish numbers. The estimates do however at least indicate the scale of the Chinese influx. Larut in north-west Perak had hardly any Chinese in 1848 when tin was first found there. In 1872 there was a Chinese population estimated at 20,000 to 25,000. In 1873 the population dropped with the secret society wars; but at the end of 1874 after a year of British administration, it recovered, and was estimated at 26,000. In Selangor, prospecting on the upper Klang began in 1857 with eighty-seven men. This was the beginning of the Kuala Lumpur fields; in 1872 the number of miners at work there was estimated at 12,000.[1]

[1] The Perak figures for 1872 are in Irving, Memorandum relative to the Affairs of Perak, 24 July 1872, C.1111, enclosure 6 in no. 52, Clarke to Kimberley, 24 February 1874; the figures for 1874 are in the Report of Assistant Resident, Perak, 2 April 1875, C.1320, enclosure in no. 20. The Selangor figures for 1874 are from the Petition of Malacca Traders to Singapore Chamber of Commerce, 27 July 1872, C.1111, enclosure in no. 1. (In 1880, a rough count by the Supt. of Police, Selangor, placed the mining population at 12,424. Sel/Sec. 11/80.) Figures for the Malays and Chinese, Perak and Selangor, in 1879 and 1884, are given below.

	Perak 1879	Selangor 1884
Malays (including unfree)	59,682	17,097
Chinese	20,373	28,236
Total population	81,084	46,568

Source: Census of Perak, 1891, and AR Selangor, 1884.

The mines were for the most part away from traditional Malay areas of settlement. The Larut valley and the upper Klang were hardly inhabited before the Chinese influx; clearing the jungle was an essential prelude to settlement and took a heavy toll of miners. The situation of the mining areas, and the close organization of the Chinese population, meant that they lived in autonomous communities under their own leadership. The nucleus of the community was the mining kongsi. It might consist of half a dozen men sharing a hut near a small mine in a lonely jungle clearing, or it might be one of many large mines grouped round a thriving township, with a market, gambling-booth, shops, theatres and secret society lodges. The remoter mines lived outside all authority, regulating their own affairs; but in the large centres the miners were organized politically in secret societies, into which immigrants were inducted. Secret societies had existed in China for centuries, and during the Manchu dynasty had taken on a political aspect, stimulating resistance to the Manchu invaders and encouraging anti-dynastic rebellions in China in the eighteenth and nineteenth centuries. In Malaya they became the harsh instruments of group control, developed by a struggling immigrant community in a strange and potentially hostile environment. Fear, isolation, the absence of all traditional authority, the complete estrangement from an alien and incomprehensible government, resulted in a deliberate withdrawal within a mutual protection society which tried to exclude external contacts altogether and itself perform the functions of government, raise revenues by the levy of protection money or by compulsory subscription, regulate the behaviour of members, arbitrate in their quarrels, punish transgressions and protect members in their conflicts with the government or with rival societies. Inevitably the society became tyrannical in its relationship with members, and hostile to all other institutions which might divert their loyalty.

The Malayan societies were offshoots of the Triad, the parent society in China, from which they derived their ritual, symbolism, cryptic signs and disciplinary codes. They were not organized on a territorial basis, and in principle they cut across territorial and even kin divisions; but the lodges came to be identified with particular territorial and kin groups. The two societies most prominent in the nineteenth century Malay states—the Ghi Hin and the Hai San— were identified in the 1870's with the Cantonese and Khehs (Hakkas) respectively, the former from the south and west, the latter from the north-east of Kwangtung Province. In the Straits Settlements from about 1850 these societies were in opposition to each other. Territorial antagonisms in China may have contributed to the hostility between the lodges in Malaya, but local economic competition for revenue monopolies and—in the Malay states—for tin concessions, certainly intensified if it did not initiate the conflicts. The secret societies were organized in Penang, Singapore and Malacca soon after the establishment of British rule and soon came to dominate the life of the Chinese; and since Chinese mining enterprise in the Malay States was initiated by the community in the Straits Settlements, it was natural that the mining colonies in the states should carry with them their secret society affiliations. The Larut colony in particular was economically and politically a dependency of the Chinese community in Penang and the Penang and Larut secret societies acknowledged a common leadership.

The secret societies dominated the life of the community in the Malay states even more than in the Straits Settlements, for in the Malay states there was no government able to challenge their authority. Leadership in the community was expressed in terms of secret society leadership. The society headmen combined political and economic power; they were the chief advancers, the importers and employers of labour and the tax farmers; and their political authority in turn provided opportunities for an immense increase in economic power. They rose from immigrant beginnings, in conditions of great hardship and violence; they were 'thrown up by the test of personal courage and force of character combined with economic success'. Their administration had a simple materialist objective—to maintain services essential to tin production. To that end they built mining tracks, kept order in the community, arbitrated in disputes, supervised markets, and opium, spirit and gambling shops and, most important of all, organized the defence of the mines.

The headmen constituted the link between the Chinese community and the Malay chiefs in whose districts the mines were established. They were officially recognized as leaders of the Chinese, and went by the historic title of *Capitan China*. The style of 'Capitan' is recorded in the time of the Malacca Sultans and the practice of treating with the Chinese community through these headmen persisted to the end of the nineteenth century, in the Portuguese, Dutch and British settlements as well as in the Malay states. The Malay chiefs negotiated conditions of mining with the Capitans, leased them the farms of monopolies, consulted with them on all matters relating to the mines and the Chinese community, and joined with them in military action. In Selangor, where the Capitan of Kuala Lumpur, Yap Ah Loy, and the Malay Ruler of Klang were thrown into close mutual dependence, the investiture of the Capitan by the Malay Raja was a formal ceremony in which Chinese and Malay ceremonial elements combined, and where the recipient appeared in Malay dress.[1]

The accounts of the times are full of references to the business contacts between Chinese and Malays, and the military alliances they established in defence of common economic interests. But their only point of contact was the tin industry—the Chinese world. Outside this they found nothing in common. Their respective areas of settlement, economic concerns, social institutions and objectives were utterly different. The Chinese in their mining kongsis and the Malays in their riverine *kampongs* lived in mutual isolation, following their separate ways under separate dispensations.

Yet though the life of the majority of Malays remained unchanged by the Chinese influx, the requirements of the tin industry, the presence of communities of Indian, Arab, and foreign Malay traders, and the influence of the business and social world of the Straits Settlements did induce certain changes in the way of life and methods of government of the chiefs with the largest stake in the mining districts. The Mentri of Perak, the district chief of Larut,[2] adopted certain western practices in his domestic and business affairs. He kept carriages in Larut (though he had only seven miles of corduroy road on which to drive them); according to report he banked his money in Penang and invested in houses and land there;[3] he retained a Penang lawyer, and in 1872 he owned or chartered two of the four steamers carrying tin from Larut to Penang.[4] In administrative matters, however, he remained a conservative. The task of keeping order

[1] See Middlebrook, op. cit. pp. 40–41, for an account of the installation of Yap Ah Loy by Raja Mahdi in Kuala Lumpur in 1869. The biography gives an invaluable account of the life of a Chinese mining community in a Malay state.

[2] See note on Mentri below.

[3] Mohammed Ibrahim b. Abdullah, op. cit. p. 76. Mohammed Ibrahim b. Abdullah (Mohammed Ibrahim Munshi) was a son of the famous grammarian Abdullah b. Abdul Kadir, author of *Hikayat Abdullah*, and like his father had been employed as a Malay teacher by the Straits Government. In 1872 he was in the service of the Maharaja of Johore, who permitted him to accompany Irving, the Straits Auditor-General, as interpreter on a mission to Selangor and Perak. This account of his travels contains penetrating descriptions of the places he visited as well as of the confidential interviews at which he assisted.

[4] Irving, Memorandum relative to the Affairs of Perak, op. cit.

was delegated in the traditional manner to Chinese leaders. In 1872 he is reported to have had forty police in Larut;[1] a visitor remarked that he was unable to say to what extent the Mentri was supposed to exercise government over these people, but his impression was that 'in the main, they governed themselves'.[2] Revenue collection was similarly delegated; until August 1873, at any rate, the Mentri was content to farm the mining rights of Larut to a Chinese headman for a fixed monthly rent, leaving him to allocate the mining land and make what profit he could.[3]

In Selangor, Tengku Zia'u'd-din, the ruler of Klang and Kuala Selangor from about 1870 to 1874, was a thoroughgoing admirer of European manners and customs, retained a European lawyer and adviser who was much in his confidence, and modelled his private life and his administration on what he saw of European methods in the neighbouring colony. His tastes included many things contrary to Islam and Malay custom; he kept two large imported dogs which scandalized a Malay visitor by running hither and thither growling 'like tigers' and covering their master with unclean caresses; he and his chief subordinate (Syed Zin b. Mohammed Puteh al-Habshi, a Penang Malay of Arab descent) drank sherry with European guests while their Malay guests drank Russian syrup; he had given all the streets in Klang English names—Beach Street, Market Street, Wharf Street, China Street, Hospital Street, Mosque Street—and when a Malay guest protested that it was a great pity, since Klang was a Malay country, not to give the streets Malay names, Syed Zin insisted that English names were good.[4]

Tengku Zia'u'd-din employed traditional methods of government where they were appropriate; his military strength came partly from

[1] Skinner, Precis of Perak Affairs, 10 January 1874, C.1111, enclosure 1 in no. 52, Clarke to Kimberley, 24 February 1874.
[2] Irving, Memorandum relative to Affairs of Perak, op. cit.
[3] Statement by the Mentri at Penang, 26 August 1873, C.1111, enclosure 6 in no. 52, Clarke to Kimberley, 24 February 1874. But there is evidence that in February 1874 he was collecting revenues on his own account. F. A. Swettenham, Report of the Larut Commissioners, 21 February 1874, Swettenham Papers, no. 72.
[4] Mohammed Ibrahim b. Abdullah, op. cit. pp. 44–46. Tengku Zia'u'd-din's purchases from a firm of general traders in Singapore between April 1872 and July 1873 included a meerschaum pipe, tobacco, two boxes of havana cigars, toothbrushes and toothpaste, a gold eyeglass, a dozen collars, six flannel shirts, a length of tweed, a bottle of port wine, a corkscrew, a microscope, a dog collar and a cheese. Edward Koek, advocate and attorney, Singapore, to Resident of Selangor, 2 November 1876, Sel/Sec. 235/76.

a large Malay following (he had 200 men from Kedah with him in Klang in 1872) and he placed his Malay supporters in charge of districts on the Klang and Selangor rivers. But his headquarters, Klang, was the scene of many innovations. On a visit to Selangor in 1872, Charles Irving, the Straits Auditor-General, was impressed by the prosperous air of Klang and by its growth since Tengku Zia'u'd-din occupied it in 1870. He found a busy wood and atap township of about 3,000 people of many races, Malay, Arab, Chinese, Eurasian, Tamil, Bengali, and *peranakan* (native-born foreigners) from Penang, Malacca and Singapore. It was growing so fast that houses were being rented before they were finished. Roads were being built, and there was a plan for Klang showing sites for a courthouse, a police station, a hospital, a gaol and a mosque. Tengku Zia'u'd-din collected his own revenues at Klang in the form of duties in cash and kind; the tin collected was sent to Malacca in his chartered steamer *Telegraph* and sold to his Malacca Chinese backer, Baba Tek Ee. He maintained a small garrison of about eighty men in Kuala Lumpur, but made no attempt to keep order among the Chinese there; this he left to the Capitan China. In Klang, however, he maintained about 230 sepoys, Tamils, Bengalis and Malays, under three or four European officers.

Tengku Zia'u'd-din's enterprise won much praise from Irving.

> He understands, what it seems so difficult for Asiatics to understand, that if the State is to be rich the people must be numerous and prosperous . . . he encourages settlers by free grants of land; he encourages the tin-mining by the moderation and uniformity of the dues; he is opening up the country by new roads; preserving order by the creation of a regular police; and is about to put the administration of justice on a sound footing under the advice of a European lawyer of Singapore of good reputation.

Irving thought he had not only sagacity and aptitude for business but certain moral qualifications as well, such as 'the desire to do justice, consistency of purpose, and a certain dignity of thought and conduct, which enabled him to hold his own and to preserve order among the very heterogeneous set of people that he has got about him'. But if Irving approved, there were others who looked at his administration with a more critical eye. Munshi Mohammed Ibrahim, who accompanied Irving in 1872,[1] was critical of the dirt and slovliness which he saw about him. He was unimpressed by the turn-out

[1] See footnote 3, p. 26.

of the sepoys; their European officers, he thought, were vagrants who could not get work in Singapore, the sepoys were all shapes and sizes, dirty and ill-clad—'some had trousers, some had sarongs, some had jackets, some did not' ('*ada berseluar ada berkain ada berbaju ada yang tidak*').[1] In 1871, on a previous visit, Irving had suggested ways in which Tengku Zia'u'd-din might improve his financial administration, but in 1874 all was still in disorder; the accounts for the last six months had not been kept systematically, receipts and payments having been made by the same person and only occasionally recorded.[2]

The chief who was most successful in adapting his administration to new needs was Raja Juma'at of Selangor, who governed the district of Lukut under grant from the Sultan until his death in 1864. With the help of advice from friendly British officials, he achieved a standard of public order rivalling that of the neighbouring settlement of Malacca. His friend the Resident Councillor of Malacca, who visited Selangor in 1860, described Lukut in the following terms:

The contrast between Lukut and Selangor is very striking; indeed the former can well bear comparison with any European Settlement; and it is equally striking and gratifying in the midst of a dense jungle to come suddenly upon the footprints of advanced civilization. The roads are well formed and macadamized; the [as yet] only street of China town is uniformly built of brick and tiled roof, kept scrupulously clean and well-drained; the godowns on the river's bank are large and massively built, and both the people and the place have an air of contentment and prosperity. . . . The Police Peons are dressed similarly to ours in Malacca, and the arrangements in the Police Station which I inspected are perfect. An object of much interest to me was the Gambling Farm; it is a large square building and there are Police Peons stationed at each of the four doors. . . . Although crowded with players the most perfect order and quiet reigned . . . Raja Jumaat's house is situated upon a hill which he is strongly fortifying; and a carriage-road, winding around, leads to the top. . . . Prisoners in chains were employed upon the work.[3]

The prosperity of Lukut was not sustained after his death. The mines were less productive, and his sons had little understanding of business

[1] Irving, Memorandum relative to a Visit in Selangor in 1872, 24 July 1872, *Papers relating to the Malay Peninsula, 1870–1882,* ANM; Mohammed Ibrahim b. Abdullah, op. cit. pp. 42–5, *passim.*

[2] Report of Assistant Resident with the Sultan of Selangor, 18 December 1874, C. 1111, enclosure in no. 75, Clarke to Carnarvon, 23 March 1875.

[3] Cited in R. J. Wilkinson, *History of the Peninsular Malays,* Singapore, 1923, pp. 143–4.

or government; by 1874 the revenue had fallen from an estimated $15,000 a month at Juma'at's death to $300 a month.[1]

In varying degrees the chiefs of the main tin districts adapted their administrative methods to new needs and opportunities. Tengku Zia'u'd-din and Raja Juma'at, in particular, established garrisons and police forces as nearly as they could on the model of the neighbouring settlements; they had begun to make roads, though not as yet beyond their own townships; and Tengku Zia'u'd-din had liberal plans for the development of Klang, though admittedly these still existed only on paper. But these limited innovations depended entirely on the initiative and vigour of individual chiefs, who had no sovereign authority, who were unable to ensure continuity of effort, and who had to work within a traditional spoils system, made anarchic by increasing rivalry for the mines.

CIVIL WAR

In 1870 the main tin centres were in Perak, in the north-west coast province of Larut; in Selangor, on the upper Klang (the Kuala Lumpur field) and on the upper Selangor, and in Sungei Ujong on the upper Linggi. The development of Larut dated from about 1850, and was controlled by the Mentri, Che Ngah Ibrahim, who had inherited the concession from his father, and who had obtained the title in consideration of his wealth and influence.[2] The Mentri ruled Larut and made his own financial and political arrangements with Chinese mining leaders, without reference to the Sultan; he was bound only by the obligation to pay to the Sultan $6 on every bhara of tin exported. In 1873 the Sultan, Ismail, lived forty miles away on the middle Perak; there is no record that he ever visited Larut or

[1] Report of the Assistant Resident, Selangor, 8 April 1875, C.1320, enclosure in no. 28, Clarke to Carnarvon, 27 April 1875. This estimate of Raja Juma'at's revenue is probably excessive. Another estimate, of $7,000 to $8,000 a month, is probably closer to the mark. Memorandum by Resident of Selangor, 23 April 1878, enclosed in Robinson to Hicks Beach, 248 of 13 August 1878, CO 273/95.

[2] The Mentri, 'Che Ngah Ibrahim, was a family connexion of the Panglima Bukit Gantang, the warden of the western approach to the Perak river valley. Larut had been part of the territory of this chief, and before the discovery of tin, had been placed under the management of his brother, the grandfather of Ngah Ibrahim. Ngah Ibrahim's father had developed Larut after the tin discoveries, and had been granted the area in written concessions from or on behalf of successive sultans in 1850 and 1856. He died in 1857, and the concession was re-issued to Ngah Ibrahim in 1858. Ngah Ibrahim was made Mentri probably in 1863 or early 1864.

that he had any financial interest in the mines there. In Selangor, the rajas themselves controlled the districts and were deeply involved in the mining investment and shared out the concessions between them.[1] Raja Juma'at, who was granted the Lukut concession in 1846, was the son-in-law of one Sultan and brother-in-law of the next; his brother, Raja 'Abdu'llah, initiated the development of the Kuala Lumpur field, the richest in the state, and in 1870 this came under the authority of Tengku Zia'u'd-din, a son-in-law of the Sultan. The Sultan, 'Abdu'l Samad, had shares himself in mining ventures on the upper Selangor, and later on the upper Langat.[2]

The chiefs had a double interest in the mines. They acted as advancers, borrowing from Straits Settlements merchants and lending to concessionaires against a supply of part of the output, and the right to buy the rest at a buyer's price; and they enjoyed tribute and taxation rights as political rulers of the area. The expansion of mining in the 1860's brought the chiefs enormous revenues, much larger than the revenues of the Sultans. The chief revenue source of the Sultan of Perak (the customs collection at the mouth of the Perak river) was leased for $26,000 in 1874; in contrast, the Larut revenue for 1874, the first year for which systematic accounts are available, was $101,554, and then the mines were in full production only in the last four months.[3] The chief source of revenue of the Sultan of

[1] The diagram following shows some of the relationships of the Selangor rajas and their interest in various concessions. It is taken from Gullick, *Indigenous Political Systems of Western Malaya*, op. cit. p. 72.

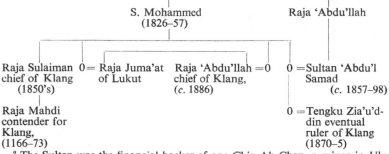

[2] The Sultan was the financial backer of one Chin Ah Chan, a miner in Ulu Selangor, who then moved to Ulu Langat and opened mines there with the Sultan's support. References to advances made by the Sultan to this man are in Sel/Sec. 426/1865.

[3] Report of Assistant Resident, Perak, for 1874, Appendix B, *SSGG*, 3 April 1875. The Mentri's revenue from the farm of the Larut mines at one time reached $15,000 per month. Statement by the Mentri at Penang, 26 August 1873, C.1111, enclosure 6 in no. 52. Clarke to Kimberley, 24 February 1874.

Selangor was the customs collection in Langat. In 1877, the second year of organized collection by British officers, the Langat revenues totalled $18,233; by contrast the revenues of Klang, the outlet for the Kuala Lumpur mines, amounted in 1874 to $114,000.[1] The chiefs owed a proportion of their collections to the Sultan, but this was not large, nor did it appear to be regularly paid.[2] A part of the mining revenue was spent on administration and war; but the revenues were still regarded as the personal estate of the chiefs, some of whom were now very much richer than their sovereigns. This, together with the scramble that now took place for a share of the tin profits, all but wrecked the Malay political structure. The Malays made some attempt to meet this challenge to the balance of their society, and to remedy the great discrepancies of income between one chief and the next; in Selangor, for example, the chiefs, prompted by their Malacca creditors, tried to come to some rational solution of the problem. In 1858 Raja Juma'at of Lukut put before the Selangor rajas a solution inspired by his friend and adviser, the Resident Councillor of Malacca; he proposed that tin duties be fixed and paid into a State Treasury which would then pay allowances equitably to all Selangor rajas.[3] But the pre-requisite for such a solution was a centralized administration, which Selangor did not have. In Sungei Ujong another sort of adjustment was attempted; in 1850 the conflicting claims of the Dato' Bandar, the Dato' Klana and the Dato' Muda Linggi were settled by the arbitration of the Yam Tuan Besar of Negri Sembilan,[4] but this settlement again was precarious in the absence of authority able to enforce it.

[1] Assistant CS for Native States, Audit Report on Native States' Accounts for 1877, C. 2410, enclosure in no. 6, Anson to Hicks Beach, 6 March 1879; Memorandum on the Financial Condition of the Native States, 6 February 1877, Paper laid before the Straits Settlements Legislative Council, Appendix 4 of 1878. Irving estimated Tengku Zia'u'd-din's revenue at $180,000 a year. Irving, Memorandum on a Visit to Selangor, op. cit.

[2] The Larut contribution to Perak in 1874, based on the traditional contribution to the Sultan, was $16,446 (Report of Assistant Resident, Perak, for 1874, Appendix B, *SSGG*, 3 April 1875). Middlebrook puts the Klang contribution to the Sultan *c.* 1870 at $6,000 a year (Middlebrook, op. cit. p. 29).

[3] Middlebrook, op. cit. pp. 23–24.

[4] Before the eighteenth century, the predecessors of the Dato' Klana and Dato' Bandar were styled Penghulu Mentri and Dato' Shahbandar respectively, and the offices they held originated in appointments of local representatives made by the Sultans of Malacca-Johore. They appear to have been co-rulers and the relative authority of the Dato' Klana and the Dato' Bandar, in consequence, has always been obscure, and the Malay sources avoid definitions. The Dato' Klana held the title of *Undang* over the whole of Sungei Ujong, and was the first of the chiefs of

The struggle for control of the mines and river outlets continued, and perpetuated old rivalries in a new form. In Perak a succession quarrel between the ruling Sultan, Ismail, who controlled the upper Perak,[1] and Raja 'Abdu'llah, a disappointed candidate whose sphere of influence was on the lower river, was given a sharper edge by the value of the revenue contribution from Larut; while Sultan Ismail

Negri Sembilan; but the Dato' Bandar was independent in his own district, and after the Klana, took precedence over all the other chiefs of the Negri Sembilan; in 1898 he joined with the Klana in signing an agreement on behalf of Sungci Ujong, accepting a Yam Tuan over the state. The territory of the Klana lay on a tributary of the upper Linggi, in the Pantai district; that of the Bandar lay on the middle Linggi, below Seremban, and included the tin port of Rasah. The Bandar was therefore in a better position to tax the tin trade. A conflict between them in 1849 was settled by the arbitration of the Yam Tuan Besar; the settlement gave the Dato' Klana, the Dato' Bandar and the Dato' Muda Linggi (a Bugis chief settled lower down the river) one-third each of the dues on ships and merchandise entering or leaving the mouth of the river (Gullick, 'Sungei Ujong', op. cit. p. 29. In 1874, however, this arrangement seems to have broken down, as the Klana complained to Pickering that he was getting none of the tin revenue, and that his main source of income was the capitation tax on Chinese miners. W. Pickering, Journal of a visit to Sungei Ujong, 4 October—29 November 1874, Swettenham Papers, no. 72.

[1] The Perak succession rotated between three branches of the royal family; on the death of each Sultan, his heir was made Raja Bendahara, while the current Raja Bendahara became Raja Muda and the Raja Muda became Sultan. On the death of Sultan 'Abdu'llah Mohammed Shah in 1857, his son Yusuf should have become Raja Bendahara; but the chiefs passed him over because of his unpopularity and Ismail, who was of Perak royal descent only on his mother's side, was made Bendahara. Ismail had clearly only a caretaker position, for he remained Bendahara at the death of the next Sultan (Ja'afar) in 1865; Yusuf was again passed over, and 'Abdu'llah was made Raja Muda. On Sultan Ali's death in 1871, both 'Abdu'llah and Yusuf were passed over, and Ismail was made Sultan, apparently by a coup of the up-river chiefs. The relationships between the various Sultans and pretenders between c.1800 and 1916 is shown in the following diagram, based on Wilkinson, op. cit. p. 97. The dates in brackets are the regnal dates.

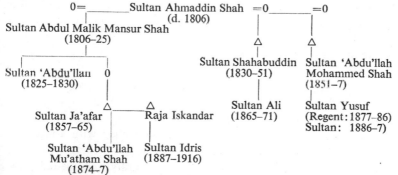

supported the Mentri and his Hai San allies, Raja 'Abdu'llah tried to secure the support of the Ghi Hin opponents of the Mentri, in return for promises of concessions. In Selangor the struggle for control of the Selangor and Klang rivers (particularly the latter), involved the whole royal family. The main struggle was between a Selangor raja (Raja Mahdi, a cousin of the Sultan), and the Sultan's son-in-law, Tengku Zia'u'd-din. Tengku Zia'u'd-din, a brother of the Sultan of Kedah, married a daughter of Sultan 'Abdu'l Samad in 1868, and was drawn into Selangor politics on the side of the Sultan's nephews by marriage, who had been expelled from Klang by Raja Mahdi in 1867. He helped the displaced heirs to regain Klang (March 1870) and he then assumed control of the Klang administration, and entered into an alliance with the Hai San headman of Kuala Lumpur, Capitan Yap Ah Loy. For the next three years, the Tengku with his Hai San allies, and Raja Mahdi with his Chinese supporters in the upper Selangor, disputed control of the Klang and Selangor rivers and their rich tin hinterlands, while the Sultan lived in the relative peace and neutrality of Langat.

In Sungei Ujong the competition for the tin revenues simply perpetuated the ancient rivalry between the Dato' Bandar and the Dato' Klana, joint holders of the office of territorial chief. The Dato' Bandar had the advantage in that he controlled the river outlet for the Linggi mines and thus controlled the revenues, and the equitable division of these between the Klana and himself was the source of constant friction. But the tin trade was damaged less by the rivalry between these two than by the exactions on its passage down the Linggi. Not only did it have to meet the legitimate claims of the Dato' Klana, the Dato' Bandar and the Dato' Muda of Linggi, but it was liable to stoppage by the Undang of Rembau, and indeed by any claimant to office who could collect a few boats and armed followers and hold up traffic. In 1872 and 1873 traffic on the Linggi was held up repeatedly by the contestants for the position of Undang of Rembau, both of whom tried to raise funds by the levy of illegal dues, while the river was also blockaded by Tengku Zia'u'd-din in an effort to stop his enemies using it as an escape route from Selangor.

It should be said that the rivalries between Malays on the west coast during the period were not as turbulent and bloodthirsty as contemporary accounts suggest. The air was filled with abuse and intrigue, but in Perak and Sungei Ujong at least, there was more noise than violence. A network of family relationships usually em-

braced both contestants for power and probably acted as a deterrent
to actual aggression; the low casualty rates may also be due to the
Malay tradition of warfare, which consisted of investing a position
and waiting for its defenders to retire. But whatever the reason for
restraint, it was possible for Sultan Ismail of Perak and his rival
Raja 'Abdu'llah (later made Sultan in his place) to live on the same
river without coming to blows. It was possible for the rivals to the
throne of Negri Sembilan (who were cousins) to live in the same state,
and for the Dato' Bandar and Dato' Klana to live on the outskirts
of the same tin field ten miles from each other—if not in friendship,
at least in suspended animosity. The hostility between the chiefs was
mainly expressed in wordy letters of complaint to the Governor or
to other British officials. In 1874, for example, word reached Singapore that the Dato' Klana was about to set out to punish his con-
tumacious fellow-chief; a Straits official was sent up to support the
Klana and to restrain him from undue violence, but he found the
Klana without men and the Bandar unwilling to fight. 'I am thankful
we came', he wrote, 'as it would have been a great disgrace to bring
a force to attack a place and find the inmates to be a childish old
man and a few followers, with women and children.'[1]

However, the Malay struggle for control of the river outlets was
sharpened and complicated by a far more bitter and serious struggle
between Chinese factions for control of the mines themselves.[2] The
Ghi Hin and Hai San societies had brought their hostilities with them
to the Malay states, and these were intensified by the competition
for mining land; and the conflicts in the states reacted in turn on the
relationships between the societies in the Straits. In Larut and Selangor, wars broke out in which each Chinese faction was heavily financed by Chinese backers in the Straits, and carried on a warfare
which showed no sign of ending while both sides in the Straits had
the resources to mount counter-offensives. In Larut the fighting was
virtually confined to the Chinese till as late as September 1873, when
Indian sepoys recruited by the Mentri came into action. The fighting

---

[1] Pickering, op. cit.
[2] The best general account of the conflicts is given in C. D. Cowan, *Nineteenth
Century Malaya; the Origins of British Political Control*, London, 1961. The
official documents bearing on the Larut wars are contained in C.1111, of July
1874. The fullest account of the fighting for Klang is contained in Abdul Samad.
Kenang2an Selangor, op. cit. from which later accounts (including Winstedt's)
are taken. The only account in English of the Chinese share in the fighting is in
Middlebrook, op. cit. *passim.*

in Selangor, on the other hand, developed out of a long-standing rivalry between Sumatran and Bugis trading communities in Klang and Kuala Lumpur. Their quarrel merged first with the struggle between the Malay chiefs for the control of mining revenues and then with the Chinese struggle for the mines. The severest fighting took place not on the rivers where Malays exclusively were involved, but in the interior round Kuala Lumpur, where large numbers of Malays and Chinese fought side by side against their countrymen.[1]

The subsidies by Chinese backers helped sustain the fighting at an intensity unknown in Malay warfare, which was usually limited by lack of funds to the sporadic raiding of stockades. The amounts poured into the Larut and Selangor wars give some indication of the extent to which Straits merchants were committed in the Malay states. The creditors of the Mentri were awarded $166,753 in settlement of debts incurred on account of the Larut wars; in Selangor the war debts of Tengku Zia'u'd-din, bonded as a state debt, amounted to $300,000.[2] These sums were equivalent to the whole revenue of Perak and Selangor for 1876, and they represent only part of the expenses of one side in the fighting. The tin at stake amounted to 7 per cent. of the total Penang imports in 1870 and 40 per cent. of the Malacca imports for that year. Malacca was especially affected by the troubles; at one stage in 1872 it was claimed that tin to the value of $300,000 was held up by the blockade on the Linggi river.[3]

The fights reached a peak of destructiveness between 1870 and 1873. In Larut in 1872 the mines changed hands twice, each time with great slaughter, and each faction on defeat retired to Penang to mount counter-offensives. In September 1873 Larut was a never-never-land where the Hai San in the mines were blockaded by the Ghi Hin on the river, who were in turn blockaded by the Hai San on their seaward side, while the Mentri on behalf of his Hai San

[1] Cowan has suggested a geographical explanation for the close Sino-Malay association in Selangor, in that the open character of the country, the greater number of river outlets for the tin and the dispersal inland of the tin fields gave the chiefs 'more opportunities of trade and contact with other areas than were available to their opposite numbers in Perak' and brought the Chinese in the mines and the Malays on the rivers into much closer mutual dependence. Cowan, op. cit. p. 67.

[2] *PCM*, 27 February 1879; Assistant CS for Native States, Audit Report on Selangor, 27 March 1880, C.3095, enclosure 1 in no. 2, Weld to Kimberley, 19 June 1880.

[3] Braddell, Report on Proceedings at Sungei Ujong, C.1320, enclosure in no. 8, Clarke to Carnarvon, 29 December 1874.

allies prepared to attack them by land. In Selangor, Capitan China Yap Ah Loy and the Malay followers of Zia'u'd-din fought for the upper courses of the Selangor and Klang rivers against the rival Sino-Malay faction, while Malay parties fought for the river mouths. Between 1870 and 1872 the Selangor river mouth changed hands three times; Kuala Lumpur was attacked twice, and in 1872 it fell, leaving the Tengku's party nothing but the Klang river mouth. The next year the picture was changed again by Malay mercenaries sent over the mountains from Pahang, who helped the Klang party to recapture Kuala Lumpur, and cleared their enemies off the whole course of the Selangor river. It is probable that the fighting would have begun again, and the situation changed once more, had it not been stabilized at this point by the intervention of the British Government.

II

THE INTRODUCTION OF RESIDENTS

THE DECISION TO INTERVENE

THE British settlements of Penang, Malacca and Singapore, collectively known as the Straits Settlements, were established by the East India Company between 1786 and 1825, and were governed by the Company till 1858, when, together with its other possessions, they came under the India Office. In 1867 they were transferred to the Colonial Office and were constituted a Crown Colony. Throughout these changes in control, metropolitan policy with regard to the native states remained consistent in principle, and so did local attitudes to the same question. The value of the Straits Settlements to the East India Company lay primarily in the commercial and strategic link they provided between the Indian empire on the one hand and the Chinese trade on the other; and the aim of metropolitan policy was, broadly, to protect the sea route without incurring territorial responsibilities which might prove uneconomic, and which might provoke the intervention of a major power.[1] Britain accordingly encouraged the two minor European powers in the Archipelago, Holland and Spain, to consolidate their position in the East Indies and the Philippines respectively, despite the fact that they were her local rivals; and since she feared to precipitate an international 'scramble for China', she refused to permit the local government to challenge Siam ('an actual feudatory of the Chinese Empire' in the judgment of the Supreme Government in India), by a forward policy in the Peninsula.

Imperial policy conflicted, as it often does, with local policy, which was to break down the obstructions to the entrepôt trade by native and European monopolies and exactions. The levies on the trade by native rulers, whether sanctioned by custom or not, were characterized as 'piracy' and naval power invoked to put them down. Commercial considerations demanded that the Siamese, who already had

[1] This analysis is developed in N. Tarling, 'British Policy in the Malay Peninsula and Archipelago, 1824–1871', *JMBRAS*, vol. xxx, part 3 (1957), pp. 9–18 *et seq.*

suzerainty over Kedah, Kelantan and Trengganu, should be prevented from extending their authority southward. The refusal of the Home Government to sanction a forward policy left the local government little room to manocuvre; but local officials did succeed in establishing Britain by treaty and in practice as the paramount power in the independent states of the Peninsula. The treaties, in general, excluded Siam from interference south of the Kedah-Kelantan boundary, prevented the states from interfering in each others' affairs, and asserted British control of their foreign relations. The intention of the treaties was to immobilize each state within its boundaries as much as possible. Treaties with Perak and Selangor in 1825 established the Bernam river as the boundary between them, provided for the recall of Selangor tax-collectors in Lower Perak, and bound Selangor not to interfere in Perak affairs. A treaty with Siam in 1826 guaranteed Perak against attack, either by Siam or Selangor, and a treaty with Perak in the same year (Treaty 2 of 18 October 1826) bound the Ruler to apply for British help if his country were disturbed. On the other side of the Peninsula, Pahang and Johore in a treaty of 1862 agreed to refer any dispute between them to the Straits Government, and undertook not to correspond with a foreign power except with the consent of that government.[1]

The Straits Government managed to maintain a balance of power on the Peninsula by using considerable diplomatic finesse, but it had no weapons except diplomacy and the occasional display of naval force; and without control over the internal affairs of the states, it could not stop dynastic quarrels or put an end to interference with the tin trade, or stop the Chinese secret society conflicts for the mines. The use of naval power gave only temporary relief. River stockades were destroyed, but the naval and police parties no sooner left the scene than the exactions began once more.[2] The Sultans could not themselves enforce order; this was demonstrated by the events of 1862, when the Sultan of Perak was called upon to make restitution for the losses of Penang Chinese forced out of Larut in the secret society clashes of the previous year. The Sultan agreed to

[1] The treaties are published in W. G. Maxwell and W. S. Gibson, *Treaties and Engagements affecting the Malay States and Borneo*, London, 1924.
[2] Braddell describes the fruitless attempts to clear the Linggi in the 1850's (Report of Proceedings in Sungei Ujong, C.1320, enclosure in no. 8, Clarke to Carnarvon, 29 December 1874). In 1871, a British sloop, the *Rinaldo*, destroyed Raja Mahdi's fort at the entrance to the Selangor river, and Tengku Zia'u'd-din occupied it; a year later it was retaken by Mahdi's party.

settle the disputes, and the Laksamana made an award to the injured parties; but nothing more was done till the British blockaded the Larut river, and forced the ruler of Larut, Che Ngah Ibrahim, to pay.

After the transfer to the Colonial Office, the Governor, Sir Harry Ord, and his *locum tenens*, Colonel Anson,[1] attempted to interfere actively in the Peninsula on their own responsibility. In 1867, the year he arrived in the Straits, Ord engaged in trade and boundary discussions with Kedah, and in 1868 he negotiated an agreement on these matters with her suzerain, Siam. The same year, he began unauthorized negotiations with Perak for the cession of territory on the mainland opposite the British-held island of Pangkor. In April 1868 he pointed out to the Secretary of State that in all the independent states except Johore, the insecurity of life and property discouraged investment and Chinese immigration, and proposed, as a remedy, the extension of British influence to that part of the Peninsula south of the Siamese-dominated Malay states. He declared, 'the subjection of these native States of the Peninsula to Powers greater and more civilised than themselves is an advantage to themselves and to all who have relations with them', and announced that he would use every opportunity that presented itself for extending British influence.[2]

Ord's despatch crossed with a Colonial Office directive on the Governor's responsibilities in relation to the native states. The directive acknowledged that the Governor might have to act independently in certain circumstances, but warned him against entering into formal negotiations with native powers, and particularly against concluding any agreement except in pursuance of a policy approved by Her Majesty's Government.[3] Ord had offended on all counts; he had acted independently, with no emergency to justify him, he had concluded an agreement on his own initiative, and his proposal to extend British influence, and indeed to add to British territorial possessions in the Peninsula, was a radical departure from established policy.

---

[1] Sir Harry St. George Ord, RE, CB, Commissioner to the Gold Coast, 1855–6; Lt.-Governor of Dominica, 1857; Governor of Bermuda 1861; Special Commissioner to West Africa in 1864; served as Governor of the Straits Settlements between April 1867 and November 1873. Lt.-Colonel Anson, RA, was Lt.-Governor of Penang from 1867 to 1882, and administered the government for periods in 1871, 1877 and 1879, in the absence of the Governor.

[2] Ord to Buckingham, 58 of 8 April 1868.

[3] Buckingham to Ord, 59 of 22 April 1868.

The Colonial Office reacted strongly. It had already received a letter from W. H. Read, a leading Singapore merchant, recounting the state of affairs in Perak, Pahang and Selangor, giving details of the trade and the importance of the area to Straits commerce, and begging for authorized intervention and 'regular government under British influence and supervision';[1] and in reply the Secretary of State had instructed emphatically that the policy of Her Majesty's Government was not one of intervention in native affairs. He now wrote to say that the government was 'not disposed to adopt the responsibility, directly or indirectly, of taking steps for the security of life and property in independent countries where this security cannot be given by the Lawful Rulers',[2] and the next year he warned Ord in particular against annexation of Perak territory, in phrases which recurred in the years that followed; 'I should not be disposed to approve of any proceedings which would extend the responsibilities of Her Majesty's Government in the neighbourhood of the Straits Settlements'.[3] As Ord complained in private, 'nothing is more difficult than to get these people [the Malay Rulers] to make treaties from which they derive no benefit, except it be to persuade the C.O. to approve of them!'[4]

In 1871 the Colonial Office was again provoked by the efforts of a local official to initiate policy in relation to native affairs. In May, Colonel Anson, while administering the government in Ord's absence, officiously appointed a committee to report on relations with the native states. His justification was the importance to Penang of the trade with the west coast of the Peninsula and with north Sumatra, the 'very unsatisfactory state of our relations with all these States and the injury to trade which is the natural result'. The committee recommended that the native authorities be induced to 'introduce into these states a European of character and ability, who while the officer of the state, would be the medium of communication between this Government and the people among whom he resides'. Anson, acknowledging that the states would not welcome such officers, and doubting whether the Legislative Council would pay for them, put forward a modified proposal for an itinerant Political Agent, whose duty it would be to visit these states frequently, and who might be

[1] Read to CO, 9 May 1868, enclosed in Buckingham to Ord, 77 of 20 May 1868.

[2] Buckingham to Ord, 92 of 4 June 1868.

[3] Granville to Ord, 157 of 10 September 1869, CO 273/30.

[4] Ord to Anson, 20 October 1870, Anson Correspondence.

employed to carry on correspondence with them.[1] The Colonial
Office did not see that there was the slightest necessity for moving,
and instructed Anson not to meddle with large matters of policy.[2]

An incident in Selangor in 1871 is worth recounting for the light
it throws on local developments and metropolitan attitudes. In June
1871, a month after the appointment of the ill-fated committee,
Anson sent the Colonial yacht *Pluto* to the Selangor river, then controlled by Raja Mahdi, to inquire into the disappearance of a Chinese
junk from Penang. It was found in the river, the missing cargo was
rounded up from the Chinese shops in the township, and a number
of prisoners were taken. While arresting them, the British officers
came into conflict with Raja Mahdi's party, and were forced to
retire. A punitive action followed; the sloop *Rinaldo* was sent to the
Selangor river, and she bombarded the forts and burnt the town. The
Colonial Secretary, J. W. W. Birch, was then sent to demand further
satisfaction from the Sultan, and to require him, among other things,
to 'place some person in the office of Governor or chief in the country
about the Selangor River, whom this Government can trust'. Tengku
Zia'u'd-din, the opponent of the Mahdi party, was clearly the person
intended. He had occupied the Selangor river immediately after the
bombardment, and Birch picked him up there and took him on to
Langat to see the Sultan. In 1868 Tengku Zia'u'd-din had received
from the Sultan an authority to 'govern and develope [*sic*] for Us
and for Our sons', an undefined territory which the Straits officials
interpreted as the whole country of Selangor, though it may only
have referred to the district of Langat, granted to the Tengku in the
same document.[3] Birch now required the Sultan to confirm this
power. The Sultan tried to procrastinate, and when that failed, he
tried to nominate two other Selangor rajas to share authority with
the Tengku; finally, under pressure from Birch, and with the guns of
a man-of-war bearing on his palace, he submitted and re-issued the

[1] Anson to Kimberley, 144 of 3 June 1871, and report of committee 19 May
1871, CO 273/47. The committee consisted of A. W. Birch, Acting Lt.-Governor
of Penang, Major J.F.A. McNair, Colonial Engineer and Surveyor-General, and
Commander George Robinson, Commander and Senior Naval Officer, Straits
Division.

[2] Kimberley to Anson, 180 of 20 August 1871, CO 273/47.

[3] Wilkinson gives the document in its English translation and interprets it
as an authority to govern Langat only, but the point is still in doubt (R. J.
Wilkinson, *History of the Peninsular Malays*, Singapore, 1923, pp. 144–5). On the
strength of this authority, the Straits officials styled the Tengku 'Viceroy of
Selangor'.

authority; and he also declared Raja Mahdi, Raja Mahmud and Syed Mashor rebels, and empowered Birch to seize them.[1] At the same time Birch pledged the Straits Government to assist 'our friend's Vakeel [Tengku Zia'u'd-din] in case any of our friend's subjects ventured to dispute his authority'.[2]

The Colonial Office reacted to this with surprising equanimity, though the whole action had provoked a strongly critical letter in *The Times* and produced an uneasy reaction from Gladstone. The Secretary of State was on firm moral ground; the Straits Government had cited 'piracy' as the cause of intervention, and the action taken had the 'apparent approval' of the Sultan;[3] more important, the government was committed to no direct responsibility. Birch's promise of support to the Tengku had caused the Secretary of State some uneasiness, but he inserted an insurance clause in his reply, warning Anson against too active a policy, while approving his support of the Tengku in principle. 'I conclude that this [promise of assistance] referred to general countenance and support, and that no promise of material assistance was given by Mr Birch.'[4] As one authority puts it, 'these transactions provoke the reflection that British policy at this time was opposed to the extension of British influence when it threatened to involve liabilities and complications, but condoned it when it did not incur technical responsibility'.[5] This generalization is applicable to Colonial Office attitudes even after heavy responsibilities had been assumed in practice.

Debarred from direct intervention, the Straits Government tried to bring about a lasting solution by intervening diplomatically on behalf of one or other of the Malay parties. There was nothing to be achieved by lending weight to the authority of the Sultans, since they were impotent to restore order, and lived by choice at a distance from the mines and the scene of the fighting. In Selangor the most eligible candidate for support was Tengku Zia'u'd-din. He wore a mantle of legitimacy, since he was fighting on behalf of the true heirs to Klang, and moreover had a commission from the Sultan to govern the

[1] Sultan of Selangor to Birch, 22 July 1871; Birch to Anson 26 July 1871, C. 446, enclosures in no. 6, Anson to Kimberley, 28 July 1871.

[2] Birch to Sultan of Selangor (July 1871), C. 466, enclosure 3 in no. 6. *Wakil:* agent or attorney.

[3] Kimberley to Gladstone, 19 and 23 September 1871, Gladstone Papers, British Museum, cited C. D. Cowan, *Nineteenth Century Malaya*, p. 95, note 81.

[4] Kimberley to Anson, 26 September 1871, C. 466, no. 8.

[5] Cowan, op. cit. p. 96.

country. He was represented in Singapore by an influential lawyer, J. G. Davidson,[1] who was his financial backer as well as his legal adviser; he was familiar with the life of the colony and paid frequent visits to Penang and Singapore; he was known to be 'Europeanized' and sympathetic to change (all the more so since he was a foreigner in Selangor and in conflict with established interests). Finally, the Mahdi party was characterized as a party of unruly adventurers (which it was) while the Tengku stood for a degree of order and organized government altogether novel in Selangor. The Selangor royal family was hostile to him, but this was rather counted to his credit; the Sultan's indifference to him was more embarrassing, but the Straits authorities explained this to their own satisfaction by attributing it to the malign influence of the court at Langat.[2]

In Perak the contestants for British support were the Mentri and Raja 'Abdu'llah, the disappointed candidate for the Perak throne; but since Raja 'Abdu'llah had no standing in Larut, and the Mentri had, and since the Straits Government was only able to intervene indirectly, and required allies of substance, it decided in September 1873 to throw its weight on the side of the Mentri. It permitted him to import arms, and to recruit sepoys from India under Captain Speedy, formerly Deputy Superintendent in the Penang Police,[3] who entered his service in July 1873; and it initiated a blockade of Larut which was in effect a blockade of the Mentri's Chinese opponents, the Ghi Hin.

To a certain extent these indirect tactics were successful. By the end of 1873, Tengku Zia'u'd-din was once more in control of the Klang and Selangor rivers, and in Larut the Ghi Hin were on the defensive, hard pressed by the Mentri on land and the British blockade by sea. But it is unlikely that the conflict could have been finally resolved without direct British intervention, either to support the winning party against the armed reaction which was sure to come,[4] or to police a settlement which would give both Chinese factions access to the mines. Before the policy of indirect support had been fully tested, however, the Colonial Office had decided to intervene.

From late 1872, Ord's despatches had dwelt at length on the dis-

---

[1] See Appendix 2.
[2] See below, p. 59–60.
[3] See below, Chapter III, p.69.
[4] The Penang authorities appeared to be powerless to stop the export of arms to Larut. Ord to Kimberley, 216 of 24 July 1873, CO 273/67.

turbed condition of the Malay states and the repercussions on the trade and internal security of the settlements. The enclosures described in detail the involvement of the Penang Chinese in the Larut wars, and included a proposal from the Acting Lt.-Governor of Penang for the annexation of Perak or at least the appointment of a Resident or Political Officer to certain of the states.[1] The Governor also forwarded requests from local merchants for a limited intervention. Chinese merchants in Malacca, supported by the Singapore Chamber of Commerce, appealed for a more active support of Ten gku Zia'u'd-din, and in July 1873 the Governor forwarded a petition from 248 Chinese traders in the three settlements, claiming, as subjects of 'our Most Gracious Majesty', protection in the half-civilized states of the Malay Peninsula, and begging for 'a moral intervention, and a determined attitude in respect of the affairs of the territories now in a state of anarchy'.[2] Before the petition arrived in London the Colonial Office had received a letter from a London businessman on the same question. In March 1873, Tengku Zia'u'd-din had granted to Davidson and another party a ten-year concession to work all the tin land in Selangor not already occupied by others. The Selangor Tin Mining Company was promoted to handle this concession, and their London representative, Seymour Clarke, applied to the Colonial Office for protection for the enterprise. He quoted from a letter Tengku Zia'u'd-din had written him, asking 'if the English, *or any other Government*' would provide security for the persons and property of traders and entrepreneurs.[3] The letter seems to have precipitated the change of policy. On 7 July, Kimberley had minuted on an account of the Larut wars, 'I think we must endeavour to put a stop to these disturbances. . . . The difficulty is how to do anything without direct interference with Perak which is very undesirable'. But a fortnight later, he minuted on Clarke's letter that the British Government could not consent to any European power assuming the protectorate of any Malay state.[4] The Colonial Office was reluc-

[1] Acting Lt.-Governor of Penang to Governor, 24 October 1872, C.1111, enclosure 3 in no. 3, Ord to Kimberley, 11 November 1872.
[2] Petition of the Malacca Traders to the Chamber of Commerce, Singapore, 27 July 1872, C.1111, enclosure 1 in no. 1, Ord to Kimberley, 6 November 1872; Petition of Chinese Traders in Singapore, Penang and Malacca, 28 March 1873, C.1111, enclosure in no. 12, Ord to Kimberley, 10 July 1873.
[3] Seymour Clarke to CO, 18 July 1873, CO 273/74, citing letter from Tengku Zia'u'd-din, 3 June 1873, CO 273/74. The emphasis is added.
[4] Minute by Kimberley, 7 July 1873, on Campbell to CO, 28 June 1873, CO 273/74; minute by Kimberley, 22 July 1873, on Seymour Clarke to CO, 18 July 1873, CO 273/74.

tant to be pushed into closer control at the instance either of local Chinese or of metropolitan British speculators; but at the point where local disturbances appeared to endanger, even remotely, British paramountcy in the Peninsula, the Home Government was ready for closer control.[1]

The change of policy was communicated to the Straits Government in a despatch of 20 September 1873. The Secretary of State referred to the prevailing anarchy in the Peninsula, the damage to trade, and the need for a remedy. He went on:

Her Majesty's Government have, it need hardly be said, no desire to interfere in the internal affairs of the Malay States. But looking to the long and intimate connection between them and the British Government, as shown in the Treaties which have at various times been concluded with them, and to the well being of the British Settlements themselves, Her Majesty's Government find it incumbent upon them to employ such influence as they possess with the native Princes to rescue if possible these fertile and productive countries from the ruin which must befall them, if the present disorders continue unchecked.

I have to request that you will carefully ascertain as far as you are able the actual condition of affairs in each state, and that you will report to me whether there are, in your opinion, any steps which can properly be taken by the Colonial Government to promote the restoration of peace and order, and to secure protection to trade and commerce with the native territories. I should wish you especially to consider whether it would be advisable to appoint a British officer to reside in any of the States. Such an appointment could, of course, only be made with the full consent of the native Government, and the expenses connected with it would have to be defrayed by the Government of the Straits Settlements.

The tone of the despatch was extremely cautious and it did no more than ask the Governor to report, in the first instance, on the steps he proposed to take. It was addressed to a new Governor, Sir Andrew Clarke,[2] who took up his duties in the Straits on 4 Novem-

---

[1] This thesis is developed in Cowan, op. cit. The original draft of the permissive despatch of 20 September 1873 brings out clearly the strategic fears that underlay the change of policy; but these sections were cut out of the final despatch. Kimberley to Clarke, 20 September 1873, in CO 273/67.

[2] Lt.-General Sir Andrew Clarke, RE, GCMG, CB, was born in 1824 and educated at the Royal Military Academy, Woolwich. He entered the Royal Engineers in 1844, and for the next twenty years held important public appointments as a professional engineer and surveyor in Britain and Australia. He was Governor of the Straits Settlements from November 1873 to May 1875, when he resumed his career as a military engineer. He had a reputation throughout his life for taking vigorous and independent action first, and reporting afterwards. His action in the Straits was inspired not only by a natural decisiveness but by a strong and patriotic personal ambition. 'I feel I have done a good stroke', he

ber. It does not appear to have been supplemented by any confidential instructions, written or verbal, empowering him to act on his own initiative,[1] but that is exactly what he did. His first report on his proceedings informed the Colonial Office that he had settled the Perak succession, had got the Sultan and chiefs to accept a Resident, and had posted an officer as Assistant Resident in Perak, to take up his duties in Larut.[2] Before he left the Straits in May 1875 he had established Residents in Selangor and Sungei Ujong as well.

The Colonial Office had stipulated that the Residents were to be introduced with the consent of the native rulers, and in the event, this was not difficult to secure. In Perak, Raja 'Abdu'llah had provided the 'key to the door' by writing to the Governor soon after his arrival, offering in effect to receive a Resident in exchange for recognition as Sultan.[3] Before he received this letter, Clarke had already arranged a cease-fire in Larut, and had summoned the Chinese factions and a number of the Perak chiefs to meet him at Pangkor Island, where the question of the Perak succession was to be settled.[4] The final settlement was embodied in the Pangkor Engagement, executed by the chiefs before the Governor on 20 January 1874. It dealt with two important questions, the succession and the appointment of a Resident. 'Abdu'llah was recognized as Sultan; the Mentri was confirmed in his title to Larut; Ismail (referred to in typical official phraseology as 'Acting Sultan') was to be pensioned off in a small territory of his own. The Engagement went on to provide: 'That the Sultan receive and provide a suitable residence for a British officer to be called Resident, who shall be accredited to his Court, and whose advice must be asked and acted upon on all questions other than

wrote after Pangkor; 'all the people here say nothing has been done so complete and equal to it since Raffles's time'. Clarke to Childers, undated, R. H. Vetch, *Life of Lieut.-General the Hon. Sir Andrew Clarke*, London, 1905, p. 154.

[1] He wrote to Anson, 'If the S. of S. does not recall me for what I have done at the Dindings I shall be lucky. If . . . the Chinese stick quietly to their mining for the next year or two and he *does* back me, I shall be luckier still'. Clarke to Anson, 1 February 1874, Anson Correspondence.

[2] Clarke to Kimberley, 14 and 15 of 26 January 1874, C.1111, nos. 39 and 40.

[3] Sultan 'Abdu'llah to Governor, 30 December 1873, C.1111, enclosure 12 in no. 39, Clarke to Kimberley, 26 January 1874.

[4] The chief Malays present (the Malay signatories to Pangkor) were Raja 'Abdu'llah; the Bendahara, the Temenggong, and the Mentri, of the chiefs of the first rank; the Laksamana, the Shahbandar and the Dato' Sagor, of the chiefs of the second rank; the Raja Mahkota of the third. The last four were all down-river chiefs. The Maharaja Lela, the Panglima Kinta and the Sri Adika Raja were absent. See Appendix 1.

those touching Malay Religion and Custom' (Article VI), and 'That the collection and control of all Revenues and the general adminis- istration of the country be regulated under the advice of these Res- idents' (Article X). The Residents and their establishments were to be a first charge on the revenues of Perak (Article VIII) and a Civil List was to be drawn up to regulate the incomes of the Sultan and officers of state (Article IX).[1] An officer was immediately appointed to reside with the Mentri in Larut. Finally, Clarke took the oppor- tunity to obtain the cessions of territory on the Province Wellesley border, and opposite Pangkor Island (the Dindings) that Ord had wanted, but had been prevented from acquiring.

In May, the Secretary of State wrote approving the proceedings at Pangkor;[2] next day he telegraphed permission to appoint Residents provisionally to Perak, Larut and Selangor, reporting the names and terms for confirmation;[3] and in a despatch of 4 September, he con- firmed this authority, with special reference to Selangor. Clarke had by this time formed his policy in relation both to Selangor and Sungei Ujong. He voiced the common opinion about Selangor royalty ('The Sultan and his Family and followers are all thoroughbred Pirates') and decided to continue Ord's support of the Tengku.[4] In February 1874 he administered a sharp correction to the Sultan on the occasion of a piracy at the mouth of the Jugra river (near the royal township) and forced him to appoint a court to try the culprits. In August, a piracy at the junction of the Langat and Labu rivers (again in the Sultan's district, though he had no part in either outrage) gave Clarke the excuse to send a junior officer, later styled Assistant Resident, to live with the Sultan; and in January 1875, intervention in Selangor was completed by the appointment of a Resident.

In Sungei Ujong the Dato' Klana proved himself a willing instru- ment of British policy; he had the advantage of seniority over his rival, the Dato' Bandar, and the latter was identified with the Selan- gor enemies of Zia'u'd-din; Clarke therefore decided to support the Klana. By an agreement of 21 April 1874, the Straits Government

---

[1] Engagement entered into by the Chiefs of Perak at Pulo Pangkor, 20 January 1874, Maxwell and Gibson, op. cit. pp. 28–30. See chapter III, note 33, for dis- cussion concerning the Malay version.

[2] Carnarvon to Clarke, 29 May 1874, C.1111, no. 59.

[3] The telegram is cited in full in a minute of 11 August on Clarke to Carnarvon 195 of 16 June 1874, CO 273/76. Clarke does not appear to have replied to it. It was referred to again by Carnarvon in a despatch of 4 September 1874, C.1111, no. 68.

[4] Clarke to Anson, 16 February 1874, Anson Correspondence.

recognized him as the legitimate authority in Sungei Ujong, and released to him a quantity of arms and ammunition which he was to use to keep the river open, and free of illegal toll-stations.[1] Since this arrangement took no account of the rights of the Dato' Bandar, it aroused his resentment; and on 24 September, the Dato' Klana wrote to say that he was in danger from his colleague and to ask for help, and he coupled this appeal with a request for a British officer to reside with him. Both requests were answered; by the end of the year the Dato' Bandar had been chastened, and an officer was left in Sungei Ujong as Assistant Resident.

THE IDEA OF A RESIDENT

The whole intervention policy centred on the appointment of a British officer to the Malay states, yet no one seemed to have any clear idea of what this appointment would involve, or what responsibilities the Resident was to discharge. A British officer accredited to a Malay court might be the instrument of any one of a number of policies: he might discharge consular functions, with extra-territorial jurisdiction over British subjects and certain foreigners; he might, as in the Indian states, control external relations and defence and exercise an informal influence over internal administration. Certainly nothing so specific as a formal control of legislative, executive and judicial processes was contemplated by the Imperial Government; and the Colonial Government, mindful of the long opposition to intervention, took care not to phrase its policy despatches in terms which suggested a radical extension of responsibility. The plan to establish Residents in the Malay states was necessarily vague and ill-formulated; it suggested, without defining, the role of the Resident—as protector of British subjects and foreigners engaged in trade; as the medium of communication between the native states and the outer world, and as a progressive influence on government organization and policy. The first essential was to establish a permanent channel of communication with the native states. The erratic intercourse between the Colony and the states was a source of concern; Clarke wrote that 'this periodical visiting, without any consistent plan or fixed policy, and on one occasion by one officer, and on the next occasion by another, have clearly never been productive of

[1] Bond entered by Datu Klana Abdulrahman and Datu Muda Lingie, 21 April 1874, Maxwell and Gibson, op. cit. p. 38.

good. . . .'[1] The chief duty of the Political Agent recommended by Anson in 1871 was to maintain communication and carry on correspondence with the states.[2]

For the local government and the unofficials, the encouragement of trade, economic development, and the provision of security for traders, were the most important functions of the Resident; and an especially important task was the protection of existing Chinese populations and the encouragement of immigration, essential to the development of the states. Clarke emphasized the scarcity of Malay population and the fact that the Chinese were 'the only industrial population' and 'the backbone of all trade and commerce throughout the Malay Peninsula'. Both officials and unofficials looked forward to a Chinese migration which would eventually swamp the Malays; at the Legislative Council debate on the Pangkor Engagement, one speaker expanded on the slow rate of Malay increase and concluded that 'to open up that country you must introduce the Chinese element' and that 'Malay States, with a large Chinese population, must be under the influence of the British flag'.[3] The Inspector-General of Police and the Colonial Engineer looked forward to a tenfold Chinese increase, 'to the manifest development of the resources of "this fine portion of the Malayan Peninsula" '. Swettenham wrote in retrospect that, 'while their first object was to benefit the Malays and make their lives easier and happier, they recognized that they must look to the Chinese as the workers and revenue producers'.[4] Until the end of the century at least, the Chinese immigration figures were, for the Residents, an index to the prosperity of the states.

The expansion of trade (which meant of course primarily the expansion of tin production), the establishment of suitable conditions for investment, the encouragement of Chinese immigration, all clearly required the Resident to be more than a means of communication or a court diplomat. The 1871 Commission had stressed the influence which such an officer might be expected to have over internal admin-

---

[1] Clarke to Kimberley, 24 February 1874, C.1111, no. 52.
[2] Anson to Kimberley, 144 of 3 June 1871, CO 273/47.
[3] Speech by W. R. Scott in *Proceedings of the Legislative Council,* 15 September 1874, C.1111, enclosure in no. 72, Clarke to Carnarvon, 5 November 1874.
[4] Proceedings of McNair and Dunlop, 15 January 1874, C.1111, enclosure in no. 39, Clarke to Kimberley, 18 January 1874; F. A. Swettenham, *Footprints in Malaya,* London, 1942, pp. 71–72. See also memoranda (undated) by members of the Executive Council on the despatch from Kimberley to Clarke of 20 September 1873, C.1111, enclosures 1—5 in no. 54, Clarke to Carnarvon, 24 February 1874.

istration, and suggested that he might give the native Rulers professional advice in opening up roads, and assist them in all matters connected with their government. The point was continually emphasized in the despatches home, and in the memoranda on the Resident's duties prepared by the members of the Executive Council immediately after the Pangkor Engagement. The stress was on informal guidance and suggestion; one official, writing in 1872, referred to the Political Agents in the Indian states, the value of the work done by a 'single well-selected British officer' in encouraging the development of communications, schools and police, and recommended the appointment of an officer to perform similar functions in the Malay states.[1]

The Pangkor Engagement, and the despatches and memoranda in which Clarke and his officials made their policy recommendations, spoke in terms of advice, guidance and persuasion when describing the influence to be exercised by the Resident at the native courts, and these references have established a long-lived myth about the nature of British intervention in the Malay states. The myth may be expressed in the words of a permanent official of the Colonial Office, seeking to explain the juridical position to the Law Officers of the Crown. '[Tell them] that about 10 years ago the Native Rulers of 3 States requested that English Residents should be placed with them to advise them on the ways of good government; that after some unfortunate disturbances the Secretary of State finally sanctioned the Residents as permanent institutions, strictly laying down that beyond the control of the collection of Revenue the Residents were only to interfere in administration by means of advice tendered to the Native Rulers.'[2] It need hardly be stressed that this representation of the Malay states administrations is false; it is not sustained even in the despatches, it is constantly belied in the minutes, and it breaks down on the most cursory survey of the government of the Malay states; indeed there is enough in the published accounts of Malay states'

[1] G. Campbell, Acting Lt.-Governor of Penang, cited Wilkinson, op. cit. p. 119.

[2] Minute by de Robeck, 12 January 1885, on Smith to Derby, 488 of 8 November 1885, CO 273/130. With occasional lapses, the officials adhered to this interpretation in their formal correspondence. In 1883 the Secretary of State disclaimed any 'desire to interfere in the minor details of the Administration of the Native States by their Rajahs' (Derby to Weld, 116 of 10 May 1883, CO 273/119). As late as 1893, the Governor, in presenting the AR for 1892, spoke of Malay Rulers as 'de facto as well as de jure the rulers of their states'. Smith to Ripon, 246 of 2 August 1893, CO 273/189.

rule, written by Governors and Residents, to cast doubts on the validity of this stereotype, without recourse to other material. It is however legitimate to argue that whatever may have been the later relationship between Resident and Malay Ruler, the original intention of Clarke and his colleagues was that the Residents should exercise a salutary pressure rather than rule directly; and that circumstances forced the assumption of a direct control that was not originally intended. The suggestion put forward here is that the creation and control of the organs of government by the Resident was essential to the purposes of intervention—the achievement of security and the guarantee of economic development; that Clarke saw this and intended his Residents to assume administrative responsibilities wherever they could safely and profitably do so; and that the representation of control as 'advice' was a concession as much to the sensibility of the Colonial Office as to that of the Malays.

Swettenham claimed in his autobiography that the system of administration called 'indirect rule', which had been introduced by British officers into Africa in the twentieth century, and which he understood to mean 'the principle of employing the people of the country to share with British advisers and their staff the direction and control of public affairs', originated with the system devised by British Residents in the Malay states in 1874 and subsequent years. It is sufficient here to say that whatever influence the philosophy of colonial government known as 'indirect rule' may have had on colonial practice in Malaya in later years, it does not appear to have played any part in the shaping of Clarke's policy. It is true that indirect rule in Africa and elsewhere was pragmatic in the sense that it found in traditional leadership a cheap and convenient means of organizing subject populations, and as the system developed, the stress came to be laid more and more on attempts to transform and modernize indigenous institutions and use them to promote change. But a powerful motive for indirect rule was a positive appreciation of traditional societies and the institutions which maintained them; and although the inevitability of change was admitted, the theory of indirect rule sought to regulate change by adapting indigenous institutions to new political and economic modes of action, instead of exposing them unprotected to the destructive impact of external forces.

This conservative sentiment was absent from the ideas of Clarke and his advisers. When they wrote of teaching the Malays good government, they were not thinking in terms of development from Malay traditions and institutions. There is nothing to show that they put any value on these institutions, either for their own sake, or as a necessary context for Malay social growth.[1] According to Clarke, 'The Malays, like every other rude Eastern nation, require to be treated much more like children, and to be taught; and this especially in all matters of improvement, whether in the question of good government and organization, or of material improvement. . . .'[2] According to Birch, the Colonial Secretary and first Resident of Perak, 'my experience as an Executive and Judicial Officer for the last twenty-seven years among an Eastern people has taught me that they are perfectly incapable of good government, or even of maintaining order, without guidance or assistance from some stronger hand than is ever to be found amongst themselves'.[3] The other officials stressed the 'absolute inability of the native rulers to maintain order without assistance' and their inability to cater to the demands of economic development. There was no question of moderating these demands. The changes that had already overtaken the Malays were to be accelerated; the external pressures which had already caused the breakdown of Malay government were to be increased. Intervention was seen to be necessary because Malay authority had proved incapable of dealing with Chinese immigration and mining activity; and it was this enterprise which the British were proposing to encourage. Considerations of economy, which might force other colonies to use indigenous authorities for want of a sufficient revenue for a European establishment, had no especial relevance to the formation of policy. There was admittedly a 'paucity of competent officers to undertake the work' (the one invariable feature of colonial expansion under any system!) but the expense of direct administration was not put forward at this stage as an argument against it, and in any case, Clarke and his officials were confidently looking forward to the rapid expansion of the economy and revenues of these states.[4] The themes and policies of indirect rule, as they were systematized half a century later in Africa, fitted neither the conditions of these states nor the motives

[1] The exception was the Auditor-General, whose views had no influence.

[2] Clarke to Kimberley, 24 February 1874, C.1111, no. 52.

[3] Memorandum by the CS regarding Native States, with reference to Secretary of State's despatch of 20 September 1873, C.1111, enclosure 5 in no. 54, Clarke to Kimberley, 24 February 1874.

[4] 'I feel persuaded that, when the country is once quiet and the revenue regularly and properly collected, it will be found that funds are available, not only for these establishments and the necessary police, but for a fair civil list to the Sultan and the Chiefs.' Clarke to Kimberley, 24 February 1874, C.1111, no. 52.

and sentiments of the utilitarian administrators in Singapore. The authorities who had to be coaxed and taught, and whose advance had to be adjusted to their prejudices, lived not in Perak or in Selangor but in Whitehall; and it was for their mental comfort that definitions were avoided, in correspondence about the functions of Residents.

Clarke did not conceal the fact that the Residents were to undertake wide responsibilities. As a later Resident remarked, the Pangkor Engagement itself covered all executive authority;[1] and in his explanatory despatch a month after Pangkor, Clarke emphasized the fiscal responsibilities of the Resident:

This watching the collection of the revenue, and controlling its expenditure, will form no insignificant part of a Resident's duties; and . . . will be about the most important portion of them.

The collection of the revenue, from whatsoever source derived, and however legitimate, is carried on at present among these States, with a perfect absence of all system . . . while it is at all times accompanied by individual instances of extortion. . . .

To check this, and to induce the Sultan to select proper men for the collection, will be the Resident's special care. . . .[2]

Clarke forestalled questions about the possible Malay reaction to these innovations by representing that the rulers themselves wanted the Residents and their advice, were anxious to reform the administration of their states, and were only waiting to be told how to do it. He had plenty of supporting documents; Sultan 'Abdu'llah, while he was still Raja Muda, had written to express the desire of himself and his great men 'to settle under the sheltering protection of the English flag'; he asked for 'a man of sufficient abilities to live with us in Perak, or at any fit place not far from us, and show us a good system of government for our dominions, so that our country may be opened up, and bring profit, and increase the revenues, as well as peace and justice'.[3] The Dato' Klana declared his wish to have his country populous, and a good straight road for traders; he declared further, '. . . we would like very much for an officer from the Great Governor, who can give good advice, so that we may do what is

[1] F. A. Swettenham, *The Real Malay*, London, 1900, p. 22.
[2] Clarke to Kimberley, 24 February 1874, C.1111, no. 52. The despatch of an Assistant Resident to Selangor in August was apparently accompanied by a proposal that British officers should collect the revenues of Selangor. Sultan 'Abdu'l Samad to Clarke, 1 October 1875, Maxwell and Gibson, op. cit. p. 35.
[3] Raja 'Abdu'llah to Clarke, 30 December 1873, C.1111, enclosure 12 in no. 39, Clarke to Kimberley, 26 January 1874.

right under that protection'.[1] Tengku Zia'u'd-din had asked for closer British protection in 1873, and the Sultan of Selangor gracefully accepted the officer sent him in 1874; 'As to my friend's request that I will enter into an agreement with my friend in order that my friend may collect all the taxes of my country, I should be very glad if my friend would set my country to right and collect all its taxes.'[2] All these communications were duly forwarded to the Colonial Office, and formed the basis of the official claim that the British went to the Malay states by invitation.

In Perak and Sungei Ujong, the request for Residents was itself a token of the isolation of the chiefs who asked for them; it is clear from their communications that Sultan 'Abdu'llah and the Dato' Klana were merely seeking British support for their disputed authority. Sultan Ismail and the Mentri in Perak, and the Dato' Bandar in Sungei Ujong, were just as clearly opposed to British interference. The fact that 'Abdu'llah had asked for a Resident, and eleven days after his request had been received, had been made Sultan, might have raised doubts about the nature of his authority, and his ability to carry out 'advice'. In his official correspondence, Clarke justified his support of 'Abdu'llah by representing him as the rightful ruler, excluded from the throne by a conspiracy, and now restored by the choice of all the chiefs except the Mentri. He took pains to emphasize that 'Abdu'llah had been 'elected' by the chiefs at Pangkor and that he (Clarke) had been a mere witness to the election.[3] The eye-witness account of the proceedings, written by his Attorney-General (Thomas Braddell) tells a different story.[4] According to Braddell, the Gov-

[1] Dato' Klana to Lt.-Governor of Malacca, 24 September 1874, C.1320, enclosure in no. 8, Clarke to Carnarvon, 29 December 1874.

[2] Sultan 'Abdu'l Samad to Clarke, 1 October 1874, Maxwell and Gibson, op. cit. pp. 35–36.

[3] Clarke to Kimberley, 26 January 1876, C.1111, no. 39; Clarke to Kimberley, 24 February 1874, C.1111, no. 52. In a private letter to the CO, he stressed that the Pangkor Engagement was not a treaty between the British Government and the chiefs, but an engagement between the chiefs themselves, which not unnaturally caused one official to wonder how in that case the clauses affecting the British Government, relating to the introduction of a Resident and the settlement of boundaries, could be enforced (Cox, minute of 11 August on Clarke to Carnarvon, 195 of 16 June, CO 273/76). It was decided to secure obedience to the Engagement by informing the chiefs that Her Majesty's Government would 'look to the exact fulfilment of the pledges which have now been voluntarily given'. Carnarvon to Clarke, 4 September 1874, C.1111, no. 68.

[4] Braddell, 'Report of Proceedings at Pangkor and Larut', C.1111, enclosure 7 in no. 52, Clarke to Carnarvon, 24 February 1874. A brief extract is printed as Appendix 2 of 'Sir Frank Swettenham's Perak Journals', JMBRAS, vol. xxiv, part 4 (1951), pp. 139–41.

ernor had decided on 'Abdu'llah, and had broken down his most determined opponent (the Mentri) before the matter was discussed with the chiefs; when they were assembled, they were asked individually whether they would support 'Abdu'llah, and individually agreed. The three surviving office-holders of the first rank—the Bendahara, the Temenggong and the Mentri—had all endorsed Ismail's succession in 1871, and now endorsed 'Abdu'llah's; but the Mentri acted under duress, and there is no record that the other two ever went near 'Abdu'llah of their own accord from the Pangkor meeting till his departure in 1876.[1] Sultan Ismail was not present, nor was Raja Yusuf, the other claimant to the throne; and of the six surviving chiefs of the second rank, only three were present, and none of the others ever endorsed the Engagement.

In his private correspondence, Clarke showed himself perfectly aware of the nature of 'Abdu'llah's elevation, and the real sentiments of the Perak chiefs towards British intervention. 'I believe in every way I was right in putting up Abdulla. Had I taken the other man, I could not have secured the peace of the coasts, or the lower parts of the rivers, my first object, as Abdulla and his party are strong there, while Ismail and his followers are high up the river where we have no trade, and where we need not go for years. . . .'[2] His rationalization of his choice, written two years after the event, need not be accepted in whole; it might have been even more useful for his purposes if the Sultan's jurisdiction had not extended over the lower river. But the passage sufficiently discredits Clarke's formal representation of 'Abdu'llah's election as a free election by the chiefs in recognition of his hereditary right. The willingness of the chiefs themselves to accept British intervention may be gauged by the fact that Clarke thought it essential to get them to Pangkor in a week, without giving them time to consult their lawyers.[3]

As to Selangor; it is notable that Clarke, anxious though he was to present his policy to the Colonial Office as in harmony with the wishes of the rulers, makes no reference in his despatches home to an actual request from the Sultan for a Resident, and though the claim has been made that the Sultan 'himself asked for a Resident', the evidence for this is slight.[4] A proclamation was issued in the Sul-

---

[1] They were present at a meeting with 'Abdu'llah at Blanja in early 1875, but this was at the insistence of Birch, then Resident.

[2] Clarke to Childers, 10 December 1875, cited Vetch, op. cit. p. 187.

[3] Ibid. p. 154.

[4] Weld in the course of a laudatory speech on the opening of the Selangor

tan's name in December 1874, referring to the presence of a British officer in Selangor (Swettenham) 'by our request',[1] and a proclamation issued by the Governor on 25 January 1875 declared that the Sultan had asked for 'an English Officer to assist him to open up and govern his country', and that a Resident and an Assistant Resident were being sent to him 'at his request'.[2] There is in existence an original letter from Clarke to the Sultan dated 18 June 1875,[3] introducing Swettenham (the bearer of the letter) as the officer who was being sent to Selangor at the Sultan's request ('*maka dengan sebab permintaan sahabat beta jadi beta sudah hantar Tuan Swettenham itu jadi wakil beta kapada sahabat beta*') and asking him to confirm acceptance of Swettenham according to a draft attached in postscript. But all these documents emanated from the Governor. Even if there were a letter from the Sultan asking for such an officer, it would still be necessary to assess it with caution, for it was common practice throughout the period to secure documents legitimizing British actions by presenting drafts for signature under pressure; but in any case, no such letter has come to light. The Sultan's letter to Clarke of 1 October 1874, reporting the arrival of Swettenham and engaging to allow the Governor to collect the taxes of Selangor, made it quite clear that this was being done at the Governor's own request.[4] Finally, Clarke's own despatch reporting the departure of Swettenham, who was 'to remain, should the Sultan desire it, at Langat', suggests strongly that the initiative came wholly from Clarke.[5]

---

railway, congratulated the Sultan on his zeal for the welfare of his people 'evidenced by his having on his own initiative set the example to Native Rulers of first asking for a British Resident to advise him.' (Weld to Granville, 319 of 23 September 1886, CO 273/141). Swettenham declared in his *AR*, Selangor, 1887, 'The present relations between the British Government and His Highness the Sultan of Selangor were initiated by Governor Sir Andrew Clarke, at the request of his Highness, in August 1874'.

[1] Proclamation by the Sultan of Selangor in English and Jawi, 18 November 1874, *SSGG* 12 December 1874.
[2] Maxwell and Gibson, op. cit. p. 36.
[3] Sir Andrew Clarke to Sultan 'Abdu'l Samad, 18 June 1875 [*sic*], Unlisted Item 4(c), Swettenham Collection, ANM. The date was filled in later, when Clarke had already left the Straits. Swettenham's Langat Journal contains an entry for 17 June 1875 saying that he delivered the Governor's letter to the Sultan on that day. 17 June is probably his mistake for 18 June, since Swettenham notes in his entry for the 19th that he has missed a day.
[4] Maxwell and Gibson, op. cit. p. 35; Swettenham's Langat Journal, entries for 30 September and 2 October 1874.
[5] Clarke to Carnarvon, 356 of 29 December 1874, CO 273/76. A few days after Swettenham arrived, he was asked by the Sultan whether he had brought

In later years, the Sultan became a pattern of complaisance and loyalty, but there is nothing to show that he wanted a Resident in 1874, indeed the evidence is to the contrary. During Birch's visit in 1871 and again during a visit by Irving in 1872, he showed great reluctance to endorse Tengku Zia'u'd-din,[1] and during Clarke's visit in February 1874, he had to be coerced into appointing a court to try the men accused of the Jugra piracy.[2] This reluctance to commit himself to support of British policies was put down by British officials to fear of assassination by the Mahdi party, who were strongly represented at his court; but even after a Resident was appointed, when presumably such fears no longer prevailed and he was free to choose his own companions, his cronies were still those who had been committed to support the Raja Mahdi.[3] Late in 1875, when there was fear of a rising in Ulu Langat, he concealed from the Resident the fact that partisans of Mahdi were collecting in the interior, and that one of them was then actually in Langat.[4] In 1882, another Resident complained that the Sultan lived 'surrounded by men opposed to British interference and averse to the policy which has led to the development and peace and prosperity of the State'.[5] In 1874, intervention in Selangor depended on the support of Tengku Zia'u'd-din, a Kedah prince and a foreigner, and on such bad terms with the royal family of Selangor (including his own wife) that between 1871 and 1874 he never went to Langat except in the company of British officers. A careful reading of the enclosures would have suggested to the Colonial Office that the anxiety for better government on the part of the Malay Rulers was not as general or as dis-

his gun, and replied that he had not, because he did not know whether the Sultan 'would care about our staying with him' (entry for 19 August 1874).

[1] Irving, who went to Langat in 1872 to get the Sultan's sons recalled from Kuala Selangor in favour of Tengku Zia'u'd-din, declared that the Sultan assented 'as I believe he would have assented to anything I had said' and 'at once ordered a letter to be written' (Irving, Memorandum relative to a Visit to Selangor in 1872 in *Papers relating to the Malay Peninsula, 1870–1882*, item 12, ANM). But according to Irving's Malay interpreter, who was a witness to the proceedings, the Sultan denied there was trouble in Kuala Selangor and put off writing the letter of recall as long as he could. Mohammed Ibrahim bin 'Abdu'l-lah, *Kesah Pelayaran*, p. 49.

[2] Vetch, op. cit. pp. 157–9.

[3] One of his closest friends was his brother-in-law, the Tengku Panglima Raja, who was suspended from membership of the State Council in 1878, among other reasons, because he had got up a petition in the Bernam district in favour of Mahdi's return.

[4] Jervois to Carnarvon, 327 of 16 November 1875, CO 273/81.

[5] Douglas to CO, 27 November 1882, CO 273/117.

interested as the despatches showed; but the Colonial Office seemed content to take the assurances of the Governor at their face value. Even if the chiefs were anxious to accept advice, it is a question whether the local officials thought them capable of carrying it out. The criterion of enlightenment was not merely that they should understand the importance of Chinese immigration (they nearly all did) but that they should attempt to rationalize their revenue collection and provide security for their foreign population. Among the Malay Rulers in the nineteenth century there were indeed a few who were alive to the political and economic changes which had overtaken the Peninsula, who realized that new administrative methods were required, and who took advice and profited by it. The most obvious example of the way in which an able ruler might profit by advice was provided by the Temenggongs of Johore.[1] They had been protégés of the British Government from the cession of Singapore in 1824, and successive rulers had assumed the sovereignty of the state and the title of *Maharaja* with the assistance of the Straits Government. In return they adapted themselves to the requirements of British policy. In 1862, by the Treaty of Pahang, Johore agreed to refer any dispute between the states to the British Government; in 1868, she accepted British arbitration in the Johore-Pahang boundary settlement, and in 1870 the Johore Government stopped an attempt by the North German Confederation to survey a naval station at the mouth of the Endau river. There was no British political agent in Johore, but such contact was hardly necessary; till 1862 the official residence of the Johore ruler was in Singapore, and after that date he kept a large private establishment there. He was in direct and constant contact with the Governor; Braddell, the Attorney-General, was his legal adviser. The aspect of Johore administration that appeared most impressive to the Straits officials, was the encouragement of Chinese immigration and the consequent economic progress of the state. Newbold guessed that the population in the 1830's was about 25,000; the Temenggong encouraged the immigration of Chi-

---

[1] The Temenggongs were court officials who administered Johore and Singapore in the latter part of the eighteenth century on behalf of absentee Sultans living at Riau. In 1819 the Temenggong Abdulrahman and Sultan Husain (a pretender whom Raffles recognized for the purpose) assented to the lease of Singapore. In 1855, by an arrangement sponsored by the Governor, the *de jure* Sultan ceded his sovereignty over Johore to Temenggong Ibrahim, and in 1868 Temenggong Abubakar was recognized as Maharaja by the then Governor, Sir Harry Ord.

nese pepper and gambier planters, and in the early 1870's the Chinese population alone was estimated at 60,000.[1] In the 1830's, the Singapore opium farmer offered $300 a month for the Johore farms; in 1857 the farms were worth $5,000 a month. In 1855 Johore Bahru was a fishing village; thirty years later, according to Winstedt, the Duke of Sutherland found it 'a gay little Malay town', with 10,000 Chinese inhabitants, and such modern amenities as 'a gaol and hospital and police-stations and schools and a steam saw-mill reported to be the largest in Asia'.

Clarke and his advisers did not fail to point to the Maharaja of Johore as an example of an enlightened Malay Ruler whose constant association with European advisers had led to the establishment of an orderly government which enjoyed the confidence of the Chinese and Europeans. But it was acknowledged that the circumstances of Johore were special. The Johore ruling house had been placed in intimate association with the government at Singapore for half a century; and in that time the Temenggongs had shown themselves outstanding among Malay Rulers for their ability and energy. The Maharaja had had an English education, had visited Europe, and entertained with magnificence and style; his hospitality was an important element in the European social life of Singapore. The most Europeanized of the Malaya rajas were clumsy imitators by comparison.[2]

In the western Malay states there were chiefs—notably the Mentri and Tengku Zia'u'd-din—who, like the Maharaja of Johore, were experienced in dealing with large Chinese populations and large revenues, and who acted extensively outside a traditional Malay context. Both of these chiefs were sufficiently sophisticated to employ European legal advisers;[3] both recruited mercenaries under European leadership to fight their wars;[4] both derived their large revenues

[1] Clarke to Carnarvon, 24 February 1874, C.1111, no. 52. The rest of the account is taken from R. O. Winstedt, 'History of Johore', *JMBRAS*, vol. x, part 3 (1932), pp. 89–117.

[2] See Emily Innes, *The Chersonese with the Gilding Off*, London, 1885, vol. i, p. 175, for an account of an unfortunate dinner party 'Government House style' given by Tengku Zia'u'd-din.

[3] Many of the chiefs whose interests brought them into judicial or economic relations with Europeans or Chinese, employed Straits lawyers. The Mentri's lawyer was R. C. Woods of Penang; Tengku Zia'u'd-din's was J. G. Davidson of Singapore.

[4] In July 1873, the Mentri employed T.C.S. Speedy, formerly Assistant Supt. of Police, Penang, to recruit and command Indian sepoys for his service, and in September, Speedy returned from India with 110 men.

mainly from duties on tin, centrally collected at the mouth of the Larut, Selangor and Klang rivers. But their control was restricted to positions en route to the mines; on the fields, where the bulk of the population lived, Malay control of any sort was non-existent.

It is conceivable that with the support of the Resident and with European police instructors, the problem of public order might have been solved, and the revenue collection systematized, without the assumption of direct control. Irving pointed out how Tengku Zia'u'd-din might be helped; by the organization of his finances (concerning which he had already consulted British officials), by a small loan, by assistance with his scheme of a road to the Pahang tin and gold mines, by inspection and advice on his fortifications. Here was a progressive chief with 'ideas in his mind on the subject of education and the administration of justice', who was eager and quick to learn. Irving, taking the policy of 'advice' seriously, and enunciating the principles of indirect rule, pleaded for an itinerant Resident;

If the policy of Her Majesty's Government were to keep pushing our influence in those countries, and becoming virtually the governing power, the appointment of permanent Residents would probably be a step in the right direction. But this I understand from the Secretary of State's despatch is not the course that is designed, and that what is desired is to interfere as little as possible, compatibly with saving the countries from open disorders, and for the rest to treat the native Governments and native institutions to be things to be improved as occasions may show to be possible, but in the main to be recognized as they are, and their self dependency rather encouraged by a wholesome neglect, than weakened by perpetual training and fostering.[1]

But though Clarke and his officials spoke exclusively of 'advising' and pointed to the example of Johore, Johore did not provide Clarke with the model he wanted. Clarke disapproved of the Maharaja's handling of his revenues,[2] just as a previous governor had disapproved of his haphazard administration of justice; and he looked to the organization of government on different principles: 'I cannot, however, conceal from myself the fact, that even there it is quite possible that, for the great future we have hardly yet received sufficient guarantees to secure the continuance of that prosperity . . . we cannot at once accept as a fact that enough has been done, and that

[1] Memorandum relative to the Affairs of the Native States in the Malay Peninsula with reference to the Despatch of the Secretary of State of 20 September 1873, by the Auditor-General, C.1111, enclosure 2 in no. 54, Clarke to Carnarvon, 24 February 1874.
[2] Clarke to Kimberley, 24 February 1874, C.1111, no. 52.

there may not be more for you or our successors to do, to secure that future in those elements of prosperity.'[1] Irving's blueprint for a genuine advisory system met with a chilly reception; his analysis of the Secretary of State's instructions went without comment, but his suggestion of an itinerant Resident was rejected outright by Clarke, Birch and Braddell as likely to confirm all the evils which had already arisen out of intermittent interference. Braddell emphasized the deficiencies in native government which must increase the Resident's responsibilities and transfer 'teaching' into direction:

> To preserve order, to do justice and prevent oppression, to collect the revenue on fixed principles, to spend a portion of it in making roads and waterworks, and in providing for the security of the people, are the simple duties required in the first instance.
>
> The native Chiefs may be said to know this, but they are indolent, self-indulgent, and averse to continuous exertion in any direction. They do not know how to commence a new line of conduct, still less how to persevere in it. . . .[2]

Clarke's private correspondence and instructions to Residents indicate that the policy to be followed was not government through native institutions but the assumption by stages of direct control; control initially of the economically important areas—the tin fields and the coasts—and *laissez-faire* in the predominantly Malay interior until a further advance might appear easy and profitable. Braddell wrote in retrospect: '. . . the interference with Upper Perak was deprecated by Sir Andrew Clarke, and advised against by me, as premature and unnecessary . . . the population was purely Malay, with a few Chinese shopkeepers and hawkers, scattered over a large territory; and although great benefit naturally would arise in time, when the proper moment for intervention should have arrived, it was felt that the time had not yet arrived in 1875.'[3] He had specified Larut, Sungei Ujong and Klang as the areas where intervention would

[1] Speech by Clarke, *Proceedings of the Legislative Council*, 15 September 1874, C.1111, enclosure in no. 72, Clarke to Carnarvon, 5 November 1874.

[2] Memorandum by the Attorney-General regarding Native States, with reference to Despatch from the Secretary of State, dated 20 September 1873, C.1111, enclosure 4 in no. 54, Clarke to Carnarvon, 24 February 1874.

[3] Braddell to Derby, 27 April 1883, enclosure in Derby to Weld, 117 of 10 May 1883. When Clarke arrived, there was no department dealing with Malay states' affairs, and Braddell, then Attorney-General, took over the duty of collating the material and reducing it to reports published in C.1111 and C.1320. He was Clarke's closest adviser, and between October 1874 and April 1875 (when he went on leave to recruit his health) he was Colonial Secretary and Secretary for Native States.

be desirable and profitable. Clarke had put things more bluntly in a letter to Birch, the first Resident of Perak, 'Limit all your efforts to the sea-coast . . . do not bother about the upper rivers where there are only Malays.'[1] A year later, when suggestions of annexation were in the air, he wrote that such a change of policy was foolish; 'till each State pays we must be patient, and not hasten too much the ideas of how things should be done. Let us know the country well, and having established our police posts, our advance, when we make it, will be easy. If you annex you must be prepared to spend money and lose many lives'.[2]

Of the instructions to Residents, there survive only a letter to Davidson, the first Resident of Selangor, and fragments of instructions to Birch;[3] but these indicate sufficiently the responsibilities which the Residents were required to fulfil. Their most important duties related to revenue collection. Birch was to 'allow the existing system to go on when not of such an irregular character as to require immediate alteration', but this licence was cancelled in the next sentence which required him to 'put down, by force if necessary, all unlawful exactions of whatever nature, so as to secure that whatever revenue is collected shall be for the state alone . . . [and] paid into the general treasury of the country'. The Residents were further instructed in a circular letter from the Colonial Secretary, that the Governor favoured 'one uniform system of revenue in all the Native States, which should be on as simple a scale as possible, putting restrictions on as few articles as possible'. Birch, who had submitted a detailed revenue scheme for Perak in December, was told that he might put it into force provisionally until reports from the other states were received, and a general scheme had been drawn up.[4] To put the matter beyond doubt, the Governor wrote to Sultan 'Abdu'-llah two months afterwards, enclosing a proclamation forbidding the collection of revenue without written instructions from the Resident or Assistant Resident, or the payment of tax to any but their officers.[5] In Selangor, Davidson was required to report as soon as

[1] Clarke to Birch, undated, cited in Vetch, op. cit. p. 182.

[2] Clarke to Childers, October 1875,, in Vetch, op. cit. p. 182.

[3] CS to Resident of Selangor, 20 January 1875, Sel/Sec. 3/175; Clarke to Birch, 26 October 1874, cited Jervois to Carnarvon, 62 of 10 February 1876, CO 273/83.

[4] CS to Birch, 12 February 1875, EPO, Appendix xiv; similar instructions were sent to Selangor in CS to Assistant Resident of Selangor, 12 February 1875, Sel/Sec. 742/1875.

[5] Clarke to Sultan 'Abdu'llah, 22 April 1875, enclosing Proclamation of 9

possible on the revenue system to be adopted, and to provide for the settlement of the Tengku's debts (now the obligation of the state). He was required to forward to Singapore a regular monthly report of progress and a monthly statement of accounts, showing the revenue and expenditure of the country, 'which you will take under your special charge, being assisted by such officers, clerks etc. as may be sanctioned by His Excellency, on your representation after arrival at Klang'.

The argument here is not that Clarke had any detailed plan for the development of the administration of the Malay states, or that he wished control to be assumed without regard for the interests or sensibilities of the rulers and chiefs. On the contrary, his letters to the first Resident of Perak convey warnings against clumsiness and haste; the Resident was told to be gentle with Ismail, the Sultan whose authority was set aside by Pangkor, and not to press him to give up anything; he was told to leave debt slavery alone for the time being. 'Have patience with them. Debt-slavery is a bad thing, but until we are prepared to compensate in full and to show a better system to secure credit, let it for the present alone.'[1] It was ordinary common sense to enjoin care and patience in instituting change, and even if common sense did not impose caution, the hesitant and qualified approval given by the Colonial Office to the policy of intervention would have warned Clarke against treating the Malays like defeated enemies. But the key to his policy and to future development was not in the advice he gave on conduct in transitory situations, but in the provision for control of revenues and general administration laid down in the Pangkor Engagement and in the instructions. These made it certain that whatever form of government was established in the Malay states, it would not be 'government by advice'.

April 1875, *EPO*, Appendices xvii and xviii. The instructions to Residents were not forwarded to the CO, but the letter to 'Abdu'llah referred to here, with its blunt assertion of authority, was sent home with a despatch of 26 April 1875 (C.1320, enclosure in no. 26).

[1] Clarke to Birch, undated, in Vetch, op. cit. p. 182.

III

THE FIRST RESIDENTS

FIRST STEPS

THE first appointment of a Resident was made at Pangkor, when Captain T. C. S. Speedy was appointed Acting Assistant British Resident at Larut. In August, F. A. Swettenham was sent to the court of the Sultan of Selangor at Langat. In November, Clarke sent his Colonial Secretary, J. W. W. Birch, to Perak as Acting Resident with Sultan 'Abdu'llah; and in December, after a police action in Sungei Ujong, Captain W. Tatham, R.A., who accompanied the ex-pedition, was left to effect settlement of the troubles. In the same month, Clarke submitted these four names to the Secretary of State for confirmation, and added to them J. G. Davidson, whom he pro-posed to send to Selangor as Acting Resident, living with Tengku 'Zia'u'd-din at Klang.[1] Speedy was at his post by the end of January; Swettenham was in Selangor by mid-August; Birch at the Perak estuary in the first week of November; and Davidson in Selangor in the first week of February 1875.[2] Though the Secretary of State had

[1] Clarke to Carnarvon, 357 of 30 December 1874, CO 273/76. In a confidential despatch of the same date, he reported at length on the qualifications of Birch and Davidson, and sought to reassure the Secretary of State as to their fitness for their appointments.

[2] Three of the Residents had been in the service of the Straits Settlements Government; all except Captain Tatham had had recent connexions with the western Malay states, though in only one case—Davidson's—did these connexions date from before 1872. See Appendix 2 for information about Birch and Swet-tenham.

Tristram Charles Sawyer Speedy had had an adventurous career as a British Agent in Abyssinia and had served in the Indian Army before joining the Straits Settlements service as Deputy Commissioner of Police in 1872. In July 1873 he resigned his post with the consent of the Governor, to enter the Mentri's service as Commander of his troops; and with soldiers recruited in India, he joined the fighting in Larut towards the end of 1873, on behalf of the Mentri and the Hai San faction. It was decided at Pangkor to appoint him provisionally to Larut as Assistant Resident, and he took up his duties at once. He was a soldier and adven-turer, not a routine administrator, and as the administration of Perak settled down into a system, relations between Speedy and his superiors became very strained. In 1876, in an effort to get him out of the service, his salary was halved and in 1877 he was moved to the very much less important district of Lower Perak. He resigned the same year.

doubts about their ability to discharge responsibilities 'so novel and delicate', and particularly objected to Davidson's financial interest in Selangor, he did not press his objections,[1] and the Residents remained in their appointments till the disturbances in Perak towards the end of 1875 disorganized the whole arrangement.

In Sungei Ujong the Malay Ruler, the Dato' Klana, lived near the mines; a single officer was sufficient to maintain communication with him and control the mining population, and he established his headquarters at Seremban, near the mines and about three miles north of Rasah, the tin port on the Linggi river. In Perak and Selangor, where the courts of the rulers were set apart from the centres of economic activity, officers were posted separately to the Sultan's township and to the tin fields or ports. The Resident of Selangor set up his headquarters at Klang, the port for the Kuala Lumpur tin and the headquarters of Tengku Zia'u'd-din, while the Assistant Resident went to the Sultan at Langat. In Perak the Resident established himself at Bandar Bahru, near the Sultan's 'palace' in Lower Perak,

---

James Guthrie Davidson was a Singapore lawyer who had been for many years the Tengku's legal adviser and financial backer. In March 1873, after the Tengku's enemies had been expelled from Kuala Lumpur with the help of Pahang troops, the Tengku granted a concession to Davidson and a partner to mine tin over a large area in Selangor. Davidson sold his share to the Selangor Tin Mining Company, floated to work the concession. There were obvious objections to his appointment to a state where he had commercial interests, objections which were not removed by the transfer of his interests to a firm in which his uncle was a partner; but his tact and experience with Malays, his knowledge of Selangor, and his close relations with the Tengku were outstanding qualifications, especially when the Governor scarcely knew where to look for suitable officers. For further details, see Appendix 2.

Walter Tatham was an officer of the Royal Artillery, and senior auxiliary officer of the troops sent to the relief of Pickering in Sungei Ujong in December 1874. He knew Malay and had often acted for officers in the civil police. He undertook an inquiry into the condition of Indian labourers in Province Wellesley in 1873. He went on sick leave in April 1875 and was replaced permanently by Commander P. J. Murray, RN.

[1] In a despatch addressed to Clarke's successor, the Secretary of State expressed doubts whether the Residents had the special qualifications necessary to carry out their tasks successfully, and instructed that the appointments should be provisional for the time being. He approved the appointments with the exception of Davidson, whom he considered unsuitable because of his financial connexion with Selangor (Carnarvon to Jervois, Confidential of 8 April 1875, CO 273/76). Jervois begged to be allowed to keep him in Selangor until he could make some other arrangement, and expanded on the difficulty of finding men of suitable quality and experience to take up the appointments (Jervois to Carnarvon, Confidential of 28 May 1875, CO 273/80). In view of the Governor's difficulties, the Secretary of State permitted the arrangement to stand. Carnarvon to Jervois, Confidential of 16 July 1875, CO 273/80.

and the Assistant Resident fixed his headquarters in Taiping, the chief town in Larut. The responsibilities of officers to the mining areas were mainly administrative; those posted with the Sultans had in the first instance the task of conciliating the Malays and getting them to accept the new dispensation; they had to travel and report on unmapped country and little-known people. 'We spent our time getting about the country, as best we could, roughly mapping it, seeking out the best points for villages, police stations, customs houses, and landing-stages, and we did what we could to meet, and make friends, with all the influential people of the country.'[1]

In all the territories, the most urgent tasks of the British officers were basically the same; to restore order after recent fighting, to disarm the Malays and Chinese and destroy their fortifications; to restore confidence and encourage the return of Malays and Chinese to their fields and mines; to make a provisional settlement of mining boundaries and get the mines going; and to take whatever administrative action was necessary to encourage tin production, whether by improving lines of communication, by regularizing conditions of tenure, or by easing the fiscal burden on the industry.

In Larut and Sungei Ujong, the Residents were posted immediately after pacification, in order to uphold an improved settlement, and restore the mines to working order. In Larut, the work of disarming the Chinese was entrusted to Commissioners who had been appointed by the Governor at Pangkor, and who accompanied Speedy on his return there;[2] they were also to settle disputed claims to the mines between the Ghi Hin and Hai San factions, and secure the return of Ghi Hin women and children captured by the Mentri and his faction. The Commissioners destroyed the stockades of both parties, and secured the return of the captives, searching for them in Larut, in Kurau and in the Perak river valley. They also inquired into the ownership of the mines and called for documents of title; they found only four papers in Malay, permitting the holders to clear jungle, but giving no right to mine. Of the 150 claimants, not one could show a written title to mining land, and no clearing permit made any reference to boundaries; and since each party laid claim to nearly all the mines, a judicious consideration of claims was out of the question. The Commissioners summarily settled the matter by drawing a line

---

[1] Swettenham, *The Real Malay*, p. 20.
[2] Report of Larut Commissioners, 21 February 1874, Swettenham Papers in ANM, item no. 72.

across the tin fields and allocating the area north of it to the Ghi Hin and that south, to the Hai San.

It was part of the Commissioners' duty to bring the Mentri and his Hai San allies to a proper understanding of their position under the Pangkor Engagement. Neither he nor they had sought the settlement which elevated the Mentri's opponent, Raja 'Abdu'llah, and in consequence appeared to favour the Ghi Hin, with whom he was associated. Much pressure had to be brought to bear on the Hai San before they would destroy their stockades, and on the Mentri before he would return the Ghi Hin women and children allocated to him as war booty. The Mentri, further, was caught taxing tin at Kota, his old stronghold; when the Commissioners remonstrated he declared that he had not understood the Pangkor Engagement to forbid his levying taxes, but if the Commissioners wanted him to stop, or even to leave Larut, of course he would obey. Speedy made him return the receipts, and the Commissioners gave him a memorable lecture on his position; the Chinese were told that they were not indispensable, and that if they would not accept the settlement peaceably, the Governor would expel them and bring in others.

The return to the mines began sluggishly after Pangkor, but accelerated with the months. By the end of the year, the district had again mushroomed into life and prosperity.[1] In February there were only 4,000 left of a Chinese population which in times of peace had reached 20,000 or more; the mines were waterlogged and choked with debris, and the tin export was only 213 piculs (about twelve tons). By the end of the year the population was estimated at 33,000, of which 26,000 were Chinese; thirty of the old mines had been drained and cleared and re-equipped, and ninety new mines opened. The tin export in December was 2,848 piculs, and Speedy hoped for more than double this monthly output in 1875. Four months after Pangkor, Larut presented 'an animated scene of industry and good fellowship'; the Chinese were opening shops and vegetable gardens and stocking the bazaars with wines and beer and tinned provisions, among other goods, and the Assistant Resident was laying out streets and building-lots. Two townships, Taiping with a Chinese population of 5,000 and Kamunting with 4,000, were established in the Hai

[1] Report of the Assistant Resident, Perak, for 1874, C.1320, enclosure in no. 20, Clarke to Carnarvon, 6 April 1875; A. Skinner, Report on a Visit to the Malay States, 22 March 1875, C.1320, enclosure in no. 30, Clarke to Carnarvon, 3 May 1875.

San and Ghi Hin areas respectively. Madras coolies were hired to repair existing roads between the landing place and the mines, and plans were made to connect Larut by road with Province Wellesley, and with Upper Perak through the Gapis Pass to Kuala Kangsar on the Perak river.

To begin with, the Larut Government was subsidized by the Penang treasury, but by the end of the year, Speedy had a small surplus of revenue, after making a grant to the newly established Residency of Perak and after paying about eight per cent of the revenues to the Mentri. The tin industry had been exorbitantly taxed in the past; the Mentri had levied $19 a bhara, of which $6 went to the Sultan, and at 1874 prices (admittedly low) this represented nearly 30 per cent. of the market price. He had levied other charges on the tin; the carriage of the tin was farmed out to a Hai San leader, and fees were charged for weighing, stamping and storing the tin at his customs house, so that altogether $22 was paid on each bhara exported.[1] From January 1875 the duty was reduced to $15 a bhara, and it was to be further reduced to $12. The second most important item of revenue, the opium import duty, was directly collected to the end of 1874; then the opium and spirits import duty collection was farmed out to a syndicate of Chinese traders and miners in Penang and Larut.

The reports show Speedy administering what was virtually a Chinese province, unhampered by Malay precedents. He had departments of Mines, Revenue, and Roads, each under a European officer, and staffed by Eurasian, Chinese and Malay clerks and interpreters. He had an establishment of 266 police, officered by three Europeans, as well as a personal guard of twenty-five sepoys; after the disarmament of the Chinese, his police constituted the only armed force in Larut. The police were concentrated in stations between the anchorage at Telok Kertang and the mines at Kamunting fourteen miles to the north-east; they guarded the custom-house, the treasury, the court-house, and kept order in the townships. To insure against future disturbance, nine of the chief Hai San fighting men were deported, and with more enthusiasm than knowledge, Speedy determined to

---

[1] The Mentri's collecting procedure is obscure. In a statement made at Penang on 26 August 1873 (C.1111, enclosure 6 in no. 52), he declared that he farmed the tin mines to a Hai San leader, Law Ah Sam, for graduated payments which reached the fixed sum of $15,000 a month, the farmer making what profit he could. At the time of the statement, however, the Mentri was getting only $1,000 a month. The Report of the Larut Commissioners suggests that in February 1874 he was collecting the revenues on his own account.

make the establishment of secret society lodges a penal offence. He claimed to have the entire support of the Chinese headmen (who were, of course, secret society leaders themselves) and of the Mentri, who was probably affiliated to the Hai San secret society.

Speedy's report makes no reference to the administration of justice among the Chinese before his arrival, and he is hardly more informative about the Malays. Each penghulu was 'Magistrate of his own petty district, and had almost unlimited power to levy fines or punish misdemeanours according to his own judgement . . . the definition of the law was of the vaguest description'. He instituted a Magistrate's court, with the Treasurer on the Bench, where he tried as far as possible to follow the Indian Penal Code, and conduct proceedings as in the Straits Settlements' courts, with warrants and subpoenas issued in the name of the Sultan.

In Sungei Ujong the Dato' Klana and the Dato' Bandar had come into conflict. The Dato' Klana was a British client, and the Dato' Bandar was in sympathy with the Mahdi party in Selangor. To secure the British position in Selangor as well as Sungei Ujong, it was necessary that the Dato' Klana's authority be established, particularly as control of the mines was at stake. In response to an appeal from the Dato' Klana, Pickering, a Singapore magistrate with a command of several Chinese dialects,[1] was sent in October to secure the Bandar's submission; failing this, he was to support the Dato' Klana in a punitive action, and keep the Chinese neutral.

The Dato' Bandar has been characterized as the aggressor in the official correspondence, but it is clear from Pickering's own account and from Swettenham's Langat Journals that it was the Dato' Klana who was attempting to upset established custom by assuming royal pretensions, asserting his supreme authority and independence of his co-ruler, and using British power for these purposes. When the Dato' Bandar failed to obey an ultimatum that he should go to Singapore and submit to the Governor, the Dato' Klana attacked and captured

[1] William Alexander Pickering, CMG (1884), was the key figure in the negotiations with the Chinese which accompanied intervention in Larut and Sungei Ujong. He began his career at sea, on a tea clipper trading to China; he then joined the Chinese Maritime Customs, and learnt Chinese. In 1871 he was appointed Chinese interpreter to the Straits Settlements Government. In January 1874 he was entrusted with the task of persuading the Hai San and Ghi Hin factions in Larut to submit to the arbitration of the Governor, and after Pangkor, went back to Larut as one of the Commissioners to enforce the agreement with the Chinese. In 1877 he became the first Protector of Chinese in Singapore. He retired in 1889.

his villages and went on to attack his stockade at Kepayang, with Pickering in train to see that he did not massacre half the countryside in a fit of aggressive zeal. The Klana's men melted away into Chinese gambling houses en route, the Klana himself lagged by the way; Pickering and a handful of men were left to do the fighting. They would have achieved their object, except that the Klana was resting on the track far behind with the only gun. The arrival of a noted Malay fighting man, Raja Mahmud of Selangor, on the other side, completed the Klana's demoralization, and he returned to his stockade much chastened, without his stage army, and utterly dependent on Pickering for protection. The Dato' Bandar eventually had to be punished by British troops; his stockade was destroyed, his tin confiscated and a settlement with the Chinese dictated by the officer in charge of reinforcements (Captain Dunlop, the Inspector-General of Police, Straits Settlements, who had been present at Pangkor and had helped to settle Larut earlier in the year as one of the Commissioners appointed under the Pangkor Engagement). Through all this the Dato' Klana hovered in the background, helpless, timid and grateful, 'the most meek and sincere Malay I ever saw . . . I never saw a Malay more amenable to counsel or more anxious to be under the Governor's advice and protection'.[1]

Although the Chinese had remained detached from the fighting, Dunlop was satisfied that two of the headmen had helped the Dato' Bandar to escape; the third, though friendly, had presumed to burn the Dato' Bandar's port of Rasah after its capture by the troops. Each of the three was made to pay a fine of $3,000 on pain of flogging and banishment, and to sign an undertaking to forget their old quarrels and return to the mines.

The rehabilitation of the mines and the regulation and development of the tin industry were taken in hand at once. The immediate consideration was the settlement of the revenue, the establishment of a secure mining tenure, and the improvement and extension of communications. In Sungei Ujong the Chinese had been given cause for apprehension by threatened changes in the revenue system; under advice from Malacca officials the Dato' Klana had proposed to farm

---

[1] Pickering, Journal of a Visit to Sungei Ujong (4 October–29 November 1874). Swettenham Papers, no. 72; Report of Captain S. Dunlop, 29 December 1874, C.1320, enclosure 18 in no. 8, Clarke to Carnarvon, 29 December 1874; Swettenham's Langat Journal, entries for 10–12 and 22 October, 24–30 November and 1–5 December 1874, and letter from Pickering dated 9 November 1874, in entry for 26 November.

the opium duty collection to a Malacca Chinese. This plan Pickering and Dunlop persuaded him to abandon, and on their advice the opium duty collection and the spirit and pawnbroking monopolies were leased to the three local Capitans jointly for six months. The poll-tax of $1 on each Chinese miner, hitherto the Dato' Klana's chief source of income (since the port of Rasah had been in the hands of his rival, he was precluded from collecting duty on tin) was replaced by a royalty of one-fifteenth on all tin exported. A twenty-year mining lease was instituted,[1] reserving control over water-supply to the government. In December, Tatham wrote to say that the Chinese had gone back to work and that everything was quiet; boats had been arriving at Rasah and there were now about seventy, laden with rice, salt fish, tobacco and salt; the duty on rice had been halved and he proposed to abolish it at the end of the year, and he asked also for instructions as to abolishing the duties on salt, salt fish, tobacco and other necessities. Rasah, the port for the tin, was being rebuilt, and a road marked from the township to the landing place; a temporary police station had already been built there. Tatham reported that through all these changes the Klana was 'most anxious to do everything in his power to assist me', and took the greatest interest in everything going on.[2]

In Selangor there was no urgent need for control. Tengku Zia'u'd-din was master of Klang, and was assisted by Davidson for part of 1874; Birch, visiting Selangor in April, found them both at Klang, busy with the problems of government.[3] Zia'u'd-din's associate, Yap Ah Loy, was in undisputed control of Kuala Lumpur, and kept the township and the tin fields orderly and peaceful. Clarke contented himself, for a start, with sending Swettenham to the Sultan at Langat, to see that his court did not again become the refuge for Zia'u'd-din's enemies. Swettenham was a gregarious young officer with tremendous energy, verve and curiosity, who liked the Malays and enjoyed their company, and whose immaturity and self-assurance no doubt amused them; and he was given a task perfectly in keeping with his tastes and interests. He had no administrative duties; he was required merely

[1] Because of lack of capital, however, the Sungei Ujong workings were small, and the miners did not take advantage of the lease, preferring to take out short-term mining licences. See *AR* Sungei Ujong, 1885.

[2] Tatham to CS, 18 December 1874, C.1320, enclosure 23 in no. 8, Clarke to Carnarvon, 29 December 1874.

[3] Birch, Journal of a Visit to Perak and Selangor in March and April 1874, Swettenham Papers, no. 72.

to establish good relations with the Sultan and other Malays of consequence, and explore the country. He pleased the Sultan, a tolerant old cynic who had for some time been content to watch from Langat while a succession of people fought over Selangor. Swettenham brought Tengku Zia'u'd-din to visit his father-in-law, and—his most spectacular success—he received the surrender of Raja Mahmud, the most noted fighting man in the Peninsula. Between August 1874 and April 1875 he went up every river in Selangor and Sungei Ujong from the Bernam to the Linggi, visited every town and village, reported on the population, native authorities, produce and revenue of each district, and he completed his travels with a journey overland on foot from the upper Langat to the upper Selangor, visiting every important tin field in the state.[1]

The most important centre, however, was Klang, the Tengku's headquarters, and the customs station for the Kuala Lumpur tin. Birch, during a visit in April, found the usual evidence of orderly administration, a police station at Klang and another at Damansara, the landing place about eighteen miles up-river; he met the Tengku's secretariat, 'all intelligent and smart young fellows'. Davidson was with the Tengku, instituting useful reforms, lowering the freight charges between Kuala Lumpur and Klang, and lowering the duty on tin.[2] But informal European advice was clearly not enough to restore order and confidence; the Pahang Malays who had retaken the Selangor river valley on behalf of the Tengku were still in Kuala Selangor, and under their leader, Che Wan Da, were burdening the countryside with exactions and acts of violence, so that people who had run away during the wars could not return to their homes. In his despatch reporting the appointment of a Resident for Selangor, Clarke declared that although the presence of Swettenham at Langat had been mainly responsible for the peace and good order of that part of the state, there had not been either in the Selangor or Klang districts 'that restoration of confidence' which he had anticipated.

These districts are still left abandoned by their former cultivators, nor have the miners returned to them in any number whilst capital to assist in opening new mines in this well known and rich mineral country is withheld, and all in consequence, I have thoroughly satisfied myself, of

[1] Report of Assistant Resident, Selangor, 8 April 1875, C.1320, enclosure in no. 28, Clarke to Carnarvon, 27 April 1875.
[2] Birch, Journal of a Visit to Perak and Selangor in March and April 1874, Swettenham Papers, no. 72.

its affairs not being subject to the control of a British officer resident with the Sultan's Viceroy, Tenku Dia Udin.[1]

Davidson, whom he chose to fill the post, was in Selangor issuing administrative instructions from Klang when he was appointed.[2]

Davidson's instructions required him to establish himself at Klang in the first instance, where he was to organize a Resident's guard and police force, applying to the Straits Inspector-General of Police for a few men from Singapore or Malacca. He was to take charge of the revenue collection, and make recommendations for changes in the fiscal arrangements, and for repayment of the debts which the Tengku had incurred during the Selangor fighting, and which now became an obligation on the state. The instructions also made certain recommendations on the subject of land policy, and suggested, as a first step in the development of communications, that a road be made from the landing place to the mines, a distance of sixteen miles. Finally, Davidson was to do his best to secure the friendship and confidence of the Sultan.[3]

Davidson's first act as Resident was to pay a courtesy visit to the Sultan, and submit for his seal certain notices recalling the fugitives from the recent wars. But his real work was in Klang and Kuala Selangor. In Kuala Selangor he left a European, Denholm, as Collector and Magistrate, with a police force of twenty, to check the activities of the Pahang men. Klang he took under his own charge. Much of 1875 was spent in checking unauthorized collections by Malay and Chinese local authorities; for example, by one Haji Kechil, who was levying duty on livestock overlanded from Pahang, and by the Capitan China, Yap Ah Loy, who was collecting $2 on each bhara of tin to make the road from Damansara to Kuala Lumpur.[4]

British control lay lightly over Selangor in this first year; it was confined to the coast stations of Klang and Kuala Selangor. Kuala Lumpur was left in the charge of the Capitan China and the Dato' Dagang, the headman of the foreign Malays who formed the bulk of

[1] Clarke to Carnarvon, Confidential of 30 December 1874, CO 273/76.

[2] The Colonial Secretary wrote informing him of his appointment on 20 January 1875 (Sel/Sec 3/75). On 19 January he was writing from Klang to forbid the illegal exactions of one Raja Legong on the trade between Klang and Kuala Lumpur. Resident to Shaikh Mohammed Taib, 19 January 1875, Sel/Sec. 2/75.

[3] CS to Resident of Selangor, 20 January 1875, Sel/Sec. 3/75. See Appendix 3a.

[4] Resident to Yap Ah Loy, 21 August 1875, Sel/Sec. 101/75.

the Malay population in the town.[1] On the Langat river, the Sultan was left to collect his own revenues for another year, despite instructions from Singapore that the method of revenue collection there was to be assimilated to that of the rest of Selangor. The Resident delayed, perhaps for diplomatic reasons, perhaps for lack of staff, and in any case Langat as a revenue producing area was insignificant compared with Klang. But early in 1876, after persistent prodding from Singapore, Langat lost its fiscal independence. A proclamation was issued by the Sultan, declaring that from 26 March all taxes in the state were to be collected by officers of the Selangor Government.[2] In 1876 the post of Assistant Resident at Langat was abolished, and Langat became an administrative division under a Collector and Magistrate.

The pressures put on Malay Rulers, and the relationships established with them, varied with the circumstances of intervention and past intercourse. In Sungei Ujong the Dato' Klana readily acquiesced in the assumption of authority by British officers and showed himself 'most anxious to do everything in his power' to assist their work and fall in with their suggestions. In Larut on the other hand, the Mentri had suffered great loss by the Pangkor Engagement, which displaced his overlord Ismail and forced him to accept a new Sultan and a British officer against his will; he was disaffected and obstructive and was excluded from association in government. The Straits Government made their distrust of him quite clear, and Speedy was under pressure to be firmer with him, though he took little enough part as it was in the administration of Larut.[3] In Selangor, Tengku Zia'u'd-din was *persona grata* with the Straits Government, and had as Resident a close and trusted adviser, and he appears to have been more closely associated in government than any other Malay Ruler. He acted for the Sultan in all business transacted with the Resident, his name was associated with the Resident's in acts of government, and even after Davidson was replaced,[4] the Tengku's influence persisted

---

[1] Kuala Lumpur remained under the control of Yap Ah Loy till 1879, when a European magistrate was stationed there. It became the headquarters of the Resident in 1880.

[2] Jervois to Carnarvon, 5 April 1876 and enclosed proclamation by Sultan 'Abdu'l Samad, 21 February 1876, C.1512, no. 58.

[3] Clarke to Birch, 16 November 1874, cited in R.H. Vetch, *Life of Lieut.-General the Hon. Sir Andrew Clarke*, London, 1905, p. 176. Jervois to Carnarvon, Confidential of 18 October 1876, CO 273/85.

[4] Affairs in Perak at the end of 1875 completely disorganized the establish-

for a time; he was consulted about changes in the method of collecting revenue, and his sanction was formally required for public works; during the Resident's absence from Selangor in 1876, Syed Zin, the Tengku's deputy, signed an execution warrant on the Resident's behalf.[1] But the position of the Tengku depended on the special relationship between himself and Davidson, and on the flexibility which this lent to their official association. When Davidson was replaced by a Resident who did not know Selangor, Tengku Zia'u'd-din's authority rapidly declined, and in 1878 he returned to Kedah.

The distinction between policy and tactics is always difficult to determine, and the clearest and most logically consistent policy must be modified by the social impacts inherent in the colonial situation. It is possible to see the differences in the treatment of native authorities in the years immediately after intervention, as variations in the application of a policy of administrative control—as the inevitable consequence of transition—and not a contradiction in the policy itself. The Straits Government set out with the object of restoring order to the western states and accelerating their economic development, and this involved them in administrative responsibilities from the beginning. Jervois was justified in his declaration to the Secretary of State, in defence of the policy he subsequently pursued: 'When I arrived here in May last I found that each Resident was personally administering the government of the state to which he was accredited, and I certainly always considered that this was understood to be the case in the Colonial Office, as it certainly was by everyone out here, from the very commencement of the Residential system.'[2]

---

ment in Selangor. The Assistant Resident, Swettenham, was on special duty in Perak for the last half of 1875 and the first half of 1876 and did not return to Selangor; Davidson, the Resident, was appointed Queen's Commissioner in Perak in October 1875, and though he did not formally take up his post till April 1876, he was present at the March trial of Birch's murderers at Bandar Bahru. Swettenham was replaced as Assistant Resident in November 1875 by Captain Bloomfield Douglas, RNR, late Second Police Magistrate in Singapore. Captain Douglas acted for Davidson during his absences from Selangor and on 1 June 1876 formally replaced him as Resident of Selangor (Sel/Sec. 186/1876, Resident to CS, 25 June 1876). The post at Langat then became a collectorate filled by a Collector and Magistrate, James Innes. For details of Douglas' career, see Appendix 2.

[1] Resident to Collector, Langat, 15 June 1876, Sel/Sec. 738/76; CS to Resident, 29 August 1876, Sel/Sec. 179/76; Tengku Zia'u'd-din to Resident, 2 September 1876, Sel/Sec. 185/76, Syed Zin to Supt. of Police, 16 August 1876, Sel/Sec. 166/76.

[2] Jervois to Carnarvon, 62 of 10 February 1876, CO 273/83.

THE RESIDENT IN PERAK

Perak, as distinct from Larut, was the last territory to receive a Resident, and it was there that the intervention policy received its most serious test. British contacts with the Perak river in 1874, after Pangkor, were confined to a mission undertaken by the Colonial Secretary, J. W. W. Birch, in April and May, to persuade Sultan Ismail to sign the Pangkor Engagement, and surrender the regalia to 'Abdu'llah. Birch visited Larut, crossed to Kuala Kangsar, and came down the Perak river to the sea, stopping on the way to visit the rival Sultan Ismail at Blanja, Raja Yusuf at Senggang, and Sultan 'Abdu'llah at Batak Rabit. The journey was fruitless in that Ismail refused to give up the regalia or adhere to Pangkor, but friendly relations were established with 'Abdu'llah, who was anxious for a Resident to support him against Ismail. In October, Birch was sent to Selama (a mining area in north Perak which was claimed by Britain under Article XIII of the Pangkor Engagement) to put down illegal taxation of the tin export, and on the completion of this task he went to lower Perak as Resident with Sultan 'Abdu'llah. He arrived at the entrance to the Perak river on 4 November; the Sultan was living in boats at Pasir Panjang, about forty-five miles up-river, and Birch established his headquarters near him, at Bandar Bahru.[1]

In the history of colonial rule there can hardly have been a more disastrous episode than Birch's tenure of office in Perak, or a more complete misunderstanding between European and native authority. Like his colleagues, Birch eagerly welcomed the extension of British influence in the Peninsula, and he badly wanted to inaugurate the

[1] Birch Journal, 1874 and 1875, covering the whole period of his Perak residence, exists in a manuscript copy in CO 273/88, Jervois to Carnarvon, 430 of 14 December 1876, enclosure 4, pp. 109–517. The enclosure contains the manuscript of evidence taken by the Commission of Enquiry into Birch's murder in November 1875. There is no heading for the item, but its identity is clear from internal evidence. The Journal was copied by many different hands, and the whole imperfectly assembled, so that there is some chronological disorder. In the text, the first entry is for 28 November 1874, and the Journal continues till 23 October 1875, with one misplacement. It then goes on in a different hand with an entry for 30 October 1875, but from internal evidence, the year should be 1874. This is the beginning of the Journal.

Parts of the Journal were reproduced in R.O. Winstedt and R.J. Wilkinson, 'History of Perak', *JMBRAS*, vol. xii, part 1 (1934); in C.1505, enclosure 3 in no. 49, Jervois to Carnarvon, 16 October 1875; and in the *EPO*. The last source contains passages not in the manuscript copy of the Journal. Another valuable source of information for Birch's activities and plans at this time is his Report of 14 December 1874, CO 273/88, pp. 518–49.

new policy in Perak. He wrote to Clarke, 'I believe I can really be of use. My whole life has been spent in opening up new country and in improving and enriching a country, and in teaching the native chiefs good government.'[1] But nothing in his experience or temperament fitted him for the task before him. Most of his official life had been spent in Ceylon. Ceylon had been a Crown Colony since 1802; in 1834 the whole island came under a uniform administration. Judicial and revenue responsibilities were discharged by British officials, and a separate judicature administered European civil and criminal law for all sections of the population. Indigenous leaders were deprived of power and even of official recognition; in 1870, the year that Birch came to the Straits, the Kandyan chiefs had been deprived of their last privilege—the right to demand personal services from their tenants. Birch's Ceylon experience had taught him that natives were 'perfectly incapable of good government, or even of maintaining order, without guidance or assistance from some stronger hand. . . .' About Perak, he wrote, 'But really it concerns us little what were the old customs of the country, nor do I think they are worthy of any consideration in dealing with the present taxation of the country.'[2] He knew no Malay, and his experience of the Malay states before 1874 was confined to a mission to Selangor in 1871, when his peremptory behaviour to the Sultan provoked the criticism of both the Governor and the Colonial Office.

Birch's character, as much as his name, exposed him to local jokes about classroom discipline and new brooms. Winstedt has given an unequalled description of the 'earnest rationalist form-master' and the Sultan.

For almost a year they faced each other, those two protagonists at the estuary of the Perak River.

One was an English gentleman with all the virtues and defects of his class period and upbringing, brave, honourable, kind, a lover of thrift and order, a strong, confident administrator . . . though he had served for years in Ceylon, [he] never clearly saw the Asiatic ruler against his historic background of Hinduism, harems and monopolies, but only as an anomaly against the very modern background of an English public school. . . . Years in the tropics had tinged his nordic energy with nervous irritability. Not far from the end of his official career, he was a man in a hurry to carry Victorian light to Perak while still he had time; for even long experience had failed to bring home to his unimaginative mind that hurry is futile in the

[1] Birch to Clarke, undated, cited in Vetch, op. cit. p. 174.
[2] Birch to CS, 14 December 1874, CO 273/88, pp. 518–49.

training of childlike chieftains. . . . He was sent to Perak to educate its chiefs in administration on lines entirely new to them but he knew no Malay and could not talk to his pupils. His pliant interpreter from the Colony had no fine public-school 'scorn of consequence' but interpreted as far as possible to avoid rebuke and give satisfaction to all parties: 'these are not the Koran,' he remarked, when posting the notices that caused Birch's murder; 'they can be disregarded as soon as the Resident leaves'.

The other protagonist was a young Malay raja with the charming manners of his class and the vices proper to the spoilt darling of a royal harem. . . . Duty was a concept entirely foreign to him. Work of a kind was a tiresome necessity for without intelligent effort it was impossible to borrow enough money for his harem, his gambling and his cock-fighting. Unpleasant business . . . must wait till tomorrow and tomorrow and tomorrow; an elementary instinct of self-preservation that European administrators and Chinese creditors seemed strangely and inconveniently to lack. . . . These were the protagonists in that long duel, when Mr Birch landed at Batak Rabit on 5 November 1874 and confronted 'Abdu'llah as Perak's first Resident, eager to pour new wine into old bottles.[1]

Birch would probably have experienced difficulty in dealing with any situation demanding tact and patience; but he was faced with extraordinary problems. The Pangkor Engagement was a piece of emergency diplomacy which secured an immediate settlement and a basis for intervention; but—full of ambiguities and contradictions as it was—it could hardly provide a stable settlement for the problems of Perak. It concealed the intended role of the Resident in equivocal phrasing, which provided for control and called it advice.[2] It took a

[1] Winstedt and Wilkinson, op. cit. p. 102.

[2] There is a possibility that the Malay version of the Engagement was watered down to exclude the obligation to follow the Resident's advice, and that Birch and 'Abdu'llah were genuinely at odds in their understanding of the Engagement. That there was a Malay version, signed and sealed at the same time as the English one, is attested by F.A. Swettenham (*Footprints in Malaya*, London, 1942, p. 33). A manuscript Malay version is reproduced in photostat in 'J.W.W. Birch; Causes of his Assassination', by M.A. Mallal, (unpublished M.A. thesis, University of Malaya, 1952), pp. 205–6. The photostat was supplied by Raja Razman b. Raja Abdul Hamid, Bukit Chandan, Kuala Kangsar, who claimed it to be taken from a copy of the original Malay version, made by Sultan Idris (ibid. p. 284), though the handwriting bears no resemblance to his own. Clause 6 makes no mention of the obligation to follow advice, though Clause 10, in directing that the revenue be collected, and the general administration of the country be carried on with the advice of the Residents, does contain the hint of an imperative (*'mahu-lah dengan bichara dan dengan nasihat Tuan2 Resident ini ada-nya'*). Other Malay versions extant do bind the Ruler to accept advice; Clause 10 of the version published in Mohammed Ibrahim, *Kesah Pelayaran* (Johore, 1956), pp. 78–80, goes even further and directs that the country be administered according to the *wish* of the Residents (*'maka pada memungut hasil itu dan kuasa*

secular view of the scope of Malay religion and custom, regarding these as separate from government, while government was in fact regulated according to custom and tradition. Taxation and justice and local controls were all sanctified by custom; yet these were the very departments which the Pangkor Engagement put under the discretion of the Resident. Finally, the settlement recognized one of three claimants without securing his acceptance by the other two. Birch found himself accredited to a Sultan whose right was denied by half his subjects, and who could not guarantee the support of the Perak chiefs for the Resident, whatever his own attitude might be.

The difficulties were increased by 'Abdu'llah's personality. Birch was in despair over his frivolity and inability to concentrate on anything beyond his immediate desires and fancies, his opium-smoking and other excesses, his changes of mind, evasions and delays.

> He is more self-vain than I ever saw him, and talks sometimes a great deal of nonsense, at the same time he listens to me. . . . The more I have to say to the Sultan the more I feel the magnitude of the task I have offered to undertake.... He is eminently silly and foolish. Opium too has become his bane again, and he is good for very little. . . . I am afraid I shall have a hard task yet with the baby down at Batta Rabit. He really and truly is only fit for a doll, or for one of those figures at a Tailor's shop to shew off coats etc. . . . [He] asked me to forgive him all his sins, large and small, and if he had done, or ever did, any fault, to correct him like a child; and he shewed himself a veritable one, for he broke off and began to try on my old cut slippers, my boots and gaiters, and caps and hats, brush his hair and oil it, and all sorts of eccentricities.[1]

'Abdu'llah's 'eccentricities', though they arose partly from his own instability of character,[2] served a purpose in that they put off discussions which always tended to the same end—the diminution of

---

pemerentah memungut-nya itu serta segala jenis perentah bagi negeri itu semua-nya hendak-lah di-aturkan dengan mengikut ka-hendak Resident2 yang tersebut-nya'). Another, slightly different, Malay version included among the papers of Raja Haji Kamaralzaman, Raja di-Hilir of Perak, in the ANM, also refers to the obligation to follow advice. From the evidence available, it is impossible to say conclusively that the Mallal version is from the original Malay, but the greater formality of the phraseology certainly gives it an air of authenticity which is lacking in the others; these appear to be later and independent translations from the English.

[1] Birch Journal, entries for 8 November and 24 November 1874, and 5 April 1875, CO 273/88.

[2] In October, after he had signed away all his powers during a week of great tension and distress, he was still able to interest himself in matters of dress and show; he asked Birch whether he might have a retinue of forty-four spearmen and a supply of gold lace caps and epaulets. Ibid. entry for 10 October 1875.

the Sultan's powers and the introduction of unwelcome reforms. 'Abdu'llah had accepted a Resident because he wanted British support and thought of Birch as a paid servant whose business was to enhance his own authority. When he realized that the British connexion might secure him recognition but would never allow him independence, he schemed to free himself of it altogether. Birch wrote optimistically, '. . . he will be a puppet, and I believe do all one advises and asks, when he once has one living near him, and sees he gets his dollars monthly'.[1] But 'Abdu'llah, unable to take a realistic view of his situation or to think or plan beyond his momentary convenience, was an unreliable puppet. Without money, without authority[2] and without the support of some of the most important chiefs in Perak, he was yet unwilling to pay the price for the Resident's backing. He spent his time in futile evasions and shifts to obtain money, and tried to counter the Resident's uncompromising and inexorable demands with obstructions and attempts at self-assertion which came to nothing.[3]

'Abdu'llah's obstinacy and lack of realism handicapped Birch greatly in dealing with Ismail,[4] who had steadily refused to adhere to Pangkor or give up the regalia, and who was not therefore implicated in the surrender of vested rights which the Malay chiefs saw to be

[1] Ibid. entry for 24 November 1874.

[2] 'Abdu'llah was forced to allow not only Birch, but his Ghi Hin backer and creditor Tan Kim Ching, to scold him like a child. 'He could not escape, and so had to sit and listen to another fine jobation, in which he was told he was not a man, that he had to give up opium and cock-fighting, set an example to his people, and make himself acquainted by constant intercourse with the Resident, with the art of governing; that, if he went on as he was doing, his country would turn him out, as other countries did their sovereigns.' Ibid. entry for 25 July. See reference to Tan Kim Ching, note 50 below.

[3] In March 1875, for example, he tried unsuccessfully to screen himself from direct contact with Birch by appointing certain chiefs to represent him (ibid. entry for 21 March 1875), and the next month without Birch's knowledge he sent a delegation to the Governor to try to persuade him to restrain the Resident. Ibid. entry for 10 May 1875; and evidence of Haji Hussein, EPO, Abridgement of Evidence, 'C'.

[4] Birch worked hard to effect a reconciliation between 'Abdu'llah and Ismail in January 1875 at which the latter would (Birch hoped) hand over the regalia to 'Abdu'llah and acknowledge him as Sultan. It does not appear from the accounts that Ismail had any intention of doing this, but in any case 'Abdu'llah did his best to sabotage the reconciliation by his own unfriendly behaviour, and there is evidence that he wrote secretly to Ismail before the meeting, asking him not to deliver the regalia or acknowledge him as Sultan, for then the country of Perak would be 'given over to the English'. Evidence of To' Nara, EPO, Abridgement of Evidence, 'B'.

inherent in the Engagement. Though he was offered a title, a pension and a small territory by Article II of the Engagement ('a regular income without trouble, larger than any my friend has ever got before with trouble'), Ismail remained aloof, and refused to endorse the Engagement. When relations between 'Abdu'llah and Birch were at their worst, Ismail made overtures to Birch, sending messengers to say that he was very glad to see the British and desired their help[1] —clearly hoping that he would be recognized as Sultan in the place of 'Abdu'llah;[2] but these overtures came to nothing. Ismail's final word was that he would accept a Resident who would 'follow my government and carry out all my laws'.[3] Ismail was as 'impracticable' as 'Abdu'llah.

The chiefs had objected to the cession of territory at Pangkor even more strongly than 'Abdu'llah,[4] who was only concerned with establishing his own position in the months following the signing of the Engagement. Their incomes and powers were threatened by Birch's proposals for reform of the revenue collection and the administration of justice, and they clashed with him sharply in their attempts to defend their customary rights.[5] In their personal dealings with him, they suffered insults and humiliations.[6] They grew to be even more hostile to him than Ismail and 'Abdu'llah, and it was probably the attitude of the chiefs that stiffened the latter in their opposition to Birch.[7] The only ally the British found among the

[1] Birch Journal, entry for 20 July 1875, CO 273/88.

[2] According to the evidence of Birch's Malay clerk, Birch indicated at the meeting that if Ismail would sign a letter declaring himself ready to accept a Resident, he might get himself recognized as Sultan (Evidence of Haji Mat Dawood, *EPO*, Abridgement of Evidence, 'C'). There is no corroboration of this in Birch's Journal.

[3] Ismail to Jervois, 13 September 1875, *EPO*, Appendix XLIII.

[4] At their urging, 'Abdu'llah sent an agent to Penang to try to get the Dindings cession rescinded. *EPO*, Precis of Evidence, p. 2.

[5] After 'Abdu'llah had given Birch powers over revenue collection in July 1875, Birch ordered that the Shahbandar, who had hitherto collected certain import duties at Kuala Perak, should no longer be allowed to do this. The Shahbandar instructed his agent to defy the order, with what result we are not told. Evidence of D'Orville, *EPO*, Abridgement of Evidence, 'G'.

[6] The Dato' Sagor was divested of his spear by Birch's order when Birch visited his village in August 1875 (Evidence of Nakhodah Trong, *EPO*, Abridgement of Evidence, 'E'). The Maharaja Lela was prevented by Birch from entering the audience hall at Blanja on the Governor's visit in September (Evidence of Haji Alli, [sic] PEP, vol. i). The Laksamana was upset when his boat was searched after Birch had taken over the revenue collection; it was not the custom to search the boats of Datos. Evidence of Nakhodah Trong, *EPO*, Abridgement of Evidence, 'E'.

[7] For the opposition of the chiefs at Blanja in September to Jervois' proposals for the cession of Perak, see *EPO*, Abridgement of Evidence, 'H'.

Perak chiefs was Raja Yusuf, who had been passed over twice for the succession, who was generally disliked and kept in ignorance of events, and whose motives in supporting the Resident were equally to establish his own position and spite his fellow chiefs.

The first object of the Pangkor Engagement—the settlement of the succession—Birch found as far from achievement as ever. The second —the establishment of a reformed administration—bristled with difficulties; and though they were not entirely of his making, and though in the matter of revenue reform he was acting under instructions, yet he approached his task in a way that made failure certain.

The right of the Governor to interfere in the revenue collection was asserted months before Birch arrived. Braddell had visited 'Abdu'llah in Perak in April and warned him not to farm the Perak taxes without consulting the Governor; but as soon as he left, 'Abdu'llah leased the collection of the Perak river revenues to the firm of his Singapore Chinese backer, Tan Kim Ching,[1] for ten years at $26,000 a year ($2,000 of this to be commission for the Laksamana and Shahbandar). Birch came to Perak with instructions to rationalize the revenue administration and abolish all the 'double inland taxes'.[2] He characterized the collections by chiefs as 'blackmail' and 'squeeze' —a perverse departure from Victorian revenue principles. Within a fortnight of his arrival, he had explained to 'Abdu'llah, Ismail and the chiefs his plan to 'have the Revenue all collected at proper and stated places, and by a fixed method, and in the name of the Sultan only'.[3] He reiterated these proposals at frequent intervals during the next few months, and was supported by a strong letter from the Governor to Sultan 'Abdu'llah, reminding him that by the terms of the Pangkor Engagement, 'not only our friend, but the other Chiefs of Perak bound themselves not to collect any taxes whatever, such taxes, and all revenues, being entirely in the hands of the British Resident'.[4]

[1] Tan Kim Ching, a Singapore Chinese and Ghi Hin leader, had sponsored 'Abdu'llah's visit to Singapore in October 1873, and tried (unsuccessfully) to bring him to the notice of the Governor, Sir Harry Ord. When Clarke replaced Ord, Tan and his European associate, W. H. Read, renewed their attempts to secure the Governor's interest on behalf of their nominee. 'Abdu'llah's letter of 30 December 1873, inviting the British Government to send a Resident to Perak, was probably written at their prompting. See *EPO*, Precis of Evidence, p. 2.

[2] It is probably these instructions which Birch received in Penang on 28 October 1874, and which he says were 'as full as I could wish'. Journal, 30 October 1874, CO 273/88.

[3] Birch Journal, 5 November and 17 November 1874, ibid.

[4] Clarke to Sultan 'Abdu'llah (22 April 1875), C. 1320, enclosure in no. 26, Clarke to Carnarvon, 26 April 1875.

In April Birch decided the time had come to act, and demanded 'Abdu'llah's *chop* (seal) on all matters of revenue.[1] At the beginning of June, 'Abdu'llah was warned that if he did not sign he would be 'put off the throne by the British Government'.[2] Under this pressure, and advised by Tan Kim Ching, he agreed to sign in return for allowances for himself and some of the chiefs. On 25 July he signed powers appointing Birch and Raja Idris judges, and Birch and the Shahbandar to manage the revenues and appoint and dismiss all headmen.[3] But 'Abdu'llah continued to make levies at the entrances of the Kinta and Batang Padang rivers, and empowered others to collect taxes, and fine those who refused to pay.

The chiefs' objection to the proposed reform was, of course, that it was an invasion of their custom and threatened their livelihood; let Birch fix allowances first, or better still, let him begin by abolishing the taxes in Ismail's territory. Article IX of the Engagement had tried to forestall their objections by providing for a civil list regulating the income to be received by the Sultan and officers of state. Birch reiterated in all his discussions with 'Abdu'llah and the chiefs that allowances would be given in lieu of abolished rights; but when 'Abdu'llah, after investing Birch with judicial and fiscal powers, submitted a civil list, he was told to refer it to the Governor.[4] Carnarvon, writing nearly a year later, noted that 'no definite settlement of allowances has ever yet been made'.[5] Money was doled out to buy support or as a reward for obedience; it was withheld when rajas or chiefs were recalcitrant, with the explanation that there would be no money for allowances till the revenues were properly collected. The chiefs were unwilling to exchange their rights for irregular and arbitrary payments, and Birch was not in a position to make fixed allowances until he had a revenue.[6] His establishment was insignificant; till the

---

[1] Birch Journal, 24 April 1875, CO 273/88. According to the evidence of Mat Rouse, Sultan 'Abdu'llah's clerk (*EPO*, Abridgement of Evidence, 'C'), Birch tried as early as January to get 'Abdu'llah to sign documents giving him control over customs collection and appointing him a judge, but there is no corroboration of this from Birch's Journal.

[2] Birch Journal, 8 June 1875, CO 273/88.

[3] Ibid. 25 July 1875, CO 273/88. Raja Idris was 'Abdu'llah's cousin and became an important ally of the British.

[4] Loc. cit.

[5] Carnarvon to Jervois, 1 June 1876, C.1512, no. 70.

[6] Birch was chronically short of money. The Perak river revenues had been farmed to Tan Kim Ching, and until August 1875 were collected by his agents and the Shahbandar, though the collections were made at Birch's customs station

middle of March he lived in a boat, and then moved into temporary quarters at Bandar Bahru, forty-five miles up the Perak river, near Sultan 'Abdu'llah's equally makeshift quarters at Pasir Panjang. Outside Bandar Bahru there was a customs house at Kota Stia with a European customs officer and fourteen police; there was besides, on the Perak river, one police station at Durian Sebatang (down-river) and three more in process of building by April 1875. In short, British influence on 180 miles of river was represented by three Europeans (Birch, d'Orville, and Birch's secretary Keyt), a Eurasian interpreter, a Malay writer and an ill-disciplined force of about forty Sikhs who ran away at the first shot. The chiefs could have had little confidence in his resources; they likened him to a Dutch sailor, 'who had nothing to fill his own belly, and came to Perak to collect the revenues of others'.

There were other sources of conflict. The system of debt-slavery in the Malay states has been mentioned. Though the enslavement of Muslims was contrary to Muhammadan law, it was sanctioned by Malay custom, and throughout the Malay territories slaves were kept, particularly by the raja class. They fell into two categories—those enslaved outright (Malayan aborigines and non-Muslim Indonesians) and debt-slaves. Men who had incurred debts, perhaps to tide them over a bad harvest, or to fulfil social obligations, or who had incurred judicial fines they could not pay, were bound to the service of their creditor till the debt was paid. In fact, payment was often refused, and not only the man, but his family, kept in a servile condition. On the marriage of his daughter, the bride-payment went to the creditor, and the girl on marriage brought her husband and children into bondage with her. The debt-slaves might be assigned to any kind of field and house service, the women particularly being valued as domestic labour, as nursemaids, and to attract the male followers necessary to the prestige of every chief. The slaves do not appear to have been used on any significant scale to develop mining and commercial agriculture; their importance was to help provide subsistence and per-

at Kota Stia, under the supervision of his clerks (Evidence of d'Orville, customs officer at Kota Stia, *EPO*, Abridgement of Evidence, 'G'). Larut, the richest part of Perak, was separately administered, and though it made a contribution to the government of Perak, this in 1874 was only $16,446, and in 1875 $29,640. In 1876 the estimate for Malay allowances alone, mostly on the Perak river, was $48,000 a year (Jervois to Carnarvon, 73 of 6 March 1877). Birch was supplied with funds by the Penang treasury. Birch to Anson, 1 September 1875, Anson Correspondence.

sonal attendance for the chief's household. The reluctance of the owners to relinquish their slaves is explained by the fact that enslavement and debt-bondage provided cheaply a large retinue of young men and women who added to the prestige of the chief, without necessarily doing any productive work.[1]

The Engagement protected the Malays from any violation of their custom; it said nothing about slavery, as Sultan 'Abdu'llah remarked.[2] Birch was humane to the point of rashness; he saw himself as the protector of the weak, and the Malay Rulers as sinister oppressors. He knew that he was on shaky ground when he interfered with slavery, but with his approval the Residency at Bandar Bahru and the customs house at Kota Stia became sanctuaries for runaway slaves; and the fact that most of the runaways were women persuaded the chiefs that Birch was stealing their slaves to provide his police with mistresses. The runaways included two from the Sultan's compound who were hidden by Birch's men and smuggled by him to Pangkor, after the Governor in September had ordered their return and promised that until the whole question of debt-slavery had been considered there would be no shelter at the Residency for escaped slaves. The chiefs were so humiliated by this interference, and by Birch's public treatment of them, that it is doubtful whether anything could have reconciled them to an administration which he headed.

There were other examples of his precipitance. Notices giving effect to his fiscal policy were prepared in May 1875, waiting the day when he was given authority to govern Perak. On that day (2 October 1875) the notices were produced for 'Abdu'llah's seal, and all except one were to come into effect from the moment of publication.[3] The exception was a notice introducing a household tax 'in the nature of the ancient "Asil Klamin" ',[4] which was not customary on the Perak river, and which was not to come into effect for two months. (Hugh Low, Resident of Perak from 1877–89, brought up the question of this tax at State Council meetings every year for six years, and then

---

[1] Minutes on Slavery in the Malay States, by Douglas, 28 May 1878; Low, 28 May 1878; Birch, 28 July 1875; Davidson, 23 August 1875; Swettenham, 30 June 1875, C.3285, enclosures in no. 2. Also W. E. Maxwell, Minute on Slavery among the Malays, 27 May 1882, C.3429, enclosure 1 in no. 4.

[2] Evidence of Edward Bacon, *EPO*, Abridgement of Evidence, 'C'.

[3] *EPO*, Appendices, lvii to lxiii. Some of the measures were proposed in his report of 14 December 1874, when he had been six weeks in Perak. CO 273/88, pp. 518–49, *passim*.

[4] Lit. 'tax on couples' but as it was generally levied on adult Malay males, it was in effect a poll tax.

did not bring it into operation, because of its unpopularity.) The notices cover the question with a completeness and detail appropriate to a highly-organized administration, but out of place in a Malay state with hardly any European establishment. The notice against smuggling, for example, restricted boats from landing anywhere except at four points on a long and unguarded coast. The revenue notices provided for the registration and taxation of every boat and canoe, and every adult male householder in Perak. Birch of course depended on the penghulus to make these rules effective, to register people and boats and help officers sent to collect the tax, in return for which they would receive a proportion of the collections and fines for non-compliance. But since some headmen recognized Ismail, some 'Abdu'llah and some neither, they could hardly be used as instruments of policy while the succession question was unresolved.

From the date of his arrival in Perak, Birch filled his official diary with complaints about 'Abdu'llah, his personal unfitness, his obstructiveness and refusal to accept advice. It may be imagined that these complaints were embarrassing to Clarke. He had chosen 'Abdu'llah, reversing the policy of the previous Governor; he had filled his despatches home with assurances of 'Abdu'llah's friendship and cooperation; Birch's reports so soon after arrival, revealed the hollowness of the settlement he had pushed through at Pangkor. Clarke would acknowledge no defects in his settlement, only in the instruments chosen to carry it through. Also, he was about to leave the Straits (he was replaced by Jervois on 8 May 1875).[1] He contented himself therefore with severe letters to 'Abdu'llah, reminding him of his obligations under the Engagement,[2] and with expressions of annoyance to Anson, the Lt.-Governor in Penang, about the 'head-over-heels' way in which Birch was doing things.[3]

[1] Lt.-General Sir William Francis Drummond Jervois, RE, GCMG, CB, FRS, was born in 1821 and educated at the Royal Military Academy, Woolwich. He was commissioned in the Royal Engineers in 1839. He was Assistant (later Deputy) Inspector-General of Fortifications, 1856–75, and during this period reported on defence works in Canada, the West Indies, and India and Burma. He was Governor, Straits Settlements, from May 1875 to February 1877, and after advising on the defence of the Australian Colonies, he became Governor of South Australia, 1877, and of New Zealand from 1882 till his retirement in 1889.

[2] Clarke to 'Abdu'llah, 22 April 1875 and 13 May 1875, EPO, Appendices xvii and xxi. When the second letter was written, Clarke was no longer Governor.

[3] Clarke to Anson, 25 March 1875, cited in A. E. H. Anson, About Others and Myself, 1845–1920, London, 1920, p. 323. Clarke did not leave Singapore till 26 May. He had therefore an opportunity of observing, critically and perhaps with some jealousy, the 'head-over-heels' way in which Jervois also was plunging into these matters. Ibid. p. 324.

Just before Clarke left, he expressed concern also about the way in which Jervois seemed to be going into the affairs of the states, and his apprehension was justified by events. Jervois early decided that the position of the Resident in Perak should be strengthened. In July he proposed in a private letter to Carnarvon that Perak should be annexed,[1] and without waiting for a reply, he put his plan into operation. In the first two weeks of September, he toured Perak with a large staff, and put his proposals forward in interviews with Ismail, 'Abdu'llah, Yusuf and the chiefs. His intention then was to annex Perak, and there was great pressure on the chiefs to sign documents inviting the British to 'give complete assistance to Perak and govern Perak'.[2] Raja Yusuf and Raja Idris[3] identified themselves with the

---

[1] Jervois to Carnarvon, 10 July 1875, PRO 30/6–40, cited in C. D. Cowan, *Nineteenth Century Malaya: the Origins of British Political Control*, London, 1961, p. 227. On 16 October he received a reply rejecting his proposals (Carnarvon to Jervois, 13 September 1875, PRO 30/6–40; Cowan, op. cit. p. 230), but by that time he had carried out his reorganization in Perak. Among the Swettenham Papers in the ANM, there is a memorandum initialled by Swettenham and dated July 1875, recommending annexation (item 83). It appears to be written in the form of answers to questions, and recounts the hostility of the chiefs, the recalcitrance of 'Abdu'llah, the need for rapid development in order to pay the Mentri's debts, and the need for a change of policy if any economic or social advance was to be made. The points are repeated in Jervois' explanatory despatch to Carnarvon of 16 October. The memorandum is probably one of a number which Jervois called for from his advisers a few weeks after arriving in the Straits, and it is a curiosity in that it shows Swettenham's early ideas on the subject.

[2] This was the prepared letter signed by Yusuf and Idris, 19 September 1875, C.1505, enclosure 9 in no. 49, Jervois to Carnarvon, 16 October 1875. The essential phrases are reproduced in 'Abdu'llah's letter to Jervois, 1 October 1875, *EPO*, Appendix LII.

[3] Raja Yusuf, Paduka Seri Sultan Yusuf Sharifu'd-din Mafthal Shah ibni almarhum Sultan 'Abdu'llah Mohammed Shah, Yang di-Pertuan Negeri Perak (reg. 1851–7), had been in the direct line of succession, but his harsh, autocratic and quarrelsome nature made him so unpopular that he was passed over in 1857 and again in 1865; he was not present at Pangkor, and none of the Straits officials realised the strength of his claim till Swettenham met him at Senggang on 21 April 1874. See C. D. Cowan, 'Sir Frank Swettenham's Perak Journals 1874–1876', *JMBRAS*, vol. xxiv, part 4 (1951) pp. 53–57. As the tensions in Perak increased, so did the understanding between Yusuf and the Resident. He undertook to persuade Ismail to sign Jervois' paper, and after much hesitation signed himself on 19 September. In the military interregnum which followed Birch's death, he gave the British active help; his information assisted the capture of Pasir Salak, and he became involved in the fighting against his old enemies, the Kota Lama people, and, in December 1876, he presided over a court which tried the main instigators of Birch's murder. On 30 March 1877, he was proclaimed the Chief Native Authority, in Perak, and in 1886 was made Sultan. He died in 1887.

Raja Idris, Paduka Seri Sultan Idris Murshidal 'aatham Shah ibni almarhum

Resident and signed; 'Abdu'llah, given fifteen days in which to sign, and threatened with ruin if he did not, capitulated at the last and signed; Ismail wrote rejecting Jervois' proposals;[1] none of the other chiefs would sign. At the end of 'Abdu'llah's period of grace, Jervois modified his original proposals; instead of declaring Perak British territory, he was prepared to let it remain under the nominal rule of the Sultan, if he would surrender the government altogether to British officers.[2] But before these letters were delivered, 'Abdu'llah had already submitted. In a letter to Jervois of 1 October 1875, he invited the British in general terms to take over the government; in a second letter of 2 October 1875, he gave 'our friend's Resident in Perak and to those officers whom our friend may send to assist him full powers to fix and collect all taxes' and full powers also 'to appoint and remove all officers in the districts and villages of Perak, and also to administer justice either personally or by deputy throughout Perak'. Two Proclamations of 2 October amplified this by prohibiting any but officers appointed by the Governor from administering justice in Perak. Cases bearing on Mohammedan religion 'such as marriage and so forth', might be dealt with by Malays appointed by British officers, after consultation with the Sultan and the *Waris Perak*.[3]

Bendahara Iskandar Shah, Yang di-Pertuan Negeri Perak, GCMG (1901), KCMG (1892), CMG (1884), GCVO (1913), was born in 1849. He was a great-grandson of Sultan 'Abdu'l Malik Mansur Shah (see table, p. 33) and Yusuf's son-in-law. He was 'Abdu'llah's cousin and had been his constant companion during 1874 and most of 1875. He had been one of a delegation sent to Clarke in May 1875 to complain of Birch's interpretation of the Engagement, and was present at meetings in July and August 1875 at which Birch's murder was allegedly plotted. But he was prepared to co-operate with the Resident, and Birch nominated him co-judge in July. He detached himself from 'Abdu'llah's party and came out with his father-in-law in support of the Resident, signing Jervois' document on 19 September. He succeeded Yusuf as Sultan in 1887, and reigned till his death in 1916.

[1] Ismail to Jervois, 13 September 1875, *EPO*, Appendix xliii.

[2] Jervois to 'Abdu'llah, 27 September 1875, *EPO*, Appendix xlix.

[3] 'Abdu'llah to Jervois, 1 October 1875, *EPO*, Appendix lii; 'Abdu'llah to Jervois 2 October 1875, *EPO*, Appendix LIII; Proclamations 'I' and 'J', 2 October 1875, *EPO*, Appendixes liv and lv. It would be of interest to compare these proclamations with those of 25 July, in which 'Abdu'llah appointed Birch and Raja Idris judges, and Birch and the Shahbandar to administer the revenue, but we have been unable to trace copies of the earlier documents, though there are plenty of references to them. The obvious difference is that by the proclamations of October the British officers were to act alone, and were given executive authority. 'Abdu'llah tried to insert a clause bringing Malay custom as well under the cognizance of Malay officers, but Birch rejected this. Journal for 2 October 1875, CO 273/88.

The new arrangement was instituted by proclamation on 15 October 1875, and under it Birch and Davidson were appointed Queen's Commissioners, the change of policy being marked by a change of title of the British representatives in Perak. They were instructed to 'carry on the Government of Perak, in the name of the Sultan, under the instructions of the Governor and with the assistance of the Malay Council'. They were to issue and enforce proclamations and orders, and generally administer the Government of Perak, consulting the Malay Council, and informing 'Abdu'llah 'whenever possible' of every action which had been taken by them.[1] The Malay Council was to sit with the Commissioners and was to consist of Raja Muda Yusuf and Raja Idris, as working members, 'from both of whom we are likely to obtain trustworthy information, valuable opinions, and a desire to benefit the community at large'. It was also to include Sultan 'Abdu'llah, Ismail and the Bendahara, from whom nothing of value was expected, but who would represent the main factions in the state.[2] The Malay Council was to deal, among other things, with questions relating to Muhammadan religion and Malay custom, not specifically protected by the Proclamation of 15 November 1875.

This advance, for which Jervois had no sanction—on the contrary, all his instructions in 1875 warned him against committing himself to 'undefined responsibilities connected with the affairs of these States'—was reported home for the first time on 16 October. He argued that 'Abdu'llah had frustrated the intentions of the Pangkor Engagement by refusing to take advice, and he drew special attention to two problems which arose out of that. First, while present conditions continued, it would be impossible to get a revenue out of Perak; the present establishment was being supported by the Straits Treasury, and was already indebted to it by £18,000, and there was no prospect of stopping the drain or getting back the money. The debts of the Mentri, which became the obligation of the state by Article XIV of the Engagement, would not be liquidated till there was financial confidence in the Perak Government. Secondly there existed in Perak the abuse of slavery, which it would be impossible to correct until the Resident had effective control. Jervois then outlined his plan for the assumption of administrative responsibilities by British officers. The burden of his despatch was that this was no

[1] Instructions to Queen's Commissioners, 23 October 1875, C.1505, enclosure 10 in no. 78, Jervois to Carnarvon, 16 November 1875.
[2] Jervois to Carnarvon, 291 of 16 November 1875, C.1505, no. 49.

departure from the intentions of Pangkor, but merely a device for carrying them out, necessary because the assurances on which the whole Pangkor structure depended were, and always had been, inadequate. It is difficult to see that he was wrong.

Jervois explained that his original plan had been to annex, but that 'on weighing well the impressions conveyed to me by my interviews with the Chiefs, it did not appear to me expedient at present that this course should be adopted'. Also, the cost of government would be less 'when carried on in the name of the Sultan than it would be if conducted on British principles,' and finally in carrying out the government of the state at present, 'it would be very inconvenient if the inhabitants of Perak all at once became entitled to the rights and privileges of British subjects'. Difficult chiefs would be easier to deal with if they did not have the protection of English law. In other words, Jervois' tour of Perak had told him that annexation would probably be resisted; he hoped that control without sovereignty might be accepted.

Jervois had sufficient hardihood to assure the Secretary of State that the new policy had been 'to a very great extent, brought about owing to the representation and requests of Perak Rajahs themselves' and that there was no need for force to carry it through. He enclosed extracts from a letter from Birch dated 13 October saying 'nothing can exceed the general good feeling', though the only feeling communicated to him at this time was that 'Abdu'llah and some of the chiefs were 'very desirous of polishing me off'.[1] Before Jervois' despatch reached the Colonial Office, they had heard by telegram that Birch had been murdered.[2] The gap between reality and official fiction can seldom have been so dramatically displayed.

Within a month of Birch's murder, troops from Penang, Singapore, Hong Kong and India had arrived in Perak.

And now up came the Buffs and the Blue-jackets; the Goorkhas and the artillery; and the Hong Kong troops and the Madras sappers and miners, all fresh from Rangoon. The electric wire, let us hope, was to the fore, and the engineers were surely not left behind. Everything seemed complete; and yet there was a want—an uncommon want. Where was the enemy? . . . Not more than thirty or fourty armed Malays were ever seen at any one time;

[1] Birch Journal, 19 September 1875, *EPO*, Abridgement of Evidence, 'G'.
[2] Birch was killed on 2 November 1875, while posting proclamations at Pasir Salak, on the Perak river a few miles above Bandar Bahru. Jervois' despatch of 16 October reached the CO on 22 November, three weeks after his telegram informing them of the murder.

and the whole number in arms in Perak throughout the so-called campaign, did not probably exceed three hundred men. [1]

Jervois had tried to recover his credit by sending for large reinforcements, but unfortunately these had arrived to find that the fighting—the taking of Pasir Salak, where Birch had been killed—had already been done by 150 men under the Straits Inspector-General of Police. There was nothing left to do but occupy Perak until Birch's murderers were captured. The real value of the troops was that they provided a demonstration of crushing strength. Their operations, and a concurrent enquiry into the origins of Birch's murder,[2] also cleared Perak of both Sultans and nearly every chief of the first and second rank. The Maharaja Lela and the Dato' Sagor were hanged for their part in the murder after a Perak trial in December 1876; the Sri Adika Raja died as a fugitive in North Perak; Ismail, 'Abdu'llah, the Mentri, the Laksamana and the Shahbandar were dealt with by executive process and banished from Perak. At the end of the military interregnum there were left, in Perak, one chief of the first rank, one chief of the second, and the lesser royalty, of whom the most prominent were Raja Yusuf and Raja Idris.

The Commission found that there had been a conspiracy to murder Birch, in which Sultan 'Abdu'llah, Sultan Ismail and the chiefs of Upper and Lower Perak were implicated, and which they had been planning since July 1875. That the chiefs were extremely hostile and —particularly in September and October—spoke of war, was certain and concealed from no one except the Secretary of State.[3] Whether there was a conspiracy will never be resolved. The Commission's findings provide the only material for a judgement; the witnesses

[1] P. B. Maxwell, *Our Malay Conquests*, Westminster, 1878, pp. 61–62. The pamphlet contains some critical notes on the evidence of the *EPO* which provide a useful balance to other writings on the subject.

[2] The Commission, appointed in March 1876, consisted of the Senior Puisne Judge, Mr Philippo, the Hon. C. B. Plunket, Acting Magistrate at Malacca, and Mr W. F. B. Paul, a former Gold Coast officer who was appointed to Perak in 1876 as Assistant Commissioner under Davidson (Jervois to Carnarvon, 129 of 21 March 1876). Their findings were published in 1876 under the title 'Enquiry into the Complicity of Chiefs in the Perak Outrages', and provide a valuable source for the events of Birch's Residency.

[3] Entries in Birch's diary for 16 September and 19 October 1875 show that he was aware of the general ill-feeling and the danger of an outbreak (*EPO*, Abridgement of Evidence, 'G'). Swettenham wrote in his diary for 16 September that 'very little would lead to a quarrel now' (Cowan, 'Swettenham Perak Journals', op. cit. p. 96). On 27 September, Jervois wrote to Anson to make discreet inquiries as to whether arms were being exported from Penang. Anson Correspondence.

were never cross-examined, and except for the Maharaja Lela, in whose kampong the murder took place, and his neighbour the Dato' Sagor, those implicated were never formally charged or questioned, and never provided with details of the evidence against them.[1] That Birch died as the result of such a conspiracy is not borne out by the manner of his death, which suggests a sudden act of passion under considerable provocation. The murder remained an isolated act of violence; Birch's companion, who was shooting snipe on the opposite bank, and Swettenham, who was posting notices up-river, were told of Birch's murder, and thus put on their guard, by Malays allegedly party to a conspiracy to kill all the Europeans. The threatened attack on the Residency never took place. Whatever the feelings of the Malay chiefs, they were neither sufficiently resourceful nor sufficiently united to offer any systematic opposition.

It seems certain that a clash of some kind must have taken place at this stage, and had Birch been better prepared and his sepoys better disciplined, the events at Pasir Salak might have developed into a routine 'row with the natives' and a trouncing for the Maharaja Lela. How the Colonial Office would have received this is open to speculation. Certainly it would not have reconciled them to Jervois' display of initiative, and the likelihood is that they would have rejected his plans and ordered—as they did eventually—a return to the vague relations established by the Pangkor Engagement; leaving it to the local officials to struggle with the problems of rival Sultans and obstructive chiefs. Birch's murder saved the Governor from such complexities. It made withdrawal from existing commitments impossible, and it also provided, with the full consent of the Colonial Office, a means of destroying resistance and disposing of obstacles to change.

The choice was between annexation and a return to the Pangkor idea of representation by a Resident—with or without Jervois' modifications. Jervois was soon hopefully pressing for annexation.[2] In a despatch of 16 November he declared a preference for governing in the name of the Sultan; but two days later he cabled proposing

---

[1] The Executive Council considered 'Abdu'llah's case on the basis of a letter from Jervois to 'Abdu'llah, 16 September 1876, specifying the charges against him, and the Sultan's reply, dated 6 October (Minutes of the Executive Council, 4 December 1876). 'Abdu'llah had previously complained that Jervois' letter did not furnish him with the names of his accusers, or with the evidence against him. Minutes of the Executive Council, 21 October 1876.

[2] Jervois to Carnarvon, telegram of 18 November 1875, C.1505, no. 54; Jervois to Carnarvon, 335 of 2 December 1875, C.1505, no. 94.

partial annexation of all that part of Perak bounded on the north by the Krian and on the east by the Perak river. He had received information that the Sultan and his advisers were implicated in Birch's murder, and though the evidence was scanty enough, it provided an opportunity to dispose of 'Abdu'llah and carry out the annexation policy which he had first contemplated.[1]

Carnarvon's response to this pressure was to refuse to hear of annexation. He instructed repeatedly by telegram and despatch that the troops must not be used for any large political object, but only to restore order and inflict punishment for outrage.[2] In the first instance, his anxiety was probably to stop Jervois from making any further advance on his own initiative, but when future policy came to be considered at greater leisure, the decision against annexation was confirmed. In the past, Carnarvon had shown himself opposed to annexation as premature, though not opposed to it in principle. In a private letter to Jervois, he had replied to proposals for annexation in these terms:

I will not say that the time may not be at hand when such a step may become necessary. I am quite aware that the change would probably be one for the benefit of the people; and it is possible that, as you say, no serious opposition or difficulty would arise on the spot. But I am clearly of opinion that this time—whether it be near or less near—has not yet come. . . . It is only within the last few months that the fact that we are establishing a very large system of indirect control over the States of the Peninsula is becoming realized by the general public in this country. We must in all these things move in harmony with that public opinion: and as a matter of wise policy I desire to see our present system somewhat more consolidated and the results of it somewhat more clearly ascertained and understood before we take the next move.[3]

After the murder, the permanent officials, though not opposed to annexation in principle, also saw no immediate need for it. Meade, who was then Assistant Under-Secretary of State, wrote in March 1876, 'I think it not improbable that annexation may be the ultimate result, but I see no reason why it should take place for some time to

[1] Jervois to Carnarvon, 2 December 1875, C.1505, no. 93 and enclosures. The information consisted of reports picked up from a Bugis trader, and statements from 'Abdu'llah's former slave girls (enclosures 63 and 66).

[2] Carnarvon to Jervois, telegram of 14 and 25 November 1875, C. 1505, nos. 42 and 55; despatch of 10 December 1875, C.1505, no. 70.

[3] Carnarvon to Jervois, private of 13 September 1875, cited in A. Hardinge, *The Life of Henry Howard Molyneux Herbert, Fourth Earl of Carnarvon, 1831–1890*, London, 1925, vol. ii, p. 137.

come and I would do nothing to precipitate it'.[1] Ord, who was in England at this time, and who, as the nearest available authority on the Malay states, was in constant touch with the Colonial Office, was consistently opposed to annexation, mainly 'on the score of the expense it must be for a considerable time, and the trouble it will give owing to the paucity of competent officers to undertake the work'.[2] He favoured a limited intervention, with the British representative acting virtually as a consular agent, providing security for the Chinese and other foreigners, and interfering not at all with the government of the state.[3] He recognized that this would be a retreat; it was in fact a retreat not only from Jervois' position but from that taken up at Pangkor.

Annexation was discredited by its association with Jervois, a strong Governor who defended his policy in able and insubordinate despatches; if ever a Governor needed to be put in his place it was he. Carnarvon realized that Jervois was trying to rush him into insufficiently considered policies, and reacted accordingly. Jervois defended his departure from Pangkor in a long despatch in which he implied that he had done no more than establish formally a control of which the Colonial Office was aware, and which it had tacitly approved. Carnarvon wrote a detailed and angry minute, concluding, 'Such a course [annexation] may or may not hereafter become necessary—but I will not sanction a great measure of State policy being adopted by a Colonial Governor without the sanction, and in opposition to the instructions of the Home Government'.[4]

Perhaps the most important consideration was the possible effect of annexation on the Malays, and the fear of further disturbances, whose suppression might fall as a burden on the Imperial Treasury. The Colonial Office 'in its ignorance and helplessness' (the phrase is Ord's) was inclined to take the Perak affair seriously;[5] and as it was followed in December by a brush with Malays on the borders of Sungei Ujong, there was a fear that country-wide resistance was about to develop. The Perak occupation had been costly; by the end of March

[1] Minute by Meade, 21 March 1876, on Jervois to Carnarvon, 62 of 10 February 1875, CO 273/83.

[2] Ord to Anson, 8 June 1876, Anson Correspondence.

[3] Ord to CO, 3 January 1876, CO 273/89.

[4] Carnarvon, minute of 22 March 1876, on Jervois to Carnarvon, 62 of 10 February 1876, CO 273/83.

[5] Minute by Meade, 21 January 1876, on Jervois to Carnarvon, 352 of 17 December 1876, CO 273/81; Ord to Anson, 28 December 1875, Anson Correspondence.

1876, £71,074 had been advanced, mainly by the Straits Treasury, towards the cost of the Indian and Hong Kong troops. But in January 1876 the Straits Treasury was empty, and Carnarvon had to empower the Governor to draw on the Crown Agents; further expenses would have to be met by a Colonial loan, as Carnarvon was unwilling to approach the Treasury for funds. The War Office, the India Office and the Admiralty all wanted to know what proportion of the total cost was likely to be repaid from Colonial funds,[1] and Carnarvon could not tell them. A policy which might require the indefinite retention of large forces in the Straits was clearly undesirable. It is true that the despatches and telegrams of December and January told of occupation of the Perak valley with little resistance; indeed the Governor was much exercised to justify, in the light of the paltry resistance offered, the presence of so large a force. But the absence of resistance was not necessarily an argument for further advance; it might be an encouragement to let well alone, and consolidate positions already gained, instead of advancing claims to formal authority and thus irritating the Malays. This is how Carnarvon saw the situation. He laid down in his policy despatch of 1 June 1876:

I fail to perceive any proof that the system under which Residents were appointed to the native States has had such a trial as to justify me in pronouncing that it has failed, or that any other course which has been indicated is not open to graver risk, larger expenditure, and more doubtful results. The obstacles which have interfered with its success are apparently such as can be removed . . . I see, therefore, no ground for an entire and abrupt reversal of existing arrangements, followed, as such reversal might be, by a further period of uncertainty and transition.[2]

The question now was whom to recognize as Sultan. It was generally agreed that 'Abdu'llah would have to go. Soon after Birch's death, suspicion had rested on him, and this had deepened with the months that followed; but whether or not he was guilty of conspiring to murder Birch, he had consistently opposed British policy in Perak

---

[1] Jervois to Carnarvon, 6 April 1876, C.1512, no. 60; Jervois to Carnarvon, 24 January 1876, C.1505, no. 111; War Office to CO, 30 November 1875, C.1505, no. 59; Admiralty to CO, 21 March 1876, C.1512, no. 19. Carnarvon intended to ask the Treasury to pay a part of the expenses of the Perak War; but before he could so do, the Treasury returned a statement which had been sent to them 'through inadvertence', with the ominous remark that 'My Lords could not admit that any of the expenditure on account of the Perak Expedition was to be charged to Imperial Funds'.

[2] Carnarvon to Jervois, 1 June 1876, C.1512, no. 70.

and thwarted the Resident, and for political reasons alone it was necessary to get rid of him. He could not be tried for conspiracy to murder Birch, since the trial of an independent Sultan raised juridical problems, and not the least of these was the difficulty of finding evidence that would stand up in court. It was decided to dispose of the case by executive action.[1] The case was considered by the Executive Council on 4 December 1876, and on the 9th, the Council decided that 'Abdu'llah, Ismail and the leading chiefs were implicated in the murder. Ismail was exiled to Johore; 'Abdu'llah, the Mentri, the Laksamana and the Shahbandar were exiled to the Seychelles in July 1877.

The obvious successor to 'Abdu'llah was Yusuf, who had supported British policy loyally ever since September 1875, and who had an unimpeachable hereditary right; and the suggestion that 'Abdu'llah might be deposed in favour of Yusuf was made soon after Birch's murder.[2] The Secretary of State, aware of Yusuf's unpopularity, demurred, and suggested that 'Abdu'llah should be replaced by the Maharaja of Johore or Tengku Zia'u'd-din:[3] Jervois, who appears to have had some informed advisers, objected that a foreigner not of royal descent would be ill-received in Perak, and made the compromise suggestion that Yusuf should be regent during the minority of 'Abdu'llah's eldest son, then eight years old, and this was accepted.[4] On 30 March 1877, by proclamation of the Governor,[5] 'Abdu'llah ceased to be Sultan, and Yusuf became Chief Native Authority in the state.

[1] Jervois to Carnarvon, Confidential of 1 September 1876, CO 273/84.

[2] Jervois to Carnarvon, 335 of 2 December 1875, C.1505, no. 94; Jervois to Carnarvon, telegram of 1 January 1876, CO 537/45.

[3] Carnarvon to Jervois, 135 of 1 June 1876. These paragraphs were omitted from the published version in C.1512, no. 70.

[4] Jervois to Carnarvon, 297 of 19 August 1876, C.1709, no. 29; Carnarvon to Jervois, Confidential of 23 October 1876, CO 273/84.

[5] SSGG 30 March 1877.

IV

DEVELOPMENT OF A POLICY

BIRCH's murder was followed by long and acrimonious despatches between Jervois and Carnarvon in which Jervois refuted the accusation that he had inaugurated an entirely new policy in Perak.[1] He pointed out that there had really been no Ruler in any of the states who had the power to carry out the Residents' advice, and that the Residents had assumed control in Selangor, Sungei Ujong and Larut in accordance with instructions issued by his predecessor. He argued that the Pangkor Engagement meant rule, not advice, and had been interpreted in that sense in Larut, but that the division of parties in Perak, and the hostility of 'Abdu'llah, nullified the intentions of the Engagement and made it necessary to formulate them in plainer terms. He cited the instructions issued by Clarke to Birch and Davidson, requiring them to take charge of the revenues and put down illegal exactions; he referred to the reports of the Residents for 1875, which made it clear that the Residents were ruling, not advising, and which had been received by the Colonial Office with 'apparent acquiescence'. He implied that the Colonial Office had known all along what was going on and by its silence had indicated consent.

The Secretary of State reacted to this despatch with an indignation which may have been enhanced by the fact that Jervois' analysis was substantially correct. He pointed out that the provisions of the Pangkor Engagement had to be considered in relation to the 'assumed

---

[1] Jervois to Carnarvon 62 of 10 February 1876, C.1512, no. 12; Carnarvon to Jervois 135 of 1 June 1876, C.1512, no. 70. The question arises whether Jervois himself regarded his policy as a great innovation, or, as he now tried to pretend, a slight modification of form. It is difficult to give a direct answer. He was certainly aware that he was placing the British officers in Perak on a new footing, and he certainly knew that he was departing radically from instructions, but the policy represented by Pangkor was sufficiently fluid to enable him to believe that the step he took was in harmony with the spirit of the Engagement. We consider that Jervois' reforms were in keeping with Clarke's Perak policy as expressed in his communications with Birch and 'Abdu'llah, and it is possible that Clarke himself would have been driven to take similar action had he remained in the Straits.

readiness of the Sultan to accept advice,'[1] and that the despatches received by the Secretary of State gave him no reason to suspect that advice would be resented or ignored. When the despatches came to describe the Residential system in operation they were equally optimistic; though they recounted difficulties (for example, the failure of Sultan Ismail to acknowledge 'Abdu'llah as Sultan or surrender the regalia) these were all represented as in course of solution, and the accounts tended to confirm the Secretary of State in the opinion that the system was working well. Carnarvon rejected the argument that Birch's report, which Jervois specially mentioned, had given him any clear idea of what was happening, or that his own acknowledgement, expressing a polite interest, could be taken as wholehearted approval. The instructions to Birch and Davidson, which he acknowledged might 'possibly give a somewhat different complexion to the Residential Schemes proposed by Sir Andrew Clarke', were never sent home, and he declined now to comment on them. Finally, he referred to numerous despatches in which he had warned the Governor against an assumption of undefined responsibilities in the states.

Carnarvon had some basis for his argument. Clarke's despatches had been consistently misleading, as the officials now realized. Carnarvon's own pronouncements on policy had consistently advised caution. In his despatch acknowledging Clarke's first reports, and in subsequent correspondence during 1874 and 1875, he had warned the Governor that the Residential system must be considered an experiment and that the appointments of the Residents were provisional.[2] He had warned Clarke against 'unduly compromising Her Majesty's Government in the internal affairs of [the] States', and he had repeated the warning in his acknowledgements of the reports of Birch, Swettenham and Davidson.[3] But these general and non-committal warnings, without a single word of guidance on the line the Resident

[1] As Meade put it in a minute of 21 March 1876, 'The Treaty of Pangkore was based on the assumption that the Residents were eagerly demanded & that their advice would be readily sought and acted upon. If therefore in process of time they should become virtual rulers of the country, it is plain from the whole correspondence that Sir A. C[larke] & the Secretary of State expected that result would follow from the influence they were represented as certain of acquiring, as the Sultan & Rajahs were said to be only waiting to have the proper road pointed out to them, to adopt it'. Minute on Jervois to Carnarvon, 62 of 10 February 1876, CO 273/83.

[2] Carnarvon to Clarke, 6 March 1874, C.1111, no. 43; Carnarvon to Jervois, 8 April 1875, C.1320, no. 70; Carnarvon to Jervois, 4 June 1875 and 15 July 1875, C.1320, nos. 34 and 35.

[3] Carnarvon to Jervois, 15 July 1875, C.1320, no. 35.

was to take, or the determination of his jurisdiction, were not policy instructions so much as a transfer of responsibility to more willing shoulders, and the Straits officials interpreted them in that sense. The Colonial Office may have been misinformed by the despatches, but the enclosures—if they were ever read—provided a sufficient corrective; and though the instructions to Residents were not sent home, Clarke forwarded in April 1875 a copy of a letter of rebuke to 'Abdu'llah, upbraiding 'our friend' for breaking the Engagement, telling him that no one but the Resident was to collect taxes in Perak, and asking him to consult the Resident if he ever wanted to visit Larut (in his own state!) or Penang.[1] At the same time, Clarke forwarded Speedy's report, describing the most complete assumption of judicial and fiscal responsibility for Larut, and with no screen of native acceptance, since the Mentri was known from previous accounts to be hostile and the Sultan un-cooperative. Carnarvon's only instruction was that the Sultan should be addressed on the subject of debt slavery, without being alarmed 'as to any undue interference with him in the internal administration of the State'.[2] It was only two months later, when a Liberal peer (Lord Stanley of Alderley) pointed out to him the degree of administrative control revealed by Speedy's report, that Carnarvon issued another general warning, and enclosed detailed instructions, supplied by a friend of Stanley's at the India Office, on the technique of taking over a government without assuming responsibility.[3]

The nearest an official came to defining what the Colonial Office thought the system to be, was Herbert's minute on a despatch from Jervois, balancing the arguments for and against annexation.

The system of governing a native country through a Resident may be so applied as to control it absolutely, as is done in the thoroughly subjugated parts of Java, where the Dutch Government governs through the native princes whom it appoints Regents with a Resident and Controleurs at the court of each—or simply to influence and advise by accrediting a diploma-

[1] Clarke to Sultan 'Abdu'llah, undated, enclosed in Clarke to Carnarvon, 26 April 1875, C.1320, no. 26. Copy in *EPO*, Appendix XVII, dated 22 April 1875.
[2] Carnarvon to Clarke, 25 May 1875, C. 1320, no. 24.
[3] The 'friend at the India Office' advised, for example, that work on the roads should be initiated by proclamation by the Ruler. This would clear the Resident of all responsibility 'as to those arbitrary measures which are sure to be resorted to in making the road, such as compulsory labour and cheating the labourers of their hire, and the appropriation of land necessary for the roadway'. Memorandum (unsigned) 28 June 1875, enclosed Carnarvon to Jervois, 27 July 1875, C.1320, no. 37.

tic officer to the independent native authorities, as we supposed we were doing in these Malay States.[1]

It is difficult to know how Herbert could have supposed this, after reading the Residents' reports. They make it clear that the English Residents were already far from being diplomatic officers, and that they had already assumed all the responsibilities of their Dutch counterparts, without the assistance of an organized indigenous executive such as had been built up in Java.

Whatever their past illusions, however, the Colonial Office now realized the true state of affairs in the Peninsula and that the administrative responsibilities assumed by the Residents or thrown upon them by the events of 1875–6 could not be discarded. It is notable that the officials, though critical of Jervois' justificatory despatch, did not condemn it outright. Meade acknowledged that effective government did not exist in Perak and that the Resident had to fill the gap. He minuted: 'I should turn out 'Abdu'llah (requiring him to reside on a pension outside Perak) and put in Raja Yusuf or some other chief to be selected by the Governor and I should govern the country in his name assisted by a mixed Malay Council. We might thus at some future day find that we have trained up a man to whom the Govt. could altogether be entrusted. . . .'[2]

The despatch instructing the Governor as to future relations with the Malay states made no concessions of principle. In paragraph 8, it continued to refer to the 'advice given by the Resident to the Chief native authority' (though paragraph 11 made it clear that the Colonial Office was aware there was no native authority capable of governing, at least in Perak), and it avoided giving a direct ruling on the role of the Residents, or direct sanction to the assumption of executive responsibility. There was, however, an implied acknowledgement and acceptance of the existing situation.

It is indeed clear that the Residents have exceeded the function of Counsellors which they were intended to discharge, but I do not think that on that account it is necessary either to withdraw them from Perak and the other

[1] Minute by Herbert (Under-Secretary of State), 20 December 1875, on Jervois to Carnarvon 327 of 16 November 1875, CO 273/81. He had minuted on the Residents' reports to the effect that the Governor ought to be very careful not to allow the 'advice which may properly be given by Residents to assume the shape of a direction as to their policy'. Minute of 27 June 1875 on Clarke to Carnarvon, 122 of 27 April 1875, forwarding the report of the Resident of Selangor, CO 273/80.

[2] Minute by Meade, 21 March 1876, on Jervois to Carnarvon, 62 of 10 February 1876, CO 273/83.

States, or to revolutionise the conditions of their political and administrative functions. A modification of the previous arrangements will probably be enough for the present, if combined with watchfulness and a great caution on the part of the Government. . . .

It is, in my opinion, undesirable that the British officers should interfere more frequently or to a greater extent than is necessary in the minor details of government. Their special objects should be the maintenance of peace and law, the initiation of a sound system of taxation, with the consequent development of the general resources of the country, and the supervision of the collection of the revenue so as to ensure the receipt of funds necessary to carry out the principal engagements of the Government, and to pay for the cost of the British officers and whatever establishments may be found necessary to support them.[1]

The Colonial Office still would not acknowledge facts, but at least it was ready to be a party to a fiction.

Two years later Jervois' successor, Sir William Robinson,[2] reported the arbitrary action of the Resident of Selangor, who had suspended a Malay member of Council for attempting to bribe a magistrate. Robinson had ordered the member of Council to be reinstated, and had issued a warning to the Residents, 'the Residents have been placed in the Native States as advisers, not as rulers, and if they take upon themselves to disregard this principle they will most assuredly be held responsible if trouble springs out of their neglect of it'.[3] The Secretary of State sent a mild reply. While approving the action of the Governor and the terms of his warning, he softened the censure of the Resident and added, 'I fully recognise the delicacy of the task imposed upon the Residents, and am aware that much must be left to their discretion on occasions when prompt and firm action is called for.'[4]

[1] Carnarvon to Jervois, 135 of 1 June 1876, no. 70. In December, Carnarvon minuted on a despatch from Jervois on the organization of the Perak police: '. . . the creation of this force for the regulation of customs and internal affairs is virtually a step—and a long one—towards the govt. of the country. I cannot perhaps refuse—the country cannot be abandoned and it must be governed. . . . But even in accepting what I cannot avoid, I think it well to note the true state of the case'. Minute by Carnarvon, 4 December 1876, on Jervois to Carnarvon 369 of 18 October 1876, CO 273/85.

[2] Sir William Robinson, GCMG (1887) was Governor of the Straits Settlements from August 1877 to February 1879. He had previously been Governor of the Leeward Islands and then of Western Australia, and subsequently returned to Australia as Governor successively of Western Australia and Victoria. He retired in 1895.

[3] CS to Residents, 17 May 1878, enclosed in Robinson to Hicks Beach, 13 June 1878, C.2410, no. 2.

[4] Hicks Beach to Robinson, 31 August 1878, C.2410, no. 3.

The Governor's circular had called forth a spirited protest from the Resident of Perak, Hugh Low. He asked what native Ruler he was supposed to advise. He had put the question to Meade before leaving for Perak: 'When I asked Mr. Meade, "who was the Raja I was sent out to advise" he said "we don't know of one, you must try to ascertain whether there is anyone fit for the position and then he will be supported." '[1] Low went on to say that his greatest difficulty in attempting to settle the country had been Raja Yusuf; that unless he could control the Raja, his position would be untenable, and that he was quite prepared to take the responsibility for the course he was pursuing. Robinson wrote reassuringly that there was nothing in Low's dealings with the Raja Muda which was inconsistent with the position the Resident should occupy. 'The advice which the Resident gives is authoritative advice and may not be lightly rejected. . . . All the same the fiction (if such you prefer to call it) that the Residents are merely advisers must be kept up, and here is just where the adroitness and ability of the Officer are so important. . . .'[2] Low wrote a satisfied and grateful reply showing that he had taken all the points in the Governor's letter and that they allowed him all the scope he needed.[3] All this correspondence was forwarded to the Colonial Office.

After Robinson had left the Straits he tried to get the Colonial Office to define the role of the Residents a little more clearly.[4] In a remarkably frank letter, he stated that the theory of government in the Malay states had no relationship to practice, and that the Residents had gone far beyond advice. Progress in the states had been brought about by 'pointing out the right path, by saying it must be followed, and by strength of will and influence obliging it to be followed, even though the question were one involving a Malay custom —a very wide term—and especially by personally dealing with every matter of detail in the administration'. The states were to all intents and purposes ruled as a colony, and natives in the states already imagined that they were British territory. He thought it wrong that Residents should be burdened with responsibility without being given formal authority. 'That government should hold the Resident

[1] Low to Robinson, 28 May 1878, enclosed in Robinson to Hicks Beach, 171 of 13 June 1878, CO 273/94.
[2] Ibid. Robinson to Low, 9 June 1878.
[3] Low to Robinson, 21 June 1878, enclosed in Robinson to Hicks Beach, 188 of 1 July 1878, CO 273/94.
[4] Robinson to CO private, 29 April 1879, CO 273/101.

responsible for the administration of the country, for its peace, the collection and proper expenditure of its revenues, the arrest of criminals, the administration of justice, and at the same time impress upon him non-interference in matters of detail, and matters of Malay custom, is a position almost impossible for any man to hold.' He asked the Colonial Office to instruct the Governor confidentially that annexation was inevitable, or at least that withdrawal was not contemplated. But the officials decided that confidential instructions to the Governor that annexation must come would be 'a very dangerous knowledge', and decided that since things seemed to be going well in the Malay states they should 'let well alone'. Robinson's letter therefore went unanswered.

The transactions between the Colonial Office, the Governor and the Residents up to 1880 had established the Residents formally as advisers; but the fact that they were administering the states was now generally admitted. It had been acknowledged by a Resident and a Governor in private correspondence, and by an authoritative statement of a Governor in a private letter to the Colonial Office; and in later years the position was to be acknowledged also in official correspondence.

In the next few years, control over policy and administration was established beyond question by the Residents and their district and departmental staffs; and their rule was justified by a great expansion in production, revenue and population. The problem of conciliating the Malays and bringing them into the administration was more difficult.

It had always been formal policy to govern through Malays, and the expediency of using Malay agencies and conciliating Malay interests had been acknowledged in some degree even by Birch and Jervois. Birch, for example, proposed to employ Malay headmen to enforce his numerous regulations, and called attention to the confusion which existed concerning their appointments and authority;[1] and Jervois' 1875 reforms had provided for the formation of a State Council on which Sultan 'Abdu'llah, ex-Sultan Ismail and three of the rajas would be represented. But Birch thought of the penghulus as revenue and police agents and was in any case thinking in terms of government through a large police force which he intended to spread over Perak; and Jervois' intention was not so much to asso-

[1] Report of the Acting Resident, Perak, 2 April 1875, C.1320, enclosure 1 in no. 26, Clarke to Carnarvon, 26 April 1875.

ciate the chiefs in government as to buy them out with pensions and empty honours. There was a strong element of bribery in the whole Malay policy of the Residents, of course; but in its later development there appeared a genuine idea of Malay participation which was absent in the discussions of Clarke and Jervois.

The idea may have been in many minds, but its most influential exponent up to 1877 appears to have been Swettenham. He formulated and developed it during his early experience of the Malay states. In his 1875 report on Selangor, he represented the lack of accredited local authorities as a serious problem, and recommended that a headman, if possible of raja birth, should be appointed by the Sultan to each district, and a penghulu placed under him in each village, to adjudicate in petty cases and collect local taxes. In a memorandum of October 1876 on local government in Perak,[1] he enunciated the familiar principles of indirect rule, which were soon to have a scriptural authority for administrators in the Malay states. He argued the case for employing native authorities from expediency as well as moral principle. As an agent of government, the penghulu would be cheaper and more effective than the police; he was influential, he was related to many of the villagers and known to all, and his office was an inheritance which could not be taken from him without causing deep resentment. He had resources at his disposal for keeping order and detecting criminals, far beyond those available to the police; and his opposition could render the police quite ineffective. The British were committed in principle to working through indigenous authorities; but this was also the most effective way, in the long run, of introducing reforms.

... it is surely a most important point in our newly adopted relations with the Native States to interest the natives themselves in the government of their own States and not to take this government out of their hands.

To preserve the accepted customs and traditions of the country, to enlist the sympathies and interests of the people in our assistance, and to teach them the advantages of good government and enlightened policy—advantages which they will be far more ready to see and admit when they themselves are instruments in the working of the plan than when they look on and see others holding the positions, which they think by right belong to them, introducing reforms which will be received with apathy and opposition because they are not their own reforms [sic].

---

[1] Swettenham, 'Some arguments in favour of governing Perak through its Headmen', 8 October 1876, enclosed in Weld to Derby, 208 of 28 May 1883 CO 273/120.

Carnarvon instructed in his policy despatch of 1 June 1876 'whatever may be the ultimate policy which it may be necessary to adopt in the Malay Peninsula it is clearly our object to make the best use of existing materials'. He approved the formation of a mixed council of chiefs and British officers and recommended its introduction into each of the Malay states, and he considered that the allowances for the chiefs should be settled as soon as possible, so that they would 'understand their interest in supporting the system of revenue devised by Mr Birch'.[1] Jervois' reply was based on these instructions. He had called for a report on allowances; he accepted the proposal to establish councils in other states besides Perak, and he also proposed to give a Colony education to the sons of chiefs, to prepare them for appointments in the state administrations.[2] Finally, in a despatch on the organization of the Perak police, he recommended that government should be carried on as far as possible through native headmen, repeating almost verbatim the arguments in Swettenham's memorandum on the subject.[3]

These points were embodied in instructions to Hugh Low,[4] appointed Resident of Perak in February 1877. Hugh Low[5] was the foremost of a small group of remarkable men who governed the Malay states in the next twenty years and gave substance to these policies. He was already fifty-three when he came to Perak, and had spent his whole official life—nearly thirty years—in the stagnant little colony of Labuan, off the north-west coast of Borneo. By all ordinary standards, his official career was a failure. It had been crippled by personal animosities which frustrated his work in Labuan and his advancement in the service, and in 1872, after twenty-four years' service, in which he had acted as Governor for long periods, he was still only a police magistrate.

Fortunately, Low had rich interests and resources outside Labuan. He had first come to Borneo as a youth of nineteen, to study tropical

---

[1] Carnarvon to Jervois, 135 of 1 June 1876, C.1512, no. 70.
[2] Jervois to Carnarvon, 297 of 19 August 1876, C.1709, no. 29.
[3] Jervois to Carnarvon, 369 of 18 October 1876, C. 273/85.
[4] No copy of the instructions has come to light, but it is clear from Low's journal that he was given a list of possible State Councillors and asked to report (E. Sadka, 'Journal of Sir Hugh Low, Perak 1877', *JMBRAS*, vol. xxvii, part 4 (1954) pp. 80–81. The source will be referred to in future as 'Low Journal'). He was instructed to proceed with the appointment of penghulus. Low to CS, 8 July 1878, enclosure in Robinson to Hicks Beach, 224 of 1 August 1878, CO 273/95.
[5] For details of Low's career, see Appendix 2.

flora and collect plants, and he stayed in Sarawak and North Borneo for two years learning Malay and other languages, and travelling widely in his botanical researches. He was primarily a naturalist, but his intellectual curiosity drew him into a study of the peoples of Sarawak, their history, customs, religions and economy. He travelled sometimes with Sarawak government officers, sometimes alone; collecting plants, studying the country's economy, moving with perfect ease and confidence among Malays and Dyaks in remote places, taking notes of everything he saw. In 1848 he published his book, *Sarawak, its Inhabitants and Productions,* the first authoritative account of the west coast of Borneo. It was the work of a typical nineteenth-century scholar-traveller, containing meticulous observations of the natural life, the economic geography, history and contemporary politics of Sarawak.

After he had entered the Labuan service, he continued to travel in Borneo on diplomatic missions and on privately organized expeditions. The most important of these were to Mount Kinabalu in 1851 and 1858. Kinabalu had not been approached by any European before Low climbed it in 1851, travelling through unexplored country, and among Dusuns and Muruts fearful of any proposals to climb the sacred mountain, and unaccustomed to foreigners. Low calmed their fears and even persuaded some of them to accompany him to the summit. In 1858 he made two more journeys to Kinabalu with Spenser St. John, then Consul-General at Brunei. All three expeditions were scientifically fruitful; Low made valuable collections of nepenthes and orchids and took copious notes of the country and its inhabitants and their dialects. He was now recognized as the chief authority on north-west Borneo; 'no man possesses more varied experience or a more intimate knowledge of the people'.[1]

Low was acquiring experiences, interests and habits of life which equipped him admirably for the solitary and responsible work of administering a new protectorate. During his Labuan service he had held nearly every office, and he had a complete knowledge of administrative method and procedure, a sense of order, and a respect for routine. He was a naturalist, intellectually absorbed in the Malaysian countries; a thoroughly experienced traveller who moved without benefit of official protection among strange peoples, unassuming, skillful in avoiding quarrels, but prompt and firm in action when

[1] S. St. John, *Life in the Forests of the Far East,* London, 1862, vol. i, Preface, p. ix.

necessary. He was well fitted for the experimental and lonely work of administering a native state, when the administrator must needs be his own ethnologist, scientist and interpreter.

Isabella Bird, who visited Kuala Kangsar in 1879, has written of Low's manner of life, perfectly attuned to his environment. His bungalow, though small and plainly designed in conventional Malayan style, was beautifully situated on a hillside overlooking the Perak river. He was silently and efficiently served, and sat down to a perfectly appointed table: 'linen, china, crystal, flowers, cooking, were all alike exquisite'. His companions were two apes, Mahmoud and Eblis, and a wild siamang that lived in the roof:

This is a curious life. Mr Low sits at one end of the verandah at his business table with Eblis looking like his familiar spirit, beside him. I sit at a table at the other end, and during the long working hours we never exchange a word. Mahmoud sometimes executes wonderful capers, the strange, wild, half-human face of the siamang peers down from the roof with a half-trustful, half-suspicious expression . . . tiffin and dinner are silently served in the verandah recess at long intervals; the sentries at the door are so silently changed that one fancies that the motionless blue turbans and scarlet coats contain always the same men; in the foreground the river flows silently, and the soft airs which alternate are too feeble to stir the overshadowing palm-fronds or rustle the *attap* of the roof. It is hot, silent, tropical. The sound of Mr Low's busy pen alone breaks the stillness during much of the day. . . .[1]

Low came to Perak after a lifetime among Malays,[2] knowing their language and customs and something of the problem of adapting a European administration to their needs and prejudices. He had seen this problem arise in Sarawak, and saw how a policy of government was evolved to meet it. Sarawak under the Brookes was known throughout Malaysia as a government which identified itself with existing Malay authorities, enlisted them in the administration, deferred to their opinion, and introduced changes at a pace acceptable to them. Malay chiefs and British officers sat together on a State Council which met monthly to consider government business, and

[1] I. Bird, *The Golden Chersonese*, London, 1883, p. 322.

[2] His first wife, Catherine Napier, was part Malay, and his daughter Kitty, whom he dearly loved, had beautiful and striking Malay features. After the death of his first wife in Labuan, he had taken a Malay mistress, Nona Dyang Loya, with whom he lived for many years, and by whom he had a child. Nona Dyang Loya, also known as Nona Tuan Low, lived with her mother and daughter in quiet respectability, and when Low joined them in the evenings, 'it was a common thing for the family to play on rebanas as they recited pantuns to each other'. James Pope-Hennessy, *Verandah*, London, 1964, p. 80.

there were district councils to advise the Residents (as the Sarawak district officers were called). Malays sat with European magistrates in the Police and Supreme Courts, and there was a Malay court to deal with divorce and inheritance cases. Raja James Brooke held that: 'Governments, like clothes, will not suit everybody, and certainly a people who gradually develop their government, though not a good one, are nearer happiness and stability than a government of the best which is fitted at random. I am going on slowly and surely, basing everything on their own laws, consulting all the headmen at every step. . . .'[1] Low was the protégé and lifelong friend of Raja Brooke, and was identified with his school of government; it was said that the relations in Sarawak between native and European had no parallel anywhere but in Perak.

Low's manner with the Malays, and the relations he established with them, impressed Isabella Bird more than anything else she had seen in the Peninsula.

In this once disaffected region he goes about unarmed, and in the daytime the sentries only carry canes. His manner is as quiet and unpretending as can possibly be, and he speaks to Malays as respectfully as to Europeans. . . . Apparently they have free access to him during all hours of daylight, and as I sit writing to you or reading, a Malay shadow constantly falls across my paper, and a Malay, with silent, cat-like tread glides up the steps and appears unannounced in the verandah, on which Mr Low at once lays aside whatever he is doing, and quietly gives himself to the business in hand. The reigning prince, the Rajah Muda Yusuf, and Rajah Dris, are daily visitors. . . .[2]

The entries in Low's journal confirm her impression. He laid it down as a first principle that officers should approach the Malays with gentleness and gain their confidence. This is not as trite as it might appear. Courtesy in addressing 'natives' did not come naturally to

---

[1] S. Baring-Gould and C. A. Bampfylde, *A History of Sarawak under its Two White Rajahs, 1839–1908*, London, 1909, p. 87.

[2] Bird, op. cit. 323–4. A French traveller who visited Perak in 1880 described him as follows: '*Un homme de grande mine et d'une physionomie originale, qu'accentue encore l'ample vêtement de mandarin chinois, à larges manches, aux pointes pendantes, dont il est vêtu dans son intérieur, et le gros jonc à pomme d'ivoire et à double pointe de fer qu'il porte comme une crosse d'évêque quand il sort de sa maison. Sa longue barbe grise, sa belle prestance, son air vénérable enfin, commandent dès l'abord le respect. Son regard est fin et pénétrant; le bout de son nez aquilin, qui remue, accompagne tous les mouvements de sa physionomie. Il pousse de temps en temps, quand il est seul surtout, de petits cris qui suivent un bâillement nerveux, probablement un reste de fiévres*'. B. de St. Pol Lias, *Pérak et les Orang Sakèys: Voyage dans l'intérieur de la presqu'ile Malaise*, Paris, 1883, p. 85.

all colonial officers,[1] and without it neither Malay co-operation nor even the appearance of it could be achieved. Low's relationship with Malays was remarkable by any standards, and his chief contribution, perhaps, was to set it up as the standard for the Malay states. Penghulus visited him from all over the state, reporting distress in their villages, complaining about the behaviour of the troops, asking that fugitives be helped to return. Dependents of executed and exiled chiefs came to ask for help, their womenfolk came to bargain with him over their allowances. He reassured them, dealt with their difficulties, lent them money—'everyone tugs at the Resident for this scarce article'—and took the opportunity to accustom them to proposals for land rent and poll tax. A week after his arrival in Perak he set out on tour of the up-river villages, holding levees of headmen wherever he went, familiarizing himself with their politics and problems and again explaining his revenue proposals. At Bukit Gantang he received a deputation of people asking for reinstatement of the Mentri:

I had a conversation with these people and told them that I had been sent here to govern the state for the benefit of all persons inhabiting it and that I thought that after a short time they would be able to trust me and would not miss the Mantri and that when I know them well [sic] I would do my best to employ [those] who deserve it under the Gov[ernm]ent in the Police, as Penghulus, and in other ways and that all men rich and poor should have free access to me whenever they had business or complaints which they were anxious I should hear.[2]

An example of Low's diplomatic ability was the way in which he secured the end of debt-slavery in Perak. He discovered when he arrived that there had been 'a strong inclination at this Residency to protect runaway slaves',[3] and decided that it would be impossible to secure the confidence of the chiefs if this practice were continued. But it was equally impossible to countenance slavery indefinitely in a state under British protection, and Low had his own scheme for abolition 'in a moderate time with the consent of the chiefs and people'. Slaves and slave debtors in possession of their masters on his arrival in Perak were to be considered as legally in that position,

[1] Low voiced his suspicion that the presence of the Assistant Resident, Maxwell, inhibited his own free intercourse with Perak Malays. 'He is a splendid fellow . . . but he is a little rough and hasty in his ways with the natives, especially the inferior classes and the part he took in the war is I expect against him with the Perak Malays for the present.' Low Journal, p. 63.
[2] Ibid. p. 30.
[3] Ibid. p. 44.

and magistrates and police were to help prevent desertion; but no free person was to be enslaved, the amount of the debt or slave price if tendered was to be accepted, and slaves who could prove ill-treatment or inadequate maintenance were to be freed.[1] In time the value of slaves would decline and the holders would be ready to consider manumission in return for compensation paid by the state. During 1881 and 1882, Low tested opinion and prepared the ground for the coming abolition. The timetable and procedures of manumission were exhaustively discussed at meetings in May and October 1882,[2] and the main differences that emerged were on minor questions of timing. Finally, Low's date for manumission—31 December 1883—was adopted, and manumission took place without incident.

It is notable that Low communicated directly with Malays of all classes, instead of approaching them through the rajas and chiefs. He used Malays of rank as his informants, but he was not dependent on them; for example, he invited the Temenggong to give him a list of villages and recommendations for penghulus, but he made a point of enquiring into penghulu appointments for himself, instead of accepting candidates proposed by the Temenggong or Raja Yusuf.[3]

[1] Low to CS, 28 May 1878, C.3285, enclosure in no. 2, Robinson to Hicks Beach, 29 July 1878. Low actually freed two slaves belonging to Raja Yusuf, and one belonging to the district chief of Kinta, because of ill treatment. Resident to Governor, 1 July 1882, C.3429, enclosure in no. 2, Weld to Kimberley, 9 July 1882; Minute by Raja Idris, 1 July 1882, ibid.

[2] *PCM*, 22 May 1882, 9 October 1882, 10 October 1882. In Selangor the population was much smaller and a large part of it recently immigrant, so that the problem was much easier to deal with. On the Sultan's advice, the Resident eliminated slavery quietly by executive and judicial process, valuing the labour of slaves at a monthly rate and deducting from this the slave price or debt till the whole was extinguished (Resident to CS, 28 May 1878, C.3285, enclosure 2 in no. 2, Robinson to Hicks Beach, 29 July 1878). In Sungei Ujong the same kind of settlement was arrived at, and the custom died out soon after Murray became Resident in 1875 (Resident to CS, 28 April 1882, C.3285, enclosure 2 in no. 8, Weld to Kimberley, 4 May 1882). In the states which came subsequently under British protection, the Dato' Penghulu of Jelebu and his waris agreed to abolish slavery from 1 January 1887 (Weld to Stanhope, 25 November 1886); the Yam Tuan Besar of Sri Menanti decided to abolish slavery as a Jubilee gift to Queen Victoria (Weld to Holland, 275 of 4 July 1887, 273/145), but died before he could carry out his intention, and it was fulfilled by his successor (*AR* Negri Sembilan, 1887 and 1888). In Pahang a ceiling was placed on the amount a slave-debtor might owe, and the value of his services, fixed at a monthly rate, was deducted, so that slavery would be extinguished in four years (*AR* Pahang, 1889); minutes of first meeting of State Council, 31 December 1889, enclosed in Smith to Knutsford, 24 of 17 January 1890, CO 273/165.

[3] Low Journal, p. 101.

He did not attempt to work through Raja Yusuf, a vindictive and violent man, for to give Yusuf even the appearance of influence would have upset the Malays and compromised his own good relations with them.[1] He was asked to keep the rajas in safe custody at Kuala Kangsar:

Shaik Ma Taib is dead against employing the Rajas and I know all the people are altogether against any native having magisterial or governing [powers]. It [is] under the circumstances very difficult to establish a native government. . . . I told Shaikh Ma Taib I intended R[aja] Idris to live at Syong which he highly applauded and recommended that all the Rajahs should be as much as possible collected there, which had also suggested itself to me, as they will be under observation and less able to be mischievous than when scattered about the provinces.[2]

Fortunately Low did not have to persuade the rajas to settle under his supervision; they were only too anxious to do it for themselves. Raja Yusuf was no fool; he realized his dependence on Low, and a few weeks after Low's arrival, Yusuf and Idris were already planning to move to Kuala Kangsar—ostensibly so that they might benefit by Low's advice, but actually so that they might derive 'an appearance of permanence' from the association.

The essence of Low's achievement is that while keeping rajas and chiefs out of executive positions, he gave them a vicarious sense of responsibility and participation in the work of the state by involving them in daily consultations on state business. He thereby secured more than the appearance of partnership. He records in his journal the value of Yusuf's comments and contributions, when his interest was diverted from his personal concerns to public business.[3] He obtained information, advice and opinions to assist him in making his decisions. So far as the balance of power was concerned, his position in relation to the rajas was not very different from that proposed by Jervois in his plan to govern Perak on behalf of the Sultan; but in spirit it was very different. Jervois and Birch would have excluded the rajas and chiefs altogether from affairs; the Perak monarchy, increasingly detached from the British executive, would probably have ended in pensioned retirement in the Malay quarter of Singapore. Carnarvon's directions and Low's policy and teaching led to

---

[1] See below, Chapter VI.
[2] Low Journal, p. 101. Shaikh Mat Taib was a Sumatran *ulama* (religious doctor) connected by marriage with Sultan 'Abdu'llah's family, and an enemy of Yusuf. Low made him a member of the State Council and State Kathi.
[3] Ibid. p. 48.

the renaissance of the sultanate within the colonial system and iden-fied the one with the other.

An important part of the Malay settlement was the preservation and development of the traditional system of local government, whereby penghulus of *mukims*[1] were employed to keep order, in preference to a large and expensive police force. Low and Swetten-ham were strong supporters of this policy, and drew up the first regular penghulu establishments in Perak and Selangor under British administration. A large number of the Selangor rajas and all the Perak headmen of the third rank were employed in this way. It was not so easy to assimilate the more important rajas, or the families of the great Perak chiefs. It was general policy to give members of the chief families in the state appointments commensurate with their dignity, but this was not easy. The administrative functions of the Malay district chiefs—revenue collection, judicial administration and control of penghulus—were now responsibilities of the European district officers; the district administration had removed the chiefs from the line of authority. The policy for the future was to educate the descendants of royal and chiefly houses in State and Colony schools, and recruit them into the administrative service; the first of such appointments was that of Raja Mansur, son of Ex-Sultan 'Abdu'llah, who became a cadet in the Perak service in 1883 and was appointed to magistracies in different parts of the state. But the survivors of the pre-British period could not be assimilated in this way. They were classified as 'Judges' and 'Native Magistrates',[2] since they had to be classified somehow, and they sat in the district and Residency courts with European officers; but with the exception of Raja Idris, who held a Malay court at Kuala Kangsar, they do not appear to have had any independent jurisdiction at a higher level than the penghulu court. Their function, undefined and unclas-sified, was to assist the Resident and the district officers in Malay affairs, to keep them informed about conditions and opinion in the mukims, to represent grievances and to help make new measures known and accepted.

The chiefs sat with the Ruler, the Resident and the Chinese Capi-tans on a State Council which had been designed at an early stage

[1] A local government division consisting of a chief village or township, and a small number of subsidiary villages or hamlets.

[2] See below, Chapter IX, for discussion of the penghulus in local administra-tion.

of British rule to assist the Resident in the business of government.[1] The Council was the legislative body of the state; it was the final court of appeal and reviewed all capital sentences; and it also decided matters relating to current administration. The Council was dominated by the Resident. He nominated its members, drew up its agenda, guided its deliberations and influenced its decisions. Independence might be expressed during the discussion, members might put forward critical opinions, but it was very rare indeed for Council members to persist in opposition to the Resident. But the Residents on the whole were intelligent administrators anxious to secure a basis of consent for their proposals. There was always the possibility of securing modifications or postponements of unpopular measures by representing the general opposition to them in Council. The Malay and Chinese members made representations and put forward suggestions that were sometimes incorporated in the final decision. Yet these qualifications do not alter the fact that the Council was essentially the advisory body of the Resident.

Despite the inadequate constitutional basis for their authority, the Residents by 1880 had become the effective rulers in the states; in the years that followed, their association with Malays developed smoothly on established principles, and the success of the Perak and Selangor administrations was reflected in phenomenal increases in revenues and populations. In consequence there was a change in the attitude of local authorities to the problems of government in the states. The years 1875 to 1880 had been spent in fruitless efforts by the Governor to get the Colonial Office to bring the states under formal control. From 1880 these efforts ceased, and Governors and Residents became the stoutest defenders of Malay sovereignty and the opponents of any measure which would bring the states formally under the control of the Colonial Office or the Government of the Straits Settlements.

The personification of this new attitude was the next Governor of the Straits Settlements, Sir Frederick Weld.[2] Weld was the complete

---

[1] In the Perak Establishment List of 1879, Raja Idris and the Temenggong were classified as Judges of the Supreme Court; in the Selangor Estimates for 1883 (and in other lists) the sons of the Sultan, Rajas Musa and Kahar, and the brother-in-law of the Sultan, Raja Laut, were classified as Native Magistrates. Sel/Sec. 215/1883.

[2] Sir Frederick Aloysius Weld, GCMG (1885), KCMG (1880), CMG (1875), was born in 1823 into an old West of England Catholic family. He emigrated to New Zealand in 1844 and began sheep farming in the Wairarapa district in the North Island. In 1854 he was elected member for Wairau in the first New

imperialist romantic. He was equally captivated by the vision of English liberty, transplanted to the colonies of settlement, and the vision of patriarchal authority, kindly and wisely exercised over the dependent Empire. This was a common dichotomy among imperialists of his generation, a definition of England's colonizing mission in terms of her traditional political genius on the one hand, and her capacity for leading backward peoples on the other. Weld would have held these attitudes whatever his experience, but they were confirmed by the circumstances of his life. He spent his middle years as a pastoralist in New Zealand, entered politics as a member of the first New Zealand representative assembly (having earlier refused a nominated seat on the non-representative Council), and he had a brief experience of office as Minister for Native Affairs and Premier. In New Zealand he was faced with the personal and national necessity of reaching an accommodation with the Maori, primarily over the purchase of land. He had the typical settler's attitude to the problem; conscious of his own rectitude and good intentions, he took it for granted that any offer for Maori land which seemed fair to him must benefit the Maori also, and concluded that those who objected in principle to land sales must be doing so for selfish personal reasons, and that it was the settlers' duty to put them down. When Maori opposition to land sales led to the wars of 1860–72, Weld preached magnanimity in victory; but it was during his government in 1864 that three million acres of Maori land were confiscated —a measure which one New Zealand historian has described as 'the worst injustice ever perpetrated by a New Zealand government'.[1]

Weld's 'old New Zealand experience' had given him a taste for native administration and a firm conviction that he was an expert on the subject; and he was captivated by the opportunities for creative benevolence which the Peninsula offered. He lived in a perpetual cloud of sentiment and patriarchal goodwill towards the peoples in his charge, and this expressed itself in an obsessive interest in the Malay states. His despatches and published letters do not reveal any great interest in the busy, sophisticated and unromantic commercial population of the Straits Settlements. He was not a professional administrator, he was impatient with routine (in his haste and im-

Zealand General Assembly. In 1860–1 he served as Minister for Native Affairs and in 1864–5 as Premier. In 1867 he left New Zealand. He was Governor of Western Australia, 1869–74; Governor of Tasmania, 1875–9; Governor of the Straits Settlements from 1880 till his retirement in 1887. He died in 1891.

[1] Keith Sinclair, *A History of New Zealand*, London, 1959, p. 140.

pulsiveness he overlooked or forgot or misinterpreted key points in communications). He was glad to leave the Colony to the Colonial Secretary and travel rough in the native states, being welcomed in villages and small towns, conferring with Residents and Malay chiefs and Chinese mine-owners, watching the Sikh 'police' on manoeuvres, shooting and fishing with Malays. (Chinese *towkays* did not fish or shoot, but they put on magnificent theatrical entertainments, and dinners with champagne, whisky, brandy and Benedictine.) He enjoyed not only the freedom and beauty of the Malay states, and the flattering deference of Malays and Chinese,[1] but the exercise of an authority and responsibility beyond anything he enjoyed as Governor of a Crown Colony. He made the final decision as to the disposal of revenues which in 1887 nearly equalled those of the Colony,[2] and he did this without reference to State Councils, Colony Councils or the Secretary of State. The last thing he intended was to permit this nearly absolute authority to be impaired by the creation of formal ties between the Malay states on the one hand and the Colonial or Imperial Government on the other. During nearly eight years of office he did everything a strong Governor could do to preserve the principle of the independence of the states.

Weld's ideas on the form of government most suitable to the Malay states were put forward in a despatch to the Secretary of State in October 1880.[3] He expressed views which were endorsed by all the Residents in later pronouncements on the subject.[4] While Robinson in 1879 had indicated only two possibilities—annexation or withdrawal, Weld indicated three—annexation, withdrawal and a continuation of the present system. The suggestion of withdrawal was merely a literary flourish, not meant to be taken seriously. Weld declared that it would result in anarchy and misgovernment worse

---

[1] Weld's susceptibility to flattery was amazing. He describes an interview with the Maharaja of Johore, soon after his arrival in the Colony. 'One of his remarks struck me. He said: "If I saw a thing as clearly as the sun in the heavens, and you saw differently, I would yield [my opinion] to you. You are my Father, and I wish always to take advice from you." Very oriental, but I think he meant it.' Diary entry for 26 October 1880, cited in A. Lovat, *The Life of Sir Frederick Weld, GCMG, a Pioneer of Empire*, London, 1848, p. 318.
[2] The revenue of the Straits Settlements for 1887 was $3,847,653, and of the states, $3,142,874. See Dickson to Knutsford, 10 July 1890, C.6222, no. 1, for figures and for a valuable review of the state administrations.
[3] Weld to Kimberley, Confidential of 21 October 1880, CO 273/104.
[4] See e.g., *PRCI*, vols. xv (1883–4) and xxvii (1895–6) for papers read by Weld and Swettenham and subsequent discussion.

than before, since British intervention had made the native rulers more and not less dependent on outside help.

Nothing that we have done has taught them to govern themselves; we are merely teaching them to co-operate with us in governing under our guidance. I have always held the theory that to teach men to govern themselves you must throw them a good deal on their own resources; we are doing, necessarily doing, the very reverse. Moreover, I doubt if Asiatics will ever learn to govern themselves; it is contrary to the genius of their race, of their history, of their religious systems, that they should. Their desire is a mild, just and firm despotism. . . .

He also rejected annexation. The existing system gave as much scope for economic development as a Crown Colony government; moreover, the Malay states required 'a somewhat elastic form of government', giving to those concerned with their affairs—the Governor, the Residents and the subordinate officers in the states—'a latitude . . . which the more rigid and complicated and expensive system of a political and legal organisation suited for a British Colony does not admit of'.

Finally, Weld hoped the Residential system would spread, and provide an example of good government to the Rulers of the Malay states still independent; but he thought it much more likely that the contrast between standards of administration in the states with Residents and those without them would lead the latter to ask for Residents too. Weld was preparing the Colonial Office for a further advance in the Peninsula. His third line of policy, which he put forward with an insinuating moderation which deceived no one, was: 'To gradually and gently increase our influence as occasion offers, over the peninsula south of Siam, not necessarily with any view of an immediate extension of the Residential system; and in respect to the protected States to determine never to relax our hold, but not to annex whilst it is possible to go on under the present system. In the meantime to work by and through the native governments by advice discreetly, but firmly administered.'

There was really no alternative to Weld's 'third possibility' and it was expressed in such general and diplomatic terms that the Secretary of State was able to endorse it without committing himself to anything. The replying despatch was confined to a guarded approval of a 'more intimate friendship' with the independent states, coupled with a warning not to institute changes without instructions from home.[1] But—as Kimberley recognized in a strong minute on Weld's despatch[2]—the extension of British control in the Peninsula was logical and inevitable. Weld devoted himself to the task of establishing Residents in the remaining independent states, and this was for the most part achieved during his governorship.[3] The territories brought under control were Pahang in 1887–8 and the remaining states of the Negri Sembilan between 1883 and 1887. In 1887, Pahang was induced to accept a joint defence treaty and a British Agent 'having functions similar to those of a consular officer'; in 1888 the murder of a British subject provided the pretext for introducing a Resident. In the Negri Sembilan two trends were discernible; the extension of British control over the little states, and their reconstitution as a confederation under the Yang di-Pertuan Besar of Sri Menanti. In 1883, an agreement with Jelebu provided for the supervision of the revenue collection by the Resident of Sungei Ujong; in 1885 a Collector was appointed to Jelebu; in 1886 an agreement with Jelebu formalized his position and duties. In 1887 a Collector and Magistrate was appointed to Sri Menanti, and extended his control over Rembau and Tampin; in 1889 the Rulers of these three territories and Johol agreed to constitute their countries into a confederation of states to be known as the Negri Sembilan (but without acknowledging any change in their relationships) and asked for the assistance of a British Resident in the government of the federation. In 1895, Sungei Ujong and Jelebu entered this curious federation, whose members continued to insist on their formal independence of one another, and whose only link was the British Resident, now placed formally in the position of adviser to all the states of the Negri Sembilan. In 1898 the constitutional position was regularized by the acknowledgment by all the states of the suzerainty of the Yang di-Pertuan Besar. The Negri Sembilan was now formally reconstituted under the aegis of the British Government.

[1] Kimberley to Weld, Confidential of 11 February 1881, CO 273/104.
[2] Minute by Kimberley, 14 January 1881, on Weld to Kimberley, Confidential of 21 October 1880, CO 273/104.
[3] The extension of British protection to Pahang and the Negri Sembilan states has been dealt with in detail in E. Thio, *British Policy in the Malay Peninsula, 1880–1910*, Vol I, Kuala Lumpur, 1968.

V

GOVERNMENT IN PRACTICE

THE COLONIAL OFFICE AND THE PROTECTED MALAY STATES

THE colonial protectorates which came within the British sphere in the late nineteenth and early twentieth centuries, though not legally part of the dominions of the Crown, were nevertheless assimilated to the Crown Colony type. Their governments were constituted by Order in Council under the Foreign Jurisdiction Act of 1890, which authorized the Crown to exercise any jurisdiction which it possessed in a foreign country in as ample a manner as if the jurisdiction had been acquired by cession or conquest; and over these territories the Colonial Office came to exercise a formal control in the same way as if they were Crown Colonies. But there were a number of protected states in which sovereign authority belonged to local rulers and in which the Crown exercised no jurisdiction. In these states British influence was preserved by resident officers whose interference in internal administration was generally confined (at any rate in name) to the tendering of advice.

The protected Malay states of Perak, Selangor, Negri Sembilan and Pahang fell within this category. The authority of the Colonial Office over these states never acquired a statutory basis. They admitted British 'advice' by local treaty and by permissive letters addressed by the Rulers to the Straits Government, but these instruments gave the Crown no jurisdiction in their territories and none was ever claimed. The instruments differed in their terminology and provisions, but their common purpose was to establish in each state a British Resident whose duty was to supervise the revenues and the general administration of the country.[1] In theory the Resident was

---

[1] In Perak and Negri Sembilan he was provided for by treaty (Engagement entered into by the Chiefs of Perak at Pulo Pangkor, 20 January 1874, W. G. Maxwell and W. S. Gibson, *Treaties and Engagements affecting the Malay States and Borneo*, London, 1924, pp. 28–31; Agreement with Negri Sembilan, 13 July 1889, ibid. p. 63). In Selangor and Sungei Ujong he was introduced by executive act, confirmed, in Selangor, by a letter of acceptance from the Sultan, and justified, in Sungei Ujong, by a previous invitation from the territorial chief (Letter from Sultan 'Abdul Samad, Selangor, to the Governor of the Straits Settlements, 1 October 1874, ibid. pp. 35–36; Letter from Dato' Klana to Lt.-Governor of

there to 'advise' the native authority by whom the government of the country was to be carried on; but by 1878 it was clear to those concerned in the government of the states that this was 'one of those fictions in which we seem to delight'[1] and that the Residents were in fact ruling. Subject only to the control of the Governor, they were initiating legislation, framing policy and carrying on the government in all its branches through state administrations directly under their authority, and manned by British district and departmental officers. It was not possible for the Secretary of State to disclaim responsibility for the Residents' actions; instances of misgovernment, oppression, official corruption and mismanagement of public funds would surely be brought home to him by the British press and Parliament.

Malacca, 24 September 1874, C.1320, enclosure in no. 8, Clarke to Carnarvon, 29 December 1874). In Pahang, the Resident was introduced in response to a letter from the Sultan inviting a British officer (Letter from His Highness Sultan Ahmad Muatham Shah to His Excellency Sir Cecil Clementi Smith, KCMG, Governor of the Straits Settlements, Maxwell and Gibson, op. cit. pp. 68–69). The best known statement of the Resident's responsibilities is of course that in the Pangkor Engagement, which was not only operative in Perak, but was acted on 'inferentially' in Selangor, and was shown to the Sultan of Pahang as indicating the powers assumed under the Resident system (Rodger to CS, 13 October 1888, enclosure in Smith to Knutsford, 451 of 15 October 1888, CO 273/155). In Selangor the primary responsibility of the Resident for revenue collection was accepted in the letter from the Sultan of October 1874. In Jelebu and Rembau it was defined in some detail by the agreements of 1886 and 1887, and these agreements also declared the control of police and the administration of justice to be the responsibilities of the British officer (Maxwell and Gibson, op. cit. pp. 51–52 and pp. 55–57). The Negri Sembilan agreements of 1889 and 1895 simply requested the 'assistance of a British Resident in the administration of the Government', and the letter from the Sultan of Pahang asked for 'a British officer in order that he may assist us in matters relating to the Government of our country, on a similar system to that existing in the Malay States under English protection'. Some of the documents excluded certain matters from the competence of the Resident or required him to administer them in association with local authorities. The Pangkor Engagement excluded questions 'touching Malay Religion and Custom'; the Jelebu agreement provided that disputes involving questions of Islamic law be settled by the proper native officers; the Sultan of Pahang expressed the hope that the British Government would not interfere with 'the old customs of our country which have good and proper reasons, and also with all matters relating to our religion'. By the Negri Sembilan agreement of 1895, the signatory chiefs undertook to follow the Resident's advice 'in all matters of administration other than those touching the Mohammadan religion'. Local land custom was safeguarded in the Jelebu and Rembau agreements, which provided for consultation between the British officers and the territorial chiefs in matters of land revenue and administration.

[1] Speech by Sir Frederick Weld, PRCI, vol. xv (1883–4), p. 281. See also F. A. Swettenham, The Real Malay, London, 1900, p. 22; and speech by Sir William Robinson, PRCI, vol. xxiii (1891–2), p. 40.

The exercise of authority over these territories by the Colonial Office, and the determination of its limits, were matters of difficulty and debate during the whole period between intervention and federation. There were problems of procedure; the channels of control whereby the Colonial Office supervised the administration of a Crown Colony, were not available. There were problems of policy; informal control, often adopted for reasons of expediency, acquired a moral justification and created vested interests whose resistance to metropolitan regulation was the more difficult to overcome because it had a legal and moral basis. The maintenance of administrative standards became a matter of delicate adjustment between ideals of non-interference on the one hand, and administrative order and integrity on the other.

To begin with, the Colonial Office was inhibited by self-imposed restraints. In the first few years after intervention it had itself tried to check the assumption of administrative control; it had prohibited annexation, had lectured Residents and Governors and warned them against extensions of responsibility, and had approved of policy statements reminding them that they were advisers and not rulers. To issue directives on matters of internal administration was inconsistent with this position. There were officials in the Colonial Office who disliked extensions of responsibility and feared to be dragged into the states' affairs at the heels of impetuous local officials; and paradoxically, those in the Colonial Office who wished for expansion also invoked the principle of non-interference, on behalf of strong and self-willed Governors and Residents who wanted a free hand in the states. Thus non-interference, preached at first by those opposed to extensions of responsibility, came to be taken up by the officials most sympathetic to strong, expansionist local administrators and most anxious to see them work unhindered by control from London.[1]

[1] Among the permanent officials, the strongest supporter of British expansion in the Peninsula was C. P. Lucas, who drafted most of the despatches dealing with the Malay states from 1878 onwards. He was a close friend of Swettenham (Resident of Selangor from 1882–9 and Perak, 1889–95), and was his mouthpiece in the Office. In nearly every case of maladministration that came before the Secretary of State between 1890 and 1895, Lucas strenuously resisted the attempts of his colleagues to interfere. He was also a strong supporter of the ambitions of Sir Cecil Smith (CS from 1878 to 1885 and Governor from 1887 to 1893) for the development of Pahang, though Pahang was financially a disaster, and Lucas' colleagues were very critical of developments there. Lucas came into endless conflict with the Assistant Under-Secretary, Fairfield, on the general administration of the states, and on Pahang. Fairfield pressed for closer control over the Residents, opposed expansion in Pahang, and aligned himself with Maxwell (Resident

The attempts by the Colonial Office to assert responsibility were also hampered from time to time by the opposition of powerful local administrators, jealous of the independence and freedom of action which they enjoyed as a result of their loosely defined authority. The Resident acted under the supervision of the Governor, who interfered with the legislative, judicial and executive processes within the states whenever he judged fit. Yet the principle of non-interference with native rulers was noisily invoked to defend the personal rule of both. Sir Frederick Weld, who had arranged with the Resident the appointment of a railway engineer to advise the Selangor government without apparently referring the matter to the Sultan (whose ideas on the matter would have been of little help) became very eloquent on the subject of states' rights when the Secretary of State vetoed the appointment. Weld's successor, Smith, who was equally assertive in his relations with the states, objected to interference with certain regulations for the registration and control of prostitutes; he declared that the Colonial Office directive on the subject would constitute 'so far as I can call to mind, an un-precedented interference with their affairs'.[1] (Legislation on this subject was actually awaiting his sanction when he wrote his despatch protesting against Colonial Office interference.) The Colonial Office had some idea of the relations between the Governors, the Residents and the Rulers, and was not much impressed by constitutional lectures on states' rights. When Swettenham objected to the cancellation by the Colonial Office of the appointment of a particular railway engineer for Selangor, complaining of interference with the Sultan's government and virtual annexation, the officials were unmoved. One of them took the lecture to mean that 'Mr. Swettenham is aggrieved, and that Sir F. Weld sympathises with him', but maintained that the Colonial Office was responsible for 'mitigating on some points the personal rule and direct influence of the Resident and the Governor'.[2] When Swettenham, then Resident of Perak, wrote, in connexion

---

of Selangor, 1889–92, and CS, 1892–5), and Dickson (CS, 1885–92). Maxwell and Dickson were strong supporters of administrative discipline; Swettenham urged the need for flexibility in the states, which meant leaving discipline to the discretion of the Residents. Between Maxwell and Dickson on the one hand, and Swettenham and Smith on the other, there was a rivalry and dislike verging on hatred.

[1] Smith to Knutsford, 406 of 29 October 1891, CO 273/176.

[2] Minute by de Robeck, 9 August 1883, on Weld to Derby, 280 of 4 July 1883, CO 273/121.

with a proposed curtailment of legalized public gaming, that the Sultan had asked him to convey 'a very strong protest against what he considered an unwarrantable interference with his rights and privileges, and an interpretation of the terms of the Pangkor Engagement which he thought could not be justified or maintained',[1] Fairfield, the Assistant Under-Secretary, thought Swettenham's letter 'a bogus piece of impertinence, mainly his (Mr. Swettenham's) own invention . . . .'[2] He minuted on another paper, 'Mr. Swettenham and the Sultan form a sort of Spenlow and Jorkins firm. Mr. Swettenham is always doing his best go get the Sultan more money, and the Sultan is always willing to come up to the scratch and express repugnance to anything proposed by the Secretary of State which Mr. Swettenham does not wish to see done.'

The Colonial Office was quite prepared to take advantage, when convenient, of the argument that the Malay states were independently administered; in 1895 the Permanent Under-Secretary thought the Colonial Office might 'use the fiction that we advise but do not govern as a reply to objections in Parliament' concerning the continued existence of legalized gambling in the states.[3] But although the formal independence of the states might be used as an argument in particular situations, the Pangkor Engagement empowered the Residents to give advice which 'must be asked and acted upon' and the Resident was acknowledged to be under the immediate control of the Governor of the Straits Settlements—a representative of the Crown. It was true that the Colonial Office had rejected annexationist policies, and formal direction of the states could not be assumed without a breach of faith. But ultimate responsibility for the Residents' advice still lay with the Colonial Office, and it accepted the principle of responsibility, and the duty of supervision, without assuming control over the details of government.

[1] Swettenham to Colonial Secretary, 5 October 1894, in Mitchell to Ripon, Confidential of 12 October 1894, CO 273/198. The Sultan wrote independently in Sultan to Governor, 20 July 1894, enclosed in Mitchell to Ripon, Confidential of 30 July 1894, CO 273/196. The Sultan's letter contains no reference to his rights or privileges or to the Pangkor Engagement but simply discusses the merits of the regulations proposed by the CO.

[2] Minute by Fairfield, 16 November 1894, on Mitchell to Ripon, Confidential of 12 October 1894, CO 273/198. Spenlow and Jorkins, characters in *David Copperfield* by Charles Dickens, are a firm of proctors to whom Copperfield is articled. Jorkins, a gentle retiring man, seldom appears, but Spenlow makes his supposedly intractable character the ground for refusing any inconvenient request.

[3] Minute by Meade, 24 March 1895, on Mitchell to Ripon, Confidential of 8 February 1895, CO 273/202.

The Colonial Office had no direct communication with the states, and there was no established category of subjects reserved for its consideration, or of material forwarded for its information. The Residents communicated officially with the Colonial Office through the Governor. Their annual estimates, council proceedings and bills were sent to Singapore for consideration and went no further;[1] before 1894 they had no newspapers which could provide a picture of unofficial opinion. The Colonial Office received the state *Gazettes*, but these were not issued before 1888 in Perak and 1890 in Selangor. But there were other channels of information available to the Secretary of State. The *Annual Reports* were forwarded and provided subjects for inquiry; disgruntled employees of the state administrations petitioned the Secretary of State about their grievances and told tales about local scandals; there were references to abuses in the states in the Colony Legislative Council. In the 1890's, the rivalry between local administrators brought a number of problems before the arbitration of the Secretary of State; local conflicts were reflected in the conflicts between departmental officials, who were turned by the pressure of controversy into Malayan specialists.

The Secretary of State used his authority to maintain standards of integrity in the public service, to keep a check on the expenditure of public funds (particularly expenditure on railways), to remedy injustice and to bring the social legislation of the Malay states as far as possible into harmony with late Victorian morality. His interference was mostly in the form of correction to administrative action taken or contemplated by local authorities; he did not interfere in the formulation of policy or the general administration of the country, though he was kept informed of important developments.

From the first days of intervention the appointments and salaries of the Residents and Assistant Residents in Perak and Selangor[2] had been decided by the Secretary of State on the recommendation of the Governor. The subordinate officers were formally considered to be servants of the Rulers, and their appointments and conditions of service were decided by the Governor without reference to the Secretary of State. The Colonial Office was reluctant to interfere with these subordinate appointments; it did not want to be answerable for a

---

[1] At the request of the CO, copies of state legislation began to be sent home in 1894. But they were forwarded for information, not for sanction.

[2] In Selangor, the office of Assistant Resident was abolished in 1876. In Perak, it was replaced by that of Secretary to Government in 1888.

'scratch lot' of officers over whose appointments it had no control. In 1876, the Secretary of State, approached privately with a request to confirm the appointment of an officer in Selangor, refused to interfere, contenting himself with instructions to the Governor to exercise some control over appointments 'whenever the Rajah or Sultan leaves the selection of officers for these posts to the British Resident'.[1] In 1878, consulted by a new Governor about a subordinate appointment, the Secretary of State referred to his earlier despatch, and went on to say that he thought it undesirable that subordinate European officers in the protected states should have any claim on the colonial government or the Secretary of State with respect to any questions arising out of their employment, as would be the case if their appointments received formal confirmation; but the Residents should 'distinctly understand' that when the selection of any European officer was left to them by the raja, they should not act without referring to the Governor.[2] In 1884, when the Governor consulted the Secretary of State about retirement terms for a former Straits officer in the service of Perak, he was told, 'The whole question . . . of gratuities and pensions to the subordinate officers of the Protected States belongs properly, I would observe, to the Governors of the Settlements and the Resident.'[3]

In the years that followed, however, the Colonial Office was drawn into an attempt to secure the tenure of the Malay states' officers and regularize their conditions of service. In theory they held office 'subject to the pleasure of the local authorities and the Governor of the Straits Settlements'[4] and while officers on the fixed establishment of the Colony had the right to an inquiry by the Executive Council and confirmation by the Secretary of State before dismissal, the dismissal of officers in the states was subject only to the discretion of the Resident and Governor. Arbitrary dismissal was not only contrary to the personal interests of the officers, it was against the interests of the public service. It was a hindrance to the recruitment of good men, and particularly men from other colonies, and as the Malay states developed, the need for men with experience of a regular colonial administration was increasingly felt. The question of securing the

---

[1] Carnarvon to Jervois, 197 of 25 August 1876.
[2] Hicks Beach to Robinson, 87 of 2 April 1878.
[3] Derby to Weld, 41 of 18 February 1884, on Weld to Derby, 531 of 31 December 1883, CO 273/123.
[4] CO to Governor of Cyprus, 14 October 1885, on Weld, private of 6 August 1885, CO 273/138.

pension rights of officers transferred from other colonies or from the Straits Settlements to the Malay states arose from time to time and caused some difficulty. Smith, acting as Governor during Weld's leave, thought that 'such service should be held to be continuous, as though it were in law, as it is in fact under one Government'.[1] The Secretary of State accordingly recommended that officers in the Malay states 'should be transferred to the service of the Colony and should be paid by and pensioned by the Colony—the Native States contributing a sufficient sum to reimburse the expense'. The proposal was not that the services should be amalgamated but that the Colony should hold itself responsible in the first instance for Malay states' salaries and pensions. The proposal broke down in the face of determined opposition from Weld, who feared that if the Colony were made responsible for the salaries and pensions of these officers, the affairs of the states would come under the scrutiny of the Legislative Council. The Colonial Office did not press the point, but it forced the adoption of a clause in the Straits Pension Regulations making the service of the Colony and the Malay states continuous for pension purposes.[2]

After Weld's departure, the Colonial Office made another attempt to get the Colony to guarantee the salaries and pensions of officers in the Malay states. It accepted the recommendation of Weld's successor, Smith, that only the Residents and Secretaries to Government should be so guaranteed. But when the bill came to be discussed in Executive Council, the Straits officials objected to placing the responsibility for Malay states' pensions on the Colony; and when the Colonial Office insisted that the Residents were not servants of the Malay Rulers, but were advisers selected by the British Government and employed by the British Government, the local officials countered strongly with the argument that 'British' in this context meant the Imperial and not the Colonial Government. The officials were furious, and Lucas minuted angrily that 'the colony might for convenience' sake identify itself to this tiny extent with the empire instead of trying to "play the colonial v. Imperial game" '. All the same, the Colonial Office refused to shoulder the responsibility, and

[1] Smith to Derby, 219 of 25 May 1885, CO 273/134.
[2] Stanley to Weld, 34 of 5 February 1886, on Weld to Stanley, 447 of 28 November 1885, CO 273/136; Weld to Stanley, 99 of 20 March 1886, CO 273/139; Stanhope to Weld, 117 of 9 December 1886, on Treasury to CO, 20 October 1886, CO 273/142.

it was settled that the Residents as well as the subordinate officers must look to the states for the payment of their pensions.[1]

The Colonial Office had tried, in effect, to smuggle the Malay states' officers onto the establishment of a colony which was not their employer in any sense, and when driven to define the actual status of the Residents, it had avoided committing itself and passed them back to the Malay states' governments. The status of the subordinate officers was clear; they were beyond doubt servants of the states. The status of the Residents typified in its ambiguity the whole relationship between the British Government on the one hand and the Malay states on the other. They were styled 'British Resident' (in the early years, 'Her Britannic Majesty's Resident') and were under the authority of the Governor; many of them—including Low, Swettenham and Maxwell[2]—had been appointed to the states from the colonial service, kept their status as servants of the Crown, and remained eligible for promotion in the colonies; yet they, like their colleagues, depended on the Malay states for their salaries and pensions. Others had come into the Malay states from private life; they had never been and never became servants of the Crown in any sense, yet as Residents they acknowledged the authority of the Governor. The obscurity surrounding the legal status of the Residents did not, however, affect administrative practice; the Colonial Office continued to make the final decision on their appointments and salaries, and when they retired, their pensions were paid through the Crown Agents on behalf of the states, after being approved by the Governor and the Secretary of State.[3]

For the Residents, legal definitions were probably of little importance, but the subordinate officers were burdened by a sense of insecurity. In 1888 the European civil servants of Perak memorialized the Secretary of State, begging to be transferred to the service of the

[1] Knutsford to Smith, 128 of 4 May 1888, on Treacher to CO, 28 of 4 March 1888, CO 273/157; Smith to Knutsford, 305 of 4 July 1888, and Knutsford to Smith, 330 of 10 October 1888, CO 273/154; Smith to Knutsford, 572 of 20 December 1889 and enclosures, and Knutsford to Smith, 68 of 27 February 1890, CO 273/162; Dickson to Knutsford, 241 of 3 June 1890 and minute by Lucas, 11 July 1890, CO 273/166; Knutsford to Smith, 44 of 4 February 1892, ibid.

[2] See Appendix 2.

[3] The forms used in bureaucratic procedure had a political significance—at least for the CO. It was only after considerable argument that it was decided that the Secretary of State should 'approve' and not merely 'acknowledge' pension arrangements. Minutes on Smith to Ripon, 192 of 16 March 1893; Ripon to Smith, 183 of 26 July 1893, CO 273/188

colony, or that the civil service of the state be recognized as a branch of Her Majesty's service, and saying that they regarded themselves as 'the servants of Her Majesty, and not of the Native Ruler of the State'.[1] The proposal was inconsistent with the recent decision on the subject and was rejected, but the Colonial Office was prepared to receive appeals from them on a variety of subjects though continuing to shelter when convenient behind the principle of states' sovereignty. A despatch stated in 1894, '. . . it is impossible for the Secretary of State to regard himself as entirely free from responsibility, where the decision, whatever its form, is virtually that of the Resident and Governor, and where it affects the interests of a public servant who is a British subject'.[2] The appeals were rare, and in the majority of cases, particularly in cases of problematical or minor grievances, the action of the local authorities was usually upheld, with some remark to the effect that the Secretary of State did not interfere in the subordinate appointments in the Malay states.[3] But where the local authorities appeared to be abusing their discretion, the Colonial Office was prepared to interfere. It upheld the claims of individuals to pensions and other benefits,[4] it awarded pensions and gratuities in response to appeals from European and local Asian staff alike and on one occasion it upheld the appeal of the Chief Magistrate of Selangor against censure by his Resident, even though the Resident was supported by the Acting Governor.[5]

[1] Memorial of European Civil Servants of Perak to Secretary of State, enclosed in Smith to Knutsford, 413 of 15 September 1888, CO 273/154.

[2] Ripon to Mitchell, Confidential of 11 July 1894, on Mitchell to Ripon, Confidential of 7 May 1894, CO 273/195.

[3] E.g., an officer complaining of reduction in position was told that the Secretary of State could not interfere as his appointment was under the Perak government. Derby to Smith, 76 of 4 April 1884, on Tuft to CO, 2 April 1884, CO 273/132.

[4] Holland to Weld, 107 of 4 June 1887, on Weld to Holland, 88 of 12 March 1887, CO 273/143, instructing that the Perak government pay the medical expenses of one of their officers; Ripon to Mitchell, Confidential of 22 August 1894, on Mitchell to Ripon, Confidential 27 June 1894, CO 273/196, instructing the Perak government to pay one of its officers a pension instead of a gratuity on abolition of office. The Acting Governor (Maxwell) had decided that the case should not be treated as abolition of office but as dismissal of an unsatisfactory officer, but the Secretary of State in a humane comment on the problem of staffing a pioneer administration, wrote that because it was sometimes necessary in new countries to appoint men of no great value when better men could not be had, they should not be treated in an exceptional or summary manner but in accordance with the rules regulating retirement.

[5] Chamberlain to Mitchell, 411 of 19 December 1895, on Mitchell to Chamberlain, 460 of 16 November 1895, CO 273/207; Ripon to Mitchell, 49 of 9 February 1894.

The Malay states' officers were recruited by nomination from a variety of sources; they were subject to general regulations closely assimilated to those in force in the Colony, but the disciplinary effect of these regulations was diluted by distance; and in pioneering governments, discipline was easier, and idiosyncrasies in administration more readily tolerated, than in old established settlements. The Colonial Office realized that there was wide opportunity for misconduct, and that it would be held responsible in the last instance for the behaviour of officers. Herbert, then Permanent Under-Secretary, minuted on a report of maladministration in Selangor, 'I would *require* and not suggest the necessary measures. . . . The fiction that we do not directly control the officers in these States is a very transparent one, and will not shield us when the misgovernment of the country becomes a public scandal.' Kimberley agreed; 'We are certainly responsible for the English officers employed in these States, and must exercise a control over them.'[1]

Of the occasional scandals that came to the notice of the Secretary of State, the most embarrassing involved Captain Bloomfield Douglas, Resident of Selangor from 1876 to 1882. His administration had been a great trial to Colony officials, who were constantly intervening to correct administrative irregularities and mistakes of judgment; finally a more serious lapse than usual was brought to the attention of the Secretary of State by a former officer of the Selangor Government, and an inquiry was instituted leading to Douglas' resignation. In the same year the Governor, Weld, forwarded a report on the Land Department of Selangor which told a story of gross mismanagement and jobbery in which the Resident and the head of the department were involved. (The latter, acting as auctioneer in a sale of town lots, knocked them down to the Resident, who happened to be his father-in-law.) The Secretary of State issued a general prohibition of such transactions, and in 1885 he issued a circular prohibiting a salaried public servant in the Colony or Malay states from occupying for profit more than twenty acres of land, or any land more than six miles from his residence.[2] The two senior Residents, Low and Swettenham, and the two Governors who successively dealt with the question, Weld and Smith, illustrated by their different reactions the conflict in the Malay states between the standards of the public serv-

[1] Minutes by Herbert, 12 July 1882, and by Kimberley, 14 July 1882, on Weld to Kimberley, 169 of 3 May 1882, CO 273/114.

[2] Kimberley to Weld, 179 of 25 July 1882, on Weld to Kimberley, 169 of 3 May 1882, CO 273/114; Derby to Weld, Circular of 2 February 1885.

ice on the one hand, and private empire-building on the other. The interest of the contrast is enhanced by the fact that all four had served in Crown Colonies, and though Weld had come into the service from political life, Low, Smith and Swettenham were career officers and had a common Colonial Service training. Low's standing, in the eyes of the Colonial Office, if not in rank or pay, was that of a Governor of a Colony; but despite his great prestige and authority, or perhaps because of it, he welcomed all instructions on the subject of land speculation without reserve. Swettenham received the 1882 instructions with a long and tendentious letter asking for clarification;[1] he thought officers in the states might be permitted to buy land and invest in enterprise in the state, provided that those interests did not interfere with work or get the officer into debt. The real point, that it was undesirable for a public servant to acquire land for profit in a state where he had the power to influence values by decisions on planning and communications, seems to have escaped him. Weld was characteristically unwilling to let any matter be determined by regulation instead of by personal decision by the Resident or himself; his supplementary instructions to Swettenham were useless as a restriction on land speculation. Smith had a more rigid attitude on these matters and in 1888 he wrote to the Colonial Office complaining that existing regulations were inadequate and proposing fresh ones. (These would prohibit any European officer in the Colony or Malay states, or any member of his family, from acquiring property other than a house or garden for his own occupation.) Low again approved this without reserve. Swettenham wrote an insubordinate minute suggesting that if an officer 'whose services were great, whose ability was undoubted, and whose honesty was unimpeachable' refused to give up his holdings, the Secretary of State might find it hard to dismiss him. Swettenham's minute was not calculated to charm the Colonial Office and the ethics of the matter were clear; the Governor was upheld.[2]

One condition of good administration was the proper conduct of the public works, and the Colonial Office established at an early date its right to be consulted before the state undertook major public works. The question arose in connexion with the construction of the Selangor railway, a line of twenty-two miles linking Kuala Lumpur

[1] Swettenham to Weld, 6 January 1883, in Smith to Knutsford, 488 of 16 December 1891, CO 273/169.
[2] Knutsford to Smith, 65 of 28 February 1889, on Smith to Holland, 536 of 5 December 1888, CO 273/156.

with its port at Klang, involving a total expenditure of more than double the Selangor revenue for 1882, and requiring to be financed by a Colony loan. Weld and Swettenham had already appointed their consultant engineer before putting the scheme up to the Secretary of State, and the first he heard of it was when the engineer appointed wrote to the Crown Agents to say he was ready to sail for the Straits, and to ask for an advance of £100. The Secretary of State cancelled the appointment (which was objectionable on other grounds) and requested that he be informed when it was proposed to construct major public works involving heavy financial liability.[1]

On technical matters the states were advised by a consultant engineer in London, Sir Charles Hutton Gregory, who was appointed with the approval of the Colonial Office, and through whom it kept in touch with construction. It was also kept informed about state undertakings by the Crown Agents, through whom (on the Secretary of State's instructions) the Residents were required to order their material. On most of the questions of construction the Colonial Office and the local authorities were not in serious disagreement; both thought in terms of a pan-Malayan system of railway communications, and both accepted uniformity of construction as a desirable principle. But the early lines were lateral lines connecting existing centres of production with the coast; the immediate need was for quick and cheap transport, and Swettenham at first thought that a light, narrow gauge railway would be most suitable for the Klang-Kuala Lumpur line. The influence of the Colonial Office contributed to the decision to adopt a metre gauge and a medium steel rail in Selangor and Perak, and the metre gauge remained the standard for the whole Malayan railway system. The influence of the Colonial Office was also used to prevent the local authorities from pledging the states to lavish railway concessions. The local and metropolitan authorities were at one in preferring construction by the state whenever profits were assured, and the Perak and Selangor railways were constructed by the state. But in Sungei Ujong, where profits were speculative, a concession with a guarantee of interest was granted to a private company to make and run the line. Weld had forgotten the Secretary of State's instructions that he should be consulted before the states were committed to large public works, and sanctioned the concession without reference home. The first intimation to the Colo-

[1] Derby to Weld, 116 of 10 May 1883, on Weld to Derby, 100 of 12 March 1883, CO 273/119.

nial Office was the despatch of the completed agreement. The Colonial Office objected to the agreement as unfavourable to the state, cancelled it, and negotiated a new one giving the state much better terms.

The Colonial Office signified its interest in the general administration of the Malay states by a ritual acknowledgement of their annual reports. Before 1888, these were acknowledged in three or four lines expressing a conventional interest; but in that year, Lucas began the practice of drafting long minutes (on which the despatches were based) bringing to the notice of the Secretary of State, the progress made by the Residents. These replies, he thought, would give 'an appearance of taking intelligent interest in these states', and would encourage the officers in their work. The replies were for the most part conventional echoes of the reports, expressing approval of progress made, regret concerning difficulties, and hope for improvement in the future. The Secretary of State noted with pleasure the rise in the land revenue of Selangor, was glad to learn that the cart road from Jelebu to Sungei Ujong was now open, and observed with satisfaction that the Selangor debt had been liquidated. He gathered that much remained to be done in respect to roadmaking, and attached the greatest importance to the spread of agriculture. As time went on Lucas' drafts grew longer and longer, and the suggestions and requests for information became more and more conscientious, detailed and irrelevant, until protests began to be heard within the department; in 1891, Fairfield thought it unwise to 'echo back' the optimism of officials, especially about Pahang, where there was already too much dangerous speculation, and in 1895 Meade begged to be spared another marathon despatch.[1] The remarks in the replies were cast in the form of suggestions which the local officials might accept or quietly ignore; and though some of them were sensible enough, they usually referred to needs already noted in the reports and already under consideration. The Secretary of State made one important policy recommendation, which he reiterated year by year; it was that agriculture be developed, as a balance to mining, by the introduction of Chinese and Indian peasant families. 'In tropical countries, immigration is so constantly synonymous with the

---

[1] Minute by Fairfield, 10 October 1891, on Smith to Knutsford, 261 of 22 June 1891, CO 273/173; minute by Fairfield, 15 March 1895, on Mitchell to Ripon, 185 of 30 June 1894, CO 273/195; minute by Meade, 4 September 1895, on Mitchell to Ripon, 253 of 24 June 1895 ,CO 273/204.

supply of indentured labour to planters and employers, or with in-
discriminate Chinese immigration, that the possibility of colonisation with selected families under some state aided system seems to
have been rather left out of sight'.[1] The Residents favoured such
colonization in principle; Swettenham in his 1888 report on Selangor
had in fact suggested that Chinese agriculturists be introduced
there. But they were too preoccupied with securing Chinese and
Indian labour for the mines and estates to spend much time on
establishing them as an immigrant peasantry, and they never had
anything to report under this head beyond minor experiments and
achievements.

In judicial matters the Colonial Office was able to interfere directly
since the Malay states, unlike most crown colonies, had no separate
judiciary; the administration of justice was a function of the executive. The final court of appeal was the Sultan in Council. No Colony
court had any jurisdiction over the Malay states, but the Governor
sometimes intervened by executive process, ordering a retrial and
modification of sentence by instructions to the Resident. The Secretary
of State in turn was able to influence judicial decisions by instructing
the Governor. The states adopted the penal code of the Colony, and
much other Colony legislation and judicial procedure, but the Residents and their subordinates for the most part had little legal training, and serious irregularities in the administration of justice were
brought from time to time to the attention of the Secretary of State.
In 1891 the Resident of Pahang had convicted a man of murder and
sentenced him to death on the basis of uncorroborated evidence from
an accomplice who had testified in the hope of improving his own
position. The Resident had reported the case to the Governor, the
Governor had asked the opinion of the Attorney-General, who had
advised that if the prisoner had been tried in the Colony, he would
probably have been acquitted. The Governor was content to direct
the Pahang State Council to commute the sentence to imprisonment
for life, whereupon the brother of the prisoner petitioned the Secretary of State. The Secretary of State called for a report, and finally
directed that the Governor take the necessary steps to secure a remission of sentence.[2]

[1] Knutsford to Dickson, 277 of 16 September 1890, on Dickson to Knutsford,
284 of 10 July 1890, CO 273/166.
[2] Gurdit Singh to Secretary of State, 17 August 1892, CO 273/185; Smith to
Ripon, 487 of 22 December 1892 and enclosures, CO 273/184, and Ripon to
Smith, 42 of 20 February 1893.

The Pahang murder case caused the Secretary of State to instruct that until more competent courts were established, British subjects charged with offences punishable by death or a long term of imprisonment should be tried either in Singapore or by Colony judges on circuit.[1] In 1894 the confidence of the Colonial Office in the administration of justice in the Malay states was further undermined by the disclosure of irregularities in two cases, one in Perak and one in Selangor, which drew attention to the abuses flowing from the executive control of justice. Both cases involved state officers, who memorialized the Secretary of State after they had failed to obtain redress from the Resident and Governor. In both cases the Colonial Office found much to criticize in the procedures adopted and the decisions reached. At the same time, Straits commercial and legal interests were agitating for judicial reform in the states; they were becoming increasingly dissatisfied with the executive control of justice, the ban on pleaders in the courts, and the absence of appeal to an independent judicial authority.

The agitation in the Straits, combined with its own increasing dissatisfaction with judicial affairs in the states, led the Colonial Office to press for radical changes in the administration of justice. In 1891, the Singapore branch of the Straits Association and the Singapore Chamber of Commerce petitioned the Secretary of State that British subjects be allowed to appeal to the Supreme Court; and the Secretary of State, advised by Swettenham, proposed that appeals should lie to a Judge of the Colony Supreme Court, travelling on circuit, and holding a commission from the Sultan in Council while in the state.[2] No action was taken on this suggestion, and in June 1894 the Secretary of State complained in a despatch that his proposal for new appeal procedures, made two years before, had gone unanswered. In September, the Governor put forward proposals for judicial reform which went beyond the question of appeals. He suggested the appointment of a single judicial authority for the Malay states, a Judicial Commissioner whose duties would be to organize and control courts of all classes, to inspect them, to hear appeals, and to advise on legislation. The proposal was approved and developed by the Secretary of State, who directed that the necessary authority be conferred by identical laws enacted in the several states; the draft to be

---

[1] Ripon to Smith, Confidential of 20 February 1893, on Smith to Ripon, 487 of 22 December 1893, CO 273/184.

[2] Smith to Knutsford, 410 of 3 November 1891 and enclosures; Knutsford to Smith, Confidential of 18 January 1892, CO 273/176.

prepared by the Attorney-General of the Colony and submitted for the approval of the Secretary of State.[1] The arrangements, in the event, became merged in the general reorganization of the state administrations under the federation scheme of 1895.

The Colonial Office was not directly informed, as a rule, about state legislation, but it occasionally gathered information from miscellaneous sources, which caused it to intervene in order to assimilate social practices in the states as far as possible to metropolitan standards of morality. As a rule the differences between the Colonial Office and the local authorities were on matters of timing, not principle. In 1875, for example, the Colonial Office picked up from Speedy's Larut report a reference to the existence of slavery and debt bondage in Perak, and subsequent inquiry showed that the institution was widespread throughout the Peninsula. The Secretary of State directed that the practice be abated 'with as little delay as is consistent with the necessary caution which is to be observed in the new relations which exist in Perak'. In 1878 the Secretary of State called for information about the practice in all the states. Action had already been taken in Selangor and Sungei Ujong whereby the value of slave labour was set against the original debt and the debt thereby liquidated; but in Perak the problem was rendered more difficult by the size of the Malay population—and therefore of resistance to change—and by the need to proceed slowly with reforms after the recent disturbances. The Colonial Office accepted the need for caution; but in 1882 it renewed its pressure.[2] By that time, however, Low had of his own accord decided that the time had come for action, and had asked the Perak State Councillors to come to the next Council meeting prepared to discuss solutions.[3] Colonial Office pressure may have advanced emancipation by two or three years, but it was clear that local authorities also were aware that these institutions could not be allowed to exist indefinitely. Again, in 1889, in a debate in the Colony legislature, an official noticed a reference to the existence of the death penalty in Perak for those convicted of organizing secret societies. The Secretary of State considered the penalty too severe, and learnt on inquiry that the Perak penalty was a dead letter; the Governor had given instructions through the

[1] Mitchell to Ripon, Confidential of 4 September 1894, and Ripon to Mitchell, Confidential of 1 November 1894, CO 273/197.
[2] Kimberley to Weld, 4 March 1882, C.3285, no. 7.
[3] *PCM*, 15 March 1882.

Resident that it should not be imposed except when murder was committed. The Secretary of State held that the law should not prescribe a penalty which would not be executed, and required that the state government be required to amend the law.[1]

On these matters the Colonial Office and the local authorities were in reasonable accord, but on others they were at odds, and it was necessary to push through reforms in the face of local resistance. Two practices continued to flourish in the Malay states after they had been abolished in the Straits Settlements and Hong Kong on the instructions of the Secretary of State. The levy of fees for brothel registration had been abolished in the Straits, but the fees continued to be levied in Perak, and in 1891 the Secretary of State noted a reference in the *Perak Government Gazette* of 8 May to the expenditure of revenue from this source on various good works, including an old people's home in Taiping. The Secretary of State learnt further that the Governor had been about to allow a Perak Order in Council for the compulsory examination and treatment of venereal disease; and as such legislation had been repealed in India and the Colonies at the insistence of Parliament, the Secretary of State felt unable to permit the Governor to sanction its introduction into the Malay states. He was instructed to disallow it, and also to bring before the State Council the objection of the Secretary of State to the levy of fees for brothel registration.[2] The sympathies of the Governor and the Resident were wholly with the legislation, and the State Council decided unanimously to retain the fees. The Secretary of State directed that an expression of his regret be communicated to the State Council, and in December, the Governor reported that the fees had been abolished.[3]

The Secretary of State also objected to the continuance of licensed public gambling in the Malay states after it had been made illegal in the Straits and Hong Kong; but here the idea of abolition aroused overwhelming opposition among the local officials. It was strongly urged, in despatches and memoranda, that the lease of the gambling

[1] Knutsford to Smith, 130 of 10 May 1889, on Smith to Knutsford, 146 of 2 April 1889, CO 273/159.
[2] Knutsford to Smith, 7 of 7 January 1892, CO 273/176. The minutes showed how the instructions were to be relayed; 'Tell the Governor to instruct the Resident to recommend the State Council. . . .' Minute by Johnson, 15 December 1891, on Smith to Knutsford, 406 of 29 October 1891, CO 273/176.
[3] Ripon to Smith, 322 of 4 November 1892, CO 273/182/18484;. Smith to Ripon, 492 of 18 December 1892, CO 273/184.

monopoly brought in a large revenue, that the experience of the Straits Settlements had shown that gambling among the Chinese did not cease on being made illegal, but simply flourished underground and contributed to the increase of crime, protection rackets and police corruption; the Governor and four of the five Residents recommended the continuance of the gambling farm and even the Sultan of Perak sent in a strong letter of protest.[1] Legalized public gambling survived in the states for another eighteen years, until it was abolished in 1912.

The Residents were able, forceful and independent men, as they needed to be in order to discharge their responsibilities, and they were supported by Governors of similar ability and independence. It is not surprising that Residents and Governors were jealous of their authority and resented the interference of departmental officials in London, or that many of them should consider the rigid discipline of the colonial service inappropriate to pioneering conditions. The Colonial Office and the local authorities were often opposed, but it would be wrong to think of them as facing each other from fixed positions in attitudes of mutual hostility. They had common standards and allegiances which cut across their disagreements in particular situations; they all wished to advance the economic development of the Peninsula and to establish orderly and solvent administrations. Residents and Governors were alike conscious that isolation carried with it the danger of demoralization; they tried to maintain standards by instituting administrative procedures and controls borrowed from colonial general orders. The Colonial Office intervened, not so much to introduce new rules, as to limit the personal discretion which the local officials permitted themselves in their interpretation of their task.

THE PROTECTED MALAY STATES AND SINGAPORE

The Residents in the Malay states acted under the direct authority of the Governor of the Straits Settlements. The treaties and engagements with the Malay Rulers, under which Residents were introduced, were negotiated by him, the first provisional appointments to

[1] Mitchell to Ripon, Confidential of 8 February 1895, and enclosures, CO 273/202; Sultan of Perak to Governor, 20 July 1894, in Mitchell to Ripon, Confidential of 30 July 1894, CO 273/196.

the Residencies were made by him, and state business was initiated and carried on under his supervision.

In his resumé of administration in the Malay states, Swettenham cited the autonomy of the Residents and the absence of effective control from Singapore, as weaknesses which the federation scheme of 1895 was designed to remedy.[1] Except for a period from 1876 to 1882, when he himself was Assistant Colonial Secretary for Native States, 'each Resident went his own way and was inclined to resent either suggestion or interference'. Transport was bad, correspondence was irregular, and Residents were isolated, unconcerned with affairs outside their own states. 'Very often he [the Resident] had no experience of any State but the one he was in.'[2]

Maxwell, who had just completed a tour as Colonial Secretary, and who had frequently crossed swords with Swettenham (then Resident of Perak) during this time, agreed as to the absence of uniformity in the states on matters where uniformity was desirable (for example, in the telegraph and railway services) and cited the 'present system of numerous small administrations' as a hindrance to development.[3] He was at one with Swettenham in criticizing the powers of Residents[4] and remarked that the Governor, unless he had specialized local information, could know little beyond what the Resident chose to report, and what he could observe during hurried tours. But he pointed out that the Governor in fact exercised a great deal more control than the Residents (particularly the Resident of Perak) cared to admit. And both Smith and Mitchell, in putting the case for federation, urged as a major argument, the immense burden of work placed on the Governor as a result of his responsibility for the protected states.[5]

[1] F.A. Swettenham *British Malaya: an Account of the Origin and Progress of British Influence in Malaya*, rev. edn., London, 1948, p. 251.

[2] This of course is nonsense; indeed the opposite is the truth. The majority of Residents had served in another state before being appointed Resident. See Appendix 2.

[3] Maxwell to CO, Memorandum on Federation, 20 March 1895, CO 273/211.

[4] One suspects that Swettenham in describing the Residents as over-mighty subjects, was pointing his criticism primarily at Maxwell, who as Resident of Selangor introduced in 1891 a controversial and ultimately definitive system of land tenure into that state; and that Maxwell in making the same point was thinking primarily of Swettenham. Of course each looked to a solution—Swettenham to the appointment of a Resident-General, and Maxwell to annexation and government from Singapore—which would be most in keeping with his own official interests and inclinations, and least to the other's taste.

[5] Smith to Ripon, Confidential of 30 June 1893, CO 273/188; Mitchell to Ripon, Confidential of 1 May 1895, CO 273/202.

Swettenham's picture of bad communications, ineffective control and independent Residents has found a ready currency among historians. 'Every Resident submitted an annual report, an annual budget and a monthly journal to Singapore. Yet want of roads and railways made supervision by the Governor ineffective to secure that uniformity of administration necessary especially for the financial development of the States.'[1] 'It was lack of these facilities [communication and transportation] . . . which allowed the residents to maintain their independence from the centralized control of the colonial government at Singapore.'[2] Certainly the Residents exercised a large measure of discretion; this was to be expected, since they mediated between new, hazardously-balanced pioneer administrations and the outside world. But the picture which has been formed of remote and little-known states conducting their affairs without interference from outside will not bear examination.

In the first place the picture of tardy and irregular communication is grossly exaggerated and is certainly not the impression the Residents sought to give in their official reports. In 1876, letters written by the Colonial Secretary to the Resident of Selangor took between one and eleven days to arrive, depending on the mails; the average was three days.[3] In 1878, the Resident of Perak replied to a letter from the Colonial Secretary on a difficult and delicate subject—slavery—a week after it was written; in 1882 he replied to a minute from the Governor (then in Penang) two days after it was written, and in the same year the Resident of Sungei Ujong replied to a letter from the Colonial Secretary, also asking for a report on slavery, eleven days after it was written.[4] Low wrote in 1883 that when he first came to Perak six years before, there was only one steamer trading between Penang and Larut, making the voyage once in five or six days; but that there were now twelve steamers trading between Penang and Perak, two or three of which arrived at and departed from Larut daily, and there were others plying between Penang and

---

[1] R.O. Winstedt, *A History of Malaya*, rev. edn., London, 1962, p. 239.

[2] N.S. Ginsburg and C.F. Roberts, *Malaya*, Seattle, 1958, p. 430.

[3] From a sample of twenty-three letters written in April, May and June 1876, Selangor Secretariat papers.

[4] Resident of Perak to CS, 28 May 1878, C.3285, enclosure 3 in no. 3, Robinson to Hicks Beach, 29 July 1878; Resident of Perak to Governor, Kuala Kangsar, 1 July 1882, C.3249, enclosure in no. 2, Weld to Kimberley, 9 July 1882; Resident of Sungei Ujong to CS, 28 April 1882, C.3285, Weld to Kimberley, 4 May 1882.

Singapore and calling at intervening ports.[1] Between Selangor and Singapore in 1885 there were three outward and three inward mails weekly.[2] In 1881 there was regular communication by steam launch between Permatang Pasir on the Linggi river and Malacca, and in 1884 there was a weekly steamer plying between Sungei Ujong and Singapore.[3] By 1893 there were six weekly steamers and two fortnightly steamers plying between Singapore, Malacca, Port Dickson and Klang. In 1890, Kuala Pahang on the east coast was connected with Singapore by a weekly steamer, and Kuantan with Kuala Pahang and Singapore by a fortnightly steamer which continued to run during the monsoon. No Resident, with the exception of the Resident of Negri Sembilan,[4] lived more than twenty-five miles from the chief port of his state, and even during the early years, when overland communication was by cart road, the journey from Telok Kertang to Kuala Kangsar, or from Klang to Kuala Lumpur, took no more than five or six hours.[5] When the Selangor and Sungei Ujong railways were opened in 1886 and 1891 respectively, the journey from the coast to the capital in each case took an hour.

During the 1880's, telegraphic communication was well advanced. The Residency at Kuala Kangsar had been connected by telegraph with Telok Kertang as early as 1876—one result of the Perak War; and in 1885 direct communication was established between Kuala Kangsar and Penang, using the Colony line. In 1886 Kuala Lumpur was connected with Klang by telegraph, and in 1890 Selangor was connected with Malacca by land line passing through Sungei Ujong, and thus placed in direct communication with Singapore. The next year the Perak line was completed as far as the Sela-

[1] AR Perak, 1883. In 1879, as one traveller records, the journey between Penang and Larut by coastal steamer took eight and a half hours. Bird, The Golden Chersonese, p. 367.

[2] AR Selangor, 1885. In 1883 the journey between Malacca and Klang took Swettenham about eight hours by coastal steamer (Swettenham Journal for 5 March, 1883, item 12, Swettenham Papers, ANM). The Singapore and Straits Directory for the same year lists three steamers plying weekly between Singapore and Klang.

[3] Singapore and Straits Directory, 1881, p. 98; 1884, p. 38; 1893, p. 260; 1890, p. 292.

[4] Kuala Pilah, the headquarters of the Superintendent for Sri Menanti (later Resident of Negri Sembilan) was fifty miles from Malacca via Tampin. By 1887 there was a good cart road all the way.

[5] In 1879, Isabella Bird took four hours to ride from Kuala Kangsar to Taiping, 'a delightful ride' (Bird, op. cit. p. 349). Swettenham regularly rode the distance between Klang and Kuala Lumpur in six hours, crossing the river at Damansara.

ngor border, so that messages could be sent from Penang to Malacca through the Malay states' lines.[1]

Communication with Singapore was conducted by various means. The most important channel of communication was the Colonial Secretariat in Singapore, which remained until the end of the period the means whereby the Residents corresponded with the Governor and the world outside their states.[2] The Secretariat was enlarged after Pangkor to deal with protected states' affairs. Early in 1874, Clarke complained that there was no fixed department for dealing with these states and no regular records, and that he was able to gather very little information from the officers who had hitherto been detached from time to time to visit the states.[3] He set the Attorney-General, Braddell, to collate information in the records, and in December 1874 he appointed him provisionally Colonial Secretary (in place of Birch) primarily to deal with their affairs.[4] In 1876, after Braddell had returned to the office of Attorney-General, the Secretariat was strengthened by the post of Assistant Colonial Secretary for Native States, and the first incumbent was Swettenham.[5] Between 1876 and 1881, Swettenham dealt with a large part of the states' correspondence in the Secretariat, building up his knowledge and reputation by office experience and frequent tours up-country. In 1879 the Governor (Sir William Robinson) wrote of the value of this office in providing expertise and continuity in the conduct of affairs, especially when both the Governor and the Colonial Secretary were new arrivals untrained in the service of the Straits.[6] Two years later, however, it was decided that a specialized office in the Secretariat was no longer necessary. The Governor acknowledged that while Swettenham was in the department, he would remain 'the principal adviser of the Government in such matters', but observed that know-

[1] *AR Perak*, 1885 and 1890; *AR Selangor*, 1886 and 1889.

[2] E.g., in 1876 the Residents were required to address correspondence with the Lieutenant-Governors of Penang and Malacca through Singapore, except in an emergency (CS to Resident of Selangor, 24 August 1876, Sel/Sec. 174/76). They communicated with the CO and the Crown Agents through the CS until 1894, when they were allowed to do business with the Crown Agents direct. Ripon to Mitchell, 138 of 9 May 1894, CO 273/194.

[3] Clarke to Carnarvon, 24 February 1874, C.1111, no. 52.

[4] Clarke to Carnarvon, 358 of 31 December 1874, and Confidential of 31 December 1874, CO 273/76. Throughout 1875, communications to the Resident of Selangor were often signed by the CS as Secretary for Native States.

[5] Jervois to Carnarvon, 100 of 6 March 1876; Carnarvon to Jervois, 103 of 28 April 1876, CO 273/83.

[6] Robinson to CO, private of 7 July 1879, CO 273/101.

ledge of the Malay states was now sufficiently diffused among officers 'from the Governor downwards' to enable a fair distribution of work of all kinds to be made.[1]

In addition to the ordinary correspondence on specific questions, the Secretariat received various official journals and returns from the Residents and their subordinates, which enabled the Governor to keep in close touch with events. In 1875 the Resident of Selangor received instructions to forward a fortnightly journal in two divisions, one for description, topography and customs of the country, and one for current events and political questions, the journal to be accompanied by special reports.[2] In 1876 the instructions were applied to district officers; the complete journal, 'an unreserved record of the events and impressions of the time', was to be kept in the writer's office for use by his successors and for consultation by the Governor, and extracts were to be copied for official notice and sent fortnightly to the Resident and through him to the Colonial Secretary.[3] When the Governor, Weld, was about to appoint a Collector and Magistrate to Sri Menanti in 1886, he wrote to him, 'I like a full journal giving information on all points, if you have time to write it. I read every journal of every Resident or District Officer in the Peninsula that reaches me, so don't be afraid of boring me by long letters.'[4] The journal was a burden to a busy Resident; Swettenham complained continually about having to write it up, but was finally silenced by the Governor's expression of interest. He conceded, '. . . tho' it seems like wasting time to record what one sees, says and hears, it is really of value to keep H.E. informed of what goes on, and the Journal is often valuable as a means of saying things informally'.[5] Towards the end of the period the Residents were still sending in their journals.[6] Other material forwarded to Singapore included the

[1] Weld to Kimberley, 339 of 22 September 1881, CO 273/109.

[2] CS to Resident of Selangor, 12 July 1875, Sel/Sec. 72/75. The extremely full and informative journal of the Resident of Perak, written between April and June 1877, has survived and has been published as part 4 of volume xxvii of the *JMBRAS*.

[3] CS to Resident of Selangor, 3 June 1876, Sel/Sec. 59/76. There were complaints that the Resident of Selangor suppressed critical passages in the journal of one of his subordinates before forwarding to Singapore (E. Innes, *The Chersonese with the Gilding Off*, London, 1885, vol. ii, pp. 197–8). That the journals were read is indicated by occasional queries about their contents. CS to Resident of Selangor, 26 April 1878 and 21 May 1878, Sel/Sec. 107/78 and 137/78.

[4] A. Lovat, *The Life of Sir Frederick Weld*, p. 392.

[5] Minute by Swettenham, 24 September 1883, on Sel/Sec. 1308/83.

[6] Dickson to Knutsford, Confidential of 28 October 1890; Sel/Sec. 771/90 and

minutes of the State Councils,[1] monthly statements of revenue and expenditure,[2] and trade, railway, medical and judicial returns.[3]

From time to time, officers of the Straits Government were sent up-country to inspect and report on state departments. Before the appointment of state auditors, Swettenham undertook the audit of accounts in Perak, Selangor and Sungei Ujong, and reported not only on the accounts but on the general condition of the states; his 1879 audit revealed abuses in the Selangor administration which formed the subject of a despatch to the Secretary of State.[4] In 1884 an audit of the Sungei Ujong accounts showed deficiencies which were again reported home.[5] Swettenham's 1879 audit report of Selangor called attention, among other things, to the state of the Selangor Lands Office, and Weld, after calling on the Resident for reports without avail, sent the Colonial Engineer to investigate; his report on the Selangor Department of Lands and Surveys formed the subject of a despatch home, and resulted in a reprimand to the Resident and the dismissal of the officer in charge.[6] In later years the Governor was occasionally accompanied by Straits officers in his tours of the Malay states, to advise him on special problems;[7]

819A/90. By 1894, however, the Residents of Perak and Selangor had been excused the duty of sending in journals, though these were still submitted by the Residents of Pahang and Negri Sembilan, the Officer in Charge of Sungei Ujong, and the Collector and Magistrate, Jelebu. Minute by the CS, 3 February 1894 on Sel/Sec. 22A/94.

[1] Sel/Sec. 675A/91 (a displaced file referring to Council Minutes for August 1877); 114/90; 382/90.

[2] CS to Resident of Selangor, 9 August 1877, Sel/Sec. 277/77; Minutes by Treasurer of Selangor on Sel/Sec. 1385/85.

[3] Sel/Sec. 21/77, 902/93.

[4] Weld to Kimberley, 60 of 19 June 1880 and enclosures, CO 273/103. Swettenham's audit tours were undertaken in 1877, 1878 and 1879. Perak had its own auditor in 1880; Selangor and Sungei Ujong shared one from 1885. Before 1885 there was no separate audit department in Selangor, and between 1880 and 1885, audits were carried out by the Treasurer.

[5] Smith to Derby, 455 of 14 October 1884 and enclosure, CO 273/130.

[6] Weld to Kimberley, 169 of 3 May and enclosure, CO 273/117.

[7] E.g., in 1882 Weld took the Protector of Chinese to Perak to investigate the causes of a recent Chinese riot in Larut (Weld to Kimberley, 296 of 16 August 1882, CO 273/115) and in 1883 he took up the Commissioner of Lands to discuss the registration of land titles with the Resident of Selangor (Weld to Derby, 90 of 12 March 1883, 273/119). In 1885 Smith, dissatisfied with what he saw of the construction of the wharves at Port Weld, took up the Colonial Engineer to report and advise (Smith to Derby, 72 of 23 February 1885, CO 273/133). The advice of the Colony officers was not always followed; in 1888 the Colonial Engineer visited Perak to examine and report on alternative routes for a railway to serve the Kinta tin mines, but the route he recommended, although supported

but while their reports and briefings were useful and often formed the basis of the Governor's decisions, these *ad hoc* inspections in particular cases did not constitute a systematic check on the state departments.

The Governor kept himself informed not only through correspondence, journals, returns and the reports of Straits officials, but also by personal tours. Every year between 1877 and 1895, the Governor or his *locum tenens* visited the states at least once, and Weld and Smith went much more frequently. In the first three years of his Governorship, and again in 1886 on his return from leave, Weld spent between four and eight weeks each year travelling in Perak, Selangor and Sungei Ujong, visiting all the outstations and travelling in the interior on foot, horseback, elephant and by canoe. He likened the position of the Governor to that of an Admiral 'commanding several squadrons at scattered ports which he must be always inspecting to keep the reins firmly and well in hand'. 'I have no hesitation in saying that my work in relation to the Malay Peninsula and external affairs is more responsible and onerous than the administration of the Straits Settlements.'[1] His successor, Smith, was hardly less assiduous; in 1891 he paid three visits to the west coast states and one to Pahang, and this despite a Colonial Office recommendation the year before that one visit only to each side of the Peninsula should be made in a single year by the regularly commissioned Governor.[2]

Weld's long despatches home about his tours contain some of the most vivid descriptions of travel in the Malay states, though his innocent pride in visiting places 'where no white man had ever been,' his amateur ethnology, his romantic delight in the colour and variety of native life, and his satisfaction at his own understanding of the Malay mind, were wickedly parodied by his subordinates.[3] He took the keenest pleasure in the river and mountain landscape of the peninsula, and in the sense of freedom experienced during long days in the forest and nights spent in a headman's house or a mountain

---

by some Perak officers, was not the one finally adopted. Kinta Valley Railway Survey, *passim.*

[1] Weld to Derby, 394 of 19 September 1883, CO 273/122.

[2] Knutsford to Dickson, Confidential of 17 October 1890, CO 273/167.

[3] There is a somewhat laboured parody of Weld's despatch style among Swettenham's papers in the ANM (No. 106). The extracts that follow are taken partly from his despatches, partly from Lady Alice Lovat's biography. Lovat, op. cit. pp. 308–9.

hut looking out over the central ranges. He described a pleasure-journey in the country estate of the Sultan of Kedah.

[We] got into a charming canoe with a small painted cabin and paddled up a tiny stream under trees and arched roots—a kind of by-lane embedded in delicate ferns, orchids, and palms. . . . Fancy paddling up the orchid or palm-house at Kew, with monkeys gambolling about, apparently quite tame, and gorgeous kingfishers and butterflies darting through the trees like animated jewels!

During a journey up the little-inhabited Bernam river, he found himself in a very different landscape, 'a wide expanse of swampy country stretching for miles, through which the river winds in various channels and meres, abounding with fish and edged with sedges and aquatic plants . . . a still huge wilderness of trees, sedges and water'.[1] Again, on a visit to Sungei Ujong, he described the view from a mountain look-out.

The Pahang Peak in the Bendahara's country on the east side of the Peninsula is visible from here, and southwards one can see almost as far as Malacca, and northwards towards Selangor. The blues, and lilacs, and pearly tints were softened in the distance with a delicate haze, and here and there a curl of white smoke, or patch of yellowish-greenish cultivated ground, relieved the brilliant green of the jungle in the middle distance. At our feet was a deep precipice overgrown with wild plaintain (banana) and fern.

In all the towns and villages, the Governor was greeted by welcoming arches, decorations, greenery, red banners and the noise of Chinese fire-crackers. Chinese and Malays put on traditional entertainments for him—processions, tableaux and dances. On Weld's first visit to Kuala Lumpur in 1880, he was entertained at the Chinese theatre with an allegorical play representing 'all the rival Rajahs, headed by the Sultan, giving up their quarrels and putting themselves under the Governor's protection and doing him homage'. The gorgeousness of the costumes, which were in the richest colours and materials, the tumblers 'executing wonderful antics in scarlet trousers and blue jackets', reminded him of a mediaeval pageant, the like of which he had not expected to see in a small township still surrounded by jungle. In 1883, on a visit to Ulu Langat in Selangor, he had a particularly memorable experience: 'At night sitting amongst palm and banana and other rich tropical foliage—intermixed with scarves and flags and quaint devices, on the banks of a mountain river lit by a full moon in a cloudless sky, we witnessed a series of dances and

[1] Weld to Derby, 514 of 15 December 1883, CO 273/123.

performances and listened to the chants of the wild Sakais, the Malays, the Menangkabau men and the Chinese.'[1] There were scarf, shawl, saucer, ring and sword dances, with instrumental accompaniments, the whole produced by villagers, peasants, miners, Malay policemen and aborigines.

Weld and his Malay hosts shared a love of picnics and shoots and fishing expeditions. On a visit to Perak in 1882 he met the Dato' Panglima Kinta, chief of the Kinta district. 'The Datoh is a thorough sportsman, and his disappointment was hardly less than the Governor's when it was found that the time at the latter's disposal was insufficient to enable him to get a chance at the big game. . . . But the Datoh promised "at least a Rhinoceros" on the occasion of the next visit.' However, Weld was entertained to fish and buffalo feasts, and thoroughly enjoyed the experience.

Reserved and somewhat dignified as the Malay seems ordinarily to be, when seen on these occasions unrestrained he is capable of thoroughly enjoying himself . . . the shouts of applause and laughter when the Governor speared a big fish, or the Assistant Resident, up to his shoulders in water, dandling one in his arms, let it jump over his head and escape, were worthy of English school boys, and when His Excellency, the 'Tuan Governor Besar'. . . lost his balance as he stood up in a frail canoe, and the Chief of the Straits Settlements and their dependencies disappeared under the water, the yells of the population were tremendous, and the cheering no less so when he re-emerged, trident and all, still ready for the fray.[2]

The tours were occasions for meetings with the Sultans, primarily ceremonial visits, though business was occasionally discussed. With the successive Sultans of Perak and the Raja Muda of Pahang, Weld was able apparently to have rational discourse on such matters as the abolition of slavery, the succession question and the Sultan's allowance, but his visits to the Sultan of Selangor appear to have put a considerable strain on both parties. At the first meeting, the Sultan ('splendidly got up, with a magnificent sword which had been presented to him by the Queen') struck Weld as being in his dotage, but the Resident thought he was only very nervous. 'However, he seemed much delighted, and after some talking he subsided, and sat chattering in a low voice to himself.'[3] Weld's reception by the Sultan the next year is worth describing as it was recorded by a Selangor

[1] Weld to Derby, 309 of 19 July 1883, CO 273/121.
[2] Weld to Kimberley, 296 of 16 August 1882, enclosure 2, C.3428. *Tuan Governor Besar* may be translated freely as 'the big chief'.
[3] Lovat, op. cit. p. 285.

observer. The Collector at Langat (Mr. Innes) told the Sultan he must wear his uniform, 'trousers with gold braid down the legs and his baju with gold braid which Queen Victoria had sent him', and also his sword. But the household was thrown into a panic by the imminent arrival of the Governor. Long after eleven o'clock, Innes went into the Sultan's kitchen to find a Malay cook holding a decapitated fowl on high and watching the drops of blood trickle from it while he said a prayer. The tiffin was very badly cooked (by Innes' own cook) and was served in the wrong reception hall in full view of the Malay population of Jugra; and the Sultan forgot to wear his uniform. Innes explained, 'The Sultan is a very conservative Malay of the old regime, and European punctuality and civilization have been brought to bear on him too late in life to change him materially.'[1]

While ceremonial and entertainment played an important part in these tours, they had a practical function in that they enabled the Governors to inspect the state establishments, meet the Residents, their officers and leading Malays and Chinese, and discuss outstanding problems. A great deal of business was transacted as a result of this personal supervision. Weld and Smith inspected public works in every district in the western Malay states; chose sites for them, judged the need for new stations and communications, and authorized special expenditures on the spot.[2] They kept in close touch with the development of communications; Weld in particular spent much of his time on tour in following the traces of proposed roads or railways, and in August 1883 he made a remarkable journey up the Peninsula from Malacca to Batu Gajah, and down the Kinta river to Telok Anson, following an inland route parallel with the central mountain range. The purpose of the journey was to examine the terrain and judge its suitability for road and rail communication, and Weld was able to report that no difficulty existed in making a good inland road and even a railway from Province Wellesley to Malacca.[3]

The business transacted with the Residents on these occasions covered a multiplicity of subjects—communications, establishments,

[1] Collector, Langat, to Resident, 8 November 1881, Sel/Sec. 459/181.

[2] E.g., Weld settled the site of a new fort and Residency at Kuala Lumpur in 1880, and Smith settled the site of the railway station at Klang in 1889 (Lovat, op. cit. p. 291; Smith to Knutsford, 234 of 20 May 1889, CO 273/160). In 1892 Smith, while on tour in Perak, approved a branch railway which he had previously rejected on paper. Smith to Ripon, 384 of 26 September 1892, CO 273/183.

[3] Weld to Derby, 361 of 5 September 1883, CO 273/122.

revenue, land administration, allowances to chiefs, the succession, slavery, forced labour. Boundary questions were settled, changes were made in the scale of tariffs, and petitions and complaints were heard. It was the Governor's practice to receive deputations of Malays and Chinese. Soon after his arrival, Sir William Robinson met deputations of Chinese miners in Perak and Selangor begging for a reduction in the tin duty;[1] Weld from his first visit to the mainland received deputations and petitions on mining matters, and Smith, who was able to dispense with an interpreter in his interviews with Cantonese, since he spoke their dialect,[2] continued the practice. In the meetings with Malays also, important business was transacted. On a journey to Jelebu in 1886, for example, Weld heard the complaints of the Dato' Penghulu and the clan heads about the alienation of padi land for tin mining, and settled the question on the basis of compensation and provision of alternative land;[3] and in 1891 Smith on a tour of Sungei Ujong attended the election of a new Dato' Klana, recognized the successful candidate and fixed his allowance.[4] The Governor also transacted business in audience with the Rulers, discussing such matters as boundary settlements, the succession, forced labour and slavery.

These channels of communication and information enabled the Governor to discharge responsibilities that were comprehensive indeed. He appointed all officers earning more than $600 a year (a category including all European officers and senior Asian clerical staff) and below the rank of Resident and Assistant Resident, and his sanction was necessary before an officer of this class might be granted long leave, suspended or dismissed.[5] Legislation required his sanc-

---

[1] Robinson to Hicks Beach, 78 of 26 March 1878 and enclosures, CO 273/93. The tin duties in both states were reduced later in the year.

[2] Smith to Ripon, 384 of 26 September 1892, CO 273/183.

[3] Weld to Granville, 93 of 15 March 1886, CO 273/139. Sometimes the Governor received independent information from these meetings which enabled him to keep a check on his Residents; while Weld was in Malacca in 1881 he heard complaints of oppressive duties being levied at Sungei Raya (a district of Sungei Ujong) and wrote to the Resident that he must be 'sold by someone'. Weld to Murray, 20 February 1881, Governor's Letterbook I.

[4] Smith to Knutsford, 288 of 13 July 1891, CO 273/174.

[5] Practice varied a little from time to time and from state to state; e.g., it was the practice in Pahang to refer every case of a few days' leave to the Governor, while in Selangor all applications not exceeding three months were dealt with by the Resident (Resident of Selangor to CS, 5 June 1895 and minutes, Sel/Sec. 373A/95). Again, in 1876 the Resident of Selangor was instructed to refer all appointments over $25 a month to the Governor (CS to Resident of Selangor, 21

tion before it could come into force.[1] In judicial matters, though the Crown had no jurisdiction in the states, the Governor received petitions relating to judicial decisions and could and did influence the course of justice by directing the Resident to vary a sentence on appeal or call for a re-trial.[2] The most important prerogative of the Governor, however, lay in his control of the state budgets.[3] This enabled him to regulate the size of the state establishments and the salaries of officers, influence the development of communications and public works, education and health services, and control fiscal policy and economic development by the exercise of his discretion over tariff rates, state borrowing and state loans to agriculturists and miners. The estimates were subject to the sanction of the Governor alone. The Selangor estimates were occasionally submitted to the

---

October 1876, Sel/Sec. 231/76), while in Perak nine years later Low wrote, 'All officers except the Residents are appointed and dismissed by the Governor of the Straits Settlements but practically those of $40 a month and under are made by the Resident who recommends and reports them to the Governor and takes his instructions as to dismissal' (Low to CO, 11 October 1885, on Weld, Private of 8 October 1885, CO 273/138). The reference in the text is to a circular of 24 June 1895 (Sel/Sec. 373A/95) defining the Resident's powers, which was a fairly close formalization of past practice. See Appendix 3b.

[1] I have not found any general instructions to this effect, but it is clear from the frequent references that it was the practice to forward legislation already passed by the State Council to the Governor for confirmation; cf., Low to Douglas, 11 June 1879, Sel/Sec. 213/79, referring to the submission of the Perak Land Regulations; Resident of Perak to CS 16 September 1891, enclosed in Smith to Knutsford, 406 of 29 October 1891, CO 273/176, referring to the submission 'as usual' of the Contagious Diseases Order in Council; SCM 27 February 1879, 18 September 1879, 31 March 1880, 25 November 1880, 11 March 1882, 14 July 1882, 31 October 1882, 27 September 1884, 17 March 1890, and minutes for 1893–5 *passim* for submission of Selangor legislation. The regulations passed at the first Pahang Council were authorized by the Governor before being put before the Council, and submitted to him afterwards for confirmation (Smith to Knutsford, 24 of 17 January 1890, CO 273/165). This was also the practice in Selangor from 1892 onwards (SCM 19 September 1892 *et seq.*), and there are earlier instances (cf., minute by Acting Governor, 29 August 1879, Sel/Sec. 292/79, approving draft mining regulations for Selangor and instructing that they be put before Council). There are instances of this from Perak: cf., Acting Resident of Perak to Acting Resident of Selangor, 13 November 1892, Sel/Sec. 5020/94, referring to the submission of a draft regulation for the collection of opium duty by Government.

[2] See Chapter VIII, on judicial administration.

[3] In 1876 the Resident of Selangor was instructed to submit for approval a yearly estimate of revenue and expenditure, and to ask for authority 'on all possible occasions' before unauthorised charges were incurred (CS to Resident of Selangor, 2 June 1876, Sel/Sec. 57/76). The estimates were considered in detail, and there were frequent applications to Singapore for approval of supplementary votes, chiefly for establishments and public works.

State Council and passed *pro forma* after they had received the Governor's sanction,[1] but this was not a regular practice, and from the minutes it appears to have ceased after 1890. It does not appear ever to have been introduced into Perak. No supply ordinance (which would have required the seal of the Sultan) is recorded in the collected ordinances of the states or in the state gazettes (where current legislation was published) and there is no evidence that such an ordinance was ever passed. On the one occasion on record when the Selangor estimates received the Sultan's seal, and arrived in Singapore thus adorned, the Resident was coldly requested to state whether he was 'acting on the authority of the Sultan's seal or in accordance with the instructions received from this government'.[2] The estimates of states receiving loans from the colony were circulated to members of the Legislative Council of the Colony and were occasionally the subject of discussion, but they did not come before the Finance Committee of Council. The Colonial Office never saw them. In short, the Residents and the Governor between them had sole control of revenues which by 1895 exceeded the revenues of the Straits Settlements.[3]

The Governor's powers enabled him, when he wished, to exercise a strict control over the Residents, and this was demonstrated during the six years from 1876 to 1882 when Captain Bloomfield Douglas was Resident of Selangor. Douglas was a poor administrator, a poor diplomat and inexperienced in dealing with Malays; and during his tenure of office, the Secretariat in Singapore possessed an officer— Swettenham—who knew more about Selangor and indeed the west coast states as a whole than any officer in the peninsula, and who was already giving proof of the administrative flair which later distinguished him as one of the great Malayan administrators. The correspondence, the diaries, the audit tours, the Governor's visits, the special enquiries kept the Secretariat informed, and Swettenham's

[1] In 1877 the Resident of Selangor was instructed not to submit financial questions, or 'other questions of considerable importance' to the State Council without first obtaining the views and instructions of the Governor (CS to Resident of Selangor, 11 September 1877, Sel/Sec. 675A/91—a displaced file). Douglas, whose Councils made up in formality what they lacked in independence, submitted the estimates (after sanction by the Governor) in 1877, 1880 and 1881. On each occasion they were passed unanimously and no discussion is recorded (see SCM 31 December 1877, 21 April 1880, and 6 April 1881). Rodger while Ag. Resident tabled the estimates in 1886 and Maxwell in 1890. SCM 27 November 1886 and 8 January 1890.

[2] CS to Resident of Selangor, 22 May 1880, Sel/Sec. 137/80.

[3] The revenue of the Straits Settlements in 1895 was $4,048,359, and that of the protected Malay states was $8,481,007.

Malay contacts enabled him to make an additional check on Douglas' activities.

In his dealings with Malays, the Resident suffered correction and rebuke. In 1878, he was forced publicly to retract his dismissal of a major chief and a few months later was again cautioned against pushing the Malays too hard, when he reported that he had rebuked the district chief of Bernam 'from the quarterdeck of H.M. ship' for conniving at debt-slavery in his district.[1] His attempts to prevent discontented rajas from bringing their complaints to Singapore were discouraged[2] and although the Governor on one occasion recorded an opinion that Malays should not visit Singapore to submit complaints without in the first instance referring to the Sultan, Viceroy or Resident, the Singapore Government continued to interview Malay rajas and chiefs and grant them favours at the expense of the Selangor treasury without prior reference to the Resident, and sometimes despite his protests.[3]

Douglas' general administration was under constant criticism. In 1882, when maladministration in Selangor was under consideration by the Secretary of State, Weld wrote that both he and the Secretariat had taken 'an immense amount of trouble to assist him and keep him right, both by word of mouth and by official and unofficial correspondence'.[4] His accounts were minutely queried,[5] and his revenue reports and estimates were criticized for general inaccuracy, persistent errors in calculation and prediction, insufficient detail and poor judgment in allocating funds.[6] Swettenham's audit report for 1879 was a comprehensive attack on the administration. He noted the inefficiency with which the chief departments (particularly the land

[1] Resident to CS, 8 August 1878, Sel/Sec. 244/78; CS to Resident, 23 August 1878, Sel/Sec. 268/78.

[2] CS to Resident of Selangor, 24 October 1876, Sel/Sec. 225/76.

[3] CS to Resident, 3 January 1878, Sel/Sec. 7/78; CS to Resident, 27 November 1878, Sel/Sec. 323/78.

[4] Weld to Kimberley, Confidential of 17 June 1882, CO 273/115. His intervention was not successful, for he wrote in his diary after a visit to Kuala Lumpur in 1882, that half the orders he had given on his last visit had been carried out badly. 'It is a singular fact that I have had to dismiss two-thirds of the staff of officials here, since I came, for inefficiency.' Extract from diary, undated, cited in Lovat, op. cit. p. 356.

[5] Cf., CS to Resident, 20 July 1878, querying payment of $5 in coroner's fees to the Supt. of Police, and payment of doctor's bills for the Resident while on leave, Sel/Sec. 220/78.

[6] CS to Resident, 4 March 1879, Sel/Sec. 83/79; CS to Resident, 8 March 1880, Sel/Sec. 61/80; CS to Resident, 26 January 1881, Sel/Sec. 29/81, requesting the Resident to prepare fresh estimates as the first draft was so unsatisfactory.

office) were carried on, and the absence of proper records; the clumsiness and inappropriateness of a taxation policy which hindered development by imposing multiple and burdensome taxes that were not worth the trouble of collecting; and the inertia of a government which sat in a melancholy and decaying little port twenty miles from the real centre of population and activity—the mining township of Kuala Lumpur.[1]

As a result of the report, the Resident was required to institute a proper system of records in the Treasury and the Lands and Courts departments. He was provided with a schedule of imports to be submitted to Council, with a view to the remission of those taxes which appeared to harass people and discourage immigration. Changes in the form and scale of excise duties were recommended, and instructions were issued with regard to court fees. Finally, the Governor intimated his wish that the Resident should move to Kuala Lumpur 'with despatch' and forward 'a detailed proposal for His Excellency's consideration' of the steps he thought necessary for establishing the Resident's headquarters there.[2]

The instructions to introduce new scales of tariffs and court fees were obeyed,[3] and the move to Kuala Lumpur took place the same year, but the administrative instructions were only partly followed. Continued dissatisfaction with the administration of the land office led to a major inquiry revealing not only culpable inefficiency but breach of public service ethics, in that sales of land had been made to public officers under questionable circumstances. The land sales were cancelled, the officer responsible (who happened to be a son-in-law of the Resident) was dismissed. It was not the first time a Governor had been forced to take note of the irregularities in the conduct of Selangor officers. In 1880 the Acting Governor learnt 'from native sources' that deductions were being made from the allowance of the Sultan for articles of furniture supplied by Selangor officers, and the Resident was instructed that in future no deductions should be made without special authority from the Straits Government.[4] His failure to carry out these instructions led to a further inquiry and to his enforced resignation in 1882.

[1] Swettenham's Report on audit of the Selangor Accounts, 1879, 27 March 1880, Sel/Sec. 80/80.
[2] CS to Resident, 10 April 1880, Sel/Sec. 80/80.
[3] SCM, 21 April 1880.
[4] Memorandum on Sultan's allowance, enclosed in Weld to Kimberley, Confidential of 24 August 1882, CO 273/115.

The relations between Douglas' administration and the Colonial Government were admittedly exceptional. The other Residents were generally respected for their ability and their success in dealing with Malays, and three of them—Low, Swettenham and Maxwell—are among the great names of Malayan administrative history; they were as able as any of their contemporaries in the Straits service. The need for active interference was therefore less. Again, after 1882, when Swettenham went to Selangor as Resident, there was no one in the Secretariat with his expertise or his Malay contacts. Relations with the states ceased to be a specialist concern[1] and became part of the general work of the department, though a considerable body of knowledge had been built up by then, and the two Governors spanning the period 1880 to 1893—Weld and Smith—had made the affairs of the states their special interest.

Swettenham's succession to the Selangor Residency is marked by a great change in the tone of correspondence with Singapore. His initiative—in land administration, road and railway construction, public works and the organization of a penghulu establishment—was received with a chorus of admiration and approval. His estimates for 1883 and 1884, proposing large projects and expenditures, were accepted in encouraging terms.[2] The Governor did not always agree with his proposals, but as Weld minuted on a scheme for a railway survey, 'he is responsible for the work being carried out, and as he thinks his way of doing it is the safe and more expeditious I approve of his proposal as set forth in his minute'.[3] In the same spirit, Smith eight years later allowed Maxwell to introduce a land code into Selangor, providing for a system of assessment and registration of title new to the state, even though he doubted the practicality of the legislation.[4]

The Residents with the greatest influence between 1882 and 1895 —Low and Swettenham—and the Governors for most of this time Weld and Smith—were agreed that the prime object of government was to get the country opened up by communications and liberal land and fiscal policies, so that for most of the period a continuity of policy was achieved, with little disagreement. Weld was temperamentally disposed to allow the maximum discretion to a subordinate

---

[1] Between 1892 and 1895, when Maxwell was CS, the department again had a specialist in Malay states' affairs.
[2] CS to Resident, 19 September 1883, Sel/Sec. 1436/83, on estimates for 1884.
[3] Minute by Weld, 19 January 1883, Sel/Sec. 68/83.
[4] Smith to Knutsford, 139 of 28 March 1891, CO 273/172.

whom he trusted, and Swettenham was not slow to take advantage of this. Yet Weld and Smith were far too interested in the Malay states, and far too jealous of the exceptional powers which had accrued to the Governor in their administration, to abandon any part of their reserve authority. Swettenham, like Douglas before him, had to report his plans in detail, and secure the Governor's sanction at each stage of their implementation; and the Governor examined the projects *in situ*, inspecting sites and plans for public works and communications on his visits to Selangor.

The reserve power of the Governor was used to some effect in dealing with Swettenham's *locum tenens*, J. P. Rodger, though he was a man of admitted ability and experience, who administered Selangor with great success between 1884 and 1888 and again in 1891.[1] Swettenham himself, when Resident of Perak, felt the force of the Governor's authority when he was confronted in 1890 by an Acting Governor unsympathetic to his policy of open-handed expenditure and unreserved support for entrepreneurs in the states. The Kinta railway extension was held up, though it had been approved in principle by the Governor and Colonial Office, and requisitions had actually reached the Crown Agents;[2] revenue farmers unable to pay their rents were denied relief despite Swettenham's plea for liberal treatment;[3] and Swettenham complained in his Perak report for 1893 that three years earlier he had been refused permission to realize certain Indian investments, and that the state had thereby been involved in a loss. The motives of the Acting Governor (Dickson) were to some extent personal, and in the matter of the Kinta railway, where a decision had already been made by the Secretary of State, his initiative was promptly discouraged. On the other two matters, however, he was acting within his authority; Swettenham's complaint over the securities, and particularly the manner of its presentation, was disapproved; and in the dispute over the farms, which reached the Colonial Office by means of a petition from the lessees, the Secretary of State refused to interfere.[4]

[1] His estimates for 1886 and 1892 were radically cut. CS to Acting Resident, 30 September 1885, Sel/Sec. 1430/85; CS to Ag. Resident, 5 November 1891, Sel/Sec. 680/92.

[2] Knutsford to Smith, 117 of 26 April 1892, on Smith to Knutsford, 83 of 20 February 1889; correspondence on Dickson to Knutsford, 369 of 22 September 1890, CO 273/168.

[3] Dickson to Knutsford, 425 of 31 October 1890 and enclosures, CO 273/168.

[4] Ripon to Mitchell, Confidential of 22 March 1895, CO 273/195; Knutsford to Smith, 393 of 23 December 1890, CO 273/168.

The delicacy and novelty of the Residents' work, their responsibility not only for governing existing populations but for peopling and developing virtually empty lands, the identity of approach and the personal accord which existed on the whole between Residents and Governors, and finally the fact that the Governors had no means of asserting themselves in the states except through the Residents—all these factors ensured that the initiative would remain with the latter and that they would retain considerable freedom in the implementation of policy. Yet the Governor's authority was no mere fiction. The Governors had at their disposal wide powers and a considerable fund of information and experience built up by full and regular correspondence and personal contact; and the states were not, after all, so large or heavily populated that an intelligent observer could not soon acquire an understanding of their problems. The Governors were able to maintain a continuous supervision which covered the major activities of the states and which became institutionalized in a regular procedure of reference and sanction at an early stage, and they were able as occasion demanded to use their authority and intelligence to check and direct the state governments.

VI

INSTITUTIONS OF GOVERNMENT: SULTAN AND STATE COUNCIL

THE SULTAN

IN the accommodation that followed the appointment of Residents, the Rulers of the protected states retired from any active part in government, and were recompensed after a fashion by increases in their wealth, ceremonial and formal honours. The decline was not so much in their actual responsibilities, which even in the days of their independence were limited by the rights and powers of the chiefs and by the narrow scope of government, but in the contrast between the enormously increased activity and responsibility of government and the Sultan's political and administrative detachment from it.

The position of the Ruler as a British client was established by the procedures followed to secure a suitable succession. Malay succession procedures, though governed by customary rules, had always been sufficiently flexible to allow of variation at the instance of interested parties. In Perak, for example, the rule of rotation between three branches of the royal family had been ignored in 1857 in order to obstruct the succession of an unpopular candidate, and in 1865 and again in 1871, the candidate from that branch was passed over. In Selangor, after the death of Sultan Mohammed in 1857, his nephew and son-in-law 'Abdu'l Samad succeeded instead of his young son Mahmud. In Pahang in 1863, the succession of Bendahara Ahmad was effected by a civil war.

Before British intervention, the major chiefs and the royal family had played an influential part in deciding the succession. In 1874 and after, British political interests dominated the choice of a Ruler. The choice, as before, was made from candidates eligible according to local custom, and usually the candidate with the most obvious natural claim was allowed to succeed; but on occasion the British power was used to impose a candidate or to remove an objectionable incumbent.

The principle that the succession must be sanctioned by the Secretary of State was established on the election of a new Dato' Klana in 1880, and there was much discussion of the question whether British influence might legitimately be brought to bear on elections in the ordinary course of events. By custom, the succession to the Klanaship descended in the female line. The late Klana had left a will securing the succession to his own descendants, and the Resident (Murray), who clearly had little appreciation of customary law, wanted the will confirmed. The Acting Governor, Anson, refused to interfere with custom; the election took place in the courthouse in the presence of the Resident and a representative of the Acting Governor. The will of the late Klana was rejected by the electors as being contrary to custom, even though some of them had put their signatures to it, and a candidate eligible according to Sungei Ujong custom was chosen by the Dato' Bandar on their behalf. The meeting had been told that the Klana elect would have to be approved by the Secretary of State, and the Dato' Bandar in fact refused to make his choice public till he had seen Anson and been assured of his approval.[1] The election having taken place, the Klana elect was approved by the Executive Council, by the incoming Governor, Weld, and finally by the Secretary of State; but Weld and Kimberley both expressed their regret that the opportunity to influence the election had not been taken,[2] and Kimberley minuted that it might be necessary to exercise 'a more decided influence' on successions in future.[3]

The clearest example of the use of this influence was in Perak. The way in which it worked to bring about the succession of 'Abdu'llah has already been described. The same power brought about his removal, and the appointment of Raja Yusuf to act for him.[4] Yusuf's official position was Regent, and it was as Regent that he presided

[1] Anson to Hicks Beach, 70 of 3 March 1880 and enclosures, CO 273/102.
[2] Weld to Kimberley, Confidential of 21 October 1880, and minute by Kimberley, 14 January 1881, CO 273/104. In later years, the Dato' Klana apparently offended the Malays and obstructed the Resident by his eccentric and scandalous behaviour, and at the instance of leading Malays (including his own kinsmen) Weld removed him to Singapore on a reduced pension in 1887. In 1891, Smith presided over a meeting in Sungei Ujong at which a new Klana was chosen according to custom. Smith to Holland, 288 of 13 July 1891, CO 273/174.
[3] Minute by Kimberley, 13 October 1880, on Weld to Kimberley, 124 of 21 August 1880, CO 273/104.
[4] The need for a Regent arose when 'Abdu'llah came to Singapore in September 1876 to face charges of complicity in Birch's murder. 'Abdu'llah was able to block the appointment of Yusuf temporarily by appointing Bendahara Osman, but his success was shortlived, for the Bendahara died a month later, and though 'Abdu'llah resisted pressure to appoint a successor, Jervois decided that in default of any special appointment, the chief authority in the country fell upon Yusuf 'by virtue of his office as "Rajah Muda" or heir apparent to the Sultanship.' Jervois to Carnarvon, 5 January 1877, C.1709, no. 85.

over the Perak State Council and gave his assent to legislation.[1] Jervois had suggested that the elder son of 'Abdu'llah be educated to succeed his father, and though the Secretary of State had not absolutely committed himself to this,[2] there remained in the minds of the officials the idea that Raja Mansur would succeed.[3] The boy was sent to Malacca, where he received an English education, and in 1883 when he was fifteen or sixteen, he entered the Perak government service as a cadet, and in 1884 he accompanied the Resident and Raja Idris on a visit to England, to broaden his experience. But all this time, Yusuf was building up a strong claim to the succession. Though in earlier years he had thrice been passed over, he had achieved in 1872 a brief understanding with 'Abdu'llah, who recognized him as Raja Muda (the title of the heir apparent) in return for recognition of himself as Sultan. Towards the end of Birch's residency, he was accorded the courtesy of this title and in 1876 and afterwards the Straits officials referred to him by this title. Low used this title in reference to him; so did various governors on their visits to Perak, and the title was consistently used in the Council minutes from 1877.[4] He had therefore the advantage of possessing the formal title of the heir apparent, and it would have been very difficult to have passed him over during his lifetime.

He consolidated his position by unwavering support for the British. From the time of his acceptance of Jervois' proposals (in itself a submission of great political value) he performed important services for the British Government—services which not only ingratiated him with the British but had the delightful advantage of enabling him to settle scores with some of his numerous enemies in Perak. He had the realism and intelligence to know that power and influence

[1] Cf., the formula in W.G. Maxwell, comp. *Land Laws of Perak, 1877–1900,* Taiping, 1906, p. 2, 'His Highness the Regent in Council has been pleased to direct. . . .'

[2] Carnarvon to Jervois, 1 November 1876, C.1709, no. 49.

[3] Minute by Cox, 19 August 1878, on Robinson to Hicks Beach, 1 July 1878, CO 273/94; also minute by Meade, 22 May 1884, on Low to CO, 21 May 1884, CO 273/132. 'The idea is to educate him to govt. employment in Perak & eventually if he turns out well, he may succeed to the position of chief ruler but of this he knows nothing.'

[4] Birch Journal, entry for 9 October 1875, CO 273/88, reporting that Yusuf had signed a warrant for construction of a road to Kota Stia by the Laksamana; Jervois to Carnarvon, 11 January 1877 and enclosures, C.1709, no. 86, reporting the trial of Birch's murderers (it was as Raja Muda that Yusuf presided over the court); Low Journal, p. 48; opening of Perak State Council, *PCM,* 10 September 1877.

depended on British favour, and the consistency of purpose to stick to a policy of support for the Resident; and he was further encouraged in this policy by the knowledge that he was universally unpopular and had no following to speak of in Perak. The accounts of contemporaries are universally unflattering. Swettenham has this to say of him:

For people with whom loyalty to their rajas is an article of faith, the dislike in which the King was held by them was extraordinary. It is charitable to suppose that early disappointment had embittered his life, for he possessed good qualities. He was undeniably intelligent, and had a wider knowledge of his country and its ancient customs than any other man in it. He knew his own mind, was determined to obstinacy, and asked counsel of few. He was a keen sportsman, courageous, and, having sought the friendship of the British, never wavered in his loyalty. If it be said that in this he consulted his own interest and knew his unpopularity with his own people, his consistency and good faith were still a merit. On the other hand, his defects and vices were numerous, and just those likely to earn him the dislike of Malays. He was incredibly mean, he was overbearing to cruelty, rapaciously grasping, jealous of the good fortune of any of his subjects, selfish, difficult of access, and unconcerned with the misfortunes of others; vindictive to those who offended him or opposed his wishes, a gambler who nearly always contrived to win, and in matters where the other sex was concerned, decidedly unreliable.[1]

Yusuf himself admitted to Swettenham in 1874 that the Perak chiefs were against him 'to a man' and had conspired to prevent him from becoming Sultan;[2] and his advice to Birch and Swettenham in 1875, to 'take violent measures with the opposition' was indicative of his relations with them. 'He says he is certain we shall have to make an example of Laxamana or Shahbandar or Maharaja Lela . . . and to burn a village or two. . . . He inveighs against all the Datus, and says not one should be allowed to remain in office.'[3]

The classic problem of British colonial administration—how to

[1] Swettenham *Malay Sketches*, p. 164. Clifford who was given the unwelcome task of shepherding him on some of his journeys outside the state, described him as 'a barbarous person of unspeakable manners and morals' and described his own agonies of embarrassment when his charge insisted on stripping in full view of a mixed European picnic party and bathing in the Penang reservoir, 'whence, with only his nose, eyes, and mouth above the level of the water, he looked up at us with all the malevolence of a bull water-buffalo'. H. Clifford, 'Piloting Princes', in *Bushwhacking and other Asiatic Tales and Memories*, 2nd. ed., London, 1929, pp. 198–9.
[2] C.D. Cowan, 'Sir Frank Swettenham's Perak Journals 1874–1876,' p. 55, also pp. 56–57 and note 65, where Cowan remarks that neither Skinner nor Irving discovered the existence of Yusuf in three years' dealings with Perak Malays.
[3] Birch Journal, entry for 19 October 1875, CO 273/88.

associate indigenous Rulers with British policies without alienating them from their own people—was reversed in Low's dealings with Yusuf. Low's problems arose not out of public dislike of the British so much as Yusuf's vindictiveness and harshness, qualities which seemed likely to involve British officers in his own unpopularity and associate them with policies which they disapproved. Low wrote:

My greatest difficulty in endeavouring to settle the Country has always been the Raja Muda who was generally hated to such an extent that he never could have succeeded, if left to himself, in establishing himself in any authority except with a few personal followers; he is a man of very good natural abilities but he has no idea of Government—except that the ryots were created to produce revenues for the Rajas and to be at their entire disposal; if I were only here to advise such a man and if he did not believe that I had authority to control his caprices when they are likely to be dangerous to the country, our hope of restoring peace to it would be vain and the position of [the] Resident untenable.[1]

Low added that the people had only been persuaded to accept Yusuf 'in the belief that the British Government intend to take care that he should be powerless for harm'. His judgment was soon confirmed by petitions for the return of ex-Sultan Ismail which had been circulated in secret in several of the districts of Perak, bore the signatures of some of the leading penghulus, and clearly had the tacit support of the Temenggong and the Dato' Panglima Kinta. Low forwarded these petitions with the remark 'I have no doubt whatever that if a petition of the character of those now forwarded were freely circulated for signature in the State, that it would be very extensively supported, indeed the Sultan Ismail seems to be the only claimant to the sovereignty of Perak who appears to have a party in the country worthy of the name.'[2]

Low had not been a month in Perak before he realized Yusuf's true position, and established over him an ascendancy which may have owed something to Low's tact and personality, but which certainly owed more to Yusuf's own ambition. At one of his earliest interviews with Yusuf and Idris, he corrected them with remarkable bluntness, and made it quite clear that their animosities were not going to prevent him from working with anyone in Perak who could be of use to him. Raja Yusuf had complained that 'the people would

[1] Low to Robinson, 26 May 1878, enclosed in Robinson to Hicks Beach, 171 of 13 June 1878, CO 273/94.
[2] Low to CS, 8 June 1878, enclosed in Robinson to Hicks Beach, 193 of 1 July 1878, CO 273/94.

not obey him, especially the Kota Lama people and the Tumongong and Sri Maharaja Lela's people and all who were influenced by Shaik Ma Taib', while Idris complained that Shaikh Mat Taib (a Sumatran religious leader and ally of the Temenggong) was interfering in his district of Kampar. Low wrote:

I told [Yusuf] that although I had not seen a man from Kota Lama, I had no fear that they would give me any trouble as he suggested; that he ought not to be surprised that people with whom he had been quarrelling all his life and with whom he still designed to keep up bad feeling himself, should have no love for him; and that I would undertake if he would only behave like a Raja instead of going into the bazaar and making himself so common as he [words illegible] and if he would do all in his power to alleviate the ill feeling that he was quite aware existed against him, things should come right at last; but that I expected on the part of the Gov[ernmen]t a good deal from him in this direction. . . . I told them that in the scarcity of useful servants the Gov[ernmen]t of Perak would be very foolish to reject the assistance of having such because they were foreigners, but that I would take care that [while] I advised the Gov[ernmen]t no-one should overstep the bounds of authority which, when I had settled with them about the Council, should be assigned to each one; but that I could not give them this advice [or discuss] as to the establishment of the Council till I have seen some chiefs who have not yet visited me, such as the Panglima Kinta. . . .[1]

Low intervened when Yusuf tried to assert his authority in objectionable ways, even when religious questions, reserved to the Malays by the Pangkor Engagement, were involved. When Yusuf made out a proclamation in the name of Resident and Raja, calling on all Muslims to attend mosque regularly on pain of fine and imprisonment, Low made Idris run his pencil through the objectionable clauses in Yusuf's presence, and write an amendment 'that in case of neglect they would be guilty of sin and certainly be punished hereafter' and later sent Idris to tell his father-in-law that he should not prepare sealed documents of this kind without consulting the Resident, and that it was foolish of him to initiate such measures when he already had such a name for severity.[2] There was no attempt to mask realities; on the contrary, public confidence depended on the knowledge that authority lay with the Resident. When penghulus came to Low to complain of harsh orders which Yusuf had issued (against Low's instructions), he told them, in effect, that they might ignore any order that did not bear his seal.[3]

---

[1] Low Journal, pp. 70–71. The word 'Yusuf' in square brackets has been substituted for 'him' in the edited text.   [2] Ibid. p. 85.
[3] Ibid. p. 98. The open assumption of power by the Resident in Selangor was

Though Low's difficulties were great, he was helped by Yusuf's acumen and consistency of purpose. Yusuf soon became aware of his dependence on Low,[1] and accepted his direction. He supported Low on the State Council, even when he himself had voiced a contrary opinion in discussion,[2] and allowed himself (though not without unwillingness) to be persuaded to give up his personal privileges in the interests of reform.[3] Low and Weld (at Yusuf's prompting) proposed that this loyalty should be rewarded by elevation to the Sultanate, that Idris should be made Raja Muda and that the state should thereby be restored to its full dignity.[4] The Secretary of State conveyed his approval, provided it was made clear to Yusuf that the change of title would not mean any difference in his political position, or 'emancipate him from any part of the control that has hitherto been exercised over him'.[5]

criticized by Raja Bot b. Raja Juma'at. He wrote to the Governor claiming the district of Lukut and offering to accept a Resident there under certain conditions. 'But as such officers have come to the Malayan States with assurances of assisting the Chiefs by advice, and have usurped the position of Rulers, acting so as to make the Rajahs small and of no account in the eyes of the people but themselves being maintained in the State and position as if they alone or the Government of Your Excellency were the Rulers of the country, thus bringing great & increasing dissatisfaction amongst Chiefs and people, I should desire, before receiving it in my Government of Lukut and Sungei Rayah, to have the footing on which such assistance should be received and given clearly defined so as to be confined to advising and not to be capable of being extended, so that the European officers might be either in fact or appearance Rulers of the country instead [of] ourselves.' Raja Bot to CS, 3 February 1879, in Robinson to Hicks Beach, 51 of 3 February 1879, CO 273/98.

[1] Swettenham has described this dependence in a piece of thinly-disguised fiction, 'The King's Way', *Malay Sketches*, pp. 161–78.

[2] Cf., *PCM*, 26 June 1878, when the Council discussed responsibility for the Mentri's debts, laid on the state by the Pangkor Engagement, but which Yusuf felt strongly should not be undertaken by the state. See also (loc cit.) discussion on the question of a pension to the widow of the Dato' Sagor, who had been executed for his part in the murder of Birch; Yusuf at first objected to the grant of a pension, but ended by suggesting a more generous sum than anyone else.

[3] E.g., on the slavery question, he agreed finally to allow the law of manumission to apply to his own household, after having attempted to secure favoured treatment (*PCM* of 9 and 10 October 1882). A little judicious coercion and bribery helped; he had been told earlier that the question of increasing his allowance would be considered when the slavery question was settled. Smith to Derby, 188 of 31 May 1884, CO 273/127.

[4] Weld to Stanhope, Confidential of 3 April 1886, CO 273/139.

[5] Stanhope to Weld, Confidential of 19 August 1886, on Weld to Stanhope, Confidential of 3 April 1886, CO 273/139. Mansur's claim was dismissed with the comment that he was young and had the power to show by his conduct that he merited advancement (minute by de Robeck, 8 May 1886). One Malay rationalization of the delay in elevating Yusuf was that he could not be installed because

There is no evidence that Yusuf was ever recognized as Raja Muda by the chiefs before he became Regent in 1876,[1] and undoubtedly he owed his career as Regent and Sultan to British support. His elevation to the Sultanate was indeed unanimously supported by the State Council, whose Malay members then included Raja Idris, one chief of the first rank, one of the second, and two of the third; but the remarkable feature of this meeting was the extent to which Low was prepared to go in order to reassure the members that the Resident's control over the Raja Muda would not be lessened by the change in status. A telegram from the Secretary of State, pointing out that the change of title would not involve relaxation of existing control, was read to the Council as well as a minute by the Governor to the same effect. Raja Idris pointed out in Yusuf's favour that he had always been in accord with the Resident as the agent of the Governor, and that he was too wise a prince to think of acting contrary to advice— a point which throws some light on Raja Idris' own idea of the proper relationship between Sultan and Resident. It is notable that at this meeting, dealing with the Malay succession, Chinese were present and spoke; one of them, Khoo Boo Ann, a Krian sugar-planter, recalled the misgovernment of rajas in former times and 'considered that precautions should be taken against the return of such misgovernment', but declared his trust in 'the support of the English Government'. Low reported that Raja Yusuf had expressed himself willing to subscribe to any oath or engagement binding him to 'fulfil the duties of Yang-de-per-Tuan in conformity with the existing administration', and the unanimous decision to recommend Yusuf's succession included a rider that he should take such an oath.[2] The oath was accordingly taken at his installation in May 1887.[3]

the state regalia was in England; and that Raja Idris went to England (the year of his visit is mistakenly given as 1886) in order to bring it back to instal Yusuf (Letter from Raja Razman, cited in Kamaruddin Ariff, 'Raja Idris, 1849–1916', B.A. Honours dissertation, University of Malaya, 1953, p. 60). Of course, Raja Idris visited England in 1884, and Yusuf's elevation did not take place for another two years. His installation took place in May 1887.

[1] Cowan suggests that he was recognized by the majority of the chiefs at some time before 1876 (Cowan, op. cit. p. 68, note 82). It is hard to imagine how this could have happened, since the loyalty of the chiefs was divided between 'Abdu'llah and Ismail till the end of 1875, and in any case they all detested Yusuf.

[2] Minutes of State Council, 7 October 1886, enclosed in Weld to Stanhope, 30 October 1886, C.4958, no. 20.

[3] 'I, Sultan Yusuf, Sultan and Iang-de-pertuan of Perak do solemnly promise and swear that I will truly and faithfully rule my Kingdom of Perak in accordance with law and the established order of Government under the protection of Her

The same Council that approved the accession of Yusuf recommended that Idris be made Raja Muda, and the next year, on Yusuf's death, Raja Idris succeeded him.[1] Once more, the throne was occupied by a man who had been outstanding in his support of British policies since he signed the letter of invitation to the British in 1875, asking them to govern Perak. Though not in the direct line of succession according to the Perak custom of rotation,[2] he was sufficiently eligible, as great-grandson of one Sultan, nephew of another, and son of a Bendahara. Clifford has left a picture of Idris in the fullness of his years and prestige, when he and other Malay dignitaries visited England in 1902 for the coronation of Edward VII. Clifford's anecdotes are mostly concerned to display the Sultan as a 'loyal and enthusiastic imperialist', but he also conveys something of Idris' intelligence, gravity, piety, and thoughtful interest in his surroundings, and one may believe that when British administrators expressed admiration for 'the clean mind, the keen intelligence, and the kind heart of Sultan Idris of Perak' they were not being merely conventional.[3] The Malays and Chinese on the Council welcomed his accession with a cordiality which had been absent in the recommendation of his father-in-law. With his accession, the unseemly spectacle of the chief Malay authority kept in semi-public restraint by the Resident came to an end, and was replaced by a picture of respectful 'advice' on the part of the Resident, and dignified royal condescension and conscientiousness on the part of the Ruler, which came close to the ideal of a constitutional monarchy. This picture took shape over a long reign of nearly thirty years,.during which Sultan Idris became the senior Ruler in point of experience, honours and wealth, of all the Rulers of the four protected states; but the background for it was filled in during his tutelage under Low.[4] Like his father-in-law, Idris

---

Most Gracious Majesty the Queen of England and Empress of India. I swear this in the presence of Almighty God' (Seal of his Highness the Sultan, witnessed by Hugh Low, 11 May 1887, enclosed in Dickson to Holland, 224 of 25 May 1887, CO 273/145). Sultan Idris signed a similar oath during his installation in 1889. Resident to Acting CS, 6 April 1889, enclosed in Smith to Knutsford, 176 of 15 April 1889, CO 273/159.

[1] Yusuf died on 28 July 1887. Sultan Idris was installed on 5 April 1889.

[2] Idris' accession virtually put an end to this tradition. Since his death in 1916, all the Perak Sultans except one have been his own descendants.

[3] Clifford, *Bushwhacking*, pp. 216–22.

[4] He was about twenty-eight when Low came to Perak. Low was then fifty-three, an old man according to Malay reckoning, and the relationship of parent or teacher would have been a natural one for him to adopt, and would have taken much of the sting out of the control he was obliged to exercise.

was a realist, and never wavered from his support of the Resident. But unlike Yusuf, he was pliable and anxious to please, and to learn.[1] His house was Europeanized, a smaller copy of the Residency—'*Trop de luxe et pas assez de confort*', as one visitor remarked.[2] He was interested in events outside Perak; he had visited England in 1884, learnt a little English and for a time employed an English tutor. His gestures were enlightened; he had freed his slaves unconditionally before manumission became general in Perak.[3]

During Birch's Residency, Raja Idris had compromised himself somewhat by his association with 'Abdu'llah, but he had made up for this by his co-operation with the British after Jervois' visit in September 1875. The elevation of his father-in-law to the position of Regent brought him further into prominence. But he was still a poor young raja looking for a berth, and dependent on Low's goodwill and good opinion.[4] Low had used Idris as a moderating influence on Yusuf,[5] and he and his father-in-law between them provided the Resident with a loyal majority at the meetings of the Perak State Council. Idris' loyalty to the British was finally demonstrated at a *Hari Raya* feast in 1885, when he made a speech 'in the name of the Regent and the people of Perak', saying that 'they had now been for ten years under the government of British officers and they wished to continue under that government and to have no other'.[6]

[1] St. Pol Lias, who visited Perak in 1880, described him as pliant and intelligent, able to understand the ideas of others, though having none of his own (B. de St. Pol Lias, *Pérak et les Orang Sakèys*, p. 177). Isabella Bird, who met him in 1879, described him as 'a very bright intelligent-looking young Malay . . . a dandy almost, in white trousers, short red sarong, black baju with gold buttons, gold watch guard and a red headdress. The expression of his face was keen and slightly scornful', Bird, *The Golden Chersonese*, p. 320.

[2] St. Pol Lias, op. cit. p. 157. Isabella Bird contrasted it unfavourably with the perfect Malay taste of the Dato' Bandar's house in Sungei Ujong. Bird, op. cit. p. 414.

[3] *PCM*, 10 October 1882, Swettenham recounts a case in which someone was accused of keeping a '*bajang*' (familiar). Idris offered to punish it if it could be produced. Swettenham, op. cit. p. 141.

[4] 'Raja Dris said he wants to serve the Gov[ernmen]t faithfully and would take no money for his services, but that if I found he deserved it he hoped I would ultimately recommend him to Gov[ernmen]t for H.E's private notice—this means payment of all arrears of salary and a good berth to be provided for him, and if he behaves well, he may deserve this. . . .They are working for the Raja Muda to be made Sultan and Dris his right [hand] man, Raja Muda or Bendahara.' Low Journal, p. 81.

[5] Yusuf and Idris tried at first to exclude all other Malays from the State Council, but gave in gracefully and approved Low's list.

[6] Acting Resident to CS, 16 July 1885, enclosed in Smith to Derby, 298 of 31 July 1885, CO 273/135. Raja Idris went on to say that 'they had first regarded the

For the years of Idris' Sultanate no records as revealing as Low's journal or the earlier council minutes have come to light, and it is impossible to penetrate the veil of official discretion which surrounds his dealings with the Resident. Perhaps the very existence of such a veil is evidence of the Sultan's own seemliness of conduct, his approximation to the ideal of enlightened royal behaviour under 'advice'; perhaps it is also evidence of an increasing sophistication in official utterances on Malay affairs. The impression gained from stray references and from the brief council minutes from 1889-95 is of an enhancement of prestige and natural authority which may be explained partly by his character and development, partly by his accession as Sultan, and partly by the retirement of his old mentor, Hugh Low. As recorded in the minutes, the Sultan's intervention was occasional and limited to a small range of subjects—Malay pensions and allowances, penghulu appointments and salaries, and Muslim marriage and divorce—but within that range it was effective in a way that had no precedent during Low's Residency; though it must be added that, as recorded, Sultan Idris over-rode the recommendations of British officers on only two occasions.[1]

In Selangor, the assumption of executive authority by the Resident (especially by a Resident who did not know Tengku Zia'u'd-din) left the Tengku with little to do except perform formal duties which could just as well be carried out by the Sultan and the Raja Muda.[2] The

British officers and British laws and customs with doubt and suspicion, but that Sir Hugh Low's administration had shewn them the change was a real gain to them'.

[1] In 1890, he blocked a proposal by the Magistrate of Kuala Kangsar that assistant penghuluships in that district be abolished, and the money used to produce the services of qualified Malay clerks to collect the land revenue. His Highness thought that the services of assistant penghulus should not be dispensed with except for gross neglect, and not even for neglect if it arose out of ignorance (*PCM*, 2 October 1890, *PGG*, 21 November 1890). Two months later, in the face of criticism from the Governor, he insisted, successfully, that increases in allowances to Malays, passed at the previous meeting of Council, should stand (*PCM*, 22 December 1890, *PGG*, 20 January 1891). On the other hand there was an occasion when the Council modified a proposal by the Sultan for transfer of a penghulu. *PCM*, 19 December 1891, *PGG*, 30 March 1892.

[2] Swettenham noted that the Tengku's position as Viceroy 'seems quite an anomaly now, whatever it was originally', and that his appointment was 'not desired by the Sultan, by his sons, by the chiefs or indeed by the Viceroy himself' (Swettenham, Memorandum on the proposed retirement and pension of Tunku Dia Udin, Viceroy of Selangor, 8 May 1878, enclosure in Robinson to Hicks Beach, 177 of 18 June 1878, CO 273/94). This assessment should be set against the charge made in 1882, that Douglas drove the Tengku out of Selangor. Innes to Kimberley, 2 May 1882, CO 273/117.

Tengku accordingly retired on a handsome pension and gratuity, and the Sultan emerged at intervals from his retirement at Langat to preside over meetings of the State Council and to perform his other ceremonial and constitutional duties under 'advice'.

The personality of the old eccentric at Langat has attracted a succession of observers and historians. He must have been nearing seventy when the first Resident was appointed,[1] though he looked younger, and retained a good deal of his physical energy into extreme old age. Swettenham found him living on a mud bank by the Langat river. There he had survived the murderous politics of Selangor, assisted by a detachment and neutrality which were probably quite genuine and not merely assumed for self-protection. He clearly had preferences but no strong feelings on the subject of Selangor politics. Swettenham has given perhaps the best illustration of this indifference:

> The Sultan asked me about Perak and I told him. He asked particularly what sort of man Ismail was, and I felt that in drawing his character, his carelessness of the affairs of state or the good of Perak so long as he himself was undisturbed I was in great measure drawing the Sultan's own character. Indeed those sitting by could not restrain their laughter. There is however one immense difference between the men. The Sultan of Selangor has no pet advisers whose opinion he either asks or follows.[2]

His disinterest in active politics went with a shrewd humanity and informality, and a lively interest in the daily life of Langat. A visitor in 1892 has described his routine. It was his practice to rise late, appearing at about four in the afternoon; then after a meal he used to go for a walk, barefoot, in simple dress and carrying a *parang*. As he walked, Malays meeting him by the roadside squatted in homage. After making a round of Malay and Chinese shops in the village, where he discussed the price of rice and opium, he returned home just before dark, and from then till the small hours, any subject who wished might see him with the minimum of etiquette.[3] Mrs. Innes (whose husband was Collector and Magistrate at Langat in the late 1870's) has described how during her walks round the village, she used to come across the Sultan seated astride a carpenter's bench, or squatting on the ground amid a crowd of dirty followers, watching

---

[1] According to a minute summarizing a letter from his successor, Sultan Sulaiman, Sultan 'Abdu'l Samad was ninety-three when he died in 1898. Minute on a letter from Sultan Sulaiman to the Governor, 6 March 1898, Sel/Sec. 182A/1898.

[2] Cowan, op. cit. p. 114.

[3] Anonymous, 'Sultan Abdul Samad', *Selangor Journal*, 23 September 1892.

a cock-fight. Clad in nothing but 'a very scanty little cotton kilt, or a pair of still scantier bathing-drawers', he was at first sight 'hardly distinguishable from an old Malay peasant'.[1] But she adds: 'Although his appearance was by no means majestic, and when skipping about in the bazaar among the carpenters he might seem to be a little wanting in oriental calm and dignity, he could assume both to perfection when he chose. I was present once on the homage-day, when all his subjects, rajas included, came crawling to kiss his hand. None of them dared approach him without grovelling on the ground. . . .'[2] As time went on, she and her husband grew to have 'not only a feeling of warm friendship, but even of respect for him', for he was invariably kind to them, and, she thought, to everybody.[3]

Swettenham appeared to get on well with him, and so did Innes, but he could be very nervous in the presence of strange Europeans. In 1892 a visitor to Langat describes an interview with him, in the company of the Resident: 'He laughed a good deal, and not always in the right place; for instance, when he heard that the Resident was leaving Selangor at the end of the year he laughed heartily, and then said his heart was very sore to hear it. And when he was told how much the Pahang war was costing the State, he laughed immoderately. Most people think that it is nothing to laugh at!'[4] His conversation with the Resident, as reported, hardly seems more intelligent: 'He seemed very interested in all the Resident talked to him about, his chief reply being "Ah, banyak bagus!" [excellent, very good].'

The complaisance of the Sultan, attested in a score of encounters,[5]

---

[1] E. Innes, *The Chersonese with the Gilding Off*, London, 1885, vol. i, pp. 38–39. Douglas describes one occasion when he discussed the matter of a pension for the Dato' Kaya with the Sultan, and was told it was 'unwise to encourage people to be idle . . . .' '. . .this remark came with considerable force as the Sultan was up to his knees in mud in a paddy field at Bandar Langat with his people around him getting in his paddy'. Resident to CS, 12 March 1879, Sel/Sec. 104/79.

[2] Innes, op. cit. p. 43. She spoils the story somewhat by saying that it was the first homage-day that he was not afraid for his life.

[3] Ibid. p. 40. Isabella Bird had the same favourable opinion. 'If Abdulsamat were not sultan, I should pick him out as the most prepossessing Malay that I have seen. He is an elderly man, with iron-gray hair, a high and prominent brow, large, prominent, dark eyes, a well-formed nose, and a good mouth. His face is bright, kindly, and fairly intelligent'. Bird, op. cit. p. 231.

[4] 'An Intercepted Letter', by 'Laetitia', Kuala Lumpur, 30 August 1892, *Selangor Journal*, 23 September 1892.

[5] 'It is difficult to lay any stress on any authority, especially verbal authority, of the Sultan's, for it is well-known in Selangor that he almost invariably says

was much abused at first by British officials in Selangor. Between 1879 and 1882, there were frequent deductions from his allowance for works at Langat which were properly the responsibility of the state, and goods of European manufacture which were pressed on him by the subordinate European officers. The articles provided included a gold watch and chain, a complete set of wine glassware, a pony and carriage, a gun, pictures of the Royal Family (which the Collector at Langat, Turney, thought would make the Istana look handsome) and a piano. The Acting Governor learnt of these deductions through 'native sources' and prohibited them for the future, but they still continued. The Resident argued in his own defence, 'It is absurd to say the Sultan did not wish for table equipage, furniture, wines and those things natives of the higher classes now provide for the entertainment of European visitors; has the Sultan to remain in the same barbarous state I found him in in 1875?' According to a former Collector, however, the Sultan had declared 'that he had never fired an English gun in his life nor wished to fire one; that he preferred walking to driving, and eating with his fingers, according to Malay custom, to the use of forks; that wine was forbidden by the Koran and that he did not know how to play the piano'.[1] After Douglas had been summoned to Singapore to await the results of an inquiry into this scandal—a move which the Governor considered necessary since he would otherwise be able to make the Sultan say whatever he wished[2]—letters arrived for him from the Sultan and his son, Raja Kahar, expressing complete confidence in him, regret at his departure, and testifying that all the goods were provided at the Sultan's own request. Unfortunately for the Resident, there arrived at the same time a letter from a Langat raja to the government Malay teacher in Singapore, saying that the Sultan had been forced to write this letter by the Collector at Langat, and asking that Swettenham (then Assistant Colonial Secretary) be informed.[3] Sultan 'Abdu'l Samad was able to make his situation known indirectly,

---

"yes" to every thing and everybody.' Swettenham, Memorandum on the proposed retirement of Tunku Dia Udin, 8 May 1878, enclosure in Robinson to Hicks Beach, 177 of 18 June 1878, CO 273/94.

[1] Innes to Kimberley, 2 May 1882, CO 273/117; Weld to Kimberley, Confidential of 24 August 1882 and enclosures, CO 273/115. Not all Western observers shared Douglas' opinion of the Sultan's taste. In 1879, Isabella Bird described his new house in Jugra as 'in the purest style of Malay architecture . . . simple, appropriate, and beautiful'. Bird. op. cit. p. 230.

[2] Weld to Kimberley, Confidential of 24 August 1882, CO 273/115.

[3] Weld to Kimberley, 327 of 6 September 1882, and enclosures, CO 273/116.

especially since there was someone influential in Singapore whom he knew and trusted; but the one thing he did not attempt was a direct opposition to the will of the British officers.[1] The continued exploitation of the Sultan, even after the directive of the Acting Governor in 1880, was exposed not through any complaint of his, but through the revelations of a retired officer of the Selangor Government with an axe to grind.

The Residents and Governors occasionally quoted the Sultans to support arguments against a line of action which they themselves disapproved, but it may be doubted whether these representations were always genuine.[2] On one occasion the Governor and the Resident gave conflicting accounts of what the Sultan was supposed to have wanted; Weld, in an attempt to persuade the Secretary of State to grant Douglas a pension or at least a gratuity on his enforced resignation, asserted that it was what the Sultan would have wished; and after the Secretary of State had agreed to a gratuity of $3,000, Swettenham, who succeeded Douglas as Resident, complained that the state had been overcharged and implied that the Sultan was displeased.[3] 'Can't pretend advice', was Swettenham's comment in his private diary.[4] Treacher, when citing examples of the acumen and independence of mind of the Sultans, referred to the two subjects— legalized gambling and the registration of prostitutes—concerning which the Residents had been in sharp conflict with the Secretary of State, neither of which were of any immediate interest to the Malays.[5] Sultan Idris' protest against interference with the gambling

[1] When Weld asked him why he had not complained about the Resident, and reminded him that he had been asked to say if anything happened that displeased him, he replied that he was not a man to make complaints. Weld to Kimberley, 390 of 27 October 1882, CO 273/116.

[2] Maxwell referred to the tendency of Residents to 'put their own arguments into the mouths of Malay Sultans' and make stalking-horses of them. Memorandum on Federation, 20 March 1895, CO 273/211.

[3] Weld to Kimberley, Confidential of 24 August 1882, and Kimberley to Weld, 304 of 9 December 1882, CO 273/115; Weld to Kimberley, 107 of 17 March 1883 and enclosure, CO 273/119. Weld tried to put the blame on the Secretary of State for allowing such a large gratuity, but as the latter was not slow to point out, Weld had tried to secure the grant of a pension, which would have borne even more heavily on the state. The whole incident demonstrates the freedom with which the Governor and the Secretary of State disposed of state funds, without consulting the Ruler or the State Council, though occasional genuflections were made in their direction.

[4] Swettenham's 1883 Diary, entry for 1 March.

[5] Discussion on Clifford's paper, 'Life in the Malay Peninsula', PRCI, vol. xxx (1898-9).

laws of the state (a rare instance of an official protest by a Ruler against British policy) does appear to have been genuine,[1] but there can be no doubt that he was encouraged to express it by Swettenham, who felt even more strongly on the subject, and who had discussed the matter with him just before his letter was written.

The Sultan of Selangor, in a realistic appraisal of his own position, once told Weld that he did not trouble himself with administration but left all that to the Resident and the Governor;[2] and this was a fair assessment of the position in the other states as well. The Residents controlled not only the European administration but also, through the district officers, the Malay penghulu establishment. The legislative bodies, the State Councils, were their instruments. The Rulers had no place in the executive chain of command, and in Perak and Selangor they lived away from the main centres of population, of administration and of economic activity. Though they presided over the State Councils, they had next to no initiative in legislation, and though they might succeed in modifying or delaying a course of action, the initiative in policy-making lay with the Resident.

This picture admitted some variation. Tengku Mahmud in Pahang and Raja Idris in Perak took an important part in judicial administration; before he became Sultan, Raja Idris held the office of 'Chief Judge' of Perak, and even after he became Sultan he continued for some time to 'sit in court on all important cases' and take 'most of the native business of the State'.[3] In the face of evidence for the existence of a judicial system based on Straits procedures and Straits criminal law and operated mainly by British officers, at any rate above the penghulu level,[4] it is unlikely that Raja Idris enjoyed sole jurisdiction in ordinary civil or criminal cases, and the few references that exist indicate that he sat with European officers when hearing such cases.[5] But he probably had an independent jurisdiction in

---

[1] He was so angry that he did not go to see the Governor when the latter visited Perak (Mitchell to CO, private, filed with Mitchell to Ripon, Confidential of 8 February 1895, CO 273/202). It is notable that the dissatisfaction of the Sultan of Selangor with the Selangor-Sungei Ujong boundary award, formally expressed in Council (SCM 16 February 1885) was not given the same prominence.

[2] Weld to Kimberley, 390 of 27 October 1882, CO 273/116.

[3] AR Perak, 1888.

[4] For discussion of judicial administration see Chapter VIII.

[5] He sat with the Assistant Resident when hearing murder charges in the late 1870's (PCM, 24 October 1878, 18 December 1878 and 20 October 1879) and at one meeting of the State Council he submitted his notes on the trial of organizers

cases relating to Muslim law. This was in fact the sphere in which the Sultan was best able to take the initiative. He was by tradition '*berkhalifah*' (endowed with the authority of God's vice-regent on earth); he 'stood at the head of the religious law and was the court of final resort in all disputes regarding Moslem law and was the court of final resort in all disputes regarding Moslem custom'.[1] The treaties with the British also left this sphere of activity to the Malays; the appointment of *kathis* and the administration of the religious law was therefore, in theory at least, solely the concern of the Malay authorities, and although the Residents intervened occasionally in the matter of appointments and had the responsibility of general supervision of the whole judicial system, including the administration of the religious law, these subjects were left to the Ruler as much as possible. In Selangor, royal interest in these matters appears to have been erratic.[2] The appointment of kathis and the general administration of Muslim law were referred to the Sultan as a matter of course, but he occasionally referred them back to the Council (and so to the Resident). Raja Muda Musa was more active, but his death in 1884 left a vacuum in Malay leadership which was not filled until his son Raja Muda Sulaiman began to take the initiative in the 1890's.[3] Sultan Idris by contrast was the undisputed authority on this question. Legislation for registration of Muslim marriages and for the punishment of adultery was passed at his instance.[4] He was in charge of the establishment of kathis; appointments of *naib* (deputy) kathis were subject to his approval; appeals against the decisions of kathis were forwarded to him for his decision as to whether grounds existed for a rehearing; kathis were required by the terms of their commissions to consult him on questions involving

---

of the Red and White Flag secret societies, when he sat with the Superintendent of Lower Perak, one chief of the second rank, and one of the third. *PCM*, 19 October 1882.

[1] R. J. Wilkinson, 'Sri Menanti', *Papers on Malay Subjects*, 2nd Series, no. 2, p. 15.

[2] See Chapter VIII.

[3] See, e.g., SCM, 5 September 1895, when he proposed the appointment of a kathi and assistant kathis to hear Muslim cases, and submitted draft rules on the subject.

[4] *PCM*, 9 December 1891, *PGG*, 30 March 1892; *PCM*, 4 June 1894, *PGG*, 14 September 1894. In 1898 he presided over a meeting of rajas and chiefs to draw up a Muslim Code, with sections relating to attendance at Friday prayers, punishment for adultery and other sexual offences, and the teaching of Muslim doctrine. Minutes of a meeting at Bukit Chandan, 20 September 1898, Sel/Sec. 111/99.

Muslim law or Malay custom.[1] Problems of religious administration were referred to him by the district magistrates,[2] and he personally inquired into charges of misconduct against the Assistant Kathi of Lower Perak and reported the case in full to the State Council.[3]

So far as the general machinery of government was concerned, the function of the Ruler was to validate state documents by the addition of his seal,[4] to advise as to feeling among the Malays, to endorse reforms by his personal example, to provide a ceremonial focus for the government of the state, and to confirm the local standing of the Resident by formal and ceremonial association with him. The documents presented to the Sultan of Selangor for his 'chop' (seal) included state bonds,[5] leases,[6] commissions (*kuasas*) for members of Council, penghulus and kathis[7] and various notices and proclamations. It was necessary to ensure that the Ruler's seal was used only on documents which were authorized by the Resident.[8] The practice in other states is not known, but in Selangor, at any rate in the early years, the Sultan's seal-box was opened by two keys, one of which

[1] See Chapter VIII.

[2] The Assistant Supt., Lower Perak, finding nothing in the records as to the time allowed for appeals from the kathi's court in cases of inheritance and marital disagreement (*herta pesaka* and *gadoh laki bini*) wrote to the secretary to the Sultan to put the matter before His Highness. He was told to allow the same as in divorce cases—forty days. Raja Ahmad to Acting Supt., Lower Perak, 15 October 1890, and minute by Acting Supt., undated, Batang Padang Papers, 257/90.

[3] *PCM*, 30 November 1894, *PGG*, 28 December 1894. Two things about this incident strike one as noteworthy; first, the painstaking manner in which the Sultan prepared his report, and second, the development of the Ruler's authority in this sphere since 1879, when the Resident pushed through the appointment of his own nominee as Chief Kathi, against the wishes of the Regent.

[4] On Yusuf's death, the Assistant Resident suggested that Raja Idris at once be appointed Regent to carry on business, since there were several leases and other documents requiring signature, which could not be long delayed without inconvenience. Asst. Resident to Resident, 2 August 1887, enclosed in Weld to Holland, 341 of 20 August 1887, CO 273/146.

[5] Kuala Langat Journal, 2 and 3 June 1882.

[6] Ibid. 17 November and 1 December 1882.

[7] Commissions appointing Raja Hassan to the State Council in 1880 and the Capitan China Yap Ah Shak in 1885 were sealed and forwarded to the Resident (Sel/Sec. 172/80 and 1051/85). The commissions for the Imam of Klang and the Imam of Kuala Selangor were sealed by the Sultan (Sel/Sec. 100/80 and 45/80). In 1885, the Collector of Kuala Langat procured the Sultan's chop to the commission for the State Kathi. Kuala Langat Journal, 25 March 1885.

[8] Soon after his arrival, Low found that Raja Yusuf was issuing 'chops' (sealed documents) threatening people with punishment if they did not attend mosque on Friday and did not return to the villages which they had deserted during the Perak War. He let it be known that no chop which did not bear his own seal was to be regarded as binding. Low Journal, pp. 85, 97, 98.

was kept in the custody of the Collector and Magistrate at Kuala Langat;[1] an arrangement which the latter found very reassuring when people arrived at Langat to ask the Sultan for penghulu appointments or other favours.[2] The documents and notices to be sealed were prepared in the offices of the Resident and forwarded to the Sultan through the Collector at Langat; even the commissions for *imams* and kathis were prepared in this way, in Perak as well as Selangor.[3]

The occasions and achievements of the new régime, such as the opening of the State Council, and the completion of important sections of railway—were dignified by the presence of the Ruler, and the symbiosis was completed by the presence of British officers on specifically Malay occasions, such as elections and installations. The election of the Raja Muda, which took place at the Sultan's request, was organized with great ceremony by the Acting Resident (J. P. Rodger) at his office in Kuala Lumpur. After the election, Rodger, in Malay dress, entertained the chief Malays and the British officers to a Malay dinner at his house; he feasted them till they were like 'ants dead in sugar' ('*semut mati di-dalam gula*') and then sent them by train and government yacht back to their homes in Klang and Langat.[4] At the installations of Yusuf and Idris, a British element was incorporated in the form of the Sultan's oath, read by the Resident after the Malay ceremonies were completed. The programme included a military salute, the attendance of a guard of honour and a military band, and a dinner at the Istana attended by the leading

[1] Collector and Magistrate, Kuala Langat, to Resident, 28 June 1880 Sel/Sec. 172/80; also Kuala Langat Journal for 25 September 1882, suggesting that the seal-box be removed in its entirety to the Collector's care.

[2] 'I feel a daily satisfaction in having the Sultan's chop under lock and key', wrote the Collector when informed that someone was pressing the Sultan to make him a penghulu (Collector and Magistrate, Langat, to Resident, 8 April 1877, Sel/Sec. 121/77). Another supplicant tried to persuade the Sultan to give him a concession to work gharu wood, gutta and rattans, 'but luckily I have the Sultan's chop'. Collector to Resident, 14 March 1877, Sel/Sec. 89/77.

[3] E.g., a commission for the Imam of Klang was drafted in the Resident's office and sent to Langat to be sealed (Minute, undated, by Resident on letter from the Collector, Langat, 20 April 1880, Sel/Sec. 100/80). There is a minute in the Batang Padang district records to the effect that kuasas (commissions, powers of authority) for the Sultan's seal were usually prepared in the office of the Secretary to Government and sent to Kuala Kangsar to be sealed. Batang Padang Papers, 307/92.

[4] *Jawi Peranakkan*, vol. xi, no. 526, 18 April 1887. I am indebted for this reference to Dr. William R. Roff, Department of History, University of Malaya.

Malays and the British officers; and the popular entertainments included races, sports, and displays by the Perak Sikhs.[1]

The Sultan's state was maintained with the help of allowances and other perquisites, partly bribes for good behaviour, partly compensation for the denial of power.[2] The Sultan of Pahang, who had expressed his disapproval of British interference by retiring to a place fourteen days up river from Pekan, thus making the conduct of business extremely difficult, was given a large increase in his allowance (from $1,500 to $2,000 a month) in exchange for an authority to his son, Tengku Mahmud, to act for him.[3] The Regent of Perak began with $12,000 a year, rising to $15,000 after the abolition of slavery in Perak, and $18,000 when he became Sultan in 1886. The allowance of his successor was doubled in four years, with Low and Swettenham pressing for ever greater increases, and in 1894, when the Resident renewed his pressure, the Sultan was given an additional $12,000 a year for expenditure on alms.[4] The Resident of Perak earned $10,800 a year in 1894, with a house, an entertainment allowance of $1,200 and various other perquisites, so that a suitable distance was maintained between the Ruler and his adviser. The constitutional relations between the Resident and the Ruler thus developed very soon into the kind of relations a twentieth-century British Prime Minister might have with his sovereign. The Ruler continued to act as the ceremonial Head of State. The Ruler in Council was the source of legislative and executive authority and the final court of appeal. Instruments of government and documents of title bore his seal. Regulations and Orders in Council were issued in his name. But in fact the Ruler had little control over the contents of

[1] Resident to CS, 18 May 1887, enclosed in Dickson to Holland, 224 of 25 May 1887, CO 273/145; Resident to Acting CS, 6 April 1889, enclosed in Smith to Knutsford, 176 of 15 April 1889, CO 273/159.

[2] As the Governor put it, 'the policy of allowing the Rulers of the Protected Native States to benefit by the results of a stable and orderly government is one which will have a good moral effect. . . .' Smith to Knutsford, 188 of 13 May 1888, CO 273/127.

[3] Smith to Knutsford, 380 of 5 August 1889, CO 273/161.

[4] Ripon to Mitchell, Confidential of 6 December 1894, CO 273/198. The Colonial Office grew restive at these repeated applications, and pointed out that the Sultan of Selangor was then getting only $18,000 a year—only $6,000 more than in 1876 (Ripon to Maxwell, Confidential of 6 February 1894, CO 273/190). Fairfield remarked that the $50,000 recommended by Swettenham was as much as the salary of the President of the United States, and suggested that Swettenham was always trying to get the Sultan more money so that he would have his support in his own battles with the Colonial Office. Minute by Fairfield, 29 November 1894, on Mitchell to Ripon, Confidential of 30 October 1894, CO 273/198.

the documents he sealed. They were drawn up in the Resident's office and presented to him for formal ratification. Apart from his validating function, his share in government was confined to giving the Resident advice and information and helping him to measure feeling in the state. The provisions of the Pangkor Engagement were reversed in practice; instead of the Resident advising the Sultan, it was now the Sultan who advised the Resident.

THE STATE COUNCILS

The State Council[1] was an essential instrument of government under the Residential system. It provided a constitutional basis for the government of a protected state administered by British officers, but not directly under the Crown; the Council proceedings illuminate the relationship between the State and the Government of the Straits Settlements, providing an invaluable source for the study of the problems and procedures of government.

The appointment of an advisory body to assist British officers first appears in 1875 as part of Sir William Jervois' proposal that Perak should be governed by the British in the name of the Sultan.[2] The Council was to consist of British officers and five Malays of the blood-royal; three—Sultan 'Abdu'llah, ex-Sultan Ismail, and the Raja Bendahara Osman—whose claims or interests might be upset by the new dispensation, and who were to be solaced by places on the Council; and two—Rajas Yusuf and Idris—who had identified themselves with the British and who were to be the 'working members', helping the Commissioners with advice and information. The Council was conceived as a compensatory device, substituting a formal connexion with government for the powers the Malays had once enjoyed. Its functions were to be purely advisory; it was to assist the Commissioners by keeping them in touch with Malay feeling, it was to give the rajas an interest in the country's affairs by involving them in discussion, and in particular it was to consider questions of Muslim religion which were not formally protected under Jervois' arrangements. Matters on which the Malay members disagreed with the Commissioners were to be referred to the Governor.[3]

After Birch's murder, when policy in Perak came to be considered

[1] The main sources for this analysis are the Council minutes for Perak and Selangor. See Note on Sources, p. 415-17.
[2] Jervois to Carnarvon, 291 of 16 October 1875, C.1505, no. 49.
[3] Jervois to Carnarvon, 62 of 10 February 1876, CO 273/83.

in detail, the idea of a Malay Council was retained and developed. The Colonial Office suggested its extension to all the states, so that the principal chiefs in each state might be associated with the government, and enabled to maintain their prestige and influence, and so that the Residents might be able to gauge local feeling about proposed reforms. Jervois suggested the expansion of the Council to include Chinese headmen, and this was accepted, though with some misgiving, by the Colonial Office. In 1877 mixed Councils met for the first time in Selangor and Perak.[1] They were small, intimate committees of Malay chiefs, Chinese headmen and British administrators. The Perak Council began with eight members: four Malays, two Chinese and two Europeans; the Selangor Council with seven: four Malays, one Chinese and two Europeans.

Under Malay rule, the power of the Sultan had been limited by the obligation to consult the chiefs and *waris negeri*[2] on important matters of state; they met in assembly on ceremonial occasions, to attend on the Sultan; successions to the Sultanate, royal installations and treaties with foreign powers required their assent and witness. An assembly of waris and chiefs was convened at Pangkor in 1874 to elect a Sultan and accept a Resident; the Engagement was signed by three chiefs of the first rank and four of the second, as well as by the Sultan. In 1875 such assemblies were called in Perak whenever the Governor, the Resident or the Sultan wished for public discussion of the important new changes involved in British intervention.

The Councils under the Residential system bore little resemblance, in their composition and function, to the traditional Malay assemblies of chiefs. Jervois' original proposal had excluded the chiefs altogether; his later suggestion that the Chinese factions should be represented by their headmen, was in keeping with changed conditions, but as the Colonial Office saw, it was 'utterly at variance with the old Perak constitution'.[3] In 1876, however, there was little left of the old Perak constitution. The murder of the Resident had led to the exile of the Sultan (now ex-Sultan) 'Abdu'llah, the ex-Sultan Ismail and most of the major chiefs, leaving in Perak, Raja Muda Yusuf as the Regent; Raja Idris as his prospective successor; one

---

[1] Carnarvon to Jervois, 135 of 1 June 1876, C.1512, no. 70; Jervois to Carnarvon, 62 of 10 February 1876, CO 273/83; Jervois to Carnarvon, 88 of 22 March 1877, CO 273/90; Anson to Carnarvon, 201 of 23 June 1877, CO 273/91.

[2] *Waris negeri* (Perak): a term applied to the male descendants of a Sultan.

[3] Minute by Round, 30 July 1877, on Anson to Carnarvon, 201 of 23 June 1877, CO 273/91.

survivor—the Temenggong—of the four chiefs of the first rank, and one survivor—the Panglima Kinta—of the eight chiefs of the second rank.[1] The Council list which Jervois drew up for Low when he went to Perak as Resident in 1877, confined the Malay membership to these four but Low crossed off the Panglima Kinta, who had not been to see him for the three months after his arrival, and whose goodwill he doubted; so the opening Council consisted of three Malays, two British officials and two Chinese.[2] The nominal head of this heterogeneous body, Raja Muda Yusuf, was on bad terms with the Temenggong and did not want the Chinese representation; he would have liked a Council consisting of himself, his son-in-law Raja Idris and the Resident, but he was over-ruled.

As Malay chiefs came back into favour, and as the state grew in economic importance, more Malay title-holders, British officials and Chinese entrepreneurs were added to the Council, until in 1895 it consisted of twelve members—seven Malays, three Chinese and two British officers. The Perak orders of rank were in abeyance for most of this period; it was not till the 1890's that the titles of exiled or deceased chiefs were restored to their descendants, and Perak once again had a resident Laksamana, Sri Adika Raja, and Mentri.[3] Until the 1890's the Malay members, though connected with royal or chiefly families, did not for the most part hold important titles.[4]

[1] In 1877, of the four chiefs of the first rank, the Bendahara was dead; the Mentri was in exile; the office of the Orang Kaya Besar was vacant. Of the eight chiefs of the second rank, the Maharaja Lela and the Dato' Sagor had been hanged for their part in the murder of Birch; the Sri Adika Raja died in 1876, a fugitive from the British army of occupation; the Laksamana and the Shahbandar were in exile. The offices of the Panglima Bukit Gantang and the Imam Paduka Tuan were vacant.

[2] Anson to Carnarvon, 201 of 23 June 1877, CO 273/91. Low had replaced the Panglima Kinta with a Sumatran commoner, Che Karim b. Ibrahim, who had been sent to open up Selama in North Perak as the agent of the Mentri and had achieved a degree of independence during the disturbances of 1875–6. Low thought perhaps that Che Karim's commercial initiative would be useful on the Council, but Che Karim kept away from Council meetings, possibly because of the difference in rank between himself and the other Malay members, and in 1880 his name was dropped from the lists.

[3] A successor to the Laksamana (a cousin) was appointed in 1891; a successor to the Sri Adika Raja (his son) in the same year; a successor to the Mentri (his son) in 1896. The new Laksamana was already on the Council as Raja Mahkota when he was raised to the title; on his death in 1894 a successor was appointed both to the title and to the Council. The new Sri Adika Raja was appointed to the Council in 1894, and the new Mentri in 1896.

[4] The five Malay members added between 1877 and 1894 (the first two of whom died soon after appointment) were the Panglima Besar (1879), the holder of the

The only title-holder of the second rank resident in Perak before 1891—the Panglima Kinta, was not made a Councillor till about 1884. No one of royal birth was added to the Council till the appointment of Raja Musa, the brother of ex-Sultan 'Abdu'llah, in 1894.

The absence of royal members (apart from Rajas Yusuf and Idris) for most of the period, the paucity of title-holders and the exclusion of the Panglima Kinta, go to show how much Perak was overshadowed by the upheaval of 1875-7, how difficult it was to reconcile considerations of security and support for Yusuf and Idris, on the one hand, with a genuine representation of influential Malays on the other. Within a certain range of influence, Malay members were chosen, as one would expect, in the order of their political reliability and not in order of rank; though in the last years of the period, a correspondence was again established between Council membership and the possession of titles.

In Selangor the situation was different in two respects. First, there was no established hierarchy of titleholders, and the control of the districts was in the hands of various members of the royal house. Second, the Residential system had been established without disturbance; opposition had been to the British protégé and not to the British Resident. There was only one dissident raja of importance—Raja Mahdi, in exile in Singapore; others, though originally disaffected and under suspicion, were either sheltered by their friendship with the Sultan, or had won their way back into favour by fighting for the British in the Perak disturbances. Representation of the influential Malays was achieved simply by appointing members of the royal family to the Council. In 1877 the Malay members were; Tengku Zia'u'd-din, the Sultan's son-in-law, as President; Syed Zin, the Tengku's chief agent; Raja Kahar, a son of the Sultan; and Tengku Panglima Raja, a brother-in-law of the Sultan. At the end of 1877, Tengku Zia'u'd-din left Selangor and was replaced as President of Council by the Raja Muda Musa, the eldest son of the Sultan, and the heir to the throne. The five Malays appointed to the

---

chief military title; Shaikh Mohammed Taib (1879), a Sumatran ulama who was connected by marriage with Sultan 'Abdu'llah's family, but who held no title; the Raja Mahkota (1880), a chief of the third rank, appointed Laksamana in 1891; the Panglima Kinta, a chief of the second rank; and Dato' Muda 'Abdu'l Wahab (1886), a subordinate Kinta chief. The Panglima Kinta is mentioned in the *AR* for 1884 as a State Councillor, but the title does not appear in the list of members in the council minutes for 1877-82, nor does it appear in the State Directory before 1886.

Council in subsequent years were all members of the royal house.[1]

The Council was the governing body of a Malay state, and Malays sat on it as state officers—as heirs to the inheritance. Official position was the bulwark of their authority, and membership of the State Council was one form of recognition of their official consequence. Council appointments therefore provided a means of honouring those whom it was expedient or safe or desirable for other reasons to honour and reassure, as well as a means of getting authoritative opinion onto the Council, and the two considerations were not always in harmony. Though councillors were valued for their influence and their capacity for representing opinion, they were not representative of the distribution of influence in the community generally. The considerations affecting the choice of Perak councillors have already been discussed. In Selangor the limitation of membership to the Bugis royal house left out of account large communities of Sumatran immigrants who had been attracted by the development of the mines, who were engaged in trade and were of some economic importance.

The Chinese sat on the Council as accredited representatives of a great foreign community, and more important, as representatives of the most important industry and the one which contributed most to the revenues. They did not hold office in the state, and though access to the source of power was no doubt always gratifying and had its material uses, Council membership did not have the same significance for them as a token of personal status. Chinese representation therefore had a utilitarian aspect; the Residents were concerned, not to distribute compensatory honours, but to get a practical representation of wealth and communal authority onto the Council. The British appointed as Chinese members the leaders chosen by the Chinese community.[2] In Perak, the two Chinese members first ap-

---

[1] They were, in order of appointment, Raja Hassan b. Raja 'Abdu'llah of Klang (1880); Raja Laut b. Sultan Mohammed (1881); Raja Sulaiman b. Raja Juma'at of Lukut (1888). The fifth member was the Sultan himself. The first President was Tengku Zia'u'd-din, but in 1877 he left Selangor. In 1879 the Sultan is recorded as attending Council meetings informally, and in 1883, after Swettenham's appointment as Resident, he began to preside over them whenever they were held in Langat. At a meeting on 7 August 1893, it was announced that the Sultan had appointed the Resident to represent him on all occasions when he was unavoidably absent. The meeting on 10 April 1894 appears to have been the last he attended.

[2] The word 'community' is here used in a general sense, to embrace those of Chinese nationality, and is not intended to indicate a unity of organization.

pointed were Chung Keng Kwee and Chin Ah Yam, who had been the acknowledged headmen of the Hai San and Ghi Hin secret societies for years before British intervention, and who had signed a separate Chinese Engagement at Pangkor in January 1874 undertaking to cease fighting. In Selangor the Chinese member from 1877–85 was the Capitan China, Yap Ah Loy. On his death in 1885, he was succeeded as Capitan China and State Councillor by Yap Ah Shak, a fellow clansman and the candidate put forward by the Hakkas and Teochiews as the successor to Yap Ah Loy. In 1889 the Cantonese leader Cheow Ah Yeok was appointed as well. All these were secret society headmen,[1] but as secret societies were illegal in Perak and Selangor, they were known, innocuously, as headmen of regional subdivisions of the Chinese community, grouped according to their place of origin in China.

Who these men represented, how they came to power, what challenges there were to their leadership within their communities, one does not know; the internal organization of the Chinese in the nineteenth century still awaits investigation. Middlebrook's study of Yap Ah Loy tells us what might be expected about leadership in a frontier mining society; those who came to power were enterprising, ruthless, and with sufficient political judgment to make useful connexions. 'The leaders of these Chinese immigrants were thrown up by the test of personal courage and force of character combined with economic success . . . this "*élite*" provided the economic and military leadership, exercising authority partly through the clan or society system.'[2] The headmen were leaders of the mining community; they were the chief advancers, the employers of labour and the tax farmers; and on the Council they represented an industry as well as a social group, and were valued accordingly.

Members of Council were appointed during the pleasure of the Sultan; in effect, for life. They were appointed by the Sultan, after their names had been approved by the Governor.[3] The evidence is

[1] In a report drawn up on the secret societies in the Malay states, by the Acting Protector of Chinese, Straits Settlements, one 'Chhiu Yok', a 'Macao' Chinese (Cantonese) is given as headman of the 'Gi-Hin kongsi in Klang', and 'Yap Shak' as headman of the Hai San kongsi there. Powell to CS, 26 May 1884, CSO Perak Correspondence 3574/1884, cited M. L. Wynne, *Triad and Tabut*, Singapore, 1941, pp. 409–13.

[2] S. M. Middlebrook and J. M. Gullick, 'Yap Ah Loy', *JMBRAS*, vol. xxiv, part 2 (1951), p. 8.

[3] Till 1885 the names of candidates were also submitted to the Secretary of State, but in that year he notified the Governor that his sanction was not re-

that they were nominated by the Resident, though the likelihood is that the choice was made in consultation with the Sultan. No appointments to the Perak State Council are likely to have been suggested by Raja Yusuf. The original list of members was drawn up in Singapore and communicated to Yusuf by Low early in 1877. Both Yusuf and Idris were opposed to the appointment of any but themselves and the British Resident.[1] Shaikh Mohammed Taib, appointed in 1879, had earned their particular dislike, and Raja Yusuf tried unsuccessfully to block his appointment as State Kathi the same year.[2] The appointments to the Selangor Council were much more likely to have been in keeping with the Sultan's own inclinations, as they were nearly all appointments of his relatives, but in one case, and perhaps in others, the Sultan merely confirmed the Resident's candidate.[3] The suspension of the Tengku Panglima Raja in 1878 illustrates the control exercised by the Resident and Governor over the Council, and particularly over the appointments. A resolution that he be deposed was put to the Council on 1 May 1878 by one of the British members, was carried unanimously and received the Sultan's assent. The Governor disapproved of this high-handed punishment of an important officer of state, for what was in Malay eyes a venial offence; the Resident was ordered to reinstate him, and on 25 May, the Council voted unanimously for his return.

The Councils met, on an average, about seven times a year, though the frequency and regularity varied, from the single meeting of the Selangor Council in 1883, to the dozen or so Councils held by Low in Perak every year from 1877 to 1882. The choice of Council meet-

---

quired, though appointments should continue to be submitted to him. Stanley to Smith, 37 of 23 July 1885, CO 273/134.

[1] Low Journal, pp. 80–81.

[2] *PCM*, 4 March 1879 and 4 May 1879. Shaikh Mohammed Taib was Low's candidate for the position of Chief Kathi, and was appointed despite Yusuf's objections. The discussion illustrates Low's handling of the Regent, the Regent's dependence on Low, and the freedom with which a strong and adroit Resident might encroach on matters which the Pangkor Engagement excluded from his competence.

[3] 'I inform my friend that my friend's letter written on the 8th September 1888 has reached me in safety. . . . Previous to the present letter I now write, I had already confirmed the proposal of my friend to make Raja Bot a member of Council, which I did with a true and sincere heart, as I do not see a more qualified person than Raja Bot whom my friend has made a member of Council. I am very much pleased with this arrangement and beg to thank my friend for the same.' Office translation of a letter from the Sultan of Selangor to F. A. Swettenham, 13 September 1888, Sel/Sec. 2649/1888.

ing-place, and the resulting pattern of attendance, reflected the different preoccupations of the Residents in Perak and Selangor. In both
states, the Residents were concerned with the interests of the Malay
population, as well as with economic progress outside the Malay
sphere; but the Malays predominated in Perak, the Chinese in Selangor; Perak had a history of Malay resistance to the Resident, Selangor had none. In Perak the Residency in the 1880's was at Kuala
Kangsar, in the heart of Malay Perak, yet only twenty-three miles
from Taiping. Raja Yusuf established himself at Sayong, on the opposite bank of the Perak river; Raja Idris lived at Kuala Kangsar,
and the Temenggong's place was at Kota Lama, about two miles
up-stream. The Resident therefore lived in close proximity to the
senior Malay members of the Council, and since the Council meetings
took place, as a rule, at Kuala Kangsar, there was a regular Malay
attendance, particularly of the senior Malay members; with the Resident they constituted an Executive Committee (so called in the minutes) which sometimes met instead of the full Council to deal with
routine business. But the frequency of Malay attendance in Perak is
not accounted for by geographical proximity, for Malays from the
south of Perak attended regularly at the Kuala Kangsar meetings,
while in Selangor, where distances and travelling times were much
shorter, members attended regularly only at meetings held near their
place of residence. The difference relates probably to the greater preoccupation of the Resident of Perak with Malay affairs; he was the
better able to devote time to them since he had a senior officer
stationed at Larut, in the midst of the Chinese population. In Perak
also the meetings of the Council had been invested with great prestige and ceremony from the earliest years. St. Pol Lias describes a
grand opening in 1880; the British officials waited to receive Raja
Yusuf in the Residency grounds, 200 Sikh police in full dress uniform
were drawn up for inspection, the band played, the guns saluted.[1]
Since the Resident—in the formative years of Perak, Hugh Low—
was the source and the originator of policy, it may be concluded
that the prestige of the Perak Council, the prominence of the Malays
and the consistency of their attendance, were due to his solicitude
and management.

In Selangor the Residency was first at Klang, then at Kuala Lumpur, while the Sultan remained at Langat, so that the Council met
on different occasions at Klang, Langat and Kuala Lumpur. Up to

[1] St. Pol Lias, op. cit. p. 176.

1887 the majority of Council meetings were held at Langat, in the Sultan's palace; after that, at Kuala Lumpur, which the Sultan hardly ever visited. Since the majority of Malay members lived at Langat or Klang, Malay attendance was fullest when the Council met in either of these places; when it shifted to Kuala Lumpur, the Malay attendance usually fell to low levels. At a third of the meetings held in Kuala Lumpur, only one Malay was present, usually Raja Laut, the Malay Magistrate there.

It was acknowledged that a large part of the Council business would not interest the Chinese population, and a separate Chinese Council at Larut (for the Perak Chinese) was once considered.[1] The idea was not pursued, and matters relating to the production and taxation of tin, the lease of the state tax farms and the regulation of labour—which after all were matters of interest to the Malays as well—continued to be discussed at general meetings. But when Councils were held at a distance from Chinese centres, attempts were made to arrange the business so that matters wholly concerning the Malay population could be disposed of without requiring the attendance of the Chinese members. The meeting of the Perak Council for 4 February 1878, concerned entirely with the appointment of penghulus and the determination of their jurisdiction, notes the absence of the Chinese members 'as it is their New Year and the proceedings concern[ed] only the Malay population'.[2] Chinese attendance was reasonably regular in Perak in the first half of the period, when Low was Resident, and in Selangor in the second half, when meetings were usually held in Kuala Lumpur. But this separation was not always possible, and the business at many of the meetings could have been of little interest to the Chinese Councillors. At one meeting in Kuala Kangsar in 1890, attended dutifully by two Chinese members, the seventeen items of business comprised twelve Malay pension applications, three items of penghulu business and two Orders in Council—one regulating the sale of poisons and the other making provision for the better preservation of oysters in the Perak river. Administrative detail and petty legislation could hardly have seemed worth the journey from Larut.

The powers and functions of the State Councils, like most other aspects of government in the Malay states, were established by practice and not by proclamation. The Council was first conceived as an

[1] Robinson to Hicks Beach, 268 of 10 September 1878.
[2] PCM, 4 February 1878.

advisory body, but from the beginning it fulfilled other functions. It was the sole legislating body; legislation took the form of Orders or Regulations passed by 'the Sultan in Council'. It was the final court of appeal; death sentences required its ratification and the Sultan's warrant before they could be carried out, since the power of life and death, according to Malay theory, was a royal prerogative. The Council was the chief executive body: changes in the tariff structure, Malay pensions and appointments, the jurisdiction and discipline of headmen and all other matters pertaining to local government, the appointment of kathis and the administration of Muslim personal law, were all dealt with by resolutions in Council.

The competence of the Council was limited by the final authority of the Governor and the Secretary of State. Two matters of importance were outside its range altogether; the annual Estimates were prepared by the Resident for ratification by the Governor, and in Perak were not submitted to the Council at all; in Selangor they were submitted occasionally (after sanction by the Governor) and were passed unanimously. It is clear from this that their submission was intended to provide the Council with information and not with an opportunity for debate or amendment. The non-Malay establishment was also outside the Council's competence, although pensions and gratuities for non-Malay, non-European subordinates were sometimes discussed.

The Governor, sometimes acting on his own initiative, sometimes under instruction from the Secretary of State, had the power to disallow or compel legislation and executive action. The Council minutes were forwarded to Singapore, and were not acted on till they had been approved by the Governor.[1] There was thus at least a retrospective check on legislation. Legislation of importance was submitted to him in draft before introduction in Council, and about 1892 this appears to have become the standard practice for all legislation. But in earlier years at any rate, there are instances of legislation submitted for the Governor's sanction after passage through Council, and disallowed after receiving the assent of the Sultan.[2]

---

[1] E.g., the appointment of an assistant kathi and a penghulu, approved by the Perak State Council in September 1891, did not come into effect till the Council minutes had been approved by the Governor. Batang Padang papers, 134/92.

[2] E.g., a fussy regulation for the licensing of washermen was passed by the Selangor State Council on 20 January 1882 and received the assent of the Sultan; it was disallowed by the Governor as contrary to public policy and rescinded at the next meeting.

The Governor also directed the Council in its executive aspect. Matters relating to fiscal policy—tariff changes, and the lease of tax farms; allowances to Malays, pensions and gratuities to non-Malays at the lower levels of the civil service; land administration, particularly special agricultural and mining concessions; public works—these were some of the matters on which the Governor might instruct the Council through the Resident.[1]

Within the Council the initiative lay with the Resident, though the Regent or Sultan formally presided. 'The Resident under the orders of the Governor, as a rule conducts or at any rate prepares the business for each meeting, carries the measures and then advises the Sultan to assent to the minutes as a mere matter of form.'[2] The agenda was drawn up from a number of subjects; death sentences awaiting review, regulations awaiting sanction, the appointments and discipline of headmen, the award of pensions and allowances to chiefs and their dependents, revenue and land matters, and all kinds of miscellaneous business. The subjects introduced had for the most part been discussed by the Resident and his officers, or the Resident and the Straits Government; usually they had also been discussed informally with Malays or Chinese. The measures for tariff reform, Malay taxation and mining leases approved by the Perak State Council on 10 and 11 September 1877 were considered and planned by Low and referred to at length in his official diary during the previous months.[3]

The Resident's initiative extended to matters of primarily Malay interest, like the grant of allowances and the appointments and jurisdiction of headmen and kathis. The responsibility for supervising and disciplining penghulus in the districts lay with the European Collectors and Magistrates, who put forward candidates for appointments,[4] suggested improvements in administration, and reported cases of neglect or corruption. Both in Perak and in Selangor the Resident and his officers put forward candidates for appointments as kathis and made recommendations for the better administration

[1] Between 1877 and 1882, during Douglas' Residency, the Selangor Council Minutes are full of every sort of instruction from the Governor, e.g., SCM 22 April 1878, 25 October 1879, 21 April 1880, 20 January 1882.
[2] Resident of Selangor to CS, 27 December 1879, Sel/Sec. 390/79. The Resident went on to say, 'At present the opinion of the people in the country is not very favourable to the value or power of the Council, as they well understand how the measures are introduced and under what influence they are carried. . . .'
[3] Low Journal, pp. 37, 88–89, 92.
[4] See Chapter IX.

of Muslim personal law.[1] In theory, Malay custom and Muslim law were excluded from the Resident's competence; in practice it was difficult for administrative responsibility to stop short of these matters when it embraced everything else of importance to the community.

The independence of the Malay members was limited, in the case of the Sultan, by the obligation to accept advice,[2] and in the case of the others, by their dependence on official appointments and allowances. All the waris negeri and titleholders in Perak received allowances or pensions in recognition of their rank; other Malays with good connexions were appointed to be penghulus of local government divisions. In Selangor every raja on the State Council except the Raja Muda had a penghulu appointment. In their dealings with the Resident the Malays suffered all the limitations of official status, without the authority and force which professional administrators might bring to bear when they tendered advice in Colony Executive Councils. Malay members had neither the responsibility of official members on the Colony legislature nor the freedom of unofficials.[3] Formally they were part of the government; in the making of policy they were a pressure group outside it. On the Council they constituted an official *bloc* on which the Resident could rely for support. On one notable occasion, the Perak State Council, in obedience to the Governor's instructions, reversed a decision it had made three months

---

[1] *PCM*, 4 March, 4 May and 20 October 1879; 26 October 1882. SCM, 14 June 1884 and 7 April 1891. It could be argued of course that while Article VI of the Pangkor Engagement did not bind the Sultan to accept advice on the administration of Muslim law, it left the Resident free to offer it. The Residents were concerned primarily with the creation of a state establishment of kathis and with the definition of their jurisdiction.

[2] An illustration of the way this compulsion worked emerged at the Selangor Council meeting of 16 February 1885, in a discussion of the boundary with Sungei Ujong. The boundary had recently been modified by the Governor, and the Sultan, while acquiescing in the award, asked that his disagreement with it be officially recorded.

[3] The anomalous position of native members is indicated in a decision by Maxwell, Resident of Selangor 1889–92, against publication of the council minutes in the Selangor government gazette. 'It seems to me that as the functions of the Council are Executive as well as Legislative there must frequently be matters which it is not advisable to make public—and I fear that by publishing the opinions expressed by particular members of Council at our deliberations, I might possibly make it difficult to get a genuine expression of opinion under special circumstances. I can conceive that sometimes a native member might be willing to support a particular policy but would rather that his countrymen did not know what his advice has been. Another might be encouraged to earn popularity by opposition.' Resident to CS, 10 March 1890, Sel/Sec. 160/90.

earlier, and voted for a 99-year agricultural lease, though the Resident, the Assistant Resident, both Chinese members and one Malay —five out of seven present—had opposed it in discussion. In the formal vote which followed—the only one on record—the Chinese and the Assistant Resident voted the way they had argued in debate; the Resident and all the Malays voted in favour, and carried the motion.[1]

If a measure was seriously opposed, the Resident sometimes refrained for the time being from pressing it to a conclusion; but once a course of action was clearly determined, by the decision of the Resident or on instructions from the Governor, overt opposition ceased. Thus the Selangor Council accepted, first the ruling of the Resident, and then the ruling of the Governor, in the case of the Tengku Panglima Raja; thus the Perak Council accepted, with obvious reluctance, the abolition of slavery.[2] Thus the Selangor Council accepted, in 1891, the Selangor Land Code though the Malays were opposed to the principles of assessment which it introduced. The Perak Council, again, accepted the liability of the state for the debts of the Mentri, though at the previous Council they had rejected, as contrary to Malay notions of right, the liability of the state for the debts of Sultan 'Abdu'llah.[3] The principles were identical, but the Mentri's debts were guaranteed by the Pangkor Engagement, and 'Abdu'llah's were not.

The hold of the Resident on the Council was maintained in various ways. In Selangor during Douglas' residency there was little pretence of discussion; Douglas could not speak Malay, the language of all the State Councils, and had to rely on his Superintendent of Police to interpret for him. There was a crude attempt to cover up the control of the Resident by resort to Western committee procedures; on the Resident's instructions the Malay members took it in turn to propose and second various measures.[4] But in Perak, and in Sela-

---

[1] *PCM*, 4 May 1879. Fifteen months later, when a new Governor sanctioned a 999-year lease, the Perak Council reverted to its original decision, though this time Raja Yusuf spoke against the motion.
[2] *PCM*, 22 May 1882, and 9 October 1882.   [3] *PCM*, 4 May and 3 June 1878.
[4] The Resident wrote to the Collector and Magistrate at Langat, 'Ask the Tunku Mudah [to propose] and Raja Hassan to second the adoption of a resolution to carry H.E. the Governor's commands into effect, then ask the Sultan to give his assent and report to me, sending me rough copies of the minutes in Council. As Collector and Magistrate you will understand that this new rule comes into force at Jugra on 1st May'. Resident to Collector and Magistrate, Langat, 25 April 1882, Sel/Sec. 174/82.

ngor after 1882, the Residents spoke Malay well, were on terms of personal friendship with Malays of rank, and proceeded by consultation. The element of discussion and persuasion is prominent in Council meetings, particularly in the reports of Perak meetings between 1877 and 1882. St. Pol Lias described the tactful control exercised by Low. He introduced the agenda, explained situations and opened the discussion, which usually consisted of agreement with his position, or a response prompted by the form of the motion. Opposition was met by persuasion, explanation, and finally by a joke which made everyone laugh and closed the subject. It was proposed to introduce a leasehold tenure of 999 years; Raja Yusuf who had been sitting in silence throughout the proceedings, chewing betel, here intervened to object strongly to alienation for so long; at Deli in Sumatra the lease established by the Dutch was for seventy-five years. No one could deny that 999 years was a long time; the Resident averted further discussion by a well-placed joke, and the Raja fell silent.[1]

Twice a Malay member persisted in his opposition to the Resident, and carried the Council, but these incidents are remarkable because they are exceptional. Both cases concerned Malay pensions, and each time the Sultan of Selangor was the chief protagonist. During the Governor's absence on leave, the Selangor Government had deducted $10 a month from the allowance of the Dato' Kaya of Klang for the support of his brother, and the Governor on his return had ordered the deductions to be restored. The Sultan declared that the pension was in the nature of an inheritance (*pusaka*) out of which the brothers and sisters were entitled to a portion; he expressed himself strongly on the subject of Malay notions of right ('*ta' patut skali dia makan sa'orang*') and declared that since he had bestowed the office to which the pension was attached, he could take it away again. He carried his point, and went on to double his grandson's allowance, despite the Resident's protests.[2] Sultan Idris was also firm on the subject of allowances; when certain increases granted by the Perak Council were queried by the Governor, the Sultan declared that he could see no reason for interfering with the decision, and the increases were allowed to stand.

The initiative of the Malay members, their contribution to discussion and their influence on policy varied with the subject. It would

[1] St. Pol Lias, op. cit. p. 176.
[2] SCM, 29 April 1886, and 13 June 1888.

be wrong to discount altogether their interest in economic matters; they had nearly all had some association with the tin industry, they knew how it operated, and it did not greatly change in technique and structure in the period; and certain fiscal practices, like the lease of tax farms and monopolies, were continued by the British administration. The economic problems discussed were well within the range of experience of the Malay members. But since they now received state allowances, most of them no longer had a functional interest in the mines, and they tended to leave matters of tariff policy and mining tenure to be discussed by the British and Chinese. They did, however, make some contributions on miscellaneous economic questions—scales of railway charges, for example, or the adoption of the Colony scale of weights and measures—and what they had to say was usually pertinent and informed. In Selangor, Syed Zin and the Raja Muda had interests in pepper, gambier and sugar plantations, and were interested in labour regulations and export duties from the employers' and producers' points of view.[1] Despite these qualifications, however, Malay discussion on mining and commercial agriculture and allied questions was not significant.

The Malay contribution was greatest, of course, on problems of Malay life and the impact on it of a foreign administrative, economic and legal order. The effectiveness of Malay opinion depended on the magnitude of the principles involved, and the extent to which external standards had to be satisfied. On questions of public morality and welfare—the abolition of slavery or the introduction of compulsory vaccination—Malay opinion might secure the delay, but not the abandonment of unpopular reforms. In one matter of major importance—land revenue—the Malays during the 1880's successfully postponed in both states, the general application of land rent, and in Perak the application of a head tax; but since the revenues were flourishing on tin, since district staffs were inadequate to deal with a proper land settlement, and since it was policy in the early years to attract population rather than seek to raise a large land revenue, Government was able to satisfy Malay wishes without sacrificing principle. When attention turned seriously to land settlement in the 1890's, opposition was no longer effective. The Selangor Land

[1] At the instance of Raja Muda Sulaiman, the remission of duty on coffee exports was extended to all agricultural produce (except pepper and gambier, which were governed by special regulations) and at the instance of Syed Zin, two clauses of the Indian Immigration Act of 1884 were altered in favour of employers. SCM, 12 September 1885, 27 September and 18 October 1884.

Code of 1891 introduced the principle of periodical assessment of holdings under customary tenure—a class composed principally of Malay smallholdings. A full Council met to consider the Code, and the Sultan, Raja Bot and Raja Kahar, and both Chinese members objected to the assessment rates as far too high, but without effect.[1]

It was on lesser questions relating to the routine of Malay life— the appointments and jurisdiction of headmen, ecclesiastical jurisdiction, the incidents of Malay farming—that Malays expressed themselves with greatest frequency and to greatest effect. How should buffalo trespass be dealt with? Should assistant penghulus be appointed by penghulus or by the state? What rents should be asked for *nipah* land? Should traders be allowed to peddle from riverboats, in competition with land-based shopkeepers who had to pay rates and taxes? And if dues were levied on shop-boats, what was to be done about the subsistence farmer who occasionally carried goods to barter elsewhere on the river? Should penghulus get a commission on the tin duty on ancestral mines? Was vaccination contrary to Islam? Should Malays be allowed to gamble? What compensation should be paid for damage done by elephants? Should marriage by abduction of a girl under sixteen be treated as an offence under the Penal Code? These are typical examples of the problems which Malay members put forward, discussed with animation and helped to solve; some of these questions were brought forward by members at the instance of villagers who were directly affected by them.

The Chinese members confined their discussion almost entirely to the mining industry. They may have made representations elsewhere on behalf of the community as a whole; it was rarely that they made them in Council. Yap Ah Loy was able to stop the levy of a door-tax on the Chinese population of Kuala Lumpur, on the ground that they had laid out and built the town without help from anyone; but most of his time on Council was spent in pressing the concerns of the mining advancers, and, in particular, his personal claims to the state farms and to land in and about Kuala Lumpur. In Perak the Capitans successfully opposed (in 1877) the imposition of a head tax on the Chinese community, only to accept it in another form two years later, when registration of every Chinese male over sixteen, with payment of a registration fee of $1, was first introduced. Registration was introduced to one district after another till in December 1881 it embraced the whole Chinese adult male population. Low

[1] SCM, 13 June 1891.

acknowledged in his official journal that registration was extremely unpopular,[1] but there is no hint in the minutes of opposition or even discussion; indeed it was left to the Magistrate of the Krian district to protest against registration and complain that Chinese were leaving his district because of it.[2]

The intervention of the Chinese magnates was directed to securing for the industry favourable conditions of tenure, minimum taxation, protection of advancers, and control of labour; and it should be remembered that the mining coolies over whom they sought this control constituted the great bulk of their own community. Many of their demands in these matters were in accordance with government policy, and there was little occasion for disagreement; indeed in fiscal matters there was little scope for it, since the tariff structure was tied in principle to the price of tin and the cost of public works. Sometimes Chinese members objected to a justifiable rise in the tin or opium duty in the spirit of hopeful bargaining; sometimes they simply acquiesced, saying that the government had always shown consideration for the industry and they would not oppose fair taxation.[3]

Matters raised in Council were often discussed in advance at unofficial meetings between the Resident and the influential men of the community, and this was an obvious method of proceeding, with Malays as well as Chinese. It is probable that these unofficial meetings, so far as the Chinese were concerned at any rate, were far more important than the Council meetings as a means of communicating with the government. On one occasion at least, an important controversy found no expression in Council, but was discussed at a private meeting. In 1879, the Resident included in the list of state tax farms to be leased for the next three-year period, the sale of *chandu* (prepared opium) throughout Perak. This was sure to be

---

[1] Low Journal, 29 September 1879, enclosed in Anson to Hicks Beach, Confidential of 18 October 1879, CO 273/100.

[2] *PCM*, 23 March 1880. Low solemnly remarked that the Chinese were very willing to pay for registration, and 'were glad to have a government which took so much care of them'.

[3] In April 1878, Low took off the $2 royalty on tin because of the low tin price; at the Council meeting of 20 February 1880, the Chinese councillors agreed to its reimposition to pay for the Taiping—Port Weld railway. It was lifted again in April because of the Taiping fires; and when the Council was asked in December to suggest ways of raising revenue to pay the state debts, the Chinese councillors agreed to the reimposition of the royalty since Government had shown itself considerate of their needs. *PCM*, 30 December 1880.

unpopular both with the miners, who feared a rise in the price of chandu, and with the labour contractors, who made a profit out of preparing chandu for sale to their men. Low expected a 'row with the Chinese' and it came in the form of a riot of miners in Taiping in October 1879. After the riot, Low called a meeting of Chinese mining leaders, including the two state councillors; they joined their compatriots in urging strongly the abandonment of the chandu farm, and Low gave in.[1] Yet no objection to the chandu farm was ever raised at Council meetings, indeed the Chinese members were not even present when the advertisement was discussed, though they must have known about it and were present at a Council meeting a week later. It is possible that representations were made—but out-side the State Council.

On occasion the Chinese contributed to general discussion, par-ticularly in reviews of capital sentences and in economic questions of wide reference, like the immigration of plantation labour, railway finance and currency questions. On the Selangor Council, Yap Ah Loy supported the Malay case for remission of land rent and Yap Kuan Seng and Cheow Ah Yeok supported Malay opposition to rates of assessment proposed under the 1891 Land Code;[2] these references may mean little, or may point to an association closer than government records can tell of. But these departures from the field of economics—and mining economics in particular—were rare. This economic preoccupation was regarded as perfectly legitimate; the value of the Chinese members to the Council and the state was judged to lie precisely in the wealth and in the enterprise which pop-ulated the state and provided the revenues, and Malay as well as British members of Council were anxious to promote the prosperity of local magnates by leasing them the state farms.

In its membership and functions the State Council represented an attempt to solve the multiple problems of the colonial situation. It sought to combine old and new sources of power, to invest each with the prestige of the other; it sought to combine traditional and modern experience and methods and turn Malay initiative in government into new channels. It sought to provide a forum where all the im-portant groups in the state might be represented and might deliberate together. The first aim was certainly realized. The Council gave to

[1] Low to CS, 6 October 1879, enclosed in Anson to Hicks Beach, Confidential of 18 October 1879, CO 273/100.
[2] SCM, 19 February 1884 and 13 June 1891.

the actions of the executive a constitutional authority, based formally on Chinese and Malay consent. It provided a means of conciliating Malay leadership and moulding it to new patterns of government. It gave Malays and Chinese a sense of participation in affairs, even if it limited their influence on decisions. They were identified with government in passing the measures which enabled government to act; they shared in the assertion of power. The power may not have been popular, but it was respected. The effectiveness of Malay and Chinese participation was limited by the overriding pressures of economic development and administrative reform, and the concentration of responsibility in the hands of the Resident, as the agent of these forces. The Council offered useful opportunities for general consultation, which contributed to the Resident's judgment of a situation and might affect decision, within narrow margins. But the Council was not, essentially, a place where decisions were made; it was a place where decisions made outside could be communicated and explained; it was yet another means of disseminating information and directing change.

The development of the Council as an unspecialized committee indiscriminately discussing routine business, as well as major policy and legislation, had the advantage perhaps that it gave Malay and Chinese members an insight into the workings of the new administration; but as government became more complex, the Council was buried under a load of administrative detail which could have left little room for discussion. The early years were years in which policy in all fields was first formulated and discussed, when the principles of taxation, of local government, of land legislation and social reform were defined, and the discussion of these principles took up most of the time of Council. The minutes of the Perak Council for 1890–5, as reported in the *Perak Government Gazette,* contrast strikingly, in their formality and dullness, with the reports of the earlier meetings. A period of consolidation is likely to be less interesting than a period of initial decisions, and gazetted abstracts of minutes are in any case a poor reflection of the original proceedings. But it is hard to believe that much discussion could have been aroused by these stereotyped agendas, which sometimes comprised twenty or so items at a sitting; two or three death sentences, four or five applications for increased allowance, half a dozen Orders in Council and a dozen penghulu appointments, retirements, and establishment questions. Though pressure of business had so much increased, the meetings were less frequent than in the earlier years, so that it cannot even be said that they accustomed the members to the rule of committees, which might have been considered an important part of their education in modern government.

During the transition from Malay to European rule, the major problems of government were problems of local adjustment to the new authority, of vital interest to Council members, even though they had no power of decision. But as solutions became stereotyped into administrative formulae, as economic horizons opened and power receded from local centres, the Councils had nothing to do but apply established principles to minor problems. The detachment of the State Councils from the centres of power and responsibility had already begun.

VII
INSTITUTIONS OF GOVERNMENT:
THE STATE ADMINISTRATIONS

THE RESIDENTS

THE instruments introducing the Residents into the various states limited their intervention to 'advice', but this 'advice' soon came to encompass all executive and legislative authority. The Sultan could not confirm death sentences, appoint a penghulu or issue a decree with penal sanctions except in Council, and as has been seen, the Council was in the Resident's hands. But while the Council was one means of controlling the Sultan, it was no check on the discretion of the Resident. Not only could he use it to validate desired legislation and action, but he acted frequently outside it in important matters. Maxwell, asked how land could be assessed and the payment of assessment enforced before the new Land Code was formally adopted by Council, replied that the Resident in a native state exercised the power of the Sultan in enforcing the payment of all dues to the state: 'What enactment is there in Selangor providing for the collection of duty on tin, for the recovery of farm-rents etc.? What legislative sanction is there for the creation of a police force at all or for the creation of particular judicial (civil) duties by the Chief Magistrate? It will never do to imagine that everything in Selangor depends upon the Council. The Sultan's power is always held in reserve.'[1] Later, when he was Acting Governor, Maxwell reiterated that as the Sultan's representative,[2] the Resident held all the powers which resided in the Sultan according to Malay political theory. When it was discovered that in Selangor there was no formal legislation imposing penalties for infringement of the rights of the gambling farmer (though such penalty was provided for in the farm contract) Maxwell minuted as follows:

The powers of the Resident are not confined to the enforcement of the few written laws which the State possesses. In special cases he may exercise in the name of the Sultan the authority which H.H. undoubtedly possesses of

[1] Minute, undated, Sel/Sec. 311/91.
[2] The Sultan of Selangor acknowledged the Resident as his *ganti* (substitute) in a letter confirming a death sentence. Sultan to Resident, 14 August 1876, Sel/Sec. 166/76.

passing any order or sentence which may seem to be just, subject to the instructions, special or general, of the Governor.

In the present instance I authorise the Resident to direct the magistrates that they may safely proceed to punish breaches of the Farmers' privileges, in connection with gaming, in the manner indicated in para. 16 of the conditions.[1]

The heart of the administration in each state was the Resident. Soon after their introduction, Residents established themselves in the places of greatest diplomatic or economic importance, according to the character of the state and the manner of intervention. The Perak Residency had been moved in 1876 from Bandar Bahru in Lower Perak to Kuala Kangsar in the north, at the point where the road from Larut met the Perak river. In the 1880's, the population of Perak was still predominantly Malay, and the Resident was still concerned with the political settlement of the Malays—a task that could not be considered completed till the establishment of Sultan Idris on the throne in 1887. During this period, a Malay centre was the logical place for his headquarters. The headquarters of the state departments, however, were situated from the beginning in the centre of economic activity, Taiping, and up to 1888 (when the post was abolished) they were in the charge of the Assistant Resident stationed in Taiping. The Resident also had an establishment at Taiping and spent much of his time there, and after 1889 (the year of Low's retirement) Taiping became his headquarters.[2]

In Selangor, Douglas clung to the original administrative base at Klang until 1880, leaving Kuala Lumpur, the main centre of population and economic activity, under the control of Capitan Yap Ah Loy. Up to June 1878 there was no establishment of any sort at Kuala Lumpur. In the second half of 1878, the *pax Britannica* was represented there by five Malay police under a corporal, quartered in the house of the Capitan China,[3] with occasional visits by the

---

[1] Minute on Resident to CS, 21 December 1893, Sel/Sec. 976/93. In 1894, however, Maxwell rejected the claim of the acting Resident of Perak to the prerogative of pardon and remission of sentence. Minute of 11 October on Resident to CS, 5 October 1894, enclosure G.6 in Mitchell to Ripon, Confidential of 14 May 1894, CO 273/195.

[2] In the Perak Administration Report for 1886, Low referred to Kuala Kangsar as the headquarters of the Resident, who lived there for half the year. His report for 1887 and Swettenham's report for 1889 and subsequent years were written from the 'British Residency, Taiping'. The Perak Directory for 1890 gives Taiping as the seat of the Resident. *Singapore and Straits Directory* 1890, p. 246.

[3] Supt. of Police, Report of a tour of inspection to the Interior, December 1878, Sel/Sec. 426/78; Supt. of Police to Resident, 30 August 1879, Report on the

Resident for the trial of serious offences. In late 1879, a magistrate was sent to reside there,[1] combining his magisterial duties with the supervision of the Public Works and Survey Department. The neglect of Kuala Lumpur was strongly disapproved of in Singapore, and was one of the subjects singled out for criticism in Swettenham's special audit report of the Selangor accounts, and in the first half of 1880 the Residency with the main departments moved to Kuala Lumpur.[2] It has remained the seat of government for Selangor to the present day.

In Sungei Ujong, as in Selangor, the Resident lived near the mines; the Residency was permanently established in Seremban. In Pahang and Negri Sembilan, both predominantly Malay, the Residency was established in or near the royal townships, the Pahang Residency at Pekan, at the mouth of the Pahang river, and the Negri Sembilan Residency at Kuala Pilah, near the royal township of Sri Menanti. In 1895, when Sungei Ujong was brought under the control of the Resident of Negri Sembilan, he moved his headquarters to Seremban.

The states were divided into a number of districts, each under an officer in general charge of the administration. The responsibilities of the district officers varied according to the depth and extent of departmental and specialist responsibility in different parts of the state, but in general they were responsible for the collection of revenue, the administration of justice, land settlement, and the supervision of headmen; and in addition they supervised departmental activities in places where there was no responsible departmental officer. The primary administrative departments were the treasury, police, public works and surveys, and land departments, and by 1880 these existed in the west coast states in varying degrees of development. As the states increased in population, revenue and communications, as new districts were opened up and sub-districts established, departments expanded and proliferated, welfare departments (health and education) were established, Chinese Affairs Departments were

Police of the Interior, Sel/Sec. 295/79. The police establishment return for the quarter ending 30 June 1878 makes no mention of Kuala Lumpur (Report of Supt. of Police, 11 July 1878, enclosed in Robinson to Hicks Beach, 224 of 1 August 1878, CO 273/95). In late 1879 the number appears to have been increased to thirteen (Sel/Sec. 326/79).

[1] Return of Resident's journeys to the interior, Sel/Sec. 377/78; Swettenham, Report on Audit of Selangor Accounts, 27 March 1880, C.3095, enclosure in no. 2.

[2] The Resident was addressing his letters from Kuala Lumpur in the beginning of May 1880. Sel/Sec. 114/80.

set up, and the great development of communications brought into existence railway, postal and telecommunications departments which by 1895 were the largest in the states.

The Residents of Sungei Ujong, Pahang and Negri Sembilan throughout dealt directly with their district and departmental officers, assisted by an office staff of clerks and Malay writers.[1] Correspondence from districts and departments, from individuals and from the Straits Government came direct to the Resident's office to be dealt with in his detailed minutes and instructions and circulated when necessary to other interested parties. For some time this was also the procedure in Perak and Selangor, but the Residents of these states soon felt the need for a competent secretariat trained in colonial administration to deal with the correspondence and relieve the Resident of routine, freeing him to spend more time in personal contact with the people of the state. Further, it was considered necessary that there should be a trained colonial official able to regularize the increasingly complex state administration and bring it into line with that of the colony. As Swettenham pointed out, in the early days of the Residential system, when the revenue was small, the officers few and the country undeveloped, a strict enforcement of administrative procedure was neither practical nor desirable; but now that the revenues and establishments had increased so greatly, and the duties of the various departments had become so important, it was essential to introduce 'those forms and regulations and safeguards which long experience and able administration has [sic] proved to be the best under similar circumstances elsewhere'.[2] In Perak, the post of Assistant Resident was abolished in 1888, and that of Secretary to Government, with headquarters in Taiping, established instead; and in 1891 a similar appointment was made in Selangor. Correspondence was now cleared through this office, and forwarded to the Resident only when it raised questions of policy; it was accompanied by influential minutes from the Secretary to Government tendering his opinion and stating precedent. The reports of district and departmental officers, however, were still sent to the Resident as a matter of course.

'I have often been asked what it is we do in the Malay States',

---

[1] In Sungei Ujong, and in Selangor and Perak before 1890, the Resident's staff also included a Chinese interpreter. *Singapore and Straits Directory* for the years 1880–95.

[2] Acting Resident of Perak to Acting CS, 20 October 1884, enclosed in Smith to Derby, 486 of 3 November 1884, CO 273/130.

Swettenham once wrote. 'The answer is that we do everything that has to be done in the administration and development of twenty-five thousand square miles of territory, inhabited by a population of over half a million people of different races, colours, religions, characters, and pursuits.'[1] Swettenham was writing of the administration as a whole, but he might well have been writing of the Residents themselves, particularly in the early days. They had to carry out the work of pacification and development in a new, unmapped country, where the administration had to be built up from nothing; they had to oversee the work of specialist departments, whose paucity of staff in the early years meant much improvization by willing amateurs; they had to make recommendations on technical questions relating to communications and public works. Their official journals are missing for the most part; but from the two that survive[2] it is possible to reconstruct the daily routine of Low and Swettenham in the early years of their service. Low's journal, covering six weeks in April and May 1877, shows him familiarizing himself with the work of every department and district, studying Malay politics and personalities, learning the economics of tin-mining, and touring the state by elephant and river-boat on two grand circuits which took him to all the settled areas. His work with the Malays has already been described. He reorganized the work of departments and dismissed and transferred staff; went over public buildings and chose new sites—it was he who recommended the site of what was to be the chief town of Lower Perak—Telok Anson—and took the first steps towards establishing it there. He gave particular attention to the Treasury, examining the accounts, arranging for them to be sent to him monthly for inspection, and ordering copies of treasury instructions and forms from Singapore so that he might 'lick the Perak accounts into shape for next year'. He discussed the economic potential of the country with Malay headmen, Chinese miners and European planters, talked about mining tenures and mine economics with the Capitan China (who was also the revenue farmer) and 'laughed him out of the nonsense about giving up the farm', collected ore samples to send out for assay, inspected mines, smallholdings and sugar estates. His decisions and recommendations and his activities generally extended over the whole field of public administration and touched on diplo-

[1] Swettenham, *The Real Malay*, p. 31.
[2] Low Journal; Swettenham Diary for 1883, item 12, Swettenham Collection, ANM. The Selangor entries run from 1 January to 5 October, when Swettenham left Selangor on leave.

macy, politics and economic development; they ranged from high policy to such minutiae as recommending dry earth 'which I have found elsewhere to be very efficient in absorbing effluvia' for the gaol latrines.

Swettenham's routine in the first year of his Selangor residency followed much the same pattern, except that he was much more closely concerned with public works and the affairs of the mines, since his headquarters were in the chief mining district and the centre of communications. His was a routine of office work and correspondence,[1] interviews with Malays and Chinese, judicial work (mostly appeals), inspections of roads and other public works, and frequent visits to Klang and other outstations. Between January and October, he was away from Kuala Lumpur once a month on an average, for fifty-four days in all; he visited Klang every two or three weeks, Jugra and Ulu Langat each three times, Kuala Selangor twice, and Ulu Selangor once; on this occasion he travelled with the Governor up the length of the state from Ulu Langat to Ulu Bernam, taking a fortnight over the journey. His diary records interviews with the Sultan about affairs in general, and with Raja Laut and Raja Kahar about penghulus and the land question. Four entries (one of them made while he was on tour) will suffice to demonstrate the variety of his work:

10 January   Went to Gomba Bridge, decided line of new road and new Bridge. Local correspondence. Gave decision in Bankruptcy case. Gave directions for clearing sites for new houses. Received mail. Went with Rodger to site of new Gambling Booth & walked over burial ground and up towards Pudu. Determined to reserve land for a diversion on the Pudu

[1] A sample of Sel/Sec. files 1–100 of 1883, all of which passed through Swettenham's hands and carried his minutes, show him dealing with the following subjects: appointments (including appointments of penghulus), requests for loans from Chinese and Malays, the preparation of estimates, rules for medical attendance on government officers, journals of district and police officers, the journal of a penghulu in a developing area (Ulu Selangor), proposals for the Klang-Kuala Lumpur railway, staff discipline, removal of Chinese bodies for burial, the establishment of an atap farm, claims for allowances. Some of the correspondence was forwarded to Singapore for instructions, but most of it was dealt with by the Resident on the spot. The files sent to Singapore deal with the appointment of officers (3/83); a land application of 6,000 acres for sago cultivation (34/83); rules for medical attendance on government officers (38/83); the land claims of the Capitan China (48/83); and Swettenham's proposals for the Klang-Kuala Lumpur railway (68/83). At the request of the Governor, the correspondence between the Residency Surgeon and the previous Resident on the hospitals and gaols of Selangor was forwarded on 74/83.

Road. Told Inspector Harper not to permit any more gambling in the old Farm. Gambling to be stopped at midnight always until 6 a.m. Returned 7.30 p.m.

17 January   Left K. Klang 1 a.m., arrived Jugra 6.30 a.m. Saw Mr Ranking & walked over proposed Road. Jugra to B. Langat. Sent for Raja Muda to sit as assessor in a Raja case. Returned 11 a.m. Inspected new station.

1 p.m. to 4 p.m. tried case with Raja Muda. Long interview with Sultan who was very animated and cordial. Left Jugra 5.45. Dropped Raja Muda at Bandar—Saw new station— went by inner passage to K. Klang. Landed 3 prisoners at Police station. Anchored for night.

5 February   Writing up Journal. Dealing with correspondence. Went over a quantity of Malay correspondence with Raja Laut[1] who is very loyal & very useful. Saw contractors about new houses & metalling roads. Saw Road overseer who complains of Mr White. Talked to the men I suspect of taking the pegs out of the Pahang Rd. Received petition mosque. Received Mail. Mr Cameron arrived. Klang revenue poor. Langat very good. Inspected housebuilding & Gomba Bridge now finished. Rode out on Pudu Road.

19 February   To Ampang 6.30. Back 10.30. In office noon to 5 p.m. Received trace of new Langat Road, sent it Langat to try for contract. Heard from Klyne, the Bandar Kanching Rd. traced but in some places his gradient 1 in 9. Contract for $800 to clear & remove stumps & make temporary bridges. Sent back to Klyne to accept contract & get on with work but to retrace road & let Hill see it. Mail from Singapore. Saw Rodger about Chinese Temple. . . . Wrote Winton, Glass, Purvis, Talbot, Hervey, [name illegible].

The Residents kept in close touch with the work of all departments through regular and frequent reports. They were particularly concerned with the development of public works and communications. They made proposals to the Governor for major public works, and decided on sites and contracts subject to his sanction. The Selangor Secretariat Papers show that in addition to these policy decisions, the Residents had the responsibility of supervising the progress of these works, receiving and commenting on plans, tracings and progress reports from the Railway Engineer and the Superintendent of Public Works. Swettenham (who had offered surveying as a subject in the Civil Service Examination) took a close interest in this branch of the administration; indeed it was probably here that he made his greatest

[1] Raja Laut was the Malay magistrate, Kuala Lumpur, and a son of a former Sultan.

contribution. 1883 saw the beginning of a tremendous drive for improved communications and government building in Selangor, and in the absence of a Superintendent of Public Works in the first half of the year,[1] Swettenham was in charge of this department. He organized its activities and regularly inspected works in and around Kuala Lumpur. After the appointment of a Superintendent, he continued to receive tracings and plans and comment on them in detail.[2]

As the work of administration in Perak and Selangor increased during the 1880's and 1890's, it became more difficult for the Residents to spare time for the long daily interviews and extensive tours which had been a part of their routine. In Perak, the move from Kuala Kangsar to Taiping must have resulted in much loss of contact with the great body of Malays, who still lived in the Perak valley.[3] But the Residents continued to visit every district in the state at least once a year, inspecting public buildings, mines, estates and Malay gardens, meeting leading Malays and Chinese and receiving deputations. Even at the close of the period, the states were not so extensively developed that personal supervision was impossible.

During this quarter of the century, the Malay states provided a field for some of the most remarkable men in the history of colonial administration. None of them equalled Raffles in imperial imagination, and their scholarship, though considerable, did not perhaps attain the breadth of the work of the great Dutch colonial scholars. But the imperial vision was there, though tempered by an intense practicality. They possessed great resources of managerial ability, judgment and power of decision; they were remarkably industrious, and indifferent to danger and discomfort; and they established an imaginative *rapprochement* with indigenous authority equal to anything achieved by those high priests of 'indirect rule', Gordon, Lugard and Brooke.

[1] The former Superintendent, D.D. Daly, had been dismissed before Swettenham's arrival as Resident in September 1882, and the new Superintendent, Bellamy, did not arrive till June 1883.

[2] E.g., Swettenham's minute on plans submitted to him, 'You must be careful about that earthwork at the new Police Barracks. I don't see that you have provide[d] any means of directing a flank fire. . . . That road deviation at the hospitals will never do—a proper road must be traced & made to come in to the public buildings. . . .' Minute of 4 October 1883, Sel/Sec. 1531/83.

[3] According to the monthly reports of the District Magistrate of Kuala Kangsar from 1890 onwards, the Resident visited Kuala Kangsar half a dozen times a year for two or three days at a time, primarily to attend Council Meetings.

Most of the Residents came from the professional middle-class and small gentry, and were educated in public schools. Four of them had gone to a university or to read law, and had taken their degrees; the others had gone from school into their chosen services, or into the adventures and experiences which were to lead finally to government service in the Far East. They had varied careers.[1] Five of the twelve Residents appointed between 1874 and 1896 came into colonial administration from other fields. Davidson's tenure as Resident was a brief interruption of a distinguished legal career in the Straits Settlements; Douglas had had a mixed experience as a naval lieutenant, a marine surveyor, and Government Resident of the Northern Territory (Australia); Murray had been a commander in the Royal Navy and had travelled a good deal in Africa; Rodger was a gentleman of means, who had been travelling in Malaya when he received his first appointment, under Swettenham in Selangor; Lister, the younger son of an earl, came to the Selangor and later the Negri Sembilan service by way of coffee planting in Ceylon and Malaya. Six of the remaining seven—J. W. Birch, Low, Paul, Swettenham, Maxwell, and Treacher, in order of appointment—were career members of the Colonial Service and had served in various crown colonies before they arrived in the states; among them were three of the most effective of Malayan administrators—Low, Swettenham, and Maxwell. Clifford, one of the most distinguished and articulate of the Residents, was the only one to spend his whole early career in the Malay states, from his first appointment in Perak as a cadet of seventeen to his first substantive appointment as Resident in 1896.

Living in an environment where so much remained to be discovered, where good administration called for a knowledge of strange languages and customs, where economic development and the growth of communications called for agricultural experiment and a first-hand knowledge of terrain, the Residents were amateur anthropologists and explorers in a small way, and their journals and reports carry much valuable topographical and anthropological information. The researches of Low and Maxwell went beyond the lively, energetic dilettantism of their colleagues; Low was a botanist of repute, and Maxwell was an encyclopaedist in the best tradition of Malayan scholar-administrators.[2] Swettenham and Clifford have

[1] See Appendix 2 for biographical notes on Residents.
[2] For a reference to Low's work, see Chapter IV. Maxwell's works include eighty-one publications in the *JSBRAS* on the history, language, folklore and ceremonies of the Malays. They include editions and translations of folk tales

some small claims to scholarship,[1] but they were more interested in imaginative writing, and both of them were moderately skilful and vigorous exponents of a late-Victorian literary genre—the semi-fictional portrayal of exotic experience. The titles of their works— *Malayan Monochromes*, *Bushwhacking and Other Asiatic Tales and Memories*, *In Court and Kampong*, *Malay Sketches*, *The Real Malay* —are sufficient indication of the general style. In these impressionistic pieces, a little nostalgic description of 'far away and long ago', a little folklore, a little history, a little patriotic tub-thumping, a little reminiscence, a little of the marvellous, the horrific and the strange are compounded into light, skilfully constructed travellers' tales, of no great literary merit, but possessing some interest and charm.

Swettenham and Clifford reveal in their writings what they thought of their surroundings, the peoples they administered, and the purpose and justification of British rule in Malaya.[2] Swettenham wrote with delight of the beauty and remoteness of the country, and he wrote of his Malay acquaintances with an extrovert, friendly familiarity. He liked them, he enjoyed their company, he respected them (more or less) and with his usual realism about humankind, he took them for what they were, and did not expect too much of them. But though he lived with them for long periods, went through many dangers with them and was dependent on them for hospitality and friendship through many lonely months,[3] he took it for granted that the Englishman and the Malay belonged to different worlds. The worlds were separated, not by gulfs of mutual ignorance and prejudice as in the later years of British rule, but by a line tacitly maintained by

and histories. The majority of his contributions are short notes, but there are some substantial and still useful papers; in particular two papers on the law and custom of the Malays relating to land, and the law relating to slavery. See Index to Journals 1–86, *JMBRAS*, vol. v, part 4 (1927).

[1] Swettenham and Clifford collaborated in producing the first half of a Malay-English dictionary (it was never completed). Swettenham also published an English-Malay vocabulary, and Clifford published a collection of Malay proverbs and notes on the Sakai dialects of the Peninsula. A Malay translation by Clifford of the Straits Settlements Penal Code evoked some criticism of style and vocabulary. Minute by Resident Councillor, Malacca, 26 March 1891, Sel/Sec. 396/91.

[2] The contrast between the two writers has already been treated in a recent analysis, and what follows here is in part a recapitulation of this. See J. de V. Allen, 'Two Imperialists', *JMBRAS*, vol. xxxvii, part 1 (July 1964) pp. 41–73.

[3] Swettenham's stories are full of his junketings with his Malay hosts. For an account of the way in which two Englishmen alone in a district become friendly with the local Malay magnate and his family. See 'A Mezzotint', Swettenham, *The Real Malay*, p. 279.

the good form and good taste of both parties. Nowhere in Swettenham's books is there any danger of the line being breached. In a story
about a romantic attraction between a Malay girl of good family and
the English district officer with whom she comes into contact, common sense prevails and each party is married off to a compatriot. If
the marriages fail and the parties go their separate ways to damna-
tion, at least the decencies are preserved; they don't travel there together. Swettenham concludes the story with a picture of a cicada
flying into the lamp as he writes, and destroying itself in the flame,
despite all his efforts to save it. It is a poetic image of the danger of
teaching a Malay to aspire to a life outside his experience. 'She
would have been wiser to remain in the cool, moonlit jungle, where,
at least, she was at home with those of her own kind; but the creatures of the forest have not yet learned the danger of giving way to
natural instincts.'

The key to Clifford's attitude is contained in a quotation from
Kipling with which he began a public lecture:

> To wait in heavy harness
> On fluttered folk and wild
> Your new-caught, sullen peoples,
> Half devil and half child.

The devils in Clifford's calendar are the chiefs whose cruelty and
greed destroyed a natural Eden, and the children are the simple and
defenceless poor. There are no amiable stories of the Resident going
picnicking with the court and being pelted with fruit by pretty women
on the ride back through the forest. Clifford's heroes (all projections
of himself) are engaged on sterner matters; frustrating a *jehad*, carrying out a rescue, putting down a riot, always single-handed, always
with a sixth sense, an uncanny knowledge of Malay affairs and Malay
psychology, and a habit of incognito perambulation through the
Malay world worthy of Harun al-Raschid himself. When his emotion
or imagination is thoroughly aroused, Clifford loses control and slips
into a fantasy in which blackest evil is overcome by a white saviour
full of love and pity. During a lecture delivered at the Royal Colonial
Institute, he gave such a gloomy picture of Malay life in Pahang
under Malay rule, that Low and Treacher felt constrained to protest
on behalf of their states and peoples. Treacher begged the audience
not to go away with the idea that life in the unprotected Malay states
was 'entirely unendurable' and reminded them that 'not very long
ago in the history of our own civilized and Christian country, women

were burned for witchcraft, people were hanged for stealing sheep, Catholics burned Protestants and Protestants burned Catholics, and slavery existed under our flag, with all its horrors, to an extent unknown to the Malays'.[1]

Yet these emotional extremes do not give the whole of Clifford's feeling about his work and environment. There are sketches—for example, 'Piloting Princes' from *Bushwhacking and Other Asiatic Tales and Memories*—written with a rare lightness of touch, which show him in close and delightful understanding with his aristocratic Malay companions. Indeed Clifford's trouble was that he felt far too strongly drawn to them, and consequently suffered deeply from invisible barriers, of the existence of which he was too well aware, and from the alienation and misunderstanding which flowed from his role as British Agent and later British Resident in the most remote and intractable of the Malay states. During the time he was in charge of Pahang (he became Acting Resident for the first time in 1890) there were two serious outbreaks against the British, and much of his time was taken up with pursuing the rebels and punishing their supporters. The hardships he was forced to inflict on the ra'ayat weighed heavily on him.

A man to go bushwhacking with a light heart should have no insight, no sympathy, no imagination. The political agent has all three. Also he loves the folk against whom he is warring. . . . It is his duty to increase the heavy measure of their troubles; he knows that by doing so relentlessly the wished-for peace will come more speedily. But they are his own people, among whom he has lived for years, and he suffers with them in spirit, groaning over the necessity which drives him to persecute them. It is an impossible frame of mind, and one that makes his days bitter to him.[2]

Clifford's consolation was the thought that by pacifying the country and providing security for the lives and possessions of the ra'ayat he was introducing a better order of things. His passionate advocacy of British intervention was perhaps intended to stifle his own growing doubt whether its benefits were worth the destruction of the natural environment and traditional ways of life. Like many of his colleagues, Clifford was driven by ambitions and aspirations completely at variance with his tastes and sympathies, but he suffered from the contradiction far more than they. Low, Swettenham, Rodger, Lister, Murray, found themselves in these remote and beautiful

[1] Clifford, 'Life in the Malay Peninsula', op. cit. pp. 369-401.
[2] *Bushwhacking and Other Asiatic Tales and Memories,* 2nd edition, London, 1929, p. 50.

places partly because they were deeply attracted to the life of solitude and independence, but also because the prospect of developing and settling these lands was an irresistible challenge. Low might live in complete contentment and peace of mind in a bungalow overlooking a magnificent stretch of the Perak river, with no company but two apes and a retriever, and he might be so attached to his surroundings as to pick out a grave-site for himself in the Kuala Kangsar cemetery (as it happened, he was buried in Alassio on the Italian Riviera) but with equal calmness of spirit, he went about the task of methodically destroying this idyll, by bringing in railways, roads, Chinese and Indian labour, and there can be no doubt of his satisfaction at the success of his schemes of development. He may have been aware of this contradiction, but he does not seem to have been disturbed by it, perhaps because he and his colleagues could rest secure in the knowledge that whatever advances they made, the conquest of the environment which they loved would not take place in their lifetime.

The same opposition of instincts existed in Clifford; the restless spirit which sought release in distant and strange places, and yet could not leave them as they were.[1] His annual reports were quite conventional in their recommendations; he appeared as anxious as his colleagues for Chinese immigration, for communications with the outside world, for the development of plantation agriculture. On the question of the future site of the state capital, he argued for Kuala Lipis, near the mines of western Pahang, against Temerloh, a centre of Malay agriculture, and he strongly recommended the incorporation of Pahang into a federation with the more advanced west coast states as a means of overcoming her financial and development problems—this in preference to a limitation of the British establishment and the scope of government in Pahang itself.[2] But he had less respect than his colleagues for 'Trade and Money and Prosperity and material comfort and Sanitation and Drains', and in the last resort the justification he sought for colonial rule was not economic development or the introduction of a superior civilization, but simply the elimination of the harsher features of Malay life—endless local wars, arbitrary rule, slavery and oppression. He did not consider it part of the British responsibility to make the Malays 'diligent by law' and abhorred the Dutch principle that 'little birds who can sing, and who

[1] See e.g., his story 'The Expeditions into the Benighted Lands', op. cit. pp. 85–6.
[2] *AR* Pahang, 1893, and also his paper 'British and Siamese Malaya', pp. 45–67.

will not sing, must be made to sing'.[1] During his Pahang career he accepted and welcomed foreign immigration and development, but when he went to Nigeria as Governor after the first world war, he confirmed the conservative 'indirect rule' policies of his predecessors, and played a leading part in excluding foreign estate agriculture and preserving cash crop agriculture as a peasant activity.[2]

Travellers have left vivid impressions of the Residents. Low appears as a judicious and calm spirit—he was already fifty-three when he went to Perak—unpretentious, but a man who knew what was due to rank; discriminating without extravagance, orderly without fuss; a completely loyal and devoted imperialist, but without bombast; humane, but without quixotry or romanticism. Swettenham's life and writings reveal a man of tremendous ebullience and energy. His great egotism, self-confidence and ambition were all well tempered by political realism, good judgment of men and situations, and a flair for easy personal relationships with European and Malay associates.[3] He was not outstandingly intelligent, and by no means original, but he was able to grasp a situation and come quickly to a rational decision. His *bête-noire*, Maxwell, had a far better intellect, and was a brilliant and energetic administrator, but his uncompromising rejection of work or conduct which fell short of the very highest standard, and his combative spirit (a family trait) made him unpopular with his colleagues.[4] Even at this distance, Maxwell's minutes sting like a whip, and one may imagine the feelings of respected and able Residents like Rodger and Treacher during Maxwell's tenure as Colonial Secretary and Acting Governor, when their recommendations were received in Singapore with curt criticisms instead of the usual sympathetic consideration. The desire to be free of the inquisitorial eye of Maxwell, then ruling the Secretariat in

[1] Ibid. p. 52.

[2] See discussion in W.K. Hancock, *Survey of British Commonwealth Affairs*, London, 1942, vol. ii, part 2, pp. 173–94.

[3] Sir Cecil Clementi Smith, then Acting Governor, paid him the following tribute in 1885; 'I never worked with anyone—and I doubt if I ever shall again,—with whom it was a greater pleasure to work . . .' (Smith to Swettenham, 25 October 1885, No. 57, Swettenham Collection, ANM). An entry in his Perak Journal in 1874 shows him whiling away a tedious hour entertaining the Laksamana with one of Hans Andersen's fairy tales. C.D. Cowan, 'Sir Frank Swettenham's Perak Journals', p. 53.

[4] Smith to Derby, Confidential of 17 April 1885 and enclosures, CO 273/134. Clifford remarks at the close of his diary for 1893, 'W.E.M.'s actions as Ag. Govr. have been things to shudder at, not to see—or feel as I unfortunately have had to do'. MSS diary, ANM.

Singapore, may have played some small part in the unanimous acceptance by the Residents of a federation likely to be headed by someone more permissive.

The Residents have testified freely to their opinion of the Malays; one would like to know what the Malays privately thought of the Residents. Their manners and social origins, on the whole, were probably good enough to satisfy a people whose national proverb demanded (according to Clifford) that 'blows should be administered by a hand that wears a ring'. The courtesy and dignity of Davidson, Low, Rodger, Paul, Lister and Clifford (to name those who have left some record of their manners) certainly came up to the high Malay standard. The prestige of the Residents was probably enhanced, in the eyes of Malays, by their style of living. The Perak residencies were run with a meticulous discipline and a certain state, and it is unlikely that others fell far short of this standard. In 1880, St. Pol Lias found the residency in Taiping as unexpected, in the civilized style of its appointments, as a castle in a fairy tale. Dinner was an elaborate meal of soup, fish, entrees, curries and side-dishes; it was served at a perfectly appointed table, laid with linen, silver, flowers, and glasses for madeira, bordeaux, burgundy and champagne; guests were waited on by two perfectly-trained servants under a grand priest of an Indian butler called Daoud.[1] A similar state was maintained at Kuala Kangsar. Sikh guards were on duty day and night at both residencies, presenting arms whenever the Resident appeared.[2]

The eccentricities of some of the Residents do not appear to have diminished their standing. What the Malays thought of Low when he sat down to meals with his two apes, Mahmoud and Eblis, is not on record, but they probably dismissed it as one of the vagaries permitted to the great. Isabella Bird has left a description of the only true eccentric among them, Captain Murray, the second Resident of Sungei Ujong, which suggests there were other means to success in dealing with Malays, besides fine manners:

He is a man about thirty-eight, a naval officer, and an enterprising African traveller; under the middle height, bronzed, sun-browned, disconnected in his conversation from the habit of living without any one in or out of the

---

[1] B. de St. Pol Lias, *Pérak et les Orang Sakèys*, p. 66.

[2] The Resident of Perak enjoyed an official state nearly equal to that of the Sultan. He had a thirteen-gun salute as compared with the Sultan's seventeen guns, but equally with the Sultan, he was entitled to a guard of honour of fifty men on arrival or departure from the state and when visiting districts. *Perak Handbook and Civil Service List, 1892*, p.60.

house to speak to; professing a misanthropy which he is very far from feeling, for he is quite unsuspicious, and disposed to think the best of everyone;
hasty when vexed, but thoroughly kindhearted; very blunt, very undign-
ified, never happy (he says) out of the wilds; thoroughly well disposed to the
Chinese and Malays, but very impatient of their courtesies, thoroughly
well meaning, thoroughly a gentleman, but about the last person that I
should have expected to see in a position which is said to require much tact
if not *finesse*. His success leads me to think, as I have often thought before,
that if we attempt to deal with Orientals by their own methods, we are apt
to find them more than a match for us, and that thorough honesty is the
best policy.

He lives alone, unguarded; trusts himself by night and day without any
escort among the people; keeps up no ceremony at all, and is approachable
at all hours. Like most travellers, he has some practical knowledge of med-
icine, and he gives advice and medicines most generously, allowing himself
to be interrupted by patients at all hours.[1]

There was one Resident, apart from Birch, whose personality must
have been entirely distasteful to the Malays, and that was Douglas.
Douglas has been made a scapegoat for many Malay dissatisfactions
which flowed from policies of which he was merely the agent. He has
been accused, for example, of driving Tengku Zia'u'd-din out of
Selangor, but the Tengku's retirement was the result of increasing
British control of government, and was fully approved by Straits officials, including Swettenham.[2] Douglas was continually in difficulties
with Raja Mahmud, the young adventurer who was Swettenham's
friend and protégé, but his minutes make it clear that he had no personal animus against the Raja; he was simply struggling with the
problem of fitting a restless, extravagant young dandy into a sober
new world where krises had to be turned into pens and fighting-
cocks into farmyard roosters.[3] If he was impatient with Malays who
continually demanded loans and increases in their allowances, his
impatience was shared by several other officers in responsible positions, Swettenham and Maxwell included. But he was less prepared than other Residents to 'temper the wind to the shorn
lamb', and preferred to administer rebukes to erring chiefs in

[1] Bird, *The Golden Chersonese*, p. 186.

[2] Anson to Hicks Beach, 308 of 16 October 1877, CO 273/91, and especially
Swettenham's memorandum describing Tengku Zia'u'd-din's position in Selangor
as anomalous, expensive, unnecessary, and not desired by the Sultan, his sons,
or the chiefs. Swettenham, Memorandum on the proposed retirement and pension of Tunku Dia Udin, Viceroy of Selangor, 8 May 1878, enclosed in Robinson
to Hicks Beach, 177 of 18 June 1878, CO 273/94.

[3] Memorandum of a conversation between Resident and Raja Mahmud, 1
March 1879, Sel/Sec. 69/79.

full Council or from the quarterdeck of one of Her Majesty's ships, rather than during a private interview in his office. After his humiliation in 1878, when he was rebuked by the Governor for securing the suspension of a Malay member of Council for bribery,[1] he again risked censure by going up to Bernam in H.M.S. *Fly* and rebuking the district chief, Raja Hitam, in the presence of seventy or eighty of his followers, for abetting a case of slavery.[2] He was rebuked several times for exercising authority without tact; one letter in which he used the royal 'we' (*kita*), and described himself as 'ruling in the town of Klang', came under the unfavourable notice of the Governor, and he was reminded of his position in relation to the Ruler and cautioned not to use such language again.[3] (But it is worth noting that Swettenham, who doubtless inspired this rebuke, himself used *kita* when he was Resident of Selangor, and so did Rodger after him.)[4] Douglas had a bullying and coarse temper which could hardly have eased his relations with Malays. In 1881 he had been reprimanded by the Governor for striking a Malay boatman, and had said in his own defence that from his knowledge of 'Malays and natives' he believed 'all of them would sooner be summarily dealt with when committing a fault than be fined or otherwise punished'.[5] He spoke in loud, authoritarian tones; one critic acidly remarked, 'I suppose it was in memory of his nautical days that he generally pitched his voice in tones which would have done admirably well for giving orders during a storm at sea.' She went on to describe the company he kept, 'The men whom the Resident usually brought with him were generally Scotch engineers of small coasting steamers, half-caste apothecaries or accountants, etc., or English policemen of the rough-and-ready order, whose " 'earts" were in the right place, according to their own account, but whose h's were decidedly in the wrong.'[6] Nothing is known of Douglas' social

[1] See Chapter IV. Swettenham once dealt with a charge of bribery against Raja Laut by quietly getting him to return the bribe, and that ended the matter. Swettenham Diary for 1883, entry for 17 April.

[2] Resident to CS, 8 August 1878, Sel/Sec. 244/78.

[3] CS to Resident, 14 November 1878, Sel/Sec. 353/78.

[4] Swettenham to Haji Mohammed Nusi appointing him a penghulu, 4 March 1884, Sel/Sec. 860/84; Rodger to Che' Ja'afar, giving him informal charge of a district, 7 April 1884, Sel/Sec. 665/84.

[5] Resident of Selangor to CS, 7 November 1881, enclosed in Weld to Kimberley, Confidential of 24 August 1882, CO 273/115.

[6] E. Innes, *The Chersonese with the Gilding Off*, vol. i, pp. 129 and 263. This delightfully acid lady had reason to dislike Douglas heartily, but Isabella Bird,

origins, but even by the provincial standards of colonial society, his career was not distinguished. Malays, who were as sensitive as any Victorian matron to the nuances of manners and social position, can have had little respect for him, especially as they knew they had only to take their troubles to Singapore to get a hearing from Swettenham in the Secretariat.

Most of the Residents had spent the greater part of their official lives in Malaya, and their associations with their states, despite the interruptions of leave, were sufficiently long and sustained to permit an intimate knowledge of what were still fairly small communities. The states were small and thinly populated, and the European community (eighty-two in the whole of Perak in 1879; 366 in 1891) was not yet large enough to interpose barriers of race snobbery and formality between the Residents and the Malay and Chinese population. The Residents knew their people and mixed with them on pleasant social occasions that have been frequently described. But the increase in population, economic activity and administrative complexity was already establishing conditions in which this spirit of informality and intimacy could not survive. It was not until the expansion of British influence in the Malay states of the east coast that British officers were once again able to enter into such easy and happy relations with the people of the state.

DISTRICTS AND DEPARTMENTS

During the nineteenth and early twentieth centuries, when British rule penetrated deeper and deeper into Asia and Africa, and extended from coastal settlements over large agricultural populations, the system of local government by district officers who discharged judicial, revenue and general executive duties came to be an accepted technique of government. An administration centralized in headquarters departments, which communicated with the local population through clerks, policemen and overseers, with no local intermediary between government and people, clearly had no adequate means of keeping itself informed of local developments, and—more important—no means of explaining its own policies and demands. The institution of district officers, usually in conjunction with a system of village headmen, was an attempt to solve the problem of communication

who had no axes to grind, said much the same thing about him. Bird, op. cit. pp. 217 and 241.

by providing a corps of officers who would be responsible for the government of a district, would co-ordinate departmental activity and would report direct to headquarters on local needs and problems. In the Malay states, district officers were introduced close on the heels of the Residents. In his first report from Selangor, Davidson mentions a Collector and Magistrate for Kuala Selangor, and when Low arrived in Perak, he found a Collector in Matang, apart from an Assistant Resident in Lower Perak and a Superintendent in Larut. Within three months of his arrival, he had established Collectors in Krian and Kinta as well. The system provided perhaps the most striking departure from current administrative practice in the Straits Settlements. In the Straits Settlements during the 1870's, administration was centralized; magistrates had no executive authority, there was no executive officer in charge of districts, and the local population came into contact with government only through police and tax-collectors. Local headmen were appointed and were required to assist in the detection of crime and in the collection of rates and rents, but they were unpaid, and responsibility for their appointments was allowed to drift into the hands of the police, so that the importance of the office declined, and there was increased danger of poor selection.[1] The model for district government in the Malay states was not, therefore, taken from the Straits Settlements—on the contrary, the Straits Settlements were indebted to the Malay states for innovations in the sphere of district administration[2]—but in all probability from India, whence the original title of the district officer —Collector and Magistrate—derived.[3] The system was also current in Sarawak, whence a number of Malay states' officers were recruited from the late 1870's onwards.

The density of administration varied according to the size and wealth of the states. The poorest and largest state—Pahang—had a sparse district administration. In 1895 the state was divided into

[1] Minute by Assistant Resident, Perak (W.E. Maxwell), 8 July 1882, enclosed in Weld to Derby, 208 of 28 May 1883, CO 273/120.

[2] Weld introduced district officers on the Malay states' model into Penang, Province Wellesley and Malacca, beginning with appointments to Balik Pulau in Penang, and Bukit Mertajam in Province Wellesley, in 1886. Weld to Stanhope, 389 of 20 September 1886, CO 273/146.

[3] In Selangor and Perak, district officers were called 'Collector and Magistrate' until 1890 and 1892 respectively. In 1890, the Selangor title was changed to 'District Officer' and in 1892 the Perak title was changed to 'District Magistrate'. In Negri Sembilan the title was 'District Officer and Magistrate'. In Pahang, Sungei Ujong and Jelebu, the title 'Collector and Magistrate' was used throughout. The term 'district officer' will be used here for convenience.

four collectorates—Kuala Pahang and Rompin, Ulu Pahang, Kuantan, and Temerloh—apart from the Residency district of Pekan; the average area of each district was 2,800 square miles. Negri Sembilan (including Sungei Ujong and Jelebu), with an area of 2,550 square miles and a total population of 65,219 in 1891, had district officers in Kuala Pilah, Tampin, Kuala Klawang (in Jelebu) and Port Dickson (in Sungei Ujong). The prosperous mining states of Selangor and Perak were much more closely administered. When Swettenham became Resident in 1882, Selangor had three collectorates—Klang, Kuala Langat and Kuala Selangor. In 1883, two more collectorates were opened, in Ulu Langat and Ulu Selangor, and between 1884 and 1895, assistant district officers were appointed to Klang, Kuala Langat, Kuala Selangor and Ulu Selangor.[1] The administration of the headquarters district, Kuala Lumpur, was under the Resident, to whom the heads of department were directly responsible, but here also land administration and the control of headmen was delegated to a district officer attached to the Land Office, so that there were in effect six districts in the state, each under the control of a responsible officer. The largest was Kuala Selangor, with 900 square miles; the smallest Klang, with 220 square miles.[2] In Perak there were eight districts by 1895, apart from the headquarters district of Larut and most of them had one or more assistant district officers. It would probably be true to say that outside Pahang, no district officer had an area larger than 1,500 square miles, or a population larger than 20,000 in his care.

The district officer was a Resident in miniature. As his original title suggested, he was primarily a judicial and revenue officer, but he was also the district land and settlement officer and was placed in charge of local headmen; and in areas where there were no local departmental representatives, he was in charge of the district work of the various departments. There are a number of commissions and instructions to district officers in Selangor, Perak, Sungei Ujong and Pahang, setting out their responsibilities.[3] The instructions of the

[1] In 1894, the post of assistant district officer, Kuala Langat, was abolished and one was established at Kuala Lumpur.

[2] *Statistical and other information regarding the Districts of Selangor, 1894.* Klang had an estimated population of 7,575, Kuala Langat 5,000, Ulu Langat 15,000, Kuala Selangor 8,500 and Ulu Selangor 16,480.

[3] Resident of Selangor to Collector and Magistrate, Kuala Selangor, 10 June 1880, Sel/Sec. 150/80; Acting Resident, Selangor, to Collector and Magistrate, Ulu Selangor, 1 December 1883, Sel/Sec. 1793/83 (circulated for the information

1880's set out their duties in simple and general terms; they defined the district boundaries (very roughly), the limits of jurisdiction, revenue duties and procedures, and duties in connexion with land administration, and they also laid on the district officer the responsibility for supervising the police, the public health and sanitation, and the public works of his district. He was also charged with the duty of familiarizing himself completely with the topography of his district, learning the customs and ways of life of the people in his care, and working in close co-operation with local headmen. The qualities needed by this Admirable Crichton were described by Maxwell in a minute of 8 May 1890:

> The District Officer should aim at possessing complete information about the condition and needs of his District—every road, path, river, village and hamlet in which he should know thoroughly. It is in his power, without in any way departing from the reserve incumbent upon a British functionary living among an Asiatic population, to acquire very detailed knowledge of the circumstances, and trading and family connections of the principal native inhabitants, and to have such an acquaintanceship among them that he will be able to judge of the value of information to be obtained from, or assistance to be afforded by each. . . . Knowledge of one or more of the native languages, of the principles of English law, and of the practice of bookkeeping are essential. . . . If he can survey, make roads, sail a boat, etc., so much the better.

Clifford, after describing the Resident's need to travel about his state in order to keep himself informed of the work of every department and every section of the community, spoke of the similar responsibilities of the district officer:

> He should know almost every soul in his district personally; should be so patient that he can listen unmoved to an hour's unadulterated twaddle in order that he may not miss the facts which will be contained in the three minutes' conversation which will terminate the interview. . . . He must, above all, be so thoroughly in touch with his people and his chiefs that it is

---

of succeeding Collectors in 1885 and 1886); Resident of Pahang to Collector and Magistrate, Kuantan, 24 June 1889, Kuantan Papers, 4/89; Minute by the Resident of Selangor for the guidance of District Officers, 8 May 1890, *SGG*, 16 May 1890. A Perak draft of revised general orders relating to District Magistrates, circulated in 1891, may be taken as a general indication of their responsibilities (Draft forwarded by Secretary to Government, 23 April 1891, Batang Padang Papers 170/91). The judicial duties of Magistrates are further detailed in Instructions to Officers Entrusted with Magisterial Duties, 7 September 1882, re-issued *PGG*, 12 October 1888, and introduced with slight changes into Selangor and Sungei Ujong. *SGG*, 25 July 1890 and Sungei Ujong Supplement, *SGG*, 28 September 1894.

impossible for any act of oppression to be perpetrated, any grievance, real or fancied, to be cherished, or any trouble to be brewing without the facts coming speedily to his ears. To do this he must rival the restlessness of the Wandering Jew, and must thereby so impress his people with a sense of his ubiquity that all learn to turn to him instinctively for assistance, sympathy, or advice.[1]

Certainly incessant travel was one of the incidents of the district officer's life. Half his time was spent visiting roadworks, mines and villages in various parts of his district. Monthly inspection journeys of a week or even longer were not uncommon, and in addition the district officer as a rule was out two or three times a week, visiting road works, mines, estates and Malay gardens. In the 1890's the work was not quite so strenuous. In Selangor, the districts were sufficiently small, and by 1895 communications were sufficiently advanced to enable the district officer to do most of his travelling in short journeys by road or rail. In Perak, districts were larger and communications more difficult, but it was still rare, after 1890, for the Perak district officer to be away travelling for longer than a week at a time, once a month.[2] It was mainly in Pahang that the size of districts, the sparseness of population and the poor communications made travelling difficult, dangerous and prolonged.

In hundreds of monthly journals, preserved in original in the Selangor Secretariat Papers or published in the *Perak* and *Selangor Gazettes,* the district officers have recorded their daily routine, and in the Batang Padang and Kuantan papers, their administration is recorded in detail. Before about 1890, there were few responsible departmental officers in the outstations, and the district officer had direct responsibility for local police, schools, hospitals and public works, as well as for his own land and court work. He inspected schools and hospitals, where hospitals existed; where they did not, he dispensed drugs and medical advice. He inspected police stations, examined their books, and occasionally drilled the men. He gave out agricultural and mining permits (and infrequently, leases), boat passes and licences for fishing stakes, and collected land rents. In the coast stations he cleared vessels, weighed tin, collected export duty and statistics of trade and immigration. He battled for money for district works; the plaintive appeal of one district officer has echoed down the years, 'Am I not to have any more money for my roads?' He

---

[1] Clifford, 'Life in the Malay Peninsula', op. cit. pp. 389-90.
[2] Information from monthly district letters, *PGG,* 1888-95.

recommended sites for public buildings and reported on the best routes for new roads. Before the appointment of a district engineer, he cut traces for roads, pegged out sites for townships, arranged contracts and supervised construction of public works. Most important, he consulted at length with leading Malays and Chinese about their problems, and forwarded reports to headquarters on projects for which they required special assistance. He made recommendations on loans for settling immigrants, for plough animals and irrigation, for building houses and opening gardens. As a rule, his staff consisted of a Malay writer and one or more English-speaking clerks, a forest ranger, and (in the coast stations) one or more tide-waiters.

The district officer was the leader of the social life of his township, a guest at Chinese and Malay celebrations, and sometimes himself involved in festival preparations for a public holiday, a Governor's visit or a Malay royal occasion.[1] In the early years, when European society was small, it could not have been easy to maintain 'the reserve incumbent upon a British functionary living among an Asiatic population', and on public holidays especially, the reserve broke down somewhat. In 1883, the district officer of Ulu Selangor—which had been formed into a collectorate only that year—described how on the last day of the year, the inhabitants of the township came in procession to his quarters bearing gifts of chickens, fruit, biscuits, liqueurs and cordials. By his own account he refused the gifts, but was told by his police and office staff that the givers had no ulterior motive, but were merely sorry for him since he was the only European in the district and so far from home, and would be insulted if their gifts were returned. So he invited them all to a party on New Year's Day, to feast on the gifts they had brought, and watch foot-racing and Malay dancing.[2] It may be doubted whether this rural informality survived the growth of communications and of the European population. Already in 1897 the favourite recreation of the eight men and one woman who comprised European society in Kajang was to

[1] In 1887, the Collector and Magistrate for Kuala Langat reported in his journal for November that he had been busy for a week, superintending decorations for the installation of the Raja Muda and keeping the Rajas from quarrelling. 'The last week has taught me many lessons & given me an insight into Malay character that I would not have missed for a large consideration. One good thing they all look upon the Magistrate as the arbitrator & rectifier of their wrongs so that my position is not a difficult one [if] friendliness is tempered with caution.' Sel/Sec. 3209/87.
[2] Collector and Magistrate, Ulu Selangor, Journal for December 1883, Sel/Sec. 51/84.

drive in to dinner in Kuala Lumpur, fourteen miles away.[1] This self-sufficiency probably became increasingly characteristic of European life in a Perak or Selangor outstation in the 1890's.

A young Perak district officer wrote to his family of his experiences and the personalities he encountered.[2] He described a legendary pioneer, 'Old Denison',[3] who never slept, but was 'always out first thing after daylight with a little short stick under his arm poking into every nook and corner all over the town', wishing every European he met was 'walking the shady side of Piccadilly'. His work with the Malays made him feel like an Irish landlord:

I go to the office from eight till eleven and generally go back there about two but very often I am only in the office just to answer letters or telegrams, but as sure as one gets there, in come a whole lot of people, teasing one, especially the old women, one will come and say her house was blown down and want Government to build a new one, it is something like dealing with the Irish only the Malays are far more reasonable but just as cunning and tell more lies. I am beginning to like the Chinese in a sort of way; they are as obstinate as pigs and are always in court with paltry cases; as to paltry cases the Klings are the worst and they are all regular lawyers and never speak the truth [except] by accident.

(Telok Anson, 5 December 1886)

He described the old solitary independence of the district officer in a remote station, 'a sort of old Raja rule that does not do now, the country is too much opened up' (Gopeng, 6 September 1891). He used to be a raja in Selama, he recalled, until the carriage road was finished, and 'with that came civilisation'. It was not only the carriage road and the telegraph that qualified the local supremacy of the district officer and complicated his life. By 1890, over most of Perak and Selangor, the Public Works, Police and Medical Departments had established district branches, many of them under European officers, and while these branches were still under the local supervision of the district officer and were required to consult with him in the discharge of their responsibilities, they brought to their work a spe-

---

[1] 'Our Out Stations', by J.M.H.R., *Selangor Journal*, vol. v, no. 26, 3 September 1897.

[2] 'British Malaya as it was', being extracts from the letters of Charles David Bowen, *The Asiatic Review*, vol. xlvi, no. 165 (January 1950).

[3] Noel Denison was recruited to the Perak service from Sarawak, where he served from 1869 to 1876. He was Collector and Magistrate, Krian, from 1877 to 1881, and Superintendent, Lower Perak, from 1881 till his death in 1893. He was the most experienced and respected district officer in Perak, and was known particularly for his settlement work in Lower Perak. *Perak Handbook and Civil Service List, 1892*, pp. 191–2; *AR Lower Perak*, 1893, *PGG*, 27 April 1894.

cialist experience which he did not possess, and could rely on their departmental heads (with whom they communicated directly) for support. The demarcation of responsibility and definition of procedures involving the district officer and the local departments were complex and delicate matters, and subjects of frequent complaint from both sides. The general principles laid down by Maxwell for the guidance of Selangor district officers in their relations with departments,[1] were valid also in Perak:

A District Officer, for instance, would not interfere in the work being performed by a gang of upkeep coolies on a road under the direction of the Public Works Department, but he should certainly communicate with the Head of the Department, if he had reason to think that money was being wasted, or that contract work was not in accordance with specification; and he should, from time to time, on passing road-gangs, check the roll and see what men are working. Again, he would not interfere with the local Apothecary or Dresser in carrying out the orders of the District Surgeon, though it is, of course, his duty to visit the District Hospital frequently, to inspect the rations occasionally, and to take notice of the absence or misconduct of any of the staff. Similarly, he would not interfere with the drill or discipline of the Police, but he is the person responsible for the suppression of crime and the maintenance of order in his District, and his orders to the Police for the furtherance of these objects must be implicitly followed.

There remained two departments over whose local branches the district officers retained direct responsibility—Treasury and Lands. In Perak and Selangor (and presumably in other states), the district officer was responsible for the conduct of the district treasury, and was required to exercise constant supervision over the books, see that the cash was balanced daily, and that the general orders relating to financial matters were complied with. In connexion with lands, his duty was to maintain a rent roll, collect land revenue and supervise demarcation. Up to 1890, most of the mining and agricultural land at the outstations was held on temporary permits or 'agreements for lease' (permits in anticipation of survey) issued by the district officer; the land so held was subject only to rough demarcation, and sometimes this formality was omitted. In 1890, Maxwell set in train a thoroughgoing reform of the Selangor land administration, the essence of which was the distinction between land held under customary tenure (a category originally confined to land held by Muslims), subject to rough demarcation and held on payment of periodical

[1] Minute by the Resident of Selangor for the guidance of District Officers, 8 May 1890, SGG, 16 May 1890.

assessment, and land held by grant or lease, subject to survey and held on payment of premium, quit rent and survey fees. A Survey Department was established to survey grants and leases, which were centrally registered in Kuala Lumpur; but the demarcation and registration of land under customary tenure, and the collection of revenue thereon, remained the responsibility of the district officer. In Perak, conditions were really not very different, despite the fact that Maxwell's reforms were ostentatiously rejected in principle. Centralization of revenue survey and demarcation increased to the extent that by 1894, revenue survey and demarcation throughout the state was co-ordinated under a Lands Department surveyor, and work sent to the central Land Office for correction and preparation of plans.[1] Registers of leases were kept in a central office, and duplicates of leases filed in the district land office. One important feature of the Selangor reforms was accepted in practice; 'promissory permits' (agreements in anticipation of survey) were abandoned in respect of native smallholdings, and the system of demarcation and registration in the district 'mukim register' was adopted;[2] the responsibility of the district officer for native smallholdings was thereby confirmed. The main work of the Perak and Selangor Lands Departments appears to have been to administer lands in the Kuala Lumpur and Larut districts, co-ordinate revenue surveys throughout the state,[3] and advise on the management of the district land offices on the few occasions when they were able to get away from headquarters and visit the districts.

The most important branch of the administration—police—was organized as a separate department in each state from the beginning, and, as might be expected, it maintained the largest establishment. The other departments—Treasury and Audit, Public Works, Lands, Surveys, Health, Education, Railways, Posts and Telegraphs—existed in varying degrees of development according to the different finances of the states. According to the Pahang Estimates for 1894, there existed on paper the following departments—Lands, Courts, Treasury and Post Office, Public Works, Medical, Education and Police. The reality, however, was much less impressive. The Medical

[1] *AR* Lands Department, 1894, *PGG*, 26 April 1895; Quarterly Report on the Revenue Survey, *PGG*, 14 September 1895.

[2] *AR* Perak, 1895. See Chapter X for fuller discussion on land administration.

[3] In Selangor the revenue surveys, which had been the responsibility of the Lands Department, were transferred to a separate Survey Department in 1891 (*AR* Lands Department, 1891, *SGG*, 19 August 1892).

Department consisted of a Residency Surgeon, a District Surgeon and three dressers, and the Education Department consisted of three teachers. According to the Pahang directory for the same year, posts were dealt with by a post office clerk under the Treasurer, and the Land Office was run by the Pekan magistrate. Conditions in Negri Sembilan were much the same. On the other hand, in Perak and Selangor (and to a lesser extent in Sungei Ujong) there was a rapid development of specialist departments from small beginnings to impressive proportions by 1895. In both states the first departmental officers to be appointed (apart from police) were revenue and public works officers. In Selangor very little was done during the locust years of Douglas' residency, and the growth of administration really dates from Swettenham's appointment in 1882; and in Perak also the early 1880's mark the recovery from the disturbances of the previous decade, and the beginning of expansion. In 1882, the Public Works, Lands and Surveys Department in Selangor (a farcical organization which had been the subject of a blistering report by the Colonial Engineer) was split into Lands and Public Works, each with its own survey staff; a Commissioner of Lands was appointed in October 1882, and a Superintendent of Public Works (a qualified engineer) in June 1883.[1] In 1891, a separate Survey Department was established to deal with trigonometrical and revenue surveys, but the Public Works Department retained its own survey staff. Also in 1883, an Inspector of Mines was appointed to survey mines, enforce mining regulations and deal with disputes. The Mines branch was part of the Lands Department until 1891, when it was briefly attached to the Chinese Secretariat; but in 1894 it was organized as a separate department under a Superintendent and Registrar of Mines. In Perak the pattern was somewhat different. There the Mines Branch, formerly attached to Chinese Affairs, became part of the Lands Department in 1889. As in Selangor, there was a Trigonometrical Survey (established in Perak in 1890) but though it did revenue and road surveys on requisition, some survey work continued to be done within the Lands and Public Works Departments. The Public Works Departments expanded rapidly in both states, but even so, the programme of building and road-making was far in excess of capacity,

---

[1] In Selangor, the appointment of Commissioner for Lands was abolished in 1890, and the Lands Department came under a Collector of Land Revenue, appointed in 1891. The Public Works department was reorganized under a State Engineer in 1891, but the changes appear to have been mainly of personnel.

and nearly all the roads and public works and much agricultural and mining survey work—especially in Kinta—were carried out by contract.

The development of railways and telecommunications in Perak and Selangor in the 1880's and 1890's brought into being large departments. In Selangor, the posts and telegraphs which had begun in 1880 with a post office clerk in Kuala Lumpur and another in Klang, developed by 1895 into an establishment of about fifty persons. The railways in 1895 employed some hundred and fifty skilled and semi-skilled people—stationmasters, drivers, guards and clerks—as well as a hundred or so porters, pointsmen, watchmen and other unskilled persons.[1] In Perak there was a similar growth. In both states, the Medical and Education Departments also developed large establishments, which made up in size what they lacked perhaps in qualifications. Finally, both Selangor and Perak organized separate departments to deal with the Chinese population.[2] Like their counterpart in the Straits Settlements, these departments registered labour contracts (the Selangor department also supervised the running of the labour depot in Kuala Lumpur), administered regulations for the protection of women and girls, arbitrated in Chinese disputes, served on Chinese hospital boards, translated letters, documents and regulations, and generally advised the government on Chinese affairs.

The importance of flexibility and freedom from red tape was preached incessantly by certain administrators, particularly Weld and Swettenham, while Maxwell and Dickson could see no reason why the state governments should not abide by rules and regulations. In fact, the states were not the happy refuge for bureaucracy that Weld or Swettenham pretended. Certainly there were pockets of irregularity, sometimes of scandalous proportions, that might persist unsuspected or overlooked for years before they were finally exposed, and some of the exposures might never have taken place but for chance acts of malice. Still, the standards of the colonial public service were generally accepted as the proper standard for the Malay states. Swettenham himself had done something to introduce better accounting methods

---

[1] *Index to List of Establishments, Selangor, 1895.*

[2] The Perak department, begun in 1883 as a Chinese Affairs Department, was styled Chinese Protectorate in 1889. In Selangor, a Chinese Secretary was attached to the Resident's staff in 1890, but till 1894, when a separate Mines Department was set up, his work mainly related to mining tenure and administration. In Perak also, the Chinese Secretary was briefly Registrar of Mines, between 1886 and 1890.

into Selangor during his yearly audit of accounts between 1877 and 1880, and Weld had initiated an investigation into the Selangor Public Works and Lands Department in 1882 and the Sungei Ujong accounts in 1884. A great many forms and procedures and establishment rules were borrowed from the Straits Settlements, and in 1885 the states acquired a common set of general orders based on the Straits Settlements revised general orders of 1884, setting out the required procedures for correspondence, establishment matters (appointments, leave, pensions, allowances), the receipt, disbursement and supervision of public funds, the administration of the courts and hospitals, and the administration of public works.[1] The additions and modifications made in each state from time to time had the effect of further refining and elaborating procedures.

In short, while the public administration may not have been as well developed and regulated as in the Straits Settlements, it was, by 1890, of the same order of size and sophistication, at least in the mining states of west Malaya. Pahang and Negri Sembilan had small administrations,[2] barely able to deal with essential tasks of revenue collection and the maintenance of order, but the density of administration in Perak and Selangor would compare well with that of much larger, older and more populated colonies. Selangor in 1895 had a fixed pensionable establishment of about 350 persons, including about sixty Europeans. In addition there were about fifty teachers, about 250 railway employees, and 750 police—making about 1,400 government employees in all, or 1 per cent. of the estimated population of the state. Though Selangor had only been under British protection for twenty years, it was more densely administered than some much older colonies; in 1895 it spent three times as much as Ceylon per head of population on establishments (excluding payments to native headmen) but only half as much in proportion to total

---

[1] *Native States General Orders*, Singapore, 1885, in Sel/Sec. 1362/85. An abridged version of the Straits Settlements General Orders was forwarded by the CS to the Residents with a view to introducing it into each state (CS to Acting Resident of Perak, 20 August 1884, Sel/Sec. 1486/84). Swettenham, who was then Acting Resident, produced his own revise, incorporating some minor changes (Acting Resident of Perak to CS, 12 September 1884, Sel/Sec. 1652A/84). The final orders incorporated such modifications by other Residents to Swettenham's revise as the Governor approved (CS to Acting Resident of Selangor, 22 August 1885 and minutes, Sel/Sec. 1362/85). The main changes concerned transport allowances, leave regulations and fees for medical attendance.

[2] The Pahang estimates for 1894 give a total establishment of 400, including about 320 police. Sel/Sec. 926/93.

revenue.[1] The work performed by the Selangor Government in 1895 included the collection and disposal of a revenue of $3,805,211; it spent $970,530 on public works, maintained 332 miles of cart and 101 miles of bridle road, and handled more than a million letters and parcels. The sophistication of the administrative services of the Federated Malay States in more recent times had a beginning in the work of nineteenth-century Residents.

THE ESTABLISHMENT

In the Straits Settlements, principles governing appointment, dismissal, leave, pension and other civil service matters were determined by Colonial Regulations, supplemented by local general orders, rules and pension laws. There was no basic regulation, however, for the civil services of the protected states. The Colonial Regulations had no force there, except in so far as particular regulations might be promulgated within a state. The *Native States General Orders* published in 1885[2] dealt on the whole with office procedures rather than basic principles in matters of appointment, leave and pension. For most of the period, the civil services in the states were regulated by precedent. Establishment procedures were informal; pensions were granted in advance of legislation, and as late as 1894 there was no formal letter of appointment for Perak civil servants. Swettenham minuted that inquiry had shown that most officers had never received any formal letter of appointment at all. 'They have simply been sent to work, and in modern times, gazetted.' He disclosed that the forms used in Perak at that time were in fact letters of nomination, and though they concerned appointments under a Malay ruler, nowhere in them was the Sultan mentioned; they were issued in the name of the British Resident. As one official wrote, 'There is no doubt that the status of officers in the Native States needs clearing up. They and their appointments have grown up, like the British

---

[1] The relevant figures are given in Ceylon rupees and Straits dollars, with the sterling equivalent in italics. Conversion has been made at the rate of 1s 4d to the rupee, and 2s 4d to the dollar.

	Revenue	Establishments	Population (est.)
Ceylon	20,982,808	5,560,329	3,298,342
	1,398,848	*370,688*	
Selangor	3,805,211	477,603	150,000
	441,941	*55,720*	

AR Selangor, 1895; *AR* Ceylon, 1895; Detailed statement of expenditure for 1895, from *Ceylon Blue Book*, 1895.

[2] See p. 224, note 1.

constitution, in unwritten style, & no one has asked too closely what is the nominal sanction for it all.'[1]

Casual establishment procedures certainly added to the difficulty of definition, but where practical realities were contrary to appearances, and where appearances had to be kept up without sacrificing realities, precise definitions were not only impossible but undesirable, and were deliberately avoided. When Mitchell, a tidy-minded incoming Governor, asked the Secretary of State to declare whether officers were to receive their appointments from the Governor, the Resident or the Sultan, and in the last case, whether the appointment should be issued by direction of the Governor or the Malay Ruler, the Secretary of State in a delphic utterance, replied that in correspondence with his own office, care would be taken to avoid language as to the status of an appointment 'which might be construed as being at variance with the facts'; but as to the formalities for completing an appointment on the spot, he wrote, 'I do not perceive that any appreciable change of practice is required, and I leave the matter to your discretion.'[2] The interests which had somehow to be reconciled, however imperfectly, were the formal independence of the states, the need to control them in the interest of British policy in Malaya, the personal security of the officers—security of tenure, salary, pension and promotion—and the integrity of the colonial establishments. So far as the Residents were concerned, there was no real problem in reconciling the first three interests. Residents might be appointed to advise a Malay Ruler, and be paid by him, and still quite properly remain servants of the Crown. This in fact is how they were regarded. They were under the direct control of the Governor, they were appointed by the Governor with the sanction of the Secretary of State,[3]

[1] Minute by Swettenham, 16 September 1894, enclosed in Mitchell to Ripon, 384 of 19 November 1894, CO 273/198; minute by Lucas, 21 December 1894, ibid.

[2] Mitchell to Ripon, 384 of 19 November 1894, and Ripon to Mitchell, 4 of 2 January 1895, CO 273/198.

[3] This assertion runs counter to a claim by Swettenham that the British Resident was appointed by the Secretary of State (Minute by Swettenham, 16 September 1894, enclosed in Mitchell to Ripon, 384 of 19 November 1894, CO 273/198). A clerk in the CO corrected Swettenham with the comment 'only "*selected*" for appt. technically' (marginal note by Johnson on minute by Lucas of 21 December 1894, ibid.). A few of the appointments were made after sanction had been received from the Secretary of State (e.g., the appointments to Perak and Selangor in 1889) but the great majority were made provisionally by the Governor on the spot and subsequently approved. The only Resident appointment which appears to have originated in the CO is that of Low. See minute by Meade, 24 May 1876,

and their salaries and other emoluments were decided by the latter. They bore the title 'British Resident', their notepaper was stamped with a crowned crest, and their personal flag was the state flag with a Union Jack in the upper canton.[1] They were considered to be 'not servants of the Sultans but servants of the Queen appointed to advise the Sultans'.[2] But they held no royal commission[3] and their position as servants of the Queen could mean little in practical terms unless they secured a footing on an establishment under the Crown. Officers who were in the Straits service to begin with had no problem; they were regarded as on secondment to the states, and their chances of promotion in the Straits were unimpaired. The difficulty was to find a base for Residents recruited from outside the colonial service.[4] In 1888 the Governor and the majority of the Executive Council strongly resisted a suggestion that they should come on to the Colony establishment, ostensibly because this would compromise the independence of the states (a worthless argument), in reality perhaps for

on Jervois to Carnarvon, 169 of 19 April 1876, CO 273/83, also marginal minute on CO draft reply.

[1] CS to Resident of Selangor, 31 January 1879, Sel/Sec. 46/79.

[2] Minute by Lucas, 21 December 1894, on Mitchell to Ripon, 384 of 19 November 1894, CO 273/198.

[3] In 1888, it was pointed out that the title H.B.M. Resident, which had been in use in earlier years, was incorrect, since the Residents were not appointed by royal commission (Acting CS to Resident of Perak, 13 September 1888, *PGG*, 28 September 1888). In 1892, Treacher defended himself against an attack on his administration by saying he had never received a commission or any instructions (Treacher to CS, 5 October 1892, enclosure G 6 in Mitchell to Ripon, Confidential of 14 May 1894, CO 273/195).

[4] The question of establishment placing was important. In 1884 a question arose concerning the pension rights of a prison warder originally in the Home service, who was transferred to the Colony and thence to Perak. The Treasury refused to accept Perak service as public employment under the Crown, and it was necessary to place the warder on the Straits establishment and transfer funds from Perak to pay his salary, in order to secure his pension rights (Treasury to CO, 6 September 1886, CO 273/142; Stanhope to Weld, 117 of 9 December 1886, on Treasury to CO, 20 October 1886, CO 273/142). In 1885, a Cyprus official, late of Ceylon, was offered the post of Secretary to Government, Perak, and warned that as Perak service was not service under the Crown, he would lose his Cyprus service for pension purposes, and strictly speaking his Ceylon service too, but that the Secretary of State would recommend to the Ceylon government that they should treat his Perak service as service under the Crown for pension purposes (CO to Governor of Cyprus, 14 October 1885, CO 273/138/14003). The Ceylon, Hong Kong and Labuan governments apparently proved more tractable than the Treasury, since officers transferred from these colonies to Perak and Selangor were treated as being on transfer from one colony to another for pension purposes. Transfers from the Straits Settlements presented no difficulty, since service in the Settlements and the states was deemed to be continuous for pension purposes.

fear of possible claims by people outside the service to promotion in the Straits Settlements. As the Colonial Office showed no inclination to assume formal responsibilities in relation to the states, the Residents were left on the state establishments and continued to look to the states for payment of their salaries and pensions. Their claim to be 'servants of the Crown' was purely rhetorical, since the Crown acknowledged no formal obligation to them.

The Residents were members of the state establishments, but not servants of the Sultan; the subordinate officers were similarly members of the state establishments, but they *were* servants of the Sultan. It requires some experience of the mental processes of British colonial administrators to perceive the essential logic of this. The appointments of subordinate officers were subject to the sanction of the Governor, and they served under a Resident who acted under the instructions of the Governor. They regarded themselves as 'members of the Resident's Staff, and as such the servants of Her Majesty, and not of the Native Ruler',[1] and some authorities also appeared to regard them in this light. Low, writing in 1879 to urge the recruitment of cadets for service in the Malay states, declared, 'I look upon all the officers here as serving the Straits Government';[2] Smith, writing in 1885 on the calculation of pensions for service by Straits officers in the Malay states, thought there was no doubt that such service should be held to be continuous with Colony service, 'as though it were in law, as it is in fact under one Government'.[3] But the official view was always that nominally, at least, they were the servants of the state government,[4] and Swettenham made it clear in so many words that this meant they were servants of the Malay Ruler.[5] The fact is that while the realities of power demanded that the state establishment be directed by the Resident, the fiction that the Resident was there to advise demanded that it be placed nominally in the service of the Sultan. An adviser's staff which consisted of the entire civil service of the state would have made an already thread-bare fiction

[1] Memorial of European Civil Servants of Perak to Secretary of State, undated, enclosed in Smith to Knutsford, 413 of 15 September 1888, CO 273/154.
[2] Low to Anson, 23 May 1879, in Anson to Hicks Beach, 190 of 5 June 1879, CO 273/99.
[3] Smith to Derby, 219 of 25 May 1885, CO 273/134.
[4] E.g., CO to Sheppard, 29 August 1881, on Weld to Kimberley, 249 of 10 July 1881, CO 273/109. CO to Treacher, 23 March 1888, on Smith to Holland, tel. of 5 March 1888, CO 273/152.
[5] Minute by Swettenham, 16 September 1894, enclosed in Mitchell to Ripon, 384 of 19 November 1894, CO 273/198.

break down altogether. When the attempt was made to smuggle the subordinate officers onto the Straits establishment in 1886, Weld's objection was not only that many of these officers would never have been appointed to the Colony in the first place, but that their transfer to the Straits establishment would be tantamount to annexation.[1]

Appointment to all offices was by nomination, in contrast to the system in the Straits Settlements, where appointments to posts in Class V and above were filled by open competition after 1882.[2] Patronage over all appointments below that of Resident and Assistant Resident and above $600 a year (a category which included all European appointments) was in the hands of the Governor, and it was the Governor also who determined salaries and approved leave applications within this range. A pension scheme presented more difficulty. Since the entire British establishment depended on future British policy in the states, neither the Residents nor the Governors felt able to introduce pension schemes on their own initiative, and it was left to the Secretary of State to declare his opinion that all European officers serving in the states should be entitled to pensions calculated in the same manner as those assigned to officers in the Straits Settlements.[3] A pensions law was not introduced into Perak till 1893,[4] nor into Selangor or Negri Sembilan till 1895, but pensions were paid in Perak and Sungei Ujong in anticipation of legislation. The introduction of pensions did not, however, secure officers against summary dismissal. In 1886, the Secretary of State reported Low as stating that while European officers were entitled to pension on the same terms as those accorded to officers in the Straits Settlements, they were liable to dismissal by the Governor without any of the formalities which were required in the case of colonial officers.[5] As

[1] Weld to Granville, 99 of 20 March 1886, CO 273/139.
[2] Between 1867 and 1869, the Straits Settlements cadetships were filled by nomination, and between 1869 and 1882, by competitive examination after nomination. In 1882 the Eastern Cadetship scheme was introduced, with a combined examination, open to public competition, for recruitment to the Straits Settlements, Hong Kong and Ceylon. Linda Tan, 'The Development of the Straits Settlements Civil Service, 1867–1896, B.A. honours dissertation, University of Malaya, 1957; Charles Jeffries, *The Colonial Empire and its Civil Service*, London, 1938, p.8.
[3] Kimberley to Weld, 63 of 15 March 1881, CO 273/107.
[4] Pensions Regulations for the Perak police were introduced in 1885, but general pensions regulations were not introduced till 1893 (replaced by Pensions Order in Council 2 of 1895).
[5] Stanley to Weld, 34 of 5 February 1886, CO 273/136.

late as 1894, Maxwell's opinion as reported by the Governor was that the services of all state officers might be dispensed with by the State Council on short notice and without compensation[1] (in fact no office held by a European was ever discussed by the State Council). Officers were dismissed by the Governor after they had had the opportunity to hear and answer charges against them. In the first decade the enquiry was usually conducted by the Resident alone; in later years, usually by a commission of fellow officers appointed by the Resident.

Two inquiries that have come to light demonstrate the power of the Resident over his establishment and the absence of proper machinery for safeguarding the tenure of officers. The first one concerned a Selangor railway engineer, Spence-Moss, who had used his knowledge of future wharf development at Klang to buy up blocks in the name of his brother-in-law. The transactions were not questioned by Swettenham, and compensation was duly paid on the resumption of these blocks by the state. Swettenham's successor, Maxwell, had the papers relating to the Klang scheme before him in August 1889, soon after his arrival in the state, but he did not then (he said) realize the implications of these transactions. He decided to investigate them when, according to his own account, his confidence in Moss had been undermined. He set up a commission of enquiry consisting of himself as president, the Chief Magistrate and the Secretary to Government, and as a result of its findings, he advised the Governor that Moss should be dismissed. By the time the inquiry was held, Maxwell had had a number of personal and professional differences with Moss, and their relations had completely broken down; as Moss pointed out, it was not possible for him to be 'an impartial and unprejudiced president of this commission'.[2] It is difficult to escape the feeling that although Moss deserved dismissal, and Maxwell's action was entirely in keeping with his own rigorous standards, yet malice against Moss (and Swettenham, whose administration was thus brought into disrepute) was not absent from his motives.

    [1] Mitchell to Ripon, Confidential of 7 May 1894, CO 273/195. A few months earlier, Maxwell, while acting as Governor, had invoked this principle when he ordered the compulsory retirement without pension of an officer whose office had been abolished and who was considered unsuitable for any other employment. The Secretary of State intervened to secure his pension. Mitchell to Ripon, Confidential of 27 June 1894, and Ripon to Mitchell, Confidential of 22 August 1894, CO 273/196.
    [2] Spence-Moss to CS, 21 April 1891, enclosed in Spence-Moss to CO, 13 September 1891, CO 273/178.

In the second case, which occurred in Perak, a district magistrate was appointed to preside over a tribunal of inquiry into the conduct of a district engineer (Fraser) with whom he had openly clashed, and whose dismissal he had already tried to bring about by forwarding charges of bribery preferred by the clerk of a local contractor who was the magistrate's own surety.[1] The correspondence reached the Secretary of State as a result of a memorial by Fraser; the appointment of the magistrate to the commission of inquiry was severely criticized, and the practice of accepting local traders as sureties for government officers was absolutely condemned, and the Governor instructed that it should be 'entirely prohibited throughout the Native States'.[2] The case had been referred to Singapore, and while the Colonial Secretary (Maxwell) had not thought the facts proven in the inquiry justified dismissal, the Governor felt that Fraser's continued employment would be against the public interest, and fell back on the argument that the Sultan had 'a perfect right, on the advice tendered to him, to dispense with the services of any officer in the State'.[3]

The Colonial Office found this continuing insecurity of tenure unsatisfactory, and an incoming Governor, Mitchell, was equally disturbed by the absence of any clear definition of the position and rights of officers in the Malay states, either in their letters of appointment or in any other way. Mitchell wrote to say that definition of the status of European officers was needed, both as regards security of remuneration and continuance of office. The Secretary of State, referring to past decisions on the subject, confirmed that officers, as servants of the states, must look to the states for payment of their salaries and pensions; as to security of tenure, he recommended that certain appointments be declared pensionable, and their holders secured against dismissal except according to well-defined procedures.

[1] Mitchell to Ripon, Confidential of 14 May 1894 and enclosures, CO 273/195. For the light thrown by this case on judicial practice see Chapter VIII.

[2] Ripon to Mitchell, Confidential of 4 March 1895, CO 273/199. The previous Governor, Smith, had already expressed his disapproval of the surety system in Perak during an investigation carried out as a result of a petition by Fraser.

[3] This is not to be taken as claiming any initiative for the Sultan. In 1877, Douglas was rebuked for consulting Tengku Zia'u'd-din about the suspension of the Collector and Magistrate, Kuala Selangor, and told, 'should similar cases arise in future in connection with superior European officers of the Salangor Government, the Resident should on no account communicate with the Salangor Government until he shall have been instructed to do so by this Government'. CS to Resident of Selangor, 14 August 1877, Sel/Sec. 285/77.

As a result of this correspondence, the Governor secured the passage of pension legislation in Perak, Selangor and Negri Sembilan in 1895 and agreed to the suggestion of the Secretary of State that it should also be introduced into Pahang.[1]

In all essentials, leave and pension regulations in the states were the same as in the Colony. Salaries, however, were much lower in the states, and they varied a good deal between one state and another. The salary of the Resident of Perak was maintained at the same level as that of the Colonial Secretary, though Low received a personal allowance in addition; the Resident of Selangor was paid about the same as the Resident Councillor of Malacca, and the Residents of Negri Sembilan and Pahang were paid roughly at the same rate as a superintendent of police in the Colony. The disparities were even greater in the case of lesser officers. The district officer of Kinta, after 1891 the richest district in Perak, earned no more than the magistrate of the Dindings (an unimportant Colony station between the Perak and Larut rivers), and the superintendent of Ulu Pahang, the chief Pahang collectorate and mining district, earned no more than a third magistrate in Singapore.[2]

The state establishments were independent of each other and of the Colony establishment, and it is clear that the different basis of recruitment alone would have made it impossible for the state and colono services to be amalgamated. But though there were obvious objections to the transfer of state civil servants to the Colony, these did not apply to a movement in reverse; the states naturally looked to the Colony as a source of trained officers and the Colony officers in their turn looked to the states as a field for professional advancement. It was established at an early stage that Colony officers on transfer to the states would not lose their chances of promotion in the Colony and the Straits pension regulations of 1887 made service in the Colony and Malay states continuous for pension purposes.[3] The

---

[1] Mitchell to Ripon, Confidential of 7 May 1894, and Ripon to Mitchell, Confidential of 11 July 1894, CO 273/195; Mitchell to Ripon, 259 of 21 August 1894 and Ripon to Mitchell, 330 of 5 October 1894, CO 273/197; Mitchell to Ripon, Confidential of 15 October 1894, and Ripon to Mitchell, Confidential of 27 November 1894, CO 273/198; Mitchell to Ripon, 486 of 10 December 1895, CO 273/207.

[2] *Native States List of Civil Establishments*, 1891; Revised Straits Settlements salary scheme, 1890.

[3] Legislative Council Paper No. 23, 15 November 1887, clause 10 (3). The main provisions of these regulations were reproduced in the state pensions laws.

Colony officers attempted to keep the higher posts in the states as a preserve for themselves, but their claims were rejected,[1] and while a few Colony officers served for long periods in the states,[2] and others went on secondment for short periods in emergencies, the majority of state officers were recruited from outside the colonial service altogether. Between the states there were occasional transfers at a high level, but these were exceptional, and below the level of Resident, the state services were virtually self-contained bodies.[3]

Before 1883, when the states were still an untried field, they attracted a strange assortment of people. There was a stiffening of ambitious career officers like Swettenham and Maxwell, who looked on their native states service as secondment from the Straits, and were secure in the knowledge that their Straits promotion would not be impaired; there were mercenaries like Speedy, solitaries like Murray, fanatics like Birch, and misfits as widely separated as Douglas and Low; the former moving restlessly from one undistinguished post to another, the latter turning a life of obscurity and bureaucratic frustration in Labuan into a triumph of personal achievement. The rank and file also had varying abilities and backgrounds. A number were simply drifters who had got to the East more by accident than design, and found themselves in the Straits in need of a job; some of these were educated men, betrayed by alcoholism or other weaknesses, others were semi-literate, barely capable of spelling English names, let alone Malay. Some of them were Straits planters or overseers, put in charge of districts for want of better men.

Low complained bitterly about the 'useless loafers whom it was formerly the fashion to send on here, insolent broken-down bankrupts, or drunkards, who all think themselves entitled to have, and to express opinions, contrary to the views of Government'.[4] His outburst should not be taken too seriously; it was obviously directed

---

[1] Kimberley to Weld, 303 of 6 December 1882, CO 273/116; Derby to Smith, 177 of 23 July 1884, CO 273/128, in which the Secretary of State rejected a memorial from Straits officers objecting to the appointment of Rodger as Acting Resident of Selangor.

[2] Apart from the Residents themselves, the most notable Straits officer to serve in the states was E.W. Birch, whose experience as Second Assistant CS and as Magistrate, Malacca, was followed by service in the Selangor Lands Department and the Perak secretariat before he went to Negri Sembilan as Resident. The Chinese Protectorate in Perak drew a number of officers from the Straits.

[3] The FMS Civil Service List, 1904 shows that transfers between the states were the exception before federation, and the rule after it.

[4] Low to Anson, 23 May 1879, in Anson to Hicks Beach, 190 of 5 June 1879, CO 273/99.

at one man—Innes—who compounded his crimes of heavy drinking and inattention to routine by a casual attitude to authority and a forthright opposition to the official toleration of slavery which he found in Perak. Low's Journal shows that he had some reason to complain of inefficient and apathetic officers, but Perak appears to have been well-off compared with Selangor under Douglas. Weld remarked after a visit to Selangor in 1882, 'It is a singular fact that I have had to dismiss two-thirds of the staff of officials here, since I came, for inefficiency.'[1] The district of Kuala Selangor was particularly afflicted, with ten changes of district officer between 1875 and 1880. There was Roberts, whose journals were confined for the most part to information about the weather ('Morning fine, evening rain') and came back from Singapore with outraged blue pencil marks under such mis-spellings as 'Mo-arum' (Moharram), 'Chinees', 'quorters' and 'voilint'. He was dismissed for flogging a policeman and also a Chinese barber who had refused to come when summoned; 'I got into a temper as I took the refusal to be as a sort of insult to me, as I being the only Englishman in the place, and I ordered the Sergeant to give him [the barber] a dozen.'[2] Then there was Perks, a paragon of efficiency, even if he was rather longwinded in his letters to the Resident, praising 'your may I state in my humble opinion very excellent system of local district Govt'. Unhappily, Perks was charged with criminal breach of trust after five years and sentenced to a term of imprisonment. There was the Ceylonese doctor, Jansz, who was found drunk and incapable in his hospital on the morning of the Resident's inspection. And so the procession continued, until Swettenham brought a fresh hope and a new spirit to the state.

Even in this early period, however, there were a number of honest, devoted officers of education and intelligence; some of them, recruited from Sarawak, knew Malay and had experience of district work. They provided a nucleus for what became a vigorous middle-class colonial service of moderate intellectual capacity and attainment, but with considerable energy and commonsense. The majority of European officers appointed between 1885 and 1895 were aged twenty-five and under on first appointment to the states, and perhaps one-quarter were aged between seventeen and twenty-one. Most of them came to the states on first appointment, and spent their whole

---

[1] Cited in Lovat, *The Life of Sir Frederick Weld*, p.356.
[2] Collector and Magistrate, Kuala Selangor, to Resident, 9 November 1878, Sel/Sec. 349/78. See also Sel/Sec. 60 and 72 of 1878, 110/80, 114/81 and 562/82.

careers there.[1] It was clear that the states had ceased to depend on the human flotsam that reached the Straits Settlements after much drifting about the Far East. The lists are silent about the school background of perhaps half the officers, but the others came from good public schools—Rugby, Cheltenham, Haileybury, Charterhouse, Sherborne, Wellington. A very few went to finishing schools in France and Germany and Spain, and perhaps one-quarter had university degrees, mostly from Oxford and Cambridge. In a service dominated by people who had never had a university education and had been put to work at twenty, a degree meant very much less than 'character', physical courage and the right background, in that order of importance. Weld thought that an upper age limit of twenty was quite sufficient for candidates for Straits Settlements cadetships, and thought little of bookwork as a preparation for the Malay states; 'no amount of cramming, or competitive examinations, will teach a man how to manage natives, or win their confidence'. It was admitted that the nomination system for appointments in the Malay states had its disadvantages. In 1896 the Acting Resident of Perak acknowledged that the Perak service, though 'a gentlemanly and high-toned service' was 'wanting in ability', but in common with his colleagues, he strongly opposed the suggestion of the Secretary of State that appointments should be made by open competition. The overriding advantage of the nomination system was that it enabled the states to recruit men of gentle birth, well-mannered, and often the sons of men who held high positions in the East:

To my knowledge it is pleasing to the Chiefs of this State to have as junior officers men who bear the name of Weld, Hose, Maxwell, and Irving. . . . It is a great recommendation to the Malay mind that a man should be a gentleman for the Malay race studies courtesy and is quick to distinguish between a gentleman and a man who is either a boor or is underbred.

For these reasons I entirely oppose the system of open competition. As a member of the covenanted Civil Service of the Straits Settlements I say without hesitation that there have been and are in that service men who if put in responsible positions in the Native States would have offended the sensitive natures and have trodden upon the ancient customs and mannerisms of the Malays.[2]

---

[1] Information from *FMS Civil Service List, 1904*, and *Native States List of Civil Establishments, 1891*.

[2] Acting Resident of Perak to CS, 6 January 1896, enclosed in Mitchell to Chamberlain, Confidential of 6 March 1896, CO 273/212.

The subordinate officers—clerks, overseers, apothecaries, dressers, station masters, guards, postmasters, draughtsmen—were Chinese, Eurasian and Tamil, in roughly equal proportions, with a sprinkling of Sinhalese and Malays. In the Selangor Establishment List for 1895, Eurasians (de Rozarios, De Silvas, De Souzas, Leembruggens) were prominent as building overseers, road inspectors, apothecaries and senior clerks, and Chinese appeared everywhere as clerks. (Kuala Langat, where the Sultan lived, was the only district office in which there were no Chinese; the clerks there were Tamils.) The Malays (outside the penghulu establishment) filled the police force, and some were employed as forest rangers and school-masters and a few as clerks. Since the posts they held were unskilled, badly-paid, or both, it will be seen that twenty years of British rule had done little to prepare them even for the lowest grades of clerical service. In the occupational caste system that had so quickly developed, they were rajas, headmen, police or peasants. The British expressed—rather tardily —some concern about this; what the Malays felt is less easily ascertained. It is possible that they looked on the state establishments as alien institutions, as indeed they were, and had not yet come to perceive that they were institutions in which Malays had a rightful place.

VIII

LAW AND ORDER

THE POLICE

AT the direction of the Colonial Office, the organization of the police was taken in hand soon after the pacification of Perak in 1876. The immediate necessity was to provide for the protection of the Resident by raising a local force and so enabling the troops from India and Hong Kong to be withdrawn. The Secretary of State asked the Governor to consider the strength and organization of the force, which would be under the orders of the Residents and responsible to them, and to consider in particular how far foreign elements should be included. 'On the one hand it may be desirable that it should not appear to the Malays to be that of a dominant power imposed on them from without; on the other a force drawn from beyond the Peninsula may be found most reliable.'[1]

The problem which then occupied the Colonial Office and the local government was to provide security for Perak, and what were considered to be the special needs of Perak imposed a military cast on the force. The first 'police' in the state consisted of Sikhs recruited by Speedy in 1873 to fight for the Mentri, as well as a detachment of sepoys who provided a guard for Birch.[2] Carnarvon visualized a force of 150 to 200 men purely for guard duty with the Resident, leaving police duties to be performed, in the main, by native authority;[3] Jervois, on the other hand, pressed for a para-military guard of 200 Sikhs, mainly in Larut and Kuala Kangsar, and, in addition, 500 Malay police distributed all over the country. In early 1877, the composition of the Perak police was in these proportions; but the inefficiency of the Malay police, combined with Low's strong representations, decided the matter in favour of a smaller and predominantly Sikh force. Low considered that much of the police work of the country—the maintenance of order and the detection of crime—could and should be done by a para-military force of 350 Sikhs, in-

[1] Carnarvon to Jervois, 1 June 1876, C.1512, no. 70.
[2] Jervois to Carnarvon, 297 of 19 August 1876, CO 273/84.
[3] Carnarvon to Jervois, 15 February 1877, C.1709, no. 88.

cluding fifty gunners, and that the Malay section should be kept down to 100 good detectives, to support the penghulus. He had already taken on himself the responsibility of reducing the force by 250 men within a few months of his arrival, by dismissing unfit or inefficient constables and not replacing them; and since his views were strongly supported by Swettenham (then Assistant Colonial Secretary for Native States) and were in accordance with Colonial Office recommendations, they finally prevailed. With an increase of fifty men in the Malay force, Low's figures were accepted as a basis for recruitment.[1]

The Perak police thus developed as a para-military force with a majority of Sikhs. In the quarter ending 1 July 1878, in a force of 477 men (including European officers and clerical staff) there were 247 Sikhs and 220 Malay land and water police;[2] and the proportion of Sikhs increased until in 1895, Sikh NCO's and men numbered 774 as against 266 Malays.[3] They were stationed in all the districts of Perak, but the largest contingent (about half the force) served at headquarters in Taiping. They performed both police and military duties, providing guards for residencies, treasuries, and customhouses, escorts for remittances between stations, and road patrols; but their essential purpose was to deal with outbreaks and disturbances in the large Chinese labour concentrations in the towns, mines and estates. They constituted in effect a small standing army, designed and trained as such. They were led by officers and inspectors transferred or seconded from British regiments, under a Commandant with the honorary rank of Lieut.-Colonel,[4] and their establishment included a small cavalry troop divided between Larut and Kinta, and a detachment of artillery. The military cast of the force

[1] Robinson to Hicks Beach, 255 of 27 August 1878 and enclosures, CO 273/95.

[2] Commissioner of Police to Resident of Perak, 17 June 1878, enclosed in Robinson to Hicks Beach, 224 of 1 August 1878, CO 273/95.

[3] Report of Inspection of Perak Sikhs, General Officer Commanding the Troops, Straits Settlements, 3 January 1896, enclosed in Mitchell to Chamberlain, Confidential of 5 March 1896, CO 273/213.

[4] Lieut.-Colonel Robert Sandilands Frowd Walker, CMG (1891), was born in 1850 and educated at the Royal Military Academy, Sandhurst. He joined the 28th Foot in 1871, saw service in Perak in 1876, and was attached to the Perak Armed Police in 1879. He became Deputy Commissioner in 1880, and Commissioner in 1882. In 1884, he was given the local rank of Major, and the title of his office was changed to Commandant, 1st Perak Sikhs. He was made an honorary Lieut.-Colonel in 1889 and was given the local rank in 1902. In 1896, he became Commandant of the Malay States Guides, a force which he organized. He retired in 1910.

is illustrated by the programme followed at an official inspection in 1888 by the Commandant, Straits Settlements; it included manoeuvres over rough ground (with artillery support), firing practice, and 'the entraining and detraining of 39 Non-commissioned Officers and men of the artillery, with half battery 7-pd. mountain guns, 1 Gardener machine gun, 1 company of infantry of 79 Non-commissioned Officers and men, with baggage, ammunition, rations for 14 days, and clothing and boots for one year'.[1]

In 1884, at the urgent request of Weld, Low, Captain Walker (the commanding officer), and the men themselves, the Secretary of State permitted the force to adopt the title '1st Battalion Perak Sikhs', but it might equally well have been called 'Weld's Private Army'. He took a loving pride in its organization and training, and well he might; it was the only force which he was at liberty to move around the Peninsula without reporting to anybody. In a moment of patriotic euphoria, he offered to send 250 Sikhs and a half battery of mountain guns (about one-third the total strength of the force) for service in Egypt or Afghanistan, assuring the Secretary of State, 'the Regent and state of Perak would I doubt not be proud & happy to shew their sense of the benefit which has accrued to Perak from British rule by this token of loyalty to Her Majesty & to the Empire'.[2] The Colonial Office declined the offer, an official minuting that India was more likely to have to help Perak than vice versa. The force was confined for the time being to action in the Peninsula and in Perak itself. A detachment of Perak Sikhs was held in readiness to go to Rembau in 1883 to deal with threatened disturbances, and detachments were sent to Pahang in 1892 and 1894 to put down Malay outbreaks. In 1883, the people of Lambor in South Perak (near the village where Birch was murdered) resisted the statutory corvée of six days in the year; refusing to listen to the arguments of Low, Raja Idris, and other Perak chiefs, they beat the mosque drum and prepared for resistance. Captain Walker with 100 police was ordered down-river, supported by Malay chiefs and their followers; the people of Lambor, overawed, submitted without a fight.[3] The other incidents reported concerned the Chinese. In 1879, Sikhs under Walker were called out to deal with threatening crowds of miners pro-

---

[1] *AR* Perak Sikhs, 1888, *PGG*, 15 March 1889.
[2] Weld to CO, private, 27 March 1885, CO 273/138. It appears from the context that he made this offer without ascertaining the opinion of the Regent.
[3] Weld to Derby, 25 May 1883, C.4192, no. 9.

testing against a proposed monopoly of the sale of cooked opium; they opened fire, and killed or wounded fifty or sixty Chinese.[1] In 1882, there was a fracas at Parit Buntar in Krian, where Chinese resisted payment of the 'hospital dollar'—a special tax collected from every Chinese over sixteen to pay for their treatment in the state hospitals.[2] In 1887, police intervened in a secret society clash at Papan in Kinta, involving some hundreds of miners belonging to the Hai San and Ghi Hin secret societies.[3]

In its ordinary police duties, also, the force was mainly concerned with the Chinese population of the state. Its services were much in demand by Chinese traders and mine-owners; the Commandant reported that during a visit to Kinta, he 'saw the towkays in every mining centre who cried out for police protection' and who provided police accommodation at their own expense.[4] According to the *Perak Handbook* for 1892, three-quarters of the police were stationed in Larut, Matang, and Kinta, leaving one-quarter for the predominantly Malay areas (though these contained half the population of the state). In these areas, again, half to three-quarters of the detachments (including most of the Sikhs) were maintained in the district headquarters, leaving the rural Malay centres to be policed, if at all, by small detachments of Malays, sometimes under a Sikh corporal.[5] A stretch of some sixty miles of river between Telok Anson and Kuala Kangsar, with a large and purely Malay population, had no police stations at all. Swettenham wrote in his report for 1889 that he had recently visited, in the company of the Sultan, all the most important mukims on the Perak river 'where the population, though large, is purely Malay and a European officer or police constable is very seldom seen'. The distribution of police was in accordance with the distribution of crime; in 1892, of 17,736 crimes reported, 13,910 were

[1] Low to CS, 4 and 6 October 1879, enclosed in Anson to Hicks Beach, 357 of 18 October 1879, CO 273/100.

[2] Weld to Kimberley, 296 of 16 August 1882, CO 273/115. The hospital dollar was first collected in 1881, and abolished from 1 January 1886. *AR* Perak, 1882 and 1885.

[3] *AR* Perak, 1887; Report of Secretary for Chinese Affairs, Perak, for 1887, enclosed in Smith to Knutsford, 347 of 30 July 1888, CO 273/154.

[4] Report of a Visit of Inspection by the Commandant, Perak Sikhs, 16 February 1893, *PGG*, 3 March 1893. During a survey of the mining industry of Perak, an official of the government of Burma was told by Chinese entrepreneurs that ten miles was too far to have to travel to a magistrate. W.T. Hall, *Report on Tin Mining in Perak and Burma*, Rangoon, 1889, p. 22.

[5] See *AR* Lower Perak, 1888, *PGG*, 31 May 1889, *AR* Batang Padang, and *AR* Selama, 1889, *PGG*, 18 April 1890 and 22 August 1890.

from Larut and Kinta.[1] Much of the serious crime in the other districts was a function of increased economic activity; it took the form of highway robbery and robbery of opium shops, gambling saloons and pawnshops. The Commandant wrote with remarkable perception about the relationship of crime to economic development:

No wonder that the crime has increased, as increase it must, with a mining population of Chinese, a race that knows no repose, that settles only for the moment where money is to be made with the greatest ease. . . . Crime with such a population as this means progress, and although a check has been given to it by raising the Force to its utmost capacity, at the sacrifice of other parts of the State, strengthening the detective branch, and paying judiciously for information, crime must arise, and as long as a fair number of discoveries are made of crimes most difficult to detect in a country where escape is so easy, and a criminal can with comparative ease conceal himself, it is all that can be expected.[2]

How the Sikh police managed to solve any crimes at all or deal in any way with populations whose languages they did not speak, remains a mystery. To begin with, the police as a whole were grossly understaffed and overworked; the Commandant in his report for 1893 complained that though the population, the revenue, and volume of crime had doubled in the last ten years, the police establishment had increased by only 17 per cent. The district officer for Kinta put the matter succinctly in his report on police and crime during 1889:

The district is noted for its want of the former and plentifulness of the latter. The Sikhs have, I believe, done hard work in the way of sentries, patrols and escorts, parades, musketry practice, etc. I do not intend to quote criminal returns, but I know they are very heavy. I can call to mind at once five or six murders, several gang robberies, cutting and wounding, and such will be the state of things till we have an efficient Police and detective force. It cannot be expected that Sikhs, highly trained as soldiers, and not knowing even Malay, can be smart policemen amongst Chinese and Malays. During an examination of some twelve men this year who presented themselves, I found only one could speak at all passably, and I doubt much if he could have made a thorough inquiry into a case.[3]

The police were strengthened by the appointment of a Superintendent of Intelligence who had served in Hong Kong and spoke several Chinese dialects;[4] there were also a number of Chinese detectives

---

[1] Figures from *AR* Perak Sikhs, 1893, *PGG*, 6 July 1894.   [2] Ibid.
[3] *AR* Kinta, 1889, *PGG* 4 April 1890.
[4] He was Superintendent Christian Wagner, Barrister of the Inner Temple, appointed to Hong Kong in 1865, and appointed to the post of Superintendent,

attached to the force, but these were few and ill-paid.[1] Yet the police were reasonably successful in dealing with crime. Excluding cases of miners absconding from their employment while under advances (5,226 cases out of 17,736 reported in 1892), the proportion of discoveries was 70 per cent. for the whole state, 66 per cent. for Larut, and 71 per cent. for Kinta.

Sikhs were disliked and feared by Chinese, but this was considered a recommendation rather than otherwise. The fact that they were also extremely unpopular among Malays was much against them, however. There was a feeling to begin with that the introduction of Asiatic aliens in positions of authority over Malays was a breach of faith. Clifford put into the mouth of a Malay an expression of distaste for Asiatic petty functionaries which he almost certainly shared:

> Your rule is just, and since we must,
> We learn to kiss the yoke;
> *You* we obey, by night and day,
> But not your dark-skin'd Folk!
> The bearded Sikh, and Tamil sleek,
> With them we will not deal,
> Nor with the throng that crowds along
> Close to the White Man's heel![2]

Of all these followers of the White Man, Clifford explained, the Sikh—convinced of his superiority to the men of any other race, Europeans alone excepted—was the most objectionable.

To other Asiatics he is as arrogant and overbearing as can well be conceived, and he displays none of the tact which helps to make a European less hated for his airs of superiority than he might be. The noisy, loud-mouthed, awkward, familiar-mannered, bullying Sikh is as unlike the courteous, soft-tongued Malay as one human being can well be from another, and his conduct and behaviour to the people of the land hurts the latter's self-respect at every turn.[3]

The point was taken up again and again by the Residents of Pahang and Negri Sembilan and by the Superintendent of Police, Selangor, during the intermittent and at times acrimonious debate

---

Intelligence Department, Perak Sikhs, in 1881. While in Hong Kong, he had passed the Higher Standard of the Hong Kong Civil Service examination for Chinese. *FMS Civil Service List, 1904; Native States List, 1891.*

[1] In 1890, there were six Chinese detectives in Kinta, earning $10 a month, less than a good mining coolie. *AR* Kinta, 1890, *PGG*, 7 August 1891.

[2] H. Clifford, *Studies in Brown Humanity, being Scrawls and Smudges in Sepia, White, and Yellow*, London, 1898, p. 122.

[3] Ibid. p. 128.

on the relative uses of Sikh and Malay police in a Malay state. The Selangor and Sungei Ujong forces, unlike that of Perak, had begun as predominantly Malay forces.[1] The Selangor police in 1875 consisted of 100 men of various nationalities and assorted dress, recruited originally for the service of Tengku Zia'u'd-din[2] and serving under a Mauritian Frenchman or Creole turned Muslim. In 1875 the force was reorganized by H.C. Syers,[3] then a private in the 10th Regiment. Fifty of the original police were retained (some of them were still serving ten years later) and 100 men recruited from Malacca. In 1878 the force consisted of about 230 NCO's and men, Malays and some Tamils,[4] under Syers as Superintendent. In 1884, Syers was prevailed upon to accept a detachment of forty Sikhs to furnish guards in Kuala Lumpur.[5] Though their numbers increased as the force grew, they remained in the minority (in 1895 there were 230 Sikhs as against 503 Malays) and until 1891 at least they were all stationed in Kuala Lumpur, where they performed purely military duties, leaving the police work to be performed by Malays.[6]

In Selangor there were no major disturbances requiring the large-

[1] A small body of Sikh police for purely military duties was organized in Sungei Ujong in 1882 (*AR* Sungei Ujong, 1882). In 1890, the last year in which Sungei Ujong figures were reported separately from Jelebu, there were 179 Malay and seventy-five Sikh NCO's and men. *AR* Sungei Ujong, 1890.

[2] These were the 'sepoys' of whom Mohamed Ibrahim Munshi wrote so unflatteringly (*Kesah Pelayaran*, p. 32). On one occasion, while visiting Kuala Selangor, he watched in great distress while the sepoys harried 'orang Islam' who were thought to have aided the Tengku's enemies. Ibid. p. 70.

[3] Harry Charles Syers was engaged by Davidson in 1875 as a temporary inspector of police (he was then about twenty-three) and was appointed Superintendent in 1875 or 1876. In 1891 he was given the title of Captain-Supt. in recognition of his services. In 1896 he became Commissioner of Police, FMS. He died in a hunting accident in 1897. He was a remarkable man. Though he had little education, he was thoroughly master of his work, and his reports were well written. In 1875 he was already fluent in Malay, and, according to Isabella Bird, in 1879 he was studying the Chinese and their language. Both she and Douglas described him as a student of the people and the country. See Resident to CS, 13 July 1875, Sel/Sec. 73/75; Bird, *The Golden Chersonese*, p. 315.

[4] Anonymous, 'An Account of the Selangor Police Force', *Selangor Journal*, vol. i, no. 6, 2 December 1892; Swettenham, Audit Report of the Native States, enclosed in Anson to Hicks Beach, 6 March 1879, C.2410, no. 6.

[5] *AR* Police Department, 1884, Sel/Sec. 195/85. In 1879 he had rejected a suggestion by the Colonial Secretary that the Selangor police should be strengthened by the addition of Sikhs, arguing that Sikhs did not understand Malays or Chinese and would be useless for police duties. Supt. of Police to Resident of Selangor, 1 December 1879, Sel/Sec. 326/79.

[6] In 1893 there were Sikh detachments at Rawang and Serendah in Ulu Selangor. For information about distribution and duties of police, see *AR* Police Department, in *SGG* from 1890.

scale intervention of the Sikhs; indeed, a remarkable feature of the Chinese society of Selangor appears to have been its orderliness—ascribed by Syers in large measure to the influence of the Chinese headmen and their readiness to co-operate with the police.[1] The Sikhs were called out on special duty nearly always in order to put down minor strikes and threatened disturbances at the mines. For example, in 1888 a number of coolies at Sungei Puteh refused to work and attacked their headman, injuring him and damaging property; they were arrested and flogged at the mine before the other coolies, in the presence of a strong guard of Sikhs.[2] No wonder the Chinese mine-owners petitioned the Resident for an increase in the Sikh contingent![3]

Syers clearly considered the Malay a better policeman than the Sikh, and until 1892 or 1893, he entrusted the general police duties of the state among both Malay and Chinese populations exclusively to Malays (assisted in Kuala Lumpur by Chinese detectives). The returns of discovered crime certainly justify his confidence, though the regularity and warmth of his tributes to the Chinese towkays suggest that much of the success of the peace-keeping operations among the Chinese was due to their help.[4] He considered Sikhs to be particularly unsuitable for dealing with Malay populations.[5] The organization of a Malay police force presented some difficulties, however. The Malays of the states themselves showed little interest in the force, and most of the recruits were drawn from Malacca, Penang, and Province Wellesley, and a few from Rembau. They were bad at drill, poor shots, more restless than the Sikhs and less amenable to discipline, and their general conduct was much less satisfactory. The more extreme among their detractors simply dismissed them as useless, and recommended in long and disparaging minutes, written after Syers' death, that the Selangor Malay police should be replaced in whole or part by Sikhs.[6] Syers had argued that Malays

---

[1] See Chapter IX.

[2] *AR* Police Department, 1888, Sel/Sec. 552A/89.

[3] Resident of Selangor to CS, 13 April 1894, Sel/Sec. 323A/94.

[4] See especially *AR* Police Department, 1885 (Sel/Sec. 1849/86), 1886 (Sel/Sec. 398/87) and 1887 (Sel/Sec. 595/88).

[5] Supt. of Police to Resident, 6 February 1889, Sel/Sec. 498/89, reporting on the organization of a police force for Pahang.

[6] Commissioner of Police (Talbot) to Resident-General, 16 March 1898; Deputy Commissioner of Police (Wagner), minute of 7 April 1898, Sel/Sec. 1546/98. Both Talbot and Wagner had served in the Perak Sikhs. Talbot knew Hindustani; Wagner, Chinese. It is not on record that either of them spoke Malay.

who were called upon to perform ordinary police duties should not be expected to drill like soldiers. 'My experience is that the best policemen make the worst soldiers, and that men who are excellent thief-catchers become perfectly useless on parade.' (He had support in the Colonial Office; a critic there once minuted that the Perak Sikhs were about as suited to police work as the Household Brigade.) The Residents of Pahang and Negri Sembilan agreed with Syers, and wholeheartedly supported the proposition that Malays, despite their defects, were indispensable for police duties in a predominantly Malay state.[1] In Negri Sembilan, where there was a largely Malay population and no security problem, the force was entirely Malay. But in Pahang, where the security problem was acute, the Sikhs— performing essentially garrison duties—eventually constituted two-thirds of the force.

The relationship between police and penghulus and the extent of police contact with the Malay population generally, are difficult to document. The whole theory of local administration in the Malay states was based on the proposition that police and judicial work among Malays would be carried out far more cheaply and effectively by their own headmen than by regular government agencies, and it seems certain that in the rural Malay areas of Perak, and in Pahang and Negri Sembilan, the peace was kept in the main by penghulus and *adat* chiefs.[2] The commissions to penghulus all instructed them to report serious crime to the nearest station or magistrate, and mean-while to inquire into the crime and try if possible to secure the of-fender. But there was in fact little serious crime among rural Malays, apart from amok cases and crimes of passion. Minor crime was dealt with by the penghulu, who had power to inquire into and hear cases and inflict small fines. The distance to police stations in many dis-tricts made it unlikely that police assistance would be invoked in

---

[1] *AR* Pahang, 1890 and 1892; *AR* Negri Sembilan, 1894. When an establish-ment for Pahang was being formed in 1888, Rodger, the first Resident, reported the strong objections of the Sultan of Pahang to the importation of a Sikh guard, and begged that they should not be sent. 'Personally I entirely agree with His Highness, as I believe that Sikhs are out of place in a purely Malay State' (Rodger to CS, 13 October 1888, enclosed in Smith to Knutsford, 451 of 15 October 1888, CO 273/155). He was over-ridden by the Governor, however.

[2] In his *AR* of 1893, the Resident of Negri Sembilan remarked that a population of nearly 40,000 Malays was controlled by three Europeans and a few police, 'the bulk of the police being required, not on account of the Malays, but in conse-quence of the Chinese immigration to mines and estates'.

petty cases, and administration reports show that in general, petty offences were dealt with by penghulus.

In Selangor, however, there appears to have been a closer association between penghulus and police. To begin with, there was a wider distribution of police stations in Malay population centres—a result perhaps of Douglas' distrust of native headmen and disinclination to leave them much responsibility.[1] They did have certain police and judicial power under Douglas, but they were not trusted, and the police were regarded as necessary checks on a bad (i.e. oppressive or neglectful) penghulu.[2] At any rate, there were at most times police stations in at least half the villages where penghulus were established. In Perak in 1879 there were some forty villages with penghulus; only four of them had police stations. For the whole length of the Perak river above Bandar Bahru—some 150 miles—there were seventeen villages with penghulus, and only four police stations. In 1892, there were about sixty villages with penghulus, and about fifteen of them had police stations.[3] In Selangor, by contrast, nine of the twelve places mentioned as served by penghulus or chiefs in 1882, had police stations. In 1893, after extensive additions to the penghulu establishment, there were police stations in twenty of the thirty-three places where penghulus were established.[4] There were thus opportunities for frequent reference to the police, and there is some evidence to show that these opportunities were used in quite minor cases, and that in general, the police and the penghulus worked together in Selangor to a degree unlikely in the other states.[5]

[1] Resident of Selangor to CS, 12 June 1882, enclosed in Weld to Derby, 208 of 28 May 1883, CO 273/120.

[2] Report of Supt. of Police, Selangor, 11 July 1878, enclosed in Robinson to Hicks Beach, 224 of 1 August 1878, CO 273/95. Low, writing at the same time, reported that it had not been possible for him to close as many stations as he would have wished, since some check was necessary on bad penghulus. Enclosure in Robinson to Hicks Beach, 255 of 27 August 1878, CO 273/95.

[3] List of Penghulus, 1879, *Perak Affairs and Despatches*, 1874–9, pp. 10–11 Return of Perak Police, 1 July 1878, enclosed in Robinson to Hicks Beach, 224 of 1 August 1878, CO 273/95; List of Penghulus and Chiefs of Perak, *PCM*, 9 December 1891, *PGG*, 30 March 1892; *Perak Handbook and Civil Service List, 1892*, p. 172.

[4] Resident of Selangor to CS, 12 June 1882, enclosed in Weld to Derby, 208 of 28 May 1883, CO 273/120; Return of Police, 31 October 1882, Sel/Sec. 317/83; *Singapore and Straits Directory* for 1894, p. 226; *AR* Police Department, in *SGG* for various years.

[5] E.g., Raja Sha'ban, undated, Sel/Sec. 103/80, reporting (among other cases) a quarrel over a woman and saying that he had called in 'Sarjan Mat' to take them to the police station; Dato' Puteh, penghulu of Jeram, reporting that two Malays had been arrested for fighting and brought in to Kuala Selangor. Sel/Sec. 229/81.

The penghulus understandably broke down sometimes under the responsibility of reporting crimes in which their fellow-villagers or kinsmen might be involved. There were many reports of cases in which penghulus who were in a position to know the author of a crime and secure him, allowed him to escape, and gave no information or help to the police. In his report for 1886,[1] Syers cited three cases of murder which had recently occurred, in all of which the murderer was known to the penghulu; in one case the penghulu had been in the village when the murder took place, saw the accused afterwards, allowed him to escape, and declared himself unable to give information; in another, the murder was actually committed in the penghulu's house while he was in residence, but the author of it was allowed to get clean away before the alarm was given. Syers recalled that under the old régime the penghulu was responsible for arresting criminals and preventing crime; now that a police force was established, less was expected of a penghulu, but, he thought, 'they ought at least to possess sufficient influence over and knowledge of their people to discover the whereabouts of a fugitive criminal who is one of their own nationality, in the case of Chinese we do not expect them to possess such knowledge'.

A clear separation between the military and civil functions of the Malay states' police forces was one of the changes which accompanied the federation of the states in 1895, but there had been important moves in this direction for some years before federation. In 1887 Weld, undeterred by earlier rebuffs, again offered a portion of the Perak Sikhs for imperial defence, to reinforce the Singapore garrison in case of emergency.[2] This offer was accepted, and despite the objections of Weld's successor, Smith (who thought that in an emergency the men would be needed where they were, and preferred in any case to look on them as police rather than as soldiers), Perak found itself committed to despatch 350 Sikhs to Singapore in the event of war.[3] A unified command of Sikh forces from Sungei Ujong, Selangor and Perak was temporarily achieved in 1892, when Sikhs from these states served under the Commandant, Perak Sikhs (R. S. F. Walker), during an outbreak in Pahang, and in 1894 Perak

[1] Sel/Sec. 398/87.
[2] Weld to Holland, Secret of 2 February 1887, CO 537/46.
[3] Smith to Knutsford, Secret of 11 September 1891 and enclosures, CO 537/47.

and Selangor Sikhs again served in Pahang under his command. In one of his despatches to the Colonial Secretary, written at the conclusion of the 1892 campaign, Walker recommended the formation of a Sikh force for the protected states, to be recruited from existing forces, put under one Commandant, and trained, armed and equipped on the same lines. 'These men would do purely military duties, no police work of any kind, and would be available at a moment's notice to move off to the scene of any disturbance.'[1] His proposals were supported by the Resident of Selangor in his report for 1892, and were given an added urgency by events in 1894, when Perak and Selangor Sikhs rushing a stockade in Pahang displayed their lack of discipline and accidentally shot one of their own officers. An inquiry into this incident and into the recruitment, organization and discipline of the Selangor Sikhs showed that their military training was quite inadequate even to deal with internal outbreaks, and strongly recommended their amalgamation with Sikhs from other states in a force with purely military duties.[2] At the same time, an inspection of the Perak Sikhs confirmed that while the force was sufficiently well trained to deal with internal disturbances, it was 'quite unequal at present to the defence of Singapore even against Asiatic troops of a foreign army'; it was in excess of the military needs of Perak, and yet too military in its organization 'for policing the Perak State in its present advanced conditions'.

The need for a Malay states' force to assist effectively in the defence of Singapore, as well as to deal with brushfire wars in the Peninsula, clearly demanded unification under a purely military command, and separation from the ordinary police, and this was effected in 1896. The new force, the Malay States' Guides, was raised by Walker (its first Commandant) from the Sikh forces of the four states, between July and October 1896; in November 1896 it consisted of 550 NCO's and men.[3] At the same time, the police forces of the states, consisting of Malays and the remaining Sikhs, were placed under a Federal

[1] Commandant Perak Sikhs to CS, 7 November 1892, from a microfilm 'Despatches, Memoranda and Proceedings relative to the Pahang Disturbances', University of Singapore Library (original print in the Perak Museum Library).
[2] Report of Major-General Jones-Vaughan, Officer Commanding the Troops, S.S., 15 November 1894, enclosed in Mitchell to Chamberlain, 399 of 4 December 1894, CO 273/199.
[3] Report on the organization of the Malay States Guides, by Lt.-Col. R.S.F. Walker, 17 November 1896, enclosure in Chamberlain to Mitchell, Secret of 23 April 1897.

Commissioner of Police, with Deputy Commissioners or Superintendents in the states. The dual organization of the police, which had resulted in units not fully effective either as police or soldiers, thus came to an end.

JUSTICE

Of all the criticisms of Malay misgovernment, the most persistent had been criticisms of the administration of justice. There has been no systematic study of judicial practice in the independent Malay states, and it is a question whether the material for such a study now exists. The scanty, uniformly disparaging references by contemporary British observers are suspect, since they are the observations of administrators committed to the introduction of a rival system, and prejudiced in any case in favour of written codes and procedures. What little we know and understand of Malay legal and judicial systems, we owe to the reconstructions of a generation of colonial officers of impartial scholarship, who worked and wrote when Malay justice, as a function of government, was receding into the past.[1]

In his study of Malay law, R. J. Wilkinson distinguished two legal systems—*adat perpateh* and *adat temenggong*—differing not so much in content as in the manner of administration. The *adat perpateh* he described as family or community custom, expressed in folk sayings which were common property and could be readily appealed to. They provided not only legal prescriptions but defined the position and powers of headmen and rulers (including their jurisdiction) and laid down right procedure. *Adat temenggong* was 'the adat perpateh administered on autocratic lines', 'an unwritten law made up of ordinary Malay custom, administered by despotic authority and supplemented by a large number of sumptuary regulations drawn up for the glorification of the court'. The adat was collected in a number of written legal digests (*undang-undang*) which became part of the hereditary possession of a chiefly family; they were not enactments, but private books of reference.[2] But the powerful territorial chiefs who

---

[1] R.J. Wilkinson, 'Introductory Sketch', Law, part 1, *Papers on Malay Subjects*, 1st Series, 1908; 'Ninety-nine Laws of Perak', edited and translated by J. Rigby, with introduction by R.J. Wilkinson, Law, part 2, ibid.

[2] According to a note in one of the copies used by the editor, the 'Ninety-nine Laws of Perak' was in the possession of the Perak Mentris, a Syed family distinguished for learning and holiness, holders of the office before its transfer to Che Ngah Ibrahim.

administered the law refused to be bound by inconvenient rules and regulations, and there was no one who had the power or the responsibility to interfere with their decisions. The administration of justice became, at best, assistance given by chiefs to their own followers. 'Litigation—in cases where the litigants did not take the law into their own hands—became a matter of diplomatic negotiation between the nobles who championed either side.'[1]

The arbitrary judgments made by chiefs, and the use of judicial powers in order to oppress the ra'ayat and profit from fines, were much emphasized in the accounts of the first years of intervention. Clifford, who had lived in Pahang as a British agent for a year before the introduction of British rule, had an opportunity to see the judicial system in operation and wrote and spoke of it in the blackest terms.[2] He described the trumped-up cases and savage fines whereby the chiefs and the Bendahara's favourites increased their wealth. He states, however, that personal law—marriage, betrothal, divorce— was administered by kathis who were mostly conscientious and hard-working, and this suggests that it was the administration of the criminal law, as well as the disputes of the wealthy Pekan traders, which gave the Bendaharas and chiefs their main opportunities for misgovernment and self-enrichment.

There was certainly a strong moral element in the criticisms of Clifford and others, but it was also true that a well-ordered judicial system was seen to be a neccessary condition of the open economic development and large capital inflow for which they hoped. The Residents' achievement was to establish a system of British courts and British criminal law, used in the main by commercially active immigrants, in the interstices of which the petty indigenous courts and indigenous personal law could continue to function. Soon after his appointment to Larut, Speedy had established a court consisting of himself and the Treasurer, following the Indian Penal Code as far as possible. A Straits official visiting Larut wrote that proceedings were conducted as in the Straits Settlements, charges under the Penal

---

[1] Low once told how a chief sitting with him in court had given a verdict of 'Not Guilty'. Low asked whether he had heard the evidence. 'What do I care for evidence? They are my people.' (Discussion on Clifford, 'Life in the Malay Peninsula', op. cit. pp. 394–5). Low adds that it was of no consequence, for they already had four votes for the conviction.

[2] Ibid. A different situation was described by a visitor to Perak in 1826 (Lt.-Col. James Low, 'Observations on Perak', JIA, vol. iv (1850) pp. 497–504). Low described the Sultan as 'a very quiet person and very indulgent to his subjects', who began the day by hearing their complaints.

Code being entered and disposed of by the magistrate.[1] In 1877, the Residents reported on courts of justice in Perak, Selangor and Sungei Ujong, in response to a request for information from the Colonial Secretary.[2] There were courts of unlimited jurisdiction in Larut and Lower Perak; a magistrate's court, with power to try criminal cases up to six months' imprisonment and $100 fine, and civil cases in claims not exceeding $200, had been established by Birch in November 1875 at Matang, under a Proclamation by Sultan 'Abdu'llah of 2 November 1875; and in 1877, Low established similar courts at Krian and Kinta under their district officers. In June 1877, the Supreme Court of the state, consisting of the Raja Muda, the Resident, Raja Idris and the Temenggong, was established at Kuala Kangsar. It had jurisdiction on appeal over all cases, and was also the ordinary court for Upper Perak. Capital sentences were submitted to the Raja Muda and the Resident (later to the Ruler in Council) for confirmation.

In Selangor, there were magistrates' courts in Klang, Langat, Kuala Selangor and Bernam, presided over by district officers, and in Klang, by the Resident and Treasurer.[3] The jurisdiction of the ordinary courts is not clearly stated, but the indications are that this was the same as the jurisdiction allowed the district officer, Kuala Selangor, in his letter of instructions in 1880—six months' imprisonment or $100 fine in criminal cases and up to $50 in civil cases. Cases beyond this jurisdiction, and appeals, were tried by the Resident. Capital sentences were referred to the Ruler in Council for confirmation—this on the Governor's instructions.[4] In Sungei Ujong there was one court, the Resident's, presumably with unlimited civil and criminal jurisdiction.

The Residents were a little vague at first about codes and procedures. In Selangor, according to Douglas, the Penal Code and other ordinances in force in the Straits were adopted in all the courts, together with 'the usual forms of Summons, Subpoena, Judgment, etc.'. In Perak, Low reported that the law administered in the courts

---

[1] Skinner, Report of a visit to the Malay States, 17 February to 13 March 1875, enclosed in Clarke to Carnarvon, 22 March 1875, C.1320, no. 30.

[2] 'The Courts of Justice in Perak, Salangore and Sungie Ujong', Straits Settlements Legislative Council Paper, 15 March 1878, Appendix 5.

[3] Before 1878, when the Resident began to hold a monthly court in Kuala Lumpur, important cases were tried by him in Klang, and petty cases by the Capitan China. Resident to CS, 5 September 1878, Sel/Sec. 293/78.

[4] CS to Resident, 25 April 1876, Sel/Sec. 34/76; CS to Resident, 12 October 1877, Sel/Sec. 346/77.

was 'the law prevalent in Mahomedan States supplemented when necessary by the laws of Great Britain'. The Assistant Resident reported that he had been furnished with no code definitely applicable to the Malay states, and had 'endeavoured as nearly as possible in consonance with Malay custom to follow the Indian Penal Code'. The Resident of Sungei Ujong wrote, with more optimism than accuracy, 'The practice in our Court is, I may say, identical with that of the Magistrates' Courts in Singapore, but without the Lawyers.' What all this meant was that magistrates in the early years administered the law according to their own ideas of equity, modified by what they knew of Malay and Chinese custom and the Indian or the Straits Penal Code. Isabella Bird was baffled in her attempts to discover anything definite about the legal system in the states. She came to the conclusion that 'a most queerly muddled system of law' prevailed; Muhammadan law existing alongside of fragments of English criminal law, the Resident's notions of equity overriding all else. She watched proceedings in the Resident's court at Seremban:

He [Captain Murray] was never still for two minutes, but was either hammering on the desk, whittling its edge, humming snatches of airs, making remarks to me, exclaiming, 'Bother these fellows!' . . . knowing that only the Malay interpreter understood him. Mr. Haywood, through whose hands the crime of Singapore and Malacca has filtered for twenty years, was very critical of the rough-and-ready methods of proceeding here, and constantly interjected suggestions such as, 'You don't ask them questions before you swear them', etc.[1]

In the next fifteen years or so, some order was brought into the administration of justice. A Chief Magistrate was appointed to Selangor in 1882, and a Senior Magistrate to Perak in 1890; the courts of justice were regulated by instructions and orders in council, defining jurisdiction and legalising codes and procedures, many of them already in use. In 1884, the powers of the Perak courts were defined by a notification issued in 1884 by Swettenham (then acting Resident)[2] and the powers of the Selangor courts by Regulation

[1] I. Bird, 'Sketches in the Malay Peninsula', *The Leisure Hour*, London, 1883, part iv, p. 148. I am indebted to Dr. William R. Roff for this reference.

[2] Perak Notification of 9 May 1884, given in Sel/Sec. 3153/88. District magistrates were empowered to impose fines up to $200 and imprisonment up to two years in criminal cases, and adjudicate in civil cases over all claims not exceeding $1,000. This far exceeded the jurisdiction of a district magistrate in Selangor, which was limited at the time by 'a sort of understanding' to claims of $100 in civil cases and $100 fine or six months imprisonment in criminal cases. Acting Chief Magistrate to Resident of Selangor, 26 September 1888, Sel/Sec. 2684/88.

1 of 1889.[1] A similar Regulation was passed in Sungei Ujong on 25 July 1889, substituting 'Resident' for Chief Magistrate and giving the other courts lesser powers.[2] Finally, legislation was introduced into Perak, Selangor, Negri Sembilan and Sungei Ujong in the 1890's consolidating and elaborating the law relating to judicial administration.[3] The model for the other two states was the Perak Order in Council. It set up as courts of first instance, the Residency court, the Senior Magistrate's court (both with unlimited jurisdiction) courts of magistrates of the first, second and third class, and penghulus' courts. The Residency court consisted of the Sultan, the Resident, and the Secretary to Government, all three, or any two, or any one separately, being competent to hold sessions; the Senior Magistrate's court consisted of the Resident, the Senior Magistrate and the Secretary to Government, any one being competent to hold sessions. The courts of first, second and third class magistrates had civil jurisdiction of $3,000, $1,000 and $50 respectively, and criminal jurisdiction of two years' imprisonment and $2,000 fine, six months and $500 fine, and one month and $25 fine respectively.[4] Penghulus' courts had jurisdiction in 'all suits brought by Malays and other Asiatics' up to $25 in civil cases and $5 fine in criminal cases. Appeals lay from courts of penghulus and magistrates of the second and third class to magistrates of the first class, from any magistrate's court to the Senior Magistrate, and from the lower courts to the Residency court. The final court of appeal was the Sultan in Council. The Order in Council also provided for courts of kathis and assistant

---

[1] This extended the jurisdiction of district magistrates to claims of $300 in civil cases, and $200 fine, a year's imprisonment and twenty-five strokes of the *rotan* in criminal cases. Certain crimes were excluded from their jurisdiction. The Chief Magistrate had jurisdiction in all civil cases and in criminal cases excepting culpable homicide amounting to murder; the Resident had power to inquire into all cases, civil and criminal. Appeals lay from the district magistrate to the Chief Magistrate, from the latter to the Resident, and finally to the Sultan in Council. (C. Kemp, ed., *Selangor Regulations, 1877–1889*, Kuala Lumpur, 1892.) The Regulation also laid down a table of court fees.

[2] Sungei Ujong Council Proceedings, CO 474/1.

[3] Perak Order in Council 11 of 1890, *PGG*, 17 October 1890; Selangor Regulation XI of 1893, *SGG*, 11 August 1893; Negri Sembilan Order in Council 1 of 1893, Supplement to *SGG*, 24 November 1893; Sungei Ujong Regulation X of 1894, Supplement to *SGG*, 4 January 1895.

[4] By Government Order 297, *PGG*, 3 July 1891, all the officers in charge of districts, and the chief assistant magistrate, Kinta, were gazetted magistrates of the first class, and other assistant district officers and assistant collectors of land revenue were gazetted magistrates of the second and third class. Raja Mansur, Raja Musa, the Dato' Raja Mahkota and the Laksamana were gazetted magistrates of the third class.

kathis with power to impose fines of $10 and $5 respectively, and jurisdiction 'in all matters concerning Mahomedan religion, marriage and divorce, and in all matters regulated by the Hukum Sharah as shall be defined in his kuasa, under the hand and seal of His Highness the Sultan, and countersigned by the British Resident'. In the legislation for Selangor and Negri Sembilan, the powers and personnel of the courts varied according to the different circumstances of the states, but the principles of classification were the same as in Perak. There was no Pahang regulation constituting the state courts, but the jurisdiction of the district officers was defined in their letters of appointment;[1] murder cases and all appeal cases were heard by the Resident.

There was one appeal procedure which was not mentioned in the legislation—appeal to the Governor. Since the Crown had no jurisdiction in the Malay states, the Governor was unknown to their legal systems, so that there could be no appeal to him in any legal sense; but he could and did intervene effectively by instructing the Resident to order a rehearing. During Douglas' tenure, even this circumlocution was dispensed with. In 1878, the Governor, while on a visit to Klang, reduced a sentence of three years' imprisonment imposed by the Collector and Magistrate, Kuala Selangor (a sentence far in excess of his powers) to six months.[2] In a dispute about the ownership of some tin, the Governor, on being petitioned by the dissatisfied litigant against a decision by the Resident, ordered a rehearing, and when rehearings both in the Resident's court and in the State Council failed to secure a reversal of judgment, the Resident was simply ordered to return the tin in dispute to the petitioner and did so, citing the Governor's instructions as his authority.[3] There is no evidence that such high-handed methods continued to be used, but review by the Governor and appeal to him by petition remained an accepted part of the legal system, both in civil and criminal cases. Swettenham, writing in 1882 to suggest the limits of jurisdiction for the Chief Magistrate, remarked that in criminal cases there would

[1] Resident to Collector and Magistrate, Kuantan, 24 June 1889, Kuantan Papers, 4/89. The magistrate's jurisdiction in civil cases extended to claims of $100 and in criminal cases to sentences of a year's imprisonment and $100 fine.
[2] Resident to Collector and Magistrate, Kuala Selangor, 10 April 1878, Sel/Sec. 3/78; Collector and Magistrate, Kuala Selangor, to Resident, 20 April 1878, Sel/Sec. 51/78.
[3] Resident to Lim Keong, draft undated, and Lim Keong to Resident, 26 May 1880, Sel/Sec. 120/80; correspondence and minutes in Sel/Sec. 225/80.

be an appeal to the Resident and eventually to the State Council
'& of course by petition to His Excellency'.[1] There is evidence to
show that reports of cases in which capital sentences were imposed
were sent by the Residents to the Governor as a matter of course.[2]

The codes and procedures prescribed were borrowed wholesale
from Indian and Straits Settlements law (the latter being often modelled on the former). A set of instructions drawn up in 1882 by the
Assistant Resident of Perak (Maxwell) prescribed the Straits Penal
Code as the guide in criminal jurisdiction; procedural details should
be as in the English Court of Petty Sessions, a manual on which was
to be furnished to every court, and the English law of evidence was
to be followed. The instructions continued, 'Native laws and customs should be allowed due rights, but as no uniform body of native
law is in the hands of Magistrates for enforcement, reference should
be made to head-quarters in cases of difficulty turning entirely on
native custom.' These instructions were re-issued in substance in
Selangor and Sungei Ujong in 1890 and 1894 respectively.[3] The
Straits Settlements Penal Code (Ordinance IV of 1871) was formally
adopted as law in Perak (1884), Selangor (1886), Sungei Ujong and
Negri Sembilan (1889), but it does not appear to have been adopted
in Pahang; the law in force there appears to have been the Indian
Penal Code, prescribed in the letter of instructions to the district
officer of Kuantan in 1889. The schedules to the Selangor and Sungei
Ujong courts regulations specify a number of Straits and Indian acts
and ordinances to be adopted as law in Selangor, notably the
Straits Penal Code (Straits Settlements Ordinance IV of 1871) the
Summary Jurisdiction Ordinance (XIII of 1872), the Oaths Ordinance
(V of 1890) and the Evidence Ordinance (III of 1893), though certain
Straits Ordinances were prescribed by Order in Council or indicated
in other ways.[4]

[1] Resident of Selangor to CS, 11 October 1882, Sel/Sec. 229/82.

[2] Acting Resident of Selangor to CS, 24 May 1892, Sel/Sec. 561A/92, offering
to 'resubmit the notes taken for His Excellency's perusal' after the Governor
had been petitioned to commute a sentence of death. See also Smith to Ripon,
487 of 22 December 1893, CO 273/184.

[3] See reference in Chapter VII, p. 215, note 3. In Selangor, the law of evidence
prescribed was the Indian Evidence Act of 1872, and for Sungei Ujong, the
Straits Settlements Evidence Ordinance of 1893.

[4] E.g., the SS Summary Criminal Jurisdiction Ordinance was adopted in
Perak by Order in Council in 1895, and the SS Evidence Ordinance was pre-
scribed for the law examination taken by junior officers in Perak in 1895. See
Notification no. 27, PGG, 18 January 1895. The books prescribed included

The senior magistrates of Selangor and Perak both had law degrees, and so did two of the Residents; Maxwell in particular held high executive position in both states and was able to influence the standard of judicial administration. In the outstations, where the level of experience was lower, the volume of crime and litigation was smaller, and demands on the courts were slight.[1] Appeals were rare, the administration of justice appeared to give satisfaction to the public, and was generally praised by Residents and Governors. But Maxwell had some hard things to say of the Selangor courts when he became Resident. He reported in November 1889: 'I have inspected the Court of the Chief Magistrate at Kwala Lumpur. Records there are none, pleadings are unknown, there is not even the "cause-paper" or statement of account used in the colonial courts of Requests, much less the plaint on stamped paper contemplated by the Indian Civil Procedure Code. A proper clerical staff is altogether wanting'. About the Kuala Lumpur police court he wrote: 'I have within the last few days introduced for the first time the use of a charge book into the Kwala Lumpur Police Court and, when the manner of entering charges is properly understood there, the same system will be extended to out-stations.'[2]

The combination of judicial and executive powers led to irregularities and injustices. In Perak and Selangor after 1890, the work of the courts came under the supervision of full time judicial officers, (senior magistrates) and after 1890 Residents seldom acted in a judicial capacity; but in the other states, the judicial work of the Residents remained an important part of their duties. Clifford, while acting as Resident of Pahang, complained in his annual report for 1894 that a man in his position, brought into intimate contact with the people, and forced to take a leading part in the suppression of disturbances, could not 'approach the trial of many of the prisoners brought before

Broome's Commentaries on the Common Law, Mayne's Penal Code, Stanley's Indian Criminal Law, and Maxwell's Duties of Magistrates.

[1] The late Sir George Maxwell, who joined the Perak service as a junior officer in 1891 and held many magisterial appointments there between 1892 and 1899, informed the writer in correspondence that the court work of a district officer took up little of his time. 'It was a rare thing for a Malay to appear as an offender in the criminal court: the accused were mainly Chinese, with a percentage of Indians. The charges mainly consisted of such things as vagrancy, drunkenness, petty thefts, criminal assault, breach of the peace and similar minor offences.' Letter to the writer, 9 January 1958.

[2] Cited in W.E. Maxwell, Memorandum on Judicial Administration in the Native States, 3 September 1894, enclosed in Mitchell to Ripon, Confidential of 4 September 1894, CO 273/197.

his court with the impartiality of a judge personally unacquainted with such prisoners, and who has not himself been instrumental in effecting their arrest'. The 'astounding obliquity of judgment', shown not only by Sir Cecil Smith (about whom the remark was made) but by others in authority in the states was revealed to the Colonial Office in successive exposures of judicial improprieties,[1] which could not always be excused by ignorance of the law. In 1889, for example, the Chief Magistrate of Selangor (himself a lawyer) had ordered the sale of the property of a convicted forger, on behalf of the person defrauded, though the matter was not before him in a civil action; and in 1892 the same man (now Senior Magistrate of Perak) obtained from the Resident an order for the return of fines imposed in a criminal court on the ground that a subsequent judgment before him (in a civil court) had the effect of reversing the earlier decision.[2] Maxwell, while Colonial Secretary, had written some very able minutes on the evils of executive interference with the judicial process, and it was unkind of the Secretary of State to correct him for supporting the same sort of arbitrary behaviour when he was Acting Governor.[3] Such inconsistencies are the very stuff of colonial administration.

In the 1890's, the administration of justice in the protected states came under criticism from commercial interests in the Straits Settlements. In 1891 the Secretary of State received a petition from the Singapore Chamber of Commerce and the Singapore branch of the Straits Association, praying for the right of appeal by British subjects in the Malay states to the Supreme Court in Singapore, in cases both civil and criminal, in suits where the sum at issue was not less than $1,500, or where the appellant was convicted of an offence carrying the maximum penalty of six months' imprisonment. The petitioners pointed out the interest of Straits traders in the Malay states, asserted that a large part of the capital invested there was the property of British subjects, and that the obvious defects in the administration of justice (in particular, the close connexion between the executive and the judiciary, the absence of legal training, and the exclusion of counsel from the courts) created misgiving in the Colony,

---

[1] See Chapter V.

[2] Maxwell, op. cit; Mitchell to Ripon, Confidential of 14 May 1894 and enclosures, CO 273/195. In the second instance, the Senior Magistrate had refused plaintiff, who was perfectly deaf, permission to conduct his case through counsel, on the grounds that pleaders were not allowed in the courts of Perak.

[3] Ripon to Mitchell, 49 of 9 February 1894, on Maxwell to Ripon, 420 of 30 December 1893, CO 273/190.

and would inhibit the flow of capital into the states.[1] In his forwarding despatch, the Governor, Smith, rejected these arguments. It was not true, he declared, that a large part of the capital invested was the property of British subjects. The European British investment was 'exceedingly small' and Asiatic investors for the most part were not British subjects. The agitation for reform was confined to a small section of the Singapore community and was supported by members of the Singapore Bar, who wished to open a new and lucrative field for themselves:[2] the actual investors in the states (mostly non-British Chinese) had no feeling of mistrust for the administration of justice. He argued strongly against the introduction of formalities and 'technicalities of the artificial system which is the growth of ages of another civilization than is to be found in this part of the world', and pointed out that in cases of difficulty, a safeguard existed in the shape of an appeal to the Governor. In the case of British subjects charged with murder, there was already provision for trial in the Colony courts.[3] When the volume of British capital and the numbers of British residents justified it, arrangements might be made for appeals to be heard by a judge duly appointed by the governments of the states.

Swettenham, who was then in England, thought that the time for this had already come, and advised the Colonial Office accordingly. He thought that the presence of banks and companies, and the construction of large railway works by contractors, might at any moment precipitate a dispute in which a state government might find itself judge in its own cause, and he suggested that a judge of the Supreme Court of the Straits Settlements should go on circuit in the states, hearing appeal cases and holding his commission from the Sultans in Council. He agreed with Smith that lawyers should be kept out of the courts, not only for reasons of principle but because 'they

[1] Smith to Knutsford, 410 of 3 November 1891 and enclosures, CO 273/176.
[2] In a private letter, Smith alleged that the prime cause of the agitation was a decision by Maxwell while Resident of Selangor, relating to the conduct of legislation by the Rawang Tin Company, which had caused losses to shareholders in Singapore, including the editor of the *Straits Times* and the Attorney-General. Smith to Bramston, private of 3 November 1891, CO 273/176, on same file.
[3] According to Victorian Act 38 of 1874, crimes and offences committed out of the Colony at any place in the Peninsula extending southward from the ninth degree of latitude, by British subjects or residents of the Straits Settlements, were cognizable in the Colony courts. In 1884, Smith had instructed the Resident of Perak to send a European accused of murdering a Chinese to Penang for trial. Smith to Derby, 256 of 12 June 1884, CO 273/128.

[the state governments] do so many things for which they would be puzzled to produce any legal warrant that the advent of educated and intelligent lawyers would be disastrous to the Native States system at the present time'.[1] But he thought that if cases went on appeal to a judge of the Supreme Court, it would be necessary to allow lawyers to appear before him.

In his answering despatch the Secretary of State put these proposals into the form of recommendations, but despite mounting dissatisfaction with judicial administration in the states, and frequent reminders from the Colonial Office, nothing was done until Mitchell succeeded as Governor. By this time the Malayan officials were deep in preparations for federation, and the judicial changes now became part of the general reorganization. The proposals finally adopted originated with Maxwell, who argued the necessity not only of an independent appeal court, but of a Judicial Commissioner competent to regulate the administration of justice in all the states, supervise the lower courts, lay down rules about procedure, advise on legislation, and generally introduce order and uniformity into state law.[2] A few months later, the Governor suggested the appointment of a separate Legal Adviser, to co-ordinate and draft legislation.[3] The Secretary of State approved these suggestions, and directed that authority be conferred on the Judicial Commissioner by identical laws enacted in each state. As it was finally passed, the enactment gave the Judicial Commissioner appellate jurisdiction from the Senior Magistrate's court in civil and criminal cases, as well as the sole right of review over all criminal courts (including that of the Senior Magistrate), and the right to transfer cases involving capital offences at his own discretion from the Senior Magistrate's court to his own. The appellate jurisdiction of the Resident's court and of the Sultan in Council was abolished, except that sentences of death were still subject to confirmation by the latter. Finally, the Judicial Commissioner was empowered to allow counsel to appear in his court.[4]

The extension of the powers of the Judicial Commissioner at the expense of the state courts met with some opposition from the Gov-

[1] Fairfield quoting Swettenham, minute of 12 December 1891, on Smith to Knutsford, 410 of 3 November 1891, CO 273/176.
[2] Mitchell to Ripon, Confidential of 4 September 1894, enclosing memorandum by Maxwell, 3 September 1894, CO 273/197.
[3] Mitchell to Ripon, Confidential of 20 February 1895, CO 273/202.
[4] 'Enactment to provide for the appointment of a Judicial Commissioner', passed in all the states in 1896.

ernor and the Residents, but they were overruled by the Secretary
of State. The opposition of the Sultan and chiefs of Perak to the
proposal to abolish the appellate jurisdiction of the Sultan in Council
fared no better. The Acting Resident, who apparently learned of
their feelings for the first time when he introduced the Order defining
the powers of the Judicial Commissioner, was shaken by the vehe-
mence of the reaction. According to his report, the Sultan and chiefs
argued that the Judicial Commissioner would come from England
'blind to the interests of this country, and full of legal principles
which he will study and give effect to without consideration for
native customs, ideas and prejudices'. They ascribed the appointment of a Judicial Commissioner, he said, to pressure brought 'by
the mercantile community in the Straits, by the press and by the
legal profession'; but, they pointed out, Singapore and Penang were
not Malay states, and the people of Perak at all events were satisfied
with the administration of justice by their own magistrates acting
under the scrutiny of the State Council. 'One of the chiefs, the Dato'
Sri Adika Raja, raised a chorus by remarking that this draft Order
appeared to set aside the country and the Sultan.' There followed a
bombardment of telegrams from the Straits, but the officials stood
firm, discounting the agitation as got up by the Resident in his own
interest, and pointing out (with considerable irrelevance, since the
states were not Crown Colonies) that in the Colony the Governor
in Council did not act as a court of appeal. They agreed, however,
that though the Sultan in Council would no longer act as an appellate court, he would continue to consider death sentences in Council
and decide whether they should be carried out or commuted; also
that the Order would not interfere with the right of subjects to petition the Sultan, or with his prerogative of pardon or commutation
of sentence in criminal cases. The matter was settled when Swettenham, now Resident-General, steered the Order through another
meeting of Council after assuring the Sultan and chiefs that these
prerogatives would not be curtailed; drawing from the Colonial
Office the satisfied comment 'Mr. Swettenham manages the natives
very well'.[1]

In recommending the appointment of a Judicial Commissioner,
Maxwell stressed the danger of divergence on subjects which could

[1] Correspondence and minutes on Mitchell to Chamberlain, Confidential of
20 February 1895, CO 273/202; Confidential of 5 May 1896, CO 273/214; and
283 of 21 June 1896, CO 273/215.

and should be dealt with by uniform legislation in all states. He pointed out that the existing statutes differed in each state, and 'as time goes on the differences may become more and more marked, without any reason for this except the individual views held by particular officers, and possibly an unacknowledged desire to exhibit originality'. There was some justice in Maxwell's remarks. The bulk of state legislation was initiated and drafted by the state governments independently, and by officers of varying professional attainments,[1] and the variable quality of the drafting operated perhaps as strongly as the inter-state jealousy cited by Maxwell, to produce gratuitous differences in legislation. Selangor legislation after 1889 (when Maxwell became Resident) was elaborate and exact; Perak legislation by contrast was 'administrator's law', expressed as a rule in ordinary language, without legal periods and somewhat lacking also in legal precision.[2] But certainly some of the differences in detail overlaying essentially similar legislation on technical subjects, appear to have been the result of parochialism and personal jealousy. And under one major policy head, there were controversial differences. The Selangor Land Regulations of 1882, introduced by Swettenham, served as the model for the Perak legislation of 1885 (introduced, again, by Swettenham while Acting Resident of Perak) and for the Negri Sembilan and Pahang legislation of 1889. The Land Code introduced by Maxwell into Selangor in 1891 destroyed this unanimity, and when officers regretted, from their different points of view, the divergences between the states, it was probably Maxwell's policy departure which was uppermost in their minds.

The extent of divergence can be exaggerated, however. Differences were usually in matters of detail and modes of expression rather than in essential provisions, and much important legislation was reproduced almost exactly in all states. A number of influences helped to bring this about. It was natural that Residents should look to Straits law to provide a model for their legislation. The adoption of the Straits Penal Code, Evidence Ordinance and Summary Criminal

[1] In Selangor, legislation was drafted by the Chief Magistrate, though Maxwell, as Resident, drew up the 1891 Land Code, and supervised the drafting of other legislation. In Perak, legislation was drafted at different times by the Secretary to Government and the Senior Magistrate. In the other states the work of drafting was presumably carried out by the Residents.

[2] E.g., Perak Order in Council 13 of 1890 and Selangor Regulation III of 1892 (Compulsory Vaccination); Perak Order in Council 4 of 1889 and Selangor Regulation XII of 1890 (Storage of Petroleum). Legislation was published in the government gazettes of the respective states. See Note on Sources.

Jurisdiction Ordinance in the three western states has already been described, and other ordinances were adopted from time to time either voluntarily by the Residents or under instructions from the Governor.[1] The smaller states borrowed freely from Perak and Selangor, and even Perak and Selangor occasionally borrowed from each other, though usually after some prompting.[2] The transfer of Residents and Chief Magistrates between the states assisted the diffusion of legislation. Finally, all state legislation was subject to the sanction of the Governor; the Singapore Secretariat became as a result a kind of clearing-house for legislation, and contrived to impose some measure of uniformity, by circulating recommended legislation, or requiring the inclusion of particular provisions. All these influences counteracted the stubborn individualism of Residents, and ensured that in major matters of policy as well as in minor technical matters, there was on the whole no great legislative divergence.

The part played by Malay authorities in the administration of justice is not easy to determine. They had had some judicial responsibilities from the very beginning of the Residential system, and it was in this sphere of government perhaps that they participated most actively, though subject to fairly close supervision. Malay rajas and chiefs held court independently in the districts before the arrival of district officers,[3] and where European courts were established, they sat regularly with the Resident or the district magistrate.[4] There

[1] E.g., legislation providing for uniform weights and measures, introduced into Perak, Selangor and Negri Sembilan in 1893, into Sungei Ujong in 1894 and Pahang in 1896; Indian Immigration Enactment, introduced into Perak, Selangor and Sungei Ujong in 1884, and Negri Sembilan and Pahang in 1889.

[2] Negri Sembilan took its Courts Order in Council, 1893, from Selangor, and its Labour, Mining and Postal Codes, 1895, from Perak (*AR* Negri Sembilan, 1893 and 1895). Selangor in turn took its Courts Regulation of 1893 from Perak. The file on this contains an interesting example of the initiative of the Governor in state legislation, and an interesting series of exchanges between the Resident and Chief Magistrate of Selangor on the subject of this legislation. See Sel/Sec. 204/92.

[3] In Selangor, Raja Kahar held court in Ulu Langat until a district officer was established there in 1883 (Sel/Sec. 426/78). Raja Indut was the Native Magistrate in charge of Bernam for many years (Kuala Selangor Monthly Report for July 1892, *SGG*, 19 August 1892). See also *AR* Negri Sembilan, 1887 and 1888).

[4] It is difficult to come to any conclusion about the effectiveness of Malay participation on a mixed bench, since few cases have found their way into the records. There was one occasion when a magistrate in Lower Perak was overruled by the two Malays sitting with him, in a case concerning an alleged breach of the pawnbroking monopoly (Batang Padang Papers, 76/90) and there may have been

were many acknowledgments of the good sense and integrity of individual Malays, but it seems clear that in serious cases at any rate, their judgment was not altogether trusted. Low described the partiality of one of his Malay colleagues towards a defendant from his own district, while the district officer of Kinta reported a different kind of partiality, displayed by the Panglima Kinta and To' Muda Wahab when they sat with him; they were unsatisfactory, he wrote, because of their deep involvement in mining and other speculations with the Chinese.[1] Malay judicial responsibility appears to have been regarded as an administrative imperfection, unavoidable in the early stages of intervention, but to be superseded by European authority as soon as possible, or circumscribed by limited jurisdiction and, in the more important cases, by the presence of a British magistrate who would be the effective dispenser of justice. In 1880, the Governor instructed the Resident of Selangor that cases of importance at Kuala Lumpur should never be tried except in the presence of the European magistrate.[2] Of Rembau, the magistrate of Tampin wrote that it had been necessary to start court work under Malay chiefs; though the ends of justice were perhaps obtained, as the decrease in crime showed, 'the means to obtain those ends were peculiar'.[3] The Resident remarked that after the establishment of a police court and court of requests under the magistrate of Tampin, no further difficulties were anticipated.[4]

In Perak and Selangor, a few Malays were gazetted magistrates of the second and third class under the courts legislation of 1890 and 1893,[5] and it is possible that some of them may have been entrusted with independent jurisdiction. It is likely that the two sons of Sultan 'Abdu'llah, Raja Mansur and Raja Chulan, both English-educated,

---

other cases, but it seems unlikely that such displays of initiative were frequent. The magistrate in question was deputizing for the Acting Supt. It is a question whether the Superintendent, Denison, would have met with such opposition.

[1] *AR* Kinta, 1889, *PGG*, 4 April 1890.

[2] CS to Resident, 2 January 1880, Sel/Sec. 6/80.

[3] *AR* Negri Sembilan, 1888.   [4] Ibid.

[5] In Perak between 1891 and 1895, seven Malays were gazetted magistrates of the third class; they were Raja Mansur b. Sultan 'Abdu'llah, Raja Musa b. Sultan Ja'afar, the Dato' Laksamana, the Dato' Raja Mahkota, the Dato' Sri Adika Raja, Raja Chulan b. Sultan 'Abdu'llah and the Dato' Sri Maharaja Lela. Raja Mansur and the Dato' Temenggong were gazetted magistrates of the second class. All these appointments were for Lower Perak or Kuala Kangsar. In Selangor there were only two such appointments between 1893 and 1895—Sheikh Abdul Mohet, penghulu of Damansara and later Klang, and 'Mr. Abdul Razak', clerk in charge of Bernam.

heard cases independently, and that the Sri Adika Raja, who was in charge of the remote northern mukims of the Kuala Kangsar district, did the same. But it would probably be true to say that for the most part, the Malays who held court independently were kathis and penghulus with minor jurisdiction. The role of the senior chiefs and rajas appears to have been to assist the European magistrate, not only by hearing and considering the evidence with him, but by advising him as to Malay custom in civil cases.[1] The judicial functions of the chiefs extended beyond the courts; in Negri Sembilan, for example, it was customary for the 'chief' (by which, presumably, was meant the lineage headman) to attempt to settle civil cases in the first instance by arbitration.[2]

The bulk of the court work among the Malays appears to have been carried out by penghulus. In Perak and Sungei Ujong, penghulus were empowered to deal with civil cases up to $25 in value, and inflict a fine of not more than $5 for petty offences; in Selangor, their jurisdiction was limited to $10 in civil cases and a $5 fine for petty offences.[3] A Pahang regulation defining the powers and duties of headmen (Regulation 1 of 1890), gave them the power to settle petty cases in their mukims, but did not specify any limits to their jurisdiction, except to say that serious offences such as homicide, stabbing, burglary, robbery, rape, arson, forgery, coining and the like were to be sent up to the district court.

In Perak and Sungei Ujong, the penghulus charged fees for court processes, and it is interesting to find the technical terms of British jurisprudence metamorphosed by them into *harga saman*, *harga sapena* and *harga notis*. The scale of fees varied from time to time and even from district to district, but the general order of magnitude is indicated by a Perak notification of 1891,[4] which empowered penghulus and kathis to charge twenty cents for every summons, postponement, service and judgment ticket, and ten cents for every

[1] *AR* Selangor, 1887; *AR* Negri Sembilan, 1887 and 1889.

[2] *AR* Negri Sembilan 1891. The report goes on to say that criminal cases were the responsibility of the police, but even in these cases, the chiefs of persons charged were required to be present.

[3] *PCM* 4 March 1879; Perak Order in Council 11 of 1890; Sungei Ujong Council Proceedings, 8 January 1884; CO 474/1; Swettenham, Minute on Local District Administration in Selangor, 6 June 1883, SS Legislative Council Proceedings, Paper 23 of 1883. The only district in Perak where penghulus had no jurisdiction was Krian (*AR* Krian, 1894). The reason is not known.

[4] Perak Notification 428 of 1891, issued 16 September 1891, *The Laws of Perak, 1877–1903*, ed. W.G. Maxwell, Kuala Lumpur, 1905.

subpoena. (The penghulu's commission on collections was 2 per cent.) The fees were a fraction of those prevailing in the ordinary courts, but they must still have made litigation in the villages unnecessarily complicated and expensive. In Selangor no fees were chargeable by penghulus.

Some officials doubted at first whether penghulus should be trusted with judicial powers; Swettenham, when drafting regulations for penghulus in 1883, was uncertain whether or not to include these powers, but was persuaded to do so after discussion with the Malays in Council.[1] Certain checks were instituted; penghulus were required to submit, monthly, a report of cases and an account of fines and fees, and it was possible to appeal from the decisions of penghulus to the district courts. With these safeguards, the system appeared to function well, and certainly it saved the European magistrates a great deal of work. The annual reports for Lower Perak and Batang Padang for 1890 show that in 1889 and 1890, the penghulus disposed of twice or three times as many civil cases as the district courts, though, in general, few criminal cases came before them.[2] In 1890 the 'penghulus and native chiefs' in Lower Perak actually disposed of more cases altogether than the district courts.

Although Malay custom and the Muslim religion were formally outside the sphere of British officers, the proper organization and supervision of an establishment of kathis who would witness marriages, administer the law relating to divorce and division of property, and punish matrimonial offences and breaches of religious observance, were matters which closely affected the peace and good order of the states, and inevitably engaged the attention of the Residents. In Pahang where (according to Clifford) the only justice to speak of in pre-British days was administered by kathis, the Resident's initiative appears not to have been necessary; a kathi, probably a pre-Residential appointment, was sitting with the Pekan magistrate in 1890, and in Negri Sembilan, two years after the appointment of a British officer, the kathi was already hearing cases in open court once a week.[3] In Perak, Low confidently took the

[1] SCM, 2 September 1883.
[2] AR Lower Perak, 1890, PGG, 24 July 1891. A return of cases settled by the penghulu of Klang in 1888 shows that out of 178 cases, 32 were concerned with quarrels, 33 with domestic differences, 91 with money matters, 13 with land, 3 with property and 2 with cattle. There were 3 abduction cases and 1 petty theft. AR Klang, 1888, Sel/Sec. 443/89.
[3] AR Pahang, 1890; AR Negri Sembilan, 1889. In Negri Sembilan, however, the jurisdiction of the kathis appears to have been limited to religious offences; in

initiative early in his tenure of office, and secured the appointment of his candidate as Chief Kathi of Perak, resident in Kuala Kangsar; Assistant Kathis were appointed to Lower Perak and Krian in 1879, and to Kinta soon after 1882.[1] The Perak estimates for 1895 carried appointments of Assistant Kathis for Sitiawan, Larut, Matang, Upper Perak and Batang Padang, as well as for Krian, Kinta, and Lower Perak.

The Chief Kathi and Assistant Kathis were salaried officers of the state and were forbidden to accept *zakat*.[2] Appointments, salaries, suspensions and dismissals of these kathis were decided by the State Council, and their powers were established by legislation and also by terms of their kuasas. According to an Order in Council passed on 8 December 1885 providing for the registration of Muslim marriage and divorce, 'Muhammadan priests' were required to keep a register of all marriages and divorces; and in 1889, an Order in Council relating to Muslim divorce made the decrees of Assistant Kathis provisional, subject to the approval of the Sultan. A proclamation issued in 1885 regulated the judicial work of the kathi; he was given power to fine,[3] and in case of non-payment an order of court would be made by the magistrate. Appeals were to be channelled through the magistrate to the Chief Kathi; cases outside the kathi's jurisdiction were to be brought by him to the magistrate, who would issue a summons and hear the case with the kathi as assessor. The kathi was to keep a record of cases and send a weekly return of decisions to the magistrate, to be forwarded to Kuala Kangsar for the information of Raja Idris and the Chief Kathi; accounts of fines and amounts collected, were to be sent weekly to the magistrate.[4]

his first report on Sungei Ujong and Jelebu, the Resident of Negri Sembilan noted that the chiefs of that state adhered to the customary law in property and inheritance cases, and failing a settlement in their courts, the cases were brought into the civil courts; while in Sungei Ujong and Jelebu, the chiefs had adopted the Mohammedan law (*hukum sharah*) in respect of such cases, which thus went to the kathi's court. *AR* Sungei Ujong, 1894.

[1] *PCM*, 4 May 1879, 3 November 1879, and 26 October 1882. Compare with names in 'A List of Penghulus and Chiefs of Perak . . .', *PCM*, 9 December 1891. *PGG*, 30 March 1892. The appointments of kathis to Krian and Kinta were requested by their respective district officers.

[2] *PCM*, 28 February 1880. *Zakat* is a Muslim tithe payable after the fasting month.

[3] The amount was unspecified, but according to Order in Council 11 of 1890 defining the constitution and powers of civil and criminal courts, assistant kathis had a jurisdiction of $5 and kathis (Chief Kathi?) $10.

[4] Rules for Kathis (undated, 1885), in 'Perak Proclamations and Notices', Perak Museum Library.

These rules were consolidated and developed in a kuasa for Assistant Kathis which was in use by 1898.[1] The Assistant Kathi was empowered to inflict fines of not more than $5, and dispose of civil claims up to $125. He was required to keep registers of marriage and divorce, though the imam of a mosque might solemnize the marriage of a woman with her guardian's consent, without the authority of the Sultan or kathi, provided it was subsequently reported to the registrar of marriages. He was instructed to report matrimonial offences, such as enticement, or re-marriage of a woman within her *edda* period, to the district magistrate; such cases were beyond the kathi's jurisdiction, and were presumably heard by the magistrate with the kathi sitting as assessor. Appeals against the kathi's decisions were to be submitted to the Secretary to Government and forwarded to the Sultan, who would decide whether there were grounds for a rehearing. Assistant Kathis were to consult the Chief Kathi or the Sultan on matters of Muslim law or Malay custom, and the district magistrate on state law.

There was in addition a class of unsalaried assistants called naib kathis. They were appointed by the Sultan, or by the Chief or Assistant Kathis subject to the Sultan's approval. They assisted at marriages and funerals and were allowed to keep the alms which they received on these occasions. They had no jurisdiction, but might settle small disputes with the consent of the parties.[2]

The orderliness of the Perak religious administration contrasts strongly with the situation in Selangor. There is very little evidence that Sultan 'Abdu'l Samad was interested in ecclesiastical matters; his son, Raja Muda Musa, was indeed so devout as to be thought a dangerous fanatic, but he confined himself (or was confined) to affairs in Langat and did not act for the state. When he died, the 'Tuan Imam' of Bandar Langat consulted the district officer about his cases.[3] It was not till the 1890's, when Raja Muda Sulaiman

---

[1] A summary of the kuasa is given in a memorandum by the government Malay writer, Taiping, 13 October 1898, Sel/Sec. 571/98. The same writer prepared a draft kuasa which he recommended for use in Selangor, and which is identical in its provisions with the summary (ibid.). It was probably a copy of the Perak kuasa. The minute goes on to say that the current form of Perak kuasa was a revised version made, it was thought, by Sultan Idris when E.W. Birch was Acting Resident (between September 1895 and July 1896). A kuasa for assistant kathis was approved by the State Council in 1895. *PGG*, 22 November 1895.

[2] Minute by Assistant Secretary to Government, Perak, 19 July 1898; minute by government Malay writer, Taiping, 27 August 1898, Sel/Sec. 571/98.

[3] 'I had an interview with the Bilal of Jugra about a divorce case; now that

began to be active in these matters, that there was a Malay initiative and leadership for the whole state. In 1875 there were in various places a number of unsalaried imams (leaders of the congregation at prayer) holding commissions from the Sultan or from Tengku Zia'u'd-din; these commissions empowered them to officiate in marriage and divorce, and to try offences against the law of Islam.[1] This system was continued under the Residents. In 1877 the Resident reported that all cases 'relating to religion or to the Mahomedan law of Marriage and Divorce' were tried by the imam in open court; the same year an imam was appointed to Jeram, with power to officiate in marriage and divorce, and fine parties committing offences against Muslim law, and in 1884 the Acting Resident rejected the request of the penghulu of Setapak for a kathi, with the explanation that the Sultan had given sole powers of acting as kathi in the Kuala Lumpur district to the imam of Kuala Lumpur, pending the appointment of a kathi for the whole state.[2]

Attempts to appoint a Chief Kathi resulted in an administrative comedy. In 1884 the Acting Resident referred in Council to the prevailing uncertainty and proposed that a kathi be appointed, to whom the imams could refer. The proposal was unanimously approved; the Raja Muda and Syed Zin promised to find a suitable person, and Syed Zin found someone and took him to Jugra to be interviewed by the Sultan. In 1885 the Kathi was duly appointed, and the first result of his activities reported to Council; the imam of Kuala Kali had resigned, pleading old age, the imam of Kuala Lumpur had decided that his business as a trader precluded him from doing justice to his religious duties and had resigned also; the imam of Jugra had been declared incapable and the imam of Klang incompetent and both had been replaced. The Sultan professed himself much pleased with the way the Kathi was carrying out his duties; but in 1886, after complaints against him had been made by the Menangkabau traders of Kuala Lumpur, the Kathi himself resigned, and the Sultan promised to look for another. In 1888 the Council was informed that His Highness was not prepared to nominate anyone; Raja Laut knew of

---

the Raja Mudah is dead, the Tuan Iman refers most of his cases to me.' Kuala Langat Journal, 14 February 1885.

[1] Minutes on the appointment of an imam at Klang, Sel/Sec. 380/78.

[2] 'The Courts of Justice in Perak, Salangore and Sungei Ujong', SS Legislative Council Paper, 15 March 1878; letter appointing Haji Osman imam at Jeram, 14 September 1877, Sel/Sec. 322/77; minute by Acting Resident, 21 August 1884, Sel/Sec. 1521/84.

no suitable person in Selangor, and it was decided that the Resident should make inquiries in Singapore. He finally procured a kathi from Penang and was thanked by the Sultan for his pains ('*dan bagitu usaha-nya paduka sahabat beta akan hendak memeliharakan nama beta muka dengan beberapa banyak-lah beta menerima kaseh*'),[1] but two years later the Resident reported complaints about the Kathi's behaviour, and it was decided to send him back to Penang. That was the end of the search for a kathi for the time being. In 1891 the Resident (Maxwell) reported to Council that he had met and consulted with the principal Muslims of the state (half of them identifiable as foreign Malays or Tamil Muslims). The sense of the meeting was that a kathi should be appointed and that cases should be heard by the kathi and Chief Magistrate sitting together. No kathi was appointed, however; in 1891 the post was taken off the establishment and in the same year, Maxwell reported that Muslim matrimonial cases were now decided by the Chief Magistrate sitting with Raja Laut and Raja Bot.[2]

One consequence of the consideration given to Islamic law was the recognition of adultery by Muslims, and certain breaches of religious observance, as criminal offences. In 1877, Low had objected to penal sanctions for non-attendance at mosque, perhaps as much from a desire to avoid repressive action at the outset of his term of office as from liberal feeling;[3] and in Selangor it was decided, apparently by the Sultan, that the imam should not levy fines for non-attendance, but should publish the names of offenders and threaten to refuse them burial.[4] In Sungei Ujong and Negri Sembilan, however, legislation passed in 1887 and 1893 respectively made non-attendance punishable by small fines. Before 1894 there was no written law in any state making adultery by Muslims a penal offence, but this did not prevent Muslims from being charged in the criminal courts with committing adultery and sentenced to terms of imprisonment. Minutes written in 1892 by the district officers of Lower Perak and

[1] Sultan to Resident, 26 December 1888, Sel/Sec. 102/89. It was the Resident who informed the imams that a kathi had been appointed to Selangor. Sel/Sec. 316/89.

[2] Selangor Estimates, 1891–5; *AR* Selangor, 1891, See SCM, various years, for details.

[3] There was a Perak Order in Council of 1885 entitled 'Muhammadans to pray on Fridays in Mosques' but it was no longer in force in 1899 (the terminal date of the Voules edition of Perak laws) and the substance is not given.

[4] SCM, 5 September 1879; draft, undated, of letter from the Sultan to the imam of Klang (in Douglas' hand), Sel/Sec. 303/79.

Batang Padang show that in both districts as well as in Kinta—in Lower Perak since 1881—adultery had been treated as a penal offence. The district magistrate of Batang Padang wrote:

When I first came to the State these cases were dealt with by the Malay Imams etc and were punished by shaving the head, flogging in public etc, this was abolished & for some time there was no recognized punishment but afterwards at the suggestion, I believe of the late Sultan (then Regent) it was ordered that cases of adultery should be tried by a magistrate sitting with an Asst. Kathi or native Magistrate & the maximum punishment was fixed at six months imprisonment of either description and (or) fine not exceeding $60/. . . . This was the custom in Kinta when I left & I introduced it here. It is also in force in Lower Perak.[1]

In 1894 the position was regularized in Perak and Selangor by legislation making adultery by Muslims punishable by fine or imprisonment.[2] Prompt arrest and punishment of offenders was not merely an authoritarian exercise; as the Sultan of Perak explained when he argued the need for such legislation before Council, most of the serious crimes by Malays were crimes of jealousy, and some action was needed to prevent people taking the law into their own hands.

The administration of the Muslim law was a source of considerable embarrassment to British officers. The existence of a dual judicial responsibility disturbed them, as it has disturbed other temporal authorities faced with the claims and pretensions of religious courts; also, they had an individualist and secular repugnance to a code which punished neglect of religious duties with fines, and adultery with heavy prison sentences. The problem was minimized by limiting the independent jurisdiction of kathis, bringing the more serious cases before the magistrate, and supervising the work of kathis in other ways; thus in Perak, reports of cases and petitions for appeal were channelled through the European officers to the Chief Kathi and the Sultan. But it was still difficult for some European officers to reconcile themselves to the temporal punishment of sin. A case from Kuala Selangor illustrates this conflict. The local Kathi, in the absence of the district officer, had sentenced a man and a woman caught in adultery to imprisonment, and asked the penghulu of Kuala Selangor to send them to prison. The penghulu would not

[1] Minute by District Magistrate, Batang Padang, 7 April 1892, Batang Padang Papers, 54/92.

[2] In Perak the punishment was fixed at simple imprisonment of up to six months or fine of not more than $250 or both. In Selangor the punishment was up to two years for the man and one year for the woman. Perak Order in Council 1 of 1894; Selangor Regulation XI of 1894.

take the responsibility, so the Kathi sentenced each of the offenders to forty blows with a stick. The Collector applied to the Acting Resident to know whether the Kathi had the right to pass such sentences and whether the gaol was to be open for the execution of his sentences. The Resident replied that the offence should be tried by the magistrate with the Kathi present, and might be appropriately dealt with by sentencing the man to three months' imprisonment; there was no gaol accommodation for women. In reply, the Collector indicated his reluctance to 'pass judgment against people who have committed no offence . . . against any law except that of Mahomet'. The Resident wrote a sharp minute: 'You are however an officer in a native Mahometan state, & consequently your strictures on the administration of Mahometan law are entirely uncalled for & improper—Instead of ignoring Mahometan law and customs, you sh[oul]d endeavour to become conversant with them, & obtain such a knowledge as is required from every Collector & Magistrate in India.'[1] He added that if the Collector agreed with the Kathi's decision, he could enforce it to the extent of a fine of $50 or imprisonment of up to three months in default; if he disagreed, or if the Kathi wished to impose a sentence exceeding those limits, the case should be adjourned and a special report sent to the Resident. The Collector had the last word, however; while apologizing, he begged respectfully 'to differ entirely on this subject'. Whether this insubordination had anything to do with his eventual disappearance is not known, but he did not remain long in Selangor. He was not the only official, however, to write minutes bristling with disapproval of the use of the state police and state courts for the arrest and punishment of matrimonial offenders.[2]

Except for the arbitration machinery provided by the Chinese protectorate in Perak, there was no separate system of courts for the Chinese. The jurisdiction of penghulus in Selangor (at least in the early years) included petty disputes in which Chinese were involved, either with people of other nationalities or with other Chinese;[1]

[1] Minute by Acting Resident, 28 July 1885, Sel/Sec. 1138/85.

[2] See, e.g., Acting Commandant, Perak Sikhs, to Secretary to Government, 19 December 1891, referring to two cases of adultery dealt with recently in the courts of Tapah and Telok Anson, and asking that if it be decided that men and women concerned in adultery be dealt with criminally, that police should not be required to act without a warrant. He added that to the best of his knowledge, cases of this kind in Larut had been consistently refused recognition in the criminal courts. Batang Padang Papers, 54/92.

[1] See, e.g., report of cases heard by Haji Mohammad Salleh, penghulu of

more serious matters were dealt with in the state courts, whose business consisted chiefly of Chinese cases. Chinese like all others were subject to the general laws of the state in criminal matters, but mining disputes had always been settled according to Chinese mining custom, and after 1890, on the suggestion of the Governor, the states agreed to follow Chinese custom in cases of inheritance and adoption.[2] Disputes affecting Chinese were often of great intricacy and involved the examination of complicated accounts, so that some specialist assistance was necessary to enable the courts to deal satisfactorily with these cases. In Selangor, the courts were helped by the Capitan China and Cheow Ah Yeok, Cantonese headman and member of Council, whose regular attendance as assessors in Chinese cases, and whose help in the examination of accounts, was frequently and gratefully acknowledged.[3] In Perak the Chinese Capitans had never been active this way; an early report of the courts of justice in Larut explained that while the 'Chinese magistrates' Ah Kwee and Ah Yam were invited to sit in any case where their advice might be useful, they rarely availed themselves of the privilege, as they were traders and had not the time.[4] Much quasi-judicial work was thrown on to the Chinese Protectorate; labour disputes, mining disputes and civil disputes generally were referred there by the courts or by agreement of the parties, and the Protector's awards were enforced as if they were orders of court.[1] In Selangor, this quasi-judicial business

---

Kanching, Sel/Sec. 289/80, and by Raja Sha'ban, Ulu Klang, Sel/Sec. 103/80, also 426/78, 273/82, 97/85 and 2028/86. The report of Panglima Garang (Ulu Selangor) for December 1881 cites instances of Chinese towkays sitting with the penghulu to decide purely Malay cases (Sel/Sec. 576/81). The Collector and Magistrate, Kuala Selangor, wrote in his AR 1890, that he had 'never had any complaints from Chinese about the Penghulus favouring their countrymen in cases of Chinese versus Malays'. SGG, 24 July 1891.

[2] Minute by Smith, 12 December 1890, enclosed in Mitchell to Ripon, Confidential of 4 September 1894, CO 273/197. Perak and Sungei Ujong passed legislation providing for the recognition of Chinese laws of inheritance (Perak Order in Council 23 of 1893; Sungei Ujong Order in Council 2 of 1891). Selangor appears simply to have followed the custom without special legislation. AR Courts Selangor, 1891, SGG 16 September 1892.

[3] There is only one instance, however, of a Chinese gazetted as a magistrate—Loh Cheng Keng, gazetted magistrate of the second class for Sepang, in Kuala Langat district (SGG, 20 July 1894). His gambier and pepper plantation, employing more than a thousand Chinese, was the raison d'être of the Sepang district.

[4] 'The Courts of Justice in Perak, Salangore and Sungie Ujong', SS Legislative Council Paper, 15 March 1878, Appendix 5.

[1] Perak Order in Council 14 of 1891, 'Reference of Chinese disputes to Arbitration'. In 1892 the Protector and Assistant Protector were given power to

appeared to form no part of the work of the Chinese Secretariat. The Residents were faced with the same problems in their administration of justice as in other branches of government; how to ensure the security of immigrant life and property and provide for the equitable settlement of commercial disputes, without disturbing indigenous custom more than they could help. The problem was dealt with by recognizing the petty jurisdiction of penghulus, and allowing it to function as informally as possible within a general system of British courts, governed by British rules of procedure and administering state law or the law of the parties, according to the nature of the case. There was sufficient flexibility in the system to provide for a great variety of needs; but it was essentially a single system, wherein judicial work was distributed according to the degree of competence of the courts, and not according to the race or law of the parties.

---

issue summonses, with penalties for disobedience (*PGG*, 12 February 1892). In 1892 the Protector of Chinese, Perak, and in 1893 the Chinese Secretary, Selangor, were gazetted magistrates of the first class. *PGG*, 3 June 1892; *SGG*, 29 September 1893.

IX

DUAL GOVERNMENT: MALAYS AND CHINESE

THE open immigration policy adopted by the state governments meant a large influx of immigrants, Malaysian, Chinese and Indian, and the growth of a population whose major elements were strongly differentiated in a number of ways.[1] The institutions of government were common to the whole population; Chinese as well as Malays were represented on the State Councils, and were subject to the authority of district officers and the jurisdiction of the state courts, including the petty courts of penghulus. But the markedly different political traditions, ways of life, patterns of settlement and economic interests of the two largest groups—the Malays and Chinese—and the different problems of government which they offered, encouraged the development in addition of specialized agencies and forms of leadership appropriate to each.

The cornerstone of policy with reference to the Malays was the preservation and use of the Malay hierarchy. Low once suggested to the disappointed tenderers for the Perak opium farm that they should take up shares in the successful syndicate, and it was somewhat in the same practical spirit that the British offered political opportunities and financial rewards to Malay rulers and chiefs after 1874. For the British too it was better, so it was argued, to legitimize the new régime, secure its acceptance and buy off disaffection by a generous policy towards Malay traditional leaders, rather than relegate them to private life and 'leave the Government to reckon with forty or fifty disappointed, embittered and impoverished men with the pre-Residential traditions and plenty of time on their hands in which to consider how best they can use their influence so as to obtain a fair settlement of scores between themselves and the Government'.[2]

The first need was to provide maintenance for chiefs deprived of their incomes by the government collection and control of revenues. The payment of allowances in lieu of revenue was provided for by

[1] See Chapter X.
[2] *AR* Perak, 1890.

the Pangkor Engagement, and Jervois had also planned a system of allowances as part of his reorganization scheme of 1875. The fiscal reforms instituted in 1876 and 1877 in the west coast states had left the chiefs almost destitute; in Perak they came to Low, begging for small loans; in Selangor, impoverished rajas quartered themselves on the Sultan and petitioned the Resident and the Governor for assistance, in order that they might be 'freed from the troubles of this world'. Between 1876 and 1880, lists of Malay chiefs with claims on the state were drawn up, and in succeeding years, new applications were considered. Descendants of Sultans to the second and third generation, and holders of offices under Malay rule were generally recognized as having claims on the state.[1]

Payments to Malay chiefs were classified under two heads—allowances and pensions. The former included 'all cases where the payee holds any office or does any real work in the service of the State such as a Magistrate, Punghulu etc.'; the latter referred to those (mostly members of the royal house) who received payments while doing no work for the state.[2] The district chiefs of Perak and Pahang were in receipt of allowances and were thus classified as working chiefs; so were the Dato' Klana, Dato' Bandar and Dato' Muda Linggi of Sungei Ujong, the Dato' Penghulu of Jelebu (and presumably the Dato' Penghulus of Johol and Rembau, though details are not to hand). They were members of the State Councils, and were supposed to help the district officers in their dealings with the Malay population; they also assisted the work of the courts. Their performance varied from one district to the next according to their own capacities and interests and the character of the district officer. Denison's reports from Lower Perak referred so frequently to long office sessions and field journeys with Raja Musa and the Dato' Laksamana as to indicate a genuine Malay participation in the government of the district. Clifford's reports from Pahang, on the con-

---

[1] See Estimates for Perak, Selangor and Sungei Ujong/Jelebu for lists of Malay allowances and pensions. A list of members of the Perak royal house entitled to payments is given in *PCM*, 26 October 1882. It includes the Regent, his two sons and daughter, four nephews and two grandsons; two sons and a daughter of ex-Sultan 'Abdu'llah; Raja Idris, his three brothers and four children; a daughter and two grandsons of the former Sultan Ali. Most of them were paid $10 or $15 a month. The Selangor estimates for 1882 included payments to four sons of Sultan 'Abdu'l Samad, three sons of the previous Sultan, Mohammed, five sons of Raja 'Abdu'llah of Klang, and four Bernam Rajas who were descendants of Sultan Ibrahim. Sel/Sec. 603/82.

[2] CS to Residents, 5 March 1879, Sel/Sec. 84/79.

trary, show that the British could hope for little active help from district chiefs, and little sympathy with the purposes of a government which deprived them of their power.

In Selangor, where the size of the pension list was the despair of the Residents, there was some attempt to make the rajas work for their money, by appointing them penghulus of mukims; of the twenty-three men appointed at the meeting of the State Council in September 1883, thirteen were rajas. This solution pleased neither the rajas, who disliked the title of penghulu and considered it derogatory to one of high rank,[1] nor the district officers, whose repeated complaints testify to the unsuitability of these appointments. They complained mostly of neglect. Raja Sah (son of the Sultan) put down as penghulu of Permatang Pasir, would not recognize the title or do any work; the Tengku Panglima Raja, penghulu of Kanchong, left his district to be looked after by a corporal of police for months on end while he stayed with the Sultan. It was acknowledged that these were political appointments and that little could be expected of the holders. In 1897 Swettenham, referring to certain rajas as underpaid, hastened to explain, 'I do not mean for their services, but for political reasons.' Rodger minuted in agreement, 'with the exception of Raja Laut at K. Lumpur & Raja Abdullah at Jeram, the value of their services is infinitesimal' and went on to remark that their sole claim to allowances rested on the fact that they were waris negeri.[2]

The rajas were by no means extravagantly paid; there were too many of them to permit that. Those whose descent, influence and loyalty secured them state appointments were relatively well off, but even they were paid no more than assistant district officers or important commoner chiefs. Those whose only claim rested on their relationship to the ruling Sultan (his consort, brothers, sisters, sons and daughters) or on their relationship to former Sultans, were given

---

[1] *AR* Lands Department, Selangor, for 1883, Sel/Sec. 334/83. But there were instances of male descendants of Sultans, bearing the title of raja, earning a humble living as fishermen and woodcutters, on land given to them by the Sultan (Collector and Magistrate, Langat, to Resident of Selangor, 2 February 1883, Sel/Sec. 75/83). Others were appointed as forest rangers; one (the son of the local penghulu) as schoolmaster at Jeram; the younger brother of Raja Indut of Bernam, as lighthouse-keeper. A raja who applied for work as a peon with the district officer of Kuala Selangor was refused, since the work was considered too menial. See *AR* Kuala Selangor, 1889, 1890 and 1893, *SGG*, 13 June 1890, 24 July 1891, and 25 May 1894; *AR* Ulu Langat, 1893, *SGG*, 25 May 1894.

[2] Minutes of 26 and 30 September 1897, Sel/Sec. 902A/97. See also reports on penghulus, *AR* Lands, 1884, Sel/Sec. 204/85.

small pensions, equivalent to the salary earned by a minor penghulu.[1] The rajas had large hospitality charges and numerous dependents; they were also unlucky in their mining and planting enterprises. They found it impossible to live within their allowances and were chronically in debt; they mortgaged their allowances and pensions to Indian moneylenders (*chetties*), a reflection not only of their financial difficulties but, more significant, of their inability to extort money under the new régime. The state governments extricated them from the worst of their difficulties by lending them large sums on the security of their allowances and sometimes their property;[2] and in order to discourage private borrowing and prevent the scandal of judgments for debt against members of the royal house, legislation was passed in Perak in 1889 and Pahang in 1893, rendering members of the royal family immune from debt actions in the courts. (In Selangor, an order dating from 1890 forbade the payment of allowances except to the payee in person.) The government's concern derived partly from self-interest; it was recognized that the weakening of the financial nexus between government and chiefs meant the weakening of loyalty:

> The influence of pecuniary interest is one of the strongest ties which ensures the loyalty of chiefs to the existing form of Government and a chief who has assigned away his allowance for a long period in advance has considerably lessened this influence, he is sure to be discontented, and having nothing to lose is likely to become disaffected and to be ready to oppose the wishes of the Resident and measures he may bring forward for the development of the country.[3]

The Residents sought conciliation, not revenge, in their relations with Malay chiefs, and even those with a record of opposition to the

[1] In 1895, the largest payment to any member of the Perak royal house, after the Sultan, was $2,400 a year to Raja Mansur b. Sultan 'Abdu'llah, then employed as a settlement officer. The allowance to the Temenggong, the most important commoner chief, was $3,600, while the Laksamana was paid $3,000. Pensions to the sons of Sultan Idris and Sultan Yusuf did not exceed $300 a year. In Selangor, allowances made in 1895 varied between $180 a year to Raja Ibrahim, penghulu of Telok Panglima Garang, and $6,000 a year to the Raja Muda. Senior rajas like Raja Bot b. Raja Juma'at, Raja Kahar b. Sultan 'Abdu'l Samad, and Raja Laut b. Sultan Mohammed were paid $1,800 to $3,000 a year. Commoner penghulus were paid $180 to $600 a year. An exceptional payment, for a commoner, was made to Haji Mohammed Tahir, a former Dato' Dagang, whose share of the duty on the tin export from Kuala Lumpur was commuted in 1877 for a pension of $2,400 a year. See State Estimates.

[2] E.g., loans of $2,000 to Raja Bot and $4,000 to Raja Laut (Sel/Sec. 496A/95 and 98A/96). These loans were frequently cancelled as acts of grace.

[3] Acting Resident of Pahang to CS, 11 June 1894, Sel/Sec. 562A/94.

British were maintained out of state revenues and they or their families were eventually restored to places of honour. It is true that all those exiled for their alleged participation in the murder of Birch were relentlessly excluded from Perak and even from the Peninsula for many years; in 1899, Sultan Ismail, exiled from Perak to the last, died in Johore a pathetic and broken old man; Sultan 'Abdu'llah was refused permission to return to the Straits until 1891 (he finally returned in 1894 with the title of ex-Sultan). The rigour of this treatment provoked criticism at the Colonial Office; when the Governor yet again raised objections to the return of the exiles from the Seychelles, an official minuted, 'It seems strange that, if our role in the Native States is as successful, popular and beneficial as it is represented to be that the officials should be afraid to let poor old 'Abdu'llah come even to Sarawak.'[1] But this hesitancy was primarily to reassure Yusuf and Idris and secure them against intrigue. The exiles were sufficiently provided for, and so were their dependents in Perak; indeed, nearly the whole of the pensions granted in 1879 consisted of payments to the exiled rulers and chiefs and their families. The brother of Sultan 'Abdu'llah, Raja Musa, was granted a pension, appointed a magistrate for Lower Perak, and made a member of the State Council in 1894. 'Abdu'llah's two sons, Mansur and Chulan, were given government appointments, and relations between the two branches of the royal house were strengthened by a marriage between Mansur and the eldest daughter of Sultan Idris in 1893. In the 1890's also, steps were taken to reconstruct the Perak hierarchy of title-holders, shattered by the events of 1875 and 1876; a Laksamana, a Sri Adika Raja and a Shahbandar were appointed in 1891, from the families of the exiled chiefs,[2] and after the death of the Mentri in Singapore in 1895, his son (who already held the post of penghulu of Bukit Gantang) succeeded to the title.[3] In Sungei Ujong, the

[1] Minute by Fairfield, 9 July 1889, on Smith to Knutsford, 252 of 3 June 1889, CO 273/160.

[2] *PGG*, 23 October 1891. The Selangor commoner titles were in abeyance for most of this period. The only title-holder still recognized in 1895 was the Dato' Kaya, who lived in Singapore and received a pension from the Selangor Government of $1,200 a year (see Chapter I, note 29). In 1898, the Resident recommended that the old titles such as To' Aru, To' Penggawa and To' Engku Klang be revived by appointing the descendants of the last holders or other relations or failing this, other Selangor Malays (Resident of Selangor, 15 June 1898, Sel/Sec. 902A/97). Swettenham, then Resident-General, approved these suggestions. 27 June 1878.

[3] *PCM*, 20 August 1895, in *PGG*, 13 September 1895.

Dato' Bandar (successor to the old enemy of the British) accommodated himself to the new régime so successfully that after the death of the old Dato' Klana Syed Abdulrahman in 1879, he became, in effect, the chief most favoured by the British, and acted as the senior chief after the retirement of the next Klana, Mohammed Yusuf, in 1887, and during the minority of his successor, Ma'amor, elected in 1891.

In theory, the British were in the Malay states partly in order to teach the Malay Rulers good government—that is to say, the virtues of order, economy and hygiene. The older chiefs might be sufficiently enlightened to give these novel principles their political support, but as might be expected, they remained somewhat detached from the actual routine of government. However, a beginning was made in the work of turning the Malay élite into a junior arm of a colonial civil service. The sons of Sultan 'Abdu'llah, who had been sent under instructions from Singapore to be educated in an English school in Malacca, entered the state service as settlement officers and magistrates. They were attached to land offices in the Krian, Kuala Kangsar and Lower Perak districts at various times (it is noteworthy that like other government servants, they were subject to transfer from one part of the state to another), and carried out the usual work of land officers; demarcation duty, rent collection and tours of inspection of mines, padi-fields and gardens.[1] The Sri Adika Raja, who was Malay-educated, and who had been trained in the Resident's office, was another recruit to the new bureaucracy, and a remarkably able one from all accounts. He was placed in charge of the northern mukims of the Kuala Kangsar district; his reports, with their detailed and orderly returns of revenue, exports, court work, mines and miners, births and deaths, are informative, methodical, and precise, and reveal a trained and energetic administrator.[2] He undertook strenuous tours of inspection, which involved days of walking over rough country; he collected rents, reported on mining and planting, assisted settlers from Patani, made bridle paths to the mines in his

[1] Kuala Kangsar monthly reports for December 1890, December 1894 and May 1895, *PGG*, 30 January 1891, 1 February and 19 July 1895; Krian monthly report for July 1895, *PGG*, 13 September 1895. Swettenham claimed in his annual report for 1890 that the two rajas were employed on the same terms as European officers. This appears to have been true of Raja Chulan; Raja Mansur's career progressed rather more slowly. See details in *FMS Civil Service List, 1904*.

[2] See *AR*, Mukims of Chegar Galah, Pulau Kamiri and Durian Pipit, *PGG*, 13 April 1894 and 15 March 1895.

own district, cut irrigation channels, enforced the quarantine regulations (his vigilance saved his district from a rinderpest epidemic in 1895)—in short, he administered and developed his district exactly in the manner prescribed for district officers everywhere in the protected states.

There is little information about the relations between the Malay ruling class and the ra'ayat under the new régime, but it seems probable that they suffered a considerable change, at least in Perak and Selangor.[1] The authority of the chiefs and rajas was broken at a number of points; they no longer had rights of taxation or justice over their districts, they could no longer keep slaves or bondmen, and their allowances did not suffice to maintain a large following. Their military functions and private armies were things of the past; their stockades fell into disrepair and were overgrown with jungle. Kerah service, while maintained by statute in Perak, Selangor and Pahang, was restricted to *kerja kerajaan* (the work of the state); the periods of service were regulated, there was provision for commutation, and although the rajas and chiefs still commanded respect and a certain degree of obedience, they had no legal right to free labour for private purposes, and no means of enforcing it. Most important of all, they ceased to have direct charge of the penghulus. All their functions in this respect were taken over by the district officers. It was the district officers who interviewed new settlers and found them land, dispensed loans and other forms of assistance, recommended candidates for penghuluships and dealt with complaints and requests.

However, the recognition offered by the British, and—especially— the conservatism of the Malays themselves, must have resulted in the preservation of a large part of the influence of the traditional Malay leaders. The recommendations of district chiefs (i.e. in the appointment of penghulus) still counted for something with the government, and their interest was worth having, even though it was no longer decisive. It was the rajas and chiefs whose help was enlisted by the government in breaking down prejudice against vaccination and education. They still gave economic assistance to the ra'ayat; there are instances recorded of the construction of irrigation works and

---

[1] It is worth recording that in Selangor, an ordinary commoner was once bold enough to lay a complaint with the Magistrate at Langat against the Sultan's son, Kahar, for abetting an abduction and rape by his son. With the Sultan's permission, Raja Kahar was fined $100. Collector and Magistrate, Kuala Langat, journal for January 1878, Sel/Sec. 60/78.

assistance with loans and plough animals;[1] the return for this was probably free labour.

A number of the Malay rajas and chiefs engaged in mining and planting enterprises, but their operations were not extensive, and for the majority, it would probably be true to say that government appointments offered the chief hope of security and status. However, a few of the Perak chiefs, particularly those of Kinta, were enabled by a freak of policy to accumulate enough wealth to engage in large mining and real estate speculations, and for them, politics and government came second by a long way to their business interests. Malay owners of ancestral mines were entitled to a royalty (*hasil tanah*) on tin obtained from their mines; further, an attempt was made to stimulate the penghulus and chiefs of Perak to encourage mining by allowing them to draw a 10 per cent. commission (*chabut*) on the duty paid on all tin exported from their districts.[2] This ill-considered concession, made in 1878 before the development of the Kinta district, meant the free distribution of large unearned sums of public money among the penghulus and district chiefs of Kuala Kangsar, Batang Padang and Kinta. In 1889, the royalty on tin from ancestral mines was estimated at $5,500 and the chabut to penghulus was estimated at $40,398 ($33,940 from Kinta). By 1893, the royalty to private mines was estimated at $2,400, but the chabut to penghulus was estimated at $74,000; $70,000 from Kinta. In 1894, the chabut to be paid to each individual was limited (the largest allowance, $900 a month, being allocated to the Dato' Panglima Kinta, To' Muda Wahab and the assistant penghulu, Ulu Kinta), but the total was still estimated at $48,360.[3] The chiefs and penghulus built large villas

[1] The district officer of Kuala Kangsar reported the construction of a canal five miles long by the Sri Maharaja Lela (Kuala Kangsar monthly report for September 1895, *PGG*, 25 October 1895); the Laksamana declared himself willing to make advances to ra'ayat in Bidor to encourage padi planting (*AR* Lower Perak, 1891, *PGG*, 12 August 1892). The district officer, Kuala Langat, wrote in his journal that he was relieved to find that the Raja Muda was helping all the men at Sungei Rambei with their *ladangs*, since he himself had 'not nearly enough money to help all the people in this District and they were rather discontented'. Kuala Langat Journal, 16 May 1884.

[2] *PCM*, 6 September 1878.

[3] The sums paid in Kinta alone amounted to $30,252 in 1888 and $41,264 in 1889. There were ten recipients; the Sultan, the Panglima Kinta, the penghulu of Sungei Raya, Papan, Sungei Trap, Kuala Teja, Teja and Kampar; the assistant penghulu, Ulu Kinta, and Raja Drahman, unidentified (*AR* Kinta, 1889, *PGG*. 4 April 1890). In 1889 the largest sums were paid to the penghulus of Papan and Sungei Trap ($7,332 and $7,560 respectively). See 1894 estimates for names of recipients of limited *chabut*.

in Ipoh and other mining townships, invested in houses and shops, and engaged in mining operations in partnership with the Chinese;[1] not surprisingly, the district officers reported that they were too wrapped up in their speculations to do any work for the government.[2]

One part of the indigenous political system which continued to function with unimpaired vitality, though in a new context and in response to new needs, was local government by penghulus. In Perak, Selangor and Pahang, this had been part of the political structure in Malay times, and the new régime built on existing foundations. In Negri Sembilan, where local government had been carried on by lineage and not territorial headmen, tradition was respected; the Resident reported, 'the tribal system existing here is more satisfactory than the Penghulu Mukim system in other states of the Peninsula',[3] and the institution was not introduced. In Sungei Ujong the penghulu system appears to have been an innovation. The Resident reported in 1883 that the system of governing through headmen in each district had been known in former times, though the headmen of the different villages had never had the same powers as the penghulus of Perak, and the system had in any case fallen into disuse; but he had found it so useful during his Perak service that he proposed to introduce it. Accordingly the State Council in January 1884 passed regulations for the guidance of penghulus, similar in essentials to the Perak and Selangor regulations, and an establishment of paid penghulus was created.[4]

In Perak and Selangor, appointments and dismissals of penghulus were made by the State Council; commissions were issued in the name of the Sultan, and the Sultan and chiefs were consulted about appointments. Penghulus from all over the state attended the ceremonies at the installation of a Sultan or Raja Muda; in 1884 the penghulus of the Kuala Kangsar district attended the Hari Raya

[1] See, e.g., Report of the district officer for Ipoh, October 1890, *PGG*, 12 December 1890; *AR* Kinta, 1889, *PGG*, 4 April 1890. They also tried to exploit the transport difficulties of the Kinta miners, by renting out elephants at exorbitant prices, until the Chinese took to using wheelbarrows. Kinta monthly report for July 1890, *PGG*, 5 September 1890.
[2] *AR* Kinta, 1890, *PGG*, 7 August 1891.
[3] *AR* Negri Sembilan, 1892. References to 'penghulus' in the Negri Sembilan reports at this time are not to mukim headmen but to the great territorial chiefs, the Undangs.
[4] Sungei Ujong Council Proceedings, CO 474/1; Sungei Ujong Estimates; references to creation of additional penghulus and good work done by penghulus, *AR* Sungei Ujong, 1889 and 1893.

celebrations held by the Regent, and in 1894, penghulus from all over Selangor attended at Jugra to celebrate Hari Raya and perform the ceremony of homage to the Sultan (*menjunjong duli*).[1] The ties of ceremony and homage were between the penghulu and the Sultan; but power and responsibility, the choice of penghulus and their supervision, lay with the Resident and the district officers. The practical realities at times overshadowed and displaced ceremony; as when penghulus received their kuasas—drawn up in the Resident's office —from the hands of the district officer or the Resident himself.[2]

One of the first duties of Low and Swettenham, when they were appointed to their respective states, was to organize a full penghulu establishment. Low spent much of 1877 investigating claims to penghuluships; at a Council meeting in 1878, penghulus of mukims in the upper and middle Perak were formally appointed, and by 1879, penghulus had been appointed to all the Perak mukims.[3] In Selangor, Douglas had had little belief in the value of Malay authorities, and at the end of his six-year tenure of office there were only a dozen Malay magistrates and headmen.[4] Half of them were rajas in receipt of allowances claimed by right of birth and whose penghuluships were clearly sinecures; the others, mostly Sumatran headmen, had been appointed by Tengku Zia'u'd-din during the Selangor wars, and confirmed by Davidson or Douglas. When Swettenham became Resident, one of his first concerns was to regularize penghulu appointments. He circularized district officers, calling for recommendations for the mukims in their districts,[5] and at a Council meeting of 2 September 1883, twenty-three penghulus were formally appointed.[6]

[1] Kuala Langat monthly report for April 1894, *SGG*, 8 June 1894; Letter from the Raja Muda to the Resident, 18 April 1894, *SGG*, 22 June 1894, giving names of penghulus who attended. According to the district officer, the ceremonial had not been 'carried out in so formal a manner for long years'.

[2] E.g., installation of penghulu of Damansara by Senior District Officer, Klang, Klang monthly report for April 1891, *SGG*, 29 April 1891. See also Sel/Sec. 1357 to 1360–83. Even in the Langat district, where the Sultan lived, one penghulu was handed his kuasa by the district officer. Kuala Langat Journal, 28 July 1884.

[3] Perak List of Allowances and Pensions, 1879, *Perak Affairs and Despatches*, 1874–9, Perak Museum Library. The list gives forty-two penghulus and twelve assistant penghulus. An establishment list for 1892 gives sixty-three penghulus, sixteen assistant penghulus, and thirty-four clerks.

[4] Resident of Selangor to CS, 12 June 1882, enclosure in Weld to Derby, 208 of 28 May 1883, CO 273/120.

[5] Minute of 4 November 1882, Sel/Sec. 597/82.

[6] In 1888 there were twenty-eight penghulus (Auditor to Resident, 22 May 1888, Sel/Sec. 552A/89). In 1895 there were forty on the estimates.

The manner in which these appointments were made reflects the primary responsibility of the European officers. Swettenham, when he was Assistant Colonial Secretary for Native States, had been inclined to use the Perak appointments to bolster the influence of Raja Yusuf; he suggested, for example, that the penghuluships of Kuala Kangsar and Kota Lama, where Yusuf had most enemies, should be given to his son; and he proposed to replace the penghulu of Bidor, Orang Kaya Mat Arshad, whose father was under sentence of exile for conspiring to murder Birch.[1] Low had no intention of filling these positions with placemen of Raja Yusuf or Raja Idris or the Temenggong; he wished to appoint men who would be acceptable to the people. He confirmed Orang Kaya Mat Arshad at Bidor, and he left Kota Lama, the village with the worst history of opposition to the British, under its old headman, To' Sri Lela. Of another penghulu appointment he wrote, 'I am afraid of being made a tool of. Chigra Galah is an important place and there are candidates in numbers and the Raja Muda supports one family and the Tumonggong and others support others. I think the best plan will be for me to go there and take a sort of plebiscite among the people and the same to some other important places down the river.'[2] In Selangor, the names of penghulus were submitted to Swettenham by the district officers after the latter had consulted with the people of the mukims and with influential Malays, and had received deputations in favour of particular candidates. The criteria of selection were local influence and popularity, measured by discussions with villagers at meetings called for the purpose;[3] activity in opening up new land and introducing settlers; tenure of office in the past, and energy displayed in assisting the district officers and police. Malay rajas and

[1] Swettenham, 'Some arguments in favour of governing Perak through its Headmen', 8 October 1876, enclosure in Weld to Derby, 208 of 28 May 1883, CO 273/120.

[2] Low Journal, p. 101. Raja Yusuf's candidate was not appointed. The successful candidate, Syed Musa, was probably the man referred to as the Temenggong's candidate, the son of the late penghulu, and the popular choice. Ibid. p. 103.

[3] See, e.g., Kuala Langat Journal for 17 and 19 August 1883. In Lower Perak, the district officer took a vote—how, he does not say (Lower Perak monthly reports for March and April 1895, *PGG*, 21 June and 19 July 1895). Sometimes the 'election' was tactfully managed by local arrangement; e.g. the district officer of Kuala Langat, arriving at Telok Panglima Garang to carry out the election of a penghulu, found only one candidate—a nephew of the Sultan—'a well-educated, sensible young fellow, who commands the respect of the people, and who, I am glad to say, was unanimously chosen as Penghulu'. Kuala Langat monthly report for December 1893, *SGG*, 20 January 1894.

chiefs living in the district were consulted,[1] and the Sultan's approval was sought for the penghulus appointed in Langat,[2] though there is no record of consultation in respect of other districts. But it is quite clear that the final decision in each case was made by Swettenham on the Collector's recommendations.[3]

The penghulu's mukim included a main village, in which he lived, and a small number of subsidiary villages or hamlets.[4] The number of people in his care was not large. The 1891 census of Kuala Kangsar, a long-established and relatively populous district inhabited almost entirely by Malays, gives a population range of 583 to 2,969 between mukims;[5] a record of Selangor in 1894 shows that most of the mukims had a population of between 500 and 2,000 (the largest being Rawang in the mining district of Ulu Selangor, with about 4,150, and the smallest Kerling, a sinecure created for a relative of the royal family, with fifty).[6] The boundaries were roughly indicated in the kuasas, but were not clearly defined till 1891, when the Selangor mukims were defined as part of Maxwell's land settlement.[7] However, approximate mukim divisions were agreed on at an early stage (they were recommended by the Collectors, together with reports on candidates in 1883) and there was probably some historical basis for most of them since they were laid down after much dis-

[1] In Lower Perak, they accompanied the district officer on his tours to ascertain opinion. Lower Perak monthly reports for January and October 1892, *PGG*, 26 February and 25 November 1892.

[2] Minute by the Resident, undated, Sel/Sec. 1255/83. Sultan Idris was apparently consulted about penghulu appointments all over Perak. A penghulu appointment in the Batang Padang district was referred to him for his comments; he minuted that he considered the suggestion a good one, the district officer having such a thorough knowledge of the affairs of his district. Minute in Malay by Sultan Idris, 22 November 1891, Batang Padang Papers, 224/91.

[3] E.g., marginal minute, undated, on appointments to two Kuala Lumpur mukims, 'Yes, I had already made up my mind to these two men' (Sel/Sec. 1186/83). See also Sel/Sec. 594/82, 633/82, 50/83, 1158/83, 1411/83. Low reported in 1878 that all the penghulus recommended by the Collector for the Krian district had been appointed. Low to CS, 8 July 1878, enclosed in Robinson to Hicks Beach 255 of 27 August 1878, CO 273/95.

[4] In 1883, a return of Kuala Selangor mukims showed that each consisted of three to eight villages; mukim populations ranged from 203 to 1,557. Sel/Sec. 55/83.

[5] *Census of Perak, 1891*. These figures exclude the three largest mukims, Kota Lama Kanan, Kota Lama Kiri and Sayong, which were subdivided for enumeration purposes. Their total population was 9,117.

[6] *Statistical and other Information regarding the Districts of Selangor, 1894*.

[7] Compare the Kuala Lumpur mukim divisions as notified in *SGG* 9 January 1891 with those in Sel/Sec. 1495/83.

cussion with penghulus. Adjustments were made with population shifts and increases; new mukims were created, old ones allowed to disappear on the death of an incumbent.

The penghulu was the agent of government in the villages. He was the source of information about daily life in the village; he chronicled births and deaths, movements of people, disputes and crimes in a monthly report for the district officer. He was the channel through which government instructions were conveyed, and also government assistance in the shape of advances to settlers. He was responsible for local obedience to government orders; he was required to collect children for vaccination and encourage their attendance at school, and see that government forestry regulations and planting timetables were followed. He was responsible for keeping public order and settling disputes. He found labour for local roadwork and river clearing and was often himself the contractor for minor public works. These were his responsibilities; though it would clearly have been an exceptional penghulu who was able to carry them all out.

Of the penghulu's multifarious duties,[1] the most important were the maintenance of order, the administration of justice, and the collection of revenue (land rent on smallholdings, passes for timber cutting and gutta collection, fishing stake licences, and the kerah tax). In Pahang, rents were collected by penghulus throughout, the penghulus drawing a commission on collections.[2] In Selangor and Perak, there were variations in practice from one district to another and one period to another. Under Douglas, some district officers entrusted collections to penghulus, others (for example, Innes at Langat) preferred to employ forest rangers or police. Swettenham instructed in 1882 that penghulus be invited to assist the district officer in the collection of land revenue,[3] but throughout the 1880's, rent collection was extremely irregular, and from 1884 to 1887, by a decision of the State Council, no rents were collected on agricultural land outside the Kuala Lumpur district.[4] In the 1890's, rents were collected by district officers, but penghulus still performed an important function in gathering the rent-payers together at the peng-

---

[1] See penghulu kuasa, Appendix 4d.

[2] Correspondence on Sel/Sec. 408A/97.

[3] Minute to Collector, Kuala Selangor, 6 December 1882, Sel/Sec. 608/82. The Collector, Kuala Langat, reported the collection of rents and timber royalty by penghulus in his journal. Kuala Langat Journal for 6 August and 11 October 1883.

[4] SCM, 19 February 1884.

hulu's house or the police station on collection day,[1] and they continued to collect timber revenues and gutta pass fees. In Perak, the penghulus collected timber and gutta revenues and land rents (except in Krian) until the 1890's; the Kuala Kangsar annual report for 1889 stated that nearly the whole of the land revenue ($9,612) was collected by penghulus, and put the total penghulu collections at $10,499 out of a total district revenue of $30,518 for that year. From 1893 however, rents were collected by district officers, the function of penghulus, as in Selangor, being to round up the rent-payers on collection day. In 1897 the Secretary to Government reported, 'It is a rule in Perak (& sh[oul]d be everywhere in Malaya) that no rents are collected by a Penghulu or Eurasian or native clerk.'[2]

In Perak, the efforts of penghulus were stimulated by a percentage of one-tenth on collections. In 1889 the tenths were estimated at $11,074, exclusive of chabut on tin duty; in 1895, with the diminution of penghulu collections, the amount estimated was $3,300. In Selangor, Swettenham introduced a complicated and unworkable system whereby penghulus could claim a percentage only on new revenues originating in their own efforts to develop their districts (i.e. paid by new settlers they themselves had introduced). Although the estimated allowances for penghulu collections were small ($300 in 1885, $700 in 1895), yet even these small sums were not distributed in the manner intended, but used to provide bonuses for deserving penghulus.[3] In some mukims, collections by penghulus were microscopic, partly perhaps because of the lack of incentive, partly because of the relatively greater ease of communication with the district centres, which encouraged people to come direct to the district offices for passes and information.[4]

The penghulus were expected to introduce new settlers and encourage the development of their mukims, and they were allocated small loans for distribution. They also played an important part in land settlement, forwarding applications for land under customary tenure, and helping to demarcate holdings and fix assessments. Applications for mining licences were often made to them in the first

---

[1] See *SGG*, monthly district reports during 1892.

[2] Minute of 25 January 1897, Sel/Sec. 408A/97.

[3] Resident to Collector and Magistrate, Kuala Selangor, 26 September 1883, Sel/Sec. 1158/83; Acting Collector and Magistrate, Ulu Selangor, 15 March 1888, Sel/Sec. 836/88.

[4] Sel/Sec. 836/88.

instance.[1] They thus had opportunities, which they sometimes exploited, for extortion and breach of trust; there were cases of penghulus appropriating loans and other public moneys for their own use, and extorting tribute from applicants for mining land; and in Negri Sembilan, where lineage headmen (*lembaga*) were initially made responsible for registering and assessing Malay holdings, it was found that the weight of their assessments had fallen most heavily on the poorer landholders.[2]

There was a contradiction in the role of the penghulu which became increasingly evident with the passing of time. His usefulness to Government lay initially in his influence, and the criteria for selection related to this; literacy and clerical ability were secondary considerations. The office itself, its material rewards (salaries, commissions, pensions, a house-site and garden free of land rent) increased his local importance, and so did the powers inherent in his judicial, revenue and developmental functions. But the proper performance of these functions demanded literacy and clerical training; he was required to submit a monthly report on his mukim, to keep accounts of revenue and make returns of births and deaths, to keep a record of land applications. The conflict of demands was resolved in Perak by the appointment of *krani* (clerks) to assist the penghulus.[3] But there was an increasing tendency to demand literacy in new penghulus, and to appoint penghulu clerks and other government clerks to vacancies,[4] and as this was done, penghulu clerkships in the smaller mukims became redundant and disappeared from the estimates. The principle of hereditary succession still had some force, particularly as a means of securing the loyalty of the more influential families,[5] but it was by no means general, and energy and efficiency

---

[1] *AR* Kuala Selangor, 1893, *SGG* 25 May 1894; *AR* Ulu Selangor, 1892, *SGG*, 4 August 1893. In Perak and particularly in Selangor they shared the responsibility for land settlement with Malay rangers attached to the district offices. In mukims where there were illiterate or incompetent penghulus, the forest rangers did most of the work.   [2] *AR* Negri Sembilan, 1893.

[3] There were no penghulu clerks on the 1879 establishment, thirty-four on the 1892 estimates, and twenty-nine on the 1895 estimates. In Selangor there do not appear to have been any government-appointed clerks, but there were some clerks employed by penghulus themselves and maintained out of their salaries.

[4] See Perak and Selangor Council Minutes and district reports in gazettes, e.g., *AR* Kuala Kangsar, 1891 and *AR* Klang, 1890. Appointment as a government clerk did not, however, exclude the possession of local influence; for example, the clerk at Sabak Bernam in Selangor, later appointed penghulu of the new mukim of Bagan Nakhoda Omar, was the son of the founder of the original settlement.

[5] The son of To' Sri Lela, penghulu of Kota Lama Kanan, claimed to have

became equally important qualifications. The majority of penghulus remained until retirement in the mukims to which they were first appointed, but transfers of penghulus were not unknown, and the appointment of government clerks to penghuluships nearly always involved transfers—usually between mukims in the same district, but sometimes from one district to another. With the decline of their revenue functions, the increasing number of clerically trained penghulus and the increasing mobility of penghulus, they began to take on a little of the aspect of a mukim bureaucracy.

The reports of the district officers on the penghulus under them were equally divided between expressions of satisfaction, and criticisms of laziness, inefficiency and indifference; and one may detect in the latter the opinions in favour of annexation and direct rule which Swettenham, Weld and others were at such pains to refute. Swettenham was probably right in saying that despite their shortcomings, penghulus and other Malay authorities justified the policy which preserved and exploited their influence. At the best, they provided an invaluable fund of local knowledge and experience; at the worst, their neutrality and abstention from active opposition was a real gain.

The dilemma of government bound to respect tradition, yet intent on revolutionizing the economy and administration, was met in yet another form when it came to devising an education system for the Malay states. The first government Malay school in Selangor was established by Davidson in Klang in 1875, the first schools in Perak in 1883,[1] but despite the interest and support of the Straits government, there was little progress; until the 1890's there was no separate department of education in any state, and the encouragement of schools was left entirely to the district officers. It was not until full-time Inspectors of Schools had been established in Perak and Selangor in 1890 that education began to make some headway in these

---

had a written promise from the government that he would succeed his father; as someone else had been appointed to Kota Lama Kanan, he was given Kota Lama Kiri (*PCM*, 19 December 1891, *PGG*, 30 March 1892). The son of To' Domba of Sungei Raya succeeded his father, the son of the Mentri was made penghulu of Bukit Gantang (his father's seat), and on his elevation to the title his brother was made assistant penghulu to help him. On the other hand, numbers of penghulus were not succeeded by their sons, though the new incumbents may of course have been relatives.

[1] Sel/Sec. 108/80; *AR* Perak, 1883. See also Report on Education in Selangor, 1880–7, Sel/Sec. 2123/87.

states.[1] Pahang and Negri Sembilan, however, continued to be without full-time trained education officers.

In principle there was no distinction between the races in the provision of education; as Swettenham put it in his annual report on Perak for 1890, 'the education of the rising generation of Malays, Chinese and Tamils is distinctly the serious duty of Government'. But the fact that the Malay population was the only one with a normal age distribution meant that the large majority of children receiving an education were Malays attending Malay vernacular schools. The only Chinese vernacular schools supported at any time by government were a Chinese school in Kuala Lumpur and an Anglo-Chinese school in Kamunting. The Selangor school was considered to be performing a useful function and allowed to survive as a government school; but in Perak, a prejudice against education in Chinese became manifest and the Chinese themselves tactfully released the government from an undertaking to maintain a Chinese class at the Kamunting school by petitioning for its abolition on the pretext that simultaneous teaching in English and Chinese was not in the best interests of the children.[2] A few government-aided Tamil and Anglo-Tamil schools were maintained in Perak and Selangor, but by 1895 the Anglo-Tamil school in Kuala Lumpur had merged with a new government-aided English school, the Victoria Institution, and there remained only four government-aided schools in Perak giving instruction in Tamil, two of them mission schools.

If there was a practical motive for furthering education, it was not at first evident. In later years, the provision of clerks, draughtsmen and apprentices, and in particular the training of Malays to fill the places hitherto taken up by aliens, were put forward as justifications for the education programme; but the initial impulse seems to have arisen from the recognition that it was the duty of an enlightened government to provide its subjects with an education. The occasional futilities of the vernacular schools were justified by Treacher in these terms:

[1] Perak in 1889 had nineteen schools with an aggregate enrolment of 626. In 1895 there were ninety-six schools with an enrolment of 4,382. Selangor in 1890 had fifteen schools with an enrolment of 505; in 1895 there were twenty-five schools with an enrolment of 981, excluding an average registration of 158 for the English-language Victoria Institution. AR Education Perak, 1891, PGG, 29 July 1892; AR Education Selangor, 1890 and 1891, SGG, 17 April 1891 and 19 August 1892; AR Selangor and Perak, 1895.

[2] AR Education Perak, 1890, PGG, 26 June 1891.

It is to be hoped that results will soon be seen in a supply of *native* subordinate officers to take up appointments which now, not without difficulty, are filled by youths educated in India and Ceylon. . . . Nevertheless, a point which the District Officers and the Inspector of Schools should lose no opportunity of impressing upon the scholars and their parents is that the vernacular education brought to their doors by a liberal Government has not for its main object the manufacture of clerks, but that a lad who has gone through the school training is likely to be a better padi planter, trader, miner or sailor than one whose early years have been passed in idleness in the village lanes.[1]

(There was a tacit recognition that a boy educated in the vernacular would probably have little alternative but to be a 'better padi planter, trader, miner or sailor', since so much of the work of the government at the higher levels was done in English.)

The people of the states appeared to have a more practical approach. In Perak, when the provision of education was discussed in Council, the Malay members suggested that elementary teaching of English, Romanized Malay and arithmetic would be more popular than exclusively vernacular education, and should be instituted to begin with in the main townships.[2] In Selangor too, Malay and Chinese leaders consulted by the Resident thought that provision should be made for the teaching of English: '. . . it was evident to me that the sense of the meeting was that nothing would tend so much to the cause of education here, as giving the people an opportunity of learning the language of those who are now appointed by His Excellency under the Residential system to administer the laws and the general functions of the Government'.[3] The proliferation of English schools in the kampongs was never seriously considered however. The staffing of such schools with trained teachers would certainly have been very difficult and three or four times as expensive as the provision of Malay vernacular teachers. English schools were confined to the towns, where the existence of an English-speaking population created an environment more favourable for the spread of English, so that the pupils were in the main Tamils, Chinese and Eurasians. They can hardly have derived much benefit from the teaching. No school taught beyond primary VI, and most of them taught up to primary II, III or IV; teaching methods were inferior

[1] 'Notes on a tour of the districts of Selangor', *SGG*, 22 June 1894.
[2] *PCM*, 20 October 1882.
[3] Resident of Selangor to CS, 24 July 1882, Sel/Sec. 122/82. The Sultan of Pahang 'expressly asked' for the establishment of an English school for the sons of Rajas and headmen, and promised his support. *AR* Pahang, 1892.

and primers were quite inappropriate. In 1889 the acting Inspector of Schools, Perak, reported that except in the Central School, Taiping (where the teaching was fairly competent) teachers proceeded by mechanically translating word for word from English into Malay, with 'very remarkable' results. The tales in the primers included 'A Week at the Farm', 'I will not hurt my little Dog', 'Mary's little Lamb', 'Spring', 'Tidy Tom', 'A willing Boy'—'all very well for little English children but . . . hardly the stuff to set before the sons of Tamil cattle-dealers and Chinese shop-keepers, who wish to learn English in order to be able to buy and sell and speculate, and transact the practical business of life'.[1]

The expense and difficulty of teaching English in a society where it was so little used, was one reason for the preoccupation with the vernacular; another reason, perhaps more important, was a political and emotional antipathy to *babus* whose imperfect knowledge of English gave them ideas above their station. Swettenham expressed a common attitude when he wrote in his Perak *Annual Report* for 1890:

> The one danger to be guarded against is an attempt to teach English indiscriminately. It could not be well taught except in a very few schools, and I do not think it is at all advisable to give the children of an agricultural population an indifferent knowledge of a language that to all but the very few would only unfit them for the duties of life and make them discontented with anything like manual labour.

English teaching even in the towns made very little progress in Perak.[2] In Selangor, there was more sympathy for English. The interest of Chinese and Indian leaders led to the formation in Kuala Lumpur of the Victoria Institution, the first liberal teaching institution in the Malay states, designed to prepare boys for the professions

---

[1] *AR* Education Perak, 1889, *PGG*, 2 May 1890. The only flaw in this criticism is that Chinese and Tamils did not need English to help them to 'buy and sell and speculate, and transact the practical business of life'. If English had a practical purpose, it was to enable them to qualify for clerkships and other government posts. There was also the social and psychological value attached to learning the language of the rulers.

[2] In 1891 there were 448 pupils in eight schools; in Taiping (three), Kamunting, Matang, Telok Anson, Bagan Serai and Parit Buntar. English was also taught in the Malay school at Kuala Kangsar. In 1895 there were 534 pupils in the same number of schools. Selangor in 1891 had sixty-four pupils in the Government English school, and about twelve in the Raja School, both at Kuala Lumpur. In 1895, the average enrolment in the Victoria Institution at Kuala Lumpur (with which all the English-language schools had been amalgamated) was 158. There was also a private Anglo-Chinese school in Klang, with twenty-six pupils. There were no English schools in any of the other states in 1895. An English school started in Seremban in 1889 was closed in 1892 as an economy measure.

as well as for clerkships.[1] Some officials were in favour of promoting English at the expense of the vernacular; the Acting Resident, E.W. Birch, argued that the practical need for 'a class of interpreters, school-masters, clerks, and policemen' could be better achieved by establish-ing a good boarding-school in Kuala Lumpur to which the pupils of the vernacular schools could be sent, than to 'scatter broadcast over the country schools for which it is difficult to find efficient masters'.[2] But the policy pursued in Selangor as in other states was to concen-trate English teaching in the towns and continue the stress on Malay vernacular education elsewhere. An English education was to remain the privilege of urban children (mostly Chinese and Tamils), the children of Malay aristocrats,[3] and those Malay graduates of the vernacular schools who were able to take up scholarships at the English schools.[4]

The village vernacular schools had little interest for Malays, at least until the 1890's, and parents had to be dragooned into sending their children there. Pedagogically the schools were bad; the teachers were untrained and miserably paid, and had to deal with up to four standards at a time in one-room schools. But good or bad, they had

[1] This school was established in Kuala Lumpur in 1894. The idea originated, it was said, with the Capitan China, Yap Kuan Seng, Loke Yew (a Chinese mem-ber of Council), and Tambusamy Pillai, an Indian miner, contractor and planter. The school was financed by an initial contribution of $5,000 from the government, $7,825 in public donations, and $3,188 standing to the credit of a Queen's Jubilee Fund collected in 1887 and still unspent. Additional finance was to be provided by an annual government grant of $3,000, an education assessment rate of 1 per cent. on houses and lands in Kuala Lumpur, and a grant-in-aid on the basis of results and attendance (Correspondence relating to the establishment of an Edu-cational Institution in Selangor, *SGG*, 7 July 1893). The school was formed in the first instance from the amalgamation of the existing English-teaching schools in Kuala Lumpur—the Government English School, the Raja School and the Anglo-Tamil School. *AR* Education Selangor, 1893, *SGG*, 25 May 1894.
[2] *AR* Selangor 1892.
[3] In 1890, on Maxwell's initiative, an English class for the children of Rajas and other influential Malays was set up in Kuala Lumpur under the Protestant chaplain and Inspector of Schools, the Rev. F.W. Haines. The number of pupils varied between ten and sixteen in the years 1890 and 1894, when the class merged with the Victoria Institution. The pupils included two commoner sons of peng-hulus in the Klang district.
[4] According to the *AR* Education Perak, 1892 (*PGG*, 28 April 1893) a free English education was offered to every boy who had passed standard IV in a Malay school. No figures are available, but the racial breakdown of pupils in English schools in that year shows that out of a total of 477, forty-five were Malays. Of the rest, thirty-nine were Europeans or Eurasians, 196 Indians, and 197 Chinese. The *AR* Selangor, 1896, announced that scholarships had been established to enable the most advanced boys from the vernacular schools to continue their education at the Victoria Institution.

no meaning for villagers who expected their children to grow up to be farmers and fishermen like themselves. A visiting Malay teacher who tried to persuade people in Kuala Selangor to send their children to school, got this reply; *'Kita punya anak kita punya suka, orang apa purduli bodoh atau pandei, tertapi jikalu handak buri gaji pada kita, bulihlah anak anak kita purgi skolah'* (Our children are our affair, who cares whether they are clever or stupid, but if we are paid to send them to school, we'll send them).[1] The personal influence of the district officers failed to increase interest; penghulus, it was claimed, were indifferent—'the majority of the penghulus decline to use their influence, and the majority of the people leave the whole question to the caprice of their children'.[2]

In the 1890's, however, there was a better response, and Malays began to ask for schools to be established in their mukims. Penghulus were more active in encouraging attendance (some of them were said to favour compulsion) and influential Malays set an example by sending their children to school;[3] the Raja Muda of Selangor established a school at his own expense at Bandar Langat, with a larger enrolment than that of the government school at Jugra.[4] There were a number of reasons for this increased interest. With the appointment of full-time education officers and visiting teachers, the schools were better organized; teachers trained in the Colony began to be recruited, classes were graded and regularly examined, syllabuses were laid down and texts prescribed.[5] Afternoon Koran classes were introduced, and played an important part in increasing interest. ('In popularising education, the Koran class in Malay schools is quite as useful as the playground in English schools.')[6] School sports and prizegivings began to be important events in the life of the commu-

[1] Report of Visiting Teacher, 3 June 1883, Sel/Sec. 892/83.

[2] *AR* Education Perak, 1889, *PGG*, 2 May 1890.

[3] The Kinta chiefs living in Ipoh sent their children to the school in Batu Gajah; the Sultan sent his sons to the school in Kuala Kangsar and later to the Government English School in Taiping.

[4] Kuala Langat monthly report for October 1892, *SGG*, 25 November 1892. It was taken over by the government in 1893.

[5] See Sel/Sec. 1026/93 for details of Perak and Selangor education systems, standards, syllabus, books, regulations etc; also Report on Vernacular Education in Perak, *PGG*, 4 January 1895.

[6] Quarterly Report on Education, *PGG*, 11 May 1894. Selangor relied also on compulsion; according to Regulation V of 1891, the parents of male Malay children between seven and fourteen living within two miles of a vernacular school were obliged to send their children to it on pain of fine up to $5 or fourteen days' imprisonment. The powers were not invoked, the regulation being 'held *in terrorem* to good effect'. No other state applied compulsion.

nity, and schoolchildren in uniform were prominent at public celebrations.[1] All this certainly played a part in raising the schools in
the public estimation. But more important was the recognition by
Malays of the value of the school as an avenue to employment, and
the recognition by European officers of the importance of recruitment to government posts as a means of increasing interest in the
schools. (In this connexion, an important innovation in the 1890's
was the teaching of Romanized Malay in the fourth standard; it was
said to double a boy's chances of employment, and was regarded as
an important step to learning English.) The levels for which the
general run of Malays were considered suitable were the lowest in
the service; one article earnestly entitled 'What can we do for the
Malay?'[2] catalogued the posts they might fill—peons and *punkah*-
pullers, process-servers, postmen, guards, ticket-collectors etc.—and
described the difficulties experienced in recruiting them even at these
low levels; the monopolies already established (for example, by
Tamils in the railways), the prejudices formed by European officers
against Malays as a result of the appointment of incompetents to
penghuluships for political reasons, the absence of specific moves
by government to encourage Malays to enter the service, and the
low wages for Malay subordinates. But Malays *were* recruited into
the service, though the numbers were small,[3] and by 1895 it was
certainly government policy to recruit them when ever possible,[4]

[1] The Kuala Langat monthly report for April 1894 (*SGG*, 8 June 1894) described their attendance at Jugra for the Hari Raya celebrations at the palace. 'The
school-boys were in various costumes; those from Telok were designated by a
blue belt from shoulder to waist, those at Bandar in yellow (royal colours) and
the Jugra contingent wore blue-and-red. The sports were really intended for the
school-boys, and they knew it, judging from their eager happy faces. One lot of
big boys from Permatang Pasir, who attend the Jugra School, were very pictur-
esquely dressed with red Scotch caps, white jackets with blue-and-red sashes,
white knickerbockers and scarlet gaiters. They had a bandmaster, dressed in
fancy blue-and-yellow uniform, who put the boys through a drill. A violin accompanied them, playing well-known Malayan tunes, and also, it is funny to say, an
adaptation of a good many modern popular English tunes, like "Ring the bell,
Watchman", "Wait till the clouds roll by" and snatches from "Pinafore", with
verses in Malay composed for the occasion.'
[2] J.H.M. Robson, 'What can we do for the Malay?', *Selangor Journal*, vol. iv,
no. 14, 20 March 1896.
[3] A breakdown of past pupils of vernacular schools in Perak in 1896 showed
that of 5,000 pupils still alive in Perak for whom returns were available, 43 were
constables, 50 were learning English, 57 were clerks, 59 teachers, 61 orderlies, 146
traders, 2,070 padi planters or gardeners and 2,177 'variously employed'. *AR*
Perak, 1896.
[4] Cf., *AR* Selangor, 1893. A directive was issued in Perak in October 1897 as

though the policy may not have been actively pursued.

The education system in the states might seem to have achieved little either in quantity or quality. In Perak, where it was furthest developed, the expenditure on education represented little more than 1 per cent. of the annual revenue, and the children at school represented about one-ninth of all those of school-going age; the highest standard in the Malay vernacular schools was Primary IV and the highest standard in the English schools was Primary VI. For the vast majority of Malays, the achievement of a government clerkship was set down as the summit of ambition. But in designing such a system, with all its crippling limitations, the state education departments were being no more unimaginative than their metropolitan counterparts. It would not be reasonable to expect the Malayan equivalent of the Victorian board-school to have been more liberal or original than its prototype. The teaching, however limited, did extend mental horizons and introduce a corporate spirit into the lives of Malay children which was in itself an important new experience. It assisted contact with the outside world in other ways, as 'a centre for the communication of news and information eagerly gleaned from the columns of the Malay newspapers supplied' and as a centre for the distribution of medicines in time of epidemic. It was already an important force for change.

The immigration of large numbers of Chinese and Indians has created in the long run serious problems of integration, and has brought on the Malays a great fear of loss of identity, not compensated in their minds by material benefits. Yet the material improvements which came to them as a result of British rule and alien immigration were genuine enough. In the first place they undoubtedly benefited from some of the more obvious consequences of an orderly administration. The wars which had depopulated whole districts came to an end. Slavery was abolished; and while the evils of slavery in Malay society have been much exaggerated by British apologists,[1]

---

follows: 'Heads of Departments and District Officers are required to note that it is the desire of Government to bring forward the Malays of the country, to educate them and to give them employment whenever it is possible, and with this object in view it is requested that employment be given to Malays in preference to strangers and, when it can be so arranged, that they be taken as apprentices in the workshops.' *Perak Circulars*, 1885–1906, ed. R.J. Wilkinson, Kuala Lumpur, 1907.

[1] Low reported in 1883 that there was a large surplus in the vote for the re-

it was a fertile source of injustice and cruelty, and its abolition was a blessing. Malays, like others, benefited from the improvement in communications; not perhaps from the railways, which were designed to serve the mining centres, but certainly from the construction of roads and bridle tracks, which now became important lines of communication and settlement. Malays did not attend government hospitals, but since medical care was poor, it is doubtful whether the Chinese gained any more from this than Malays did from vernacular education. The only clear social improvements which, by demographic accident, Malays did not enjoy, were the services provided in the towns—metalled roads, piped water, street lighting and scavenging—but as the great majority of Chinese and Indians lived not in towns but in mine or estate dormitories, their lives also were innocent of these amenities.

The benefits of an orderly administration and development of communications were enjoyed by the Malays at no great cost to themselves. There was little pressure on them to provide labour for economic development, and they thus escaped perhaps the most brutal and demoralizing of the pressures of colonial rule. The revenues were sufficient to pay for labour on public works, and Chinese and Indians were recruited to work on the mines, estates, roads and railways, often under brutal conditions.[1] The kerah or corvée, due formerly to the raja and the district chief for personal as well as state service, was continued for a time, but in a greatly modified form. In Perak it was enforced by regulation in 1882 as an alternative to land rent; it was limited to six days a year, and commutation fixed at twenty-five cents a day, those paying land rent (virtually all Malays outside the Perak river valley) being exempt.[2] About half of those liable chose to commute their services.[3] The tax was the only considerable

demption of slaves and bondmen in Perak, in consequence of 'the great and unexpected liberality of the owners of slaves in refusing to accept compensation for them, but freeing them in the hope of the "mercy of God", and as being unwilling to sell dependents who had been born in their houses and were looked upon as part of the families of their masters'. *AR* Perak, 1883.

[1] In a paper to the Royal Colonial Institute, Clifford contrasted the freedom of Malays 'to lead their own lives in the fashion which most completely commends itself to them' with the position of Dutch subjects in the East Indies, 'where the white rulers hold the opinion that an indolent brown population must be made diligent by law. . . .' 'British and Siamese Malays', op. cit. p. 52.

[2] *PCM*, 18 October 1882.

[3] The number of adult Malay males in Perak in 1879, exclusive of those living in Larut, Krian, Kurau and Selama (5,524) was about 14,000. $10,450 in kerah commutation was collected in 1884. *AR* Perak, 1884.

revenue payment made by the Perak river Malays till the late 1880's, but there was much pressure for its abolition; in 1885 Swettenham, then Acting Resident, wished to abolish it, and finally did so in 1891, after he became Resident.[1] Selangor Regulation XV of 1890 revived the obligation to customary service on communal or state works in terms which suggested that it had not recently been enforced for these purposes.[2] The service was limited to community works for which Malays were by custom expected to contribute their labour, such as 'any work for the purpose of clearing or burning jungle or of irrigation or drainage . . . usually executed by the joint labour of the cultivators of a certain village or area'; it also included attendance on district officers on tour. Labour was to be paid a minimum of thirty cents a day (the rate paid by the Public Works Department for free Tamil labour in Kuala Lumpur)[3] and the obligation to service might be commuted for an annual payment of $2, which represented a week's work at the minimum rate. The relatively high rate of wages alone would have been sufficient to ensure that the regulation was not abused. In Pahang the burden of kerah was certainly much heavier; according to Regulation V of 1889, it might be enforced for a maximum of two months in a year. But here also there was provision for commutation; food or an alimentary allowance was to be provided, and liability was to be limited to work for the state or for government officers.

The incidence of taxation fell lightly on the Malays. Import taxes had been abolished at an early stage (except on opium and spirits) and the main revenues were derived from the export duty on tin and the import duty on opium, both primarily contributed by the Chinese. Other important sources of revenue such as the farm of opium, gambling and spirits, railway receipts and fines and fees of court, mainly affected alien immigrants and alien enterprise, primarily Chinese. Malays did not drink spirits and were not allowed to gamble;

[1] AR Perak, 1891. In 1889 the estimate of kerah collection had fallen to $1,485. This fall probably relates to the great increase in the land revenue which took place about this time.

[2] The people of the Langat mukims still went off en masse to help the Sultan clear his land (and probably harvest his padi), but there is nothing to show that they were now subject to any force beyond the force of custom. Collector, Kuala Langat Journal for May 1887, Sel/Sec. 1467/87.

[3] Report of the Commission of Enquiry into the State of Labour in the Straits Settlements and Protected Native States, 1891, Appendix A, Evidence, p. 161. This report, published as an SS Legislative Council Paper in 1891, will be referred to henceforth as 'Labour Commission Report, 1891'. See also Resident of Selangor to Selangor Planters, 19 February 1891, Sel/Sec. 44A/92.

the railways, which provided an increasingly important element of the revenue, ran between the mining districts and the coast, and a majority of the passengers were probably Chinese (this is borne out by the preponderance of Chinese clothing and utensils in the lists of unclaimed goods left on the railways). The land revenue was derived partly from rents on Malay smallholdings, but half at least must have come from premia and rents on estate and mining land and town lots. Judicial fines and fees derived mostly from Chinese litigation, since Chinese were the people most frequently in the courts and their disputes involved the largest sums. Clifford, the first of a long line of vicarious Malay nationalists, calculated that the Malays paid no taxes except a land rent and duties on forest produce. He estimated that half the land revenue and three-quarters of the forest revenue represented virtually all that was paid by Malays—about $600,000 of the 1901 total of $17,541,507 for the four states, or some 3.4 per cent.[1] Clifford's estimate is probably too low, but his general argument is sound. The alien contribution preponderated even in Negri Sembilan and Pahang, where there was little mining, and where Malays were very much in the majority.[2]

*   *   *

[1] Clifford, op. cit. pp. 49–50. An attempt has been made to calculate the Malay contribution to the Perak revenues for 1895. The Malay contribution to Customs (tin and opium duty) has been calculated at 5 per cent. of the total for that item, in proportion to the occupational distribution in the 1891 census, where the number of Malay and Chinese miners is given as 2,217 and 47,444 respectively. The Malay shares of 'licences' (farm of spirit, gambling and pawnbroking for the state, coast chandu farm, farm or duty on firewood, timber, atap and forest produce) has been estimated at 5 per cent. (the Malays contributed substantially only to the last-named item). Municipal receipts have been calculated in proportion to the Malay element of the urban population. For other revenues, district totals have been the basis of calculation, and the Malay share calculated in proportion to their numbers in the district. On this basis, the total Malay contribution has been estimated at about $430,000, or just over 10 per cent. of the total revenue of $4,033,611. (The numbers of Malays and Chinese in the state were roughly equal in 1891.) It is impossible to assess their share of the expenditure, but it is noteworthy that the expenditure in districts with predominantly Malay populations was considerably in excess of revenue; for example, Kuala Kangsar, with a Malay population of about 80 per cent. of the district total, earned $82,968 in 1894 and spent $230,000, of which $73,491 is accounted for under Malay allowances and pensions. Upper Perak, with Malays numbering about 93 per cent. of the population, earned $4,432 and spent $25,655. The figures for 1894 have been taken, since the large receipts under 'licences' were credited to districts in that year, giving better district figures for revenue. Sources of information are Appendixes to *AR* Perak, 1894 and 1895, CO 438/1 and *Census of Perak, 1891*.

[2] A detailed statement of revenue for Negri Sembilan for 1890 shows that of

The spinning world of government and development turned on the work and pleasures of the Chinese. They were recognized as 'the bone and sinew of the Malay States', 'the labourers, the miners, the principal shopkeepers, the contractors, the capitalists, the holders of the revenue farms, the contributors of almost the whole of the revenue'.[1] The large-scale immigration of Chinese was thought of as 'only a subject of congratulation'. Indeed the Residents year by year cited the number of Chinese immigrants as an index to prosperity. Chinese, like other immigrants, came in without restriction and in large numbers. Nearly all of them were adult male labourers, the great majority bound for the mines, a large minority for Chinese sugar, gambier and tapioca estates. But while the accepted pattern was of migratory bachelor labour, entering temporarily to work for limited periods, there was no policy objection to permanent settlement by Chinese as a fixed agricultural community, and though there was no government-sponsored plan of settlement (with the mines exerting such a powerful attraction, any such plan would have been a waste of time and money) individual Chinese initiative and interest in agricultural settlement, and particularly in padi-planting, was warmly welcomed and encouraged.[2] The only sour note was struck by Weld, whose interest in encouraging Indian immigration arose partly out of his anxiety to limit the dependence of the country (and particularly the Malay states) on the Chinese.[3]

---

the total revenue of $107,033, $39,600 came from the farm of the opium import duty, and $31,320 from the export duty on tapioca (a Chinese cultivation). Of the land revenue of $20,842, $8,909 represented the registration fee on Malay holdings, at that time the only Malay land-tax (*AR* Negri Sembilan, 1890, Appendix B, CO 437/1). A statement of revenue and expenditure for Pahang for 1894 shows that out of a total revenue of $100,220, opium and spirit farms gave $24,000 and royalties on tin and gold (predominantly Chinese-worked), $35,904 (*AR* Pahang, 1894, Statement of Pahang revenue, CO 435/1). Deficits in Pahang and Negri Sembilan were made good by borrowing from the Straits Settlements, Perak and Selangor.

[1] Swettenham, *The Real Malay*, pp. 39–40. See also Clifford's remarkable tribute to the 'incalculable debt' owed by the Federated Malay States to 'the courage, persistency and ability of their Chinese citizens'. Clifford, op. cit. p.56.

[2] *AR* Perak, 1889; *AR* Kuala Selangor, 1893, *SGG*, 25 May 1894. The district officer for Krian reported that he had 'persuaded Chinese to take up padi land in one or two places' (monthly report for August 1891, *PGG*, 11 September 1891). See also reports of alienation of some three thousand acres to Chinese for padi planting in Lower Perak. *AR* Lower Perak, 1891, *PGG*, 12 August 1892; Lower Perak monthly reports for April, May and June 1892, *PGG*, 20 May, 1 July and 29 July 1892.

[3] 'I consider that it will be a political advantage for the Colony and for the

The difficulty of governing a population of migratory male labourers, living in what were essentially labour camps, was increased by the barriers of language, by the Chinese distrust of government, and by the xenophobia which added to distrust when the government was a foreign one. On the whole, this dislike was heartily reciprocated. Under certain circumstances, the relations of the Chinese with British and Malays were easy and pleasant; in the smaller communities, Chinese traders and shopkeepers were well-known, spoke Malay, and fitted easily into their environment, and between the big towkays and the British (and Malays) intercourse was made smooth by lavish hospitality and the mellowing effects of great wealth. Yet even here there were reservations in the relationship between European and Chinese which did not exist between Europeans and Malays.[1] The feeling towards the common Chinese labourer was expressed by Low when he described how the Chinese were coming into Perak in crowds. 'Having been imported direct from inland districts in China, they were of all men the most rude, conceited, and ignorant, with no confidence in Europeans, easily oppressed and misled by their own countrymen who employed them, and who were themselves greatly influenced by the secret societies of Penang, especially on the coast districts.'[2]

The state government did little enough to bridge the gap between themselves and the Chinese. Swettenham's dictum—'The first requirement was to learn the language of the people to be ruled'—did not apply to Chinese. Swettenham was the only one of the Residents known to have a little knowledge of the language. Cadets were required to pass a certain standard of conversation, reading and writing in a native language before appointment to a substantive post, but no particular inducement was held out to them to learn the more difficult language, and most of them elected to learn Malay,[3]

Native States to encourage the immigration of our own subjects from British India and to make them less dependent than heretofore on Chinese labour.' Weld to Holland, 195 of 11 May 1887, CO 273/145.

[1] Cf., Swettenham's remark 'It is almost hopeless to expect to make friends with a Chinaman, and it is, for a Government officer, an object that is not very desirable to attain'. Swettenham, op. cit. pp. 38–39.

[2] AR Perak, 1882. In 1880, the Supt. of Police, Selangor, complained 'there are a large number of Chinese in this country who think the only form of government worthy of attention is that of their own headmen'. Supt. to Resident, 7 September 1880, Sel/Sec. 272/80.

[3] They knew enough Malay for administrative purposes, but it is doubtful whether many knew it well. A Malay translation of a Selangor Regulation, made

and went on to govern mainly Chinese districts with no other language qualification. In 1895 there were probably no more than half a dozen Chinese-speaking European officers in all the states, and half of these were recruited from the Straits Settlements or Hong Kong.[1]

The agencies employed to maintain order among the Chinese were the Chinese leaders themselves, the police (whose role has already been discussed) and the special Chinese affairs departments set up in Perak and Selangor. In Selangor it was the Capitans on whom the administration relied and who were effectively in control of the Chinese; in Perak their influence, though still great, appears to have been less explicit, and the Chinese Protectorate played a much larger part in conducting relations between the Chinese and the government. The reason for this was probably the greater homogeneity of the Chinese in Selangor[2] and the immensely strong hold on the Kuala Lumpur Chinese established by Yap Ah Loy in the days before intervention.

The practice of recognizing Capitans, who would relieve the host governments of the cost and difficulty of directly administering and communicating with the Chinese, was continued by the British in the states with large Chinese populations. In Perak, the headmen of the rival secret societies, Chung Keng Kwee (Hai San) and Chin Ah Yam (Ghi Hin) were recognized as Capitans.[3] In Sungei Ujong the

by Turney, the senior District Officer, was submitted by Maxwell to Raja Bot and was criticized as obscure and crude ('*kasar bunyi-nya*'). Maxwell, regretting that that he had no officer who was a 'competent Malay scholar' translated it himself in collaboration with Raja Bot (Sel/Sec. 181/91). It is amusing to find Turney a year later passing five young cadets in Malay and reporting with a patronizing nod of approval that they showed promise of becoming 'good sound Malay scholars'. *SGG*, 1 April 1892.

[1] Information from *FMS Civil Service List, 1904; Perak Handbook and Civil Service List*, 1892; and notices of language examinations, *PGG* and *SGG*.

[2] In his report for 1891, the Resident of Selangor suggested that the good order maintained in the mines was due to the predominance of Khehs. In Perak, the returns of Cantonese, Khehs and Hokkiens in 1891 were 35,978, 24,739 and 17,856 respectively, out of a total Chinese population of 94,345 (*Census of Perak, 1891*). In Selangor, 32,411 Khehs were returned out of a total Chinese population of 50,844; 24,575 lived in the Kuala Lumpur district. The next largest group, the Cantonese, numbered 7,861 (*Census of Selangor*, 1891, *SGG*, 11 December 1891). According to the Census report for Larut, there was reason to believe that many Khehs had returned themselves as Cantonese or Hokkiens, according to the district in which they had lived in China before migrating; it is suggested that this in itself indicates a somewhat looser organization within the community than existed in Selangor.

[3] According to one authority, Khaw Boo Ann, sugar-planter, Teochiew leader and one-time Ghi Hin headman, was 'accorded the same honorific title of

first Capitans were Chin Woh and Chong Fong Chong, the latter identified as a Ghi Hin headman.[1] In Selangor, three Capitans were appointed in succession before the office was abolished in 1902.[2] In Pahang, the appointment seems to have lapsed, and in Negri Sembilan it was decided not to appoint a Capitan for the whole state, but to appoint headmen for each dialect group.[3]

The post of Capitan China was not merely an informal recognition of influence; it was a formal state appointment. It carried membership of the State Council, and except in Perak, a small allowance.[4] At least one of the Capitans recognized by the British—Yap Ah Loy—is known to have been previously installed by Malay authorities with full ceremony.[5] The manner in which his appointment

---

Kapitan on his appointment to the Perak State Council in 1886' (C.S. Wong, *A Gallery of Chinese Kapitans*, Singapore, 1964, p. 81) but he is not referred to as a Capitan in the gazetted minutes of the Council in subsequent years, though Ah Kwee and Ah Yam are so described.

[1] M.L. Wynne, *Triad and Tabut: a survey of the origin and diffusion of Chinese and Mohamedan Secret Societies in the Malay Peninsula, A.D. 1800–1935*, Singapore, 1941, p. 412, citing report by Chong Bun Sui, a Chinese interpreter who had worked in Selangor, Perak and Sungei Ujong.

[2] The first, Yap Ah Loy, died in 1885; Yap Ah Shak was appointed the same year, and died in 1889. Yap Kuan Seng was appointed in 1890 and died in 1902. He was the last Capitan China of Selangor. All three were Khehs and all bore the Yap surname, but there is no evidence that they were related.

[3] *AR* Negri Sembilan, 1887. The Capitan China in other states was always ex-officio a member of the State Council, but there was no Chinese member either in Pahang or in Negri Sembilan before its amalgamation with Sungei Ujong. In Pahang there was an ex-Capitan who received a pension of $360 a year. Pahang Estimates for 1892, enclosed in Smith to Knutsford, 129 of 23 March 1892, CO 273/179.

[4] The allowance granted to Yap Ah Loy was in consideration of the abolition from 1 January 1878 of his special duty of $1 a bhara on all tin exported from Kuala Lumpur, and was first fixed at $200 a month. In response to his urgent request, and in consideration of his services to Selangor, the Governor raised the allowance to $400 a month (Sel/Sec. 38/79). His successor was paid $100 a month, and Yap Kuan Seng received $200 a month, rising to $225 in 1895. The payments were probably of some material importance to Ah Loy, since they came at a time when he was in financial straits. They could have meant nothing to his successors, except in token of their office. The Capitans of Sungei Ujong were paid $420 a year each from 1886. In Perak, Chin Ah Yam was paid a small personal allowance from 1890, but the reason is not known. No allowance was paid to his colleague, Chung Keng Kwee. State Estimates, various years.

[5] Yap Tet Loy (also known as Yap Mao Lan) was a Kheh, born in 1837 in the Fui Cheu prefecture of Kwangtung province. He sailed from Macao for Malacca in 1854, and after working as a shop assistant, a mine cook and a dealer in pigs around the mines of Lukut and Sungei Ujong, he became a principal fighting man under the Capitan of Sungei Ujong. His chief was killed in a faction fight, and his successor, the gambling farmer Yap Ah Shak, made way for Ah Loy. Ah Loy was

(and those of the Capitans of Perak and Sungei Ujong) were confirmed by the British is not known, but there is some information about the appointment of his successors, Yap Ah Shak and Yap Kuan Seng. In the case of Yap Ah Shak, the papers relating to the appointment were tabled before the Council by the Acting Resident. They consisted of communications from various dialect groups; the Hokkiens left the matter to the Resident (perhaps a polite way of expressing reservations about Ah Shak); the Cantonese, more explicit, left it to the Governor but wanted a Cantonese; the Khehs asked for Ah Shak. There was some discussion as to getting Ah Shak and Cheow Ah Yeok, the Cantonese headman,[1] to act jointly, but it was decided that because of the preponderance of Khehs and the difficulties of divided control, Ah Shak should be appointed, with a salary of $100 a month and a seat in Council. The Resident was asked to communicate this to the Governor with the recommendation

---

now Capitan at the age of 26. At each stage of his career he was helped with loans, shelter, or employment by clansmen of the Yap surname. In 1862, one of the Kheh chiefs of Sungei Ujong, with whom Ah Loy had been closely associated, moved to Kuala Lumpur and became Capitan; Ah Loy followed him, managed his mines, and in 1868 succeeded him as Capitan China, with the approval and support of the Chinese and Malay leaders in Kuala Lumpur. In 1869 he was formally installed in this position by Raja Mahdi, then ruler of Klang. The same year, Mahdi was driven out by Tengku Zia'u'd-din, and Ah Loy began an association with the Tengku which lasted the rest of his life. Between 1870 and 1872, he fought for Kuala Lumpur on the side of the Tengku; he was driven out in 1872 and restored in 1873 by the Tengku's Pahang allies. In 1873, the Tengku installed him afresh as Capitan. (All this information has been taken from S.M. Middlebrook, 'Yap Ah Loy', *JMBRAS*, vol. xxiv, part 2 (1951), and is based on Chinese sources.) When a British administration was formed, Ah Loy was recognized as Capitan and appointed to the State Council. From 1875 to 1879 there was no British officer resident in Kuala Lumpur, and Ah Loy governed with little interference. In 1880, the Resident moved to Kuala Lumpur, and Ah Loy's power began to suffer a series of checks. He died on 15 April 1885.

[1] Little is known about Ah Shak except that he was one of the leading miners in Selangor and a trusted associate of Ah Loy. He had been with him in Sungei Ujong and had preceded him as Capitan about 1860 (see note 1 above). In a report on Chinese secret societies in the protected states, cited by Wynne (op. cit. p. 412) he is mentioned as one of the headmen of the Hai San. Cheow Ah Yeok (Cheow Yeok Wing) was a Cantonese, born about 1843. At the age of 17 he followed his brother to Malaya, going first to Malacca and then to Selangor, where he settled as a miner in Sungei Puteh. He became one of the largest miners in the state, with interests in the Kuala Lumpur and Ulu Langat districts. In the report on secret societies cited by Wynne, he is mentioned as a headman of the Ghi Hin. During the Selangor wars, however, he appears to have supported Ah Loy, and Middlebrook (op. cit. p. 99) mentions him as a friend of Ah Loy's in the 1880s. He died on 2 November 1892. See obituary, *Selangor Journal*, vol. i, no. 5, 18 November 1892.

that Ah Yeok be appointed 'a magistrate for the Chinese'.[1] The next Capitan, Yap Kuan Seng, was appointed by the Resident (Maxwell) with the sanction of the Governor, and the Council merely notified. There is an account by Maxwell of the manner in which the decision was made. The appointment was one of the first things he had had to consider on his arrival in Selangor in August 1889. The choice lay between Yap Kuan Seng, a Kheh miner, and Cheow Ah Yeok, and after studying them both and their positions in the community, Maxwell decided that Yap Kuan Seng would make a 'stronger and more useful Captain of the two'.[2] There was another candidate, Yap Hon Chin, a son of Ah Loy who had been too young to succeed on his father's death and whose candidature was now pushed by the Hokkiens and Teochiews,[3] but not, apparently, by the Khehs. He was very young, personally insignificant, without business ability, and was said to be dissipated and extravagant, and Maxwell had no difficulty in rejecting him. The appointment of Yap Kuan Seng was approved by the Governor, communicated to the State Council and gazetted.[4] During a visit to the Sultan in 1889, Maxwell had settled with him the terms of a letter of authority to the Capitan under the Sultan's seal, 'not that this was really necessary, but I thought that it would give additional éclat to the appointment'. The Capitan was formally presented to the Sultan on his appointment,[5] and may have received his kuasa at the same time.

[1] SCM, 23 May 1885. Ah Shak was given a letter of appointment sealed by the Sultan. Sel/Sec. 1051/1885.

[2] Resident to CS, 6 March 1890, Sel/Sec. 157/90. A deleted portion of the draft reads as follows: 'He is a Kheh, which is numerically far the strongest tribe of Chinese in Selangor—Cheow Ah Yeok is a Macao man—he is rich, influential and of a strong character. I doubted Ah Yeok's capacity to hold his own in the face of a discontented Kheh faction.'

The correspondence throws light on the Resident's role in the appointment of a Capitan, on his relations with the Sultan, and on the relations between members of the royal house. It is concerned mainly with the efforts of Raja Mahmud (Tengku Panglima Raja) to interfere in the appointment by canvassing the claims of various candidates at Langat. According to him, the Sultan had supported Yap Hon Chin, and the Raja Muda had promised that he would not be a party to any appointment without previous consultation with the chiefs or in Council. When Yap Kuan Seng's appointment was announced, Mahmud withdrew his allegiance from the Raja Muda. Despite Maxwell's assurances that the choice was the Resident's and had been accepted by the Sultan, Mahmud persisted in his attitude and was banished from Selangor, though he continued to receive his allowance. Maxwell suggested that his resentment was assumed in a calculated attempt to destroy the position of the Raja Muda with the Sultan.

[3] Sel/Sec. 2406/89 and 2407/89.

[4] SCM, 8 January 1890; SGG, 24 January 1890.

[5] Kuala Langat monthly report for January 1890, SGG, 7 March 1890.

The power of the Selangor Capitans, though still great twenty years after the appointment of the first Resident, had been eroded by the extension of British rule, and in any case was now held by the grace of the British authorities. None of them were as independent as the first Capitan, who negotiated with the Selangor government almost as an equal, knowing how much the state depended on his enterprise and leadership. Ah Loy was born to govern. Chung Keng Kwee, when reminded of the Larut Wars by an inquiring visitor, dismissed the subject with an expression of distaste—'*Banyak rugi!*' (Big loss). What Ah Loy would have answered one does not know, but his Chinese biographers at any rate had no doubt that the Selangor Wars, when he ruled and defended Kuala Lumpur, constituted the period of his greatness. For five years after the appointment of a Resident, there was no British administration in Kuala Lumpur, and Ah Loy governed without interference; the representatives of the state government—a few policemen and a fire-engine—were lodged in his compound. He owned every large enterprise in Kuala Lumpur; the gambling booth—which stood in the central square in front of his house—the market, the brothels, and more than half the town property. He was the largest mine-owner and had in addition a tapioca concession of 12,000 acres outside Kuala Lumpur. He was said to have 4,000 men employed in his various enterprises. He had built twenty miles of road round Kuala Lumpur,[1] and his admirers even credited him with a 'hospital' (a grandiose name for a shed where shelter and food allowance—but no medical attention—was provided for twenty-eight inmates).[2] The Superintendent of Police told Isabella Bird that the Capitan's control of Kuala Lumpur was so firm that 'during many years not a single serious crime has been committed'. Swettenham was not slow to contrast his effectiveness with the feeble government at Klang.[3]

[1] Ah Loy's descendants estimated his expenditure on roads at $65,000, which is probably fairer than Swettenham's estimate of $20,000 (Middlebrook, op. cit. p. 121; Resident to CS, 17 May 1883, Sel/Sec. 661/83). Ah Loy may well have spent more money on roads than Swettenham's predecessor (who spent $18,993 in 1882) and laid it out to better purpose, but no private road-building programme could have compared with the work of the state in this field after 1883. In that year the expenditure on roads in Selangor totaled $134,785.

[2] State Apothecary to Resident, 27 July 1880, Sel/Sec. 201/80. The hospital had been supported by a tax of $1 on every pig imported into Selangor; when the tax concession ceased, so did the hospital. Resident to CS, 21 May 1883, Sel/Sec. 315/83.

[3] Audit Report on Selangor, 27 March 1880, C. 3095, enclosure 1 in no. 2. Swettenham's eulogy should not be accepted without reserve. While his admira-

At the same time, the unfettered control exercised by Ah Loy over the most important and populous district of Selangor could not be tolerated indefinitely. He claimed all the land within a radius of two miles of Kuala Lumpur and resisted the application of land regulations to his holdings; no one dared compete with him for the state farms, and he held them for years at a fraction of their value;[1] and he very naturally opposed the introduction of a magistrate to Kuala Lumpur, since it meant the presence of a rival authority.[2] The challenge he presented became explicit in 1879, when a police escort taking two Chinese prisoners to Kajang was attacked en route by Chinese miners, the prisoners freed, and the police led bound and in torn clothes through the streets of Kuala Lumpur to be delivered to Ah Loy.[3] The move to Kuala Lumpur was already a foregone conclusion, but this incident made certain that it would not be long delayed.

The move was made in 1880, and in 1882, Douglas was replaced by Swettenham. Ah Loy for the first time came up against a personality and an authority which matched his own. Swettenham immediately set in motion plans to reform the land administration and rebuild Kuala Lumpur, but proposals for widening roads, re-siting the town's gambling booth and rebuilding the market interfered with Ah Loy's interests and were resisted. Swettenham's admiration of Ah Loy was now tempered with criticism. The gambling booth in its central position was represented as a public offence, the filth and the hazardous construction of the 'very insecure shed called a market' were described in detail.[4] Swettenham tried to persuade him that the planned improvements would benefit himself as the largest property-owner in Kuala Lumpur, but the Capitan was probably more interested in power than in property values. In the final settlement,

---

tion was sincere, this particular manifestation of it appeared in an audit report of the Selangor accounts, which was intended as a grave criticism of the whole administration, and the references to Ah Loy were intended to deepen the discredit of the Resident by unfavourable comparison.

[1] In 1880 Ah Loy leased the Kuala Lumpur gambling, pawn and spirit farms for $450 a month. In 1881 he was forced by Malacca competition to raise his bid to $1,000 a month (Koh Hoon Boh to Resident, 7 December 1881, and minute by Resident, 9 December 1881, Sel/Sec. 528/81). In 1883 he was paying $51,612 a year for these farms. Resident to Governor, 17 May 1883, Sel/Sec. 661/83.

[2] CS to Resident, 18 November 1879, Sel/Sec. Misc./79.

[3] Supt. of Police to Resident, 16 October 1879, Sel/Sec. 326/79.

[4] Resident to CS, 10 November 1882, Sel/Sec.-/82. The file cover with the Resident's office number is missing. The file was in the 701–800 bundle, the only identifying number being Native 8044/82.

the administration gained its objects, but acknowledged Ah Loy's unique position and the value of his enterprise by special concessions. His Kuala Lumpur holdings were granted to him free of premium and subject only to payment of quit rent (waived in respect of his personal accommodation). He was also granted 12,000 acres of agricultural land free of premium or quit-rent, and he held the Kuala Lumpur market free until his death.[1]

These were substantial concessions but no more than he deserved. The prosperity of Selangor probably did not depend on him as much as some people imagined; it was impossible that such a rich field could have been long overlooked by Chinese miners. But strong government played its part in creating confidence and attracting investment, and Ah Loy had provided this at great cost to himself. He received no compensation for the money expended during the wars, unlike the creditors of the Mentri and Tengku Zia'u'd-din, and all the concessions made to him probably did not repay the expenses he had incurred in defending and maintaining Kuala Lumpur at that time.

After the death of Ah Loy, the nature of Chinese leadership changed. His successors 'existed to interpret the two dissimilar elements in the new composite leadership of the community'.[2] They sat on State Councils and sanitary boards, sponsored vaccination campaigns (in 1890, Yap Kuan Seng gave up his office one day a week for vaccination purposes) and endowed schools and hospitals. The day of the secret society headman and war chief was over. His features softened into the stereotype of the wealthy community leader under colonial rule, the monument of civic virtue, the inveterate committee member,[3] contributor to charities and sponsor of progressive activities and good works. But if Ah Loy's successors lacked his authority and independence, their influence among the Chinese must still have been very great. Year after year, the police reports acknowledged their indispensable assistance in keeping order. In

[1] Resident to Governor, 17 May 1883, and Resident to Capitan China, 9 June 1883, Sel/Sec. 661/83. Swettenham pointed out that the Taiping market had been let for $5,196 in 1882.

[2] J.M. Gullick, 'Kuala Lumpur, 1880–1895', *JMBRAS*, vol. xxviii, part 4 (1955), p. 127.

[3] In 1894 Yap Kuan Seng, already a member of the State Council and the Kuala Lumpur Sanitary Board, was also Chairman of the Cooly Depot Committee, a member of the Board of Examiners in Chinese, Chairman of the Tai Wah Fund Committee (to provide a home for decrepit Chinese paupers) and a visiting justice. *SGG* for 1894, index.

1886, the Acting Superintendent reported that Capitan Yap Ah Shak saw him every day at the police office and seemed ready to assist 'at all times ... upon any subject, re catching runaways or preventing crime'. Syers described a religious festival held during November 1887 and attended by 40,000 Chinese; the headmen themselves organized a force of Chinese police to help the regular force, and personally visited the gambling farm every night to help keep order. He acknowledged that it was largely thanks to their exertions that everything passed off without a single crime of violence.[1]

The Capitans were the largest entrepreneurs and employers of labour in the state,[2] and in a community whose *raison d'être* was the search for wealth, economic success was an essential element of leadership. Ah Loy's wealth appears to have been the consequence of his force of character and powers of leadership; for his successors, who did not have or need his qualities, influence seems to have derived from wealth. Their appointment as Capitans and their mediation in economic matters must in turn have strengthened their own economic position and their hold on their fellow-countrymen; for example, in 1890, a year of tight credit, the government lent Yap Kuan Seng $50,000 to distribute in loans to miners at his own discretion, and in 1892, loans were made on his recommendations and security.[3] The public position of the Capitans may also have had some bearing on the fact that they were commonly the successful tenderers for the most profitable of the state revenue farms.[4]

[1] *AR* Police Department Selangor, 1885 and 1887, Sel/Sec. 1849/86 and 595/88. The Capitan was authorized to issue passes to Chinese leaving Selangor (a procedure discontinued in 1894) to prevent labourers absconding under advances, and received a small allowance for this. Sel/Sec. 548A/92.

[2] Of 182,236 pikuls of tin exported from Selangor in 1889, the largest amount —14,907 pikuls—was exported by Yap Kuan Seng. Next came Yap Ah Shak with 14,400 pikuls (*AR* Land Department Selangor, 1889, Sel/Sec. 892/90). Yap Ah Shak was reputed to have left $1,000,000 (*Lat Pao*, 10 July 1889. I am indebted to Mr Yen Ching Hwang for the reference). Yap Kuan Seng informed the Labour Commission that he had recruited 7,000 labourers for his mines in 1889. *Labour Commission Report*, 1891, p. 174.

[3] Sel/Sec. 385/90 and 104/92.

[4] Chung Keng Kwee held the opium import duty farm for Perak between 1886 and 1888 (inclusive) and between 1892 and 1894. He also held the Kinta general farm (gambling, pawnbroking and spirits) between 1892 and 1894, and in association with others, the general farm of the whole state between 1895 and 1897. He held other smaller farms at other times (*SSGG*, 20 November 1885, *PGG*, 22 December 1891 and 26 October 1891). Yap Kuan Seng, either alone or in association with others, was the successful tenderer for the general farm, Kuala Lumpur, between 1890 and 1898 and for the opium duty farm between 1892 and 1894. *SGG*, 10 January 1890, 16 October 1891, 11 November 1892 and 6 December 1895.

The history of the Chinese in Perak was much more turbulent and was punctuated by large-scale secret society riots, put down by the police without any assistance from the Capitans. The Chinese of the coast districts, mostly woodcutters and fishermen belonging to the Ghi Hin and Ho Seng secret societies, lived practically outside any authority but their own; and after a riot in the coast village of Tanjong Piandang (in protest against enforcement of the revenue farm regulations) and an attack on the district officer at Pangkor, measures were taken to bring them under control. An order passed in the State Council on 1 March 1879 required the registration of all Chinese living on the coast between Larut and Bruas, on pain of fine or imprisonment. Registration was extended by degrees, so that by the end of 1881 it applied to every adult Chinese male in Perak.[1] The registration fee of $1 was used to finance hospitals for sick Chinese, mostly beri-beri sufferers. Swettenham, who was a liberal in his economics at least, and who had a rational distaste for any taxation that discouraged immigration and development, abolished both tax and registration in 1885, bringing in new regulations for the control of Chinese labour.[2]

A Secretary for Chinese Affairs (later called Protector) was appointed in Perak in 1883, but in Selangor, a similar appointment was not made till 1890, probably because the Capitans were such useful intermediaries between the government and the Chinese. Maxwell, who proposed the appointment, conceived of it in narrow terms; he wanted, not a Protector, but an adviser on Chinese affairs attached to the Resident's office.[3] Between 1891 and 1894, when he was relieved of this responsibility, the Chinese Secretary was also in charge of mines, and this work took up most of his time. He wrote in his annual report for 1892 that next to nothing of the work of a Chinese Protectorate had been done in his department; 'Selangor has got on very well without a Protector of Chinese.'[4] It was not till a new Resident arrived in 1893 that the department turned its attention exclusively to Chinese affairs.

The Chinese departments in Perak (and later in Selangor) dealt generally with all matters particularly affecting the Chinese, but the

[1] *PCM*, 3 November 1879, 30 December 1880, 17 December 1881.
[2] *AR* Perak, 1885. See *AR* Police Department Perak, 1888, *PGG*, 15 March 1889, giving 1885 as the last year in which the Kinta miners were numbered by registration.
[3] Resident to CS, 11 August 1890, Sel/Sec. 546/90.
[4] *SGG*, 26 May 1893.

bulk of their work related to three subjects; the control of Chinese labour, the protection of women and girls,[1] and the supervision of Chinese societies. The basis of Chinese labour relations at this time was the credit-system. The *sinkheh*[2] or new recruit was initiated into this system on first leaving China, when he incurred a debt for his passage and advances which he contracted to repay to his employer out of his first year's wages. In fact he received no wages (except for overtime work) but worked for his food and shelter. At the end of the year he was deemed to have paid off the cost of his importation, but he might well have incurred further debts to his employer in the meanwhile, binding him to a further period of service. A labourer who had worked off his indentures was free to engage himself wherever he wished, and did so under a variety of arrangements; on time-wages, piece-work, or under the co-operative system, whereby he received a share of the tin after a proportion had been paid to the advancer and the contractors for labour and plant. All these arrangements had certain features in common which made them disadvantageous to the labourer, restricted his earnings, and often plunged him into debt. First, settlement of wages was customarily made twice a year, so that the labourer was forced to receive his supplies from the advancer on credit; secondly, these supplies were provided at 20–30 per cent. over the market price, while money advances carried interest of 10 per cent. a month.[3] Clearly the labourer had every incentive to abscond from an unprofitable contract, which came very

[1] One consequence of the great discrepancy in the ratio of Chinese women to men was that a large number of the Chinese women in the states at this time were prostitutes; e.g. of 4,687 adult Chinese women in Perak in 1891, 923 were prostitutes or brothel-keepers (*Census of Perak*, 1891). To secure them from forcible detention and ill-treatment, the registration and regular inspection of brothels and prostitutes was instituted in Perak and Selangor. But the regulations were thought to give countenance to prostitution, and in accordance with a policy enforced earlier in the Straits Settlements and Hong Kong, the Secretary of State instructed that registration be discontinued. In 1895, new regulations were introduced into Perak and Selangor, requiring prostitutes to take the initiative in approaching the Protector for help, and thus withdrawing effective assistance from them. See *AR* Chinese Protectorate, Perak, 1894, *PGG*, 24 May 1895, for comments on the 'middle class morality' that forced this action on the state governments.

[2] Lit. 'new guest'. The term was used for credit-ticket or indentured recruits. *Laukheh* (old guest) was the term used for an old hand.

[3] This summary is taken from a number of sources, in particular, W.T. Hall, *Report on Tin Mining in Perak and Burma*, Rangoon, 1889; *Labour Commission Report*, 1891; W.L. Blythe, 'Historical Sketch of Chinese Labour in Malaya', *JMBRAS*, vol. xx, part 1 (1947); J.C. P[asqual], 'Chinese Tin Mining in Selangor, ii, 'Labur and Labour', *Selangor Journal*, vol. iv, no. 3, 18 October 1895 and vol. iv, no 6, 29 November 1895.

close sometimes to debt-bondage, and in a time of great expansion of the industry, he had every opportunity to do so.

The concern of the government was to stabilize the available labour supply by securing the labourers their wages, and seeing that they fulfilled their contracts and did not abscond while under advances. Orders in Council passed in Selangor in 1882 and elaborated in 1888 provided for the issue of certificates to labourers on first entry into the state, and for discharge certificates to be issued by employers on completion of contract and repayment of advances. Minimum hours of work were laid down, and labourers who absconded or otherwise broke their contract were liable to imprisonment and whipping. Employers who took on labourers without discharge tickets or failed to provide them on termination of a contract were liable to a fine.[1] In 1886, an Order in Council was passed in Perak, providing for the control of labour by similar means.[2] In addition, both Selangor and Perak adopted Straits Settlements Ordinance 1 of 1882, limiting the duration of verbal contracts to one month and requiring longer contracts to be executed in writing before a magistrate before they could be considered valid. Breach of contract was made punishable by fine or imprisonment in the case of labourers, and by fine in the case of employers.[3]

Some attempt was made to protect the labourer. Selangor Regulation VIII of 1888 placed a limit on the advances which might be given, and bound the sinkheh to work off only those in his original contract. Perak Order in Council 3 of 1891 required the form of indentures to be 'as far as possible' in the form sanctioned by the British Resident (the legislation is full of these escape clauses) and provided penalties for employers who failed to comply with the conditions of the in-

[1] Selangor Order in Council 4 of 1882, summarized in SCM, 31 October 1882; Selangor Regulation VIII of 1888, C. Kemp, *Regulations, Rules and Orders, Selangor, 1877–89*, Kuala Lumpur, 1892. The latter regulation was passed at the instance of the mining capitalists, and was based on their original draft (Sel/Sec. 1295/88). In 1890, a 'Cooly Depot' (a registration centre and labour exchange) was set up in Kuala Lumpur in connexion with this regulation, and administered by a committee of five Chinese under the chairmanship of Yap Kuan Seng. Sinkhehs were lodged there by coolie brokers to await employment; laukhehs might lodge there of their own free will for the same purpose. The depot acted as the registration centre for the purposes of the Regulation. See *AR* Selangor, 1890.

[2] *AR* Perak, 1886. This was an amended form of an Order in Council introduced by Swettenham while Acting Resident in 1884, and based on his Selangor Order in Council 4 of 1882.

[3] Selangor Regulation IV of 1892, *SGG*, 23 May 1892; Perak Order in Council 22 of 1889, *PGG*, 20 September 1889.

denture. The specimen sinkheh contract laid down the maximum advances and deductions which might be made, and stipulated that the contract might be prolonged only until the original advances were paid off (these reservations did not appear in the general contract). Both sinkheh and general contract stipulated for the provision of free shelter, food, clothes and medical attention. A record of tasks worked and an account of transactions were to be posted on the wall of the kongsi-house for the information of labourers, visiting police, and officers of the Protectorate. But these regulations did not directly limit the period of the contract, and did not affect the source of exploitation—the six-monthly settlement in arrears, and the practice of advancing at exorbitant rates. Legislation to protect labourers by limiting advances and restricting the legal duration of verbal contracts was ignored by employers, labourers, and apparently by government as well. In his annual report for 1894,[1] the Perak Protector wrote that under the 'heterogeneous and self-contradictory set of Labour regulations' which had grown up around the discharge ticket system, 'a coolie on a merely oral contract was practically compelled to serve his employer as long as he owed any money to him; a system, in fact, of debt-slavery tempered by wholesale absconding'. As to Selangor, Yap Kuan Seng himself admitted in evidence before the Labour Commission of 1890 that he and his predecessor had required Hai-Lok-Hong sinkhehs (a composite term for the Hai Hong and Lok Hong districts in Kwangtung province) to pay back twice the amount of their real debt.[2] The Labour Code of 1895 limited verbal contracts to thirty days and laid down that no contract made in the Straits Settlements or the Malay states was to exceed two years under any circumstances, but the Resident wrote in his annual report for 1896 that although the portions of the Labour Code dealing with sanitation and hospital treatment of labourers had worked well, the provisions for the registration of contracts and definition of their terms had 'practically remained a dead letter in Selangor'. Yet in previous years, labourers in Selangor had been required to get discharge certificates to free them from contracts whether verbal or written, and had been liable to prosecution if they sought work without these certificates.

[1] *PGG*, 24 May 1895.
[2] *Labour Commission Report*, 1891, p. 174. He went on to say that Inspectors of police who visited the kongsi-houses inquired about health and sanitation but never about wages.

Where the government had failed to improve conditions of work, economic and technical change succeeded. One important factor was the change in marketing practices attendant on the development of European smelting.[1] The traditional Chinese practice was to smelt at long intervals at or near the mine, and settle wages after smelting. The establishment of a European smelting works buying ore from Perak, Selangor and Sungei Ujong, and paying good prices in cash, lessened the dependence of the miners on long-term credit at high rates of interest. Even more important was the effect on Perak labour of the development of the Kinta tin fields in the late 1880's. The wealth of the fields, the demand for labour, the dispersal of the mines and the early lack of communications encouraged absconding. The introduction of a sluice-box of about eight feet for washing the ore, capable of being operated by a small stream of water, in place of the old thirty-foot box which required a large head of water and a large pump, meant the profitable entry into the industry of men of small means.[2] By 1893 it was recognized that the discharge ticket system had failed to prevent absconding and it was abolished.[3] It remained in Selangor for another year, until it was abolished there also by the terms of the Labour Code, passed uniformly in the three western states in 1895.

Whatever its hardships, the mining industry had one powerful attraction for the Chinese labourer—the element of speculation. A man who survived his indentures and was lucky enough to become a share-labourer in a paying mine might return to China after a few years the richer by three or four hundred dollars. But the number of men who succeeded in this way was outweighed by those who did not long survive their introduction to Malaya. A death rate of 10 per cent. per annum for the Chinese would probably not be too high an estimate,[4] and it must be remembered that this was a population

[1] See Chapter X.
[2] AR Perak, 1891; AR Kinta, 1893, PGG, 27 April 1894.
[3] PGG, 24 November 1893.
[4] Returns of births and deaths were first compiled in Perak in 1884 and Selangor in 1885, in both states by the police. In Perak the registration of births was made compulsory by the provisions of the Vaccination Order in Council 13 of 1890, but the registration of deaths remained voluntary. In Selangor the registration of births and deaths was made compulsory by Regulation II of 1892. Throughout the period, both in Selangor and Perak, Malay returns were supplied by penghulus, Chinese returns by the manager of the kongsi-house where labourers lived, and Indian returns by the managers of estates. Hospital deaths were returned separately in Selangor (AR Selangor 1888, AR Medical Department

of young adult males, with no infants or old people to swell the statistics of mortality. To put it another way, Chinese deaths in Perak and Selangor in the twenty years after intervention were probably equivalent to four or five times the Chinese population of these states in 1875, taking the latter at approximately 30,000. Mortality of this order of magnitude would go far to explain the large discrepancy between the total gain by immigration and the increase of population recorded in the census returns.

The diseases responsible for the largest number of hospital deaths were beri-beri, intestinal disorders (classified as 'diarrhoea' and 'dysentery') and pulmonary diseases. The incidence of malaria and the dreaded epidemic diseases—smallpox and cholera—was insignificant. The scourge of the mines was beri-beri. Though the mortality from intestinal diseases was greater, both proportionately to cases and in absolute terms, beri-beri was the commonest disease, and one with a consistently high mortality. By 1881, the Perak Government had gone far towards establishing a connexion between beri-beri and the inferior diet of the mines (rice and salt fish).[1] Low claimed in his report for 1885 that repeated attempts had been made 'to induce the towkays to introduce and the coolies to make use of a more nourishing regimen, and to keep their barracks in a better

Selangor 1893, *SGG*, 30 March 1894. That this was the case in Perak also is indicated from a comparison of the Perak and Selangor figures. It is not clear, however, whether the totals given in the *AR* Selangor, 1894 and 1895, included hospital deaths). Death returns in Selangor rose sharply after the introduction of compulsory registration, but this was reported in 1895 to be 'still very imperfect'. The Selangor authorities were agreed that the returns were likely to be more reliable for Malays than for Chinese. The Chinese population was migratory in the extreme, there were a number of remote mines far from police stations, and there was no network of indigenous authorities required to make returns as part of their office. It was suspected that mine headmen often did not report deaths (perhaps to evade inquiry). If this was true of Selangor, it was even more likely to be true of Perak, where registration was voluntary, and where despite all the rigour of the discharge ticket system, it was possible for thousands of miners to abscond every year without trace. The Selangor return for 1893, giving a death rate (including hospitals) of 7.8 per cent. on the 1891 census return, must be short of the real figures; 10 per cent. would probably not be an over-estimate. In some years the mortality rate must have been even greater; Low wrote in his 1882 report that since 1879 not less than 3,000 immigrants had died every year of beri-beri. The Residency Surgeon, Selangor, reported that in 1888 the miners had 'succumbed by thousands', and that losses of 40 and 50 per cent. in the mines seemed to be common. There were 1,199 deaths in the pauper hospital at Kuala Lumpur alone. Sel/Sec. 559/89.

[1] Acting on information from the Madras Government, the Perak Government introduced a better diet into the gaol, whereupon beri-beri disappeared. *AR* Perak, 1881, 1882 and 1885.

state of sanitation', but that neither group was interested in reform, and that both regarded the government's endeavours as 'unwarrantable interference'. (Did the labourers really object to attempts to vary their diet, one wonders? and how were their feelings ascertained?) In later years the connexion with diet was lost sight of; indeed was rejected in 1894, when an investigation into the high death rate, ordered by the Governor, elicited from the Residency Surgeon of Selangor the claim that the miners' food was 'excellent in quality and abundant in quantity'.[1] Doctors sought an explanation of the disease in the 'miasmatic poisons' emanating from newly-cleared land, and the beri-beri cases came to be regarded as the unfortunate casualties of the first stages of pioneering.

The great mortality among Chinese migrants stimulated the development of medical departments and hospitals at an early stage in the western Malay states, and later, to a much smaller extent, in Pahang. The first public hospital of Perak was the 'Yeng Wah', established in Taiping in 1880 exclusively for Chinese. It remained a hospital for Chinese till 1894, when it became a general hospital for the district. There was no exclusively Chinese hospital anywhere else, but the pauper hospital in Kuala Lumpur and the hospitals established in the mining districts were largely attended by Chinese. (From the late 1880's, an increasing number of Indian estate labourers also attended the government hospitals, but they remained a small minority. Malays hardly ever used them.) The general complaint of medical departments was that the men were brought to hospital only in the last stages of illness;[2] employers wished to work them as long as possible, or were afraid of their labourers absconding from hospital, or the hospitals were too far, or the men themselves preferred Chinese methods of treatment. Employers of mining labour were required to send sick men to hospital, but the regulations do not seem to have been enforced,[3] and it is difficult to know how they could

---

[1] AR Medical Department Selangor, 1894, SGG, 28 March 1895.

[2] The Residency Surgeon, Selangor, calculated from a sample of 200 consecutive cases that the average duration of an illness before admission was between six and seven weeks. Minute of 28 May 1894, Sel/Sec. 353/94.

[3] A Selangor notification dated March 1886 and republished in January 1895 (SGG, 4 January 1895) providing for the sanitation of mining kongsis, required all sick labourers to be sent to the nearest government hospital, but this was not enforced (minute by Residency Surgeon, 28 May 1894, Sel/Sec. 353/94). In Perak, the form of contract scheduled in Order in Council 3 of 1891 (Protection of Indentured Chinese Labourers) had a similar provision. Medical attention for sick labourers and removal of serious cases to hospital was made obligatory by

have been enforced; in the absence of regular and frequent inspection, the removal of the sick clearly had to be left to the discretion of the sick persons themselves, their friends, or employers. Not least of the difficulties of enforcement lay in the fact that the hospitals would have broken down had the regulations been carried out. The delay in forwarding cases was put forward as a reason for the high hospital death rate,[1] and no doubt it was, but when the miners showed greater readiness to use the hospital, the strain on accommodation was so great that only the most serious cases could be admitted.[2] The overcrowding and lack of trained staff meant that little medical treatment could be given; the hospitals were in effect shelters where the sick could rest until they either died or recovered. For some employers they were simply dying-houses, which saved the expense of burial or the nuisance of a police enquiry.

It was not the indifference of state governments, however, that was responsible for overcrowded hospitals and high death rates. The ratio of hospital beds to total population was about 1 : 200 in Selangor in 1890, and 1 : 100 in 1895; in Perak it was about 1 : 170 in 1895.[3] Such figures place these governments—quantitatively at least—among the most progressive of their day in respect of hospital services. Their failure to stem the tide of sickness is a comment on a completely abnormal situation, compounded very largely of the indifference and greed of employers[4] and the ignorance of the men

the 1895 Labour Code. Perak Order in Council 4 of 1895, Selangor Regulation VI of 1895, and Negri Sembilan Order in Council I of 1895.

[1] The percentages of deaths to numbers treated in Perak and Selangor be tween 1886 and 1895 is given below.

	Selangor		Perak	
Year	Nos. treated	% of deaths	Nos. treated	% of deaths
1886	3,175	15.2	9,585	13.4
1887	7,324	18.3	11,867	14.6
1888	8,493	19.8	14,042	15.4
1889	7,504	16.9	13,432	16.4
1890	6,722	14.3	11,922	13.6
1891	6,401	16.5	12,499	12.9
1892	10,511	13.9	17,353	11.7
1893	13,870	17.1	20,528	15.4
1894	12,322	16.7	20,313	16.9
1895	14,860	16.5	20,992	14.2

AR Medical Department Selangor, 1892, SGG, 28 April 1893; Appendices to AR.
[2] AR Medical Department Selangor, 1892, SGG, 28 April 1893.
[3] There were 456 beds in Selangor hospitals at the end of 1890, and 1,552 at the end of 1895 (AR Medical Department). There were 1,468 in Perak, exclusive of beds in the gaol and quarantine hospitals. AR Perak, 1896.
[4] The larger employers did contribute towards the construction of government

themselves. If the state governments were to blame, it was because they preferred to treat the results of labour exploitation rather than deal effectively with causes. The latter course would have led them into direct conflict with mining entrepreneurs and perhaps have affected the importation of labourers and the rate of development, and this was something to be avoided at all costs.

The period of British expansion in the Malay states was also one during which officials in the Straits became increasingly aware of the threat of the secret societies to public order. The societies represented the only system of authority in the Straits which the Chinese understood or respected; they provided a strong and cohesive organization which could if necessary be used to frustrate the government, and was designed in particular to protect members from the law. They were organized for violence and operated in a highly volatile and excitable population, possessing none of the balances and restraints normally supplied by kin groups and family responsibilities. The objections to secret societies which led to their suppression in the Straits Settlements in 1890, applied with even more force in the Malay states, where British intervention had been preceded by secret society wars of great intensity. While the Straits Government tolerated secret societies under certain safeguards till their suppression in 1890,[1] the

hospitals (e.g., the Chinese of Kuala Lumpur contributed $2,500 to a new ward of the pauper hospital in 1885) and they built small hospitals on their own account, but their efforts were not of much practical significance. In 1893 Loke Yew, a leading Selangor miner and a member of the State Council, built a hospital at Serendah for eight to twelve patients, the government supplying a dresser; another Selangor miner, Khoo Mah Lek, built a hospital for his labourers at Sungei Puteh; Loh Cheng Keng, a pepper planter employing some 1,000 men, put up a dispensary on his estate and offered to pay $15 a month towards the cost of a government dresser. The largest private hospital in the states, the T'ung Shin in Kuala Lumpur with 100 beds in 1895, was begun in temporary premises by the Capitan China and associates in 1892, and moved to permanent quarters in 1895. It employed Chinese methods of treatment and was established and maintained from private contributions. The Tai Wah home for incurables, opened in Kuala Lumpur in 1894, was mainly financed from an impost on tin, which paid also for four ambulance carts put into operation in the same year.

[1] By SS Ordinance XIX of 1869, all associations of ten men or more, except commercial companies and lodges of freemasons, were required to be registered. The Registrar of Societies had the power to refuse registration, but this power was not used till 1882, when the Hai San society of Singapore was suppressed. Ordinance IV of 1882 took suppression further by abolishing the Mohammedan Red and White Flag societies, and prohibiting British-born Chinese (who could not be banished) from membership of secret associations. Finally, by Ordinance I of 1889, societies were deemed unlawful unless registered or exempted from

protected states prohibited them from the inception of British rule. Speedy reported in 1875 that secret societies had been forbidden in Larut, and in 1881, at the instance of the Resident, the Selangor State Council resolved that the establishment or existence of secret societies in the state was contrary to law.[1] The introduction of Residents to Negri Sembilan and Pahang was followed shortly after by proclamations declaring these societies illegal.[2] Further legislation passed in Selangor in 1888 and in Perak in 1889 declared all Chinese secret societies to be 'absolutely prohibited' and rendered organizers and members liable to large fines, long periods of imprisonment, and deportation.[3] In 1894 and 1895, Selangor and Perak successively adopted new regulations based on Straits Ordinance I of 1889, requiring all societies to be registered before they could lawfully operate, and giving the government the power to refuse registration.[4]

In 1884, in the course of a well-known correspondence first cited by Wynne and republished by other writers, Powell, the Acting Protector of Chinese in the Straits Settlements, forwarded to the Colonial Secretary a memorandum on the secret societies of the protected Malay states, prepared by a Supreme Court interpreter who had firsthand knowledge of Chinese affairs in the three western states. The memorandum gave details of the leadership of the Ghi Hin and Hai San societies in the various districts, citing the Capitans and leading towkays—Chung Keng Kwee, Chih Ah Yam, Yap Ah Loy, Yap Ah Shak, Cheow Ah Yeok and Chong Fong Chong among others—as headmen.[5] This immediately brought disclaimers from the Superintendent of Police and the Acting Resident of Selangor,

registration, and heavy penalties were provided for persons convicted of being managers or members of an unlawful society. The legislation was followed (in 1890) by the publication of a list of unlawful societies.

[1] SCM, 28 February 1881. The Resident informed the Council that in Tengku Zia'u'd-din's time, a secret society meeting-house in Klang had been closed by order of the Viceroy, and that the Capitan China and other principal Chinese were 'all opposed to the establishment of secret societies'.

[2] AR Negri Sembilan, 1887; AR Pahang, 1890. The Pahang proclamation was based on Selangor Regulation II of 1888.

[3] Selangor Regulation II of 1888; Perak Order in Council 24 of 1889. The Perak order brought within its scope the large numbers of Chinese enrolled in societies in the Straits (where they were still legal before 1890). Hitherto they had been immune, perhaps because the Straits government objected to penal action against them while the societies were still legal in the Straits.

[4] Selangor Regulation X of 1894; Perak Order in Council 8 of 1895.

[5] Wynne, op. cit. pp. 410–13; Gullick, op. cit. pp. 133–7, citing Sel/Sec. 1335/84; L.F. Comber, *Chinese Secret Societies in Malaya; a Survey of the Triad Society from 1800 to 1900*, New York, 1959, pp. 214–16 and 226–7. Powell's in-

and denials from Ah Kwee and Ah Yam that they had ever been headmen, though they both admitted to past membership of the Penang society; Ah Kwee's claim that he had resigned earlier in the year was corroborated by the Secretary for Chinese Affairs in Perak. The replies of the Perak and Selangor authorities have been taken to indicate their ignorance of the true position in their own states, and the ease with which they could be fooled by the Chinese headmen, but there was perhaps less margin of disagreement between Powell and his adversaries than is generally assumed. Powell agreed that the societies in Selangor and Perak were not distinct societies but 'part and parcel' of the Penang and Malacca societies; Syers for his part conceded that nearly all the Chinese in Selangor belonged to secret societies in the Straits Settlements, that in the case of one society at least, there had been an attempt to establish local branches and enrol new members (2,000 had been enrolled and paid their subscriptions before the attempt was frustrated by the police) and that although there was no local headman of the Hai San society, the members regarded Ah Shak as one of their principal men, and appealed to him when any difficulty arose. (A year after his letter was written, Ah Shak became Capitan China of Selangor.) What the state authorities were unable to accept—at least in public—was the possibility that recruiting tours by visiting organizers did not represent the sum total of secret society organization in the states; that there were permanent state lodges, headed by the very community leaders whom they recognized and trusted.

In later years, the existence of secret society organization was freely acknowledged by district, police and Chinese affairs officers. The clearest evidence was provided by outbreaks of rioting in Perak in 1887 at the Salak mines in Kuala Kangsar district, and at Papan in Kinta. The Kinta riots involved hundreds of men of the Ghi Hin on the one hand, and the Ho Seng and Hai San on the other.[1] In 1888 the Commandant of the Perak Sikhs visited a number of kongsis in the Kinta district and made a return of the labourers according to their probable society affiliations; in 246 kongsis visited he found 13,841 miners of whom 8,447 were probably Ghi Hin and 5,394 Hai

formant was writing of conditions over a period of some twenty years, and in one place (in describing the Kanching societies) he wrote of a past situation in the present tense. It is difficult therefore to be sure that when he gave the names of headmen, he was referring to an existing situation.

[1] Report of Secretary for Chinese Affairs, Perak, for 1887, enclosed in Smith to Knutsford, 347 of 30 July 1888, CO 273/154.

San.[1] In the same report, he estimated that half the Chinese in Perak were secret society members—their tickets were found on them whenever the police had occasion to search them—but could not be touched so long as they were sworn in the Straits Settlements. The district officer for Kinta stated bluntly that secret societies influenced nearly the whole of the Chinese population, suppressing cases and preventing evidence from being brought in the courts; meetings were held regularly, at which thousands of new members were initiated each year.[2] In Selangor the police were more reserved. They frequently reported attempts to organize and recruit (mostly by Ghi Hin but occasionally by Hai San) but these attempts were usually ascribed to immigrant organizers from Penang, Malacca and Deli; in his annual report for 1888, for example, the Superintendent of Police blamed two Hai San immigrants from Deli for starting a quarrel over mining land. The district officers were more outspoken, the assistant district officer, Rawang, reporting in 1893 that he had not the slightest doubt that the district was 'honeycombed with secret societies'.[3]

Both the Perak and Selangor authorities represented the secret societies as being mainly organizations for crime and extortion, responsible for gang and highway robberies, attacks on gambling farms and extortion from brothel-keepers and the like, and were at pains to insist that the influential Chinese were entirely opposed to them.[4] The Superintendent of Police, Selangor, was particularly emphatic about this. The Resident of Selangor, echoing the Superintendent, wrote in his annual report for 1892, '. . . the advantages of law and order are so apparent to the richer and more respectable members of the Chinese community that they generally give information to the authorities whenever their lawless brethren combine, and so long as this feeling exists no great danger can arise'. Syers paid tribute to the Capitans for the assistance they gave in suppressing these societies, and acknowledged the helplessness of the police themselves. 'It is extremely difficult to obtain any information as to the existence or otherwise of these illegal institutions; our great safeguard

[1] *AR* Police Department Perak, 1888, *PGG*, 15 March 1889. He estimated the total Chinese mining population at double the number given.
[2] *AR* Kinta, 1888, *PGG*, 3 May 1889. He reported that there had been cases where men had collected a large crowd simply by giving a sign of the hand, and that he had had certain people flogged and sent out of the district for threatening others with violence from their secret society friends.
[3] *AR* Rawang sub-district, Ulu Selangor, 1892, *SGG*, 4 August 1893.
[4] Kinta monthly report for February 1889, *PGG*, 29 March 1889; *AR* Police Department Perak, 1893, *PGG*, 6 July 1894; *AR* Selangor, 1890.

is in the fact that the Capitan China and all the best men here are opposed to them.'[1] But it is noteworthy that the assistance of the Capitans invariably ended in the frustration of the attempts of the rival society—the Ghi Hin—to organize in Kuala Lumpur.[2]

Did the Selangor Capitans really detach themselves from these secret societies after they were proscribed by the government, or did they continue their association with them? And in the latter case, how much did the British know or suspect? Here we can only speculate. First, it is clear that the establishment of British-run administrations rendered the political functions of the secret society obsolete.[3] It was no longer necessary or possible to resort to self-help in protecting life and property, nor was it possible to use the secret society organization to exclude economic rivals by force. The British were prepared to tolerate much, but they did not take kindly to monopolistic practices which threatened the state revenues. Again, it was not necessary to use the secret society organization to control labour when the towkays were able to call in the police—nor to administer justice, when the erstwhile secret society headmen sat in British courts as examining magistrates. It may well have been the case that while the secret societies continued to be of importance to the rank and file, as providing a sense of group security, they became increasingly an embarrassment to the entrepreneurs, who now had other and safer instruments of control at their disposal.

Still, it is unlikely that the Capitans could have detached themselves at will from the secret society organization, or that they would have wished to do so, since their retirement would have left a vacuum of leadership for others to fill. The probability is that they continued for a time to act as headmen of these societies. Yap Ah Loy's early association with the Hai San must have been known to Davidson

---

[1] AR Police Department Selangor, 1892, SGG, 12 May 1893.

[2] E.g., AR Selangor, 1891 and 1892.

[3] One authority, writing of the Chinese of nineteenth-century Singapore, has argued that while, in their earliest phase, 'the Singapore Chinese bound all their solidarities together . . . the secret society acting as the knot', in later times 'increasing complexity and growth of scale forced individual principles of grouping to crystallise in different types of association' (M. Freedman, 'Immigrants and Associations; Chinese in Nineteenth-Century Singapore', Comparative Studies in Society and History, vol. iii, 1960–1, p. 45). After 1890, as a result of penal legislation, societies which had hitherto been secret only in a ritual sense became really secret and degenerated into small-scale criminal associations. It is likely that the same process took place in the Malay states at the turn of the century, and that the role of the secret society in promoting group welfare and cohesion was taken up by surname, dialect and occupational associations.

and Swettenham and probably to Syers, who had been in Selangor from 1875 and who had known Kuala Lumpur under Ah Loy. It is hard to believe that, knowing the strength of the secret societies as they did, they can have expected Ah Loy or his successors to shake off their attachment and still maintain their influence; or that they were not able to draw conclusions (so obvious to historians) from the fact that the Capitans laid information only about rival societies. It may be that they knew of the continuing connexion between the Capitans and the secret societies, and because of their very great dependence on the ability of the Capitans to keep order in Kuala Lumpur, were prepared to turn a blind eye to their secret society affiliations so long as the formalities were preserved and disorder and scandal avoided. This *entente*, if it existed, would have required a great deal of discretion, ability and spirit of co-operation on the part of the Capitans, but it is clear that these qualities were not lacking. It may be objected that it would have been superfluous, in that case, to ban secret societies at all. But if the British wished to stamp them out in the long run—and they did—penal legislation was in itself a warning and discouragement, and gave a power which could be applied at will; and it would not have been out of keeping with the intensely pragmatic style of British colonial government to have secured this power and at the same time retained some flexibility in its application. The circumstances of government in the protected states made such discretionary and indeed arbitrary action possible.

The reproach often cast at the British—that they deliberately kept the communities apart as a matter of policy, is a distortion of historical facts. The British simply accepted, as a matter of administrative convenience, the plural organization of society which they found on their arrival. If they confirmed and developed this by establishing special departments to deal with the Chinese, it was because it seemed an appropriate way of dealing with communities which continued to be sharply differentiated in patterns of occupation and settlement, as well as in cultural values. The principle of communal leadership might in another age become a political weapon rather than an administrative tool, a means of preserving barriers which were in danger of being eroded by social and economic change; but this still lay in the undisclosed future.

X

THE ECONOMY:
POLICY AND DEVELOPMENT

*He that can establish a large trade, Heaven will surely bless
with a long life.**

SITUATED within a day's sail of a world port, rich in a mineral already
known and partially exploited, provided with labour and entre-
preneurial skills through the immigration of Chinese, the Malay
states in the 1870's offered exceptional opportunities for economic
growth. While encouraging the existing labour-intensive, technically
limited mining enterprise of the Chinese, the governments aimed in
the long term at encouraging the development of plantation agriculture and the entry into the mining industry of highly capitalized
European companies who would introduce machinery and improved
techniques. These objectives were to be achieved by a variety of permissive policies and by the active development of public works and
communications. The scarcity of population presented a labour problem, but one which could be solved by an open immigration policy;
the expanses of jungle constituted both a challenge and an opportunity, making it possible to adopt a liberal land policy without disturbing indigenous interests; and the revenue provided by tin made
it possible to lift the taxation burden from every other sector of the
economy, and still provide the communications and administrative
foundation necessary for realizing the mineral and agricultural potential of the states.

It was taken for granted that labour for large-scale mining and
agriculture would have to be imported, not only because the Malay
population was so small, but because Malays would not offer themselves as a permanent labour force. The living conditions that estate
managers and contractors considered appropriate and economically
viable—the crowded labour barracks, where there was sometimes no
separate accommodation for women or married couples, the hard
monotonous daily round, the watchful supervision and petty bully-

* Farewell address presented by the Chinese merchants of Larut to Sir
Hugh Low on his retirement in 1889.

ing[1]—would have seemed to the Malay peasant a great deal worse than the debt-bondage from which his new rulers were so anxious to rescue him. Since the standard of living offered to their labour by planters and miners was inferior in every social value to that already enjoyed by Malays, and so low in material values that Malay standards could hardly have been worse, it followed that Malays could not be recruited for continuous field or mine labour except by force, and such an idea was never entertained. Malays did play some part in the new economic development, but in a way that suited them, as casual short-term labour on clearing, woodcutting and collection of jungle materials for the temporary buildings that mushroomed with the spread of mining and agriculture. For regular routine work, labour had to be imported.

As we have seen, the immigration of Chinese was self-regulating in accordance with the vicissitudes of the economy and the demand for labour. Recruiters in China, coolie-brokers, and depot-keepers in the Straits formed the links in a chain of supply and profit which finally terminated in the delivery of the labourer to his employer in the Colony or the Malay states. In the Colony, the government intervened at the point of entry, where immigrants were interviewed and assisted immigrants were required to sign contracts before an officer of the Chinese Protectorate; and in the states, contracts might be validated by execution before a magistrate or Chinese Affairs officer. Both in the Colony and the states, the general labour laws provided for enforcement of contracts, but there was in practice little difference between the treatment of indentured labourers on the one hand and free labourers under advances on the other.

The supply of Indian labour also was left to private enterprise, despite much clamour for government intervention to secure more immigrants; but as a result of the pressures and demands of the Indian government, Indian labour was subject to much closer government supervision. The promotion of Indian immigration was the subject of negotiations leading to the passage of identical legislation in the Colony and protected states in 1884, regulating the employment of indentured labourers (or 'statute' labourers, as they were called), setting out their maximum advances, length of service, minimum wages, and hours of work. The obligations of the labourer were enforced by a battery of penal clauses which rendered him liable

---

[1] See *Labour Commission Report*, 1891, especially Appendix B, pp. 1–24.

to fines, deductions from wages, and imprisonment for neglect to labour, disobedience and desertion; the employer on his part was bound to provide rations at current market prices, 'sufficient and proper' accommodation, medical attention, and hospital care. The working of the ordinance was supervised by the Indian Immigration Agent in Penang, and Assistant Indian Immigration Agents in the states. They were required to visit estates, muster the statute labourers, inquire into their condition, and inspect accounts and returns of sickness, mortality, desertions and arrests. The effectiveness of supervision was limited by the fact that the Assistant Agents were required to combine this work with heavy full-time duties; in Perak and also in Selangor, the Agent was a district officer, and in Sungei Ujong he was the Residency Surgeon. The elasticity of interpretation of the clauses relating to 'sufficient and proper' accommodation, sanitary arrangements and medical care was revealed during a tour of inspection of estates by the Labour Commission of 1890.[1]

The control and supervision thus provided, together with a subsidy for a line of steamers bringing Indian immigrants to Malaya,[2] represented the sum total of the assistance provided by the state governments to Indian immigration. It barely kept pace with the rapid economic development which took place after 1880. The large programme of government works and road and railway construction created intense competition for labour, so that the removal of restrictions on the emigration of Indian labour to the Malay states did not result in a substantial lowering of labour costs, though it kept them within economic limits. The Indian indenture system was of some importance to the economy of the sugar industry of northern Perak, but it had drawbacks which made it unpopular with employers who could afford free labour; acclimatization took a heavy toll of life, there were frequent desertions, and the special regulations imposed on employment of this type of labour (in particular, those requiring the provision of hospital accommodation and medical care) were disliked by employers. By 1895, the recruitment of indentured Indian labourers in the Malay states had virtually ceased, except in Perak,

---

[1] *Labour Commission Report*, loc. cit.
[2] The subsidy operated from 1887 to 1892, and provided for a steamer to carry immigrants fortnightly to west coast ports. Between 1887 and 1890, the subsidy of $30,000 per annum was divided between the interested governments as follows: the Straits Settlement and Perak, $10,000 each per annum, Selangor $7,000 and Johore $3,000. In 1890, Johore ceased to be a party to the arrangement, and the share of the other governments was increased by $1,000 each.

THE ECONOMY: POLICY AND DEVELOPMENT   327

where they continued to be imported in hundreds for employment on two Krian sugar estates.[1] Coffee planters began to recruit their labour direct from India through *kanganies* (head coolies). However, the flow of free Indian immigrants did increase markedly after 1884, and though the population was highly mobile, with a large yearly outflow, there was a large net increase in the Indian population and labour force.[2] Without this increase, the development of the coffee industry and the growth of communications would not have been possible.

Immigration was regarded not only as a means of providing labour for mines, estates and public works, but of getting a permanent population on to the soil; so that while the immigration of an agricultural or industrial labour force was the active concern of government, the settlement of thousands of Malaysian subsistence farmers from the archipelago, with their wives and families, was also encouraged. In principle, the permanent settlement of Chinese and Indian families in smallholder agriculture was equally welcomed, but apart from small settlements of Tamil Christians in the Krian district and in Lower Perak,[3] there was little settlement of this kind. In general, settlement patterns were sharply differentiated according to race; the Indians immigrating to work on estates, roads and other public works, the Chinese to work in a variety of industries, but mainly in the mines, and Malaysians from the peninsula and archipelago to settle as small cultivators.

The immigration of Malaysians was encouraged by rent remissions and small loans, but while settlement schemes were carried out on the initiative of individual district officers, there was no regular gov-

[1] The Indian indentured labour force in Selangor declined steadily from 404 at the end of 1888, to 267 at the end of 1895, and 129 at the end of 1896, out of a total Indian labour force of 2,600 for that year. In Sungei Ujong the indentured labour force declined from 185 at the end of 1889 to 44 at the end of 1895. Only in Perak did the number of indentured immigrants remain fairly constant, and most of them were employed on sugar estates from the beginning. *AR* states, and Indian Immigration Agents, various years.

[2] E.g., of 14,885 Indians in Perak in 1891, 3,277 were agricultural labourers and 3,473 industrial labourers. In 1879, the Indian population was 937.

[3] A Tamil Christian agricultural colony was started by the French Roman Catholic Mission near Bagan Serai in 1882. In 1889 there were 101 families (430 people in all) with 450 acres of cleared land (translation of an account written by Father Fee, founder of the mission, and kindly supplied by Dr. R.K. Jain). A Tamil agricultural colony was started by Denison in Lower Perak in 1886, and twenty-four families brought in under government advances (*Labour Commission Report*, 1891, Appendix A, p. 155). A Tamil settlement was started by the district officer, Ulu Langat, in 1885 (*AR* Selangor, 1886). There were about fifty planters in 1886.

ernment-assisted scheme of immigration. Families of settlers came singly or in small groups, sometimes independently, more often with the assistance of a leader who had previously negotiated with a district officer and secured land and an advance on the harvest, to be distributed among his followers. There was also a small intake of indentured labourers from Java and elsewhere in the archipelago, imported by coolie brokers and lodged in Colony depots before engagement, in the same manner as Chinese immigrants. They were employed chiefly in such work as felling and clearing, drain-cutting and road-building, and frequently settled with their wives and families on the completion of their indentures.[1] Malaysian settlers came from all over the peninsula and archipelago. Javanese settled in the Klang and Kuala Langat districts of Selangor, and in Lower Perak and Krian; Banjarese in Kuala Selangor, Krian, Selama and Lower Perak; Sumatrans in the Ulu Langat district and in Kinta, where they were reported in 1894 to outnumber the indigenous Malays in the Kampar, Kuala Teja and Sungei Raya mukims.[2] There was a large inflow of Malays from other states in the Peninsula; from Kedah and Perlis into Krian, Kurau and Selama, from Patani into Ulu Krian and Ulu Perak, from Kelantan (stimulated by a famine in 1888) into Pahang, Selangor (mainly Kuala Selangor) and nearly every district of Perak.[3]

Population counts made in all the states in 1891 give details of population distribution by sex, race and (for the Chinese) dialect group, and the fuller returns for Perak and Selangor give details of age and occupational distribution by districts, and distribution as between town and country divisions. The significant feature of the general return is the size of the non-Malay element. The Chinese constituted 39 per cent. of the total population, and about half the total population of Perak, Selangor and Sungei Ujong. The percent-

[1] *Labour Commission Report*, 1891, p. 34. The numbers who signed contracts with the Protector of Chinese, Singapore, between 1886 and 1890 were given in the report as follows—1886: 2,741; 1887: 3,589; 1888: 4,931; 1889: 4,974; 1890: 5,133.

[2] The district officer for Kinta reported in his monthly letter for April 1894 that there had been a large (Hari Raya) gathering of 'foreign Malays' at Gopeng, at least 2,000 being present. Several hundred families had come in from Sumatra the previous year, and they were expected before long to form the majority of the Malay population of Kinta (*PGG*, 25 May 1894). In his monthly letter for November 1892, he had reported the entry of numbers of Mandelings (*PGG*, 6 January 1893). In Selangor, it was estimated that about two-thirds of the Malay population in 1886 consisted of natives of Netherlands India. *AR* Selangor 1886.

[3] District reports, various years.

ages of Malays (including Malays of the archipelago but excluding aborigines), Chinese, and Indians (of whom the great majority were Tamils), are shown in the following table:

	Malays	Chinese	Indians
All states	53	39	5
Perak	46	44	6
Selangor	31	62	4
Sungei Ujong and Jelebu	47	42	4
Negri Sembilan	86	13	2
Pahang	90	5	1

The only group which had a normal sex ratio and a normal ratio of children to adults was the Malay.[1]

Population counts taken by penghulus and police in Perak in 1879 and Selangor in 1884 enable some sort of time-comparison to be made for these two states,[2] and show the phenomenal expansion of all groups. The percentage of increase for Perak was 164 per cent., and for the Malays, Chinese and Indians, 74 per cent., 363 per cent. and 1,488 per cent. respectively. The Selangor increases between 1884 and 1891 were almost as dramatic, allowing for the shorter time-span: the percentage of increase for the whole state was 75 per cent.; and 48 per cent., 80 per cent. and 902 per cent. for the Malays, Chinese and Indians respectively.[3] There were large increases in every district. In Perak, the percentage of increase ranged from 75 per cent. for the Lower Perak and Batang Padang district to 561 per cent. for Kinta, and in Selangor, from 50 per cent. for Kuala Langat

[1] The figures are as follows:

	Ratio of women to men (excluding Pahang—no figures)	Ratio of children to adults (Perak only)
Malays	1: 1.1	1: 1.7
Chinese	1:15.5	1:40.6
Indians	1: 3.9	1: 6.0

Persons under 15 years are returned as children.

[2] Census of Perak, 1891, containing 1879 returns; AR Selangor 1884. A study of the population of Selangor, using the 1884 and 1891 figures, has been made by J.C. Jackson, 'Population changes in Selangor State, 1850–1891', Journal of Tropical Geography, vol. 19 (1964).

[3] Jackson, op. cit. p. 46. The relatively small Chinese increase, compared with Perak, puzzled the Selangor authorities. It was about 22,000 less than the estimate for 1887, while the Perak figure was 17,000 more. Yet the increase in tin duty—a safe guide to the size of the Chinese population— was proportionately greater in Selangor over the same period. Even if the 1887 estimate is rejected as too large for Selangor, the Chinese population in 1891 estimated in proportion to the tin duty and taking the Perak population as a base, should have been about 70,000.

to 204 per cent. for Ulu Selangor. (In both states the higher percentages were accounted for by Chinese migration.) The Malay gain was fairly evenly distributed between the older settlements and the new mining areas.[1] The largest Malay increase of all, both in absolute terms and in proportion to earlier figures, was in Krian, where the Malay population increased by 120 per cent. over 1879. Since five-sixths of the Malay population of Krian and Kurau was returned as 'foreign Malay' in 1879 (as well as the entire Malay population of Selama) it appears that nearly all the Malays in this district in 1891 were born outside the state.[2]

By opening the doors wide to immigrants, by negotiating with the Indian government to remove restrictions on the entry of Indian subjects, by establishing a legislative and judicial apparatus for the control of labour (largely, it must be said, in the interests of employers), the state governments did what they could to improve the labour supply and populate the states. The main attraction, however, was the rapid economic development; the growth of communications and the liberal fiscal and land policies pursued also probably played a part in bringing about the spectacular increase in population.

*   *   *

[1] The Malay increase in various districts of Perak and Selangor between 1879–91 and 1884–91 is given below. In making these calculations, 'Malays' are taken to include natives of the archipelago, but not aborigines. The figures arrived at for Selangor therefore differ from those given by Jackson. The district returns for Lower Perak and Kuala Kangsar for 1879 have been adjusted to correspond with the slightly different arrangements of mukims in the 1891 census.

Malay increase, Perak

	1879	1891	Increase
Lower Perak	13,654	21,499	7,845
Batang Padang	2,304	4,557	2,253
Kuala Kangsar with Upper Perak	19,420	26,237	6,817
Kinta	7,863	14,635	6,772
Larut	7,671	13,041	5,370
Krian and Kurau	6,852	14,991	8,139
Selama	1,918	3,215	1,297

Malay increase, Selangor

	1884	1891	Increase
Kuala Langat	2,819	3,257	438
Klang	2,702	3,654	952
Kuala Lumpur	4,454	6,039	1,585
Ulu Langat	1,808	3,000	1,192
Kuala Selangor	3,343	5,976	2,633
Ulu Selangor	1,971	3,396	1,425

[2] That these districts had been settled only recently and not brought under Malay traditional authority to any great extent is indicated by the fact that they had no slave population in 1879.

Swettenham remarked in connexion with land policy, 'we do not seek revenue but population', and while this remark was possible, paradoxically, only because the revenue was so large, it does provide a pointer to fiscal policy. The presence of mineral wealth, the scarcity of population and the absence of agricultural enterprise, indicated a tax structure based on taxation of tin output and miners' luxuries, with minimal burdens on agriculture, and the avoidance of customs or poll taxes which might discourage settlement. The Malay taxation pattern had been a patchwork of local produce, land, labour and poll taxes, varying in incidence and method of collection according to local circumstances and privileges; its main features were the import duties on all goods, and royalties on all exported produce. One of the earliest circulars from the Governor to the Residents recommended the replacement of this system by one based on liberal principles:

Where possible, the duties on imports should be diminished, so as to induce traders to visit the country, and there should be one uniform system through all the Native States, which should be on as simple a scale as possible, putting restrictions on as few articles as possible, and keeping a free communication of every kind by land and water, as far as may be done without affecting the necessary police supervision.[1]

It took some ten years for these recommendations to be implemented in the western states. In Perak, import duties (except on spirits, tobacco and opium—by far the most important imports) were abolished from 1 January 1878, and export duties retained only for tin, gutta and jungle produce.[2] In Selangor and Sungei Ujong, despite criticism from Singapore, Douglas and Murray were allowed to pursue fiscally conservative policies for much longer, for reasons which are not clear. In Sungei Ujong, the tariff on sundries was in operation at least till 1882 (it was abolished by 1885) and in Selangor, the duties on tea, salt and salt fish were retained till 1884, and those on tobacco and oil till 1885, though the revenues they produced were insignificant.[3] From the beginning of 1886, however, all import duties were abolished in Selangor, except for those on opium and spirits. In Pahang, duties on imports, other than opium and spirits, were abolished from July 1889, when the Resident began to collect the revenue.[4]

[1] CS to Assistant Resident, Selangor, 12 February 1875. Sel/Sec. 8/75.
[2] *PCM*, 10 and 11 September 1877.
[3] In 1883, the duties on these imports were estimated at $8,340, as against an estimate of $90,000 for opium import duty alone. Sel/Sec. 215/83.
[4] *AR* Pahang, 1889.

Agricultural exports were selectively taxed, according to the nature of the crop and its place in the economy of the state. The earliest large-scale cultivations, all of them in the western states and all pioneered by Chinese in the 1870's, were tapioca, pepper and gambier in Sungei Ujong and the Negri Sembilan (and, from the mid-1880's, in Selangor), and sugar in Perak. In the 1880's, important experiments with coffee also took place in the western states. Pepper and gambier paid duty in all the states; tapioca, apparently, only in Sungei Ujong and Negri Sembilan (in Selangor an early duty on tapioca was removed by 1883, probably by Swettenham, and apparently not re-imposed). Perak sugar does not appear to have been taxed. Coffee, a crop from which much was hoped, paid no tax in Perak and Selangor until 1894, though it was taxed in Sungei Ujong —the state where the cultivation was first introduced—by 1884.[1] Revenue from agriculture was also obtained in the form of premia and rents on land, but as the revenue figures indicate, until the 1890's the total land revenue for all the states, including revenue from town lands and mining leases and licences, was not more than 10 per cent. of the duty on tin.[2]

Undoubtedly it was the productivity of the mines and the exploitation of the miners for revenue purposes which made it possible to ease fiscal burdens on trade and agriculture. Tin was heavily taxed; a calculation of the average *ad valorem* rate of tin duty in Perak and Selangor shows that between 1880 and 1896, the rate varied between 9 per cent. and 15.3 per cent. in Perak, and between 8.1 per cent. and 14.6 per cent. in Selangor.[3] The tin duty represented the largest element in the combined revenues of the states. Next in importance was the revenue from 'licenses', derived from the sale of monopolies chiefly affecting the Chinese. In Perak and Selangor, the revenue from licenses between 1885 and 1895 was roughly equal to the revenue from tin and in some years it was much larger. During this decade, the receipts from tin and licenses in these two states amounted in most years to roughly four-fifths of their combined revenues.[4]

[1] Return of exciseable imports and exports, *AR* Sungei Ujong, 1881; Memorandum on the Mode and Incidence of Taxation in the Native States, by J.F. Dickson, 31 January 1891, enclosed in Smith to Knutsford, 70 of 19 February 1891, CO 273/172; Estimates, Sungei Ujong, Selangor and Perak, various years; *AR* Negri Sembilan, various years.

[2] See Table 2, pp. 411–12.

[3] Wong Lin Ken, *The Malayan Tin Industry to 1914*, Association for Asian Studies, Monograph and Papers, no. xiv, Tucson, 1965, p. 253.

[4] See Table on facing page.

The farming of revenues, practised by the British both in the Settlements and the Malay states, enabled government to avoid some of the trouble of revenue collection and to minimize the possibility of loss through smuggling and other kinds of fraud. The farms leased at various times included a whole range of privileges, such as the right to collect export duty on atap, firewood and jungle produce, to license opium shops and manufacture and sell toddy; but far and away the most valuable were the right to manufacture and sell spirits, to keep gaming-houses and pawn shops, and in particular, to collect the duty on opium and (in the coast districts) to prepare and sell chandu or cooked opium. The pawn, spirits and gambling rights were farmed in all states from the beginning of British rule; but the most important monopoly of all—the opium duty collection—was not farmed till the 1880's. It was carried out by government up to 1880 in Perak, 1883 in Sungei Ujong and mid-1886 in Selangor.[1]

The economic significance of the farming system was that it provided, at least in theory, a means of attracting Chinese capital and labour to the states. The success of the farmer's speculation depended, of course, on the consumption of opium and spirits and the volume of business in the gambling houses, and he therefore had an incentive to increase consumption by investing in mines and other enterprises and introducing labour into the state. Estimates of the economic initiative to be expected from applicants for the farms played an important part in the calculations of government when farm tenders

Revenue from Licenses (in Straits dollars), 1886–95

Year	Perak	Selangor
1886	750,979	311,038
1887	744,196	458,938
1888	752,807	456,580
1889	1,388,816	648,961
1890	1,154,395	681,807
1891	1,000,478	607,750
1892	1,020,867	621,585
1893	1,031,771	752,655
1894	1,054,331	770,946
1895	783,222	424,955

Source: Appendixes to *AR*.
The drop in returns after 1895 was due to the fact that the opium import duty was collected by the government in Perak and Selangor that year and so came under 'Customs'.
[1] Schedule of Perak revenue farms, 1880–91, enclosed in Dickson to Knutsford, 425 of 31 October 1890, CO 273/168; Smith to Derby, 4 April 1884, C.4192, no. 21; *AR* Selangor, 1886.

were being considered; Low, describing his negotiations with Penang capitalists over the Perak revenue farms, wrote in his journal:

They [the Penang farmers] will afford this very well indeed, but of course it requires a large capital and bold speculation. Ah Kwee told him he wanted 5,000 more coolies put in at once, and this is the only way to make it successful, but Tean Tek talks of 2 or 3 hundred coolies at a time at which fiddling game of course they could not develop the tin industry sufficiently to make it worth my while to let it to them.[1]

Capitalists who already had a large stake in the country were in a strong position when it came to tendering for the farms, for a number of reasons; they were in a position to expand their enterprises if their applications were successful, and restrict production and immigration in an attempt to break the farm if they were not; and since their prosperity was of some importance to the state, there was an incentive to support them financially by giving them the farms. Sometimes, in order to break a local ring, or to encourage new capital to enter the state, the farms were given to outside interests, with varying results. In 1885, in an attempt to attract Penang capital, the Selangor Government gave the principal farms, including the pawn and gambling farm of Kuala Lumpur, to a Hokkien syndicate from Penang. The syndicate introduced a large number of Hokkiens into the state; the previous holders, who were Khehs, failed to break the farm and took shares in it after a few months of opposition.[2] Ten years later, however, a Penang firm withdrew its tender for the Selangor opium farm because no local entrepreneur would take up shares.[3] There is reason to believe that the large farms—the general farms of Larut, Kinta and Kuala Lumpur, and the opium duty farms of Perak and Selangor—were held as a rule by local men in partnership with Singapore or Penang interests or both, though the existence of such partnerships is not always revealed by the published lists of tenderers.[4]

[1] Low Journal for 30 September 1879, enclosed in Anson to Hicks Beach, Confidential of 18 October 1879, CO 273/100. Low refers here to Chung Keng Kwee, the Capitan China of Perak, and Khoo Thian Tek, Penang secret society leader and lessee of the Penang farms. There were secret society and business affiliations between Khoo Thian Tek and Chung Keng Kwee.

[2] *AR* Selangor, 1885. The Kuala Lumpur farms were restored to the Khehs, in the person of the Capitan China, in 1887. Sel/Sec. 2012/86.

[3] Sel/Sec. 752A/95.

[4] On the occasion of the letting of the Selangor farms for 1890–2, there was an understanding between the local applicants, Cheow Ah Yeok and Yap Kuan Seng, and a Penang applicant, Cheah Chen Eok, acting on behalf of the Singapore opium farmer, Cheah Tek Soon, that whoever was successful should admit the

The importance of the farms in the credit structure of the state was brought out by Swettenham in a report on the Perak farms, in connexion with a petition for relief by the farmers in 1890:

... the failure of the signatories to the contract means almost invariably the ruin of a large number of people who are interested in the Farm or who depend upon the Farmer's assistance in their various industries, it means financial depression and the weakening of confidence, the stoppage of supplies and the closing of some avenues to capital; it means a fall in the value of real property, possible immediate loss to the Revenue and an almost certain reduction at the next reletting of the Farms.[1]

He recommended that the farmers, who were suffering severe losses both on account of the general decline of trade and because they had overbid for their contracts, should be treated gently, and referred to concessions which had been made in similar circumstances in the past. In 1885 and 1886, for example, loans totalling $8,000 had been made to the Larut gambling farmer (Chin Ah Yam) to enable him to continue paying the farm rent; repayment was not expected, and eventually the loans were written off with the Governor's consent. The farmers were clearly in a position to profit from the economic growth of the states with little risk to themselves. If the price of tin was high and immigration boomed, they made large profits; if trade was depressed and they were unable to meet their commitments, they were able to plead for relief, usually with some success, since the government could not afford to risk the financial collapse of large local interests.

The collection of the opium duty by farmers was a comparatively brief experiment; adopted in the 1880's, it was abandoned by the several states, and the duty once more collected by government, between 1895 and 1901.[2] The large profits made by farmers,[3] their relative immunity from the consequences of over-bidding, their con-

---

other two into the partnership. Minute by Resident, 23 September 1889, Sel/Sec. 23/89.

[1] Swettenham to CS, 28 September 1890, enclosed in Dickson to Knutsford, 425 of 31 October 1890, CO 273/168.

[2] In Perak, government collected the duty from 1895, and in Selangor from 1900, after a year's trial in 1895. The government of the old Negri Sembilan collected the opium duty directly from 1892; Sungei Ujong and Jelebu followed suit in 1895. In 1898 the combined states (the new Negri Sembilan) reverted temporarily to the farm of the duty because of the decline of opium imports. The farm was finally abolished in 1901. Pahang alone continued to farm the duty after 1901.

[3] E.g., in 1893 the Selangor opium farmers made a profit of about 35 per cent. on their contract, and in 1894, about 70 per cent. Sel/Sec. 120B/94 and 176/94, and 752A/95.

spiracies to keep down tenders, scepticism about the real extent of their contribution to economic development, increasing confidence in the ability of Chinese Affairs officers to deal with smuggling, a growing sense of professional discomfort at the discharge of an important government function by powerful private interests—all these contributed to the decisions taken at various times to assume responsibility for collection.[1] The Home Government was at this time under pressure to limit the exploitation of opium smoking for revenue purposes in the colonies, and in 1891, the Secretary of State called on the Governor to consider whether the farming system could be dispensed with or existing arrangements modified 'so as to diminish the evils of the opium traffic without seriously crippling the revenue'.[2] The changes in collection initiated by the states therefore took place in an atmosphere of mounting metropolitan criticism of the whole system. In face of the objections of the Straits officials, however, the Secretary of State declined to meddle for the time being with the opium farm in the Straits,[3] and it is clear from the correspondence that the decision of Negri Sembilan, Selangor and Perak to collect the duty directly was reached independently, and that no pressure from the Colonial Office had been brought to bear. The states were perhaps the more inclined to risk these changes since by the end of the century, the opium farms had served their purpose; the mining industry was firmly established, western capital was entering the field, and it was no longer necessary to look to the farming system as a means of attracting investment to the states.

In addition to these measures for attracting capital, the state governments gave direct assistance to enterprise by making loans from public funds to individual miners and planters. In Selangor, the

[1] In 1892, the Resident of Negri Sembilan, already restive at the failure of the farmer to invest in the state, decided to collect the opium duty directly after a conspiracy to force down the farm rents. The results were successful, the government receipts in 1893 being $36,760 for opium duty and $7,920 for the spirit farm, as against the highest tender of $33,600 for both farms (*AR* Negri Sembilan, 1893). The Selangor Government experimented with direct collection in 1895 because it was decided, in the light of the farmer's profit for the previous three years, that the state was losing too much by farming the duty (minutes by Resident, 3 January 1896, and Treasurer, 18 December 1895, enclosed in Mitchell to Chamberlain, 17 or 18 January 1896, CO 273/212). The pros and cons of collection by farmers were fully ventilated on Sel/Sec. 1473/99, when proposals for reverting to government collection came under consideration.

[2] Knutsford to Smith, 264 of 18 August 1891, No. 20 in CO Confidential Print Eastern 63, CO 882/5.

[3] Chamberlain to Mitchell, 352 of 1 November 1895, on Mitchell to Ripon 70 of 8 February 1894, CO 273/194.

practice of lending large sums to Chinese miners at the New Year, to enable them to settle accounts with their labourers, was in force in Douglas' time.[1] When Swettenham became Resident, he obtained a blanket authority to make loans to 'respectable persons' for various purposes, reporting any large advances. In September 1883, he reported 'No less than $52,000 has been advanced in this manner at different times during the current year and I consider that this assistance has contributed not a little to the large increase in the revenue'.[2] Maxwell continued the practice; in his annual report for 1889, he wrote that the maintenance of tin exports at the 1889 level would probably depend on the readiness of government to make advances. In 1890 he obtained permission to make loans to miners totalling $57,000, exclusive of $50,000 lent to the Capitan China to enable him to assist miners.[3] Loans to miners on a similar scale were made in 1891, 1892 and 1893; they were suspended in 1894 and 1895 because of pressure on balances, but in 1896 a loan of $50,000 to the Capitan China and Loke Yew was approved by the Governor.[4] It is possible that similar loans were made in Perak, but of this there is no record.

Both Perak and Selangor made large loans on easy terms to European planters.[5] Loans were also made to Malays to assist them in mining, trading and planting, and to cover the initial costs of settlement; with a few exceptions these loans were individually insignificant, but reached a substantial aggregate sum, at least in Selangor. There were other loans for special purposes, for example, to assist victims of flood and famine, and to enable town dwellers to replace their atap shops and dwellings with brick.

The loans to Chinese miners were for short periods (usually three to six months) at interest of 10 per cent. per annum. Those to European and Malay planters were for two, three and sometimes five years at interest rates of 5 or 6 per cent. Most loans were secured by

[1] E.g., in 1878 the Capitan China was lent $5,000. In 1880 he was again lent $5,000 and Yap Ah Shak $3,000. Sel/Sec. 220/78 and 239/80.
[2] Sel/Sec. 502/82; Resident to CS, 10 September 1883, Sel/Sec. 1331/83.
[3] Sel/Sec. 32/90 and 385/90.
[4] Sel/Sec. 1208/96.
[5] In the AR Perak 1888, it was stated that sums of $2,000 to $40,000 [sic] had been lent to pioneer European planters. A Selangor loan account of 1889 shows $5,000 lent to Hill and Rathborne, pioneer coffee planters of Kuala Lumpur, and an account of loans outstanding in 1896 shows loans totalling $21,000 to European coffee and pepper planters, the largest being a loan of $15,000 to Stephenson Brothers, pepper planters of Klang. Sel/Sec. 598/89 and 4937/96.

real property or a personal guarantee; but small loans to penghulus for the development of their mukims were usually secured by a lien on their salaries and paid no interest. The formation of agencies of the Chartered Bank in Perak and Selangor in 1888 did not stop the government's loan business, but it was probably responsible for the stricter conditions which Maxwell tried to impose on mining loans in Selangor in 1890.[1] After 1890, also, the misgivings of the Singapore Government as to this unorthodox use of public funds increased; but this was probably due less to banking pressure than to the dislike of career administrators like Smith, Mitchell and Dickson for these annual speculations. However, the advice of the Residents as to their economic usefulness continued to be accepted.

The largest development expenditure was on communications. River transport was expensive and hazardous, and it was vitally important to make roads to connect existing mines with their natural outlets, and to open new mining and agricultural country. In 1886, Kuala Lumpur had a railway to Bukit Kuda, on the right bank of the Klang river, and in 1890 the line to Klang was completed. In October 1894, an extension from Kuala Lumpur to Kuala Kubu (about forty miles), serving the whole Ulu Selangor mining district, was completed. The Ulu Langat extension from Kuala Lumpur to Kajang was completed in 1897. In Perak, a railway completed in 1885 connected Taiping with Port Weld on the Larut coast, and by 1895 a railway fifty miles long linked the mining districts of Kinta with the port of Telok Anson on the Perak river. In Sungei Ujong, a railway twenty-four miles long, completed in 1891, linked Seremban with Port Dickson on the coast. The railways complemented and in certain instances paralleled an extensive road system; by 1895, Perak and Selangor together had 1,500 miles of roads and bridle paths, of which 500 miles were metalled cart roads.[2] The immediate and urgent need for links between centres of production merged in a long-term design for a trunk road and railway running the length of

---

[1] Maxwell limited the loan period to three months, and raised the rate of interest to 12 per cent. (24 per cent. on overdue loans), but a depression and general tightness of credit forced a relaxation of these rules in 1891. The loans of 1893 and 1896 were again at 10 per cent. Sel/Sec. 32/90, 103/92 and 1208/96.

[2] Exact figures for Negri Sembilan, Sungei Ujong and Jelebu are not to hand, but in 1893 these states had 360 miles of roads, including 170 miles of metalled and unmetalled cart road. Pahang had about sixty miles of bridle path, apart from a few miles of cart road made by mining companies in the vicinity of their own mines. (*AR* all states, and Memorandum Regarding Roads in Selangor, *SGG*, 7 December 1894.

the peninsula. By 1895 there was a cart road the whole way from Malacca through Negri Sembilan, Sungei Ujong, Selangor and Perak to Province Wellesley, except for fifty miles on the Perak-Selangor border, where a six-foot bridle path was in process of conversion into a cart road. In 1903 the rail link from Seremban to Prai in Province Wellesley was complete.

The wealth of Perak and Selangor encouraged a confident and liberal development policy which influenced even the poorer states. In Selangor, the expenditure on roads and railways between 1883 and 1895 amounted to nearly half the total expenditure for these years; and in Perak, there was a comparable activity and scale of expenditure after 1889. With the exception of a railway loan of $300,000 (out of a total capital expenditure of $3,844,594) borrowed by Selangor in the early years of her railway development, Perak and Selangor paid for their communications out of revenue. The success of their railways and the rapidity of their economic growth encouraged the development of the poorer states by large-scale borrowing. Colony loans paid for a cart road from Malacca to Kuala Pilah, begun before an administrative officer was appointed to the Sri Menanti states; the Sungei Ujong railway, the only railway in the protected states to be privately constructed, involved a guarantee of interest which was, again, met by borrowing from the Colony; and the chief work in Pahang, a road eighty-five miles long and estimated to cost $1,250,000, was financed by Selangor at a time when Pahang was over a million dollars in debt. That there was still a readiness to speculate on this undertaking, in a state which had consistently shown large annual deficits and was not even able to pay for her ordinary administration, sufficiently testifies to the strength of the belief in communications as the sovereign key to economic development. Swettenham, who more than anyone else was the moving spirit in this field, expressed his belief in a policy of expansion in his Perak report for 1894. After declaring his satisfaction that there was now nothing left of the balance of $1,800,000 built up by his predecessor, he wrote:

The lesson to be learnt from these facts and figures, is, I think, a very plain one. It is, that in the administration of a Malay State, revenue and prosperity follow the liberal but prudently-directed expenditure of public funds, especially when they are invested in high-class roads, in railways, telegraphs, waterworks, and everything likely to encourage trade and private enterprise. . . . The Government cannot do the mining and the agriculture, but it can make it profitable for others to embark in such speculations by giving them every reasonable facility, and that we have tried to do.

The existence of a productive mining industry able to finance state expenditure and development, and the abundance of land in relation to population demand, provided extremely favourable conditions for the development of a rational land policy. Because of the ready availability of virgin land,[1] it was easy from the beginning to differentiate between the various purposes of occupation and lay down conditions of tenure appropriate to each; it was possible also to permit the alienation and occupation of land on liberal terms both for subsistence and plantation agriculture, with little danger of collision between the two interests. It was not till the late 1890's that the destruction of forest for shifting subsistence and commercial agriculture began to cause concern; it was then also that the development of schemes for rice irrigation areas in the coastal regions of Perak began to confront the authorities for the first time with serious problems of competition for land.

Under Malay rule, ownership of the soil was vested in the Sultan. The cultivator enjoyed a heritable, transferable right of occupation on condition that he continued to cultivate his land, pay his taxes, and meet his labour obligations. The abundance of land, and the scarcity of population, made the land itself valueless until it was occupied and developed. In the four states here discussed, the land generally bore no tax obligation, either in the form of land rent or levy on produce, though there might be a tithe on grain or a capitation tax in rich rice-growing areas, of which the Krian district of Perak was one example.[2] Some of these principles were perpetuated by the British administration. Ownership of the soil was vested in the state, and land was alienated by grant or lease conditionally on payment of land rent, *bona fide* working of the land, and (where this

---

[1] E.g., by the end of 1896, 208,254 acres had been alienated in Perak for agriculture, and 67,553 for mining. The area of the state was 5,087,360 acres. *AR Perak*, 1896.

[2] Reports by Residents and others on Land Taxation in the Native States, enclosed in Smith to Knutsford, 405 of 28 October 1891, CO 273/176; Low to Lucas, 15 December 1891, CO 273/178. According to Low, a tenth of the rice crop had been formerly collected by the Mentri in Krian, in addition to a capitation tax, but in other parts of Perak, 'contributions from the cultivators were raised in an irregular manner by fines and exactions, by compulsory unpaid labour and forced contributions, but no settled liability in the notion of rent seems to have been claimed or acknowledged'.

was required) payment of export duty on produce. The idea that land was valueless *per se* and that the object of policy was to get it taken up on practically any terms, continued to hold good with the majority of officials.[1] Swettenham spoke for them when he wrote in his annual report on Perak for 1890:

The present object of the Government is to give the greatest possible encouragement to agriculturists and miners of all nationalities. The unoccupied lands (especially those distant from lines of communication) are really of very little actual value, and it is of more importance to get in capital and labour, especially a fixed agricultural population, than to worry people who are easily frightened away by a quantity of regulations that under other circumstances would be not only excellent but necessary.

The land regulations passed in all the states between 1882 and 1889 were based, with minor modifications, on the Perak land regulations of 1879 drawn up by Maxwell while he was Assistant Resident.[2] These 1879 regulations provided for the division of the state lands into four categories; waste land (described in subsequent regulations as 'land available for agricultural purposes'), land in the occupation of natives under Malay tenure, building land in towns and villages, and mining reserves. The form of tenure envisaged for all agricultural land, whether under Malay subsistence cultivation or plantations, was the lease for 999 years, giving a permanent, heritable and transferable right on payment of premium, survey fee and a fixed land rent. The regulation provided for the issue of permits and certificates of title (called 'agreements for lease' in subsequent legislation) in anticipation of survey.

The intention of providing every Malay landholder with a lease in this manner was defeated by the expense of survey and preparation of title. The laying out of towns, the survey of roads, large agricultural blocks and mining leases, all took precedence of Malay smallholdings, and the majority of these were held on permits and certificates of title in anticipation of survey, while much land was occupied without being registered or paying any rent at all.[3]

---

[1] Reports on Land Taxation in the Native States, enclosed in Smith to Knutsford, 405 of 28 October 1891, CO 273/176.

[2] The Selangor regulations were promulgated in 1882; the revised Perak regulations in 1885; the Negri Sembilan regulations in 1887, and the Pahang regulations in 1889 (*SSGG*, 17 November 1882, 10 July 1885, 14 October 1887 and 27 January 1890). The Sungei Ujong regulations, passed in 1887, are reproduced in the Sungei Ujong State Council Minutes, CO 474/1.

[3] Maxwell wrote in his *AR* Selangor, 1890, that 250 out of 585 holdings in the mukim of Setapak in the Kuala Lumpur district were occupied without any

Maxwell was appointed Commissioner of Lands Titles, Straits Settlements, in 1882, and for the next five years was engaged on the reorganization of the Lands Department of the Colony. His investigations convinced him that the confusion into which the land administration had fallen was a result of applying formal English instruments of title, based on expensive surveys, to all types of land in occupation, including native smallholdings. In a series of ordinances passed in 1886, he brought about a reform of the Malacca land system, establishing new regulations for land occupied by Malay smallholders. Such land was deemed to be land held under customary tenure; continuous occupation over ten years entitled the occupant to the status of 'customary land-holder' and to a permanent, heritable and transferable right of use and occupancy, subject to cultivation and payment of assessment. The land was demarcated by native agency, and entered in a 'mukim register' which served as a revenue record, and in effect though not intention, as a record of title. The revenue obligation of the occupant consisted of an assessment based on the value of the crop. It was this tenure which he introduced into Selangor in 1891 and prescribed as suitable for the other Malay states.

The features to which Maxwell drew particular attention were the recognition of right by occupation, the replacement of survey by demarcation, and the substitution of periodical assessment for a fixed rent. The survey of every smallholding was so clearly beyond the resources of the government (and of the smallholder) that Maxwell's point on this was quickly conceded; by 1893, smallholdings in Perak were being demarcated by native agency as part of a permanent settlement, and the mukim register system had been introduced.[1] The point of controversy, debated by Swettenham and Maxwell through many years and many hundred pages of repetitious and arid argument,[2] concerned Maxwell's proposal to replace a fixed rent by periodical assessment. Maxwell argued from the history of the Colony that fixed rents bore no relation to land or crop values, and meant the permanent alienation of land for nominal sums, to

---

written authority. In 1893, Swettenham confessed the difficulty of applying the 1885 Perak regulations to smallholdings. Resident, Perak, to CS, 4 August 1893, in W.E. Maxwell, *Memorandum on the Introduction of a Land Code in the Native States in the Malay Peninsula*, Singapore, 1894, pp. 59–60. See ibid. p. vi for further information relating to Selangor.

[1] *AR* Perak, 1895.
[2] Maxwell, op. cit. *passim*.

the great loss of the revenue. The principle of rent revision was not introduced into Selangor in respect of grants of town lands, or country lands over 100 acres, which were presumed to bear export crops liable to duty; but it was applied to agricultural grants of less than 100 acres and to lands under customary tenure.[1]

Maxwell argued in defence of his proposals that the system of tithing the crop was traditional in Malaya as in other Muslim countries. Swettenham objected, with strong support from his fellow officials,[2] that whatever the Muslim prescription, payment of land revenue in the form of a tithe (or in any other form) was not general Malay practice, at least in the protected states. But the main argument was one of policy. For Swettenham and his supporters, the chief need was to attract population, whose productive efforts would be an asset to the state and produce indirect revenue; while Maxwell took a directly opposed view of the desirability of Malay settlement, holding that the Malay cultivator was a revenue liability and that a policy of low fixed rents and rent remissions to attract Malay settlement would permanently impoverish the state.

In 1897, two years after Maxwell's departure from Malaya, a Land Enactment repealing existing legislation was passed in all four states. Though it was framed at Swettenham's instance, it was a qualified victory for Maxwell, in that it provided a simplified form of tenure for smallholders, free of premium and the costs of survey and preparation of title. It made no explicit distinctions between the land under 'customary tenure' and other agricultural land (these distinctions had in any case been rendered meaningless by amendments to the Selangor Code opening land under 'customary tenure' to non-Malays) but it provided for the tenure of agricultural land under 100 acres (a category which included smallholdings) under extract from the mukim register after demarcation in lieu of survey. It made a grudging concession, also, to the principle of periodical revision of rent by enabling the Resident to declare future alienations liable to such revision after a minimum period of thirty years.

The effect of the land legislation of the protected states, so far as it concerned land in Malay occupation, was to provide a simplified form of tenure free of the cost of premium, survey and preparation of title, but to make such land transmissible in the same way as land

---

[1] Selangor Regulation III of 1891, *SGG*, 10 July 1891.

[2] Maxwell's only influential supporter in this controversy was the CS, Dickson, who died in December 1891.

held by grant. This had not been Maxwell's intention. He had thought to confine the 'customary tenure' and its special provisions to land held by Muslims—in effect, Malays—and to make such land transmissible to Muslims only. The purpose of these restrictions was to prevent Malay smallholders from charging their land to Chinese and Indian money-lenders and traders as security for advances; though it was open to Malays who wished their land to be readily marketable, to take out land grants. These restrictions were in the original Selangor Land Code (Regulation III of 1891) but in 1892, after Maxwell had left the state, amending regulations were passed throwing open the customary tenure to non-Malays, with the express purpose of making the land more marketable. The 'customary tenure' thus became simply an alternative method of holding agricultural blocks of under 100 acres.

While the state governments hoped for some extension of commercial agriculture through the enterprise of smallholders, it was to estate agriculture that they looked for a significant development of commercially valuable crops. Loans were made to pioneer planters, roads cut to serve outlying estates, and taxation of export crops postponed. Land was offered on especially liberal terms; in Selangor and Perak, regulations passed in 1884 and 1885 offered land for gambier and pepper cultivation without premium and free of rent for the first three years of occupation (in Sungei Ujong, similar conditions prevailed until 1891, when rent began to be charged from the first year of occupation). Special regulations and notices were passed from time to time, offering land on especially liberal terms,[1] and concessions going beyond the regulations were offered to individual applicants;[2] liberal extensions of time were allowed for payment of

[1] Special regulations for the leasing of waste land were passed in Perak and Selangor in 1879, offering land for 999 years on payment of $1 premium and 10¢ an acre quit rent, or $2 premium and no rent. In the 1890s, notifications issued by the Perak and Negri Sembilan governments offered land to a limited number of applicants without premium and free of rent for the first two years. *PGG*, 5 June and 11 September 1891; *SGG*, 9 June 1893.

[2] E.g., in Selangor Yap Ah Loy was allowed a concession of 12,000 acres for tapioca planting free of premium and quit rent; Syed Zin on behalf of the Selangor Padi and Sago Company was granted 6,000 acres free of rent; Messrs. Hill and Rathborne obtained a concession of 12,000 acres in Perak at 50¢ an acre and no rent, and leases totalling 8,000 acres in Selangor, mostly free of rent (Kuala Lumpur leases 518, 519, 673, 701, 706 and 815 and Klang lease 130, Registry of Titles, Selangor State Secretariat, Kuala Lumpur; Memoranda on Alienation of Land in Perak, by G. Hose, 8 November 1895, and J.A. Swettenham, 17 March 1896,

premia and rents and these were sometimes waived altogether; cultivation conditions were not strictly enforced.

Agricultural exports did not begin to be significant items of trade till about 1888, and then did not approach tin exports in importance; still, their value in proportion to total exports increased steadily, and by 1895, commercial agriculture was no longer a negligible factor in the economy of the states.[1] The chief commercial crops were sugar, gambier and pepper, coffee, tapioca, coconuts and areca nuts.[2] The last two were traditional Malay cultivations, planted for the most part on smallholdings; though there were some Malay plantations of 100 acres or more in the Klang and Kuala Langat districts, growing areca nuts and coconuts among other crops. Sugar, gambier, pepper, tapioca and coffee were estate crops, cultivated commercially by Chinese or Europeans, though some successful planting of coffee was carried out on Malay estates in the Klang district, and a little pepper was grown on smallholdings throughout the western states.

Gambier and pepper had been grown by Chinese in Singapore and Johore since the 1820's and 1830's. The two crops were generally

in CO 273/213). In 1895 the area of European estates in Selangor amounted to 38,642 acres, of which 5,396 were cultivated, as against 40,000 acres held under 'customary tenure'. *AR* Selangor, 1895.

[1] A table showing tin and agricultural exports in relation to total exports for the years 1890 and 1895 is given below. The chief products were areca nuts, coconuts (including coconut oil and copra) coffee, indigo, gambier and pepper, sago, tobacco and tapioca. Exports of rice and padi are not included as the states, on balance, were rice importers. Amounts are given in dollars.

1890	Agricultural exports	Tin and tin ore exports	Total exports
Perak	415,527	7,605,668	9,985,713
Selangor	134,262	5,423,449	6,467,564
Sungei Ujong†	313,521	819,662	1,148,816
Negri Sembilan	no figures		
Pahang	no figures		
1895			
Perak	916,583	13,712,718	15,596,225
Selangor	492,216	12,774,821	13,955,803
Sungei Ujong	571,167	709,086	1,295,464
Negri Sembilan	no figures		
Pahang	10,381	517,867*	775,313

Source: Appendixes to *AR*.
†Excludes Jelebu,   *Includes gold exports.

[2] The account which follows is taken largely from annual state and district reports, and from estate lists in the *Singapore and Straits Directory*. I am indebted also to J. C. Jackson, *Planters and Speculators: Chinese and European Enterprise in Malaya, 1786–1921*, Kuala Lumpur, 1968, for a full and valuable study of the subject.

cultivated in association, since they were complementary in their use of labour and in other ways. Gambier had been grown by Chinese in Sungei Ujong before the arrival of a Resident, and was subsequently encouraged in Sungei Ujong and Selangor by large concessions and special regulations. (The two largest concessions in active production in the protected states throughout this period were blocks totalling some 25,000 acres on both sides of the Selangor-Sungei Ujong boundary, employing 2,000 Chinese labourers, leased to a single Chinese gambier and pepper planter.) European coffee planters grew pepper experimentally on their estates in Perak, Selangor and Sungei Ujong, and in the 1890's, Malays began to grow it on smallholdings in the western states, but the crop, in association with gambier, remained predominantly a Chinese interest.

Large-scale tapioca cultivation was introduced into the protected states by Chinese from Malacca. In the late 1870's and early 1880's, it expanded into Sungei Ujong and the old Negri Sembilan states, principally Rembau; most of the area taken up for this crop in Negri Sembilan by 1891—some 76,800 acres—had been granted before protection. Under protection, a large Chinese tapioca estate was opened in Selangor in the late 1880's, but Negri Sembilan continued to be the main centre of production.

The Chinese were also pioneers in the large-scale cultivation of sugar, first in Province Wellesley and then in the neighbouring Krian district of north Perak. In 1888 there were twenty-one Chinese sugar estates in Krian, occupying 16,414 acres; of this area, half had been taken up between 1877 and 1880. By 1894, 31,000 acres had been alienated for sugar planting, 25,000 acres to Chinese. A European company entered the industry in Perak in 1882, opening the Gula estate; this became the largest and most important of the Krian estates, but until 1893 it was the only European sugar undertaking in Perak.[1]

Coffee was introduced by Europeans into Perak, Selangor and Sungei Ujong between 1879 and 1881, and continued to be largely a European interest. It was developed by Ceylon planters seeking new fields when the coffee industry of Ceylon was threatened by the spread of a fungus disease. Till the late 1880's, the chief European pioneers were Hill and Rathborne, a firm of planters and contractors with large grants in the three states; though some planting was also

[1] *AR* Krian, 1888, *PGG*, 8 February 1889.

carried out by the Perak Government on its experimental station near Kuala Kangsar, and Malays successfully introduced the cultivation into the coastal lowlands of Selangor, in the Klang district. During the 1880's however, the acreage under coffee was insignificant, and coffee planters depended for a living on other activities; Hill and Rathborne, for example, were important road contractors in the western states, and were indeed employed as contractors for bridle tracks to their own estates. After 1890, estate cultivation of coffee developed rapidly, partly because of rising prices, partly because of the easing of the labour situation with the growth of Indian immigration (while the tapioca, gambier and sugar estates mainly employed Chinese, coffee depended almost entirely on Indian labour). In 1890 there were about 1,200 acres under coffee in all the states, 550 in Hill and Rathborne's plantations; in 1895 there were 5,396 acres cleared and planted in European estates in Selangor, mostly under coffee.[1]

Tapioca, gambier and pepper, particularly the first two, rapidly exhausted the soil, and the fuel required for processing denuded the forest. The Chinese preferred to break new ground sooner than incur the expense of maintaining fertility by manuring, so that these were essentially shifting cultivations, leaving a waste of abandoned and exhausted land. Tapioca was particularly destructive since no more than four crops at most (more often only three) could be taken in succession from the same piece of ground. Coffee by contrast was a permanent crop; it was a means of developing the uninhabited highlands, and of attracting European capital, management and technical skill—all objects much desired by the state governments. In Perak, the advertisements of special terms to pioneers appealed directly to coffee and tea planters even though the concessions were not specifically limited to these crops; and coffee was not only lightly taxed in respect of premium and rent, but paid no duty in Perak and Selangor till 1894. But though coffee was perhaps favoured by a slight margin, agricultural policy generally was still encouraging and permissive in respect of all export crops.[2] The interest shown in coffee both by

[1] Return of Liberian coffee crops for estates owned by Hill and Rathborne, showing acreages and planting dates, *SGG*, 10 June 1892 and *PGG*, 16 August 1895; *Singapore and Straits Directory*, 1890, pp. 386–408; List of Coffee Estates owned by Europeans in Selangor, Appendix H, *AR* Selangor, 1895.

[2] Except in Negri Sembilan, which had the largest acreage alienated for agriculture in proportion to total area. Gambier was discouraged (*AR* Negri Sembilan, 1888 and 1894) and restrictions placed on tapioca planting. An Order in

estate owners and small-holders in the 1890's had more to do with price rises than government encouragement; the Resident of Selangor, while noting the supremacy of coffee in his annual reports for 1894 and 1895, remarked that there was a whole range of tropical products which flourished in the state, and that market fluctuations might at any time cause a change in the relative areas under each crop.

As it happened, the advent of rubber at the end of the century banished interest in all other crops, and sugar, tapioca, gambier, pepper and coffee all gave way to it. These enterprises had more than a temporary value, however. In the generation since the beginning of protection, the foundations of an export agriculture had been laid by a generous land policy, and by the development of communications and the establishment of an efficient administration; and these facilities had attracted capital, management and labour to agricultural enterprise, despite competition from mining. When the opportunity came for a really profitable development, the states were ready for it.

The encouragement of European agriculture was one important policy objective. Another, equally important, was the encouragement of European mining; not for political reasons especially, though there was some favouring of Europeans as such, but because it was hoped that their entry into the industry would lead to the modernization of techniques, both in the European and Chinese sectors.[1] In the 1870's, European interest did not go beyond company-mongering, which the British authorities, anxious for the productive development of the industry, were at pains to discourage; in 1874 for example, an attempt to secure the approval of the Secretary of State for a ten-year monopoly of all tin mining and prospecting on unoccupied land in Selangor, failed in its object and the concession was never ratified. From the 1880's, however, *bona fide* applications from Europeans for mining land were encouragingly received, and large blocks on especially favourable terms were granted, on the understanding that the mines would be scientifically worked and the tin smelted in the

Council of 1892 declared that only two crops might be taken from the same piece of ground, so that the forest might still have a chance to renew itself, instead of giving way altogether to the rank grass (*imperata cylindrica* or *lalang*) which took hold of exhausted soil.

[1] For a full account of the development of tin mining in nineteenth-century Malaya, see Wong Lin Ken, op. cit.

state.[1] The demands of the European companies tried the patience of officials, who compared them unflatteringly with Chinese mining enterprises. In contrast with Chinese mining leases in Selangor, which were seldom for more than fifty acres,[2] European concessionaires were allowed to select up to 500 acres in one block, and were, predictably, unable to fulfil the conditions requiring the working of a proportionate area each year. Applications for concessions were usually accompanied by requests for tax remissions, sometimes without justification, as when a company formed to buy the Ampang mine of the Capitan China of Selangor, a rich mine in full working order, applied (unsuccessfully) for a remission of $1 per bhara on all tin produced.

During the 1880's and 1890's, the performance of European companies was disappointing, especially in Selangor. Of the ventures begun there in the early 1880's, only one was still working in 1885. The Ampang mine bought from the Capitan China in 1884 was resold to him the next year for a fraction of the sale price, having produced, on a monthly average, less than one-third the output of the mine in 1883.[3] In Perak, the European companies were more successful; in 1890, four companies (apart from two lode mining companies which soon failed) were still in operation, and one of them— the Société des Étains de Kinta—introduced steam fans and machinery for pumping and washing the tin. But the mines worked principally on the tribute system—that is, they were let to Chinese in return for a proportion of the tin raised. This ensured their profitable working, but not the technical advances which were expected from European companies.

The early failures of the European companies resulted largely from the misuse of capital and the faulty application of technical knowledge. While Chinese sank trial pits to determine the richness of the ground, Europeans depended on boring tools which might carry

[1] E.g., in Selangor, two concessions of 1,000 acres each were granted in 1882, with rebates of $2 per bhara tin duty (about 20 per cent. on prevailing rates) and two more concessions of 500 acres each were granted in 1883 and 1884, with rebates of $1 per bhara tin duty. Sel/Sec. 142/82, 589/82, 196/84 and 1024/84.

[2] Of 365 mining leases issued to Chinese in Selangor between 1883 and 1887, about half were for twenty-five acres or less. There were six over 100 acres, and thirty between fifty and 100 acres. The largest was for 342 acres, and the minimum work force stipulated was 1,200 men. Kuala Lumpur Mining Lease Book I, Registry of Titles, Selangor State Secretariat, Kuala Lumpur.

[3] Return of tin on which duty is paid by European mining companies, 1884, Sel/Sec. 2229/84.

down with them particles of ore and so show traces of tin through a much greater depth than the actual ore-bearing stratum. There was heavy outlay on plant, buildings, and housing for European staff before operations were even begun, and it might then be found that the land selected was useless for alluvial mining. The Chinese system on the other hand, using cheap, simple equipment and a co-operative plan of working, was flexible and mobile and involved much less risk for the advancer.[1] In addition, Chinese entrepreneurs had advantages denied to Europeans; the revenue farms enabled them to accumulate capital for investment in the mines, and they profited from their role as suppliers of provisions (particularly opium) to miners. The European miners also found Chinese labour difficult to obtain or control, since Chinese disliked working for any but their own countrymen, and neither Malays nor Indians were satisfactory substitutes.

There were, however, two significant technical advances achieved at this time as a result of European participation.[2] One was the introduction of hydraulic mining in Perak in the mid-1890's. This process, whereby the tin sand was disintegrated by a jet of water at high pressure, provided a profitable entry for Europeans into the industry, since it required a heavier capital outlay than most Chinese advancers were able or willing to provide; it required little labour, and could be made to pay on poor ground which could not be economically worked with the labour-intensive Chinese methods. The other was the introduction of modern smelting methods by the opening of coal furnaces, first in Telok Anson in Perak and then on Pulau Brani off Singapore, by the firm of Sword and Muhlinghaus (converted in 1887 into the Straits Trading Company). In 1886, the firm was given the exclusive right of exporting tin ore from Selangor and Sungei Ujong for smelting in their works. The monopoly ran for eight years in Selangor and three years in Sungei Ujong, and was accompanied by fiscal concessions; while the metallic content of the ores averaged 70 per cent., the company paid export duty in Selangor only on 60 per cent. (and in the last three years of its monopoly, on 65 per cent.). Restrictions in Perak and Selangor on the use of charcoal furnaces burning hard woods, imposed in the interests of conservation, also benefited the company's operations in that they raised the cost of Chinese smelting. By 1895, the company was smelting about 30 per

[1] F.A. Swettenham, *About Perak*, Singapore, 1893, p. 34.
[2] Wong Lin Ken, op. cit. 150–3; 160–7.

cent. of the tin exports of Perak and Selangor. On the whole, the competition offered to Chinese smelters had a beneficial effect on the mining industry. The company offered cash payment and fair prices after accurate assays, thus helping to end the delays in wage settlement and the consequent wage-indebtedness associated with the traditional smelting cycle. Further, by offering cash advances to the smaller mines, it freed them of the need to obtain supplies from advancers at exorbitant rates of interest.

The only important technical innovation generally accepted by Chinese at this time was the portable steam pump for draining the mines. It was first introduced into the protected states by Low in 1877, and after its usefulness had been demonstrated in Ah Kwee's mines, pumps were installed in the larger mines in Perak, Selangor and Sungei Ujong, enabling work to be carried on at deeper levels, and overcoming the problem of flooding which had periodically immobilized the mines. Apart from this, Chinese mining continued with little change, its limitations and wastefulness offset by the abundance of rich surface soil which could be profitably worked by traditional methods. While these rich, accessible deposits were readily available, the Chinese maintained their grip on the industry. It was only when the surface deposits became impoverished in the period between the end of the century and the First World War, that Western mining, with its superior technology and capital resources, came into its own.

The first economic priorities were the provision of labour, communications, and institutional arrangements for mining and estate agriculture; but the establishment of a large self-employed agricultural population (as distinct from plantation labour) was also considered desirable, and the encouragement of Malay agriculture and settlement had a place, though a minor one, in the plans and allocations of the state governments. The staple food and chief subsistence crop of the Malays was rice. Rice was grown wherever Malays settled; in the swamps of Krian, Lower Perak and Kuala Selangor, and along the coasts and river valleys; it was grown in hill clearings or ladangs, usually abandoned after two or three years of cropping, and in inundated fields, or bendangs. The bendangs were usually permanent, but in the Kuala Langat district of Selangor, there was a form of cultivation to which the district officer gave the name of 'wet ladang', to signify shifting cultivation of wet rice, in swamps which were only partially cleared, and were abandoned after a period in the same way as dry-rice clearings.[1] Skills, equipment, and productivity varied greatly from place to place. In general, immigrants from Sumatra, Kelantan, Kedah and Patani were reputed to be more systematic and skilful cultivators than indigenous Malays. Among the latter, the most popular cultivation was hill rice, which required no ploughing, irrigation or manuring, and could be grown on partially cleared land.[2] For wet rice cultivation, plough animals (buffaloes and oxen) were in general use, particularly in the old-established settlements in the Perak and Pahang river valleys and in Negri Sembilan; they were less common in the newly settled districts of Krian and Lower Perak. It is unlikely that they were in general use in Selangor, except perhaps in Ulu Langat. In Kuala Selangor, they had become a memory. According to local tradition, this district had produced a large surplus of rice in earlier times, and 'all the planters' then possessed buffaloes, but years of war and neglect had wiped out the herds, and they had to be reintroduced in the 1890's by purchase of animals from Jelebu.[3]

Some irrigation was practised, but it was by no means general or popular, especially among the indigenous Malays of Perak, Selangor and Pahang. The Resident of Pahang wrote in his annual report for 1891 that although the padi-swamps were for the most part irrigated by artificial means, Kelantan Malays were often hired to dig the irrigation trenches, as the Pahang Malays were too lazy to do it themselves. In Selangor, the only district where irrigation appears to have been systematically practised was Ulu Langat, then the major rice-producing area of the state, settled mainly by Sumatrans. In Perak, irrigation works had been constructed by district chiefs in former times,[4] and large works were constructed by the wealthy Kinta chiefs in the 1890's, but little is heard of such activities under British rule. In 1880, when a proposal was put to the State Council to construct an irrigation canal 4,000 yards long in the Kuala Kangsar mukims

[1] For descriptions of padi-planting in Selangor, see reports and minutes on Sel/Sec. 722/91, 108A/92, 261/92 and 513/92; Kuala Selangor monthly report for August 1892, *SGG*, 23 September 1892. See also *AR* Pahang, 1891 and description of padi-planting in Kuala Kangsar district, Kuala Kangsar monthly report for April 1894, *PGG*, 25 May 1894.

[2] *AR* Kuala Langat, 1891, *SGG*, 2 September 1892; *AR* Pahang, 1891.

[3] *AR* Kuala Selangor, 1892 and 1893, SGG, 21 July 1893 and 25 May 1894.

[4] The Mentri had made an irrigation channel from Matang to the sixth mile on the Kuala Kangsar road; it had become overgrown with jungle, but was cleared and repaired by the district officer, Matang, in the 1890's. Matang monthly report for May 1894, *PGG*, 17 August 1894.

of Kampong Gajah and Pasir Panjang, it was thought that Javanese might have to be employed to undertake the work.[1] Sumatrans and Banjarese in the Kinta and Krian districts made dams and canals in the 1890's, bringing many hundreds of acres under cultivation, but in the Kuala Kangsar mukims inhabited by Perak Malays, there was little attempt at irrigation.[2]

The reports on padi cultivation are a dismal tale of poor harvests, relieved occasionally by bumper crops which clearly owed more to good luck than good management. The chief cause of failure was unfavourable weather, from which irrigation clearly gave insufficient protection; any climatic irregularity might result in a damaged or ruined crop. The system of synchronized planting under the direction of penghulus existed only in memory and was not revived until the 1890's; and without simultaneous clearing and burning, insect pests and vermin flourished. Between 1884 and 1889, Krian had a succession of bad harvests; in 1889 the people of Negri Sembilan had to buy rice for half the year because of a poor harvest, and in 1891 the Resident reported the complete failure of the crop. The rice crop in Pahang was reported to be scanty and insufficient even in good seasons, because of inferior seed and insufficient attention to irrigation. The district officer of Kuala Selangor reported that there were only about fifty acres of healthy padi in his district at the end of 1890; in 1891 the rice crop failed over most of the state.[3]

Despite these repeated failures, no hardship was reported. Malay subsistence cultivation appears to have been sufficiently flexible to provide alternatives to rice, chiefly tapioca, maize and plantains;[4] the traditional sources of income—mining and the collection of jungle produce—continued to provide money which might be used to buy imported rice. Economic growth under the new régime provided a whole range of employment opportunities of the kind which Malays found congenial; though they refused to commit themselves to sustained wage labour, they welcomed casual work over short periods, and the extensive clearing and construction programmes provided this. The greater part of the road and railway construction was car-

---

[1] *PCM*, 25 February 1880.

[2] See especially Kuala Kangsar monthly report for April 1894, *PGG*, 25 May 1894.

[3] Krian monthly report for January 1889, *PGG*, 22 February 1889; *AR* Pahang, 1890; *AR* Kuala Selangor, 1890, *SGG*, 12 June 1891; *AR* Selangor, 1891.

[4] *AR* Negri Sembilan, 1891; *AR* Kuala Selangor, 1890 and 1891, *SGG*, 24 July 1891 and 2 September 1892.

ried out by Chinese and Indians, but the clearing of rivers and the construction and repair of bridle paths were frequently allocated to small Malay contractors working with local Malay labour; it was a matter of policy to provide this employment for Malays in the districts, especially to assist new settlers.[1] Malay labour was in demand to clear land for mines and plantations:[2] the construction of kongsi-houses and mine equipment provided a welcome market for bamboo, rattans and atap;[3] and the fast-growing townships used quantities of timber, cut and rafted by Malays to Chinese sawmills.

Improved communications and the growth of mining and urban populations provided accessible markets for foodstuffs, and while much of the rice consumed was imported, and the vegetables supplied by Chinese market-gardeners, Malay subsistence farmers also found an outlet for their surplus produce. The bulk of the population in Kuala Selangor depended not on rice but on coconuts and fishing; the latter flourished partly because there was now security from pirates, and partly because the construction of the Klang-Kuala Lumpur railway made it possible to supply fish packed in ice to the Kuala Lumpur market. Taiping in 1893 imported $18,000 worth of vegetables and $30,000 worth of fish from the Matang district. The sale of fruit, especially durians, was an important supplement to income; in the 1890's, the land rent for the Kuala Kangsar district was paid for out of the sale of durians.[4]

Undoubtedly, the encroachments of mining played some part in discouraging rice culture. Mines competed for water with padi *sawah* (irrigated fields); mine tailings silted up streams and washed over

---

[1] E.g., Kuala Selangor monthly reports for March and August 1895, *SGG*, 26 April and 27 September 1895; Ulu Selangor monthly report for May 1895, *SGG*, 5 July 1895; Lower Perak monthly report for August 1891, *PGG*, 25 September 1891; Kuala Kangsar monthly report for November 1893, *PGG*, 2 February 1894.

[2] The district officer of Ulu Langat reported in 1893 that the Chinese were offering $8 an orlong (about one and a third acres) to clear mining land, and that in one district, Sungei Lui, 600 orlongs had been given out in three months and were waiting to be cleared. The Malays however were holding out for more money. Ulu Langat monthly report for March 1893, *SGG*, 28 April 1893.

[3] E.g., *AR* Selangor, 1885.

[4] The district officer reported that thirty or forty carts left the Kota Lama mukims daily during the season, each loaded with 500 durians which sold for 10¢ each in Ipoh. There were two or three other mukims in the district which grew as much fruit as Kota Lama (Kuala Kangsar monthly report for August 1895, *PGG*, 27 September 1895). The export of fruit from Lower Perak during the 1890 season was worth $9,035 (Lower Perak monthly report for January 1891, *PGG*, 27 February 1891). Negri Sembilan exported cart loads of fruit to Malacca. *AR* Negri Sembilan, 1887.

agricultural holdings, and land under cultivation, known to contain tin, was bought up by Chinese miners, or resumed under compensation for mining. The advance of mining at whatever cost to existing cultivation was considered by some officials to be a positive good, by most others a regrettable necessity which could however be tempered by payment of compensation,[1] or by the grant of equivalent areas of land. Mining encroachment was resented by indigenous Malay agriculturists, and no compensation scheme appeared to work satisfactorily; a lump sum payment was soon spent, leaving the cultivator with neither money nor land, while payment of royalties from the mine was only profitable if the mine was successful.[2] But though mining encroachment caused hardship to some, it opened up economic opportunities for others. The immigrant Malays of Ulu Langat left the district when mining fell off, and with it the market for jungle produce; the Beranang padi-planters, warned that the advent of Chinese miners would interfere with the water supply for their sawah, said that they preferred to have Chinese mining going on than be able to plant padi, for with the advent of mining they expected work in supplying atap, rotan and other jungle produce.[3] The district officer for Kinta remarked in 1889 that there were not ten well-cultivated acres of rice in his district, because the Malay cultivators preferred to grow plantains which they sold at high prices to the Chinese.[4]

A criticism commonly made of colonial rule in Malaya—that it tried to force Malays into rice-growing and excluded them from commercial crops—is certainly not true of this time. The district officers in charge of large rice-growing areas, and the Residents of the largely Malay-populated states of Pahang and Negri Sembilan, were concerned about rice-growing, not because they had any sentimental preference for rice as the traditional and proper crop for Malays, but

[1] E.g., Swettenham, in correspondence with the district officer of Ulu Langat, expressed his dislike of the alienation of good padi land for mining, but was prepared to sanction it on payment of heavy compensation (Sel/Sec. 509/88). An interesting discussion of the economic and social consequences of such alienation is to be found in an argument between the Officer-in-Charge, Sungei Ujong, and the Collector and Magistrate, Jelebu, on Sel/Sec. Sungei Ujong 11A/1894.

[2] AR Sungei Ujong, 1893.

[3] Ulu Langat monthly report for March 1895, SGG, 26 April 1895.

[4] AR Kinta, 1889, PGG, 4 April 1890. Of 7,400 adult male Malays in Kinta, including natives of the Archipelago, 3,322 described themselves as cultivators, and of these, 1,160 were padi-planters. There were 1,532 miners. Census of Perak, 1891.

because rice happened to be the chief cultivation and the staple food of the people in their care. They had no prejudice against cultivation of commercial crops; indeed, the encouragement of such crops was an important part of their settlement work. But they could provide no insurance against a fall in the market, and they had experience of the distress which resulted from a dependence on production for the market, to the exclusion of agriculture for subsistence.[1] Again, access to the market was generally in the hands of Chinese middlemen, and the system of advances, combined with the improvidence of Malays themselves, led sometimes to perpetual debt.[2] Also, the presence of large rice-consuming populations in the mining areas and on the sugar, tapioca and gambier plantations, promised a sure market for the cultivation which lay nearest to the hands of Malays.

It was recognized, however, that rice-growing was not nearly as profitable as other enterprises open to Malays. In 1894 Treacher, then Resident of Selangor, remarking that Liberian coffee planting was coming into great favour with Malays, calculated that an acre of rice (assuming a harvest of 400 gantangs to the acre) would be worth about $30, while an acre of coffee would be worth about $150 to $200 at the high prices then prevailing.[3] The district officer of Ulu Selangor wrote in 1894, 'It seems to me hopeless to look forward to any large increase in the area of land cultivated for padi, where such lands yield so small a return in cash for the labour expended on them'.[1] If rice was not especially profitable to the cultivator, neither

---

[1] See, e.g., Lower Perak monthly report for September 1891, *PGG,* 23 October 1891, for effect of fall in the price of atap on the economy of the Malays.

[2] Clifford wrote of gutta collection as the curse of the Pahang Malays. They were given advances on collections, squandered them on expensive imported rice, put off the search for gutta, neglected their fields, and when the time of reckoning came, were without rice, money or gutta. *AR* Pahang, 1894.

[3] Resident's tour of Ulu Langat, *SGG,* 23 February 1894. Lister gives 400 gantangs as the average return on a holding (*AR* Negri Sembilan, 1892). In 1891, the district officer of Ulu Langat, measuring the crop in ten sawahs, found that the average yield was a little over 500 gantangs to the acre—a good crop, he thought (Ulu Langat monthly report for February 1891, *SGG,* 3 April 1891). The district officer for Kuala Selangor, reporting on the 1894 crop, wrote that in the mukim of Jeram, the average size of the rice plot was an acre and a half; the harvest per acre was 215 gantangs, giving a 35-fold return on seed. The mukim of Api Api, where the planters were settlers from Kelantan, gave a similar return per acre, though a better yield in proportion to seed. He considered these 'excellent crops'—in contrast no doubt with previous harvests. Kuala Selangor monthly reports for May and June 1894, *SGG,* 22 June and 20 July 1894. The gantang is a measure of capacity. One gantang of padi would equal about six pounds.

[1] *AR* Ulu Selangor, 1894, *SGG,* 10 May 1895.

did it profit the state; it paid only a small land rent, while a commercial crop was liable to export duty as well. The state governments had therefore no particular reason to favour rice-growing in preference to other forms of agriculture, and in general the encouragement of rice was only one part—and not the most important—of the agricultural extension work of the district officers. There were no rice cultivation conditions on land alienated to Malays; in Selangor, land under customary tenure, originally under rice, was planted with coffee in perfect freedom from restriction. Remission of land rent on newly cleared land applied to plantations of commercial crops as well as to rice. Assistance to settlers was given without distinction between subsistence and commercial agriculture, and individual Malay entrepreneurs were allowed large loans for the cultivation of commercial crops. Plants of commercial value were distributed to Malays from government nurseries, some of them maintained by district officers on their own initiative; for example, in his annual report for 1889, the district officer of Batang Padang stated that he had distributed over 30,000 Liberian coffee plants to Malays living in his district.[2]

In the 1890's attention began to be directed to the question of increasing the rice supply of the Colony and the Malay states. In 1891, a circular from the Colonial Secretary to the Residents called for reports on the land available, and the steps necessary to get it opened up, and asked that the matter be brought before the State Councils.[3] Government-assisted irrigation works were constructed in a number of districts, and reports prepared for large schemes in Krian and Kuala Selangor.[4] Synchronized planting under the direction of penghulus—a procedure long fallen into disuse in Perak and Selangor —was re-introduced in an attempt to minimize loss through disease and pests. The interest in increased rice output appears to have derived from strategic rather than economic considerations; the government of the Straits Settlements was at the time engaged in a prolonged correspondence with the Secretary of State on the subject of the local defences, and the food supply of the peninsula was an

[2] *AR* Batang Padang, 1889, *PGG*, 18 April 1890.
[3] CS to Residents, 18 December 1891, SS Legislative Council Paper 6 of 1893.
[4] In 1895, work began on a scheme for the irrigation of 50,000 acres in Krian, at a cost of $350,000 (*AR* Perak, 1894 and 1895). In 1896, a survey was made of a similar scheme in Kuala Selangor, but the scheme was not adopted, as the cost was considered excessive in relation to the revenue which could be expected. *AR* Selangor, 1896.

important subject of discussion. Improvement of output by better cultivation and irrigation would no doubt benefit the Malays as the chief rice-growers, and the officers in charge of rice districts welcomed an interest which they had tried in vain to arouse for many years; but on the whole, officials were unenthusiastic about the profitability of rice-growing, and sceptical about the possibility of achieving a substantial increase with the existing Malay population.[1] Encouragement of rice culture was still regarded as an experiment in agricultural development, one of the many under trial, and did not exclude support of commercial cultivation by Malays.

The encouragement of agriculture and new settlement (the two were closely related) was effected by rent remissions for the first year of occupation or longer, by assistance with employment and seed, and by small loans. These were made initially to the penghulu or the headman of a settler group for one year or more, without interest, and on the security of his government salary, his land, or a personal guarantee. In Selangor, rent on all agricultural land outside the Kuala Lumpur district was remitted in 1884 for three years, and from that year, $1,000 was placed at the disposal of each district officer, to assist agriculture and settlement. The loans were to be distributed through the penghulus, and were to be spent on providing subsistence for new settlers until they had cleared, planted and harvested their crop.[2] In addition to this vote, special assistance was given to chosen settler colonies, in both Selangor and Perak. The majority of settlers, especially in the mining districts, probably came on their own initiative, attracted by economic opportunities and low taxation, but many settler colonies were directly helped by government, on the initiative of individual district officers. The largest and best known was the colony of Achinese, Banjarese and Kelantanese established at Sitiawan in the Perak Dindings by Denison between 1886 and his

[1] In his *AR* Selangor, 1888, Swettenham had advocated the introduction of Chinese rice-growers, with government assistance if necessary, to increase rice production. In 1892, the district officer of Kuala Langat advocated the introduction of large numbers of Burmese and Siamese for the same purpose. District officer, Kuala Langat, to Government Secretary, 4 January 1892, Sel/Sec. 108A/92.

[2] Minute by Acting Resident of Selangor to Collectors and Magistrates, 25 December 1883, Sel/Sec. 1938/83. See also details of loans, Kuala Langat, and form of bond used, Sel/Sec. 206/84. The amount on this vote in 1895 was $5,000 for the whole state (*AR* Selangor, 1895). In Negri Sembilan, advances amounting to $3,925 in 1888 included 'small loans to native chiefs for good objects, such as opening mines and developing new rice lands'. *AR* Negri Sembilan, 1888.

death in 1893. In 1888 the colony numbered 800, and by 1891, there were about a thousand settlers growing rice, fruit, pepper, patchouli, coconuts and coffee. The incentive offered there (as in Krian in earlier years) was rent remission for three years, and under this system about 5,000 acres were alienated between 1886 and 1891. In some cases, the government also helped with passages and a rice allowance in the early stages of settlement. (The advances to settlers in Sitiawan amounted to $1,300 by 1893, and the total cost of colonization experiments in Lower Perak between 1886 and 1893 was $7,189.) The penghulu was required 'to see that labour equivalent to the advance given is expended on the land, and that the land which is held on security for the advance is enhanced in value to this amount'.[1] Elsewhere in Perak and Selangor, small colonies of a hundred or so families were helped in the same way by rent remissions, subsistence allowances and employment on road construction and river clearing in the early stages of settlement.[2]

The money allocated to district officers for encouraging settlement and cultivation could hardly have gone far,[3] but it was not the only money available to Malays for these purposes. In Selangor, of a total of $34,899 in loans outstanding on 1 January 1889 (much of it lent on authorities dated one, two or three years earlier), $27,499 represented loans to Malays.[4] The purpose of the loans is not stated, and some of it (for example, $1,000 lent to Raja Bot and $720 to Raja Laut) must have been paid simply to extricate important Malays from their perennial financial difficulties; but large sums were lent

[1] AR Lower Perak, 1888 and 1891, PGG, 31 May 1889 and 12 August 1892; Swettenham, Memorandum on Correspondence concerning the Cultivation of Rice in the Protected Malay States, 16 March 1893, PGG, 9 August 1893.

[2] See, e.g., reference to settlement of about a hundred Javanese families at Kelanang in Kuala Langat, AR Kuala Langat, 1889 and 1890, SGG, 11 July 1890 and 10 July 1891; settlement of ninety Kelantanese at Api Api in Kuala Selangor, Kuala Selangor monthly report for April 1893, SGG, 26 May 1893; settlements at Kampong Jawa, Telok Pulai and Kapar in Klang, senior District Officer to Government Secretary, 15 April 1893, SGG, 7 July 1893.

[3] It was estimated that $300 would only help twenty settlers (Collector and Magistrate, Langat, minute of 14 February 1884, Sel/Sec. 206/84). In 1892, 100 settlers in Kuala Selangor received between $10 and $15 each. Kuala Selangor monthly report for August 1892, SGG, 23 September 1892.

[4] Return of loans outstanding on 1 January 1889, Sel/Sec. 598/89. The district accounts are as follows: Kuala Lumpur $9,745 ($4,495 to Malays); Klang $8,705, in three large loans to Malays; Kuala Langat $4,600 ($4,100 to Malays); Ulu Langat $1,535 ($1,485 to Malays); Kuala Selangor $2,389 (all to Malays); Ulu Selangor $7,925 ($6,325 to Malays). Haji Tahir was lent a further $4,000 in 1891 (Sel/Sec. . . . /92).

to individual Malays engaged in mining, trading and agriculture. The largest loan went to Haji Mohammed Tahir, formerly Dato' Dagang of Klang and Kuala Lumpur, agricultural pioneer and small contractor; he was lent $4,000 on the Klang account, and a further $1,000 on the Kuala Langat account in conjunction with Haji Kel Kadir, headman of the Javanese settlers at Kelanang in Kuala Langat. Haji Tahir, 'our most enterprising Malay planter', began planting in the Klang district in 1884; by 1888 when he obtained his government loan, he held about 600 acres of land, planted with indigo, areca nuts, coconuts, fruit and coffee. A return of estates of 100 acres or more in the Klang district in 1894 showed that of 2,786 acres under cultivation, 507 acres belonged to Haji Tahir, and of these, 308 acres were under coffee; the total area planted by Malays was 1,152 acres, under coffee, areca nuts and fruit.[1] Haji Tahir's discovery that Liberian coffee could grow in wet lowlands encouraged both Malays and Europeans to embark on this cultivation and diverted planting interest from Kuala Lumpur to Klang, a development welcomed by the government since it relieved pressure on mining land in the interior.[2] The largest Malay planting enterprise in Perak was that of Syed Musa, penghulu of Chegar Galah in the Kuala Kangsar district. Assisted by a government loan of $8,000, he opened a pepper plantation of sixteen acres, cultivated on a share-cropping basis by Achinese and Javanese labour. Here, as in Klang, the example of a pioneer stimulated Malay enterprise in the district.

The majority of state officials wholeheartedly supported the policy of encouraging settlement and agriculture by rent remissions and judicious loans.[3] Denison spoke for them and repeated their argu-

[1] Notes on the Resident's Tour of the Klang district, *SGG*, 22 June 1894; Return of estate of 100 acres and over, *AR* Klang, 1894, *SGG*, 26 April 1894. Haji Tahir had the second largest area under cultivation, the largest being the Jeang Eng Hin tapioca estate at Batu Tiga. Other Malay entrepreneurs were not so successful. The Selangor Padi and Sago Planting Company Ltd., in which Tengku Zia'u'd-din had an interest, and which obtained an advance of some $1,700 from the government in 1885, was a failure; a sugar and coconut plantation of about 1,000 acres, started by Raja Muda Musa, fell into difficulties after his death. The total number of Malay estates over 100 acres is not known, but apart from Raja Muda Musa's estate, there were probably none outside Klang.

[2] The first export took place in December 1891, and the first repayment was made four years later. *AR* Kuala Kangsar, 1889, 1890 and 1891, *PGG*, 28 March 1890, 14 August 1891 and 26 August 1892; Kuala Kangsar monthly report for December 1891 and September 1895, *PGG*, 29 January 1892 and 25 October 1895.

[3] See, e.g., Swettenham's *AR* Selangor, 1887, and his Memorandum on Cor-

ments when he defended the policy against its critics, pointing out that land was valueless until it had been rendered productive by the labour of immigrants; that the loss of rent to the government in the first three years was amply compensated by the drainage and cultivation of swamp and forest; and that for poor peasants, immigration was a serious speculation, not to be undertaken without some encouragement and help. In a brief history of the Sitiawan settlement, he pointed out that in 1889 and 1890, while he was on leave, the period of rent remission was cut to one year, and only 120 acres were taken up, in contrast with an average of 1,200 acres a year under the system of three-year remissions.[1] The target of these remarks was clearly Maxwell, who was then tightening up land administration in Selangor, and campaigning against fiscal relaxation elsewhere in the states. Maxwell was opposed to any form of concession to settlers; he had 'no faith in colonisation schemes which begin with bribing Malays by advances and loans to take up land and at the end of a few years leave a deficit which has to be written off, while the new Malay community, if any is permanently established, becomes a source of expense to the State in respect of roads and police protection, without making any adequate contribution to the revenue'.[2] Loans, he thought, were meant to be repaid, and the 'infinity of trouble' he had experienced while Resident of Selangor, in recovering loans made by his predecessors, prejudiced him entirely against this form of assistance—at least to Malays; he was more generous in his dealings with European planters, and judging by the length of time these loans were outstanding, his successors must have had as much difficulty in recovering them as he experienced with the loans granted by his predecessors. The senior district officer of Selangor, in a palpable hit at his former superior, contrasted the small advances to Malays with the large sums granted by Maxwell to Europeans. 'When we look at the large advances that have been made to European coffee and pepper planters by the Government, in places within reach of commercial and financial circles where they had all facilities for obtaining the means for starting planting enterprises, the very modest request from Langat in the name of the sons of the soil, without

respondence concerning the Cultivation of Rice in the Protected Malay States, 16 March 1893, *PGG*, 9 August 1893; minute by Treacher, 9 May 1894, Sel/Sec. 194B/94.

[1] *AR* Lower Perak, 1891, *PGG*, 12 August 1892.

[2] Maxwell cited by Swettenham in his Memorandum on Correspondence concerning the Cultivation of Rice in the Protected Malay States, op. cit.

means at hand to beg or borrow except at the hands of the Government, should, I venture to think, receive consideration'.[1] One may sympathize with Maxwell to some extent; the loans *were* difficult to collect, and it must have set him back somewhat to come to Selangor in 1889 and find a large sum of public money in outstanding loans to about seventy-five individuals. At any rate, in 1894 he had the support of a Governor who was a rigid economist and had conventional views about the expenditure of public funds; in reply to an application for permission to lend more money to Kelantan settlers in Kuala Selangor, Mitchell refused, saying, 'As at present advised, I decline to authorize advances to agriculturists'.[2] A return of outstanding loans on 30 June 1896 shows how the pattern of lending had changed; of $43,071 lent to individuals, $21,000 was lent to three European planters ($15,000 in loans dating from 1890 and 1891) and the rest mostly to Chinese shop-keepers at high rates of interest to enable them to erect brick houses in the towns.[3]

The British authorities were economic pragmatists, bent on furthering the exploitation, by whatever race or nationality, of the fine property that fell to them to administer. But the emphasis on development meant the distribution of assistance on the basis not only of present performance but future promise, and in the calculation of this, there was a clear bias in favour of European enterprise. Political considerations also played a part in deciding allocations. Loans to Chinese were strictly business transactions, amply secured, for short terms, paying high rates of interest, and giving immediate returns in the shape of augmented tin output. Loans to European planters were made in the spirit of great expectations; results were hoped for in the long term, and meanwhile the government could expect (and indeed require) a satisfactory level of capital expenditure by those receiving them.[4] Loans to Malays were made partly for economic, partly for political reasons. Those to entrepreneurs were

---

[1] Senior District Officer, Selangor, to the Government Secretary, 15 April 1893, *SGG*, 7 July 1893. Since assistance was given indiscriminately to indigenous Malays and to immigrants (and more willingly to the latter) it is clear that the term 'sons of the soil' then as now possessed considerable elasticity and was taken to mean all those of Malaysian race, wherever born, resident in the Peninsula.

[2] Minute of 18 May 1894, Sel/Sec. 194B/94.

[3] Return of loans outstanding on 30 June 1896, Sel/Sec. 4937/96

[4] Stephenson Brothers, pepper planters at Klang, had spent $30,000 on their plantations before applying for a government loan (Sel/Sec. 224/94). Payment of loan instalments to F.A. Toynbee, coffee planter of Kuala Lumpur, was made after inspection of expenditure as shown in his estate books. (Sel/Sec. 25/16/89.

made in the spirit of cautious speculation and were restricted in proportion to the small initial size of Malay enterprises and capital resources. The bulk of assistance to Malays, however, consisted of small loans to cultivators, distributed through district officers and headmen; they were probably spent largely on subsistence agriculture in the first instance, they did not as a rule have any appreciable effect on the development of cultivation for the market, or on the growth of revenues. Nor did they provide a source of wage labour. They had an economic value, in that they provided for the clearing and drainage of the land, and introduced a rent-paying population, and the economic motive certainly played a part in the distribution of this assistance. But equally important perhaps was the sense of obligation—limited though its expression—to those in whose name protection was established.

There was, broadly, a differentiation of economic function between the various communities; the conventional picture of the Malays as engaged in subsistence cultivation, while the Chinese and the British threw themselves into production for the market, very roughly fitted the circumstances. But this picture needs modification. Malays, especially immigrant Malays, did contribute to the market economy and adapt themselves to innovation, even though the majority of them remained in fringe activities. There was no attempt by the highly practical and *laissez-faire* state governments—instinctively averse to doctrinal interference with economic development—to limit or direct economic activity beyond the general regulations which might be imposed in the interests of orderly development. The beginnings of protection and economic segregation may be discerned perhaps in Maxwell's attempts to limit customary tenure to Malays, and in the rice irrigation schemes adopted towards the end of the century; but the great need at this time was seen to be the general encouragement of enterprise, and so long as the enterprise was productive, it mattered little to the authorities whence it came.

XI

FEDERATION

SUGGESTIONS for the closer association of the states under protection began to be made soon after the residential system had proved itself in the western states, and gained seriousness and point when the acquisition of Pahang and the extension of protection to the borders of Siamese influence invited a stocktaking and consolidation of existing positions. In 1885, Lucas at the Colonial Office tentatively threw out a suggestion, on a paper concerning a salary increase for Low, that it might be worth while considering 'whether he should be made a sort of Resident general for the Malay states', but the idea was shelved with a minute that when they had a Governor ignorant of native affairs or too lazy to travel, the suggestion would be worth considering.[1] In 1889, Low recommended in a private letter that British influence be extended to the other states of the Malay Peninsula, and that those already protected be combined in a 'confederation' so that policy in all might be uniform, and the states might assist each others' development; he also envisaged the appointment of a 'specially qualified officer' to assist the Governor in his task of supervision.[2] In a lecture to the Royal Colonial Institute in 1891, Maxwell proposed a confederation of the states in order to rationalize the administration and assist development.

In putting the case for federation, much was made of the growing divergencies between the states; but it is arguable that the pressure for a closer association arose as much out of their similarities as their differences. The ideal of uniformity had always been pressed by Singapore, and though it frequently provoked a jealous and unco-operative response from Residents, and much insistence on the unique problems of their own states, a considerable degree of institutional and legal uniformity had been achieved. The state establishments remained separate, each providing a virtually closed system of appointments and promotions, but they were run on similar prin-

[1] Lucas, minute of 8 October 1885, on Low to Weld, 5 October 1885, CO 273/138.
[2] Low to CO, 6 July 1889, CO 273/164.

ciples, and at the higher levels there was movement of officers between the states. Tax structures varied only in detail; tin exports carried much lower duty in Pahang, Negri Sembilan and Jelebu than in the two major mining states, but the principle underlying these differences—relief to backward areas—applied also to different districts of a single state. Between Perak and Selangor, duties on opium, tin and agricultural produce differed hardly at all after 1890, and identical changes in the tariff regularly came into effect at about the same time in both states. The states had much legislation in common; when it was necessary to impose identical laws, as with the Indian Immigration Enactment, they followed directives from Singapore; at other times similarities were achieved by suggestion or simple imitation. There were essential similarities in the organization of the police and justice, the system of district administration, and the functioning of the State Councils.

But although the states had so much in common institutionally, their administrative structures remained obstinately separate, and it was perhaps because of their institutional similarities, as well as their developing communications, that their continuing structural isolation appeared anomalous. It was absurd, as Maxwell pointed out, that there should be a multiplication of state departments—for example, the audit department—to carry on work which could be done more efficiently by a single department for all the states.[1] It was unsatisfactory that there should be three separate telegraph departments controlling the state sections of the line from Malacca to Province Wellesley; or that there should be separate railway administrations, applying different tariff rates, for small railway systems in Perak and Selangor which were certain soon to be connected. The amalgamation of the state services, with uniform rates of pay, pensions secured by a central fund, and a larger field for transfers, would provide a more attractive service generally than any which the individual states could offer.

By the 1890's, also, the need for judicial, legal and police reform had become apparent. The pressure for judicial reform, arising out of increased European business activity in the Malay states, has already been described; also the way in which the use of the combined Sikh military forces in Pahang, and the weaknesses in their existing organizations, stimulated proposals for their separation

---

[1] Maxwell, Memorandum on Federation, 20 March 1895, CO 273/211.

from the civil police, and amalgamation into a purely military force for the defence of the Peninsula.[1] The urgent financial embarrassments of the Pahang administration, added to the liabilities of Negri Sembilan and Sungei Ujong, now created powerful arguments for a combined exchequer, which would lift the responsibility for them from the Colony and place it on Perak and Selangor.

The extension of the residential system to the small states of the Negri Sembilan and to Pahang had involved yearly loans from the Colony for administration, communications and public works. The loan to the Sri Menanti states stood at $90,000 in January 1887; it had been spent mainly on making roads, and to some extent in subsidies (in plain English, bribes) to the chiefs. In subsequent years, the annual excess of expenditure over revenue (between 1887 and 1895 there was an excess every year except one) meant continued loans from the Colony, so that by the end of 1891, the loan to Negri Sembilan stood at $210,000, excluding accumulated interest at 4 per cent. At the same time, the precarious balance which Sungei Ujong had been able to maintain between revenue and expenditure, was upset by the failure of the Sungei Ujong Railway Company to show a profit, and the consequent obligation on the state to find the money for a yearly guarantee of interest. By the end of 1891, the Sungei Ujong debt to the Colony stood at $199,000. But the state which did most to turn happy dreams of wealth into a Colonial Treasurer's nightmare was Pahang. By the end of 1891 this state, which was thought by powerful defenders (including Weld, Smith, Swettenham and Lucas) to have mineral deposits as rich as those of Perak and Selangor, had cost the Colony nearly $600,000 in loans, and the annual excess of ordinary expenditure over revenue was running at $150,000. In 1892, a rebellion by a major chief added another $57,000 to the debt to the Colony, and a further debt of $100,000 to Perak and Selangor for the costs they had incurred in sending assistance. At the end of 1892, despite rigorous economy and a virtual standstill in public works, the debt to the Colony stood at about $800,000, exclusive of war expenditure.

During the 1880's, the Colony Legislative Council had willingly voted these sums; revenues were flourishing, it was anticipated that assistance to the states would bring rewards in the form of increased trade and investment opportunities, and some of the unofficial members had a personal interest in enterprises in the states. In the 1890's,

[1] See Chapter VIII.

however, the situation changed. A trade depression brought the Straits revenue down from $4,268,000 in 1890 to $3,652,877 in 1892; the military contribution payable to the Home Government doubled from a little over £50,000 in 1890 to £100,000 in 1891, and the effect of this increase was intensified by a fall in the rate of exchange to the dollar from 3s 5d in 1890 to 2s 6d in 1893. In 1891 and again in 1892, expenditure was three-quarters of a million dollars in excess of revenue. The Colony, itself forced to postpone important public works, was no longer in a position to subsidize the states; the un-officials, sore at the imposition of mining regulations on European companies in Pahang, and at the refusal of the Secretary of State to sanction a loan for the construction of a Pahang railway, refused to co-operate in making further loans. A motion for a $200,000 loan to Pahang, brought before Council in January 1891, had a rough passage. In March 1892, a proposed loan of $175,000 to Pahang was cut in Council to $100,000, and in August 1893, a proposed loan of $120,000 was cut to $50,000. Both times the Governor voted with the unofficials.

The difficulties of the poor states increased pressure for rational-ization of their administrations. More important, the financial straits of the Colony made it necessary to find some way of shedding at least part of the responsibility for them. The obvious way out of the difficulty was to raid the balances of Perak and Selangor, which stood at about $2,200,000 at the end of 1891. But here, the Colonial Office intervened. In August 1891, Smith wrote to the Secretary of State to say that further assistance must come from Selangor and Perak; the Secretary of State objected that the Pahang debt would not be a good asset for them, and that in any case their balances were pledged for important public works. However, he was prepared to allow Selangor to take over Sungei Ujong's debt to the Colony ($199,000) thus enabling the Colony to carry Pahang for another year.[1]

The official proposals for federation were made in the context of the deepening Pahang crisis. In March 1892, the problem of financing Pahang was raised again by the refusal of the unofficials to vote the full loan of $175,000 for the year; at the same time the Resident, forwarding the 1892 estimates, gave a discouraging picture of the condition and prospects of the state. In September, Smith, in reply

[1] Smith to Knutsford, 335 of 21 August 1891, and Knutsford to Smith, Con-fidential of 13 November 1891, CO 273/174.

to a call for a report on the future of Pahang, bleakly refused to pledge further help from the Colony, and maintained that help would have to come from the other states, or in the form of a loan floated for the purpose. In December, a report on the Pahang estimates for 1893 continued the story of economic standstill and retrenchment, but the Secretary of State was still averse to financial impositions on the other states, and made his views clear in a despatch strongly criticizing an unauthorized raid by the Governor on Selangor funds.[1]

During 1892, the future administration of Pahang came under urgent consideration. Three possibilities were put forward by the Resident; that a large loan be raised to provide for expenditure on public works and communications, or that Pahang be attached to Selangor for administrative purposes, or that the general administration and collection of the revenues be handed back to the Sultan, leaving the Resident with only a Sikh guard to protect Europeans in Pekan and at the mines. Fairfield added to these the suggestion that the most productive mining district, Ulu Pahang, be attached to Selangor, and the rest of the country handed back to the Sultan. Smith argued strongly for bold solutions, for raising a loan, building a railway or at least a road, allowing the richer states to carry Pahang. He was supported by Swettenham, who thought that the same economic miracles which had taken place in Perak and Selangor would take place in Pahang once communications were easier and more Chinese induced to enter the state. From his retirement, Low gave support, proposing that Pahang should be attached to and financed by the western states in a general federation.[2] The Colonial Office was divided, Lucas arguing with a strong optimism for raising a loan, spending large sums on Pahang communications and levying contributions from Perak and Selangor, and Fairfield arguing with equal force against a speculation unfounded on evidence of great mineral wealth.

The first official proposals for federation appeared in a memorandum by Lucas on a despatch relating to Pahang finances.[3] It was

[1] Smith to Knutsford, 129 of 25 March 1892, CO 273/179; Smith to Ripon, Confidential of 30 September 1892, CO 273/183; Smith to Ripon, 465 of 3 December 1892, CO 273/184; Ripon to Smith, 25 of 2 February 1893, on Smith to Ripon, 489 of 27 December 1892, CO 273/184.

[2] Swettenham to CO, private, November 1892, CO 273/185.

[3] Memorandum, undated, enclosed in Ripon to Smith, Confidential 'A' of 19 May 1893, on Smith to Ripon, 455 of 29 November 1892, CO 273/183. According to Swettenham, Lucas wrote it in March. British Malaya, rev. ed. 1948, pp. 363–4.

clear from the minutes—which were now, on balance, in favour of an aggressive policy in Pahang—the covering despatch and the memorandum itself that the federation scheme was being put forward in immediate consequence of the difficulties over Pahang. A union or federation of states, with a common administration and a common purse, would not only result in greater efficiency and economy, but 'would afford an obvious and reasonable justification for a policy, by which the stronger states may at the outset help the weaker, and those which are more prosperous for a time subsidise the less developed'. As to the scheme itself, it was suggested that the Governor's control should be maintained and formalized by some title such as High Commissioner; but the increasing responsibilities imposed by the Colony and the states were held to be beyond the powers of one man. There should be a Resident-General, responsible to the Governor, who would be 'the Chief British Officer of a united or Federated Protectorate' and who would 'visit, inspect and supervise' the states. The revenues might be wholly or to a large extent combined; departments of police, public works, posts and telegraphs should be placed under a single head; there should be a high court for all the states; and they should be administered by a unified civil service, classified, recruited and organized on a single system. It was suggested that Selangor, Sungei Ujong and Negri Sembilan should be federated in the first instance.

It appears, however, that the Pahang crisis was only the occasion for floating a scheme which had originated much earlier with Swettenham, and had been developed in discussions with Lucas ('a close personal friend') while Swettenham was on leave in 1892.[1] In a memorandum of 1889 entitled 'Suggestions for the future Administration of the Malay States',[2] Swettenham proposed that Sungei Ujong and Jelebu be attached to Selangor, and Selangor and Perak placed under a Chief Resident who would be responsible for the administration of the states under the general control of the Governor. Such an arrangement would relieve the Governor of much routine work, would provide for uniformity of administration, and would enable the stronger states to assist in the development of the weaker. These ideas appear again in another memorandum dated 25 January 1893,[3] in which he proposes the entry of Pahang and the creation of a

[1] Swettenham, *Footprints in Malaya*, p. 104.
[2] Swettenham Papers, ANM, item 67.
[3] Ibid. item 14.

unified Sikh police, a Chief Railway Engineer, a single department of posts and telegraphs, a unified civil service, and a bench of judges. In a series of articles which appeared in the *Straits Times* in August and September 1893, later published in book form, he argued fluently for the federation of the states under a Resident-General, stressing the need for uniformity, pooling of resources, unification of the civil service, and common arrangements for defence.[1] Criticizing the independence of individual Residents, he wrote: 'There are now too many valuable interests at stake, too large an official service, too many important legal questions to decide, too many different industries, and too many laws required to protect or control too large a population for all these matters to be left practically in the hands of one man. . . .'

It should be noted that the essence of the scheme as propounded by Swettenham was the creation of a chief executive officer, the Resident-General, who would be over the Residents and co-ordinate their activities. He continually stressed the dangerous independence of the Residents and the consequent divergencies in administration, and his prime remedy for these weaknesses was the creation of a chief executive officer who would ensure uniformity.[2] There was justice in these proposals; if certain functions of government were to be centralized, there had to be a central executive, either in the states or in Singapore, and centralization in Singapore was anathema to those who, like Swettenham, saw increased Colony control as a threat to the special position of the states. But it does not escape notice that in 1889 and even more in 1893, the most likely choice for the post of Resident-General was Swettenham himself. Indeed, when the scheme had once been put forward, Lucas speedily staked a claim on his behalf.[3] Among the pressures which gave momentum to the federation scheme, the ambition of Swettenham played no small part.

Centralization under a Resident-General was not the only form of rationalization proposed. The eventual annexation of the states had been freely taken for granted in earlier years, and had found sup-

[1] Swettenham, *About Perak*, pp. 76–78.

[2] In the account he gave, almost half a century later, of his discussions with Lucas, his preoccupation with this aspect of the scheme is very marked (*Footprints in Malaya*, op. cit. p. 104).

[3] On a proposal to raise his salary, Lucas minuted that if a Resident-General were to be appointed, 'Mr. Swettenham would be the obvious man'. Minute of 30 June 1893, on Smith to Ripon, Confidential of 4 May 1893, CO 273/187.

porters even among state officials.[1] In the 1890's, it was pushed by business and legal interests in the Straits Settlements, who felt they could operate more securely and freely in the states, and bring their influence to bear more effectively, if the states became British territory. Swettenham devoted some paragraphs of his Perak report for 1890 to demolishing the annexationist argument, and repeated the case against it at length in articles published in 1893:

> To enable members of the Straits Bar to practise in the Native States Courts, to be able to compel the Native States to contribute to the cost of Imperial Troops stationed in Singapore, to induce English speculators to invest money and safeguard their transactions by English laws . . . these are some of the grounds advanced for breaking faith with the Malays, who are now perfectly satisfied with existing arrangements wherein they have an influence and interest of which they would certainly be deprived by annexation.[2]

Annexation was not a serious possibility, however. It would have had to be imposed in the face of strong Malay opposition, and it would have frightened off the independent Malay Rulers and prejudiced the extension of British influence; not least, it would have been opposed by most of the Governors and Residents associated with the establishment of the residential system, and their knowledge and influence made them powerful partisans. They had, and knew how to exploit, a strong moral argument; that annexation would be a breach of faith with the Malay Rulers.

There was a third possibility—a federation without a Resident-General. In March 1895, Maxwell proposed a limited confederation under the Governor, who would be assisted by a council of four, consisting of a Secretary for Native Affairs, a Judicial Commissioner, a Financial Comptroller and a Consulting Engineer to be stationed

---

[1] In 1885, W.E. Maxwell, writing of the need for land reforms, urged that the states should be regarded as 'non-regulation provinces of the Colony, which are certain, sooner or later, to form parts of it' (minute of 14 December 1885, *Memorandum on the Introduction of a Land Code in the Native States in the Malay Peninsula*, Singapore, 1894, p. 27). In 1886, an official minuted on a matter of pensions 'annexation of the States to the Colony must be the final end' (minute by Johnson, 1 November 1886, on Treasury to CO, 20 October 1886, CO 273/142). In 1889, a Perak district officer thought that Perak, Selangor, Sungei Ujong and Johore were 'certain to become British as soon as their respective Sultans die'. Letter by C.D. Bowen, 21 June 1889, cited in 'British Malaya as it was', *The Asiatic Review*, vol. xlvi, no. 165 (January 1950).

[2] Swettenham *About Perak*, op. cit. p. 19. A critic retorted that if Swettenham were 'instructed to advise the Sultan to agree to the annexation of his dominions . . . there would be no difficulty and no breach of faith'. *Pinang Gazette*, 5 October 1893.

in Singapore. Such a federation would provide for common action in the departments where it was immediately needed. There would be an amalgamated civil service. The State Councils would cease to have legislative functions, though they would continue to act as consultative bodies. Drafts would be settled by the Judicial Commissioner in consultation with the Residents; disputed points would be settled by the Governor, and the law when finally approved would be sent to each state for promulgation by the Ruler on the advice of the Resident. There would be meetings of Rulers under the presidency of the Governor, 'annually if possible', but these would be advisory (and, one would imagine from their frequency, largely decorative).[1]

Despite its typically brusque exclusion of all but official voices from the formulation of policy, this proposal had much to recommend it, in that it would achieve common action in essentials far more cheaply and modestly than the federation scheme as finally adopted. But as Maxwell himself confessed, the Residents would oppose this centralization in Singapore and would persuade their Sultans to oppose it too (though the latter would hardly need persuasion against an increase of external control). The scheme had no support from either of the Governors concerned with federation; both Smith and Mitchell welcomed the creation of an executive officer who would rid them of a great burden of administrative detail, while leaving them control of major policy. Swettenham's plan, as expounded by Lucas, had a surface simplicity; it appeared the least likely to disturb existing forms or the *amour propre* of Sultans or Residents, and there was an officer immediately available to whom it could be entrusted. Not surprisingly, it was the only plan accorded serious consideration, and remained the basis for discussion in the years that followed.

The despatch recommending federation for the consideration of the Governor was accompanied by another of the same date, making various proposals for dealing with the immediate problem of Pahang. The Secretary of State asked whether the Colony was prepared to go on helping the state, adding a warning that a reduction in the military contribution was unlikely, and suggesting as an alternative that the whole or part of Pahang be attached to Selangor for administrative purposes, and that the chiefs be used to a greater extent in the administration. He also indicated his willingness to sanction a

[1] Maxwell, Memorandum on Federation, op. cit. 20 March 1895, CO 273/211.

Colonial loan not exceeding £100,000 for making roads in Pahang.[1] Smith forcefully rejected these proposals. He reported that the unofficial members of council refused to consider further assistance to Pahang, either by making advances or by raising a loan, unless the military contribution were reduced; that the chiefs were already used in the administration to the fullest extent compatible with good government; and that the Sultan would object strongly to the attachment of any part of Pahang to Selangor for administrative purposes.[2] In a confidential despatch written a few days later, he warmly welcomed the memorandum on federation, indicating that he had been about to address the Secretary of State on the same subject,[3] and proceeding to elaborate a scheme so like Lucas' that it was necessary for the latter to disclaim any 'friendly collusion' between them. He developed Lucas' suggestions by proposing a complete and not a partial federation. He outlined the functions of the Resident-General, who should reside in Kuala Lumpur (not Singapore) and whose duty should be to supervise and control the state administrations under the general direction of the Governor, acting as a channel of communication between the Governor and the Residents, and relieving him of his present burden of routine administration. He accepted Lucas' suggestions for a common purse, a unified civil service, and a common judicial authority, and proposed that the uniform working of certain services be ensured by placing the state departments under a single head.

In the next six months, the urgency was temporarily removed from the Pahang crisis by the surrender of the Colonial Office on the principle of assistance by the other states. The chief opponent of this policy—Fairfield—made a tactical retreat on this point; much as he disliked subsidizing Pahang at the states' expense, he disliked even more the prospect of a federation with Swettenham at its head, and he hoped that the removal of the problem of financing Pahang would mean the quiet collapse of the federation idea.[4] But there

[1] Ripon to Smith, 119 of 19 May 1893, on Smith to Ripon, 455 of 29 November 1893, CO 273/183.
[2] Smith to Ripon, 182 of 12 June 1893, CO 273/188.
[3] Smith to Ripon, Confidential of 30 June 1893, CO 273/188. Swettenham claimed that Smith's ideas on the subject derived from his own memorandum of January 1893, which he claimed to have shown to Smith in January or February. *British Malaya*, pp. 363–4.
[4] Fairfield, minute of 15 July 1893 on Smith to Ripon, 182 of 12 June 1893, CO 273/188; minute of 3 August 1893 and C.O. tel. of 8 August 1893, on Smith to Ripon, tel. of 3 August 1893, CO. 273/189.

were obvious objections to the indefinite levy of contributions from Perak and Selangor on very poor security and in the absence of any political connexion between them and the other states.[1] Also, federation had a logic, a purpose, and by now a momentum of its own. It was carried forward in minutes by Lucas and in discussions at the Colonial Office with the retiring Governor, Smith, and the incoming Governor, Mitchell, during the second half of 1893. When Mitchell left for Singapore in January 1894, he took with him copies of the correspondence on federation between the Secretary of State and his predecessor, as well as a further memorandum by Lucas on the proposed structure of federation, and a memorandum embodying the views of the Secretary of State.[2] Lucas endorsed Smith's recommendations as to the relationship that should exist between the Governor and the Resident-General, and again pressed Swettenham's claims to the post; and he took the proposal for a unified civil service a good deal further by recommending a covenanted civil service filled by open competition and amalgamated with that of the Straits Settlements and Hong Kong. The second memorandum indicated the general approval of the Secretary of State for the scheme outlined, without committing him or the Governor to its acceptance.

When he finally reported eighteen months later, Mitchell accepted the desirability of federation and forwarded a detailed scheme.[3] His arguments were related to the need for administrative reform; he did not mention the Pahang problem, and it appears on the surface that by this stage federation had become a separate question to

[1] There were hints of a possible future resistance in Swettenham's responses to requests for help. While expressing his willingness to help, he entered the reservation that this assistance should not be such as to embarrass Perak or interfere with her 'legitimate aims'. Drawing attention to the fact that Perak had 'at present no very direct interest in or intercourse with Pahang', he remarked that in the circumstances it was necessary to look to the security offered. Both he and Treacher (Resident of Selangor) made it clear that assistance would be conditional on the opening of Pahang by means of roads and the cancellation of concessions which were locking up large areas and discouraging the entry of Chinese. Swettenham to CS, 28 August 1893, in Maxwell to Ripon, 4 September 1893, CO 273/189; Swettenham to CS, 14 May 1894, and Treacher to CS, 24 May 1894, enclosed in Mitchell to Ripon, Confidential of 12 June 1894, CO 273/196.

[2] i.e., Ripon to Smith, Confidential 'A' of 19 May 1893; Smith to Ripon, Confidential of 30 June 1893; Memorandum by Lucas, 30 October 1893 (based on a minute of 16 August 1893), and Memorandum of 22 December 1893, on Smith to Ripon, Confidential of 30 June 1893, CO 273/188.

[3] Mitchell to Ripon, Confidential of 1 May 1895, enclosing 'A Proposal for the Administrative Federation of the Protected Malay States', draft instructions to Swettenham, and draft federation agreement, CO 273/202.

be decided on its own merits. But a decision taken in 1894 to maintain the British position in Pahang undoubtedly strengthened the case for a permanent financial solution, which could hardly be achieved except by associating the other states politically with Pahang. In June 1894 Mitchell, sceptical of the economic future of the state and reluctant to pledge Selangor or Perak to further advances, was prepared to recommend partial withdrawal from Pahang, retaining control only of Ulu Pahang and Kuantan (the two mining districts) and leaving an agent with the Sultan at Pekan.[1] A rebel raid in the same month made such retreat undesirable, as it would have appeared a confession of weakness. It was agreed that the residential system should be continued another year, the deficit met by a loan from Perak or Selangor, and that a road be built from the Selangor frontier to Ulu Pahang.[2] Before the year of grace was out, however, he had recommended in favour of federation.

Mitchell's scheme, which was finally approved by the Colonial Office, was in essentials the same as that put forward by Lucas. It interposed a Resident-General as an intermediate authority and channel of communication between Residents and Governor. It recommended the unification of certain departments under federal heads, who would secure uniformity of practice in the departments in all states. The appointments made during the initial stages should include a Judicial Commissioner, who would hear appeals and capital cases in all states and assimilate judicial procedure as far as possible to one standard; an Attorney-General, who would draft legal enactments and other important documents, and advise the Governor, the Resident-General and the Residents on any legal question that might be referred to him; a Commandant, Malay States Sikhs, who would be in charge of the amalgamated Sikh military force; and a Chief Commissioner of Police. Other appointments might follow; a Chief Commissioner of Lands and Mines, an Inspector of Schools, a Chief Engineer in charge of Public Works, a Chief Railway Engineer, a Chief Surgeon, a Chief Auditor, and a Chief Surveyor.

Much of the scheme was taken up with a clarification of the relations that should exist between the Governor, the Resident-General and the Residents, and a definition of the limits of their authority in matters of patronage and expenditure. Annual estimates and draft

---

[1] Mitchell to Ripon, Confidential of 12 June 1894, CO 273/196.
[2] Mitchell to Ripon, Confidential of 2 October 1894, and Ripon to Mitchell, Confidential of 6 November 1894, CO 273/197.

legislation would be forwarded to the Governor for his sanction, through the Resident-General. Each Resident would continue to carry on the work of his state as hitherto, except that the Resident-General would have full power to issue instructions to him; and while a Resident would have the right of appeal to the Governor in case of difference, he would be bound to act on instructions till a decision was arrived at. The Resident-General might, while travelling or residing in any state, communicate direct with anyone on any subject, but he should issue no instructions except through the Resident, and if addressed on any subject by anyone in the states, he should send his reply through the Resident; except that in matters of urgency, he might use his discretion, informing the Resident later of his action and the circumstances.

The 'Chief Officers' whose appointments were recommended under the scheme would be 'generally responsible' for their departments in each state, the local head being directly responsible for the department within the state. The Chief Officers would correspond direct with the Resident-General and take their instructions from him; but they had no power to issue orders to their departments in states that were opposed to the rulings of the Resident. When a difference arose between a Resident and the Chief Officer of a department, it must be referred to the Resident-General, and till a decision was received from him or from the Governor, the Resident's ruling must stand.

Mitchell's recommendations differed from those of Lucas and Smith in two respects. He advocated a retention of the state councils, which would meet and conduct their business as hitherto. There might, he thought, also be an annual assembly of Rulers, Residents, and members of the State Councils under the presidency of the Governor, with purely consultative and advisory functions. Secondly, there should be no common purse. Each state would collect and spend its own revenues, and all money advanced to other states would be classed as loans, to be repaid by mutual arrangement. Federal charges would be divided between the states in proportion to their revenues, and would form a first charge on them.

The scheme was in effect a proposal for administrative centralization under the Resident-General, with arbitration machinery (appeal to a still higher authority) to deal with disputes between the state officers and the central executive, and elaborate procedures for maintaining the appearance of autonomy while securing uniformity. Whatever it might be called, it is clear that it was not a true federation. There was no delimitation of state and federal spheres of action; no federal body was envisaged, except the consultative assembly of chiefs. There were to be a number of 'federal' officials but there was no clear differentiation of function between them and the state officials; there was instead a graduation of powers between executive officials on the same ladder of authority—the Residents, the Resident-General and the Governor. It is doubtful whether, in using the word 'federation', the authorities knew or cared much about terminological accuracy; indeed Lucas in one memorandum used the words 'union' and 'federation' interchangeably, and in a minute on Mitchell's scheme, he suggested that in time the status of Residents should be diminished, 'bringing the present separate States as near as may be without offending native prejudice to the level of districts of the same State'.[1] But if this was not a federation, neither was it a union, though it was certainly closer to a union in spirit. The scheme went to elaborate lengths to preserve the nominal autonomy of each state, by preserving the separate existence of the state councils, rejecting the idea of a common purse, and interposing the Residents between the 'Chief Officers' and the state departments. The wish to achieve centralization of authority without sacrificing any part of the appearance of separate identity, meant that although power was ultimately concentrated in the hands of a central executive, the values of speed and efficiency attributed to this type of organization would be partly dissipated by the circumlocution and delays imposed by the need to deal with the states through the Residents. The federation scheme meant in effect an uneasy equilibrium between Residents in danger of losing their states and Chief Officers in search of their departments, with the Resident-General holding the balance between them.

Mitchell had been warned on his departure that in working out a uniform system of administration, he should avoid any step which might 'in any way wound the susceptibilities of the various native rulers'; earlier, Smith had reported his promise to the Sultan of Perak 'that the integrity of his country would be preserved, and that there would be no radical changes in the system of administration of which he did not approve'.[2] Whether the detailed scheme was ever

[1] Minute of 8 November 1895 on Mitchell to Ripon, Confidential of 1 May 1895, CO 273/202.

[2] Memorandum of 22 December 1895, on Mitchell to Ripon, Confidential of 1 May 1895, CO 273/202; Smith to Ripon, Confidential of 30 June 1893, CO 273/188.

discussed with the Malay rulers is not known. Swettenham was entrusted with the task of obtaining their assent to the Treaty of Federation, but his itinerary did not give him time to discuss the scheme on that occasion, though he may have discussed it earlier with the Sultan of Perak.[1] Certainly, nothing of the scheme found its way into the Treaty, which rivals the Pangkor Engagement for brevity and ambiguity on the meaning and significance of the changes proposed. In the first two paragraphs, the Rulers severally placed themselves and their states under British protection, and agreed to constitute their countries a federation, to be administered under the advice of the British government. The third paragraph declared that no one Ruler or chief should exercise any power or authority in any state other than his own. In the fourth, the Rulers agreed 'to accept a British officer to be styled the Resident-General, as the agent and representative of the British Government under the Governor of the Straits Settlements . . . and to follow his advice in all matters of administration other than those touching the Muhammadan religion'. In the fifth, they pledged themselves to give to those states which required it such assistance as the British government might advise, and to provide a body of armed and equipped Indian troops for service in the Straits Settlements on the outbreak of war. The sixth clause was pure bromide. 'Nothing in this agreement is intended to curtail any of the powers or authority now held by any of the above-named Rulers in their respective States, nor does it alter the relations now existing between any of the States named and the British Empire.'[2]

The question arises whether the federation scheme made any practical difference to the position of the Ruler in his own state, and whether there was in fact a breach of faith in omitting from the Treaty any mention of the administrative changes proposed. After all, Rulers had always had to follow advice; Residents and state administrations had always been subject to direction of the Governor, open and acknowledged. Rulers and Councils had never had any voice in the collection or distribution of the revenue; inter-state

[1] The Treaty, dated July 1895, was taken round to the rulers separately for their signatures in June and July 1895. Swettenham's journey took about ten days in all, giving him a few hours in each state capital. Swettenham, Report of a visit to Pahang, 21 June 1895, and Report of a Visit to Selangor, Sungei Ujong, Negri Sembilan and Jelebu, 28 July 1895, in Mitchell to Ripon, Confidential of 7 August 1895, CO 273/205.

[2] W.G. Maxwell and W.S. Gibson, *Treaties and Engagements affecting the Malay States and Borneo*, London, 1924, p. 70.

loans had been made at the Governor's direction, and military police ordered out at a moment's notice for service outside state borders; and the Ruler's permission for all this had been sought, if at all, purely as an act of courtesy. Was it necessary to enlarge on a scheme which meant, in effect, a rearrangement of the way in which direction was brought to bear on the state executive?

Though it might be argued with some force that the powers of the Rulers in their own states were already so limited that they could hardly be diminished by federation, the federation scheme did place them several removes further from the source of power. There were now to be two authorities above the Resident, and each of the state departments was to be responsible to an officer outside the state. It was to be expected that the amount of influence the individual Ruler could bring to bear on the affairs of his own state would diminish in proportion to the number of federal officers with responsibility for state departments. The autonomous state civil services were to give way to a unified service, with transfers freely made between states. These changes were of importance to Rulers, who might hitherto have had little power, but who had at least been able to identify certain services and officers as belonging to their own states, and derive some reassurance from long acquaintance with them. In omitting all reference to these material changes, however, the Treaty was in accord with Malayan constitutional precedents. Like the Pangkor Engagement and the other instruments providing for Residents, it was designed to soothe fears and prejudices and conceal reality, not to provide a frame of reference for administrative practice.

During the twenty years after intervention, a colonial government, ruling its own populations through colonial departments and recognizing no native authority as an executive instrument, had brought into being a system of rule in which the native authority was sovereign, native hierarchies preserved, and native institutions used as agencies of government. We have seen the part played in this development by the traditional preference of the Imperial Government for informal control, by the ambitions of local authorities, some of whom tried in the early stages to formalize control, but nearly all of whom later came to defend the nominal independence of the states; and by the character of the native Rulers, whose weakness invited intervention but at the same time made it safe to preserve them as nominal rulers. But the development of the Residential system was not entirely the result of circumstance. One essential feature—the early centralization of government in the hands of a highly organized European executive—was determined by economic conditions and objectives; the other—the preservation of indigenous forms and institutions—depended much more on contingency, but this feature also can perhaps be related to economic factors. Economic development took place largely outside the Malay sector; it was therefore possible to encourage it without making demands on Malay land, labour or revenue contributions which would disrupt Malay society.

Of all the achievements of government in the Malay states—and they are many—perhaps the most remarkable was the perpetuation of the illusion that states whose populations, industries, administration and chief towns had become predominantly alien were nevertheless Malay worlds. The illusion was maintained not merely by associating the Malays in government but by the identification of British officials with the Malay life and spirit. Speaking Malay, selected for their attraction to Malay manners and ways of life, understanding the power of appearances, ritual and forms, British officers inhabited the Malay world as well as their own. They became honorary members of the Malay élite; the rituals of colonial government and Malay authority complemented each other. This identification of the British with the Malays has often been explained in terms of policy and power relationships, and particularly as a mutual alliance against the Chinese. Such an explanation is too simple, and whatever application it may have to the 1920's and 1930's, it does not fit this early, intensely pragmatic period when administrators measured their success by the number of Chinese they induced to migrate to the states. The relations between the British and the Malays may have been inspired originally by policy, but it was a policy which released natural sympathies and affinities. The early British administrators were enchanted by the beauty of the country in which they worked; thrown on the company of Malay aristocrats by the scarcity of their own kind, they found them hospitable country gentlemen who combined courtesy and reserve in the right proportions and who loved field sports; their households were open and friendly, and they did not despise foreigners. It is not hard to understand why British officials felt drawn to them and found friends among them.

The Malay states provide a particularly clear-cut example of the organization of government to deal with a divided society. The intrusion of the world economy was accompanied by the growth of a large and highly-developed administration, directed and staffed by non-Malays, paid for by non-Malay taxation and largely serving non-Malay commercial interests, while district administration and local government were left to Malay local authorities and a growing cadre of Malay district officers. The British administration provided the link between these two interests and undertook to hold the balance between them. To the administrators of the nineteenth century the immediate problem was economic; how to fill empty lands, develop mining and commercial agriculture and establish a modern system of communications. It was only in the twentieth century that the danger to Malays posed by unrestricted immigration and increasing centralization of power in non-Malay hands, became apparent. The theory of Malay sovereignty, Malay proprietary interest and special Malay claim to government office, now came to have a strong moral sanction and came to be regarded as the first defence of Malay interests against alien encroachment. These principles, given new life by the Malay nationalism of the twentieth century, and surviving to some degree in modern constitutional forms, owe something of their vitality and practical application to their preservation and growth during seventy years of British protection. The ideas and policies developed to deal with the problems of a dual society in the Colonial period continue to find expression in modern Malaya.

APPENDIX 1

a. THE PERAK CONSTITUTION

An account of the Perak Constitution *c*. 1874 is given in Winstedt, 'History of Perak', *JMBRAS*, vol. xii, part 1, pp. 119–76, Appendixes A–K. The titles, genealogies, functions and revenues of the chiefs are given in Appendix D, pp. 134–58. In Winstedt's list, the chiefs of the second rank are given in the order assigned to them by the Perak State Council of 1905. Except for a change in one title, and slight differences in the order, the list is the same as that given by C. J. Irving, Memorandum on a Visit to Perak, 24 July 1872, C.1111, enclosure in no. 52.

The titles below are in the order given them by Winstedt, and are followed by summaries of (nominal) functions, revenues and territorial affiliations, taken partly from Winstedt and partly from other sources. The expression of power in terms of formal survivals from more highly developed political systems is characteristic of Malay society, and it has therefore seemed worthwhile, by way of illustration, to give the functions traditionally attached to the four great offices of state (orginally court offices) even though they had a largely antiquarian interest by 1874, and even though their holders lived in their own districts and not with the Sultan.

The titles or elements of the titles of nearly all the chiefs occur in histories of the Malacca Court of the fifteenth century. According to tradition, the offices of the Four Great Chiefs and five of the Eight Major Chiefs, were held by members of the family of Malacca Bendaharas; but by the nineteenth century only the titles of the Sri Adika Raja, the Panglima Kinta and the Panglima Bukit Gantang remained in the hands of this family. All the title-holders of the first rank, and the Laksamana in the second, were signatories to treaties executed between Perak and the Dutch East India Company in 1650 and 1655; but some of the titles of the second rank appear to be eighteenth century creations, and it was only in the eighteenth century that the titles of either rank came into the hands of the families holding them in 1874.

THE RAJAS

1. *The Sultan.*
2. *The Raja Muda* (heir presumptive).
3. *The Waris Negeri* (male members of the royal house in the line of succession. An elastic category).

ORANG BESAR EMPAT (THE FOUR GREAT CHIEFS)

1. *Raja Bendahara*
   Before the eighteenth century he was the greatest commoner chief and the Sultan's chief minister, but about the middle of the century the office came into the royal family. The Bendahara then stood next to the Raja Muda in succession to the throne. On the death of a Sultan, the Bendahara became Regent, and took possession of the regalia. After seven days he invested the Sultan with it, and superintended his installation.
   His revenues came mainly from duties on trade on the Kinta river. In 1874 the Bendahara (Osman) lived at Sayong in Upper Perak. He died in 1877, and some time later the title was assumed by Raja Idris, son-in-law of Raja Yusuf, who had become Regent in 1877.

2. *The Orang Kaya Besar (Orang Kaya Besar Sri Maharaja 'diraja Penghulu Bendahari)*
   The Sultan's 'treasurer, secretary and chamberlain'; a great palace official. The office was vacant at this time.

3. *The Temenggong (Orang Kaya Temenggong Paduka Raja)*
   A military and police officer, in charge of defence works and prisons and chief of executioners. He was also in charge of markets and weights and measures.
   He derived his revenue from a monopoly of the sale of salt and atap, from fees on weights and measures, and from fines. In 1874 (and throughout the period) the Temenggong lived at Kota Lama, near Kuala Kangsar in Upper Perak.

4. *The Mentri (Orang Kaya Mentri Sri Paduka Tuan)*
   Nominally the State Justiciar, but in 1874 chiefly notable as the governor of Larut.

ORANG BESAR DELAPAN (THE EIGHT MAJOR CHIEFS)

1. *The Maharaja Lela (Orang Kaya-Kaya Maharaja Lela Tuan Lela Putra)*
   A chief above the law, and entrusted with the protection of the Sultan at court ceremonies. He was territorial chief of Pasir Salak, and drew revenues from his district and from tolls on the Sungei Dedap.

2. *The Laksamana (Orang Kaya-Kaya Laksamana Raja Mahkota)*
   The Laksamana had charge of the sea-coast and of the tidal reaches of the Perak river. Together with the Shahbandar, he collected customs duties for the Sultan at the mouth of the Perak river, and was entitled to a share of collections. He also had a customs station on the Batang Padang. His village was Durian Sa-batang, at the confluence of the Perak and the Bidor.

3. *The S'adika Raja (Orang Kaya-Kaya Sri Adika Raja Shahbandar Muda)*
   Territorial chief of Upper Perak, from Kuala Temong to the Siam boundary. His revenues came from taxes on tin and gutta exported from his district, and from a rice levy on each household.

4. *The Panglima Kinta (Orang Kaya-Kaya Panglima Kinta, Sri Amar Bangsa' 'diraja)*
   Territorial chief of Kinta, and warden of Perak's eastern frontier. He received a tenth of all the tin produced in his district.

5. *The Panglima Bukit Gantang (Orang Kaya-Kaya Bukit Gantang Sri Amar 'diraja)*
   Territorial chief of Bukit Gantang, in the pass between the Perak and Larut valleys, which he guarded. The office was eclipsed by the rise of the Mentri (himself one of the Bukit Gantang family) who succeeded to the territorial influence of the family in northwest Perak. The title lapsed in 1871, and was not revived till the twentieth century.

6. *The Shahbandar (Orang Kaya-Kaya Shahbandar Paduka Indra)*
   A Lower Perak chief who acted as harbour master and customs officer. He was joint collector with the Laksamana of customs revenue on the Perak river, and took a commission on collections.

7. *The Dato' Sagor (Orang Kaya-Kaya Sri Agar 'diraja)*
   Territorial chief of the district between Kampong Gajah and

Pulau Tiga, on the Lower Perak.

8. *Imam Paduka Tuan (Orang Kaya-Kaya Imam Paduka Tuan Sri 'diraja)*
The chief religious dignitary in the state, deriving his income from the contributions of the pious. The office was vacant in 1874.

b. THE PERAK REVENUE SYSTEM

Details of the revenues of the Sultan and major chiefs of Perak may be found in Mohammed Ibrahim Munshi, *Kesah Pelayaran*, pp. 73–74, based on information collected during a visit to Perak in 1872; in the evidence of Che Mida, 14 October 1876, before the Commission of Enquiry into the Perak Outrages, and in the Administrative Report on Perak by J. W. Birch, 14 December 1874, both enclosed in Jervois to Carnarvon 430 of 14 December 1876, CO 273/88. The material has been summarized in Winstedt, 'History of Perak', *JMBRAS*, vol. xii, part 1 (1934), Appendix D, pp. 134–55. All these accounts relate to conditions in the years immediately before British intervention, and it is apparent that some of the taxes at least were recent impositions and that innovations had been introduced in the collection of others, but in its main outline the revenue system appears to have been traditional and in keeping with practice in the other protected states.

The sparse population, the low level of productivity, and the importance of mining in the economy explains the general absence of land rent and taxes on subsistence agriculture, and the importance of taxes on trade in the revenue system of the state. Both Sultan and chiefs derived their main revenues from customs taxes and taxes on production for export. The poll tax was not commonly levied, though there are references to a poll tax of fifty cents on every male in Perak, levied by the Bendahara, a poll tax of $2 on every married man in his district, levied by the Maharaja Lela, and a tax of $2.25 levied by the Sultan on every household in the Krian, which was a royal district. There were no land taxes as such, though there were taxes on produce for export, often and most conveniently levied as export duty. There was no levy on production for subsistence, except in Krian and Upper Perak, where the Sultan and the Sri Adika Raja respectively levied an annual padi tax of seventy gantangs a household. The special treatment of the Krian district is explained by the fact that the district was cleared and planted by migratory cultivators from

Penang, Province Wellesley and Kedah, who stayed long enough in the district to take a yearly crop and then returned to their original homes. They were not subject to kerah service and the padi and household tax constituted their only revenue contribution.

The Sultan derived revenue mainly from the customs duties on the Perak river, and a share of the duties on the rivers of Larut. Customs duties were imposed on all imported articles; the most important of these being opium, tobacco, textiles, rice, oil and salt. Export taxes were levied on tin, gutta and other wood gums, atap, rattans and hides. During Birch's residency, the Perak river export duties were partly farmed out to Chinese, partly collected by the Dato' Shahbandar and a lesser chief. According to Winstedt, not only the Shahbandar but the Laksamana (also from Lower Perak) drew a commission on the Perak river collections; and according to Mohammed Ibrahim Munshi, the two last-named were allowed to export specified quantities of tin free of duty—a privilege worth $600 a year in the case of the Laksamana and $300 a year in the case of the Shahbandar. The Temenggong also derived part of his income from a share of the Perak river dues; he had the monopoly of the import duty on salt, and one tenth of the export duty on atap.

Birch gives details of customs stations maintained by the chiefs on the other rivers. There was one at the mouth of the Kinta, kept by the Bendahara and levying duties on the principal imports and exports; one at the mouth of the Batang Padang, levying duty on tin on behalf of a syndicate of six, including the Sultan and the Laksamana; another tin station at the mouth of the Bidor, farmed out by the Bendahara to a son of the Laksamana. The chiefs taxed boats passing up and down their stretches of river—'every chief in his own place took something'. But the main income of the chiefs was probably derived from taxes on tin, gutta and other export produce obtained in their districts. The Mentri, the Maharaja Lela, the Panglima Kinta, the Panglima Bukit Gantang, the Dato' Sagor and the Sri Adika Raja derived tribute in this way; the tribute was paid in consideration of their political position and did not constitute private rent or profit from business undertakings.

APPENDIX 2

BIOGRAPHICAL NOTES ON RESIDENTS

James Woodford Wheeler Birch
He served as a midshipman in the Royal Navy before going to Ceylon in 1846 to serve in the Department of the Commissioner of Roads. From 1853–6 he was a Commissioner of Requests and Police Magistrate, and from 1858–67 was Assistant Government Agent in various provinces before becoming Government Agent for the Eastern Province in 1868. In 1870 he became Colonial Secretary, Straits Settlements, and in 1874 he became British Resident, Perak. He was murdered in Lower Perak in November 1875.

Sir Hugh Charles Clifford, GBE [1925], GCMG [1921], KCMG [1909], CMG [1900], FRGS
Born in 1866, he was educated at Woburn Park and passed for Sandhurst with a Queen's Cadetship in 1883, but instead he joined the Perak service in the same year. In 1887 the Governor sent him on a special mission to Pahang, to obtain the assent of the Sultan to a treaty of protection, and on conclusion of the treaty he became British Agent in Pahang, 1887–8. He became Superintendent, Ulu Pahang, in 1889; Acting Resident, Pahang, at various times between 1890 and 1895, and Resident 1896–9; was nominated by the Colonial Office to the post of Governor of North Borneo, but resigned and was reappointed Resident, Pahang, in 1901; became Colonial Secretary, Trinidad and Tobago, 1903; Colonial Secretary, Ceylon, 1907; Governor of the Gold Coast, 1912; Governor of Nigeria, 1919; Governor of Ceylon, 1925; Governor of the Straits Settlements, High Commissioner for the Malay States, and British Agent for Borneo, 1927. He resigned in 1929 and died in 1941. He wrote numerous essays, short stories and articles about life in Malaya and his own experiences.

James Guthrie Davidson
Born about 1838, he came to Singapore in 1861 to practise law. He became the legal adviser and financial backer of Tengku Zia'u'd-din,

and in 1875 was appointed British Resident, Selangor. In 1876 he was appointed British Resident, Perak, but resigned in February 1877, and returned to his legal practice in Singapore. He died in Singapore in 1891. He was a nephew of James Guthrie, of the Singapore commercial house of Guthrie and Co.

Captain Bloomfield Douglas, RNR

He served in the Royal and Indian Navies, and was for a time in command of Sir James Brooke's schooner *Royalist*. He was mentioned by Admiral Sir H. Keppel and Admiral Sir E. Belcher for services against the pirates in Borneo in 1843–4. He served in the English coastguard between 1847 and 1852, when he joined the merchant navy. In 1854 he was appointed naval officer and harbour master, South Australia, and carried out a survey of part of the South Australian coast. In 1858 he was also appointed collector of customs, and in 1860 he became superintendent of the Marine Board and stipendiary magistrate. In 1870 he was appointed Government Resident of the Northern Territory, but resigned in 1873 and in 1874 was employed by the South Australian Government to introduce Chinese labour for the development of the Northern Territory. He acted as Police Magistrate, Singapore, 1874–5, and in November 1875 was appointed Assistant Resident, Selangor. In 1876 he became Resident. He resigned in 1882, and after serving for some years as Naval Adviser to the Canadian Marine and Fisheries Department, he died in Ottawa in 1906.

The Hon. Martin Lister

The second son of the third Baron Ribblesdale, he was born in 1857 and educated at Cheltenham College. He worked for a time as a clerk in the Bank of England, and then went to Ceylon where he worked on a coffee estate. He came to Malaya about 1879, at about the same time as two other Ceylon planters, Thomas Heslop Hill and Ambrose Rathborne, and in partnership with them opened coffee plantations in Sungei Ujong and Selangor. He entered the Perak service in 1884 as secretary to the Resident, and between 1884 and his death in 1897, he filled various posts in Perak, Negri Sembilan, and Selangor, at the same time retaining his planting interests. In 1885 he became Collector and Magistrate, Ulu Selangor, and in 1887, Superintendent of the Sri Menanti states. In 1889 he became British Resident, Negri Sembilan. He died in 1897. He was deeply interested in Malay culture; while he was in Ulu Selangor, he paid for a *ma'yong* troupe to visit and perform in the district.

Sir Hugh Low, GCMG [1888], KCMG [1883], CMG [1879]

Born in 1824 at Clapton, England, he came of a family with horticultural interests. He was educated in private schools. At the age of nineteen he went to Borneo on a botanical tour, and there came under the patronage of Rajah James Brooke. In 1848 he was appointed Secretary under Brooke to the newly formed government of Labuan, and held various posts in the Labuan administration (including that of Acting Governor) for the next twenty-nine years. In 1877 he was appointed British Resident, Perak, an appointment he held till he retired in 1889. He died in 1905. He was a Fellow of the Linnaean Society and of the Zoological Society. He was a well-known naturalist and traveller, and the first European to climb Mount Kinabalu (in 1851; he climbed it twice more in 1858). His publications include *Sarawak, its Inhabitants and Productions*, London, 1848, and 'Selesilah (Book of the Descent) of the Rajas of Brunei', *JSBRAS*, no. 5 (1880), pp. 1–35.

Sir William Edward Maxwell, KCMG [1896], CMG [1885]

The son of Sir Peter Benson Maxwell (jurist and Liberal polemical writer and Chief Justice of the Straits Settlements, 1867–71), he was born in 1846 and educated at Repton. He was employed as a clerk in the Supreme Court of Penang and Singapore from 1865–9, and qualified as an advocate of the local bar in 1867 (he was called to the English bar in 1881). Between 1869 and 1878, he served as a magistrate in various posts in Singapore, Malacca and Province Wellesley. On Birch's murder in November 1875, he became Deputy Commissioner with the Larut Field Force operating in northern Perak, and in August 1876 he became acting Assistant Resident in Perak, and Assistant Resident, 1878–82. In 1882 he was appointed Commissioner of Lands, Straits Settlements, and was entrusted with the task of reforming the land law of the Colony. In 1883 he became a member of the Executive and Legislative Councils of the Straits Settlements, and in 1884 he was employed on two missions to Acheh, which resulted in the release of the crew of the *Nisero*. He acted as Resident Councillor, Penang, 1887–9, and in 1889 became British Resident, Selangor. In March 1892 he became Colonial Secretary, Straits Settlements (acting as Governor from September 1893 to January 1894), and in 1895 he became Governor of the Gold Coast. He died in 1897.

Commander Patrick James Murray, RN

He was born about 1837. He joined the Royal Navy in 1856 and retired in 1872. He was appointed acting Assistant Resident, Sungei Ujong, in 1875, and was subsequently confirmed as Resident. He died in Malacca in 1881 after a short illness.

William Francis Bourne Paul

He was born in 1844 and was educated at Eton. He served in Sarawak, 1860–72; in the Gold Coast 1873–6, first as Civil Commissioner, Accra, and then as District Commissioner, Elmina; and in Perak 1876–81, as Deputy Commissioner (1876), Superintendent Larut (1877) and Superintendent, Lower Perak (1878–81). While he was in Perak he served also on the Commission of Enquiry into the Perak Outrages. He was appointed British Resident, Sungei Ujong, in 1881, and retired in 1893. He was an accomplished Malay linguist, and accompanied the Governor, Sir Frederick Weld, as interpreter on a mission to Brunei in 1887.

Sir John Pickersgill Rodger, KCMG [1904], CMG [1899]

Born in 1851, he was educated at Eton and Christchurch, and was called to the bar in 1877. In 1882, while travelling in Malaya, he accepted the post of Chief Magistrate and Commissioner of Lands, Selangor. He acted as British Resident, Selangor, for long periods between 1884 and 1888, when he became Resident, Pahang. He became Resident, Selangor, in 1896, and Resident, Perak, in 1902. He retired in 1903. He spoke Malay well and was considered equally effective in his dealings with Malays and Chinese. He had spent some time working in the East End of London, which was considered at the Colonial Office to be 'not a bad training for a man who is to look after natives'.

Sir Frank Athelstane Swettenham, GCMG [1909], KCMG [1897], CMG [1886]

He was born in 1851. Appointed a cadet in the Straits Settlements Civil Service in 1870, he passed his final examination in Malay in 1872, and accompanied the Governor as interpreter on visits to the east coast, Johore and Kedah. In the same year, he went to Klang and Kuala Lumpur as Davidson's guest, and was entertained by

Tengku Zia'u'd-din and Yap Ah Loy. In 1873 he was Collector of Land Revenue, Penang and Province Wellesley, and in May 1874 he was appointed Magistrate and Commissioner of the Court of Requests, Penang. During 1874 he was engaged on several missions in the Malay states; in January he was sent to Larut to summon the Chinese headmen to the Pangkor meeting, and immediately after it he returned to Larut as one of the Commissioners to enforce the agreement with the Chinese. In April he accompanied Birch as Malay interpreter on a mission to Perak, and in June he went back on another, and partly successful, mission to persuade Sultan Ismail and Raja Yusuf to meet the Governor to discuss the Pangkor settlement. In August he was sent to reside with the Sultan of Selangor, and was appointed Assistant Resident, Selangor, in December. In September 1875 he accompanied Jervois on his tour of Perak. He was in Perak posting proclamations in an up-river village when Birch was murdered, and in the same month, was appointed Deputy Commissioner with the southern column of the Perak Expeditionary Force. He became Assistant Colonial Secretary for Native States, 1876; Assistant Colonial Secretary, 1881; British Resident, Selangor, 1882; Acting British Resident, Perak, 1884–6; Resident, Perak, 1889; Resident-General of the Federated Malay States, 1896; Governor, Straits Settlements, and High Commissioner for the Malay States, 1901. He retired in 1904 and died in 1946. He wrote numerous essays and short stories about the Malay Peninsula (for a list of his publications see C. D. Cowan, 'Sir Frank Swettenham's Perak Journals, 1874–1876', *JMBRAS*, vol. xxiv, part 4 (1951).

Sir William Hood Treacher, KCMG [1904], CMG [1890], MA [Oxon]
He was born in 1849. He entered the Labuan service in 1871, and in 1881 obtained leave without pay to become the first Governor of British North Borneo. He became Secretary to Government, Perak, in 1888; British Resident, Selangor, 1892; British Resident, Perak, 1896; acted as Resident-General, Federated Malay States, 1902–4, when he retired. He died in 1919.

APPENDIX 3

a. INSTRUCTIONS TO A RESIDENT OF
SELANGOR (SEL/SEC. 3/75)

Colonial Secretary's Office,
Singapore, 20 January, 1875.

To:
J. G. Davidson Esq.,
Her Majesty's Resident,
Salangor.

Sir,
I am directed to inform you that the Governor has been pleased to appoint you, subject to confirmation by the Secretary of State, to be Her Majesty's Resident to the Sultan of Salangor, and to communicate to you the following instructions for your guidance in the duties of that office.

2. His Excellency desires that you will proceed at once to Klang, where you will establish yourself at first, making such arrangements for your personal accommodation as the nature of the case will admit of, and proceeding as soon as possible to organise a Resident's guard and Police of such force as you may think proper under the circumstances, applying to the Inspector General of Police for a few men from Singapore or Malacca in the first instance as a commencement.

3. His Excellency desires that you will at once publish notices far and wide, not only in Salangor, Klang, Langat, Lookoot, Lingie, and other places in Salangor, but also in Perak, Malacca, Singapore, and Penang, recalling all fugitives, promising them protection, and taking special steps for having such of them as possessed property restored to the possession of their property, and providing all of them with waste land to cultivate if they wish to cultivate.

4. His Excellency attaches much importance to success in inducing these people to return to Salangor, and trusts that you will give your best attention to the matter.

5. You are requested to make a report at your earliest convenience on the general subject of the Revenue System which you think should be adopted.

6. His Excellency is of opinion that waste lands should be freely granted to bona fide intending cultivators on terms free of State tax for 3 years, and after 3 years to be liable to 5% on estimated produce on lands cleared and cultivated subject to be commuted to a yearly money payment, but large grants of land should be sparingly given without guarantee of intended cultivation or of large sums being spent in the erection of machinery etc. or that they should be given liable to a small tax of so much an acre, if not cultivated within a reasonable time, and kept in a state of cultivation.

7. The lands will be liable however to taxation for road making to be managed by the occupiers, and also for expenses required at any time for an extra Police Force made necessary in any District by crimes of violence.

8. One of the first of these roads should, His Excellency thinks, be made or rather improved, from the landing place at Klang to the mines, a distance it is said of 16 miles.

9. The system of collecting revenue on imports, such as Opium, tobacco, rice etc., and on exports, mineral and vegetable should occupy your early attention, and His Excellency will be prepared to receive a report from you on this important matter, so as to have the system settled as soon as possible.

10. Tuanku Dia Oodin's debts should however be enquired into at once, and a well authenticated statement of his affairs submitted for settlement, by a sinking fund calculated at the rate of 6% on all bona fide debts due by him, incurred for the benefit of the country, and from your previous knowledge of the Tuanku's affairs, His Excellency doubts not that you will be able to send in a statement and scheme for settlement at an early date.

11. As is usual in such cases you will keep a careful diary of all your proceedings, a copy of which should be sent to this office by every regular opportunity from Klang, and you will send in a regular monthly report of progress, and a monthly statement of account showing the revenue and expenses of the country, which you will take under your special charge, being assisted by such officers, clerks etc. as may be sanctioned by His Excellency on your representation after arrival at Klang.

12. A steam launch will be provided for you at once, to enable

you to visit the several places of trade and population in Salangor, and His Excellency desires that you will take an early opportunity of seeing the Sultan of Salangor at Langat, and that you will enter into such relations with His Highness as will enable you, in gaining his confidence, to be of real service in securing the progress and prosperity of his country.

13. Mr. Swettenham, the Assistant Resident at Langat, has been instructed to correspond direct with this office for the present, sending copies of his letters to you for your information.

Braddell,

Col. Sec. S.S.

b. INSTRUCTIONS TO RESIDENTS (SEL/SEC. 373A/95) *CIRCULAR.*

Colonial Secretary's Office,
Singapore, 24 June 1895.

INSTRUCTIONS TO RESIDENTS.

His Excellency the Governor has been pleased to direct that the following Standing Instructions shall be observed in all the Protected Native States:-

I. *Authority for Expenditure.*—No new appointment on the Fixed Establishment or Provisional and Temporary Establishment can be made, and no increase of salary can be granted, without the sanction of the Governor, while, as regards other expenditure not provided for in the Estimates, the authority of the Residents is limited to a sum of $500 on any one account, and a return of all such excess warrants must be rendered quarterly, in the form of the Schedule attached, to the Governor.

Where any sum beyond $500 is urgently required, full particulars must be given and reference made to the Governor for authority to spend the amount required.

In the same way, no transfer of any amount exceeding $500 can be made from one vote to another without reference to the Governor.

Exception.—In Perak and Selangor, in the case of Works, Railway Works and Roads, the authority of the Resident may extend to the transfer or allowance of $2,500 on any one item.

II. *Re-votes for Works.*—In the case of works unexpectedly left unfinished in the year in which provision for their execution is made in the Estimates, re-votes to the extent of the unexpended balance may be allowed by the Resident, but the amount of such re-votes must be immediately reported through the Colonial Secretary.

No re-vote may be made in respect of a provision for a work which has not been begun or in respect of the unexpended balance of an open vote.

III. *Appointments.*—The Residents will deal with all appointments and promotions carrying salaries on the Fixed or Provisional and

Temporary Establishments not exceeding $600 per annum, or, where paid from an open vote, not exceeding $1,200.

Exception.—In Perak and Selangor, the Residents will deal with appointments and promotions to offices on the Fixed or Provisional and Temporary Establishments carrying salaries of over $600 and not exceeding $1,200 per annum, also in the case of posts carrying salaries exceeding $1,200 but not exceeding $1,800 per annum paid out of open votes. All other cases must be referred to the Governor.

IV. *Dismissals.*—No dismissal of an officer on the Fixed Establishment whose salary exceeds $600 can be made without reference to the Governor.

In the case of officers on the Provisional and Temporary Establishment, or paid out of open votes, reference to the Governor is only necessary if the salary exceeds $1,200 per annum, but in all cases of dismissal it is absolutely necessary that the officer concerned should first be called upon to give a written reply to the written charges of which he is accused.

V. *Leave.*—The Residents may grant vacation leave up to six weeks to any officer entitled to it under the General Orders.

Exception.—Beyond six weeks, and up to a total of three months, leave of absence may be granted, either vacation or on half-pay, or without salary, by the Residents of Perak and Selangor only.

Application for leave exceeding three months in duration must be referred to the Governor, as also all leave for even a shorter period should an officer be proceeding to Europe who desires to draw salary from the Crown Agents, or who, while at home, may visit or address the Colonial Office.

VI. *Loans.*—No loan of public money is to be made by a Resident without the previous sanction of the Governor.

Exception.—An exception may be admitted to this rule, in Perak and Selangor, where the Resident is authorized to make loans in no case exceeding one thousand dollars and in the aggregate not exceeding five thousand dollars (including all previous loans) to Malays—

(a) for *bona fide* agricultural enterprise, or the purchase of seed-corn or buffaloes; or,

(b) for the *bona fide* development of mining or other land;

provided that security to the satisfaction of the Resident for the repayment of the loan and interest is given, and that interest of at least 6% per annum is charged.

In Negri Sembilan the Resident is authorized to make loans in no case exceeding two hundred dollars and in the aggregate not exceeding one thousand dollars (including all previous loans) for the above stated objects.

VII. The Auditor of the State is directed to report to the Colonial Secretary through the Resident any breach of these Instructions.

VIII. The Instructions of May 27th, 1892 (C.S. 3230/92) and all modifications thereof are hereby cancelled.

By His Excellency's Command,

J. A. SWETTENHAM,

Colonial Secretary.

c. MINUTE, BY THE RESIDENT, FOR THE GUIDANCE OF DISTRICT OFFICERS
(*SGG*, 16 May 1890.)

No. 105. MINUTE, BY THE RESIDENT, FOR THE GUIDANCE OF DIS-
TRICT OFFICERS.—In reviewing the administration of the State of
Selangor in 1889, I have become convinced that the duties and functions of a District Officer are not sufficiently understood in this
State. I have noticed in almost all the Districts a want of initiation
on the part of the Officers in charge, who seem to think that reforms
and improvements in the administration of their Districts must be
suggested from head-quarters. There has been also a tendency in
some cases to disclaim responsibility for, or interest in, matters controlled by the professional Departments at head-quarters, and, even
in financial matters coming within the cognisance of a District Officer
as Sub-Treasurer, it has not always been recognized that the Officer
in charge of a District Treasury has to insist on adherence to the
General Orders, and that Departmental irregularities should be
checked, and, if necessary, reported by him. I doubt if proper efforts
are being made to utilise the services of the Penghulus, and to instruct
them in their duties; and there is little in the diaries and monthly
letters of the Officers in charge of Districts to shew me that they are
using their powers and opportunities to interest the native inhabitants in the well-being and advancement of their District. I do not
learn much from them of the Penghulus and other influential natives.
In judicial matters, existing enactments and regulations have seemed
in some cases to be imperfectly understood, and the procedure of
the Courts leaves much to be desired. I am hopeful that, in 1890,
much that I now criticise will be corrected, but I am convinced that
the first thing to do is to place before District Officers, in clear and
unmistakeable language, my view of what their duties are. The Regulations at the foot of this Memorandum are, therefore, issued for
their information and guidance.

I look to a District Officer to exercise general control and supervision over every thing that goes on in his District. He has no legislative functions, a statement which it would be unnecessary to make,
but for the fact that I have known instances where District Officers
have prescribed certain things by notice or proclamation, and have

treated a breach of their directions as a punishable offence. The District Officer should be able, through his headmen, with whom he should be in touch and in constant communication, to give the Resident information about any local matter; and while avoiding anything like unnecessary interference in professional details, which are properly left to the direction of Heads of Departments at Kwala Lumpor, he can contribute to Departmental efficiency, and render important assistance to the Inspecting Officers, by exercising a vigilant superintendence over local subordinates. A District Officer, for instance, would not interfere in the work being performed by a gang of upkeep coolies on a road under the direction of the Public Works Department, but he should certainly communicate with the Head of the Department, if he had reason to think that money was being wasted, or that contract work was not in accordance with specification; and he should, from time to time, on passing road-gangs, check the roll and see what men are working. Again, he would not interfere with the local Apothecary or Dresser in carrying out the orders of the District Surgeon, though it is, of course, his duty to visit the District Hospital frequently, to inspect the rations occasionally, and to take notice of the absence or misconduct of any of the staff. Similarly, he would not interfere with the drill or discipline of the Police, but he is the person responsible for the suppression of crime, and the maintenance of order in his District, and his orders to the Police for the furtherance of these objects must be implicitly followed.

The District Officer should aim at possessing complete information about the condition and needs of his District—every road, path, river, village, and hamlet in which he should know thoroughly. It is in his power, without in any way departing from the reserve incumbent upon a British functionary living among an Asiatic population, to acquire very detailed knowledge of the circumstances, and trading and family connections of the principal native inhabitants, and to have such an acquaintanceship among them that he will be able to judge of the value of information to be obtained from, or assistance to be afforded by each. Every additional qualification acquired by a District Officer adds to his efficiency, and life at an outstation should usually afford ample time for study. Knowledge of one or more of the native languages, of the principles of English law, and of the practice of book-keeping are essential; and no District Officer can be considered to be competent who has not given much time to these subjects. If he can survey, make roads, sail a boat, etc., so much the better. The varied demands upon the knowledge and resource of the chief officer of a District are the best test of his efficiency. He may be sure that the manner in which he responds to such demands is closely watched at head-quarters, and that his success in the public service depends upon it.

SELANGOR,   W. E. MAXWELL,
   April 11th, 1890.   *British Resident.*

REGULATIONS.

1. The District Officer is subject to the orders of the Resident, in general executive charge of the district assigned to him. His principal duties are—

A.—To hold Courts, both Civil and Criminal, at the chief station of the district, and at the out-lying stations, on days fixed by the Resident, and to act as Coroner.

B.—To superintend the Land Office of the district.

C.—To collect revenue of all kinds, and to manage the Sub-Treasury of the district.

In the Coast districts he is also Harbour Master.

A.

2. The practice of the District Courts shall follow generally that of the Police Courts and Courts of Requests of the Colony of the Straits Settlements, and all accounts shall be kept, and fees collected, in the manner prescribed there.

3. The District Officer will hold an inquest in all cases of sudden or violent death, reported to him by the Police, within his district, with as little delay as possible. When absent from his station, he will leave information as to the place at which such a report may be sent to him.

B.

4. The duties of a District Officer, in connection with the Land Office, are as follows:—

   (*a*) To collect Land Revenue (current and arrears), according to the existing Rent-Roll.

(b) To prepare and keep up a new Rent-Roll, classified according to *Mukims*.
(c) To supervise the Demarcation and Survey staff (if any).
(d) To receive and report on applications for Waste Land.
(e) To issue licenses to cut timber and collect jungle produce.
(f) To protect Waste Lands from encroachment.
(g) To register transfers, etc.

5. The revenue records, namely, the original Rent-Roll and the Duplicates of Titles will be kept at the District Office. Agreements for grants and leases must be drawn up in duplicate at the District Office, numbered in consecutive order, and signed by the District Officer and the licensee, and counter-signed by the Resident; they will be entered in a temporary Rent-Roll kept for the purpose; one copy will be delivered to the licensee and one filed in the District Office for record. Land Grants can be prepared in the District Office, if a surveyor is attached to it, but where this is not the case, a requisition must be transmitted to the Land Office, Kwala Lumpur, for the preparation of a title plan. The Grant or Lease will in this case be completed in the Land Office, and sent to the District Office, when ready for issue.

6. The District Officer has no authority to decide upon applications for Waste Land. He must forward all such applications for the orders of the Resident. But the District Officer is authorised, subject to the Resident's instructions, where there has been at least five years' occupation of Agricultural Waste Land by a squatter, to recognise the squatter's right to receive a title, on payment of a reasonable premium and back rent.

7. The District Officer must, on, or as soon as possible after, the 1st of each month, send to the Resident a return of the Land Revenue collected in the District in the month just ended, classified under the headings in the Estimates.

8. The District Officer should, as long as the demarcation of his District is incomplete, apply, from time to time, for authority to employ as many demarcators as he can conveniently supervise, and he shall push on the demarcation of holdings, land revenue settlement, and the preparation of a territorial Rent-Roll.

9. The Mukim Rent-Rolls, as prepared successively, shall be examined by an Officer of the Audit Department, and authority must be obtained to adopt them and write off all entries in the old Rent-Rolls.

10. Every Penghulu or other Sub-Collector employed in the collection of Land Revenue shall give subsidiary security. He shall be required to pay in all moneys in his hands, weekly, and to produce his counter-foil books to be checked with the cash.

11. Each District Officer shall be a Sub-Treasurer for his District, and he is empowered to retain revenue collections in his Sub-Treasury to the amount of $3,000. Any sum in excess of this should be paid into the Treasury, Should the sum in his hands at any time exceed this amount, he must, at once, report the fact by telegraph or letter to the Resident, who will direct him as to the disposal of the money.

12. In making disbursements, the District Officer, as Sub-Treasurer, has the same powers and responsibilities as the Treasurer at Head-quarters, subject to any special orders contained in these instructions, or to be given by the Resident from time to time. He is to be guided in all respects by the General Orders. For every disbursement entered in the Cash Book, a duly authorised bill or voucher must be retained.

13. No payment is to be made by the Sub-Treasury of one District on account of that of another District, unless the bills are first countersigned by the Officer in charge of the District to which the expenditure is chargeable.

14. No bill is to be paid without the special authority of the Resident, which causes the expenditure in any one month on any open vote to exceed one-twelfth of the total provision for the year.

15. The District Officer shall keep a Cash Book in the form of that kept in the Treasury, in which all receipts and disbursements shall be entered.

The Cash Book shall be balanced and initialled at the close of each day's transactions by the District Officer, or, in his absence, by his Chief Clerk. The money in each District Treasury shall be kept in the chest, which shall be secured by two different locks. The keys shall be in the custody of the District Officer, and his Chief Clerk, respectively.

16. I.—The Chief Clerk is responsible for the correctness of the daily collections and disbursements; every receipt and payment should pass through his hands.

II.—At the close of business, daily, he must compare the cash with the counterfoils, and, if correct, hand it to the District Officer, obtaining the usual receipt.

Any difficulty in arriving at the exact collections for the day should be reported to the District Officer, but in no case should deficits be made good by the Chief Clerk without the express orders of the District Officer.

III.—Any amount collected in excess, in error, should be treated as a *Provisional Receipt*, until otherwise disposed of, on the instructions of the Auditor.

17. After paying in the day's collections, the Chief Clerk must write up the Cash Book (Receipts), which must be examined every morning by the District Officer; and to enable the figures to be properly checked, the daily total should be carried out in the column for *Head of Service*, when its correctness can be easily proved by reference to the Chief Clerk's daily receipt book.

18. All Remittance Statements should be entered at the end of each month.

19. Clerks and Forest Rangers entrusted with certain collections are responsible to the Chief Clerk for the same, and the latter on receiving cash from them must initial the counterfoils as an acknowledgment that the money has been received.

20. I.—All disbursements should be made from the safe, and not from the cash collected each day, except when the District Officer is absent, and the Chief Clerk has to make a payment from the daily collections in his hands.

II.—When the Chief Clerk is entrusted with the payment of bills, he should obtain from the District Officer an order in the Form A attached.

III.—He should prepare the Vouchers, making a short entry of them on the back of the order, and then present the bills and order to the District Officer, who, after satisfying himself as to their correctness, and after signing the bills, may issue the amount to the Chief Clerk, retaining the order in the safe.

21. The Cash Book should be written up as payments are made.

22. There must be a receipted voucher in the Office for every payment, and vouchers must not be sent out of the Office for signature before entry in the Cash Book. Where completed vouchers cannot be obtained, an advance may be made on a temporary receipt headed *Advances to Heads of Departments*. On the completion of regular vouchers, subsequently, the accounts should be adjusted by *contra* entries.

23. The Cash in the safes should be examined by the District Officer, and a balance struck at least once a week.

24. Stamps should be regarded as Cash, and when received from Head-quarters should be treated in the same way as a Cash remittance. The District Officer is responsible for the Stamps standing to the credit of his cash balance. When Stamps are sold, no credit entry is necesssary.

Post and Telegraph Clerks, at out-stations, must pay for Stamps received from District Officers, keeping a Stamp Stock Book detailing sales. The District Officer should for his own private information keep a record of Stamps sold.

II.—At stations where there are no Post and Telegraph Clerks, one of the District Officer's Clerks should, on giving a written receipt for the same, be supplied with a limited quantity of Stamps for sale, and must account for the Cash to the Sub-Treasury as the Stamps are sold.

25. Within five days after the close of each month, the District Officer shall send a copy of the Cash Book entries for the month, together with all vouchers to the Auditor.

26. I.—Subject to the Conservancy Regulations of Government, the District Officer shall perform in respect of the villages, and so far

as regards supervision of all the roads in his District, the duties assigned to Municipal Commissioners in a town in the Colony of the Straits Settlements.

II.—He must pay attention to sanitation, inspect the Government Hospitals in his District, take all proper precautions on the out-break of infectious disease, whether among men or cattle, and enforce vaccination.

27. The District Officer must visit all Vernacular Schools in his District, from time to time, and encourage education among the people.

CORRESPONDENCE.

28. A copy of every letter despatched must be kept.

29. Letters and Minutes received must be registered in a correspondence-register, and a complete copy of every important minute-paper received from the Resident's Office must be kept. These must be filed according to their registered numbers.

30. The *Selangor Government Gazette*, and all newspapers subscribed for officially, must be filed regularly and bound up in volumes at the end of every year.

31. A complete list of all Government furniture and other property in the District Officer's charge must be kept and maintained up to date, and a stationery stock-book, shewing receipts and issues, must be kept.

W. E. MAXWELL,

THE RESIDENCY, SELANGOR,   *British Resident.*
     May 8th, 1890.   ————

d. PENGHULU COMMISSION, PERAK
Kaulul—Haq

Bahawa maka ada-lah kita Sultan Idris Murshidil-a'adzam Shah KCMG Ibnu Al-Marhom Iskandar Shah Yang Di-Pertuan Negeri Perak Daru-r-ridzuan serta Tuan2 Ahli Meshuarat Council Kerajaan Perak maka kita telah menaroh harap dan perchaya di-dalam mengerja dan menjalankan atoran yang telah kita izinkan maka ada-lah kita menjadi-kan To' Muda Ab. Rahman bin Raja Setia Penghulu daerah Batang Padang serta kita kurniai gaji kapada-nya $25.00 sa-bulan dengan tiada mendapat chabut.

Yang pertama: Shahadan maka ada-lah kita menjadikan To' Muda Ab. Rahman Penghulu daerah Batang Padang maka kita telah memberi kapada-nya dengan sa-chukup kuasa supaya boleh ia menyelesaikan perkara aduan yang kechil 2 di-dalam daerah-nya serta kita benarkan boleh ia mendenda di-atas perkara itu tiada lebeh daripadi lima rial, maka rial denda yang tersebut hendak-lah di-hantar serahkan kadalam perbendaharaan tempat perhimponan rial di-dalam daerah mukim-nya ia-itu di-Tapah.

Yang kedua: Kalakian maka ini-lah kita memberi kapada Penghulu To' Muda Ab. Rahman dengan sachukup kuasa boleh ia mengutipkan segala hasil2 yang telah kita benarkan, maka rial yang tersebut mahu-lah di-masokkan ka-dalam perbendaharaan tempat perhimponan rial di-dalam daerah.

Yang ketiga: Maka jika sakira-nya ada perkara yang besar2 di-dalam daerah-nya ia-itu saperti penyamun dan berbunoh2an atau mati terkejut saketika itu maka yang demikian itu hendak-lah ia tangkapkan yang membuat-nya dan dengan segera-nya-lah ia mahu mendapatkan serta di-beri tahu darihal perkara itu kapada kepala yang memerentahkan daerah-nya dan jika ada orang yang di-kenai penyakit yang berjangkit2 ia-itu saperti ketumbohan atau lain2-nya maka hendak-lah penghulu asingkan dengan berjauhan tempat-nya tiada boleh bersama2 dengan orang yang lain.

Yang keempat: Demikian lagi pekerjaan penghulu itu hendak-lah menyimpan satu buku register nama-nya ia-itu-lah buku di-tulis nama2 orang yang di-dalam ta'alok daerah-nya baik daripada tanah atau galian dan yang punya dan lain perkara bagi yang tersebut di-dalam list yang telah di-beri kapada-nya serta hendak-lah penghulu memberi nasehat segala orang2 di-dalam mukim-nya menyurohkan berbuat bendang supaya meninggalkan perkerjaan ladang kerana ada-lah pekerjaan berladang itu tiada-lah kekal kepenyudahan-nya dan lagi menjadi kebinasaan jua kapada negeri demikian jua mana2 orang yang belum kena penyakit ketumbohan itu hendak-lah penghulu ikhtiar serahkan ia kapada Tuan Doctor bertanam beneh ketumbohan kerana beberapa banyak yang kita kctahui mana2 yang sudah di-tanam beneh itu tiada lagi di-kenai oleh penyakit itu.

Yang kelima: Maka ada-lah saperti segala orang2 di-dalam mukim-nya mahu-lah mengikut dan menurut bagi pcnghulu yang tersebut ini di-atas surohan-nya yang patut hendak-lah segala orang tulong kerjakan atas yang berpatutan dengan segera-nya.

Yang keenam: Jika siapa2 orang yang engkar daripada surohan-nya nyata-lah orang itu mendapat kesalahan yang besar tertentu-lah kita jatohkan denda atas bagi yang demikian tiada lebeh daripada lima ratus rial atau ikut sabagaimana keputusan hakim mempenjarakan akan bekerja berat yang tiada lebeh daripadi dua tahun.

Yang ketujoh: Jika ada mereka2 di-dalam daerah-nya itu menaroh kuasa daripadi segala raja2 yang dahulu menjadikan ia penghulu di-dalam daerah itu maka sekarang telah kita batalkan tiada boleh di-pakai dan tiada berguna dan mahu-lah di-serahkan surat kenyataan itu kapada penghulu.

Yang kelapan: Demikian lagi jika ada siapa2 mengaku diri-nya jadi penghulu di-dalam mana2 mukim dengan tiada ketetapan daripada kita atau tiada dengan kebenaran daripada British Resident nyata-lah di-kcnakan satu denda bagi yang demikian tiada lebeh daripada lima ratus rial atau di-masokkan ka-dalam penjara tiada lebeh daripada dua tahun.

Yang kesembilan: Jika penghulu membuat perkara yang tiada kebenaran daripada kita atau mengutip chukai atau menyuroh orang tiada dengan sapatut-nya atau anyaya pada ra'ayat kita penghulu itu nyata-lah kita murkai dan kita jatohkan hukum yang berat di-atas-nya demikian-lah kita beri ketahui supaya jangan-lah di-perbuat saperti yang tersebut di-atas ini hubaya2 jangan di-lalui ada-nya.

Termaklub di-dalam Office Secretary Government kapada 8hb. December 1894.

(*Translation*)

The Word of Truth

We, Sultan Murshidil-a'adzam Shah, KCMG, Ibnu al-Marhom Iskandar Shah, Yang di-Pertuan of Perak, the Abode of Grace, together with the members of the Council of Perak, in whom we place our confidence and trust in conducting the business [of the state] in the manner we have sanctioned, hereby appoint To' Muda Ab. Rahman bin Raja Setia to be Penghulu of Batang Padang with a salary of $25 a month without commission.

First: We appoint To' Muda Ab. Rahman to be Penghulu of Batang Padang with power to settle small cases in his district and impose fines of not more than $5, the said fines to be delivered to the treasury of the district in which his mukim is situated, that is, at Tapah.

Second: Furthermore we grant Penghulu To' Muda Ab. Rahman authority to collect such revenues as we sanction, the collections to be delivered to the district treasury.

Third: Should there be an important occurrence in his district, such as robbery, homicide or sudden death, he should arrest the culprit and immediately inform the district officer [lit: the head of the administration of the district]. And if there should be someone suffering from an infectious disease, such as smallpox, he must isolate the sick person.

Fourth: It is the duty of the penghulu to keep a register book in which he should enter the names of the people in his district, with details of lands, mines, and owners thereof, and such other information as may be specified in the return furnished to him. He should advise and instruct everyone in his mukim to plant wet padi and to cease shifting cultivation, since it is not permanent and ruins the country. He should take steps to bring people who have not yet had smallpox to the doctor to be vaccinated, since according to our knowledge, whoever has been vaccinated is thereafter immune from the disease.

Fifth: All persons in his mukim must follow his lawful instructions, and promptly assist in carrying out lawful tasks.

Sixth: Disobeying the instructions of a penghulu is a serious offence, punishable by a fine of up to $500, or, should the magistrate so direct, by up to two years' imprisonment with hard labour.

Seventh: Should there be anyone in his district holding an authority from a raja in former times, appointing him a penghulu, such authority is hereby cancelled and should be surrendered to the [lawful] penghulu.

Eighth: Should anyone claim to be a penghulu in any mukim without our confirmation or the sanction of the British Resident, he will incur a fine of up to $500 or imprisonment up to two years.

Ninth: Should a penghulu act without our sanction or collect taxes or give orders unlawfully or oppress our people, he will incur our wrath and will be severely punished.

Written in the office of the Secretary to Government, 8 December 1894.

Note. This document has been transliterated into Rumi from a Jawi original in Batang Padang Papers, 10/95. There is room for confusion in the use of the word *daerah* (district). Batang Padang was the name of an administrative district as well as of a penghulu sub-division (mukim) and it is the latter word that is commonly used to describe the area of a penghulu's authority. Daerah has therefore been used in this sense when it appeared appropriate. The main provisions of this penghulu authority are contained in the Selangor penghulu commission drawn up by Swettenham in 1883 and based on the form promulgated in Perak in 1879; this Selangor commission was still in use in 1891 (Swettenham Minute on Local District Administration in Selangor, 6 June 1883, S.S. Legislative Council Paper 23 of 1883; Sel/Sec. 2256/91). It was replaced by a new commission in 1892.

TABLES

1. RETURN OF REVENUE AND EXPENDITURE, MALAY STATES, 1875–96

Year	REVENUE					EXPENDITURE				
	Perak	Selangor	Negri Sembilan	Pahang	Total	Perak	Selangor	Negri Sembilan	Pahang	Total
	$	$	$	$	$	$	$	$	$	$
1875	226,333	115,656	67,405	—	409,394	256,831	111,305	68,736	—	436,872
1876	273,043	193,476	94,478	—	560,997	289,476	191,174	104,539	—	585,189
1877	312,872	226,853	97,707	—	637,432	292,711	232,090	97,338	—	622,139
1878	328,608	189,897	75,898	—	594,403	291,473	187,624	76,802	—	555,899
1879	388,372	184,387	76,632	—	649,391	369,707	185,729	75,252	—	630,688
1880	582,496	215,614	83,800	—	881,910	521,995	202,806	70,143	—	794,944
1881	692,861	235,227	97,665	—	1,025,753	652,938	234,383	73,469	—	960,790
1882	905,385	300,423	109,412	—	1,315,220	918,914	259,081	121,458	—	1,299,453
1883	1,474,330	450,664	117,144	—	2,042,138	1,350,610	448,703	153,686	—	1,952,999
1884	1,532,497	494,483	121,175	—	2,148,155	1,481,470	514,948	142,292	—	2,138,710
1885	1,522,084	566,411	120,214	—	2,208,709	1,316,625	826,526	118,803	—	2,261,954
1886	1,688,276	689,401	123,364	—	2,501,041	1,465,325	683,876	137,338	—	2,286,539
1887	1,827,476	1,153,896	161,355	—	3,142,727	1,550,489	885,931	179,948	—	2,616,368
1888	2,016,240	1,417,998	223,435	—	3,657,673	1,709,260	1,055,373	249,310	—	3,013,943
1889	2,776,583	1,828,427	377,600	30,390	5,013,000	2,090,116	1,394,181	464,161	142,620	4,091,078
1890	2,504,116	1,888,928	384,944	62,077	4,840,065	2,555,793	1,996,544	387,236	297,702	5,237,275
1891	2,324,981	1,825,585	344,358	77,386	4,572,310	3,146,129	1,724,338	446,159	238,174	5,554,800
1892	2,689,565	2,135,448	472,132	50,044	5,347,189	3,094,855	2,044,115	473,044	271,393	5,883,407
1893	3,034,093	2,765,351	530,002	83,688	6,413,134	3,401,086	2,605,588	508,629	282,235	6,797,538
1894	3,542,114	3,334,468	535,007	100,220	7,511,809	3,587,224	2,817,292	508,760	249,120	7,162,396
1895	4,033,611	3,805,211	535,442	106,743	8,481,007	3,757,007	3,083,386	510,247	231,913	7,582,553
1896	3,960,871	3,756,936	555,329	160,947	8,434,083	3,989,376	3,572,583	573,569	462,619	8,598,147

Source: *AR* Federated Malay States, 1896, Special General Return.
Note: The return for Negri Sembilan includes returns for Sungei Ujong and Jelebu.

2. DETAILED RETURNS OF REVENUE, 1875–96

Year	Duty on Tin					Land Revenue				
	Perak	Selangor	Negri Sembilan	Pahang	Total	Perak	Selangor	Negri Sembilan	Pahang	Total
	$	$	$	$	$	$	$	$	$	$
1875	—	—					866			866
1876	—	—					406			406
1877	140,292	—			140,292		605			605
1878	245,512	111,920			357,432	10,998	1,326			12,324
1879	281,823	107,558			389,381	21,637	943			22,580
1880	298,805	100,586			399,391	38,388	456			38,844
1881	387,642	126,038			513,680	32,499	2,957			35,456
1882	457,410	161,832			619,242	58,365	1,810			60,175
1883	619,809	180,002	—		799,811	56,479	25,738	—		82,217
1884	641,351	—	27,901		669,252	48,535	30,905	15,467		94,907
1885	547,648	255,254	28,392		831,294	61,504	16,000	14,012		91,517
1886	611,869	302,530	32,703		947,102	73,148	21,575	13,304		108,027
1887	720,247	450,365	46,020		1,216,532	72,710	46,626	30,960		150,296
1888	851,420	526,742	58,595	—	1,436,757	85,623	50,214	53,253	—	189,090
1889	937,293	750,634	60,171	1,910	1,750,008	82,109	43,271	54,197	10,961	190,538
1890	860,730	672,667	71,381	4,623	1,609,401	75,387	33,155	37,945	19,567	166,054
1891	812,956	672,633	78,707	9,145	1,573,441	92,603	41,674	43,168	22,235	199,680
1892	1,124,931	828,326	135,284	8,733	2,097,274	152,901	81,975	52,030	13,774	300,680
1893	1,333,890	1,082,004	176,164	10,322	2,602,380	149,629	104,521	69,103	24,347	347,600
1894	1,648,981	1,402,174	169,275	17,570	3,238,000	235,667	122,697	70,531	28,367	457,262
1895	1,669,707	1,520,927	164,712	24,467	3,379,813	226,345	142,092	75,960	23,842	468,239
1896	1,541,442	1,377,325	181,260	26,947	3,126,974	280,738	134,313	66,379	29,807	511,237

Source: *AR* Federated Malay States, 1896, Special General Return.

2. DETAILED RETURNS OF REVENUE (continued)

Year	POSTAL AND TELEGRAPH REVENUE					RAILWAY RECEIPTS				
	Perak	Selangor	Negri Sembilan	Pahang	Total	Perak	Selangor	Negri Sembilan	Pahang	Total
	$	$	$	$	$	$	$	$	$	$
1875	—	104	—	—	104	—	—	—	—	—
1876	—	76	—	—	76	—	—	—	—	—
1877	—	76	—	—	76	—	—	—	—	—
1878	—	68	—	—	68	—	—	—	—	—
1879	—	85	—	—	85	—	—	—	—	—
1880	206	27	—	—	233	—	—	—	—	—
1881	520	—	—	—	520	—	—	—	—	—
1882	676	—	—	—	676	—	—	—	—	—
1883	552	465	—	—	1,017	—	—	—	—	—
1884	3,538	403	357	—	4,298	—	—	—	—	—
1885	4,149	528	255	—	4,932	23,873	—	—	—	23,873
1886	6,334	1,109	366	—	7,809	55,015	9,726	—	—	64,741
1887	8,426	3,485	527	—	12,438	60,953	141,570	—	—	202,523
1888	9,252	7,638	798	—	17,688	78,759	289,594	—	—	368,353
1889	10,994	13,333	1,436	264	26,027	82,791	276,234	—	—	359,025
1890	21,890	12,678	1,956	1,218	37,742	88,764	317,268	—	—	406,032
1891	24,810	15,300	2,639	1,537	44,286	99,338	315,551	—	—	414,889
1892	30,136	18,920	2,972	1,602	53,630	82,940	381,199	72,972	—	537,111
1893	31,478	37,765	3,565	1,133	73,941	117,906	521,386	84,642	—	723,934
1894	40,756	40,469	6,631	1,934	89,790	244,447	660,794	81,376	—	986,617
1895	56,006	43,655	8,282	2,850	110,793	443,877	770,074	80,439	—	1,294,390
1896	54,134	76,182	7,274	2,640	140,230	509,063	750,519	85,412	—	1,344,994

3. RETURN OF IMPORTS AND EXPORTS, 1875–96

TRADE

Year	IMPORTS					EXPORTS				
	Perak	Selangor	Negri Sembilan	Pahang	Total	Perak	Selangor	Negri Sembilan	Pahang	Total
	$	$	$	$	$	$	$	$	$	$
1875	—	—	—	—	—	—	—	—	—	—
1876	831,375	—	—	—	831,375	739,972	—	—	—	739,972
1877	965,894	—	—	—	965,894	1,075,423	—	—	—	1,075,423
1878	1,311,140	—	—	—	1,311,140	1,256,163	—	—	—	1,256,163
1879	1,781,980	—	—	—	1,781,980	1,465,547	—	—	—	1,465,547
1880	2,231,048	—	—	—	2,231,048	1,906,952	—	—	—	1,906,952
1881	2,936,893	—	352,373	—	3,289,266	2,566,592	—	465,877	—	3,032,469
1882	3,866,425	1,188,417	614,236	—	5,669,078	3,267,907	1,707,331	563,403	—	5,538,641
1883	4,772,332	1,525,614	669,908	—	6,968,854	5,164,311	2,253,639	625,592	—	8,043,542
1884	6,047,694	1,824,859	668,481	—	8,541,034	5,393,996	2,124,307	578,265	—	8,096,568
1885	5,811,605	2,275,391	580,429	—	8,667,425	6,569,465	2,544,947	577,373	—	9,691,786
1886	5,586,563	4,178,856	648,455	—	10,413,864	8,674,032	3,741,642	786,708	—	13,202,382
1887	6,951,963	5,052,112	899,414	—	12,903,489	12,249,334	5,901,785	1,056,760	—	19,207,879
1888	7,998,364	8,207,105	1,121,923	—	17,327,392	11,799,653	6,779,357	1,205,100	—	19,784,110
1889	7,048,046	7,029,406	1,576,004	—	15,653,456	10,812,673	7,764,007	1,144,009	—	19,720,689
1890	7,173,617	7,005,496	1,264,696	—	15,443,869	9,985,713	6,467,564	1,148,816	—	17,602,093
1891	7,913,357	5,670,098	1,306,487	—	14,889,942	10,655,332	6,560,324	1,279,898	—	18,495,554
1892	9,628,051	7,393,668	1,797,767	341,673	19,161,159	12,387,024	8,060,416	1,883,723	331,196	22,662,359
1893	10,188,448	9,274,649	2,069,186	363,834	21,896,117	14,499,475	10,271,808	2,234,922	367,555	27,373,760
1894	9,262,396	12,139,686	2,309,674	787,859	24,499,615	17,184,836	12,925,602	1,933,056	659,653	32,703,147
1895	9,581,372	10,759,123	2,366,279	946,497	22,653,271	15,596,225	13,955,803	1,295,464	775,313	31,622,805
1896	8,713,940	9,131,195	2,123,572	1,180,188	21,148,895	14,289,680	12,006,108	1,234,787	865,280	28,395,855

Source: *AR* Federated Malay States, 1896, Special General Return.

4. CENSUS OF PROTECTED STATES, 1891: ABSTRACT OF POPULATION

	Perak	Selangor	Sungei Ujong and Jelebu	Negri Sembilan	Pahang	Total
Europeans	366	190	46	15	102	719
Eurasians	289	167	40	28	41	565
Chinese	94,345	50,844	9,880	5,511	3,241	163,821
Malays, and other natives of the archipelago, including aborigines	103,992	26,578	12,532	35,948	53,122	232,172
Tamils and other natives of India	14,885	3,592	1,037	80	583	20,177
Others	377	221	67	35	373	1,073
	214,254	81,592	23,602	41,617	57,462	418,527

NOTE ON SOURCES

THE main source for the initiation of the Residential system is the correspondence between the Governor and the Colonial Office, useful also for the light it throws on the growth of policies and institutions in later years. The enclosures to these despatches contain material of importance not available elsewhere, including correspondence between the Singapore Secretariat and the Malay states. The gaps in the CO 273 series of despatches have been filled in by reference to the complete set in the National Library of Singapore. Where despatches have been published (i.e. in Command Papers) reference is to the published form.

The main sources for the internal administration of the states are the records of the state governments, housed in the Arkib Negara, Malaysia, (National Archives of Malaysia). The Resident's files have survived for Selangor and Negri Sembilan, but for Perak and Pahang the only files available are for the districts of Batang Padang and Kuantan respectively. It was not possible to deal adequately with the whole of this large body of material, and the writer has therefore concentrated on the Perak and Selangor records. The Selangor records date from the first appointment of a Resident in 1875, till 1940. They consist of correspondence and papers from the Colonial Secretary of the Straits Settlements and from outstations, departments and individuals to the Resident. In 1890, a Secretary to Government was appointed and thereafter the correspondence was addressed to him. For three months in 1890, and again from 1893–5, Sungei Ujong was placed under the supervision of the Resident of Selangor, and the records contain correspondence with the Officer in Charge, Sungei Ujong. There are some gaps, especially in the first ten years, and the contents of certain files are missing, but on the whole, they constitute a full and invaluable record of the government of the state.

The Batang Padang records are the office files of the district officer, Batang Padang, and contain correspondence and reports relating to the affairs of his district. They are reasonably full, but the contents of some files—district reports, returns, and instructions—are missing. The Negri Sembilan records, like those of Selangor, are the Resident's files and date from 1887 to 1941. The Kuantan District records run from 1889 to 1920 though there are a few files from 1888.

In addition to the official correspondence, there are a number of valuable unpublished journals kept by Residents and Collectors. Birch's journal, covering the whole period of his Residency, was forwarded to the Secretary of State in 1876 together with other material on his assassination, and is contained in CO 273/88. Swettenham's Langat journals, kept from the day of his arrival in Langat in August 1874 until his departure in September 1875, have now come to light and are shortly to be published. They give valuable information about contemporary Selangor, and about Swettenham's early contacts with the Sultan. The affairs of the Langat district are further documented by a letter-book and case-book, kept principally by James Innes, between 1876 and 1880, and a series of journals written by various Collectors between 1882 and 1885.

Council proceedings are available for three states, Selangor, Perak, and Sungei Ujong. The Selangor Council Minutes represent the official record of proceedings from the first council meeting on 18 April 1877. The original record of the Perak Council has not come to light. The minutes of meetings from 1877 to 1879 and 1880 to 1882 have been edited by C.W. Harrison and R. J. Wilkinson respectively, and published as History III (1907) and History IV (1909) of Series 1 of *Papers on Malay Subjects*, under the general editorship of R. J. Wilkinson. Abstracts of the minutes from 1889 to 1895 have been published in the Perak Government Gazettes for those years. The minutes of the Sungei Ujong State Council, 1883–93, are contained in CO 474/1.

The manuscript records are supplemented by government gazettes. Gazettes were first published in Perak in 1888 and Selangor in 1890, the Selangor gazette carrying a Sungei Ujong supplement from 1893. They were published fortnightly, and contain government notifications, legislation, Council minutes (Perak only) and district and departmental reports. They are particularly useful as a source for state legislation, since the standard editions of state laws (see List of Sources) do not give details of obsolete legislation.

There is a fair amount of statistical information, mostly from about 1888, in the appendices to annual reports (see List of Sources). It includes abstracts of revenue and expenditure, returns of trade, court cases, immigration, births and deaths, hospitals and schools. In addition, there are detailed estimates for Perak, Selangor and Sungei Ujong/Jelebu for certain years. The 1891 census of all states is published in Merewether, *Census of the Straits Settlements, 1891*, Singapore, 1892. (The Sungei Ujong figures include those for Jelebu; separate figures are to be found in the state reports for 1891.) The *Census of Perak, 1891* includes returns of an earlier census in 1879.

The information on establishments is taken from a great variety of sources. The main source for Selangor is the *Index to List of Establishments, Selangor, 1895*. It gives an alphabetical list of officers in the service, with the exception of police constables and certain categories of unskilled workers—e.g. labourers in the Railway Department. It also gives a detailed list of establishments, with salaries, the appointments being divided into 'fixed' and 'provisional' categories. The main source for Perak is the Government of Perak List of Establishments, available for the years 1884 to 1895, and the *Perak Handbook and Civil Service List, 1892*. The former contains a list of officers in the Perak Service and a detailed list of establishments, salaries and dates of first appointment; the latter, details of service of all European and some non-European officers. There is no comparable information for Sungei Ujong, Negri Sembilan or Pahang, though the *Sungei Ujong Estimates* for 1886–8 and 1890–5, and the Pahang Estimates for 1894 (Sel/Sec. 962/93) contain useful information, and there is also information about the European establishments in all the states in the *Native States List Containing the Civil Establishments, 1891.* In 1895, lists of fixed, pensionable appointments were drawn up for each state; the Selangor and Sungei Ujong lists were published in the *SGG*, 22 November 1895, and the Perak list in the *PGG* of the same date. The Singapore and Straits Directories contain much information, but the entries for any particular year usually relate to the year preceding, when the information was collated. Information given in annual state and departmental reports has been used to qualify or correct information in the directories.

LIST OF SOURCES
OFFICIAL RECORDS

Official Correspondence

Correspondence between Governor, Straits Settlements, and Secretary of State, 1867–98. CO 273.

Correspondence between Governor, Straits Settlements, and Secretary of State, Secret, 1873–98. CO 537.

Governor's Letter Books, 1877–81; 1881–93; 1881–94. National Library Archives, Singapore.

Perak Despatches, 1874–9 (with lists of penghulu appointments and state allowances, 1879). Perak Museum Library.

Batang Padang District Office files, 1888–95.

Selangor Secretariat files, 1875–99.

Journals of F. A. Swettenham at Langat, 13 August 1874 to 3 September 1875. (To be published.)

James Innes, Letter Book and Journal, Langat, 1876. CO Library.

Kuala Langat Journals, 1882–5. Typescript in University of Singapore Library.

Parliamentary Papers (Great Britain)

Command Paper 466 of 1872, *Papers relating to Salangore.*

C.1111 of 1874, *Correspondence relating to the Affairs of certain Native States in the Malay Peninsula.*

C.1320 of 1875, *Further Correspondence relating to the Affairs of certain Native States in the Malay Peninsula.*

C.1503 of 1876, *Further Correspondence relating to the Affairs of certain Native States in the Malay Peninsula.*

C.1505 of 1876, *Further Correspondence relating to the Affairs of certain Native States in the Malay Peninsula.*

C.1512 of 1876. *Further Correspondence relating to the Affairs of certain Native States in the Malay Peninsula.*

C.1709 of 1877, *Further Correspondence relating to the Affairs of certain Native States in the Malay Peninsula.*

C.2410 of 1879, *Instructions to the British Resident and Other Papers relating to the Protected Malay States.*

C.3095 of 1881, *Papers relating to the Protected Malay States* (with *AR* 1879)

C.3285 of 1882, *Correspondence respecting Slavery in the Protected Malay States.*

C.3428 of 1882, *Correspondence respecting Slavery in the Protected Malay States* (*AR* 1881).

C.3429 of 1882, *Further Correspondence respecting Slavery in the Protected Malay States.*

C.4192 of 1884, *Correspondence respecting the Protected Malay States* (*AR* 1882 and 1883).

C.4958 of 1887, *Further Correspondence respecting the Protected Malay States* (*AR* 1884 and 1885).

C.5566 of 1888, *Further Correspondence respecting the Protected Malay States* (*AR* 1886 and 1887).

C.5884 of 1889, *Further Correspondence respecting the Protected Malay States* (*AR* 1888).

C.6222 of 1890–1, *Papers relating to the Protected Malay States* (*AR* 1889).

House of Commons 378 of 1890–1, *Extracts of Correspondence with reference to the case of the Ex-Sultan Abdullah of Perak.*

C.6576 of 1892, *Further papers relating to the Protected Malay States* (*AR* 1890).

C.6858 of 1893, *Further papers relating to the Protected Malay States* (*AR* 1891).

C.7227 of 1893, *Reports on the Protected Malay States for 1892.*

C.7456 of 1894, *Reports on the Protected Malay States for 1893.*

C.7877 of 1895, *Reports on the Protected Malay States for 1894.*

C.8257 of 1896, *Reports on the Protected Malay States for 1895.*

C.8661 of 1897, *Reports on the Protected Malay States for 1896.*

Council Proceedings

Minutes of the Straits Settlements Executive Council, 1875–93. National Library Archives, Singapore.

Proceedings of the Straits Settlements Legislative Council, 1874–95. CO 275.

Perak Council Minutes
  1877–9 (see under Harrison, C. W.).
  1880–2 (see under Wilkinson, R. J.).
  1888–95 (see in *Perak Government Gazette*).

Selangor Council Minutes, 1877–95.

Proceedings of the Sungei Ujong State Council, 1883–93, CO 474.

Government Gazettes

Straits Settlements Government Gazette, 1875–95. CO 276.

Perak Government Gazette, 1888–95. CO 467.

Selangor Government Gazette, 1890–5. Containing Sungei Ujong Supplement from 1893. CO 469.

Reports

State Annual Reports (see under Parliamentary Papers).

Appendices to *State Annual Reports*, 1888–95. CO 435 (Negri Sembilan, Sungei Ujong and Jelebu), CO 437 (Pahang), CO 438 (Perak), CO 439 (Selangor).

Annual Reports, Perak, 1874–9. Typescript. Perak Museum Library.

Enquiry as to the Complicity of Chiefs in the Perak Outrages, Singapore, 1876.

420   THE PROTECTED MALAY STATES

Perak Enquiry Papers, 3 vols, 1876. National Library Archives, Singapore.
Proceedings of the Commission appointed to enquire into matters relating to the use of Opium in the Straits Settlements and the Federated Malay States, vol. 1 (Command Paper 4521 of 1909).

Establishments, Directories

Straits Settlements Civil Service List, 1884.
Federated Malay States Civil Service List, 1904.
The Native States List Containing the Civil Establishments, 1891, Singapore 1891. ANM.
Government of Perak, List of Establishments, 1884–9, 1891–5. Perak Museum Library.
List of Establishments, Selangor, 1895. ANM.
Perak Handbook and Civil Service List, 1892, Taiping, 1892. Colonial Office Library, London.
Straits Calendar and Directory, 1874.
Singapore Directory, 1877, 1879 (entries for Selangor for 1879).
Singapore and Straits Directory, 1880–95 (with entries for Perak and Sungei Ujong from 1880, Selangor from 1881, Jelebu from 1887 and Pahang and Negri Sembilan from 1888).
Statistical and other Information Relating to Selangor, 1894. Kuala Lumpur, 1894. ANM.

Statistical

Census of the Straits Settlements, 1981, by E. M. Merewether, Singapore, 1892.
Census of the State of Perak, 1891. Taiping, 1892.
Appendices to *States Annual Reports,* (See under *Reports.*)
Estimates, Jelebu, 1889. ANM.
Estimates, Perak 1877–95. Perak Museum Library.
Estimates, Selangor, 1889–95. ANM.
Estimates, Sungei Ujong, 1886–8. ANM.
Estimates, Sungei Ujong and Jelebu, 1890–5. ANM.

Laws, Regulations, etc.

The Laws of Negri Sembilan; Orders in Council, regulations and enactments, together with rules thereunder having the force of law, 1883–1902. 2 vols. Singapore, 1904.
Pahang Laws passed by the State Council between the 31st December 1889 and 8th January 1896, with a chronological table and an index to the short titles of the laws. Kuala Lumpur, 1897.
Pahang Laws passed by the State Council between the 18th September 1896, and 24th December 1897. Kuala Lumpur, 1898.
The Laws of Perak; Orders in Council and enactments passed by the State Council, 1877–1896, comp. A.B. Voules. Taiping, 1899.
The Laws of Perak, from the 11th September 1877 to the 31st December

1903, comp. W.G. Maxwell. 3 vols. Kuala Lumpur, 1907.
The Land Laws of Perak, 1877–1900, comp. W.G. Maxwell, with an index by F.A.S. McClelland. Taiping, 1906.
Perak Circulars, 1885–1906, ed. R.J. Wilkinson. Kuala Lumpur, 1907.
Perak Proclamations and Notices, 1880–5. Perak Museum Library.
The Laws of Selangor, 1877–1899; Orders in Council, regulations and enactments passed by the State Council, together with the rules thereunder having the force of law, comp. A.B. Voules. Kuala Lumpur, 1901.
Regulations, Rules and Orders, Selangor, from 18 April 1877 to 31 December 1889, ed. C. Kemp. Kuala Lumpur, 1892.
Native States General Orders, 1885. Singapore, 1885.

UNPUBLISHED PRIVATE PAPERS

Anson Correspondence
1. Ord to Anson, 1867–80,
2. Birch to Anson, 1873–4,
3. Clarke to Anson, 1873–7,
4. Jervois to Anson, 1875–7,
5. Robinson to Anson, 1877–9,
6. Weld to Anson, 1880–2.
National Library Archives, Singapore.
Diary of Hugh Clifford, Pahang, 1888, 1893. ANM.

Jervois Correspondence, Nov. 1875–March 1876 (concerning Perak operations). National Library Archives, Singapore.

Swettenham Papers (papers and books in print, typescript and manuscript, 1874–1942, serial numbers 1–126, including Swettenham's 1883 Diary, kept in his first year as Resident of Selangor, item 12). ANM.

Journal of Collector and Magistrate, Kuala Langat, 1882–5. Typescript in University of Singapore Library.

BOOKS, ARTICLES, ETC.

Published Works
ABDUL AZIZ b. KHAMIS and SHEEHAN, J.J., 'Adat Kuala Pilah', *JMBRAS*, vol. xiv, part 3 (1936).
ABDUL SAMAD b. AHMAD (ed.), *Kenang2an Selangor*, by Wan Mohammed Amin b. Wan Mohammed Sa'ad, Kuala Lumpur, 1937.
ALLEN, J. DE V., 'Two Imperialists', *JMBRAS*, vol. xxxviii, part 1 (1964).
ANDERSON, JOHN, *Political and Commercial Considerations relative to the Malayan Peninsula and the British Settlements in the Straits of Malacca*, Prince of Wales' Island, 1824.
ANSON, Sir A. E. H., *About Others and Myself, 1845–1920*, London, 1920.
BARING-GOULD, S. and BAMPFYLDE, C. A. *A History of Sarawak under its Two White Rajahs, 1839–1908*. London, 1909.

BEGBIE, Capt. P. F., *The Malayan Peninsula; embracing its history, manners and customs of the inhabitants, politics, natural history, etc. from its earliest records*, Madras, 1834.

BERTRAM, Sir ANTON, *The Colonial Service*, Cambridge, 1930.

BIRD, ISABELLA L. [Mrs Bishop], *The Golden Chersonese; and the Way Thither*, London, 1883.

BLAND, R. N., 'Currency of Negri Sembilan', *JSBRAS*, no. 18 (December 1886).

—— 'Aturan Sungei Ujong', *JSBRAS*, no. 28 (August 1895).

BLYTHE, W. L., 'Historical Sketch of Chinese Labour in Malaya', *JMBRAS*, vol. xx, part 1 (1947).

BOWEN, C. D., 'British Malaya as it was', *The Asiatic Review*, vol. xlvi, no. 165 (January 1950).

BRADDELL, ROLAND, *The Legal Status of the Malay States*, Singapore, 1931.

BRADDELL, T., *Statistics of the British Possessions in the Straits of Malacca; with Explanatory Notes*, Penang, 1861.

BROOKE, Sir C., *Ten Years in Sarawak*, 2 vols. London, 1866.

BROWN, C. C., *Malay Sayings*, London, 1951.

BUCKLEY, C. B., *An Anecdotal History of Old Times in Singapore*, 2 vols. Singapore, 1902.

CALDECOTT, A., 'Jelebu Customary Songs and Sayings', *JSBRAS*, no. 78 (June 1918).

CAMERON, J., *Our tropical possessions in Malayan India, being a descriptive account of Singapore, Penang, Province Wellesley and Malacca; their people, products and government*, London, 1865.

CLIFFORD, Sir HUGH, 'A Journey Through the Malay States of Trengganu and Kelantan', *Geographical Journal*, vol. ix (1897).

—— 'Life in the Malay Peninsula; as it was and is', *Proceedings of the Royal Colonial Institute*, vol. xxx (1898–9).

—— *Studies in Brown Humanity; being Scrawls and Smudges in Sepia White, and Yellow*, London, 1898.

—— 'British and Siamese Malaya', *Proceedings of the Royal Colonial Institute*, vol. xxxiv (1902–3).

—— *Malayan Monochromes*, London, 1913.

—— *In Court & Kampong*, London, 1927.

—— *In a Corner of Asia*, London, 1928.

—— *Bushwhacking and Other Asiatic Tales and Memories*, London, 1929.

COMBER, L. F., *Chinese Secret Societies in Malaya: a Survey of the Triad Society from 1800 to 1900*, New York, 1959.

COOPE, A. E., 'The Kangchu System in Johore', *JMBRAS*, vol. xiv, part 3 (1936).

COWAN, C. D. (ed.), 'Sir Frank Swettenham's Perak Journals, 1874–1876', *JMBRAS*, vol. xxiv, part 4 (1951).

—— *Nineteenth-Century Malaya; The Origins of British Political Control*, London, 1961.

DALY, D. D. 'Surveys and Explorations in the Native States of the Malayan Peninsula, 1875–1882', *Proceedings of the Royal Geographical Society* (July 1882).

DE LA CROIX, J. E., *Les Mines d'Etain de Perak*, Singapore, 1881.

—— 'Some account of the mining districts of Lower Perak', *JSBRAS*, no. 8 (1888).

DE MORGAN, M. J., *Explorations dans la presqu'ile Malaise*, Paris, 1886.

DE MOUBRAY, G. A. DE C., *Matriarchy in the Malay Peninsula and Neighbouring Countries*, London, 1931.

DENISON, N., 'The Kurau district of Perak', *JSBRAS*, no. 18 (December 1886).

DEW, A. T., 'The Fishing industry of Krian and Kurau, Perak', *JSBRAS*, no. 23 (December 1890).

DOYLE, PATRICK, *Tin Mining in Larut*, London, 1879.

FREEDMAN, MAURICE, 'Immigrants and Associations; Chinese in Nineteenth-Century Singapore', *Comparative Studies in Society and History*, vol. iii (1960–1).

GAMMANS, L. D., 'The State of Lukut', *JMBRAS*, vol. ii, part 3 (1924).

GRIST, D. H. (comp.), *An Outline of Malayan Agriculture*, Kuala Lumpur, 1936.

GULLICK, J. M., 'Sungei Ujong', *JMBRAS*, vol. xxii, part 2 (1949).

—— 'Captain Speedy of Larut', *JMBRAS*, vol. xxvi, part 3 (1953).

—— 'Kuala Lumpur, 1880–1895', *JMBRAS*, vol. xxviii, part 4 (1955).

—— *Indigenous Political Systems of Western Malaya*, London, 1958.

HALE, A., 'Mines and Miners in Kinta, Perak', *JSBRAS*, no. 16 (December 1884).

HALL, HENRY L., *The Colonial Office; a History*, Imperial Studies, No. 13, London, 1937.

HALL, W. T., *Report on Tin Mining in Perak and Burma*, Rangoon, 1889.

HARDINGE, Sir ARTHUR, *The Life of Henry Howard Molyneux Herbert, Fourth Earl of Carnarvon, 1831–1890*, 3 vols. London, 1925.

HARRISON, C. W., 'Council Minutes, Perak, 1877–1879', *Papers on Malay Subjects* (ed. R. J. Wilkinson), 1st Series, History III, 1907.

HERVEY, D. F. A., 'Rembau', *JSBRAS*, no. 13 (June 1884).

HORNADAY, W. T., 'A naturalist's visit to Selangor', *JSBRAS*, no. 3 (July 1879).

HUGHES, T. W. H., *Preliminary Sketch of the Mining Industry of Perak and Burma*, Rangoon, 1889.

INNES, EMILY, *The Chersonese with the Gilding Off*, 2 vols. London, 1885.

JACKSON, J. C., *Planters and Speculators: Chinese and European Enterprise in Malaya, 1786–1921*, Kuala Lumpur, 1968.

JENKYNS, Sir HENRY, *British Rule and Jurisdiction Beyond the Seas*, Oxford, 1902.

JOSSELIN DE JONG, P. E. DE, *Minangkabau and Negri Sembilan; Socio-Political Structure in Indonesia*, The Hague, 1952.

LEECH, H. W. C., 'About Kinta', *JSBRAS*, no. 4 (December 1879).

—— 'About Slim and Bernam', *JSBRAS*, no. 4 (December 1879).

LIAS, BRAU DE St. POL, *Pérak et les Orang-Sakèys: Voyage dans l'intérieur de la presqu'ile Malaise*, Paris, 1883.

LINEHAN, W., 'A History of Pahang', *JMBRAS*, vol. xiv, part 2 (1936).

LISTER, HON. M., 'The Negri Sembilan: Their Origin and Constitution', *JSBRAS*, no. 19 (1887).

—— 'Malay Law in Negri Sembilan', *JSBRAS*, no. 22 (December 1890).

LOVAT, Lady ALICE, *The Life of Sir Frederick Weld, GCMG; a Pioneer of Empire*, London, 1914.

LOW, Sir H., *Sarawak, its Inhabitants and Productions*, London, 1848.

[LOW, H.], 'Notes of an Ascent of the Mountain Kina Balow', *Journal of the Indian Archipelago and Eastern Asia*, vol. vi (1952).

MCNAIR, J. F. A., *Perak and the Malays: 'Sarong and Kris'*, London, 1878.

MAKEPEACE, W., BROOKE, G. E., and BRADDELL, R. St. J. (eds.), *One Hundred Years of Singapore*, 2 vols. London, 1921.

MAXWELL, Sir P. B., *An Introduction to the Duties of Police Magistrates in Prince of Wales' Island, Singapore and Malacca*, Penang, 1866.

—— *Our Malay Conquests*, Westminster, 1878.

MAXWELL, Sir W. E., 'A Journey on Foot to the Patani Frontier in 1876', *JSBRAS*, no. 9 (June 1882).

—— 'The Chiri', *JSBRAS*, no. 10 (December 1882).

—— *Straits Settlements: Present and Future Land Systems*, Rangoon, 1883.

—— 'The Law and Customs of the Malays with reference to the Tenure of Land', *JSBRAS*, no. 13 (June 1884).

—— 'The History of Perak from Native Sources', *JSBRAS*, no. 9 (June 1882) no. 14 (December 1884).

—— 'Titles and Offices of the Officers of the State of Perak', *JSBRAS*, Notes and Queries I, (December 1884).

—— 'Malay Titles in Ulu Perak', *JSBRAS*, Notes and Queries III (December 1885).

—— 'The Law Relating to Slavery Among the Malays', *JSBRAS*, no. 22 (December 1890).

—— 'The Malay Peninsula: its Resources and Prospects', *Proceedings of the Royal Colonial Institute*, vol. xxiii (1891–2).

—— *Memorandum on the Introduction of a Land Code in the Native States in the Malay Peninsula*, Singapore, 1894.

MAXWELL, Sir W. G. and GIBSON, W. S., *Treaties and Engagements affecting the Malay States and Borneo*, London, 1924.

MIDDLEBROOK, S. M., ed. GULLICK, J. M., 'Yap Ah Loy', *JMBRAS*, vol. xxiv, part 2 (1951).

MILLS, L. A., 'A History of British Malaya, 1824–1867', *JMBRAS*, vol. iii, part 2 (1925).

MOHAMMED IBRAHIM b. ABDULLAH, *Kesah Pelayaran*, Johore, 1956.

MUHAMMAD GHAZZALI, DATO' BENTARA LUAR, 'Court Language and Etiquette of the Malays', *JMBRAS*, vol. xi, part 2 (1933).

NEWBOLD, T. J. *Political and Statistical Account of the British Settlements in the Straits of Malacca*, 2 vols. London, 1839.

PARR, C. W. C., and MACKRAY, W. H., 'History of Rembau', *JSBRAS*, no. 56 (December 1910).

Perak State Railways, 1881–1901, Kuala Lumpur, 1956.

PICKERING, W. A., 'Chinese Secret Societies', *JSBRAS*, no. 1 (July 1878); no. 3 (July 1879).

PURCELL, VICTOR, 'Chinese Settlement at Malacca', *JMBRAS*, vol. xx, part 1 (1947).

—— *The Chinese in Malaya*, London, 1948.

RATHBORNE, A. B., *Camping and Tramping in Malaya*, London, 1898.

[Read, W. H.] *Play and Politics; Recollections of Malaya by an Old Resident*, London, 1901.

RIGBY, J., 'The Ninety-nine Laws of Perak', *Papers on Malay Subjects*, (ed. R. J. Wilkinson), 1st Series, Law II, 1908.

RUNCIMAN Sir STEVEN, *The White Rajahs: a History of Sarawak from 1841–1946*, Cambridge, 1960.

SADKA, EMILY (ed.), 'The Journal of Sir Hugh Low, Perak, 1877', *JMBRAS*, vol. xxvii, part 4 (1954).

St. JOHN, SPENSER, *Life in the Forests of the Far East*, 2 vols. London, 1862.

—— *The Life of Sir James Brooke, Rajah of Sarawak*, Edinburgh, 1879.

SCHLEGEL, GUSTAVE, *Thian Ti Hwui; The Hung-League, or Heaven-Earth-League. A Secret Society with the Chinese in China and India*, Batavia, 1866.

SKINNER, A. M., 'A Geography of the Malay Peninsula', *JSBRAS*, no. 1 (July 1878).

SONG ONG SIANG, *One Hundred Years' History of the Chinese in Singapore*, London, 1923.

SWETTENHAM, Sir F. A., 'Some account of the Independent Native States of the Malay Peninsula', *JSBRAS*, no. 6 (1880).

—— 'Journal kept during a journey across the Malay Peninsula', *JSBRAS*, no. 15 (1885).

—— *About Perak*, Singapore, 1893.

—— 'British Rule in Malaya', *Proceedings of the Royal Colonial Institute*, vol. xxvii (1895–6).

—— *The Real Malay; Pen Pictures*, London, 1900.

—— *British Malaya; an Account of the Origin and Progress of British Influence in Malaya*, New edition, London, 1948. (First published in 1907.)

—— *Malay Sketches*, 4th ed. London, 1913.

—— *Footprints in Malaya*, London, 1942.

TARLING, NICHOLAS, 'British Policy in the Malay Peninsula and Archipelago 1824–1871', *JMBRAS*, vol. xxx, part 3 (1957).

TAYLOR, E. N., 'The Customary Law of Rembau', *JMBRAS*, vol. vii, part 1 (1929).
—— 'Malay Family Law', *JMBRAS*, vol. xv, part 1 (1937).
THIO, EUNICE, *British Policy in the Malay Peninsula, 1880-1910*, vol. 1, Kuala Lumpur, 1968.
VETCH, COL. R. H., *Life of Lieut.-General the Hon. Sir Andrew Clarke*, London, 1905.
WELD, Sir F. A., 'The Straits Settlements and British Malaya', *Proceedings of the Royal Colonial Institute*, vol. xv (1883-4).
WILKINSON, R. J. (gen. ed.), *Papers on Malay Subjects* (see under Harrison, Rigby, Wilkinson, Winstedt).
—— *Malay Beliefs*, London, 1906.
—— 'Law; Introductory Sketch', *Papers on Malay Subjects*, 1st Series, Law I (1908).
—— 'Council Minutes, Perak, 1880-1882', *Papers on Malay Subjects*, 1st Series, History IV (1909).
—— 'Notes on the Negri Sembilan', *Papers on Malay Subjects*, 1st *Series*, History V (1911).
—— *A History of the Peninsular Malays, with chapters on Perak and Selangor*, 3rd. edn. revised, Singapore, 1923.
—— 'Some Malay Studies', *JMBRAS*, vol. x, part 1 (1932).
WINSTEDT, Sir R. O., 'Malay Arts and Crafts', *Papers on Malay Subjects* (ed. R. J. Wilkinson), 1st Series, Industries I, 1909.
—— 'Some Rembau Customary Sayings', *JMBRAS*, vol. vi, part 4 (1928).
—— 'A History of Johore (1365-1895 A.D.)', *JMBRAS*, vol. x, part 3 (1932).
—— 'Negri Sembilan: The History, Polity and Beliefs of the Nine States', *JMBRAS*, vol. xii, part 3 (1934).
—— 'A History of Selangor', *JMBRAS*, vol. xii, part 3 (1934).
—— 'Kingship and Enthronement in Malaya', *JMBRAS*, vol. xx, part 1 (1947).
—— *The Malays; a Cultural History*, London, 1953.
—— and WILKINSON, R. J., 'A History of Perak', *JMBRAS*, vol. xii, part 1 (1934).
WONG, C. S., *A Gallery of Chinese Kapitans*, Singapore, 1964.
WONG LIN KEN, *The Malayan Tin Industry to 1914*, Association for Asian Studies: Monographs and Papers, no. xiv. Tucson, 1965.
—— 'Western Enterprise and the Development of the Malayan Tin Industry to 1914', in *The Economic Development of South-East Asia*, ed. C. D. Cowan, London, 1964.
WYNNE, M. L., *Triad and Tabut: a Survey of the Origin and Diffusion of Chinese and Mohamedan Secret Societies in the Malay Peninsula A. D. 1800-1935*, Singapore, 1941.

Journals

Journal of the Indian Archipelago and Eastern Asia.

Journal of Eastern Asia (one issue, 1875).
Journal of the Royal Asiatic Society (*Straits Branch*).
Journal of the Royal Asiatic Society (*Malayan Branch*).
Selangor Journal, 1892–7.
Proceedings of the Royal Colonial Institute.

Unpublished Works

KAMARUDDIN ARIFF, 'Raja Idris of Perak, 1849–1916', B.A. honours dissertation, University of Malaya, 1953.
MALLAL, M. A., 'J. W. W. Birch: Causes of his Assassination', M.A. thesis, University of Malaya, 1952.
TAN, LINDA, 'The Development of the Straits Settlement Civil Service, 1867–1896', B.A. honours dissertation, University of Malaya, 1957.
THIO, EUNICE, Ph. D. thesis, University of London, 1956. 'British Policy in the Malay Peninsula, 1880–1909', vol. 2.

INDEX

INDEX 429

363, 385; commercial, 85, 344–5, 356, 357, 358, 363; Colonial Office suggests that Chinese and Indians be encouraged to take up, 132–3; immigrants and, 132–3, 300, 327; plantation, 208, 324, 332, 340, 344, 351; almost untaxed, 331, 340; revenue from exports produced by, 331; Malays and, 351; mining encroaches on, 354–5 (see also Cultivation: Land: Plantations).
A History of Malaya, 139.
A History of New Zealand, 115.
A History of Sarawak under its Two White Rajahs, 1839–1908, 109.
A History of the Peninsular Malays, 29, 33, 42, 51.
Ah Kwee, 272, 303, 320, 334, 351.
Ahmad, Bendahara of Pahang, 156.
Ahmaddin Shah, Sultan of Perak, 33.
Ahmad Muatham Shah, Sultan of Pahang, 15–17, 120.
Ali, Sultan of Perak (1865–71), 33, 275.
Allen, J. de V. (cited), 205.
Allowances: for Rajas, 84, 106, 148, 175, 201, 211, 274–5, 280, 283, 299, 305; for Capitan China, 303, 309 (see also Pensions).
Amok, 10, 245.
Ampang, Selangor, 202; tin-mine at, 349.
Anderson, J. (cited), 3.
Anglo-Dutch Treaty (1824), 15.
Annual Reports, 124, 132, 139, 416.
Anson, Colonel A. E. H. (later, General Sir Archibald), 40, 41–3, 92, 157; (cited), 87.
Api Api, Kuala Selangor, 356, 359.
Appeals: to territorial chiefs, 7; to Governor, 133–4, 149, 254–5, 258; from penghulu, 253, 265; to Senior Magistrate, 253; to Resident, 253, 254, 255, 259; from District Magistrate, 253; to Chief Magistrate, 253; from Chief Magistrate, 253, 254–5; to Judicial Commissioner, 259; from Senior Magistrate, 259; from kathi, 267.
Arabs, 5, 26, 27, 28.
Arbitration: among chiefs, 9, 32, 33; among Chinese, 24, 25, 223, 271, 272–3; by chiefs in civil cases, 264; between state officials and central

executive under federation, 376.
Areca nuts, 345, 360.
Assistant Colonial Secretary for Native Affairs, Swettenham as, 141, 150–1, 169, 213, 238, 284.
Assistant Residents: appointment of, 3, 48, 54, 57, 63, 65–7, 72, 75, 110, 214; their posts abolished, 75, 124, 197, 199; salaries of, 124.
Atap: trade in, 6, 355, 356; used in building, 22, 28, 108, 354; farm for, 201; duty on, 299, 383, 386.
Attorney-General: in Singapore, 55, 59, 62, 133, 135, 141; for Malay States, 375.
Audit: Swettenham's audits of states' accounts, 143, 198, 223–4, 306–7; separate audit departments in each state, 365; post of Chief Auditor proposed, 375; state departments for, 397, 402–3, 404.
Australia, 46, 87, 102, 115, 204, 388.

BACON, EDWARD (cited), 86.
Bagan Nakhoda Omar mukim, Selangor, 288.
Bagan Serai, Perak, 292, 327.
Balik Pulau, Penang, 214.
Bandar, Selangor, 295.
Bandar Bahru, Perak, 66, 76, 77, 85, 86, 197, 246.
Bandar Kanching, Selangor, 202.
Bandar Langat, Selangor, 267, 294.
Banjarese settlers in Malay States, 328, 353, 358.
Baring-Gould, S. and Bamfylde, C. A. (cited), 109.
Batak Rabit, Perak, 77, 79, 80.
Batang Padang district, Perak: kuasas in, 174; district records of, 217, 262, 415; penghulus in, 265, 285, 406–9; assistant kathi of, 266; adultery among Muslims treated as a crime in, 270; commission on tin paid to penghulus and chiefs in, 281; increase in population of, 329–30; coffee grown in, 357.
Batang Padang river, 21, 84, 384, 386.
Batu Gajah, Perak, 147, 294.
Batu Tiga, Selangor, 360.
Bebar, Pahang, 16.
Bellamy, Mr., 203.
Bendaharas: of Malacca, 10, 18, 382;

growers of, 361, 362.

Collector and Magistrate: of Kuala Langat, 74, 75, 76, 147, 167, 173–4, 188; of Jelebu, 118, 143; of Sri Menanti, 118, 142; of Kuala Selangor, 214, 231, 254, 270–1; of Matang, 214; of Krian, 214; of Kinta, 214.

Collectors and Magistrates: supervise *penghulus*, 186; in Pahang, 214; in Sungei Ujong, 214; in Jelebu, 214; in India, 214; in Sarawak, 214; official names for, 214 (*see also* District officers).

Colonial Engineer, 50, 143–4, 222.

Colonial Office: Straits Settlements transferred (1867) from India Office to, 38, 40; Ord and, 40–1, 44–5, 95; intervention in Malay States, 40–2, 44–8, 51–2, 55, 58–9, 64, 76; Anson and, 41–2; and Birch's visit to Selangor, 43; and role of Residents, 47–8, 98–102, 103–4; and Pangkor Engagement, 48, 55; deceived by Clarke's despatches, 56, 99–100; Jervois and, 76, 90–1, 93–5, 98–100; and annexation of states, 94–5, 104, 114, 121, 123; and cost of occupation of Perak, 95–6; Weld and, 117–18; and colonial protectorates, 119; its anomalous jurisdiction over Malay States, 119–24, 176, 228; and states' civil servants, 124–8, 226–9, 231, 235; and land speculation, 129–30; and public works, 130–2; and states' administration, 132–7; and development of agriculture, 132–3, 357–8; and administration of justice, 133–5, 257–60; Residents' correspondence with, 141; and Governors' tours, 144, 364; not consulted about states' loans, 150; and Kinta Railway, 154; and succession to sultanates, 157, 162; and sultans' allowances, 175; and State Councils, 177; and states' police, 237–8, 245, 251; and exiled Rajas, 278; and opium-smoking, 336; refuses European tin monopoly, 348; and federation, 364, 372–4; and states' indebtedness, 367–8; Governors' correspondence with, 415.

Colonial protectorates, 119.

Colonial Regulations, 225.

Colonial Secretary, 116, 134; Birch as, 4, 42, 53, 65, 77; Maxwell as, 138, 153, 209, 231; Braddell as, 141; district officers' journals sent to, 142; salary of, 232; and police, 243; Residents report on law-courts to, 251; Swettenham as, 397.

Colonial Service: states' officials seconded from, 125–6, 227, 233; some Residents selected from, 127, 204; Low, Smith and Swettenham in, 130; cadetships in, 229, 235; proposal to transfer states' civil services to, 374.

Colonial Treasurer, 366.

Comber, L. F. (cited), 319.

Commission of Enquiry as to the Complicity of Chiefs in the Perak Outrages (1876), 92, 385.

Committee to report on relations with the Native States (1871), 41, 50.

Communications: Swettenham criticizes, 138–9; Weld and Smith inspect sites and plans for, 148, 154; development of, 198–9, 218, 222–3, 297, 324, 330, 338–40, 354; Residents and, 200, 202–3; Clifford and, 208; no central control of, 365; states' debts due in part to cost of, 366.

Compensation: for freeing slaves, 111, 296–7; for mining encroachment, 148, 354–5; dismissed officials and, 230.

Consulting Engineers, 131, 371.

Coolie-brokers, 22, 325, 328.

Cooly Depot, Kuala Lumpur, 308, 312.

Coromandel Coast, tin exported to, 18.

Correspondence: Residents' with Straits Settlements, 138, 139, 141, 199, 415; Governors' with Colonial Office, 141, 415; Residents' with district officers, 199; rules for district officers on, 405.

Courts: *penghulus*', 70, 105, 245, 253, 264–5, 271–2, 406, 408; first British, 70, 250–1; in Ceylon, 78; in Sarawak, 109; mixed benches, 113, 171, 262, 264, 265, 269, 270, 272; appeals, 114, 133–4, 149, 253–5, 258–60, 265, 267; irregularities in, 133–4, 251–2, 256–8; lawyers not allowed to appear in, 134, 252, 257–9, 371; court-fees, 152, 253, 264–5, 298–9; Courts Department in Pahang, 221; civil and crim-

448 INDEX

permits for, 217, 220; Chinese and, 272; European improvements in, 350–1.

Mining Code, 262.

Miscegeny, 22, 206.

Missions, 290, 327.

Mitchell, Sir Charles: and federation, 138, 372, 374–8; and status of officials, 226, 231; and reform of administration of justice, 259; and loans, 338, 362; and Pahang, 375.

Mohammedan law, custom and religion: inheritance, 8, 173, 265, 266; Pangkor Engagement and, 47–8, 89–90, 120, 161, 187, 265; religious cases, 89, 109, 250, 254, 265, 267, 268, 269, 270; marriage, 89, 172, 250, 254, 266, 267, 268; Malay Council and, 90, 185; divorce, 109, 250, 254, 265, 268; attendance at mosques, 161, 172, 173, 269; adultery, 172, 269–71; Idris and, 172–3; Residents and, 187, 265; marriage and divorce registers, 266; British officials and, 270–1; under federation, 378.

Mohammedan secret societies, 318.

Mohammad Salleh, 271.

Mohammed Ibrahim bin Abdullah (cited), 5, 26, 27, 28–9, 58, 79, 243, 385, 386.

Mohammed Nusi, Haji, 212.

Mohammed, Sultan of Selangor (1826–57), 19, 31, 156, 275.

Mohammed Tahir, Haji, 14, 277, 359, 360.

Mohammed Taib (Mat Taib), Shaikh, 112, 161, 179, 182.

Mohammed Yusuf, Dato' Klana of Sungei Ujong, 156–7, 279.

Moneylenders, 19, 31, 32, 36, 277, 344.

Monopolies, 78; Sultans and, 11; Portuguese and Dutch monopoly in tin, 18; secret societies and, 25, 322; Malay chiefs lease to Chinese, 25–6; local policy is to break down, 38; in spirits and pawnbroking, 72; local officials urge retention of gambling monopoly, 136–7; State Councils and, 190; in jobs, 295; large revenue from, 332; Europeans want tin monopoly, 348, 350; in pre-British times, 383.

Monsoon, steamer services and, 2, 140.

Muar river, 1, 3.

Muhlinghaus, Herman, 350.

Mukims: penghulu in charge of, 113, 276, 282, 283, 284–6, 287, 288–9, 338, 407, 409; the Sri Adika Raja in charge of some, 279; schools in, 294; registers for, 342, 343, 406, 408; rent rolls in, 402.

Murder cases, 133–4, 247, 253, 254, 258, 259, 264.

Murray, Commander Patrick James: replaces Tatham, 66; Resident of Sungei Ujong, 111, 157; career of, 204, 390; attracted by Malaya, 207–8; Miss Bird on, 210–11, 252; a solitary, 233; in court, 252.

Musa, Raja Muda, of Selangor: the Sultan's son, 114, 179; a Magistrate, 114; a devout Muslim, 172, 267; becomes President of the State Council, 179; plantation of, 360.

Musa, Raja, of Perak: brother of ex-Sultan 'Abdu'llah, 179, 278; a member of the State Council, 179, 278; a magistrate, 253, 263, 278; works with Denison, 275; is granted a pension, 278.

Musa, Syed, 284, 360.

Muslims: adultery and, 172, 269–71; land tenure amongst, 343, 344.

NAKHODA ALLANG, DATO' DAGANG, 14–15.

Nakoda Trong, 5, 82.

Napier, Catherine, 108.

Native States General Orders, 225.

Negri Sembilan Land Code (1889), 261.

Negri Sembilan (former); extent of, 1–2; area of settlement in, 3; population of, 4; immigrants in, 6; political system of, 6–9; its Ruler known as Yang di-Pertuan Besar, 8; tin-mining in, 18, 20, 21; rivalries in, 32–3, 35; lineage headmen in, 282, 288; Chinese in, 303; plantations in, 332, 346, 347; duties levied in, 332; opium duty in, 335; land regulations (1887) in, 341; revenue and expenditure, 410–12; imports and exports, 413.

Negri Sembilan (later): extent of, 1, 215; a confederation (1889) of small

DATE DUE